Essential Study Skills

Fifth Edition

Essential
Study
Skills

LINDA WONG

HOUGHTON MIFFLIN COMPANY   Boston   New York

Publisher, Humanities: *Patricia A. Coryell*
Senior Sponsoring Editor: *Mary Finch*
Development Editor: *Shani B. Fisher*
Editorial Associate: *Andrew Sylvester*
Senior Project Editor: *Fred Burns*
Editorial Assistant: *Brett Pasinella*
Senior Manufacturing Coordinator: *Marie Barnes*
Senior Art and Design Coordinator: *Jill Haber*
Senior Composition Buyer: *Sarah Ambrose*
Marketing Manager: *Elinor Gregory*
Marketing Assistant: *Evelyn Yang*

Cover image by Leigh Wells.

Photo Credits:

Page 9: © David Joel/Getty Images. **Page 22:** © Bonnie Kamin/PhotoEdit.
Page 34: © Michelle D. Bridwell/PhotoEdit. **Page 48:** © Getty Images.
Page 73: © Michael Newman/PhotoEdit. **Page 75:** © Michelle D. Bridwell/PhotoEdit.
Page 93: © Patrik Giardino/Corbis. **Page 103:** © Gary Connor/PhotoEdit.
Page 116: Stewart Cohen/Getty Images. **Page 124:** © Lori Adamski Peek/Getty Images.
Page 150: © Mary Kate Den/PhotoEdit. **Page 159:** © Olivia Baumgartner/Corbis Sygma.
Page 178: © Spencer Grant/PhotoEdit. **Page 183:** © Michael Newman/PhotoEdit.
Page 199: © Amy Etra/PhotoEdit. **Page 218:** © Corbis.
Page 241: © Tom Stewart/Corbis. **Page 252:** © Gary Connor/PhotoEdit.
Page 265: © Bob Daemmrich/The Image Works. **Page 283:** © Duomo/Corbis.
Page 295: © Richard Pasley/Stock Boston. **Page 314:** © Grant LeDuc/Stock Boston.
Page 328: © Gary Connor/PhotoEdit. **Page 351:** © Aaron Haupt/Photo Researchers.
Page 368: © Bonnie Kamin/PhotoEdit. **Page 381:** © Corbis.
Page A-17: © Esbin/Anderson/The Image Works. **Page A-18:** © Esbin/Anderson/The
Image Works. **Page A-21:** © Reuters/Allen Frederickson/Archive Photos.
Page A-25: © Reprinted with special permission of King Features Syndicate.
Page A-27: © David Alan Harvey/Woodfin Camp. **Page A-30:** © Lauren
Greenfield/Corbis Sygma. **Page A-35:** © Esbin/Anderson/The Image Works.
Page A-37: © Huntly Hersch/Index Stock Imagery.
Page A-38: © Tedrussellphotographer.com. **Page A-40:** Courtesy of American
Psychological Association. **Page A-41:** © Leslie O'Shaughnessy/Medical Images.

Printed in the U.S.A.
Library of Congress Control Number: 2005921859

ISBN: 0-618-52883-0
4 5 6 7 8 9—KDL—09 08 07 06

Dedication

The fifth edition of *Essential Study Skills* is dedicated to Daniel L. Hodges, Ph.D., former director of assessment and testing at Lane Community College in Eugene, Oregon, for his insightful contributions, critiques, and expertise in the areas of educational psychology and research-based learning strategies. His personal interest, dedication of time and resources, valuable feedback, and commitment to student success are embedded in the pages of this fifth edition. Daniel Hodges, Ph.D., has retired from the community college, but he has not retired from actively contributing to the field of education.

Contents

UNIT THREE: Developing Effective Textbook Reading Strategies

UNIT FOUR: Using Effective Notetaking Techniques

Preface

The fifth edition of *Essential Study Skills* is a textbook appropriate for all post-secondary students interested in learning powerful study strategies to increase academic performance. The step-by-step supportive approach used in this textbook makes the text especially helpful for adults returning to school for the first time in many years, for underprepared students, and for students interested in a direct approach to learning powerful study skills strategies. The fifth edition includes the contemporary working memory model, which lays the foundation for and allows the development of *metacognition* (the process of knowing about one's own memory system and selecting appropriate learning strategies to tackle intellectual tasks). Using the metacognitive approach enables students to assume responsibility for their own learning and realize that academic success is a product of skills and behaviors they can acquire, customize, and effectively implement. This textbook provides students with versatile, practical, and meaningful strategies and exercises that will lead to higher grades, more thorough learning of information, and increased confidence, self-esteem, and sense of empowerment.

Student-Oriented Features in the Fifth Edition

Essential Study Skills focuses on the study skills essential for college success. As shown by the Contents for this textbook, students will learn to understand how they process information (Unit One, Chapters 1 and 2), prepare themselves for optimal learning (Unit Two, Chapters 3 through 6), develop effective textbook reading strategies (Unit Three, Chapters 7 and 8), use effective notetaking techniques (Unit Four, Chapters 9 through 11), and strengthen their test-taking skills (Unit Five, Chapters 12 and 13). Consistent student-oriented features appear in each chapter to guide students through the process of learning new strategies and skills. The optional online practice exercises and tests offer students additional opportunities to master the textbook content.

The following textbook features that appear in each chapter promote active learning, provide step-by-step instruction and examples for implementing strategies, captivate student interest, and promote student participation in the learning process.

- **The Quick Start Checklist** at the beginning of the textbook presents essential study skills that students can implement at the beginning of the term to familiarize themselves with registration, campus resources, computer access, textbook organization, syllabi, and other successful study strategies.
- **Chapter visual mappings** use a graphic form to show the main headings of each chapter.
- **Terms to Know** listed at the beginning of each chapter help students easily identify the key terms they will need to learn in the chapter.
- **Chapter profiles** provide students with a self-correcting tool to assess their current attitudes and behaviors. To show progress and changes made through the course of the term, students complete the profiles again at the end of the term. Students record their scores on the Master Profile Chart located in Appendix A.

■ **Boxed information** provides students with highlights of key points to use while previewing, reading, and reviewing the chapter for tests.

■ **Ample exercises** provide guided practice in applying the skills of the chapter whether in class, in small groups, with partners, as individual homework assignments, or independently for enrichment.

NEW

■ **New excerpts** for exercises throughout the textbook include multidisciplinary topics, with emphasis on science, social science, math, and personal development materials.

NEW

■ **Online practices** referred to throughout the textbook provide students with drill, practice, and enrichment options. Many of the online practices are interactive, self-correcting objective questions that are corrected online; students also receive feedback that explains and reinforces the correct answer. Some of the exercises provide students with text boxes in which to write their responses; they may then print or e-mail their responses to you. You may assign students these online practices or encourage them to complete the practices independently.

■ **Case Studies** provide students with the opportunity to recommend specific skills or solutions to student situations presented as case studies. Answers are open-ended and involve using critical thinking and problem-solving skills. The textbook case studies and additional "online only" case studies are available on the student website for this textbook; students may print or e-mail their responses directly to you.

■ **LINKS exercises** connect content in the chapter to skills, concepts, and excerpts presented in previous chapters or to the psychology chapter in Appendix D.

NEW

■ **Essential Strategies charts** for specific study skills appear in each chapter to draw students' attention to essential strategies that lead to the acquisition of new skills and greater success. The **Set Learning Goals** section that appears before each *Essential Strategies* chart encourages students to identify effective strategies they already use and strategies they plan to make a concerted effort to use for specific study skills areas. The **Class Discussion question** following each *Essential Strategies* chart provides an opportunity for class discussions that integrate the strategies with other study skills topics and personal applications.

■ Three **Reflection Writing Assignments** provide students with the opportunity to personalize the chapter content, discuss current skills and attitudes, integrate the chapter's skills with other study skills, and apply the chapter content to personal experiences.

■ **Group Processing—A Collaborative Learning Activity** in each chapter provides a small-group activity that enhances student interest; creates a forum for student interaction through brainstorming, discussion, and cooperative work; and promotes critical thinking skills.

■ **Photographs** in each chapter are accompanied by discussion questions that integrate the content of the chapter with real-life situations and applications.

NEW

■ **Culminating Options** at the end of each chapter provide students with comprehensive review activities for the chapter: an online flash card activity to practice definitions for chapter terminology; four ACE practice tests using fill-in-the-blank, true-false, multiple-choice, and short-answer questions; and portfolio and project options listed in Appendix C Learning Options.

■ **Chapter summaries** review the main points in succinct lists that students can use when previewing and reviewing a chapter.

■ **Review questions** at the end of the chapter assess students' understanding and application of the chapter content.

The **appendixes** in *Essential Study Skills,* Fifth Edition, offer the following student-oriented materials.

■ **Appendix A** includes the Master Profile Chart and answer keys for the chapter profiles.

■ **Appendix B** includes convenient forms for student use. A Learning Options Assessment Form, time management forms, Cornell notetaking assessment forms, and a Personal Insights form to use as a culminating activity at the end of the term can be removed from the textbook for easy use.

NEW

■ **Appendix C** includes *seven Standard Learning Options* that are appropriate to use for every chapter in the textbook. These seven options are followed by *three* additional learning options tailored to the specific content of each chapter. The *Learning Options* in Appendix C offer students assessment activities and projects that promote creativity, offer choices based on learning styles and preferences, create motivation, and increase interest. These activities and projects may be used for individual assignments, extra credit projects, class presentations, or portfolio development.

NEW

■ **Appendix D** includes a full excerpted chapter, *Health, Stress, and Coping* from an introductory psychology textbook. Use of the chapter in Appendix D results in direct application of chapter skills to a full psychology chapter, and exercises and references appear within the text to encourage this application. As with all the exercises in the chapters, instructors can choose to use some or all of the exercises that relate to the Appendix D chapter.

Teacher-Oriented Materials for the Fifth Edition

Essential Study Skills, Fifth Edition, is designed to provide both instructors and students with a wide array of learning activities and exercises. We encourage you to identify and select activities, exercises, and assignments that are appropriate for your students and your classroom format. **You do not need to use all of the materials in the textbook or online in order to teach the essential skills in this textbook.** Students can use the textbook activities or online activities that you do not include in your course outline to explore topics in greater detail, reinforce the textbook skills, and create independent enrichment activities to further their understanding. The following ancillary materials for the Fifth Edition facilitate the development of course content, selection of appropriate materials, presentation of content to students, and assessment of student performance.

■ **Instructor Resource Manual (IRM),** which is organized chapter-by-chapter, provides you with the following materials:

1. Course syllabus, course outlines, assignment sheets, grading rubrics, and record-keeping forms
2. A chapter overview that lists sections in the chapter to use for reading assignments
3. A list of the textbook activities and exercises available for partner or small group work, full class activities, and homework assignments
4. A list of instructional materials available on the Class Prep CD
5. Step-by-step teaching tips to use as you move through each chapter
6. Answer keys for exercises and chapter review questions
7. Masters for overhead transparencies
8. Optional student forms or worksheets (for some chapters)

The Instructor Resource Manual is available on the ClassPrepCD and on the Instructor's Website. **For a printed version, please contact our Faculty Service Center at 800-733-1717, Extension 4032 to request the printed IRM for Wong's** *Essential Study Skills,* **5th edition.**

■ The **Class Prep CD** provides you with a convenient way to use your computer to access the following additional instructional materials.

1. For instructors transitioning from the Fourth Edition to the Fifth Edition, a list of changes and new materials provided by the Fifth Edition
2. The complete Instructor Resource Manual in a format that allows you to modify or customize the materials and place them online for online instruction.
3. A summary of the online practices and online tests available on the student website
4. Additional enrichment activities and printable worksheets
5. A comprehensive chapter-by-chapter test bank that you can use to create your own chapter, unit, midterm, or final exam tests
6. Ready-to-use unit tests, a midterm exam, and a final exam, which you can also modify by using Test Bank questions.
7. PowerPoint slides for each chapter

■ The **Instructor Website** for the Fifth Edition provides you with the instructional materials listed below, following the colored box. For details, go to:

1. http://college.hmco.com/collegesurvival/instructors
2. Go to the section *Study Skills*.
3. Scroll down to *Essential Study Skills 5e*. Click Go.
4. You will be on the homepage. Bookmark this page.
5. Click on the materials you wish to use.

1. Materials from the Class Prep CD, including PowerPoint slides
2. Access to an Instructor Discussion Group for networking with other *Essential Study Skills* instructors and the author
3. Material for Houghton Mifflin's Student Success video materials
4. Additional Houghton Mifflin resources available for classroom, department, and institutional use
5. Links to other websites.

Optional Resources, Consulting, and Support Services to Accompany This Textbook

For information on including the following products with your order of *Essential Study Skills*, Fifth Edition, contact your College Survival consultant (1-800-528-8323), your local Houghton Mifflin sales representative, or visit the Houghton Mifflin website at http://college.hmco.com/instructors.

Student Success Planner: Our week-at-a-glance Student Success Planner includes a "Survival Kit" of helpful success tips for students.

Myers-Briggs Type Indicator (MBTI) Instrument®: This widely used personality inventory determines preferences of four scales: Extraversion-Introversion, Sensing-Intuitive, Thinking-Feeling, and Judging-Perceiving. Qualified schools may purchase this inventory.

Retention Management System College Inventory: The Noel Levitz College Student Inventory identifies students with tendencies that contribute to dropping out of school. This instrument works with campus advisors as an early-alert intervention program.

Correspond with the Author: Visit the instructor website for this textbook to locate the author's e-mail address. The author welcomes the opportunity to correspond with you.

College Survival Consulting Service: Expert consultants as well as this textbook's author are available to provide your campus with training programs and materials for designing, implementing, and administrating student success and first-year courses.

Acknowledgments

Appreciation is extended to the following reviewers who contributed valuable ideas to further strengthen the effectiveness of this textbook for college students.

Karen Fenske, Kishwaukee College, IL
Richard Grossman, Tompkins Cortland Community College, NY
Phyllis Guthrie, Tarleton State University, TX
Leslie King, SUNY-Oswego
Gary Laird, Lamar University, TX
Joanna Leck, Full Sail Real World Education, FL
Patricia Malinowski, Finger Lakes Community College, NY
Teresa Massey, Chemeketa Community College, OR
Joan Nealy, Spokane Falls Community College, WA
Alison Parry, Capilano College, BC, Canada
Margaret Peck, College of Southern Idaho
Lois Washington, Southwest Tennessee Community College
Susan Wickham, Des Moines Area Community College, IA
Ramona Williams, East Tennessee State University
Carla Young, Community College of Allegheny County, PA

I applaud the outstanding editorial and production staff that has worked with me through the stages required to develop and produce this book. I extend a very special attitude of gratitude to Shani Fisher, Melissa Kelleher, Fred Burns, and Andrew Sylvester for their expertise, team spirit, and dedication.

—*Linda Wong*

To the Student

Essential Study Skills, Fifth Edition, is designed to provide you with skills that will unlock your learning potential. By consistently using the skills presented in this book, you will learn information more thoroughly and remember it more easily. This section tells you how to get the most out of *Essential Study Skills.*

How to Start the Term

As soon as you purchase your book (and read this), read the Quick Start Checklist section preceding the text chapters. As you complete each task designed to prepare you for an excellent start to the term, check off the item. Continue through the checklist until you complete all the items.

How to Start Each Chapter

1. Read the paragraph on the first page for a glimpse of the skills you will learn in the chapter.
2. Study the visual mapping on the first page of the chapter. This mapping is a picture form of the main headings or topics in the chapter.
3. Read through the Terms to Know to familiarize yourself with the chapter vocabulary.
4. Answer honestly the chapter profile questions on the second page of the chapter. This will not be graded; it will be used to show your current attitude, habits, and knowledge of skills that will be presented in the chapter. If you prefer, you can complete the profile online at the website for this textbook.
5. Follow the directions for scoring your profile. If you complete the profile online, you will receive your score automatically. Chart your score on the Master Profile Chart on page A-2 in Appendix A.
6. Complete the Reflection 1 Writing assignment—even if your instructor does not assign it.
7. Prepare your mind for the content of each chapter by surveying the chapter before you begin the careful reading. Survey, or preview, the chapter by
     Reading the headings and subheadings.
     Reading the highlighted boxed information.
     Noticing the key words in bold blue print.
     Reading the chapter summary.
     Reading the chapter review questions.
8. Begin the process of thorough, accurate reading. Read one paragraph at a time and think about what you have read. Your goal should not be to race through the chapter reading quickly; fast reading is not a reading approach that will lead to comprehension or retention of the information.

**How to Use the
Special Features in
the Chapter**

Introductory Paragraph The introductory paragraph on the opening page of each chapter helps you formulate a "big picture" of the topics you will be studying in the chapter.

Visual Mapping The visual mapping at the beginning of each chapter provides you with an overview of the main topics in the chapter. The chapter title is in the center of the mapping. The chapter headings branch out from the title, beginning in the upper left corner at the "11:00 position." To read the headings in order, move in a clockwise direction. After you finish reading the chapter, *copy the visual mapping on your own paper. Expand the mapping by adding key words for each heading. See Appendix C for an example.* Expanding the chapter mapping provides you with a concise study tool to review before a test.

Terms to Know The list of terms at the beginning of each chapter introduces you to the vocabulary you will need to learn to define. As you survey and later read the chapter, note that the *Terms to Know* appear in bold blue print throughout the chapter. *Copy the list on your own paper; use the chapter information to write a short definition for each term. Upon completion of the chapter, you should be able to write and recite the definitions for these terms.*

Chapter Profiles Complete the ten-question chapter profile to show your current attitudes and habits. You can also complete this profile online and receive your score. Follow the directions to score and record your score on the Master Profile in Appendix A. At the end of the term, you can repeat these profiles to show the changes you have made throughout the term.

Boxed Information As you preview, read, and review a chapter, pay special attention to the boxes throughout each chapter. Read each box carefully; then read the text following, which discusses each point in detail. Review the boxes when you prepare for tests.

Textbook Exercises This textbook contains a wide variety of exercises to practice the skills and techniques presented in the chapter. Your instructor will assign some of the exercises in class or outside of class as homework. Your instructor might not assign all of the exercises, so pay close attention to the assignments given to you in class. Work carefully and thoughtfully to complete each assignment so your work reflects the quality of work you are capable of producing. For practice and personal enrichment, you can complete on your own any of the exercises not assigned by your instructor, including the special exercises related to the psychology chapter in Appendix D in the back of your book.

Case Studies The *Textbook Case Studies* describe student situations that ask for your suggestions for improving the situation. After you read each case study, answer the question by using strategies and skills you learned in the chapter. These questions are open-ended, meaning there are many possible answers, but your answer must focus specifically on the situation. Check your answers to be certain that they address the problem or situation discussed in the case study. You may complete these case studies online and then print or e-mail your responses to your instructor. *Online Case Studies* provide you with additional case studies to examine and respond to with suggestions; the *Online Case Studies* are available online for each chapter.

Online Student Practices Many of the *online practices* that appear throughout each chapter consist of true-false, multiple-choice, or fill-in-the blank questions; when you complete the practices, you will receive your score and get feedback that helps you understand the correct answers. Other practices use text boxes so you can write your responses and then use the option to print or email your responses to your instructor. These companion practice exercises provide you with extra practice and reinforce the skills in the chapter.

Set Learning Goals, Essential Strategies Charts, and Class Discussions
Essential Strategies charts for specific study skills appear in each chapter to draw your attention to essential strategies that you can begin to use immediately. Follow the directions for *Set Learning Goals* that appear before each chart; identify the strategies you already use and set learning goals to include the other strategies in your study method or routine. Read the *Class Discussion* question; ponder answers to the questions and be prepared to respond in class. Participating in class discussions demonstrates an interest and effort on your part, promotes critical thinking skills, and presents you as a productive member of the class.

Reflective Writing Assignments Three *Reflective Writing Assignments* appear in each chapter. Your instructor may assign one, two, or all three writing assignments as individual assignments, entries in a journal, or as a cumulative set of responses as a portfolio project. You can also complete the writing assignments online at this textbook's website if you prefer. If your instructor does not use the *Reflection Writing Assignments,* you have the option of writing responses for your own records and your own benefit.

Culminating Options The *Culminating Options* at the end of each chapter provide you with review activities to reinforce the skills and concepts you learned in that chapter, give you feedback about the accuracy and thoroughness of your learning, and help you prepare for upcoming tests. Your instructor may assign one or more of these options, or you may want to select your own options for independent review and personal benefit.

■ The **online flash card review** gives you the opportunity to practice and to review definitions for defining the terminology in each chapter.

■ The **ACE Practice Tests 1, 2, and 3** are interactive and scored online for immediate feedback.

■ The **ACE Practice Test 4** provides you with the opportunity to respond to short-answer questions involving critical thinking.

■ **The Learning Options** (located in Appendix C) are activities or projects that provide an alternative form of assessment to show how well you understand the concepts and skills in the chapter and how effectively you can apply them in new ways. Learning Options add excitement, interest, and creativity to the learning process. Your instructor may assign specific Learning Options, allow you to select your own learning option from the Appendix C list of options, or use Learning Options for group or extra credit assignments. (An Assessment Form of Learning Options appears in Appendix B, page A-4.)

Additional Online Materials   The website for each chapter offers additional online materials, such as *Student Forms, Worksheets, Student Discussion Groups,* and *Links to Other Websites.* You can explore all the materials available on the Essential Study Skills website by following these directions.

1. Type: http://college.hmco.com/collegesurvival/students
2. In the section *Get Online Materials,* click *List of Sites by Author.*
3. Scroll down to Wong, *Essential Study Skills 5e.* Click on the title.
4. If you are working on your own computer, bookmark the website for quick access throughout the term.
5. Click on the chapter you wish to explore.

Summary   The summary at the end of each chapter provides you with a brief list of key points in the chapter. Read the summary when you first preview a chapter, and again after you have read the chapter thoroughly. Practice expanding the summary's points by adding additional details you have learned. Use the summaries as review tools to prepare for tests.

Review Questions   The questions at the end of the chapter will help you check how well you have learned and applied the chapter's study skills. You should be able to complete the questions without looking back at the chapter or your notes. Read the directions carefully before answering the questions. Additional practice tests are available at this textbook's website.

How to Use the Special Features in the Appendixes

In the back of *Essential Study Skills,* Fifth Edition, you will find four appendices. Take time to examine the contents of each appendix before the term begins. *Appendix A* contains the materials you will need to score and record your chapter profiles. *Appendix B* contains forms that you may need to use during the course of the term. *Appendix C* contains the *Learning Options* that may be used for special assignments or portfolio projects. *Appendix D* consists of a full psychology chapter, *Health, Stress, and Coping;* many exercises in the textbook provide you with the opportunity to apply the study skills directly to this psychology chapter. In addition to using Appendix D for applying skills, you will find that the information in the chapter is important, meaningful, and beneficial for your personal health and well-being.

A Note From the Author

Your goal is not to learn *about* study skills, but to learn *to use* powerful study skills to consistently be able to accomplish other goals and achieve success. Learning is a lifelong process. Each time you are faced with a new learning situation—whether at school, at home, or at work—you can draw upon the skills you have learned in this textbook. By applying the skills of goal setting, time management, concentration, processing information, strengthening memory, and acquiring new knowledge to any new task at hand, you will be prepared to experience the rewards of success . . . again and again and again. May my commitment to you, belief in you, and support of you in the learning process be reflected in the pages of this textbook.

—Linda Wong

Quick Start Checklist for the First Week of Classes

❏ **Register for your classes before the term begins.**

❏ **Obtain a printout of your classes.** Complete the Class Schedule in Appendix B, page A-5.

❏ **Become familiar with the campus and the locations of key departments, services, and facilities.**

If campus tours are not available, use a campus map to explore the campus and its facilities. Take time to locate the following areas:

1. Your classrooms and closest restrooms
2. Most convenient parking areas or bus stops
3. Financial Aid office
4. Career Counseling, Counseling/ Advising offices
5. Student Records or Registrar's office
6. Student Health
7. Library
8. Computer labs
9. Bookstore
10. Tutoring centers
11. Student Activities/Student Government
12. Cafeteria

❏ **Inquire how to access computer labs, an e-mail account, and the Internet.**

❏ **Visit the library.**

Learn the procedures for locating and checking out materials, the hours the library is open, and the availability of library orientation workshops.

❏ **Organize your notebooks.**

Use dividers to set up a three-ring notebook with sections for each of your classes. If you need to use more than one notebook, consider a notebook for the MWF classes and another for the T/Th classes. In each section of your notebook, organize the following materials:

1. Your weekly schedule of classes (See the Class Schedule form in Appendix B.)
2. The course *syllabus* (which is an outline of the class and the requirements)
3. A list of names and phone numbers of other students in class whom you may want to call to discuss homework assignments or meet for a study group
4. All of your class notes, handouts, and completed assignments arranged in chronological order

❏ **Create a term-long calendar.**

Locate a month-by-month planner or use a regular calendar to record all scheduled tests, midterms, due dates for projects, study-group meetings, conferences, and final exams. Begin by carefully examining each course syllabus for important test dates, project dates, and final exam dates. Also, refer to your college calendar for the term for additional dates of importance (holidays, last day to change grade options or drop courses, and special college events). Keep the monthly calendar in the front of your notebook. Plan to update it throughout the term.

❑ **Decide on a system to use to record all homework assignments.**

Select an easy-to-use system for recording your homework assignments. While some instructors provide students with daily assignment sheets, most do not. The system you select should provide you with a list of tasks or assignments that need to be done.

One system that works effectively is to title a sheet of notebook paper "Assignments." Place this Assignments page in the front of each section of your notebook. Use this page *every time* an assignment is given. Write the date the assignment is given, the specific assignment, the date it is due, and a place to check that the assignment is done. Your assignment sheet will look like this:

Assignments—Math 60

Date	Assignment	Due	Done
10/3	Read pages 110–125	10/5	x
	Do odd-numbered problems on 112, 115, 118, 125	10/5	x
10/5	Study for quiz on Chapter 3	10/7	

A second system involves using a commercial daily or weekly planner that has enough room for you to write assignments and their due dates. Check off the assignments as you complete them. A week in your weekly planner would show the assignments on the days they were given.

You can create your own weekly planner page using unlined notebook paper. Make six columns (one for each school day of the week and one to list your classes) and enough rows to show all of your classes. Each time an assignment is given, write the assignment on your planner page. Assignments can be checked off after they are completed. Your weekly planner page would look like this:

classes	Mon.	Tues.	Wed.	Thurs.	Fri.
math					
writing					
theater					
psych.					

❑ **Become familiar with your textbooks by surveying each textbook.**

Before you begin attending classes, get a head start by surveying your textbooks. Surveying a textbook involves becoming familiar with the features of the book by previewing or looking through specific sections in the textbook before you begin reading. Surveying, which often takes fifteen minutes to half an hour per book, will enable you to use the book more effectively and more efficiently throughout the entire term. Take time to complete the following six steps to survey your textbooks.

Step 1: Look at the title page, copyright page, and table of contents in the front of the book.

Step 2: Locate and read the introductory information. This section may also be labeled Preface, To the Teacher, or To the Student. This introductory material often provides valuable background information on the book and the author and clarifies the book's purpose.

Step 3: Look in the back of the book for an *appendix* or appendixes. An appendix provides you with supplementary materials that were not included in the chapters. You may find answer keys to exercises; additional exercises; practice tests; additional readings; frequently used charts, formulas, or theorems; maps; or lengthier documents.

Step 4: Look to see if the textbook has a *glossary* (a mini-dictionary that defines key terms used in the textbook).

Step 5: Look to see if your textbook has a section in the back of the book titled *References* or *Bibliography*. This section provides you with the names of authors and the books, magazines, or articles that were used by the author as sources of information. This list of references can also be used if you wish to research a topic further.

Step 6: The last step of surveying is to locate the *index* in the back of the book. The index is an alphabetical listing of subjects used throughout the textbook. An index can be used to quickly locate page numbers when you want to

    1. review a specific topic that was discussed in class.
    2. locate a topic for a class assignment or discussion.
    3. review specific information for a topic for an essay.
    4. clarify information written in your notes.

❑ **Show up the first day of class ready to learn.**

Many students know that the term begins more smoothly when they are in class the first day and are ready to work. This is the day that the syllabus is usually discussed, introductions are made, and class expectations are explained. The following suggestions can help you get off to a good start:

1. Be on time.

2. Sit toward the front of the classroom rather than "hiding" in the back row. You will be able to see better, will concentrate more easily, and will show you are interested in the course.

3. Come prepared with your notebook, paper, pencils, pens, the textbook, and any other materials that you might need.

4. Be friendly! Show others that you are approachable and willing to be a part of the group. Your friendliness can help set a positive tone in the classroom.

5. Plan to listen carefully and be attentive.

6. Use a highlighter to highlight important information discussed on the syllabus.

7. Plan to take notes. Later in the term, you will learn an effective notetaking system. For now, the format you use for notes is not as important as the habit of writing down information as it is presented. Your notes should also include a record of your homework assignments.

❑ **Make a commitment to dedicate sufficient time each week to studying.**

One of the most common mistakes students make involves allocation of time. *Time on task,* or time devoted to studying, is highly correlated to academic success. Students who spend too little time reading, studying, memorizing, and applying information in a variety of ways often struggle with the process of learning. In addition to completing reading assignments, written work, papers, and problems, you should dedicate some time each week to reviewing information that has been covered. Time management will be covered later in the term, but for now, you can use a time-management technique called the 2:1 ratio. For most or all of your classes that involve textbook reading assignments and written work, plan to study two hours for every one hour in class. Therefore, if one of your classes meets for three hours a week, plan to study six hours a week for that class. The six hours of study time can be spread throughout the week. You can use your weekly planner or schedule to identify the total hours you plan to study during the week for each of your classes. Your classes and study blocks for each class can be planned on the Weekly Time-Management Schedule in Appendix B, page A-6.

❑ **Plan to ask questions about the class, the expectations, and the assignments.**

Becoming an *active learner* is important. Be willing to show your interest by asking questions in class. Most instructors are very willing to expand directions or give further explanations about classroom or textbook topics. Student questions also help promote interesting classroom discussions.

❑ **Monitor your stress levels.**

Some stress is normal. Normal stress is manageable and can even be a motivator. New or unfamiliar situations are commonly linked to feelings of self-doubt, lower confidence levels, and lower self-esteem. These feelings are part of the "learning cycle" and weaken or dwindle as you gain familiarity with and "settle in" to the new routine, expectations, and tasks to be completed. Chapter 5 introduces you to a variety of concentration, relaxation, and stress-reduction techniques that will assist you in keeping your stress at a comfortable, manageable level. In addition, this course itself will reduce stress levels as you gain skills and confidence by learning strategies designed to strengthen your ability to do well academically.

Stressors, or occurrences in the process of life that cause stress, can occur unexpectedly. Most colleges or universities have counselors, support groups, workshops, or courses that can help individuals with stress reduction and with periods of transition. Schedule a time with a counselor to explore the resources and options available on your campus.

CHAPTER 1

Discovering and Using Your Learning Styles

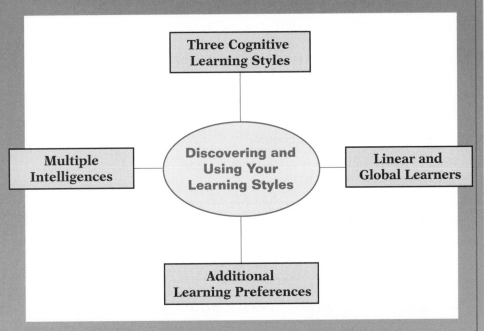

Understanding your individual style of learning can help you become a more effective learner. In this chapter, you will examine your preference for using your visual, auditory, or kinesthetic modality for learning new information. You will also become familiar with a wide range of multisensory strategies to use when you study. These new learning strategies capitalize on your strengths, add interest and motivation to studying, and actively engage you in the learning process. After completing a linear and global learners inventory, and reading about learning environments and interactive versus reflective learners, you will gain additional insights about yourself in different learning situations. Finally, you will learn about the eight intelligences that you already possess. Through this process of understanding more about yourself as a learner, you will quickly discover that you already have many skills and abilities that will contribute to your college success.

1

Chapter 1 Learning Styles Profile

ANSWER each profile question honestly. Your answers should reflect what you do, not what you wish to do. Check YES if you do the statement always or most of the time. Check NO if you do the statement seldom or never.

SCORE the profile. To get your score, give yourself one point for every answer that matches the answer key on page A-3 in the back of your book.

RECORD your score on the Master Profile Chart on page A-2 in the column that shows the chapter number.

ONLINE: You can complete the profile and get your score online at this textbook's website.

	YES	NO
1. I am aware of my learning style preference as a visual, auditory, or kinesthetic learner.	_____	_____
2. I can describe four or more effective learning strategies for each learning preference: visual, auditory, or kinesthetic.	_____	_____
3. I tend to use identical study methods for all of my classes.	_____	_____
4. I usually study new information in a straightforward manner without spending time making creative study or review tools.	_____	_____
5. I know whether my thinking patterns reflect global (right-brain) or linear (left-brain) learning patterns.	_____	_____
6. I use a variety of learning strategies when I study.	_____	_____
7. I have difficulty adjusting my learning strategies when my learning styles do not match my instructor's teaching styles.	_____	_____
8. I use study strategies that capitalize on my learning styles and preferences.	_____	_____
9. I recognize which of Howard Gardner's eight intelligences are strongest in me.	_____	_____
10. I am confident that I can adjust my learning strategies to meet the demands of new learning situations or tasks.	_____	_____

Reflection Writing 1
Chapter 1

On separate paper, in a journal, or online at this textbook's website, respond to the following questions.

1. What is your profile score for this chapter? What does it mean to you?

2. In general terms, how do you tend to proceed when learning something new? How do you begin to tackle the new task? What approaches do you use to work your way through the new learning process? What learning techniques generally work best for you?

Three Cognitive Learning Styles

Learning is an individualized process; different educational and background experiences, personality traits, levels of motivation, and numerous other variables affect the way you learn. The term *cognitive* refers to thinking and reasoning processes, so **cognitive learning styles** refers to the general way people *prefer* to have information presented in order to problem solve, process, learn, and remember new information. Three commonly recognized learning styles (also called **learning modalities**) are *visual, auditory,* and *kinesthetic.* You can lay a strong foundation for learning thoroughly and effectively when you understand your preferred learning style and select study strategies that capitalize on your learning preferences and personal strengths.

Common Characteristics of Visual, Auditory, and Kinesthetic Learners

The following chart shows common characteristics of each of the three types of learners or learning styles. A person does not necessarily possess abilities or strengths in all of the characteristics but may instead "specialize" in some of the characteristics. Some of this may be due to a person's educational or personal background. For example, an auditory learner may be strong in the area of language skills but may not have had the experience to develop skills with a foreign language or music.

Common Characteristics

Visual	• Learn best by seeing information • Can easily recall information in the form of numbers, words, phrases, or sentences • Can easily understand and recall information presented in pictures, charts, or diagrams • Have strong visualization skills and can look up (often up to the left) and "see" information • Can make "movies in their minds" of information they are reading • Have strong visual-spatial skills that involve sizes, shapes, textures, angles, and dimensions • Pay close attention and learn to interpret body language (facial expressions, eyes, stance) • Have a keen awareness of aesthetics, the beauty of the physical environment, and visual media
Auditory	• Learn best by hearing information • Can accurately remember details of information heard in conversations or lectures • Have strong language skills that include well-developed vocabularies and appreciation of words • Have strong oral communication skills that enable them to carry on conversations and be articulate • Have "finely tuned ears" and may find learning a foreign language relatively easy • Hear tones, rhythms, and notes of music and often have exceptional musical talents
Kinesthetic	• Learn best by using their hands ("hands-on" learning) or by full body movement • Learn best by doing • Learn well in activities that involve performing (athletes, actors, dancers) • Work well with their hands in areas such as repair work, sculpting, art, or working with tools • Are well coordinated, with a strong sense of timing and body movements • Often wiggle, tap their feet, or move their legs when they sit • Often have been labeled "hyperactive"

EXERCISE 1.1   Learning Styles Inventory

Complete the following Learning Styles Inventory by reading each statement carefully. Check YES if the statement relates to you all or most of the time. Check NO if the statement seldom or never relates to you. There is no in-between option, so you must check YES or NO. Your first, quick response to a question is usually the best response to use.

	YES	NO
1. I like to listen and discuss information with another person.	_____	_____
2. I could likely learn or review information effectively by hearing my own voice on tape.	_____	_____
3. I prefer to learn something new by reading about it.	_____	_____
4. I often write down directions someone gives me so I do not forget them.	_____	_____
5. I enjoy physical sports and exercise.	_____	_____
6. I learn best when I can see new information in picture or diagram form.	_____	_____
7. I am easily able to visualize or picture things in my mind.	_____	_____
8. I learn best when someone talks or explains something to me.	_____	_____
9. I usually write things down so that I can look back at them later.	_____	_____
10. I pay attention to the rhythm and patterns of notes I hear in music.	_____	_____
11. I have a good memory for the words and melodies of old songs.	_____	_____
12. I like to participate in small-group discussions.	_____	_____
13. I often remember the sizes, shapes, and colors of objects when they are no longer in sight.	_____	_____
14. I often repeat out loud verbal directions that someone gives me.	_____	_____
15. I enjoy working with my hands.	_____	_____
16. I can remember the faces of actors, settings, and other visual details of movies I have seen.	_____	_____
17. I often use my hands and body movements when explaining something to someone else.	_____	_____
18. I prefer standing up and working on a chalkboard or flip chart to sitting down and working on paper.	_____	_____
19. I often seem to learn better if I can get up and move around while I study.	_____	_____
20. I prefer pictures or diagrams instead of paragraph explanations to assemble something, such as a bike.	_____	_____
21. I remember objects better when I have touched them or worked with them.	_____	_____
22. I learn best by watching someone else first.	_____	_____
23. I tend to doodle when I think about a problem or situation.	_____	_____
24. I speak a foreign language.	_____	_____
25. I am comfortable building or constructing things.	_____	_____

	YES	NO
26. I can follow the plot of a story when I listen to a book on tape.	_____	_____
27. I often repair things at home.	_____	_____
28. I can understand information when I hear it on tape.	_____	_____
29. I am good at using machines or tools.	_____	_____
30. I enjoy role-playing or participating in skits.	_____	_____
31. I enjoy acting or doing pantomimes.	_____	_____
32. I can easily see patterns in designs.	_____	_____
33. I work best when I can move around freely.	_____	_____
34. I like to recite or write poetry.	_____	_____
35. I can usually understand people with foreign accents or dialects.	_____	_____
36. I can hear many different pitches or melodies in music.	_____	_____
37. I like to dance and create new movements or steps.	_____	_____
38. I participate in activities that require physical coordination.	_____	_____
39. I follow written directions better than oral ones.	_____	_____
40. I can easily recognize differences between similar sounds.	_____	_____
41. I like to create or use jingles/rhymes to learn things.	_____	_____
42. I prefer classes with hands-on experiences.	_____	_____
43. I can quickly tell if two geometric shapes are identical.	_____	_____
44. The things I remember best are the things I have seen in print or pictures.	_____	_____
45. I follow oral directions better than written ones.	_____	_____
46. I could learn the names of fifteen medical instruments more easily if I could touch and examine them.	_____	_____
47. I remember details better when I say them aloud.	_____	_____
48. I can look at a shape and copy it correctly on paper.	_____	_____
49. I can usually read a map without difficulty.	_____	_____
50. I can "hear" a person's exact words and tone of voice days after he or she has spoken to me.	_____	_____
51. I remember directions best when someone gives me landmarks, such as specific buildings and trees.	_____	_____
52. I have a good eye for colors and color combinations.	_____	_____
53. I like to paint, draw, sculpt, or be creative with my hands.	_____	_____
54. I can vividly picture the details of a meaningful past experience.	_____	_____

Turn to the next page to score your Learning Styles Inventory.

Scoring Your Profile

1. Ignore the NO answers. Work only with the questions that have a YES answer.
2. For every YES answer, look at the number of the question. Find the number in the following chart and circle that number.
3. When you finish, not all the numbers in the following boxes will be circled. Your answers will very likely not match anyone else's.
4. Count the number of circles for the Visual box and write the total on the line. Do the same for the Auditory box and Kinesthetic box.

Visual					Auditory					Kinesthetic				
3,	4,	6,	7,	9,	1,	2,	8,	10,	11,	5,	15,	17,	18,	19,
13,	16,	20,	22,	32,	12,	14,	24,	26,	28,	21,	23,	25,	27,	29,
39,	43,	44,	48,	49,	34,	35,	36,	40,	41,	30,	31,	33,	37,	38,
51,	52,	54			45,	47,	50			42,	46,	53		

Total: _____   Total: _____   Total: _____

Analyzing Your Scores

Highest Score	=	Preferred learning style
Lowest Score	=	Weakest or least developed modality
Scores >10	=	Frequently used modality
Scores <10	=	Less frequently used modality

Your highest score is your preferred way to receive and process new information. If your two highest scores are the same, you can work equally well in each of the modalities. You may find yourself alternating between these two modalities, depending on the learning situation. Your lowest score is your least frequently used or your weakest modality. Scores higher than 10 indicate that you use the modality frequently, even if it is not your preferred modality. Scores lower than 10 indicate modalities that you do not use frequently. Your weakest modality and any modalities with scores lower than 10 may be the result of little or no training in techniques to strengthen these modalities, or they may be due to a physical or neurological impairment (such as a learning disability) that makes using the modality difficult. In such cases, students can learn to capitalize on their strengths and to use alternative learning strategies to process information.

Learning Style Preferences

The Learning Style Inventory indicates your **learning style preference**. This basically reflects your tendency to use the cognitive learning style or modality with the highest score when you have a choice of how to learn or process new information. It also reflects the way you would prefer to have information presented to you. For example, if you are in a work situation, and your employer asks you to learn a new process on a computer or the operation of a new piece of equipment, you would learn most comfortably if you used your strongest modality. A **visual learner** may prefer to read the manual or learn from pictures, charts, or graphs. An **auditory learner** may prefer to be told how the new process or equipment works. A **kinesthetic learner** may prefer to be shown how the process or piece of equipment works and then be given an opportunity to try each step during the training session.

Cognitive Learning Style Preferences

1. **Visual learners** learn and remember best by *seeing* and *visualizing* information.
2. **Auditory learners** learn and remember best by *hearing* information.
3. **Kinesthetic learners** learn and remember best by using large and small body *movements* and *hands-on experiences*.

The tendencies toward your preferred learning style started in your childhood. If you are a visual learner, you may have been fascinated by books, pictures, colors, shapes, and animation. If you are an auditory learner, you may have been perceived as a nonstop talker who frequently asked questions, sang, or recited nursery rhymes. If you are a kinesthetic learner, you very likely were a bundle of energy and actively explored your surroundings—running, jumping, rolling around, taking things apart, and building things out of whatever objects were available.

As you matured, entered into the educational system, and were exposed to new learning situations, you learned to use, strengthen, and integrate all of your modalities. The modality preference still exists, but you have broadened your skills so that you are able, in most situations, to learn even when information is presented in a form that is not based on your preferred method of learning. An essential goal for you as an adult learner is to continue to develop skills that enable you to receive and process information regardless of the form in which it is presented. Strive to become increasingly more comfortable and confident working outside your preferred learning style. By using a variety of learning strategies, some that capitalize on your learning preference and some that will help you strengthen your weaker modalities, you will increase your ability to perform well in a wide range of learning situations. Modifications in learning strategies as well as college accommodations for students with learning disabilities can often be implemented to help students learn to process information successfully. In each of the following examples, notice how each student could implement alternative learning strategies to process and learn the information.

1. Patrice had a low score in the visual category of the Learning Styles Inventory. She has more than average difficulty reading a map or following a set of directions drawn in the form of diagrams or pictures. She has difficulty interpreting charts and diagrams in her textbooks. She has weak spatial skills that are necessary to understand information in pictorial forms.

   Alternative Strategies: Participate in discussion groups or work with a tutor to receive verbal explanations of the graphic material. After discussing the material, make lists of the important points or write a summary to explain the graphic material.

2. Mandy had a low score in the auditory category of the Learning Styles Inventory. She has problems following and comprehending lectures. The information gets scrambled, and she finds following the sequence of ideas difficult. Mandy does not have a hearing loss, but she does have difficulty with auditory processing.

   Alternative Strategies: Explore possible accommodations for lecture classes. Perhaps the lectures could be taped and reviewed outside of class. Perhaps a classmate could provide copies of lecture notes. Meet with the instructor to explore the possibility of getting copies of overheads used in the lecture.

3. Ralph had a low score in the kinesthetic category. He readily admits that he has always had poor coordination skills. He finds detailed work that requires the use of his hands difficult to complete to his satisfaction. He has poor—sometimes almost illegible—handwriting. In his science lab, he feels as though he is "all thumbs" and that his finished products look immature and incomplete.

Alternative Strategies: Use a computer for written assignments. Ask a tutor or another student to help identify the steps that need to be done to complete a lab project. Allocate more time to work through each step carefully and slowly.

Now that you are aware of your learning style and learning preference, you can begin to combine learning strategies, selecting some that utilize your strengths and some that will help you "stretch" and strengthen your other modalities. Using a variety of learning strategies benefits you in many ways. First, it adds variety, motivation, and interest to the learning process. Second, you will gain confidence in your ability to handle information regardless of the form in which it is presented. In addition to these benefits, as you will learn in the next section and in Chapter 2, your ability to recall information from your memory will be strengthened when you process information by using more than one sensory channel.

Group Processing: A Collaborative Learning Activity

Form groups of three or four students. Then complete the following directions.

Create a chart with three columns. Label the columns *visual, auditory,* and *kinesthetic.* As a group, brainstorm different learning strategies or "things you can do when you study" that capitalize on each of the learning modalities. Use your own experiences and ideas for study strategies on the chart; do not refer to your textbook. You may use the following examples to begin your chart.

Group scores:		
Visual	*Auditory*	*Kinesthetic*
Use colored pens to highlight	Talk out loud to study	Make wall charts to review

Effective Learning Strategies

Using effective learning strategies will affect your memory and your ability to recall information. As you take in and process information, your brain uses visual, auditory, and motor (kinesthetic) codes (encoding) to accept and move the information into different locations in your memory system. When you use your strongest modality or your preferred learning style, you may notice that you can take in and process information more easily and smoothly. Recognize, however, that you use all of your secondary channels to learn, so to some degree you are a visual, an auditory, and a kinesthetic learner.

Visual learners prefer to have information presented to them in a visual form, which includes pictures, graphs, or charts as well as information printed in lists or paragraphs. Visual learners also favor creating and using visual strategies when they study. Having something that they can *see*, examine for details, and even possibly memorize as a mental image is important and effective for visual learners.

Auditory learners prefer to have information presented to them verbally. They learn by listening to others explain, debate, summarize, or discuss information about topics they are studying. Auditory learners, however, are not passive. Auditory learners like to *talk* and *listen* as they learn. They often get involved with discussions and learn by explaining information in their own words, expressing their understanding or opinions, and providing comments and feedback to other speakers.

Kinesthetic learners prefer to have information presented to them in some form of movement. They learn best by *doing*. Kinesthetic learners often process information more clearly when they are involved in activities that use large muscles or body movements, such as working at large charts, role-playing, or dancing. They also may prefer learning situations that require small muscle activities in a hands-on environment. They are able to remember and recall information more readily if they have the opportunity to feel, handle, use, manipulate, sort, assemble, or experiment with concrete objects. Large and small muscles hold memory, so involving movement in the learning process creates muscle memory.

Knowing how to use a variety of learning strategies for each of the modalities enhances your ability to store and recall information from your memory system. The following chart shows a variety of learning strategies that you can incorporate into your tailored approach to learning.

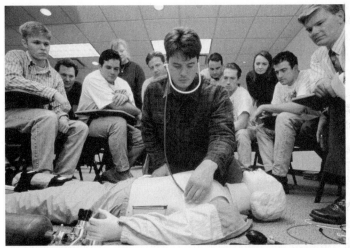

Does this learning strategy work with your strengths? Consider trying it out before you make a decision.

Learning Strategies

Visual

- When you read, use different-colored highlighter pens to **highlight** important information such as facts, definitions, formulas, and steps. Colors often stand out better and create stronger visual images in your memory.
- Take time to **visualize** pictures, charts, graphs, or small sections of printed information. Follow this with time to practice recalling the visual memories when you study and review.
- Create **movies in your mind** of information that you read or hear. Use your visual memory as a television screen with the information moving across the screen in an organized way.
- Create **visual study tools** such as visual mappings, hierarchies, and comparison charts to represent information that you are studying. Show several levels of detail on your visual study tools.
- Expand the **chapter mapping** at the beginning of each chapter. Add details next to each chapter heading. Add colors, shapes, or pictures next to main ideas or key details.
- Enhance your notes, flash cards, or any other study tools by adding **colors** and **pictures** so that the information stands out more clearly in your memory.
- **Copy** information in your own handwriting. Practice looking away and visualizing the information you copied.
- Use your keen visual skills to **observe** people to pick up clues that tell you the importance of what they are saying, their attitude or feelings toward the subject, and what you are expected to know.
- **Carry a pen and notepad** with you so you can write down information or directions. You can study or memorize the information at a later time.

Auditory

- **Talk out loud** to explain new information, express your ideas, paraphrase another speaker, or summarize a lecture or a conversation.
- **Read out loud.** Reading out loud (verbalizing), with a normal voice or with exaggerated expression, often increases comprehension and clarifies confusing information. The natural rhythm and patterns in language often group information automatically into meaningful units.
- **Ask questions** to show your interest, seek clarification, and interact with others. Asking questions opens the door for receiving verbal information and encoding information into your memory system through your auditory channel.
- Work with a **tutor,** a **study buddy,** or in a **study group.** Studying with others provides you with the opportunity to ask questions, articulate answers, explain to others, and express your ideas.
- **Recite** frequently when you study. Reciting involves recalling information, stating the information out loud, in your own words and in complete sentences, without reading or referring to printed information. Reciting provides you with instant feedback about your level of understanding.
- **Tape the lectures.** For lectures in a difficult class, take notes in class, but back up your notes by taping the lecture. (Ask for the instructor's consent before taping.) After class, review only the sections of the lecture on tape that you found unclear or confusing.
- **Make your own study tapes** by either reading or reciting the main ideas, facts, or significant details that you need to learn. Study tapes that have your own voice often strengthen auditory memory and recall.
- **Explain** information that you are learning to another person or even to an imaginary person. Being able to explain information clearly can provide valuable feedback about your level of understanding.
- Create **rhymes, jingles,** or **songs** to help you remember specific facts.
- Use **technology** with audio features or voice-activated software. Spell checkers, calculators, and CD-ROM programs are a few examples of products available to auditory learners.

Learning Strategies, *continued*

Kinesthetic

- **Handle** objects, tools, or machinery that you are studying. For example, handle the rocks in a geology class or repeat computer applications several times.
- **Create manipulatives** (study tools that you can move around with your hands). Flash cards or index cards, for example, can be created and then shuffled, spread out, sorted, or stacked into categories.
- **Cut charts or diagrams apart** so that you can practice assembling them in their correct order.
- **Use exaggerated movements and hand gestures** when you study. Drama, dance, pantomime, and role-playing use large muscle movement. Moving or pointing fingers and expressing information and emotions through hand gestures involve small muscle movement.
- **Use a computer** to type information and access muscle memory through keyboard strokes.
- **Walk** as you recite or practice information. Pacing or walking with study materials in hand helps some people learn without being distracted by the discomfort of sitting too long.
- Work at a **chalkboard, flip chart,** or **large poster paper** to create study tools. List, draw, practice, or write while you stand up and work on a large surface.
- Learn through **creative movement and activities.** For example, if you are studying perimeters in math, tape off an area of a room and walk the perimeter.
- Create **action games.** Convert the information you are studying into a game, such as Twenty-One Questions, Jeopardy, or Concentration. Review the information by playing the game with another student or group.

Multisensory Learning

As you experiment with the various learning strategies shown in the previous charts, strive to design **multisensory strategies,** strategies that combine two or more modalities. Explore combinations that help you *see* the information in new ways, *say* the information you are learning, and *interact* with the information through some form of movement or hands-on activities. For example, **verbalize** (read out loud) as you copy the steps used to solve a math problem, color-code each step, and **recite** (talk out loud as you recall *information from memory*). As a second example, assume that the instructor in your computer class assigns a complex project to be done in the computer lab. You decide to discuss the lab project with another student, take notes on important points or steps, reread the notes out loud to check their clarity, and highlight key points or steps. You perform the operation on the computer to your satisfaction and then reinforce the learning by completing the process a second time. In this example, you *see* your color-coded notes, *talk* about the information, plus *write* and perform the hands-on learning.

As you take on new learning tasks, make a conscious effort to incorporate all three modalities in your learning approach. Using multisensory strategies when you study boosts your memory and provides you with multiple ways to access and recall information. It also provides you with options so that you can adjust or modify your strategies to fit the requirements of various courses. By "mixing and matching" visual, auditory, and kinesthetic learning strategies, you can find the most effective combinations of strategies to succeed in each course.

EXERCISE 1.2   Group Discussion, Part 1

Select the strategy you would prefer to use in the following learning situations. Then discuss your choices with the members of your group.

1. To learn the steps to use to solve a specific kind of math problem, I would
   a. refer to the steps and the example in the textbook, read through the steps several times, copy the steps on my paper, color-code each step, and rework the example at least one time.
   b. work with a tutor or a study partner, explain each step to the person, tell why it is important and how it works, apply the steps to new math problems, get feedback from the tutor or compare my answers with my partner's work.
   c. write the steps on a piece of paper (without the number of each step), cut the list of steps apart, practice placing them in the correct order, and rework the examples in the textbook, placing the strips of paper with each step next to the steps in the problems.

2. To learn the fourteen key terms and definitions in the Appendix D chapter (see page A-44), I would
   a. work with a study partner to take turns quizzing each other by reciting the definitions and giving each other feedback.
   b. use any available software with a flash program to practice the definitions and check my accuracy.
   c. use index cards to make my own flash cards, self-quiz with the cards, check my accuracy, and make a pile of the cards I need to study further.

Group Discussion, Part 2

As a group, solve the following problem. Pay attention to the approach your group uses to reach the final answer.

A parent and a child are standing together on the sidewalk. They both start walking at the same time. Each person begins the first step with the right foot. The child must take three steps for every two steps the parent takes. How many steps must the child take until they both land again on the same foot?

1. How many steps did the child need to take? _____

2. Did they both land on the right foot or the left foot? _____

3. How did your group solve this problem? _____

You can use the following space to solve the problem.

EXERCISE 1.3 **Using Cognitive Modalities**

Work by yourself, with a partner, or in a small group to complete parts 1 and 2.

Part 1: *Read each statement below. Circle **V** (visual), **A** (auditory), or **K** (kinesthetic) to indicate the most dominant modality used by the person.*

V   A   K   1. Without reviewing his textbook, Mark can see details of pictures he studied in a previous chapter.

V   A   K   2. Jorge may distract others, but jiggling his legs and tapping his pencil on the desk actually help him maintain his concentration.

V   A   K   3. Lori is studying interior design, for which she seems to be well suited; she has always had a good eye for coordinating colors, fabrics, and accessories.

V   A   K   4. In our Acting 1 class, James amazed us with the messages he could convey with his refined movements and facial expressions during his mime performance.

V   A   K   5. LinLee recounted her conversation with her grandfather; she described the tone of his voice and specific words of advice that he shared with her.

V   A   K   6. Leroy wants to capitalize on his talent for working with lighting, shading, angles, and composition, so he is majoring in photography.

V   A   K   7. Raina has notebooks filled with original poetry; she participates in a poetry reading group that meets twice a month.

V   A   K   8. Maggie won a blue ribbon for her bronze sculpture at the mayor's art show; several of her pieces of pottery also received recognition.

Part 2: *The following learning strategies may involve using one or more modalities. Circle **V, A,** or **K** to indicate the modality or modalities each strategy emphasizes.*

V   A   K   1. Within the first week of every class, Sharon finds a "study buddy"— someone who wants to meet on a regular basis to discuss class work and topics.

V   A   K   2. Simon learns shapes for his geometry class by tracing over them several times with his finger and then repeating the process on his desk.

V   A   K   3. Liz types all her papers on a computer and then asks a tutor or a friend to read each paper out loud so she can listen to the way she expressed her ideas.

V   A   K   4. Cindy is an excellent notetaker. After each class, she uses three different colors to highlight main ideas, terminology, and important details.

V   A   K   5. Mark loves history and gets excited thinking about the relationships among different events. He tacked a long piece of paper across his bedroom wall so he can chart all kinds of events on a continuous time line.

V   A   K   6. Kathryn enjoys reading, but no one likes to be around her when she reads. She reads everything out loud and uses a lot of hand gestures.

V   A   K   7. Lily loves to make flash cards for all her classes. She color-codes them by chapter. She practices reciting the information and then shuffles all the stacks together to create a variety of interesting review activities for her study group.

V   A   K   8. After Paula reads each literature assignment, she closes her eyes and tells her friends she is studying. At first they did not believe her, but then she told them that she creates an entire movie in her mind about the literature she just read.

ONLINE PRACTICE 1

Visit the *Essential Study Skills*, Fifth Edition, website and go to Chapter 1. Click on **Practice 1: Cognitive Learning Style Preferences**. Complete the ten-question interactive multiple-choice quiz. Upon completion of the quiz, you will receive your score. You can exit at that time, or you can print or e-mail your results to your instructor.

Reflection Writing 2
Chapter 1

On separate paper, in a journal, or online at this textbook's website, respond to the following questions.

1. What have you learned thus far about your learning style and learning style preferences?

2. Give two or more examples of learning situations in which your learning style preference affected the way you approached a new learning situation.

3. Make a chart with two columns. In the first column, list the strategies from the charts of learning strategies on pages 10–11 that you currently use. In the second column, list the strategies that you will strive to learn to use this term.

Currently use	Goals to learn to use

Linear and Global Learners

The cognitive learning styles model with three basic modalities (visual, auditory, and kinesthetic) is but one of many learning styles models that encourages individuals to identify their preferred ways to receive and process new information. The goal behind every learning styles inventory is for you to increase your awareness about the conditions and the strategies that work most effectively for you to learn information. Remember in all cases that no one learning style is better than another; each style is simply a distinctive way of learning, interacting, or responding.

Research beginning in the late 1960s discovered that the human brain consists of two hemispheres or cortices that are connected by a complex network of nerve fibers called the *corpus callosum*. Though the two hemispheres are linked together neurologically, each hemisphere dominates specific kinds of mental activities and learning patterns. People tend to have a preference for initially processing information through the left hemisphere (also referred to as the left brain) or the right hemisphere (the right brain). However, once they receive and start processing information from one side of the brain, the information is then shared with the other side of the brain for total processing. The **brain dominance theory,** another cognitive model, identifies specific functions of each hemisphere.

The *left hemisphere* of the brain processes mental activities that involve logic, sequences such as lists or steps, verbal language (words), numbers, and analytical thinking. Because the left hemisphere deals with logic, structure, and predictable patterns, people who begin the initial learning or intake process by activating the left hemisphere first are referred to as left-brain or **linear learners**. They prefer information that provides them with specific details, clearly defined steps, words, numbers, and logical arguments. Because of this linear preference, they tend to master information in the structured sequence in which it is presented. In courses that require problem solving, such as science or mathematics, they learn the fundamentals, such as problem-solving steps, and then proceed to apply the steps to solve problems or answer questions. They tend to do well in straightforward, detail-oriented lectures and with textbooks that present information in a sequential, structured, and clear manner.

The *right hemisphere* of the brain processes mental activities that involve spatial skills, pictures, colors, visual memories (visualizations), imagination, creativity, intuition, and rhythm. Because the right hemisphere deals with information in more generalized or big-picture patterns, people who begin the initial learning or intake process by activating the right hemisphere first are referred to as right-brain or **global learners**. They prefer information in the form of pictures, charts, diagrams, and colorful visual stimuli. They enjoy using their creativity and intuition to process information, its meaning, and its applications. Because of this global preference, they tend to learn details in random order; they may not understand the details clearly until the *light bulb turns on*, and all the details come together to form a whole picture. In problem-solving situations, they tend to take intuitive leaps to find solutions, sometimes creating their own problem-solving steps. They may be unable to explain to others how they arrive at their solutions. Global learners do well in classes that involve discussions, group activities, creative problem solving, and creative interpretations such as literature, poetry, creative writing, or personal development. To learn from textbooks, global learners often find that reading a chapter introduction, skimming through the entire chapter, and reading the summary help to create a big picture for them before they begin learning specific details.

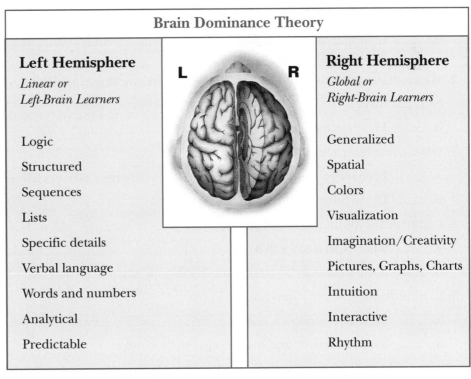

Brain Dominance Theory

Left Hemisphere *Linear or Left-Brain Learners*	**Right Hemisphere** *Global or Right-Brain Learners*
Logic	Generalized
Structured	Spatial
Sequences	Colors
Lists	Visualization
Specific details	Imagination/Creativity
Verbal language	Pictures, Graphs, Charts
Words and numbers	Intuition
Analytical	Interactive
Predictable	Rhythm

Source: Douglas Bernstein and Peggy Nash, *Essentials of Psychology,* 2nd ed. (Boston: Houghton Mifflin Co., 2002), p. 59. Copyright © by Houghton Mifflin Co. Used with permission.

As previously mentioned, one hemisphere is *dominant* and begins the mental processing activity. The information is then shared with the other hemisphere, so both sides work to process information—but in different ways. For example, consider the mental activities involved in the process of composing music. Initially, you might assume that the composer is a global learner with right-brain dominance because composing involves rhythm, creativity, intuitive feelings, and imagination. After the initial process begins, however, the left-brain or linear learner skills are activated in order to apply specific musical conventions such as writing the music in a logical, recognizable format. Could a composer be a linear learner? Yes. The composer could begin by identifying a specific style or format for the composition and by analyzing the required elements. With a logical structure in mind, the right hemisphere is activated to bring creativity and imagination to the work.

To think of yourself as only a *linear learner* (left brain) or only as a *global learner* (right brain) limits your perception of yourself and your mental processing skills. Instead, think of yourself as a *whole-brain learner,* a person who has a brain hemisphere dominance for the initial intake of information, but who then combines learning activities that activate both brain hemispheres. Making a conscious effort to use a wide variety of study strategies, some linear and some global, will strengthen you as a whole-brain learner and enhance your ability to learn new information.

EXERCISE 1.4   Brain Dominance Inventory—Left/Right, Linear/Global Dominance

Answer all of these questions quickly; do not stop to analyze them. When you have no clear preference, choose the one that most closely represents your attitudes or behaviors.

1. When I buy a new product, I

   a. _____ usually read the directions and carefully follow them.

   b. _____ refer to the directions but really try and figure out how the thing operates or is put together on my own.

2. Which of these words best describes the way I perceive myself in dealing with others?

   a. _____ Structured/Rigid

   b. _____ Flexible/Open-minded

3. Concerning hunches:

   a. _____ I generally would not rely on hunches to help me make decisions.

   b. _____ I have hunches and follow many of them.

4. I make decisions mainly based on

   a. _____ what experts say will work.

   b. _____ a willingness to try things that I think might work.

5. In traveling or going to a destination, I prefer

   a. _____ to read and follow a map.

   b. _____ to get directions and map things out "my" way.

6. In school, I preferred

   a. _____ geometry.

   b. _____ algebra.

7. When I read a play or novel, I

   a. _____ see the play or novel in my head as if it were a movie/TV show.

   b. _____ read the words to obtain information.

8. When I want to remember directions, a name, or a news item, I

   a. _____ visualize the information or write notes that help me create a picture, maybe even draw the directions.

   b. _____ write structured and detailed notes.

9. I prefer to be in the class of a teacher who

   a. _____ has the class do activities and encourages class participation and discussion.

   b. _____ primarily lectures.

10. In writing, speaking, and problem solving, I am

   a. _____ usually creative, preferring to try new things.

   b. _____ seldom creative, preferring traditional solutions.

Scoring

For items 1 through 5, give yourself one point for each B answer: _____

For items 6 through 10, give yourself one point for each A answer: _____

Total Points: _____

Circle your total points on the following scale.

Left _____ Right

    1   2   3   4   5   6   7   8   9   10

Interpretation

Scores of 1 or 2:	Left-brain tendency; highly linear
Scores of 3 and possibly 4:	Left-brain or linear tendency
Scores of 4 through 7:	Possibly no dominance; flexible in learning patterns
Scores of 8 and possibly 7:	Right-brain or global tendency
Scores of 9 and 10:	Right-brain tendency; highly global

Berko, *Communicating*, 1998, pp. 75–77.

SET LEARNING GOALS

The following *Essential Strategies for Linear and Global Learners* chart highlights nine important strategies to use to capitalize on two learning styles. Place a star next to the strategies that you already use. Highlight the strategies that you plan to make a conscious effort to begin using to strengthen your ability to be a *whole-brain learner*.

Essential Strategies for Linear and Global Learners

▶ **Use your understanding of your linear or global preference to analyze and adjust to learning situations.** The following strategies promote making adjustments in your learning strategies as you strive to become a *whole-brain learner*.

▶ **Ask for a summary or list of significant points** in classes that seem too open-ended without clear conclusions, such as a poetry or literature class.

▶ **Organize a list or chart of important points** made in discussions that feel too disorganized or random to create a meaningful unit of information.

▶ **Take time to organize information logically** when dealing with information from different sources (lectures, discussions, textbooks, and multimedia sources).

▶ **Add your own heading and subheadings** to textbooks that lack a detailed organizational structure.

▶ **Ask for specific examples or anecdotes** in straightforward lectures that seem to contain only series of facts, data, or technical information.

▶ **Add color, pictures, or diagrams** to lecture notes when information is presented in a linear manner.

▶ **Ask instructors and other students questions** about connections, relationships, trends, or themes when details seem detached from a whole picture.

▶ **Get an overview of a topic before a lecture** on it by reading the introduction, skimming through the chapter, and reading the summary of the textbook chapter to get the big or whole picture.

CLASS DISCUSSION

Question: From what you can tell so far this term, what aspects of this course are compatible with linear learners? What aspects of this course are compatible with global learners?

Additional Learning Preferences

How humans process information and the factors that affect learning are areas of study that continue to expand. Theories, models, and inventories exist to assess and analyze thinking styles and emotional intelligence as well as behavioral, personality, and psychological styles. The array of inventories and learning styles at times may overwhelm you; however, keep in mind that learning style inventories are mere indicators of the way you prefer to learn. The main goal behind these inventories and styles is for you to understand yourself and the ways in which you process information, deal with people, and handle situations most effectively. As you become more aware of your preferences, you may also notice that some preferences are *situational*, meaning they will vary in different situations. For example, preferences in college may vary for different courses based on your familiarity, background knowledge, and interest in the subject. These indicators provide you with options so that you are able to modify, personalize, and tailor your approach to learning tasks.

In the following student examples, learning preferences focus on classroom environment, class structure, and teaching style. As you read through the examples, compare your own preferences with those of the following students. In Exercise 1.5 on page 20, you will have the opportunity to identify your situational preferences for nine different kinds of college courses.

1. Brandon learns best in a traditional, **teacher-directed environment**, which typically involves structured lectures and multimedia materials such as overhead transparencies, slides, graphic materials, and videos. Brandon likes the deductive approach used in lectures: the teacher presents the important concepts and terms, followed by applications or uses. The teacher presents the information in a straightforward manner; classroom discussions or interactions are minimal. Brandon has effective listening and notetaking skills and takes responsibility for learning the information and completing the assignments in a timely manner.

2. Lorraine learns best in an active **student-directed learning environment** that involves cooperative learning, group activities, team or group projects, and learning communities that link two or more courses. In a student-directed environment, Lorraine is able to use her leadership skills to organize, motivate, and interact with other students. She thrives on the inductive approach to learning, which involves putting pieces of information together to form larger pictures, solutions, or conclusions. She enjoys exploring information in creative ways; discussing, explaining, brainstorming, and problem solving with others; experimenting in labs, on campus, or in the community; and having a sense of belonging to a community of learners.

3. Skip is an **interactive learner** who learns best by interacting with others, getting personally involved with the subject matter, and bringing high energy to group activities or projects. Skip retains information better when he participates in group activities; gets involved in role-playing or skits, panel discussions, debates, and interviews; and has hands-on experiences in labs or out in the field. In a teacher-directed environment, Skip often breaks the flow of information by asking questions and encouraging more interaction between the teacher and students. When he cannot exhibit his active learner preferences in class, he uses active learner strategies outside of class.

4. Marissa is a **reflective learner** who learns best in an environment that allows her to process information on her own, in her own way, at her own pace, and in her own space. Marissa likes to reflect, ponder, contemplate, or think seriously about topics she is studying. She often finds that she comprehends new ideas, integrates information, sees relationships and trends more readily, and understands applications more easily when she works by herself. She retains information better by examining information introspectively without the input or influence of others. Marissa has learned that she becomes impatient, frustrated, and uncomfortable in group activities, so whenever possible, she chooses independent study, online courses, or courses that do not involve extensive interaction inside or outside the classroom.

As you sit in your classrooms, you can be assured that you are a member of a diverse group of learners. Students with visual, auditory, kinesthetic, linear, global, interactive, and reflective learning style preferences sit side by side, taking in and processing information differently. The teaching styles used to organize and present information often reflect teachers' own learning styles. Historically, the American approach to education favored the visual and linear learners. However, by implementing new teaching methods that address the needs of a diverse group of learners, more and more teachers are breaking away from or altering their teaching and learning style preferences.

Even though many teachers are using a greater variety of instructional approaches in the classroom, mismatches between teaching styles and your preferred learning styles will occur. Before enrolling in a course that offers several sections with different teachers, talk to other students, teachers, and counselors to learn more about the teaching and classroom styles of each teacher. *If you have a choice,* enroll in the section with the teacher who seems most compatible with your learning styles and preferences. Realize, however, that throughout your college career, you will find yourself in classes that do not match your preferred ways of learning. Since you cannot expect instructors to modify their approaches to meet your needs, strive to adjust to the teaching style of the class. You can begin by informally analyzing the teaching style and learning style differences that might exist in a specific class and with a specific teacher. Identify the classroom skills (such as notetaking, working in a group, participating in discussions, or maintaining your concentration) that you will need to succeed in the course. Identify strategies that you can use outside of class to compensate for learning needs that are not being met within the classroom. For example, an interactive learner in a teacher-directed, lecture-style class may want to form a study group outside of class to benefit from more discussions and interactions. A reflective student in a student-directed class may want to schedule time after each class to be alone to ponder and summarize what occurred in the last group activity or session. Your ultimate goal as a student is to be able to function effectively in any learning environment, even when the teaching style does not match your preferred learning styles.

EXERCISE 1.5   Learning Preferences Chart

In the following chart, check the box that shows your situational preference. Decide whether you have one specific learning style preference or pattern for all subjects or if you vary the preference among different courses or content areas.

Situational Preferences Chart

Class	In class: teacher-directed / Outside class: interactive learner	In class: teacher-directed / Outside class: reflective learner	In class: student-directed / Outside class: interactive learner	In class: student-directed / Outside class: reflective learner
reading				
foreign language				
writing				
sociology				
math				
computer				
science				
literature				
health				

ONLINE PRACTICE 2

Visit the *Essential Study Skills*, Fifth Edition, website and go to Chapter 1. Click on **Practice 2: Additional Learning Preferences**. Complete the ten-question interactive multiple-choice quiz. Upon completion of the quiz, you will receive your score. You can exit at that time, or you can print or e-mail your results to the instructor.

EXERCISE 1.6   Textbook Case Studies

Read each of the following student situations carefully. Then, on your own paper and in complete sentences, answer the question that follows each case study. You can also answer these questions online at this textbook's Chapter 1 website. You can print your online responses or e-mail them to your instructor.

1. Elaine is usually an outgoing person. She started college in the middle of the year and does not know anyone on campus. After she received her midterm grades, she became concerned because she knew her work did not reflect her abilities. She knows she has strong auditory skills and is an interactive learner and a global thinker. She studies three or four hours every day alone in the library. She turns in her assignments on time but has difficulty retaining information. She also has trouble motivating herself and getting interested in her classes. What changes can Elaine make to combat the problems she has encountered in the first half of this term?

2. Conor is enrolled in a poetry class to complete one of his program requirements. He has never enjoyed or really understood poetry. He had hoped that this class would provide him with specific methods to analyze, interpret, and respond to poetry. Instead of providing ways to learn specific steps or guidelines, the class time consists of open-ended discussions that seem to be nothing more than a lot of different opinions. He is frustrated with the instructor and the lack of structure, direction, or specific answers. He is not comfortable talking to other students about this because they seem excited about the class, the instructor, and the content. He is doing well in all of his other classes, which include math and advanced physics, and is afraid that this class is going to lower his GPA. What are Conor's learning styles, and how do they contribute to the problems and frustrations he is experiencing in the poetry class?

ONLINE CASE STUDIES

Visit the *Essential Study Skills*, Fifth Edition, website and go to Chapter 1. Click on **Online Case Studies**. In the text boxes, respond to four additional case studies that are only available online. You can print your responses or e-mail them to your instructor.

Multiple Intelligences

Learning styles provide one framework for understanding how people learn. Howard Gardner's **Theory of Multiple Intelligences** provides another framework for understanding cognitive development. In 1983, Gardner, a noted Harvard University psychologist, presented his theory in his book *Frames of Mind: The Theory of Multiple Intelligences*. This Theory of Multiple Intelligences (MI) challenges the traditional intelligence quotient (IQ) tests, which measure intellectual abilities in the areas of verbal, visual-spatial, and logical mathematics. In his more recent book, *Intelligence Reframed* (1999), Howard Gardner defines intelligence:

I began (in 1983) by defining *an intelligence* as "the ability to solve problems or to create products that are valued within one or more cultural settings." I called attention to key facts about most theories of intelligence: namely, they looked at problem solving and ignored the creation of products, and they assumed that intelligence would be evident and appreciated anywhere, regardless of what was (and was not) valued in particular cultures at particular times. . . . I now conceptualize an intelligence as *biopsychological potential to process information that can be activated in a cultural setting to solve problems or create products that are of value in a culture.* This modest change in wording is important because it suggests that intelligences are not things that can be seen or counted. Instead, they are potentials . . . that will or will not be activated, depending upon the values of a particular culture, the opportunities available in that culture, and the personal decisions made by individuals and/or their families, schoolteachers, and others. [From Howard Gardner, *Intelligence Reframed: Multiple Perspectives for The 21st Century*, 1999, pp. 33–34. Copyright © 1999 Howard Gardner. Reprinted by permission of Basic Books, a member of Perseus Books, L.L.C.]

What are the different intelligences a director and an actor rely on to work together to produce a play?

When Howard Gardner first presented his Theory of Multiple Intelligences, he identified seven distinct intelligences. In order to be classified as **an intelligence,** a specific aptitude, capability, or set of skills (also referred to as *faculties*) had to meet eight clearly defined scientific criteria. All of the original seven intelligences met all eight of his defined criteria. In 1996, Gardner added an eighth intelligence, the naturalist, and contends that very likely additional intelligences will be identified in the future. (*Special Note:* In his book *Intelligence Reframed,* Gardner discusses spiritual and existential capabilities and whether or not they qualify as new intelligences. Gardner concludes that neither spiritual nor existential capabilities meet all eight criteria; neither at this time may be classified as a ninth intelligence. In *Intelligence Reframed,* Gardner states: "Despite the attractiveness of a ninth intelligence, however, I am not adding existential intelligence to the list. I find the phenomenon perplexing enough and the distance from other intelligences vast enough to dictate prudence—at least for now. At most, I am willing . . . to joke about "8½ intelligences" [p. 66].)

The Eight Intelligences in Howard Gardner's MI Theory

Linguistic	Logical-Mathematical	Musical	Bodily-Kinesthetic
Spatial	Interpersonal	Intrapersonal	Naturalist

Subintelligences

Gardner notes **subintelligences** (core abilities) under each of these eight intelligences. For example, people can exhibit many different talents and abilities under the category of musical intelligence. A person with a high musical intelligence may not have all of the subintelligences of music well developed. Singing, playing different instruments, composing, conducting, critiquing, and appreciating a variety of music require different skills, abilities, and processes. The level of accomplishment or degree of mastery will vary within an individual among the subintelligences, but the *potential exists* to process information that can be activated to solve problems or create products that are valued.

Linguistic Intelligence

Linguistic intelligence includes verbal and written language abilities. Common characteristics of this intelligence include a love of language—a curiosity and fascination with words, meanings (semantics), and structure (syntax). Sensitivities to how words are used, how they sound (phonology), and how they evoke feelings are other characteristics. People with these developed abilities may exhibit sharp, detailed, vivid memories about written or spoken language; excel in word games such as crossword puzzles or Scrabble; enjoy creating and reciting puns, jingles, or poetry; and show an ability to learn languages. They may exhibit the ability to express ideas well in public presentations, storytelling, or debates and may express ideas well in writing, whether in journals, prose, or poetry.

Logical-Mathematical Intelligence

Logical-mathematical intelligence involves the use of logic, sound reasoning, problem solving, analysis, identification of patterns, sequential thinking, and mathematical calculations. People with logical-mathematical intelligence think concretely and abstractly, understand and apply abstract numerical symbols and operations, and perform complex calculations. They may use systematic, logic-based, sequential problem-solving techniques and scientific methods to measure, hypothesize, test, research, and confirm results.

Musical Intelligence

Musical intelligence consists of an acute sensitivity to and appreciation of musical patterns and elements such as pitch, timbre, and harmony. People with these developed abilities may exhibit strong auditory memories and may use vocal or instrumental music to express creativity, imagination, and the gamut of human emotions. They may be skilled in reading and writing music. Other characteristics that reflect musical intelligence include an understanding of music theory and symbols; a passion for different types and structures of music; and an enjoyment of singing, chanting, humming, or drumming.

Bodily-Kinesthetic Intelligence

Bodily-kinesthetic intelligence encompasses fine, precise body rhythms, body movements, motor coordination skills, an acute sense of timing, balance, dexterity, flexibility, and possibly strength and speed. People with well-developed gross (large) motor skills are able to judge how their bodies will respond to certain situations and are able to fine-tune and train their bodies to perform at higher levels. People with well-developed fine (small) motor skills work well with their hands to create or modify the objects they work with. They can "sense" through their hands. For example, a mechanic unable to see inside an engine may be able to locate and fix a problem using only his or her hands. People with developed bodily-kinesthetic intelligence often enjoy physical exercise, sports, dancing, drama, role-playing, inventing, building, and repairing things. They prefer "hands-on" or activity-oriented tasks.

Spatial Intelligence

Spatial intelligence involves keen, accurate, precise perceptions of patterns in the physical world, including sizes, shapes, textures, lines, curves, and angles. People with developed spatial intelligence are able to present their ideas graphically. They often possess strong visual imagery or visualization skills, creativity, and active imaginations. For example, a gifted chess player can play a challenging game of chess blindfolded, or an architect can picture the floor plans of a building before drawing them. People with strong spatial intelligence often enjoy the arts, such as painting, sculpting, drawing, drafting, or photography.

Interpersonal Intelligence

Interpersonal intelligence emphasizes effective interpersonal communication skills, social skills, leadership ability, and cooperative teamwork. Such individuals participate actively in groups, create bonds with diverse groups of people, and feel a sense of global responsibility toward others. Other characteristics include the ability to interpret nonverbal clues that appear in the form of facial expressions, gestures, or general body language and the ability to interpret the behavior, motivation, and intentions of others. People with these developed abilities often enjoy socializing, helping others, sharing their skills, tutoring or teaching others, and contributing to the development of positive group dynamics.

Intrapersonal Intelligence

Intrapersonal intelligence focuses on personal growth, self-understanding, personal reflection, intuition, spirituality, and motivation to achieve personal potential. People with this developed ability enjoy exploring their feelings, values, goals, strengths, weaknesses, and personal history. They often use life experiences as lessons and guides to change aspects of their lives and to give their lives meaning. They frequently project a sense of pride, self-esteem, confidence, self-responsibility, control, and empowerment; they tend to be self-regulating, self-motivated, and goal-oriented. People with strong intrapersonal intelligence are usually able to adapt to a wide variety of situations and circumstances; consequently, they succeed in many fields of work.

Naturalist Intelligence

Gardner identified the eighth intelligence, **naturalist intelligence,** in 1996. People with a naturalist intelligence are sensitive to the physical world and aware of the balance (or imbalance) of plants, animals, and the environment. They are keen observers of nature's elements—such as daily, seasonal, and cyclical changes—and of the relationships in nature. People with developed naturalist intelligence often demonstrate detailed knowledge and expertise in recognizing and classifying plants and animals. They may exhibit the ability to organize, classify, arrange, or group items and ideas into logical units or categories. The strong pattern-recognition talents or abilities of naturalists may also be activated outside of the plant-animal world as artists, poets, laboratory scientists, and social scientists use patterns to solve problems or create products that are of value in their culture.

Applications of the MI Theory

The Theory of Multiple Intelligences serves as a reminder that we are all "evolving beings." We have the potential to expand our abilities and intelligences to reach greater levels of performance and fulfillment. We can also consciously make choices to capitalize on our abilities and intelligences and strive for ways to cultivate and enhance them. Not surprisingly, many people seek and find success in careers that emphasize their stronger intelligences. The following chart shows a sampling of typical careers that capitalize on the abilities associated with each of the intelligences.

Intelligence	Careers
Linguistic	author, journalist, editor, poet, newscaster, television announcer, motivational speaker, playwright, politician, consultant, lawyer
Logical-mathematical	mathematician, math or business teacher, scientist, computer programmer, accountant, tax expert, banker, researcher
Musical	music teacher, composer, conductor, performer, sound engineer, filmmaker, television crew or director, marketing or advertising personnel
Bodily-kinesthetic	dancer, athlete, actor, musician/instrumentalist (guitarist, drummer, pianist), dance teacher, choreographer, photographer, mime artist, painter, sculptor, surgeon, inventor, craftsperson
Spatial	architect, designer, interior decorator, artist, painter, sculptor, fashion designer, landscaper, carpenter, contractor, graphic artist, advertiser, cartographer, inventor, pilot, surgeon
Interpersonal	parent, tutor, teacher, therapist, counselor, healer, social activist, motivational speaker, workshop leader, religious leader, sociologist, actor, political organizer, salesperson
Intrapersonal	psychiatrist, spiritual or personal counselor, self-help or motivational writer or speaker, philosopher, biographer
Naturalist	meteorologist, geologist, botanist, herbalist, biologist, naturopath, holistic healer, medicine man, gardener, environmentalist

Howard Gardner's Theory of Multiple Intelligences has opened a new door to understanding individual differences, skills, abilities, and interests. This theory recognizes that most people have some degree of each of the intelligences, but that some intelligences are more developed than others in the individual. Through effective training, experience, and conducive environments, people have the potential to develop and strengthen each of the intelligences. Many educators and leaders of the educational reform initiatives in the United States use Gardner's research and philosophy to create or modify classroom teaching methods and curricula. Many educators are exploring both practical applications for classroom teaching and assessment of student performance based on the understanding that students' abilities are diverse and that students will excel in the areas of academics and personal growth when their wider range of talents or intelligences are recognized and nurtured.

Although educators have discovered ways to modify classroom approaches, curricula, and activities, they have not yet successfully found ways to assess the eight intelligences in people. Many MI inventories, in reality, assess people's *preferences* for using certain intelligences, and this "assessment" through inventories occurs through a linguistic or logical paper-pencil test, not through the intelligences themselves. Since intelligence is defined as *the potential to process information that can be activated in a cultural setting to solve problems or create products that are of value in a culture,* valid assessment procedures require that testers place individuals in settings where the individuals are required to activate specific intelligences. As Gardner explains in *Intelligence Reframed,* "If one wants to assess spatial intelligence, one should allow people to explore a terrain for a while and see whether they can find their way around it reliably, perhaps even when they have to enter or exit at an unfamiliar point. Or, if one wants to examine musical intelligence, one should expose people to a new melody in a reasonably familiar idiom and determine how readily they can learn to sing it, recognize it, transform it, and so on" (pp. 80–81). "I would recommend that any intelligence be assessed by a number of complementary approaches that consider the several core components [subintelligences] of an intelligence. Thus, for example, spatial intelligence might be assessed by asking people to find their way around an unfamiliar terrain, to solve an abstract jigsaw puzzle, and to construct a three-dimensional model of their home" (p. 82).

From Howard Gardner, *Intelligence Reframed: Multiple Perspectives for the 21st Century.* Copyright © 1999 Howard Gardner. Reprinted by permission of Basic Books, a member of Perseus Books, L.L.C.

EXERCISE 1.7   Discussing Multiple Intelligences

Work with a partner or in a small group to complete this exercise. After each learning activity listed below, use the following codes to indicate which intelligence or intelligences are most activated to produce a product of value. Write each answer on the line provided.

L	= Linguistic	BK	= Bodily-Kinesthetic
M	= Musical	INTRA	= Intrapersonal
S	= Spatial	INTER	= Interpersonal
N	= Naturalist	LM	= Logical-Mathematical

_____ 1. Work as a group to create a student handbook for incoming freshmen.

_____ 2. Perform a scene from a book in a literature class.

_____ 3. Compile the results of four interviews conducted with people who work in the career field of interest to you.

_____ 4. Select appropriate plants to use for experiments in an existing greenhouse on campus.

_____ 5. Collect and organize samples of music from five different cultural or ethnic groups.

_____ 6. Use a computer graphics program to create an eye-catching presentation.

_____ 7. Write a poem about your heritage or cultural ties.

_____ 8. Create a collage of international flags to hang in the library.

_____ 9. Construct a 3-D model that shows your idea about how to make better use of an existing space on campus.

_____ 10. Write a paper contrasting American English and British English terms for common objects.

_____ 11. Role-play a conflict resolution strategy.

_____ 12. Keep a daily journal or log to record your progress in reaching a specific goal.

_____ 13. Organize a small group of students to tutor elementary school students.

_____ 14. Attend a movie and then write a critique to present to the class.

_____ 15. Design a tee shirt for an organization on campus.

EXERCISE 1.8 LINKS

The three cognitive learning styles (visual, auditory, and kinesthetic) provide a framework for ways people prefer to process and learn new information. Howard Gardner's Theory of Multiple Intelligences provides a framework for understanding human potential and intelligences that can be cultivated and strengthened to problem-solve or create new products of value. Which cognitive learning styles are actively used in each of the eight intelligences? Outline your response in the following space. Then, on separate paper, write your response in one or more paragraphs, or in the form of a chart.

ONLINE PRACTICE 3

Visit the *Essential Study Skills*, Fifth Edition, website and go to Chapter 1. Click on **Practice 3: Multiple Intelligences**. Complete the ten-question interactive true-false quiz. Upon completion of the quiz, you will receive your score. You can exit at that time, or you can print or e-mail your results to your instructor.

Reflection Writing 3
Chapter 1

The primary goal of learning style, personality, or other kinds of inventories is to help you become aware of the way you operate, identify approaches to learning that are effective, and acquire the tools to adjust your strategies so you can perform on a higher level and achieve your goals. As part of this process, you are also strengthening your *intrapersonal skills*.

On separate paper, in a journal, or online at this textbook's website, summarize what you learned about yourself in each of the following areas. Then briefly explain how you can use this information in your courses this term.

1. Cognitive learning styles

2. Linear and global learners

3. Teacher-directed and student-directed environments

4. Interactive and reflective learners

5. Multiple intelligences

SUMMARY

- Three main cognitive learning styles or learning modalities determine how individuals prefer to learn: visual, auditory, and kinesthetic.

- Most adults have a learning style preference but are able to function using all three modalities.

- Effective study strategies are those that are compatible with your visual, auditory, or kinesthetic strengths and are multisensory.

- Weak learning modalities may be due to lack of experience or training or to physical or neurological conditions.

- The brain dominance theory groups thinking patterns into right-hemisphere and left-hemisphere thinking. Linear learners are left-brain learners. Global learners are right-brain learners.

- Additional learning preferences include working in a teacher-directed environment or a student-directed environment. The teacher-directed approach works with information in a straightforward, deductive, and often lecture-style format. The student-directed approach works with information in an interactive, inductive, and often group-oriented format.

- Interactive learners learn best through interaction with others and activity-based personal involvement. Reflective learners learn best through personal time, space, and pace to think about, ponder, and comprehend new information on their own.

- Howard Gardner's Theory of Multiple Intelligences proposes that intelligences are human potentials that can be learned and strengthened.

- Gardner defines intelligence as *biopsychological potential to process information that can be activated in a cultural setting to solve problems or create products that are of value in a culture.*

- Gardner identifies eight intelligences that people possess: linguistic, logical-mathematical, musical, bodily-kinesthetic, spatial, interpersonal, intrapersonal, and naturalist. Gardner has examined other talents or abilities but has not added them as additional intelligences because they do not meet all of the criteria used to qualify as new intelligences.

- Each of the eight intelligences has subintelligences. A person may not exhibit developed abilities in all of the subintelligences.

CULMINATING OPTIONS FOR CHAPTER 1

1. Visit this textbook's website and go to Chapter 1 to complete the following exercises:
   a. Flash card review of Chapter 1 terms and definitions
   b. ACE Practice Test 1 with ten fill-in-the-blank questions
   c. ACE Practice Test 2 with ten true-false questions
   d. ACE Practice Test 3 with ten multiple-choice questions
   e. ACE Practice Test 4 with short answer–critical thinking questions

2. Go to Appendix C in the back of this textbook for more Learning Options to use for additional practice, enrichment, or portfolio projects.

Chapter 1 REVIEW QUESTIONS

True-False

Carefully read the following statements. Write T *if the statement is true and* F *if it is false.*

_____ 1. *Cognitive learning styles* refers to the way people interact in a group setting.

_____ 2. The three cognitive learning styles are *hands-on, visual,* and *kinesthetic.*

_____ 3. All adults are capable of developing all three cognitive modalities to equally high levels of functioning.

_____ 4. Learning styles indicate people's preferred ways of learning and processing new information, but students cannot always use their preferred modality in every learning situation.

_____ 5. A study strategy that uses a multisensory approach incorporates more than one cognitive learning style or modality.

_____ 6. *Visual learners* have strong memories for printed material or pictures, diagrams, and charts.

_____ 7. *Auditory learners* often have strong language skills and auditory memories.

_____ 8. *Kinesthetic learners* would most likely prefer a teacher-directed environment that consists of mainly straightforward, well-organized lectures.

_____ 9. *Interactive learners* would likely benefit from discussing course work with others, participating in a group project, or using a hands-on approach to learning.

_____ 10. *Linear learners* often prefer using intuition, visually graphic materials, interactive approaches, and structured, predictable formats to learn new information.

_____ 11. *Global learners* tend to be more creative, interactive, and effective at visualizing information than are linear learners.

_____ 12. *Reflective learners* are self-directed, prefer to work alone, and use their own methods of studying and reviewing information.

_____ 13. Students should only enroll in courses in which their learning style preferences match the teaching styles used by the instructor.

_____ 14. Howard Gardner has identified eight intelligences; each intelligence consists of different categories of talents or core abilities called *subintelligences.*

_____ 15. The skills or abilities exhibited by a person with a well-developed logical-mathematical intelligence reflect characteristics of linear learners.

_____ 16. A person with a well-developed naturalist intelligence may exhibit strong pattern-recognition skills, the ability to organize and classify objects in the plant and animal world, or a sensitivity to the cycles and balances in nature.

_____ 17. To be considered intellectually strong in any one of the intelligences, a person must exhibit special talent or abilities in all the subintelligences related to that intelligence.

_____ 18. Through a variety of traditional paper-pencil tests, individuals can be evaluated to determine an accurate intelligence level (score) for each of the eight intelligences.

Short Answer and Critical Thinking

Use complete sentences to answer each of the following questions.

1. The Theory of Multiple Intelligences is based on the premise that traditional IQ tests are too limiting. What intelligences did Howard Gardner add to expand the concept of traditional intelligence and include a wider range of talents and abilities?

2. Teaching styles frequently reflect a teacher's own learning styles and preferences. Choose and describe a student with a specific type of learning style and a teacher with a specific type of teaching style. Discuss the kinds of difficulties the student might encounter in a class with that specific teacher.

3. What would be an ideal classroom environment and instructional approach for you that would allow you to capitalize on your various learning styles and preferences? Use specific details to describe the classroom and the instructional approach.

Processing Information into Your Memory System

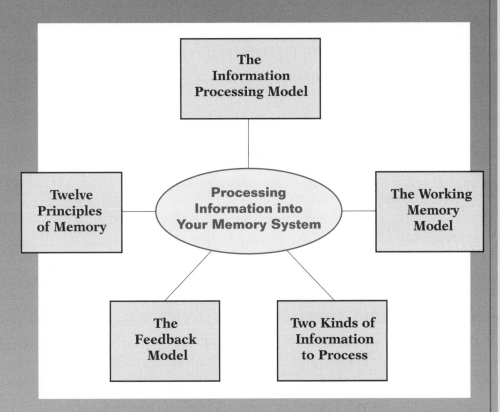

For centuries people have been fascinated by the workings of the human mind. In this chapter, you will learn about two learning theory models: the traditional Information Processing Model and the contemporary Working Memory Model, which evolved from the traditional model. You will learn about two kinds of information you process frequently: declarative knowledge (factual) and procedural knowledge (processes). The series of steps in the Feedback Model provides you with a method to verify and correct information that you are learning. The Twelve Memory Principles lay a strong foundation for many study skills strategies. This chapter will help you gain a better understanding of your learning process and will empower you to become a more effective, successful student.

Chapter 2   Information Processing Profile

ANSWER, SCORE, and **RECORD** your profile before you read this chapter. If you need to review the process, refer to the complete directions given in the Profile for Chapter 1 on page 2.

ONLINE: You can complete the profile and get your score online at this textbook's website.

	YES	NO
1. I use study methods that give me feedback so that I know whether I am learning.	_____	_____
2. I take time to relate or associate new information to information I already know.	_____	_____
3. I have problems identifying and pulling out the information that is important to study.	_____	_____
4. I rearrange information into meaningful units or clusters so it is easier to learn.	_____	_____
5. I wait until close to test time before I practice the information that I previously read.	_____	_____
6. I talk out loud to myself as I study because reciting seems to help me learn.	_____	_____
7. I use the same method of learning information for everything I need to study.	_____	_____
8. I frequently use rote memory by memorizing specific details exactly as they are presented in the book.	_____	_____
9. I make movies in my mind about the information I am learning.	_____	_____
10. I am confident in my ability to use effective strategies to learn factual information and steps to complete specific processes or procedures.	_____	_____

Reflection Writing 1
Chapter 2

On separate paper, in a journal, or online at this textbook's website, respond to the following questions.

1. What is your profile score for this chapter? What does it mean to you?

2. How do you feel about your memory? Is it usually vivid, strong, and accurate, or is it often unclear, weak, and inaccurate?

3. What do you see as your greatest memory strengths and your greatest problem areas?

The Information Processing Model

This chapter introduces you to important processing models and strategies that lay a strong foundation for many study skills strategies in later chapters. Brain research and learning theories are more complex than the information that you will encounter in this chapter. However, the technical information in this chapter will equip you with basic knowledge about *how* your mind processes information, *how* your memory works, and *how* you can use this information to increase your learning potential and to tailor or personalize your approach to learning different kinds of information.

Psychologists frequently use the **Information Processing Model** to help explain how we receive, process, and learn information. The Information Processing Model consists of six main parts. Although each part has its own distinct functions, the parts do not work independently. Each part has an important role to move information through your memory system as you learn.

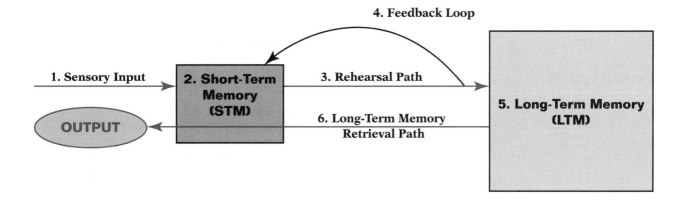

Sensory Input

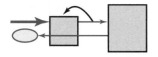

In the Information Processing Model, we receive information through our five senses (sight, sound, smell, taste, and touch); this information is called **sensory input**. Such input comes in the form of **sensory stimuli**, which can be letters, numbers, words, pictures, and sounds.

Short-Term Memory

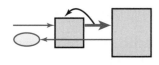

Trap door

Short-term memory (STM) is a temporary *storage center* that is very limited in time and capacity (up to seven items at one time). Sensory input first moves into short-term memory and remains there for a few seconds. Within that short time, a "decision" is made by the person receiving the stimuli to dump the information or process it further. This decision may be made consciously or subconsciously. If attention is not given to the stimuli, the automatic response will be to "dump" it through an imaginary trap door. This imaginary *trap door* discards unwanted or unattended-to information before it has the chance to be processed in memory.

Rehearsal Path

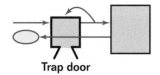

Once you decide that particular information is important to learn, that information moves on to the **rehearsal path**. It is on this "learning path" that you select effective learning techniques to move the information into your long-term memory. The rehearsal path is an *active path* where practice, comprehension, and learning take place. It carries the sensory stimuli in a coded form that long-term memory can recognize. The type of **encoding** depends on the type of information being transmitted. Following are the four most common types of encoding.

1. *Linguistic coding,* also called *acoustical* or *auditory coding,* carries verbal information. Learning or remembering information by recalling the speaker's exact words, seeing something and describing for yourself what you see, or reading and reciting information by explaining it out loud in your own words are examples of encoding information linguistically. With effective techniques you can move spoken information into your memory in its encoded linguistic form, or you can convert information from other codes into a linguistic code.

2. *Visual coding,* also called *imaginal coding,* carries information in visual images such as pictures or diagrams. When you look at an object and pay attention to its shape, colors, size, and location; when you read a history passage and try to see people and events in your mind; or when you create a chart, a visual mapping, or a picture of printed information, you are using visual coding. As with linguistic coding, you can convert information encoded in a different form into a visual form.

3. *Motor coding,* also called *physical* or *kinesthetic coding,* carries information through muscle memory. Riding a bike, typing, driving a car, and skiing are examples of skills learned through motor coding; without consciously thinking about moving various body parts, your muscles send messages to the section in the brain that coordinates and moves muscles. If you watch a football linebacker make a tackle, and you imagine how he moved and how the parts of his body responded, you are encoding the information in motor terms even though you yourself do not perform the action.

4. *Semantic coding* carries information in the form of its general meaning and emotional responses of a specific experience. When you recall a personal experience and the feelings or emotions involved in the experience, when you listen to a lecture, or when you watch a movie and then translate the events into their general meanings along with your emotional responses, you use semantic coding. Semantic coding can occur even if you are not the person performing the action. For example, if you watch a hockey player collide with an opponent, and you imagine how the opponent knocked off his skates feels, semantic encoding occurs. These semantic codes of personal experiences and events that happened when you were present are stored in a special kind of memory, your *episodic memory,* as one chunk or unit of information.

The rehearsal path is an extremely important part of the Information Processing Model, for the way you rehearse will affect how clearly, effectively, and efficiently the information will be placed in your long-term memory system. A powerful way to rehearse information is to use **elaborative rehearsal**. *Elaborative rehearsal* involves active thinking processes and often involves multisensory learning strategies. When you use elaborative rehearsal techniques, you give time and effort to understanding the information, seeing how it relates to other information, associating or linking it to information you know, and identifying how it can be used to complete a task, solve a problem, or get desired results. Elaborative rehearsal usually includes a *self-quizzing* technique, which provides *feedback* so that you know whether or not you are understanding and remembering the new information. When you learn information through elaborative rehearsal, you will be able to explain it, show that you understand it, and apply it as needed in learning situations. (See the *Memory Principle Elaboration* on page 53.)

What problems does the survival technique of cramming create in a student's memory system?

Feedback Loop

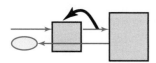

When you rehearse and find out that you do not understand or know the new information, you receive **feedback** that you need more rehearsal or practice. Through this awareness, information "zips" through the **feedback loop** and returns to short-term memory. The feedback loop is an *inactive path*. It does nothing but immediately send the information back into short-term memory for further rehearsal.

Long-Term Memory

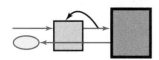

Long-term memory (LTM) is an enormous *storage system* that permanently "files away" learned information. This storage facility has unlimited capacity; it never runs out of storage space. Information that is carefully encoded and rehearsed is *imprinted* in your brain and stored in your long-term memory. Unless information has been learned as random items not associated with other existing information, the encoded information is routed to clusters of related information called **schemas**. Schemas consist of large concepts or frameworks in which other related ideas, facts, and details are attached. The number of schemas in a person's memory system is also unlimited. The more you learn, the more schemas you create, or the larger the existing schemas become. (As an interesting note, with advanced technology, brain scans can actually show which sections of the brain are activated when a person learns specific kinds of information.)

When you start to learn something new and unfamiliar, the learning process at first is challenging, frustrating, and full of errors. The initial learning process of an unfamiliar topic or information may be difficult because you are just beginning to construct a new schema for this knowledge. Later, after you have learned this information or skill, learning additional information is easier and smoother because a schema for that concept already exists. This concept of schemas helps explain why learning is so much easier and sometimes effortless when there is an interest, a background, and perhaps even some expertise in a specific field.

Another way to look at long-term memory is to think of your brain as a filing system with many different files and many different drawers filled with different kinds of information. When information is carefully placed in the file cabinet, you can locate it when you need it. If any drawer is opened and a file stuffed in without organization or logic, the file may be difficult to find at a later time. *Elaborative rehearsal* organizes information carefully and logically so that it is easier to locate at a later time in long-term memory. The Essential Strategies on page 37 provide you with eight strategies to help you process information into your long-term memory.

Long-Term Memory Retrieval Path

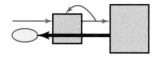

The **long-term memory retrieval path** is an *active path* that carries information from long-term memory back into short-term memory. Once the information is in short-term memory, you can give a response or show some type of output that indicates you were able to locate and retrieve information from your long-term memory. *Long-term memory retrieval* is the process of accessing, or finding, information stored in long-term memory. When you have a conscious need and make a conscious effort to recall information, retrieval efforts begin. Sometimes you can locate information quickly and directly. More often, however, you need to conduct a **memory search** that involves linking together a series of ideas, concepts, or previously learned associations in order to locate information stored in your long-term memory. When you use *elaborative rehearsal*, you intentionally create links or associations that serve as **memory cues** (also referred to as *retrieval cues*); recalling one idea or image links you to another piece of information and so on until you locate the desired information.

Retrieving information from long-term memory is a process you use often. Every time you try to recall specific facts or processes you have learned or attempt to relate new information to previously learned information, you actively use the retrieval path. By reviewing learned information on an ongoing basis, you practice locating and retrieving information more readily and with less effort.

Learning a foreign language is a good example of the necessity to practice retrieval. Imagine that you spent time learning a foreign language but have not practiced it for many years, so you probably no longer speak that language fluently. You may remember the sentence structure but may have forgotten the vocabulary needed to express your ideas. If you do not retrieve information for years at a time, you will no longer have access to that information in memory. However, by "brushing up" with a few lessons, you may find that the vocabulary comes back to you fairly quickly. You will definitely "relearn" the language faster than you learned it the first time.

Output

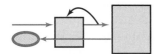

Output is the end result or the "proof" that learning has taken place. Output is the result of successfully encoding, processing, storing, and retrieving information from long-term memory. Some form of demonstration occurs in this final stage of the Information Processing Model. The following are examples of output:

- Responding with a correct answer
- Solving a math question
- Explaining information logically and accurately
- Arguing a point or an opinion and using supporting details
- Writing an effective essay or paper
- Creating or constructing a product

SET LEARNING GOALS

The following *Essential Strategies to Process Information* chart highlights eight important strategies to use when you work with new information. Place a star next to the strategies you already use. Highlight the strategies you plan to make a conscious effort to begin using to improve your information processing.

Essential Strategies to Process Information

▶ **Pay attention to incoming sensory input.** Concentrate and focus on the incoming stimuli and block out distractions that disrupt your concentration. Make a conscious effort and set a goal to be receptive to the incoming information. Failure to be alert and attentive to the incoming stimuli often results in stimuli dropping out of your short-term memory.

▶ **Limit the number of items and the speed at which you take in stimuli.** To avoid overloading your short-term memory, do not attempt to take in too much information too quickly. Cramming for tests or reading complex textbooks quickly, for example, are ineffective strategies due to the limited capacity and duration of your short-term memory.

▶ **Find meaning, significance, and interest in new information.** If you automatically label something as meaningless, irrelevant, or boring, you send a message to your short-term memory to discard the information. Your attitude and intent to learn make you open and receptive to incoming information.

▶ **Use elaborative rehearsal techniques.** As you practice new information, look for relationships and create associations to link together pieces of information. Think about the new information and its relationship to information you have already learned. Work with the information in new ways, such as reorganizing it, making multisensory study tools, or attaching pictures or diagrams to the information.

▶ **Use self-quizzing when you rehearse. Self-quizzing,** the process of testing yourself and receiving feedback about the accuracy and completeness of your answers, helps you gauge the effectiveness of your rehearsal and learning strategies. Reciting, writing from memory, discussing, reproducing visual materials, and demonstrating how to complete a process are examples of self-quizzing activities that provide you with valuable feedback.

▶ **Avoid using rote memory when you rehearse. Rote memory** is the process of using repetition to learn information *in the exact form* in which it was presented. Rote memory does not lead to thorough understanding or provide you with the skills to manipulate or apply the information in new ways. Rote memory works to memorize a phone number, the spelling of a new word, or an interesting quotation, but often it is ineffective for mastering academic material.

▶ **Make a conscious effort to think about related categories and to create associations.** Information is linked in networks or organized around clusters of related information (schemas) stored in long-term memory. To strengthen your ability to learn and to recall information, organize details you are learning into categories. Take time linking information to categories of information you already know. Create associations so that thinking about one item in the association serves as a memory cue to trigger recall of the second item.

▶ **Allow ample time to practice frequently.** To learn any skill thoroughly requires time, effort, and ample practice. If you know how to ski, play an instrument, or prepare a gourmet meal, you learned the skill through practice. Learning academic material requires frequent practice, so schedule time in your study blocks each week for ongoing review.

CLASS DISCUSSION

Question: Which of these strategies specifically refer to short-term memory, which refer to the rehearsal path, and which refer to the retrieval path?

ONLINE REVIEW

Visit the *Essential Study Skills*, Fifth Edition, website and go to Chapter 2. Click on **Information Processing Model** to review the functions of each part of this cognitive learning model. No responses are required.

ONLINE PRACTICE 1

Visit the *Essential Study Skills*, Fifth Edition, website and go to Chapter 2. Click on **Practice 1: The Information Processing Model**. Then type responses to the six questions. After you type your responses, you can print or e-mail your responses to your instructor.

ONLINE PRACTICE 2

Visit the *Essential Study Skills*, Fifth Edition, website and go to Chapter 2. Click on **Practice 2: Processing Problems**. Complete the ten-question interactive multiple-choice quiz. Upon completion of the quiz, you will receive your score. You can exit at that time, or you can print or e-mail your results to your instructor.

The Working Memory Model

Understanding how we learn is an evolving study and area of extensive research. A number of models have been proposed to help us visualize the process. The **Working Memory Model** is a contemporary learning model that evolved from the Information Processing Model. The Working Memory Model, proposed by Alan Baddeley, a British researcher and psychologist, suggests that the activities frequently associated with short-term memory, rehearsal, feedback, and retrieval in the Information Processing Model all occur in the active, *conscious mind* called **working memory (WM)**.

Instead of dividing information processing into individual parts (short-term memory, rehearsal path, feedback loop, and retrieval path), the Working Memory Model shows *all* of these activities and parts working together, and in various sequences, in a larger processing unit called the *working memory*. Unlike the Information Processing Model, which shows a linear or straight-line flow of information, the Working Memory Model shows a more active, integrated, multidirectional flow of encoded information, and greater interaction with information in long-term memory during the learning process. Another way to grasp the scope of *working memory* is to understand that *anything that you are aware of doing occurs in working memory*. The following chart shows the scope of working memory in relation to the Information Processing Model.

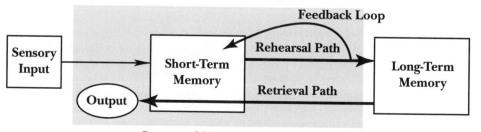

Scope of Working Memory

The Parts of the Working Memory Model

In the Working Memory Model, instead of one temporary (short-term) storage center, there are *two* temporary storage centers called the *visuo-spatial scratchpad* for visual stimuli and the *phonological loop* for auditory stimuli. A third part of the Working Memory Model is called the *central executive*. Because this model represents all the activity in our *conscious mind*, stimuli rapidly move back and forth to different sections of the brain and in and out of long-term and "short-term" (working) memory. The role of the *central executive* is to receive, organize, coordinate, and integrate the flow of information throughout the working memory system. It initiates and controls deliberate actions and goal-directed behavior. The *central executive* is thought to be the decision maker of the conscious mind; it initiates and manages attention, planning, and decision-making functions. The following diagram shows the three main components of working memory and their relationship to the overall memory system.

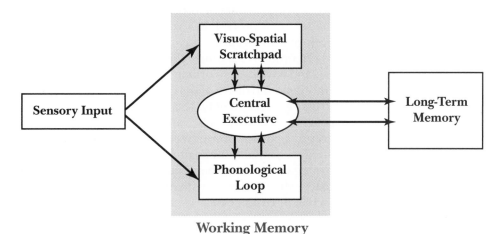

Working Memory

Note: The single-direction arrows represent a *serial process* in which information is accessed or processed by a linear search of all active subjects, one item or chunk at a time. The double-direction arrows represent a *parallel process* in which information can be accessed rapidly from different places at the same time through the use of memory or retrieval cues (associations).

Important Points to Know About Working Memory

The following are key points about working memory. Study skills strategies throughout this textbook use these working memory functions to help you process information more effectively and efficiently.

1. Sensory stimuli are held or stored briefly, for a matter of seconds, in the temporary storage centers *unless* you pay attention to the information and act on the information with an intent to learn it. Information that you do not pay attention to fades quickly and drops out of working memory. (Chapter 6, pages 139–141, explains causes of forgetting.)

2. Information held in working memory with the *intention* (goal) to be learned activates chunks of related information located in your long-term memory. This related information is pulled back into working memory, where it is integrated with the new information.

3. Rehearsal and retrieval activities involve active movement of information throughout the working memory and long-term memory. Encoding infor-

mation for long-term memory frequently occurs through the use of associations, or links between ideas or chunks of information. Recalling information from long-term memory schemas often involves conducting memory searches and using memory cues, self-quizzing, and feedback techniques. The *Essential Strategies to Process Information* on page 37 apply to the Working Memory Model.

Freeing Up Your Working Memory

As with the traditional short-term memory, working memory requires your undivided attention. Shifting your attention away from the learning task interferes with working memory processes. Giving undivided attention to incoming sensory stimuli will prevent the stimuli from fading. Your mind needs to be attentive and alert in order to activate information in long-term memory, find associations among items, and retrieve information from schemas. Integrating new information and previously learned information, rehearsing the new patterns or associations, and sending this information back into long-term memory schemas are active processes that you need to do consciously. Finally, when the learning process has your undivided attention, faster and more accurate performance occurs.

In order to maximize the abilities of working memory, perform on high levels, and have more working memory space, strive to remove intrusive thoughts, emotions, and distractions that disrupt your undivided attention. Daydreaming, stress, general anxiety, test anxiety, negative self-talk statements such as "I'll never be able to do this," and shifted attention due to distractions around you occupy a portion of your working memory, thus reducing the amount of working memory available for cognitive (thinking) processes. In Chapter 5, you will learn strategies to strengthen your concentration and reduce your levels of stress. Later, when you work with Appendix D, you will learn about the effects of stress on cognitive processes.

EXERCISE 2.1   Working with Learning Models
In a group or with a partner, complete the following directions.

1. If you are working in a group, use large chart paper; if you are working with a partner, use notebook or legal paper. Draw and label the parts of the Information Processing Model.

2. Insert the following words in the appropriate places where they occur in the model.

practice path	*inactive path*	*schemas*	*outcomes*
imprinting	*review*	*sensory stimuli*	*unlimited capacity*
self-quizzing	*trap door*	*limited capacity*	*learning path*

3. Draw a large box around the sections of the Information Processing Model that reflect the activities included in the Working Memory Model. On the *rehearsal path* and *retrieval path,* add arrows to show the flow of information in both directions between short-term and long-term memory.

4. As a group, create a way to show on your chart the *two* short-term sensory storage centers (the visuo-spatial scratchpad and the phonological loop) and the central executive. Be ready to explain your chart to the class.

O N L I N E   P R A C T I C E   3

Visit the *Essential Study Skills*, Fifth Edition, website and go to Chapter 2. Click on **Practice 3: Using Your Working Memory**. Complete the ten-question true-false quiz. Upon completion of the quiz, you will receive your score. You can exit at that time, or you can print or e-mail your results to your instructor.

Two Kinds of Information to Process

Understanding the two different kinds of information you will need to process helps you select effective strategies to rehearse and retrieve information from your long-term memory. The following chart shows the two kinds of information you will frequently work with as you learn new information.

Two Kinds of Information to Process

1. **Declarative knowledge** consists of specific facts, details, concepts, events, or experiences that you can be consciously aware of and talk about to others.
2. **Procedural knowledge** consists of a series of steps or a sequence of rules you apply to complete a procedure, solve a problem, or create a specific product.

Declarative Knowledge

Every time you learn a specific piece of information, you are working with **declarative knowledge**. Learning a specific fact (*one meter equals 100 centimeters*), a set of details (*three kinds of cognitive learning styles*), a definition (*A chronic stressor is a stress-producing event that continues over a long period of time*), a concept (*the Theory of Multiple Intelligences*), an event (*the 9-11 terrorist attack*), or an experience (*a first job interview*) all involve declarative knowledge in your working memory. You learn declarative knowledge through reading, observing, listening, and experiencing. This learning often involves elaborative rehearsal, creating associations and memory cues, and ongoing review.

Procedural Knowledge

Every time you perform a series of steps (*surf the Internet*), apply a sequence of rules (*subtract a double-digit number from a triple-digit number*), unconsciously perform a procedure (*ride a bike or rollerblade*), or repeat a habit without having to consciously think about the individual steps (*skim through a test before answering questions*), you are working with **procedural knowledge**. Procedural knowledge involves acquiring the skills necessary to complete a procedure, solve a problem, or create a specific product with accuracy and speed. Your goal is to become so familiar with the steps or procedure that your actions become automatic.

We often learn procedural knowledge through a trial-and-error approach:

1. We watch someone do the process and then copy the person's actions.
2. We try to do the process ourselves by reading a set of directions.
3. We get feedback about whether or not we completed the process correctly. We correct our actions or make adjustments as needed.

4. We repeat the same process over and over until it becomes automatic, and we increase our speed and accuracy.

When you are aware that the information you need to learn is *procedural knowledge,* plan to practice the process or procedure *multiple times* over a period of several days and often over several months. Your goal is to develop a performance skill and to build speed and accuracy over time. Practice of this skill may involve *many* repetitions before it becomes automatic. Additional practice may be required to blend this new procedural knowledge with other parts of a larger procedure and to attain expertise. Strategies to develop procedural knowledge always include more repetition and feedback than are necessary to learn declarative knowledge.

The Feedback Model

Whether you are learning declarative knowledge (factual) or procedural knowledge (process), your outcome involves learning accurate information that you can use in some way. In order to transfer information into your long-term memory in a logical, organized manner, the information must first be accurate and complete. When we are in the beginning phases of learning, we use feedback to check the effectiveness of our learning strategies while the information is still fresh in our minds. At later stages of learning, we use feedback to check our memories hours, days, or weeks after the initial learning. Including feedback activities *as you rehearse, learn,* and *review* gives you opportunities to correct errors and strengthen your memory skills.

The following **Feedback Model** shows the steps of using feedback effectively: *Learning Goal, Action, Feedback, Comparison, Results.*

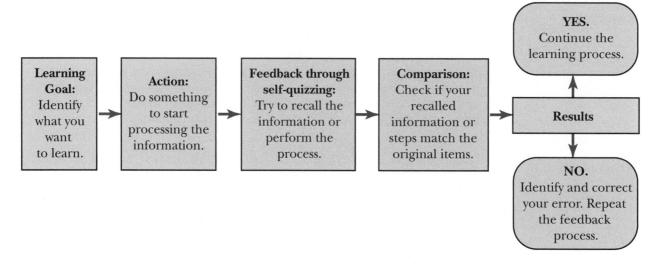

The following example demonstrates how you can use feedback when you read and work math problems. In your math class, you are learning how to calculate compound interest rates (*learning goal*). You read a section in the textbook that explains how to perform these calculations (*action*). After you read the explanation, *you look away from your textbook* and try to recall what you just read (*feedback through self-quizzing*). You look back at the textbook to compare your memory of the explanation with the textbook information (*comparison*). You pay attention to the *results.* If the result is YES, your recall matches the textbook information. You then continue on to repeat the same process with the textbook's worked examples and later with the assigned homework problems. If the result is NO, your recall does not match the textbook information. You reread the information for better understanding (*learning goal*), and try another technique such as highlighting the key points (*action*). You repeat the *feedback* and the *comparison* processes and then examine the results of your effort.

Group Processing: **A Collaborative Learning Activity**

Work in groups of three or four students. Complete the following directions.

1. Copy the following chart on large chart or poster paper.

Course	Declarative	Procedural	Feedback
Writing			
Science			
Computer			
Math			

2. Brainstorm specific examples of *declarative knowledge* that you would need to learn for each type of course. Then, do the same for *procedural knowledge* that you would need to learn. List your ideas in the appropriate boxes in the chart.

3. In the final column, list activities you could do to receive feedback when you study for each kind of course. Your list should include activities with feedback for both declarative and procedural knowledge.

EXERCISE 2.2   Memory Principles Inventory

You will soon learn about the twelve principles of memory that enhance the learning process. First, complete the following inventory by answering YES or NO to each question. The letter in the upper left corner of each box will be explained later.

S		YES	NO
1. Do you spend a lot of time studying but seem to study the "wrong information" for tests?		_____	_____
2. Do you get frustrated when you read because everything seems important?		_____	_____
3. Do you tend to highlight too much when you read textbooks?		_____	_____
4. Do your notes seem excessively long and overly detailed?		_____	_____
5. Do you avoid making study tools such as flash cards because you are not sure what information to put on the study tools?		_____	_____

A	**YES**	**NO**
1. Do you tend to memorize facts or ideas in isolation?	_____	_____
2. When you try to recall information you have studied, do you sometimes feel "lost" because there is no direct way to access the information in your memory?	_____	_____
3. Do you feel that you are memorizing numerous lists of information but not really understanding what they mean or how they are connected?	_____	_____
4. Do you "go blank" on tests when a question asks for information in a form or context different from the way you studied it?	_____	_____
5. Do you lack sufficient time to link difficult information to familiar words or pictures?	_____	_____

V	**YES**	**NO**
1. When you finish reading, do you have difficulty remembering what paragraphs were even about?	_____	_____
2. Do you have difficulty remembering information that appeared in a chart your instructor presented on the chalkboard or on a screen?	_____	_____
3. Do you find it difficult to get a visual image of printed information?	_____	_____
4. When you try to recall information, do you rely mainly on words rather than pictures?	_____	_____
5. When your instructor explains a new concept by giving a detailed example or anecdote (story), do you have difficulty recalling the example or anecdote after you leave class?	_____	_____

E	**YES**	**NO**
1. Do you learn individual facts or details without thinking about the schema in which they belong?	_____	_____
2. Do you frequently attempt to use rote memory to memorize facts, definitions, or rules?	_____	_____
3. Do you complete a math problem and immediately move on to the next problem?	_____	_____
4. Do you study information in the same order and in the same form in which it was presented?	_____	_____
5. Do you avoid creating new study tools that involve reorganizing information?	_____	_____

Continue the Inventory on page 45.

C		YES	NO
1.	Do you often experience divided attention because too many unrelated thoughts disrupt your thinking?	_____	_____
2.	Do you have so many interruptions when you study that you are not quite sure what you have accomplished at the end of a study block?	_____	_____
3.	Do you miss important information during a lecture because your mind tends to wander or daydream?	_____	_____
4.	When you are reading, do you find it difficult to keep your mind focused on the information in the textbook?	_____	_____
5.	Do you study with the television, radio, or stereo turned on?	_____	_____

R		YES	NO
1.	When you review for a test, do you do all or most of your review work silently?	_____	_____
2.	Do you have difficulty defining new terminology out loud?	_____	_____
3.	Do you have difficulty clearly explaining textbook information to another person?	_____	_____
4.	When you rehearse information out loud, do you often feel that your explanations are "fuzzy," unclear, or incomplete?	_____	_____
5.	Do you feel awkward or uncomfortable talking out loud to yourself?	_____	_____

I		YES	NO
1.	When you sit down to study, do you set a goal to complete the assignment as quickly as possible?	_____	_____
2.	Do you always have the same purpose in mind when you sit down to study?	_____	_____
3.	Do you lack curiosity, interest, or enthusiasm in the course content for one or more of your classes?	_____	_____
4.	When you begin learning new information, do you find setting a specific learning goal difficult to do?	_____	_____
5.	Do you study declarative knowledge (facts, details, concepts) in the same way that you study procedural knowledge (steps, processes, habits)?	_____	_____

B		YES	NO
1.	Do you have problems distinguishing between main ideas and individual details in textbook passages?	_____	_____
2.	Do you understand general concepts but oftentimes have difficulty giving details that relate to the concept?	_____	_____
3.	When you begin working with new information, do you begin by focusing your attention on learning the details and then later shift your attention to concepts and schemas?	_____	_____
4.	Do your lecture notes capture main ideas but lack details?	_____	_____
5.	Do your notes include running lists of details without a clear method of showing main ideas?	_____	_____

F		YES	NO
1.	Do you use tests as your main means of getting feedback about what you have learned?	_____	_____
2.	Do you keep taking in new information without stopping to see whether you are trying to learn too much too fast?	_____	_____
3.	When you are rehearsing, do you "keep on going" even if you sense that you have not clearly understood something?	_____	_____
4.	Do you tend to use self-quizzing only when you are preparing for a test?	_____	_____
5.	If you get feedback that you did not complete a math problem correctly, do you ignore your original answer and try working the problem again?	_____	_____

O		YES	NO
1.	Does information from lectures often seem to be one continuous stream of information without any apparent organization or structure?	_____	_____
2.	Do you have difficulty remembering the sequence of important events or the steps of a process?	_____	_____
3.	When you try to do a "memory search" to locate information in your memory, are you sometimes unable to find the information?	_____	_____
4.	Do you spend most of your time trying to learn information in the exact order in which it is presented?	_____	_____
5.	Do you feel unsure about rearranging, reorganizing, or regrouping information so that it is easier to learn and recall?	_____	_____

T		YES	NO
1.	When your assignment is to read and study a specific chapter, do you spend a lot of time on the assignment so that you will not need to make contact with it again for several weeks?	_____	_____
2.	When you are studying, do you often feel as though you are trying to study too much information too quickly?	_____	_____
3.	When you study, do you change to a second subject as soon as you complete the assignments for the first subject?	_____	_____
4.	Are some of your study blocks more than three hours long?	_____	_____
5.	In at least one of your courses, do you spend less time studying that subject than most other students in class do?	_____	_____

O		YES	NO
1.	Once you have completed an assignment, do you put it aside until close to the time of the next test?	_____	_____
2.	Do you have problems remembering or recalling information that you know you learned several weeks earlier?	_____	_____
3.	Do you need to add more review time to your weekly study schedule?	_____	_____
4.	Do you study fewer than two hours per week for every one hour in class?	_____	_____
5.	Do you sit down to study and feel that you are all caught up and have nothing to study?	_____	_____

About the Inventory

1. The letters in the upper left corner of each of the boxes on the inventory represent one of the principles of memory. Return to the inventory and label each of the boxes with the following principles of memory:

Selectivity	**C**oncentration	**F**eedback
Association	**R**ecitation	**O**rganization
Visualization	**I**ntention	**T**ime on Task
Elaboration	**B**ig and Little Pictures	**O**ngoing Review

2. Now look at your answers. A NO indicates you are already using the principle of memory when you study. If you gave NO answers to all the questions within one memory principle box, you are using the principle of memory consistently and effectively. A YES answer indicates that you will benefit by learning to use this principle of memory more effectively when you study. The more YES answers you have, the greater the need to add this principle of memory to your learning strategies or study techniques.

Reflection Writing 2
Chapter 2

On separate paper, in a journal, or online at this textbook's website, respond to the following questions about the Memory Principles Inventory.

1. Which principles do you use effectively on a regular basis?

2. Which principles do you use only sometimes or only on occasion?

3. Which principles have you not yet used effectively and need to learn to use on a more consistent basis?

EXERCISE 2.3   Learning the Basics

Before you begin reading the details about each memory principle, try learning the basic labels for each of the twelve principles of memory. This will help you "set up the schema" for the information you will be reading. Use the short clue below each line and the initial letter of the word to help you list the twelve principles of memory. Try to complete this without looking at the list of principles.

S _____
(Picking and choosing)

A _____
(Linking ideas)

V _____
(Seeing it in your mind)

E _____
(Working with information)

C _____
(Focusing)

R _____
(Explaining out loud)

I _____
(Identifying a purpose or goal)

B _____
(Concepts and details)

F _____
(Self-quizzing)

O _____
(Structuring logically)

T _____
(Using minutes and hours)

O _____
(Repeated practice)

Twelve Memory Principles

Learning, as you have seen, is a complex process. Many mental processes are involved in moving information into long-term memory and then retrieving that information when you need it. The following twelve memory principles can help you process information more efficiently through your memory system. The memory words SAVE CRIB FOTO will help you remember all twelve principles; each letter in the words represents one of the memory principles.

Twelve Memory Principles (SAVE CRIB FOTO)

1. **S**electivity: selecting what is important to learn.
2. **A**ssociation: associating or linking new information to something familiar.
3. **V**isualization: picturing in your mind the information you are learning.
4. **E**laboration: working with information to increase understanding and recall.
5. **C**oncentration: staying focused and attending to specific stimuli.
6. **R**ecitation: repeating information verbally in your own words.
7. **I**ntention: having a clear goal to learn.
8. **B**ig and little pictures: recognizing levels of information.
9. **F**eedback: self-quizzing to check your progress and understanding.
10. **O**rganization: reorganizing information in logical ways.
11. **T**ime on task: dedicating and scheduling ample time to learn.
12. **O**ngoing review: practicing retrieving information from memory.

Which Principles of Memory could a marketing expert use to prepare a polished presentation to her (his) clients?

On the following pages, for each of the twelve principles of memory you will find a definition, a learning goal (a purpose) to keep in mind as you apply the principle, an explanation, and basic strategies to apply as you study and review academic information. Read this information carefully, for it lays the foundation for many study skills strategies discussed in later chapters. Complete Exercise 2.4, **A Brief Summary Chart**, to record key information. These principles, when used consistently throughout the learning process, result in a stronger, more efficient memory.

EXERCISE 2.4   A Brief Summary Chart

After you read about the first four Principles of Memory, *pause to add summary notes to the following chart. Continue this process after you read each group of four* Principles of Memory.

Principle	Your Brief Summary
Selectivity	
Association	
Visualization	
Elaboration	

Principle	Your Brief Summary
Concentration	
Recitation	
Intention	
Big/Little Pictures	

Principle	Your Brief Summary
Feedback	
Organization	
Time on Task	
Ongoing Review	

Selectivity

SAVE CRIB FOTO

Definition: **Selectivity** is the process of identifying and separating main ideas and important details from a larger body of information.

Learning Goal: To identify the information to keep for further processing and to discard the information that is not relevant or significant to learn.

Explanation: Learning everything—every detail, every example, every word—is not possible and certainly not reasonable. All the stimuli would overload your working memory by requiring your undivided attention for too much information in a short period of time. Important information would fade or be dumped before you could process it. Without selectivity, you also risk the chance of processing insignificant information along with important information. The result could lead to cluttered, disorganized, and ineffective schemas of information in your long-term memory.

Application: You will use the principle of selectivity frequently in study strategies discussed in Chapters 6 through 11. Selectivity will help you decide what to survey in a book or a chapter, what to highlight or mark in your textbook, what information to write in your notes or to include in study tools that you create, and what information to study for tests. Each time you use selectivity, you will be honing your skills in identifying and pulling out main ideas and supporting details. The following are three basic study strategies based on the *principle of selectivity*.

1. Use your course syllabus, the introduction in your textbook, and your lecture notes to help you identify the main ideas, concepts, or themes. Notice the topics that receive frequent or repeated emphasis.

2. Use the special features in textbook chapters to help you identify the important details to learn. Special features include course-specific terminology, information that appears in the margins or in boxes, chapter summaries, and chapter questions or problems to solve.

3. As you read or listen to lectures, identify information that provides you with background information, refers to familiar information in order to warm you up to a new topic, or appears in the form of stories or examples designed to capture your attention. Recognize that these kinds of details help information flow smoothly and provide a setting for understanding the main ideas and important details, but they are not the details that you need to memorize or learn thoroughly.

Association

sAVE CRIB FOTO

Definition: **Association** is the process of linking or connecting together two or more items or chunks of information.

Learning Goal: To create a strong, vivid association between two or more items so one can serve as a memory cue to recall the other.

Explanation: Associations are made between two or more items. These items may be single words, pictures, or numbers, or they may be chunks of information that are grouped under one category. By quickly associating the items with previously learned information, a personal experience, a familiar object, or a schema, you hold the new information longer in your working memory and reduce the chance that the information will fade or be dumped out of memory. By using elaborative rehearsal to encode the information in a new way, such as linking it to a picture, explaining it out loud, or actually performing the action or process, you create associations that can later serve as *memory cues*, and you send a stronger coded message to your long-term memory. With clear, strongly coded messages, you can sometimes recall information instantly. More often, however, to locate information in your long-term memory, you need to conduct a **memory search** that involves activating your long-term memory and thinking your way to the information by linking ideas or associations until you find the necessary information.

Application: You can use many kinds of associations in the learning process. The following is a beginning list of possibilities for creating associations.

1. Associate new information with previously learned information. Ask yourself questions such as the following: *What do I already know about this? How is this similar or different from something I have already learned? When have I experienced this before? What schemas does this belong in? What does this look like or sound like?*

2. Associate study questions you create with their correct answers.

3. Associate printed or spoken information with a picture or a diagram that is in the book, presented in class, or created by you.

4. Associate new words or terminology with their definitions.

5. Associate individual items with a specific category, schema, or list you create.

6. Associate the information you learned with the setting in which you learned it. Ask yourself questions such as these: *Did I learn this from the textbook? Did I learn this by doing a lab project? Did I learn this through my homework assignment? Did I discuss this with a partner or a tutor? Did I learn this from a lecture?*

7. Associate the steps of a process with ways you can use the process. Ask yourself questions such as these: *Where else can this be used? What other products could I create by using these steps? What other kinds of problems can I solve by using this same process?*

Visualization	**SAVE CRIB FOTO**

Definition: **Visualization** is the process of making pictures and sometimes "movies" in your mind.

Learning Goal: To create a strong visual image of important information that can be recalled as needed from long-term memory.

Explanation: Visualization is a powerful memory tool that you can use when you rehearse and retrieve information. The effectiveness of visualization may be linked to the way our brains are structured. Because so many stimuli are visual, our working memory has a special storage center designed to manage visually encoded information. For many students, information presented in a visual or graphic form, such a picture or a diagram, is often easier to process than information presented in printed form such as paragraphs. Some visual learners can see "in their mind's eye" printed words, numbers, or formulas as they have seen them previously on textbook pages, on flash cards, in their notes, or on a screen in class. The ability to recall visual information is strengthened by the fact that many visualization strategies include verbalizing or explaining the information out loud. Consequently, the information becomes encoded and carried along two sensory paths (visual and linguistic or auditory), which boosts the ability to retrieve information from long-term memory.

Applications: Visualizing involves creating vivid, colorful, detailed pictures in your mind and recalling the pictures *without looking at the visual form itself*. To visualize, you can close your eyes and strive to visualize the picture, the graphic, or the movie "on the inside of your eyelids." Or you may prefer to look up, *to the left*, toward the ceiling to visualize. Looking up and to the left can be interpreted as a signal that you are accessing visual information from the right hemisphere of your brain. Once you have pulled your visualization back into your working memory, check the accuracy of the image by referring back to the original visual form. The following are four examples of ways you can use visualization.

1. Visualize (picture) yourself achieving specific goals, creating a mindset to concentrate on a task, or studying productively for a test. Visualizations provide you with incentive and motivation to make changes and perform on higher levels.

2. Examine, stare at, and visually memorize important objects you need to know such as medical instruments, a skeleton, rock samples, a 3-D science model, an electronic component, or a work of art. Focus on the size, shape, color, and specific details of the object and think of the function or uses of the object. Close your eyes or look away to practice visualizing the object; check your accuracy and strengthen the image if necessary.

3. Use mnemonics (memory tricks) that involve the use of colors and pictures to learn information that is difficult to remember. You will learn about mnemonics in Chapter 6.

4. To improve your reading comprehension, create *movies in your mind* as you read. Visualize the characters, the setting, the details, and the unfolding action as soon as you begin reading. If the process of *making movies in your mind* does not occur automatically, slow down your reading rate and make a concerted effort to activate your visual skills to "get the camera rolling" to create a movie in your mind.

Elaboration

SAV**E** CRIB FOTO

Definition: **Elaboration**, also called *elaborative rehearsal,* is the process of thinking about, pondering, or working with information in new ways in order to increase understanding, learning, and recall.

Learning Goal: To work with and practice information while it is fresh in your working memory.

Explanation: As soon as you begin the learning process, personalizing the information and working with the information make the information more meaningful. You can use a variety of encoding systems (visual, auditory, motor/kinesthetic, semantic) to lay a strong foundation of understanding that allows you to transfer meaningful, logically organized units or chunks of information to your existing schemas. Working with the information, clarifying meanings, attending to details, and focusing on steps forces you to move beyond *rote memory.* As with all the memory principles, activating the principle of elaboration also activates other thinking processes and memory principles.

Applications: Elaboration works for both *declarative knowledge* and *procedural knowledge.* However, determining whether new information involves declarative knowledge or procedural knowledge can help you select the most effective learning strategies to use. The following are five basic strategies that promote elaboration.

1. Ask yourself questions about the information you are learning. Explain or recite a complete answer. Later, when you want to retrieve the information from long-term memory, ask the same question again. For example, ask, *Does this make sense? How can I use this? When does this apply? When does this not apply? How is this like/different from (name another concept)? What schema does this belong to?*

2. Identify what type of encoding you used when you first received the stimuli or the information. Choose a different form of encoding when you rehearse. For factual information, typical options include talking, discussing, explaining/reciting, writing, or converting the information to pictures or a graphic form. Draw diagrams, label the parts, and describe how the parts in the diagram flow together. For steps and processes, use the previous suggestions plus repetitive practice. Rework the same problem several times; talk about or write the steps, mentally summarize the steps, and notice the key elements of the problem so that you can recognize those same elements in new problems.

3. Pay attention to details. For factual information, notice similarities and identify the minor differences among items. For procedures or processes, notice the details of the individual steps.

4. Weave big ideas or concepts together with their related details. Creating visual mappings, such as those at the beginning of each chapter in this textbook, is ideal for connecting different levels of information.

5. Generalize the information. Think about ways you can use the information, its functions, or its applications.

Concentration	**SAVE** **C**RIB **FOTO**

Definition: Concentration is the process of focusing the mind on only one task or item at a time, without interruptions to the thought process.

Learning Goal: To have a focused mind and undivided attention by blocking out disruptive thoughts and distractors.

Explanation: Concentration is essential for working memory to attend to stimuli and operate smoothly. The central executive function of your brain needs to perform multiple tasks organizing information, coordinating a variety of encoding systems, integrating information, and making decisions about information. It does not need extraneous or unrelated activities to add to its workload. In addition, you want to free up your working memory from distractions so that its full abilities can be used on the immediate learning task.

Applications: In Chapter 5, you will learn many techniques to strengthen your ability to concentrate, reduce the tendency to procrastinate, and reduce stress. In addition to the strategies in Chapter 5, you can use the following three strategies to create an environment and mindset for giving undivided attention to the process of learning.

1. Choose an environment that is conducive to concentrating and achieving undivided attention. Studying in a room with the door closed or in a quiet lab or library area is a conducive learning environment. Learning environments such as a noisy cafeteria, a grassy knoll in the sun, or a home area with active children tugging at you for attention are ineffective and contribute to poor concentration.

2. Be an **active learner**. Learning involves activities that work with the information and keep you actively involved in the learning process. Study with a pen in hand; be ready to jot down notes, make diagrams, create study tools, write comments in the margins of textbooks, and highlight text. Being actively involved decreases the likelihood that you will switch into *automatic pilot,* a state of mind in which you mechanically go through the motions without information registering in your memory.

3. Limit unnecessary stimuli that can interrupt your thought patterns. Studying with the television, stereo, or radio turned on brings unrelated stimuli into your working memory.

Recitation

SAVE C**R**IB FOTO

Definition: **Recitation** is the process of explaining information clearly, out loud in your own words, and in complete sentences.

Learning Goal: To explain information clearly and in an organized, knowledgeable manner without looking at printed information.

Explanation: Recitation encodes information linguistically and places information in an auditory channel to your long-term memory. Reciting by converting formal textbook information into your own form of expression helps you personalize the information. It also helps you hold information in your working memory longer, increase concentration, and improve comprehension. Perhaps the greatest benefit of recitation is that it provides you with immediate feedback on your level of understanding. When you recite as a part of a review process, you activate your auditory channel to schemas in long-term memory and bring that information back into your working memory.

Applications: Researchers, teachers, and students recognize the benefits of reciting. If you are initially uncomfortable reciting because you are not used to talking out loud to yourself, push yourself to include this memory principle in your study strategies. The more frequently you recite, the more comfortable you will become with this powerful activity. The following are four strategies for using the principle of recitation.

1. To prepare for class discussions, practice reciting information about the class topic *before* you enter the classroom. This provides you with the opportunity to familiarize yourself with the material, use course-related terminology effectively, practice putting ideas together coherently, and express yourself clearly.

2. Spend time each week reciting to yourself or to someone else the definitions for key terms in your textbook and from lectures. Understanding course-related terminology is an essential foundation skill you will want to master.

3. Recite important ideas, details, and procedures you encounter during the reading process and you capture in your textbook or lecture notes. Explaining them clearly strengthens your memory and ability to recall information.

4. Use self-quizzing to prepare for upcoming tests. Ask yourself questions and then practice reciting complete answers out loud. Reciting creates a linguistic association to the information. In testing situations, you can call upon your auditory memory to help you search for answers and "hear" yourself saying the correct information.

Intention

SAVE CRIB FOTO

Definition: **Intention** is the purpose or goal to act or perform in a specific way.

Learning Goal: To put yourself in a learning mode that includes a determination to accomplish a specific task or goal.

Explanation: Intention is knowing what you want or need to do (goal) and how you intend to do it (plan of action). Your working memory can be very active and efficient when you set the stage for learning. You make a commitment to organize yourself, your materials, your environment, your activities, and your thinking in order to optimize the learning situation. When your intent is to learn, you prepare yourself to receive incoming sensory stimuli, attach meaning to the information, activate related information in your long-term memory, and integrate information before you send it on to long-term memory. When your intent is to review, the same kinds of activity occur. If you approach a learning situation with a negative attitude, a lack of motivation or interest, or an unwillingness to apply effort, your working memory will accommodate your wishes by letting information fade within fifteen seconds and drop out of your working memory. By actively setting learning goals, you give yourself a purpose and motivation to achieve a specific outcome, and you create a receptive mind that is ready to engage in complex thinking processes.

Applications: Take time to identify your intentions by stating a learning goal and a course of action for your desired outcomes. The following three strategies use the principle of intention.

1. Create a list of your priorities and then organize the items on the list either by their degree of importance or by a logical sequence. Working with a priority list can help you avoid wasting time or procrastinating.

2. Identify a *specific* learning goal by stating exactly what you intend to accomplish. For example, your learning goal might be to survey the chapter to get an overview before starting to read the chapter thoroughly; to reread your notes or highlighted text to gain a fuller understanding; to rework previous problems to increase problem-solving speed and accuracy; to create study tools (flash cards, visual mappings, notes) for a specific chapter; to review materials in a specific chapter by self-testing or self-quizzing; or to review class notes, reorganize them, and work with them further.

3. Create a plan of action. Outline on paper or in your mind the steps you will work through to achieve your desired outcome. Knowing *how* you will achieve your goal before you begin the actual process increases your efficiency. For example, if your learning goal is to review a specific section in one of your math chapters, your plan of action could begin with categorizing or grouping the textbook examples according to the type of problem or the problem-solving method required. Then, your plan of action could be to recite the steps used to solve each kind of problem. Finally, your plan of action could be to rework the textbook examples and several of the math homework problems and to check the accuracy of your answers.

Big and Little Pictures

SAVE CRI**B** FOTO

Definition: **Big and Little Pictures** is an understanding that concepts and details are different levels of information: the *big pictures* are the schemas, concepts, or main ideas, and the *little pictures* are the supporting details.

Learning Goal: To identify the main ideas or concepts as well as the important supporting details (facts, definitions, functions, causes, effects, or steps in a process).

Explanations: This principle is sometimes referred to as seeing "the forest and the trees." If you focus only on the forest, you miss the meaning and beauty of individual trees. If you focus only on a few individual trees, you do not see how all the trees form together to make the forest. Learning new knowledge is similar to the idea of the forest and the trees. If you place too much emphasis on the details, you may fail to see their relationships to each other and to the larger concepts. If you focus only on finding main ideas, you lack specific details to support or prove the main idea. The principle of big picture–little picture serves to remind you to think actively about the various levels of information and to use your understanding of the structure of long-term memory: details are organized in clusters of related information (schemas). Each time you use associations, conduct memory searches, or activate retrieval cues, you access your memory bank by putting in or pulling out both concepts and details.

Applications: Many study strategies in this textbook emphasize the importance of identifying and responding to levels of information. The following three strategies use this principle of memory.

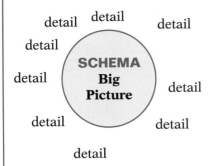

1. After you read textbook information or listen to a lecture, convert the information into a basic picture as shown on the left. Place the concept, topic, or main idea (the "big picture") in the center of your paper inside a circle. Surround the circle with details ("the little pictures") or items of information that develop or support the "big picture." Creating this quick visual graphic demonstrates your awareness and understanding of levels of information.

2. Convert textbook or lecture information into a list with the "big picture" (category or topic) as a heading. Then, write the "little pictures," the details that belong under this topic.

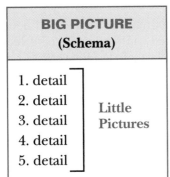

3. Use self-quizzing strategies. (Review page 37.) When you encounter new information or review previously learned information, ask yourself questions about the level of the information: *Is this a main idea? Was this the heading in a chapter? Was this the main topic for the lecture? Where does this detail fit or belong? What main idea or topic is it related to? What other details belong with this one?*

| Feedback | **SAVE CRIB FOTO** |

SAVE CRIB FOTO

Definition: **Feedback** is the process of verifying how accurately and thoroughly you have or have not learned specific information.

Learning Goal: To check your accuracy of remembering facts or processes and to correct any inaccuracies.

Explanation: As you learned from the **Feedback Model** (page 42), using feedback activities *as you learn* and *as you review* gives you opportunities to correct errors and strengthen your memory. Accurate information in working memory leads to accurate information in your long-term memory schemas. Using the steps of feedback is essential: *Learning Goal, Action, Feedback, Comparison, Results.*

Applications: Feedback is built into most study skills strategies. Regardless of the strategy you use to read, take notes, rehearse, or review, do not skip using the recommended feedback step. The following are four ways to give yourself feedback.

1. Recite often. Simply reading something out loud does encode the information linguistically, but it is not the same as reciting; reading does not provide feedback. Reciting techniques are built into most reading comprehension, note-taking, and study tool methods such as flash cards or visual notes. Self-quizzing techniques, such as the techniques you use to recite definitions from flash cards, emphasize reciting for feedback.

2. Use **Look-Away Techniques**. When you read, pause during the intake process of receiving new information by looking away and mentally rehearsing (or reciting) the information. When you study a process, pause, look away, and then review the steps involved. When you study a visual graphic, pause, look away, and then visualize the information. Look-Away Techniques keep information active in your working memory and provide you with time for the information to gel or integrate with other information.

3. Write summaries. When you reach the end of a section in a textbook chapter, *without looking at the textbook,* practice writing summaries that capture the main ideas and the important details. If you are learning the steps to a process, write the steps from memory and then check your accuracy. Writing summaries helps you check the accuracy of your learning and helps you prepare for short-answer and essay tests.

4. Rework math problems in the textbook and on homework assignments. Procedural knowledge needs to be practiced multiple times. For feedback, check your work with the textbook or homework answers.

Organization

SAVE CRIB F**O**TO

Definition: **Organization** refers to a meaningful, logical structure or arrangement of *ideas* or information.

Learning Goal: To organize information into meaningful chunks and to create associations that connect levels of information.

Explanation: Organizing information in new, meaningful ways forces you to examine information; identify main ideas, concepts, or themes; and connect important details to those "big ideas." It helps you personalize the information, hold information longer in your working memory, and then transfer the information into your long-term memory as chunks of related information to add to existing schemas. Taking time to reorganize information also increases comprehension, concentration, interest, and motivation.

Applications: In Chapters 6 through 11, you will learn to extract main ideas and important details, work with information in new ways, reorganize it, condense it, and create study tools to use for rehearsing and retrieving information. The following are three strategies that you can use to organize and work with information in new ways.

1. Categorize information by making lists. To avoid working with isolated details, group related details together under one category. Use the subject, main idea, theme, or concept as the heading for your category. *Twelve Principles of Memory*, for example, is a category heading for twelve different items. Studying and recalling lists of information is much easier than trying to locate random, isolated items scattered throughout your long-term memory.

2. Categorize information by making charts or tables. When you are working with more than one subject or main idea, a variety of charts and tables works effectively to represent the information as a unit or a chunk. You will learn more about visual charts and tables in Chapter 11. (See Chapter 11, page 298, for a visual mapping of the Twelve Principles of Memory.)

3. Organize the information chronologically, or by time sequence. Creating a chart or a time line for a series of events (such as in history or social science courses), the development of a product (such as in business or marketing courses), or a process involving steps in a given sequence (such as in math or science courses) gives you a visual representation of the information. The Feedback Model on page 42 is an example of a chronological chart.

Time on Task

SAVE CRIB FO**T**O

Definition: **Time on Task** refers to the amount of time and the spacing of contact time used to process information.

Learning Goal: To use time to your advantage by allocating sufficient time to the learning process and using spaced practice.

Explanation: If you overload your memory system by trying to study too much information at one time or for a period of time that is too long, the ability to comprehend and remember what you have studied decreases. By using *time on task* effectively, you will drastically reduce the need to *cram* or use *marathon studying.* (See Chapter 3, page 77.) Also, there is a high correlation between the amount of time spent studying and the grades earned in a course. Students who dedicate sufficient time to studying, which includes rehearsing, creating associations, bringing information back into working memory, and using retrieval cues efficiently, show greater success. Students who spend too little time studying or who cram to learn new information quickly tend not to do well or to show their true abilities.

Applications: In Chapter 3, you will learn many techniques for managing your time effectively and scheduling effective study blocks. The following are four techniques you can use to promote effective use of the *time on task* memory principle.

1. Use **spaced practice** (also called *distributed practice*) by making multiple contacts with new information and spreading those contacts over several days or weeks. Using spaced practice cuts down on your total learning time. (See Chapter 3, page 76.)

2. Use the **2:1 ratio** for your classes. The 2:1 ratio states that in most cases you will have ample time to learn and review course information when you schedule *two hours of studying for every hour in class.* (See Chapter 3, page 76.)

3. Plan to study one subject at a time in a fifty-minute block of time. Working with only one subject for fifty minutes keeps your working memory active and your mind focused on a specific set of concepts and details. After a fifty-minute period, take a short break to give your working memory time to finish processing and to free up space for new information.

4. Identify the kind of information you are working with when you study. If you are working with procedural knowledge (steps and processes), your time on task to master the steps in the process will be greater that the time you will need to master declarative knowledge (facts).

Ongoing Review

SAVE CRIB FOT**O**

Definition: **Ongoing Review** is the process of practicing previously learned information.

Learning Goal: To use time and effort each week to review previously learned information.

Explanations: Even though information in long-term memory is considered to be permanent, without ongoing review, access to the information can be blocked or denied. To remember, recall, and access information stored in long-term memory, you need to reactivate the paths to that information, practice using retrieval cues and associations, and revisit the information frequently to keep it active in your working memory.

Applications: Ongoing review is the final step of most reading, notetaking, and study skills strategies. In addition to the strategies you will learn in later chapters, the following four strategies use the principle of ongoing review.

1. When you have difficulty recalling or retrieving information, strive to recall the encoding system you used during the initial learning process. If you encoded the information visually, try to remember what visual form you used. If you encoded the information linguistically, try to recall the conversation, discussion, or lecture. If you used dual encoding, encoding with more than one sensory system, you have two possible ways to recall the information.

2. Be patient when you need to do a memory search. Use associations to move from one idea to another until you locate the information in your long-term memory. Think of related items, where you were when you learned the information, examples you used to connect ideas, questions you asked yourself, or study tools you created.

3. For procedural knowledge, rework problems with the goal to increase your accuracy and your problem-solving speed. With frequent practice and ongoing review, many of these procedures can become more automatic.

4. Conduct a final review right before you know you will need to use the information: before a test, a class discussion, a speech, or a performance task.

ONLINE PRACTICE 4

Visit the *Essential Study Skills*, Fifth Edition, website and go to Chapter 2. Click on **Practice 4: Twelve Principles of Memory**. Complete the twelve questions by typing in the name of the memory principle described in the question. Upon completion of the quiz, you will receive your score. You can exit at that time, or you can print or e-mail your results to your instructor.

EXERCISE 2.5   Matching Principles to Descriptions

Match the principles below with the descriptions at the right. On the line, write the letter from the list at the right to show your answer.

———— **1.** Selectivity

———— **2.** Association

———— **3.** Visualization

———— **4.** Elaboration

———— **5.** Concentration

———— **6.** Recitation

———— **7.** Intention

———— **8.** Big Picture–Little Picture

———— **9.** Feedback

————**10.** Organization

————**11.** Time on Task

————**12.** Ongoing Review

a. I practice and review information by saying it out loud, in my own words, and in complete sentences.

b. I use self-quizzing to verify that I am learning new information.

c. I create learning goals to focus on what I plan to accomplish.

d. I link new information to old information, to other concepts, or to pictures.

e. I use strategies to keep my mind focused on the material I am studying.

f. I schedule ample time to study, rehearse, make study tools, and review.

g. I practice retrieving information from memory on a regular basis.

h. I make pictures or movies in my mind for the information I study.

i. I carefully select the main ideas and important details to study.

j. I look for the larger concepts and the smaller details of information I study.

k. I personalize the learning process by rearranging information in logical, meaningful ways.

l. I think about, work with, and encode information in new ways.

EXERCISE 2.6   Textbook Case Studies

Read about each of the following student situations carefully. Then, on your own paper and in complete sentences, answer the question that follows each case study. You can also answer these questions online at this textbook's Chapter 2 website. You can print your online responses or e-mail them to your instructor.

1. By the end of the week, Curtis needs to read a thirty-page chapter and be prepared to discuss it in class. Curtis does not enjoy this textbook or course, so he tends to procrastinate. The night before class he reads quickly through the chapter to get an overview. He jots down a few words, phrases, and main ideas and shoves the list in his book so he will be prepared for the class discussion the next day. Instead of a class discussion, however, the instructor gives a short quiz. Curtis answers only two out of ten questions. What principles of memory did Curtis ignore when he read the assignment?

EXERCISE 2.6 continued

2. Damon knows he learns best when he can discuss information with others. He will have a midterm in one of his classes in two weeks. Damon asks other students in class to join him in a study group. His enthusiasm and understanding of the subject attract many students to his study group. What principles of memory does Damon implement in this approach to prepare for his midterm?

3. Mary has been on the Honor Roll twice in the last two years. This term she faces many challenges and conflicts in her personal life, which make studying and focusing on her classes difficult. Seeing her grades decline adds more concerns to her life. Mary knows she has to find ways to free up her working memory, but she is not sure where to begin. What strategies would you suggest that Mary use to free up her working memory and get her academic performance back to its previous level of success?

ONLINE CASE STUDIES

Visit the *Essential Study Skills*, Fifth Edition, website and go to Chapter 2. Click on **Online Case Studies**. In the text boxes, respond to four additional case studies that are only available online. You can print your responses or e-mail them to your instructor.

 EXERCISE 2.7 LINKS

Work with a partner or a small group. Discuss answers for the following questions. Be prepared to share your answers with the class.

1. Are the Twelve Principles of Memory more applicable to specific kinds of learning styles, or are they applicable to all learning styles? Explain your answer with specific details.

2. What relationship do you see between using working memory effectively and strengthening multiple intelligences?

Reflection Writing 3
Chapter 2

On separate paper, in a journal, or online at this textbook's website, respond to the following questions.

1. What did you learn about working memory that will help you become a more powerful learner?

2. Which Principles of Memory would bring about the greatest changes in your study methods if you used them on a regular basis? Explain.

SUMMARY

■ The Information Processing Model is one model that explains how we receive, learn, store, and retrieve information. The six parts of the model lead to a final outcome or product that demonstrates successful learning: *sensory input, short-term memory, rehearsal path, feedback loop, long-term memory,* and *long-term memory retrieval.*

■ Sensory input gets encoded into a recognizable form to transmit to long-term memory. The four most common encoding systems are *linguistic, visual, motor,* and *semantic encoding.* You can strengthen the path to long-term memory by translating information from one encoded form to another as you rehearse.

■ *Elaborative rehearsal* involves transferring information into long-term memory by thinking about and working with it in new ways. Self-quizzing and feedback are essential components of rehearsal.

■ Long-term memory is organized around clusters of general information called *schemas.* Schemas contain main ideas or concepts as well as important related details. Retrieving information from long-term memory often involves conducting *memory searches* and using *memory cues* to locate information stored in the schemas.

■ The Working Memory Model is a contemporary model that explains the activities and processes that occur in the conscious mind (working memory). This model, which incorporates the key elements from the Information Processing Model, shows a multidirectional flow of information and more interaction and activity occurring between working and long-term memory.

■ In the Working Memory Model, sensory input is transmitted to two short-term storage centers. Another part of the brain, the *central executive,* attends to, coordinates, and organizes information from the storage centers and the processing of information in and out of long-term memory.

■ Working memory, to work efficiently, requires undivided attention. You can free up your working memory by removing intrusive thoughts, emotions, distractions, and stress.

■ Learning involves two kinds of information: *declarative knowledge* (facts, concepts, and experiences) and *procedural knowledge* (steps in a process to complete a skill).

■ The Feedback Model, which provides information about how well you are learning or recalling information, has five steps: *learning goal, action, feedback through self-quizzing, comparison,* and *results (yes or no).*

■ Using the Twelve Principles of Memory helps you process information more efficiently through your memory system. The mnemonic *SAVE CRIB FOTO* represents the twelve principles: *selectivity, association, visualization, elaboration, concentration, recitation, intention, big and little pictures, feedback, organization, time on task,* and *ongoing review.*

CULMINATING OPTIONS FOR CHAPTER 2

1. Visit this textbook's website and go to Chapter 2 to complete the following exercises.
   a. Flash card review of Chapter 2 terms and definitions
   b. ACE Practice Test 1 with ten fill-in-the-blank questions
   c. ACE Practice Test 2 with ten true-false questions
   d. ACE Practice Test 3 with ten multiple-choice questions
   e. ACE Practice Test 4 with three short answer—critical thinking questions

2. Go to Appendix C in the back of this textbook for more Learning Options to use for additional practice, enrichment, or portfolio projects.

Chapter 2 REVIEW QUESTIONS

Matching

Match the terms below with the descriptions at the right. On the line, write the letter from the list at the right to show your answer.

_____ **1.** Schemas

_____ **2.** Long-term memory

_____ **3.** Self-quizzing

_____ **4.** Declarative knowledge

_____ **5.** Procedural knowledge

_____ **6.** Goal-action-feedback-comparison-results

_____ **7.** Working memory

_____ **8.** Rote memory

_____ **9.** Spaced practice

_____ **10.** Elaborative rehearsal

a. Factual information

b. Any technique that tests your understanding

c. Spreading contact with material over time

d. Conscious memory or mind

e. Knowledge of steps to use for a procedure or process

f. Memorizing without emphasizing understanding

g. Clusters of related information in long-term memory

h. Permanent memory with unlimited capacity

i. Thinking about and practicing information in new ways

j. Steps in the Feedback Model

True-False

Carefully read the following statements. Write T if the statement is completely TRUE. Write F if the statement or any part of the statement is FALSE.

_____ **1.** Short-term memory and working memory hold all sensory stimuli until information is thoroughly learned.

_____ **2.** Linguistic, motor, visual, and semantic codes can be used to send information into long-term memory.

_____ **3.** The memory principles of association, intention, and organization are usually used in elaborative rehearsal techniques.

_____ **4.** Self-quizzing, reciting, and Look-Away Techniques are ways to get feedback about how well you are learning information.

_____ **5.** More repetition and practice are often required for declarative knowledge than are required for procedural knowledge.

_____ **6.** When you conduct a memory search for information, associations often work as memory cues to locate information.

_____ **7.** The memory principle of organization refers to organizing your work area, your notebook, and your study materials so that they are easy to use.

_____ **8.** Spaced practice is the opposite of distributed practice.

_____ **9.** All information stored in schemas is stored in the form of pictures.

_____ **10.** Information in long-term memory can be activated by sensory stimuli in working memory.

Short Answer—Critical Thinking

Use complete sentences to answer each of the following questions.

1. Why does some information drop out or fade from your working memory?

2. How does working memory use associations to rehearse and retrieve information?

CHAPTER 3

Managing Your Time

Terms to Know

pie of life
Increase–Decrease Method
term schedule
weekly schedule
fixed study blocks
2:1 ratio
spaced practice
marathon studying
trading time
flex study blocks
daily schedule
task schedule

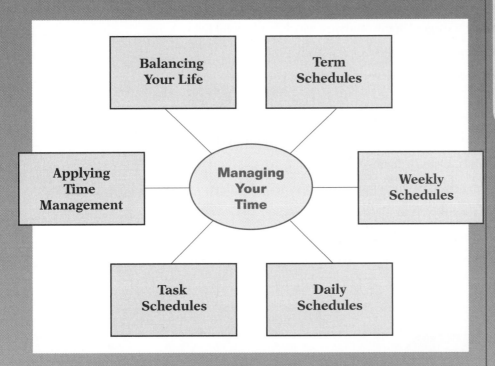

Time management, perhaps the most essential of all study skills, is an organized method for planning the use of your time to achieve goals. Learning to use time management to balance your academic, work, and leisure time leads to greater productivity, more successes, and less stress. Using four different kinds of schedules, including a comprehensive weekly schedule, puts you in control of your life.

Chapter 3 Managing Your Time Profile

ANSWER, SCORE, and **RECORD** your profile before you read this chapter. If you need to review the process, refer to the complete directions given in the Profile for Chapter 1 on page 2.

ONLINE: You can complete the profile and get your score online at this textbook's website.

	YES	NO
1. I use a weekly schedule to organize my studying, work, and social lives.		
2. Friends and family often take priority over my study time.		
3. I try to make each scheduled day different so I do not get bored.		
4. I often study for three hours or more in a row so I can stay current with my reading and homework assignments.		
5. I usually study two hours during the week for every one hour in class.		
6. I schedule specific times to study during the weekend.		
7. I know the times during the day when I am the most mentally alert.		
8. I study my least favorite subjects at night.		
9. I avoid time management because I prefer to be spontaneous.		
10. I am confident that I have the skills necessary to manage my time well.		

Reflection Writing 1
Chapter 3

On separate paper, in a journal, or online at this textbook's website, respond to the following questions.

1. What is your profile score for this chapter? What does it mean to you?

2. How do you currently feel about time management? What successes and problems have you had with time management? Give details.

Balancing Your Life

As a student you will need to continually balance three main areas in your life: school, work, and leisure. *School* includes attending classes; completing homework assignments; studying on your own, with a partner, with a tutor, or in a study group; developing study tools; using ongoing review; and preparing for tests. School may also include involvement with athletics, student government, or student organizations. *Work* includes a part- or full-time job, volunteer work, and any personal responsibilities such as parenting, household chores, and running errands. *Leisure* includes time with family and friends, recreational activities, personal hobbies, or personal time to relax or pursue special interests. How you spend your time in these three main areas depends on your goals, needs, and interests. Feeling confident, fulfilled, happy, challenged, and in control are signs that you have achieved an effective balance in your life. Frequent bouts with negative feelings, self-doubt, resentment, or a sense of a lack of control are signs that you need to examine and rebalance the three areas of your life.

Pie of Life

The **pie of life** is a graphic representation that shows how much time you dedicate to each of the three main areas of your life: school, work, and leisure. A balanced pie is not necessarily divided into three equal parts; the amounts of time dedicated to school, work, and leisure vary according to an individual's circumstances, goals, and values. A student who is not working or not living with family members will have a different pie of life than a student who has a job or family responsibilities. The first circle below shows a pie of life divided into three equal parts. Divide the second circle into a pie that shows the estimated amount of time you spend per week in each of the three areas of life. In the last circle, adjust the lines to show your ideal pie of life.

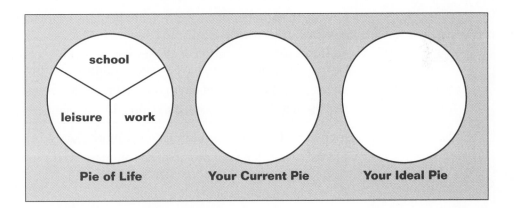

Achieving your ideal pie of life requires a willingness to examine the ways you currently use time and a commitment to try new strategies that will improve your time management and goal-setting skills. Change is not always easy, but the benefits of having a more balanced life make it rewarding.

Increase–Decrease Method

There are only so many hours in a week. If your pie is unbalanced, you have two choices. First, you can learn new strategies to use your time more efficiently. Using strategies in this textbook can result in more effective studying, thus reducing or eliminating time wasted using ineffective techniques. They can also result in performing tasks such as shopping, household chores, or errands more effectively and efficiently. Second, you can use the **Increase–Decrease Method** to change the boundaries in the *pie of life* by expanding or increasing any section of the pie that needs more time. To do this, you will need to decrease one or both of the remaining sections of the pie. The following chart provides you with options for adjusting the boundaries and getting you closer to the balance you seek.

Using the Increase–Decrease Method to Balance Your Pie

Problem	Possible Solutions
Too Little Time for Family or Friends	1. Reduce the amount of time spent on leisure activities that exclude family or friends. 2. Reduce or change work hours, if possible. 3. Reduce the hours spent on chores by seeking more help from other members in the household or by using goal setting to do chores more efficiently. 4. Reduce school hours by taking fewer classes, if possible. 5. Reduce nonproductive study time by learning more efficient study techniques.
Too Little Time for School	1. Reduce social time; make school a greater priority. 2. Create more "meaningful" or "quality" social time and eliminate the less significant time spent with friends or family. 3. Reduce work hours, if possible, to make more time for studying. 4. Apply for scholarships, financial aid, grants, and/or loans to replace income if you reduce your work hours. 5. Reduce the number of classes you are taking so you have enough time to do well in fewer classes. 6. Examine the combination of classes you are taking; consider alternative classes if all your classes have heavy reading or writing requirements. 7. Learn time-management techniques to make better use of your time. 8. Use the self-discipline needed to study during planned study blocks.
Too Much Leisure Time	1. Increase school time by adding one or more classes. 2. Increase work hours, if possible, or volunteer your time at a local agency, community program, or organization. 3. Pursue new hobbies or set new goals. 4. Get involved with campus groups, organizations, or work-study programs.

ONLINE REVIEW

Visit the *Essential Study Skills*, Fifth Edition, website and go to Chapter 3. Click on **Online Review: Pie of Life,** an interactive review of key concepts about the three areas of the pie of life. This is a read-only website; you will not be required to answer questions.

ONLINE   PRACTICE   1

> Visit the *Essential Study Skills*, Fifth Edition, website and go to Chapter 3. Click on **Practice 1: Increase–Decrease Method**. Then type responses to the four questions. After you type your responses, you can print your responses or e-mail them to your instructor.

EXERCISE 3.1   How You Use Time

Complete Parts 1 and 2 to show your use of time for a three-day period.

Part 1: *Keep a log of how you spend your time for three complete days. Begin your log by writing time blocks down the left side of a sheet of paper. Begin with the time you wake up and continue with half-hour blocks throughout the day until you go to bed. (Example: 7:00, 7:30, 8:00, 8:30, . . . 11:30 PM) For each time block, write what you did during that time. Be specific. After you have collected your data for three days, count the number of hours for each of the categories shown in the following chart. Some activities may fit in more than one category, but you must count each activity only once, so select the most appropriate category to classify the activity. Your total hours for all three days should equal seventy-two hours.*

Three-Day Time Log

Categories of Time	Hours Spent
• How many hours did you spend on school? (Include class time, reading and studying, school activities and meetings, tutors, study groups, and lab times.)	
• How many hours did you spend on work? (Include employment, household chores, preparing meals, and errands.)	
• How many hours did you spend on leisure? (Include time with friends, family members, talking on the phone, watching television, listening to music, using the Internet, recreation, exercise, hobbies, and other similar leisure-time activities.)	
• How many hours did you spend sleeping and napping?	
• How many hours did you spend on things other than those listed above? (Include time spent getting ready in the morning, commuting, and miscellaneous.)	
Total Hours:	72

Part 2: *On separate paper, answer the following questions.*

1. Were you surprised by the amount of time you spent in one or more of the categories? Explain.
2. Does the data reflect your desired *pie of life*? Explain.
3. What activities do you feel show excessive or ineffective use of your time?

Term Schedules

Well-designed schedules serve as road maps to guide you through the term, through the week, and through each day. Rather than being at the mercy of time, you take control of it. With schedules, *you* create goals and plans for how you wish to spend your time.

A **term schedule** is a month-by-month calendar that shows important events and deadlines for the entire term. You can use a regular calendar or a monthly planner, or you can create a monthly calendar on a computer and run enough copies for each month in the term. At the beginning of each term, create your term schedule by adding the following items to your calendar:

Items to Include on Your Term Schedule

1. Important deadlines for special projects, reports, and writing or lab assignments that appear on your course syllabi
2. Scheduled tests, midterms, and final exams
3. Special events, meetings, workshops, or conferences
4. Holidays
5. Scheduled times for tutors, study groups, or other support services
6. Personal appointments on or off campus

Keep the term calendar in the front of your notebook so you can refer to it on a regular basis. Update the calendar throughout the term with deadlines for new assignments or significant events. A term calendar is an effective tool that provides you with an overview of the term, reduces the chances that you will overlook or forget an important date, and serves as a guide when you create your weekly schedule.

⊙ EXERCISE 3.2   Term Schedules

Use your campus calendar, the syllabus from each of your courses, and your personal calendar of events to create a term schedule. Include the six items listed in the box above. If your instructor does not provide you with calendar pages, use any month-to-month calendar, planner, or computer software program. A monthly calendar is also available online at this textbook's website.

Weekly Schedules

A **weekly schedule** is a detailed plan that serves as a guide for creating a comfortable, manageable routine in which you can be productive and bring greater balance to your life. Using a weekly schedule can help you maintain a focus and help you organize, monitor, and regulate your use of time for various activities and obligations. By learning to use time-management skills effectively, being your own time manager becomes a rewarding lifelong skill.

The example of a weekly schedule on page 74 shows many characteristics of an effective time-management schedule. The schedule is organized logically and realistically so it is easy to follow. Adequate time blocks are set aside for class assignments and studying, work (employment, errands, and chores), and leisure time. The schedule also plans time for getting ready in the morning, commuting, eating meals, and sleeping. Unlike a time log made *after* you complete activities or tasks, a weekly time-management schedule is made *before* you engage in the activities. The weekly schedule becomes your *plan*, your guide, and your structure for the week.

Characteristics of an Effective Weekly Schedule

Consider the following characteristics of an effective weekly schedule when you create your own schedule. Strive to include as many of these characteristics as possible in your weekly schedule. If you are not able to include some of these characteristics in your weekly schedule this term because of personal situations or class schedules, strive to include them in your weekly schedule the following term when you have new classes or changes in other personal situations. The following are the characteristics of an effective weekly schedule:

- **The schedule reflects a realistic *pie of life* balance.** By planning seven days at a time, you can schedule sufficient study and review time spread out throughout the week. You can plan how much time to devote to studying rather than studying only when you have an assignment due or have an upcoming test. On your schedule, you can set aside blocks of time for employment, household chores, errands, and time for family, friends, and recreation.

- **The schedule includes time for specific goals you wish to achieve.** For example, if you want to work at a job three times a week, meditate for twenty minutes every day, or spend time in the park with your children twice a week, demonstrate the importance of the goal and your commitment to it by scheduling blocks of time for your goals each week.

- **The schedule has strong patterns that can easily become routine.** Consistent patterns for certain days of the week or times of the day make learning your weekly schedule easier. The following are examples of strong patterns you can use in your schedule:

  - If you have classes that meet Monday, Wednesday, and Friday, use the same daily schedule for each of these three days.
  - Set a specific time each day or on alternating days to show when you plan to study for a specific course. For example, study *writing* from 2:00 to 3:00 PM Monday, Wednesday, and Friday. Study *history* from 7:00 to 9:00 PM Tuesday, Wednesday, and Thursday.
  - Plan for *social and leisure activities* and *dinner* every day from 4:00 to 7:00 PM.

- **The schedule reflects your individual learning styles, preferences, and lifestyle.** Schedule time for personal preferences such as working in study groups, with a study partner, or with a tutor. When possible, schedule study blocks during the time of the day when you are most alert, not when you tend to be physically fatigued or have a lower level of concentration. Schedule study blocks before classes, between classes, or after classes to allow more time later in the day to spend time with children at home.

- **The schedule provides time for meals, exercise, and adequate sleep.** To keep your energy high and your physical and emotional health strong, plan time to enjoy three relaxing, nutritious meals a day and to participate in some form of exercise. Establish a routine time to go to bed so that your internal clock and your sleep-awake patterns will be stable and will provide you with adequate rest each night.

In addition to computers, what other electronic devices can a person use to manage time and create schedules?

WEEKLY TIME-MANAGEMENT SCHEDULE

For the week of _____

Time	Monday	Tuesday	Wednesday	Thursday	Friday	Saturday	Sunday
12–6 AM	SLEEP ———————————————————————→						
6–7:00	SLEEP ———————————————————————→						
7–8:00	Get up, get ready, eat breakfast ————→					SLEEP	SLEEP
8–9:00	Commute to school ————————————→					Get up	Get up
9–10:00	PE Class	Study Math	PE Class	Study Math	PE Class	breakfast	breakfast
10–11:00	Math Class	Math Class	Math Class	Math Class	Study Math	Career Class	Get ready
11–12 NOON	Study Math	LUNCH	Study Math	LUNCH	with TUTOR	Study Career	CHURCH
12–1:00	LUNCH	Computer Class	LUNCH	Computer Class	LUNCH	ERRANDS	CHURCH
1–2:00	Reading Class	Computer Class	Reading Class	Computer Class	Reading Class	LUNCH	LUNCH
2–3:00	Study Reading	Lab-Study Computer	Study Reading	Lab-Study Computer	Study Reading	CHORES	LEISURE
3–4:00	Study Reading	Lab-Study Computer	FLEX	Lab-Study Computer	FLEX	CHORES	LEISURE
4–5:00	Commute home ————————————————→					CHORES	LEISURE
5–6:00	DINNER ————————————————————→						LEISURE
6–7:00	LEISURE	LEISURE	LEISURE	LEISURE	WORK	WORK	DINNER
7–8:00	Study Reading	WORKOUT	Study Math	WORKOUT	WORK	WORK	Study Math
8–9:00	Study Reading		Study Computer		WORK	WORK	Study Computer
9–10:00	LEISURE		LEISURE		WORK	WORK	FLEX
10–11:00	LEISURE		LEISURE		WORK	WORK	PLAN WEEK
11–12 AM	SLEEP ————————————————→				WORK	WORK	SLEEP

Five Steps for Creating a Weekly Time-Management Schedule

Each Sunday spend a few minutes planning your schedule for the upcoming week. Keep this schedule in the front of your notebook. Refer to this schedule whenever you wish to make new plans or set up appointments. By using the following steps to create your weekly schedule, you can feel confident that you will have a more balanced weekly routine.

Creating a Weekly Time-Management Schedule

1. Write in all your fixed activities.
2. Write in your fixed study times for each class.
3. Add several flexible study blocks.
4. Add time for personal goals and other responsibilities.
5. Schedule leisure, family, and social time.

Step 1: Write your fixed activities.   Fixed activities are those activities that do not change from week to week as well as special appointments that cannot easily be rescheduled. On your weekly calendar, write the following fixed activities in the appropriate time blocks:

1. Class times

2. Work schedule (employment)

3. Meals

4. Special appointments

5. Sleep

Step 2: Write your fixed study times.   After learning about the importance of the memory principles of time on task and ongoing review, you should understand the importance of making study blocks a high priority on your weekly schedule.

How should these athletes schedule their practice time for the term? Do you think athletes should consider athletics as part of school, work, or leisure?

By using the following time-management principles for scheduling **fixed study blocks**, you will be able to allot sufficient time to complete your reading and homework assignments, create study tools, use elaborative rehearsal, and practice retrieving information through ongoing review.

■ Use the 2:1 ratio for all of your classes. The **2:1 ratio** recommends studying two hours for every hour in class, for all of your classes that require reading and homework assignments. For example, if your writing class meets for three hours each week, schedule six hours of studying *for the writing class* each week. The following points about the 2:1 ratio are important to know.

 ■ When you first begin using the 2:1 ratio, you may think it gives you too many study hours per week. Remember, however, that studying in college means much more than just doing the reading or the assignments.

 ■ On some occasions you may have classes that truly do not require the use of the 2:1 ratio; you can perform well in the classes and have sufficient study and review time with fewer fixed study hours.

 ■ You may also on occasion have classes that require more than the 2:1 ratio; perhaps you will need a 3:1 ratio for an extremely demanding class.

 ■ In other words, the 2:1 ratio is a standard college expectation for the amount of *quality* time you spend studying, but the ratio is not necessarily the most appropriate for all classes.

■ Use spaced practice to space your learning over different study blocks and different days of the week. **Spaced practice,** also known as *distributed practice,* is a time-management and learning technique that involves allowing sufficient time for your brain to process information by limiting the length of a study block and spreading study blocks out over time. The following points about spaced practice are important to know.

 ■ When you use spaced practice, your ability to understand and recall information occurs with less difficulty.

 ■ The breaks or rest intervals between study blocks give your memory system time to sort, process, and connect information.

 ■ Spaced practice can also increase your interest, motivation, level of concentration, and overall attitude toward a subject. For example, you would better understand and recall information that you are studying for a history class if you studied it for one hour six times a week or two hours (fifty minutes with a ten-minute break between the two hours) three days a week rather than studying it for six hours at one time or for six hours on the same day.

 The following chart from Tony Buzan's *Use Both Sides of Your Brain* shows the amount of recall *during the learning process.* The following points about this recall chart are important to know.

 ■ When short breaks (such as reflection time) occur during a one-hour study block, understanding and retention of information remain high.

 ■ When no breaks are taken during a two-hour period, the recall drops below 60 percent.

 ■ When no breaks are taken during a learning period that is longer than two hours (in other words, when spaced practice is not used), recall drops below 40 percent.

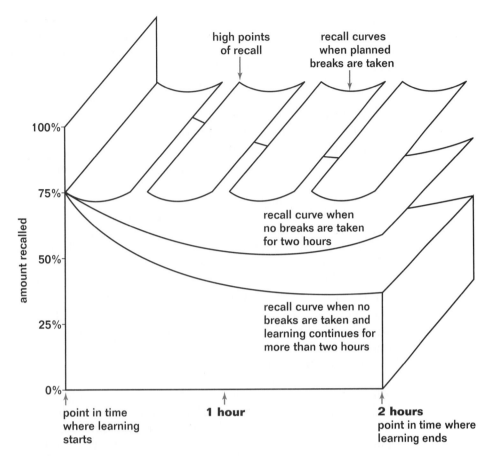

high points
of recall

recall curves
when planned
breaks are taken

100%

75%

amount recalled

recall curve when
no breaks are taken
for two hours

50%

25%

recall curve when no
breaks are taken and
learning continues for
more than two hours

0%

point in time
where learning
starts

1 hour

2 hours
point in time where
learning ends

Recall during learning — with and without breaks. A learning period of between 20–50 minutes produces the best relationship between understanding and recall. If a period of learning from a lecture, a book or the mass media is to take two hours, it is far better to arrange for brief breaks during these two hours. In this way the recall curve can be kept high, and can be prevented from dropping during the later stages of learning. The small breaks will guarantee eight relatively high points of recall, with four small drops in the middle. Each of the drops will be less than the main drop would have been were there no breaks. Breaks are additionally useful as relaxation points. They get rid of the muscular and mental tension which inevitably builds up during periods of concentration.

Source: Tony Buzan, *Use Both Sides of Your Brain,* figure from p. 61. Copyright © 1974, 1983 by Tony Buzan. Used by permission of Dutton, a division of Penguin Group (USA) Inc.

■ Avoid marathon studying. **Marathon studying,** also known as *massed practice,* occurs when you study more than three hours in a row. Three or more continuous hours of reading to comprehend, practice, and memorize course information often results in lower productivity, concentration, retention, and effectiveness. The following points about marathon studying are important to know.

■ You will see better results by studying for one to three hours and then changing to a different kind of activity.

■ Stepping away from studying gives your mind time to mull over, work with, and process information.

■ Marathon studying, however, can be effective in learning situations that involve a flow of creativity, such as sculpting, constructing a model, or writing a research paper. In fact, staying with the learning process for more than three hours in these kinds of situations may be a better course of action than leaving the process and trying later to tap back into the same channel of creativity.

■ Use trading time sparingly. **Trading time** is a time-management technique that allows you to trade or exchange time blocks for two activities within the same day. For example, if you want to participate in an unexpected social activity that will occur during your 7:00–9:00 PM study block, you can trade the study block with a 2:00–4:00 block of time you had set aside to spend with friends. Trading times, or switching time blocks, gives you some flexibility to respond to unexpected events; however, use trading time sparingly. If you trade time blocks too frequently, you will lose the sense of routine, and your self-discipline to follow your schedule may decline.

■ Use the entire study block for one subject. Jumping from one subject to another within an hour block does not provide you with adequate time to get involved with the material, to create a "mindset" for the subject matter, to establish an effective level of concentration, or to allow time for information to consolidate or register in your memory. Begin the study block by reviewing previous work and then work on the current assignment. If you complete the assignment, use the remaining time to review the information, take notes, create special study tools, recite what you learned, and think about the information, its importance, and its applications.

■ Study during your most alert times of the day. You will be more mentally sharp and able to concentrate without too many distractions. For many students, studying early in the day is the best time for high concentration and productivity. Studying right after lunch or in the late afternoon after a busy day is not effective or productive. Some students claim that they study most effectively late at night, but research shows that in most cases this assertion is not accurate. People's bodies and eyes may be physically fatigued and their levels of concentration may be affected by the day's events. If you notice a pattern of having trouble concentrating during certain times of the day, use those times to complete chores or engage in social or family time.

■ Use the *Essential Strategies for Scheduling Study Blocks* on page 79. These additional strategies will help you create an effective weekly schedule.

Step 3: Add several flexible study blocks.   Identify two or three hours each week that you can hold in reserve in case you need additional time to study for a specific class, prepare for a test, or complete a special project. On your weekly schedule, write *flex* for these time blocks. Unlike fixed study blocks, which you should use each time they appear on your schedule, **flex study blocks** are flexible blocks of time that you use only when you need them. Flex blocks are *safety nets* for extra study time. If you do not need flex blocks, convert them to free time.

Step 4: Add time for personal goals and other responsibilities.   Any important goals should have time allotted on your weekly schedule so you can work on them. If you do not specifically set aside time, you may find yourself postponing the goals or any other personal responsibilities or dabbling at them instead of making steady progress.

Step 5: Schedule leisure, family, and social time.   After you complete steps one through four, the remaining time on your schedule can be labeled *family, social,* or *leisure.* You can include specific plans such as "family skating," "movie," or "go fishing," or you can leave the time open and flexible to whatever you are in the mood to do at that time. Having family, social, and leisure time is important for mental and physical health and strong relationships. If you do not have adequate time on your schedule for these activities, look for ways to use the Increase–Decrease Method to find a more comfortable balance in your week.

SET LEARNING GOALS

The following *Essential Strategies for Scheduling Study Blocks* chart highlights seven important strategies to use to create a weekly schedule with effective study blocks. Place a star next to the strategies that you will be able to use this term. Highlight the strategies that you cannot use this term because they do not fit your existing schedule.

Essential Strategies for Scheduling Study Blocks

▶ **Label each study block** to show specifically the course you intend to study during that time block. Labeling a block "study" does not provide you with a plan to implement the 2:1 ratio; instead, you will find yourself studying whatever you feel the most urgency to get done. Use specific labels such as *Study English*, *Study Math*, or *Study Psychology*.

▶ **Schedule at least one study block every day of the week.** By spreading your study times throughout the entire week, you will have time during the weekdays to enjoy leisure activities. This method provides a better balance and creates less stress than using a typical student pattern of studying long hours during the weekdays and then engaging mainly in leisure activities on the weekend.

▶ **Schedule a math study block every day.** On the days when you have a math class, if possible, schedule a math study block right after the class. Studying math on a daily basis provides essential time for ongoing review and application of math problem-solving skills. Multiple contacts with the same material over the course of several days results in fewer mistakes and stronger memory. To bring current principles and processes into your working memory, begin each math study block by reviewing current notes and textbook pages. Rework examples and use self-explanations to restate the steps or equations needed to solve the problems. Use the remainder of the study block to begin new assignments.

▶ **Schedule your hardest or least-liked subjects early in the day.** Do not delay studying for your hardest or least-liked subjects until the end of the day. By placing the hardest or least-liked subjects first on your study priorities, you are able to use a more alert mind and focused attention to tackle the assignments and process new information.

▶ **Schedule a study block right before a class that involves discussion or student participation.** This puts you in the mindset for the course, refreshes your memory of key concepts, and provides you with time to rehearse as needed. For example, you will feel better prepared and more confident walking into a foreign language class or a speech class if you are able to study and review the information the hour before the class.

▶ **Schedule a study block right after a lecture class.** During lecture classes or teacher-directed classes, one of your main tasks is to take lecture notes. For some lecture classes, the amount of information disseminated in one hour can be overwhelming. By scheduling a study time right *after* the class, you can review your notes, compare them with other students' notes, fill in missing details, and reorganize your notes in more meaningful ways.

▶ **Color-code your class and study times** so that they stand out from the other activities on your weekly schedule. You can use different colors to show work and leisure activities.

CLASS DISCUSSION

Question: The Memory Principle of Time on Task applies to the *Essential Strategies for Scheduling Study Blocks*. What other Memory Principles do you actively use when you implement these strategies?

EXERCISE 3.3   **Creating Your Weekly Schedule**

Use the weekly schedule form on page 81. (An additional form is available in Appendix B and online at this textbook's website.) Then complete the following directions.

1. **Complete the five steps below** to create a weekly time-management schedule. Use a pencil at first so you can rearrange time blocks as needed to create a manageable and realistic schedule.

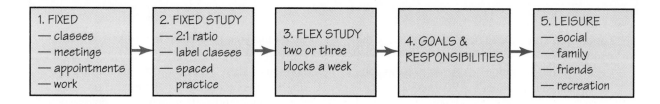

1. FIXED
 — classes
 — meetings
 — appointments
 — work

2. FIXED STUDY
 — 2:1 ratio
 — label classes
 — spaced practice

3. FLEX STUDY
two or three blocks a week

4. GOALS & RESPONSIBILITIES

5. LEISURE
 — social
 — family
 — friends
 — recreation

2. **Mentally walk through each day** on your schedule to determine whether it is realistic. Then answer the questions on the Weekly Time-Management Checklist (page 82). Adjust your schedule if you discover areas that you can strengthen or improve.

3. **Color-code your schedule** so it is easier to see at a glance. Use one color for your classes; another for study times; and a third for leisure, family, and social time. Use a fourth color for work or leave the spaces without color coding.

4. **Make a copy of your schedule** to keep in the front of your notebook if your instructor asks you to turn in pages 81 and 82 for comments.

5. **Begin following your schedule** as soon as possible. Several times during the day, indicate on your schedule how often you followed it as planned. Create a code system such as using stars for blocks that worked as planned and checks for blocks that you did not follow according to the plan.

6. **Use your schedule for a full seven days.** After that, be prepared to turn in your first schedule and the Weekly Time-Management Checklist.

In the box below, write any questions about your weekly schedule that you would like to discuss with your instructor.

WEEKLY TIME-MANAGEMENT SCHEDULE

For the week of _____ **Name** _____

Time	Monday	Tuesday	Wednesday	Thursday	Friday	Saturday	Sunday
12–6 AM							
6–7:00							
7–8:00							
8–9:00							
9–10:00							
10–11:00							
11–12 NOON							
12–1:00 PM							
1–2:00							
2–3:00							
3–4:00							
4–5:00							
5–6:00							
6–7:00							
7–8:00							
8–9:00							
9–10:00							
10–11:00							
11–12 AM							

Name _____

Weekly Time-Management Checklist

Use this checklist to evaluate your weekly time-management schedule and to strengthen it by adding any items that you may have overlooked. Write *Y* for yes or *N* for no.

Study Blocks

_____ Do you have enough study blocks set aside to study for each class? (Use the 2:1 ratio when it is appropriate.)

_____ Do you specifically label "study" and name the class?

_____ Are your study blocks spread throughout the week?

_____ Are you spending some time studying on the weekends?

_____ Do you avoid marathon studying so that you do not study more than three hours in a row?

_____ Do you avoid studying late at night?

_____ Do you include flex time in your schedule?

Fixed Activities

_____ Do you schedule time for three meals each day?

_____ Do you schedule sufficient time to sleep each night?

_____ Do you keep a fairly regular sleep schedule throughout the week?

Balancing Your Life

_____ Do you plan time specifically to be spent with your family and friends?

_____ Do you plan time for exercise, hobbies, or special interests such as clubs, organizations, and recreational teams?

_____ Do you plan specific time to take care of household chores and errands?

_____ Do you plan time to work on specific goals?

Will the Schedule Work?

_____ Can you "walk through each day" in your mind and see that your schedule is realistic?

_____ Are your peak energy times used wisely?

_____ Do you feel that your life would be more balanced if you followed what you have planned on your weekly schedule?

Other

_____ Have you used color codes in the schedule?

_____ Have you referred to the term schedule for special deadlines or events?

Comments or Questions:

Daily Schedules

A **daily schedule** is a specific list of tasks that you plan to achieve over the course of a day. This list can include specific homework and review activities; chores or errands; and family, social, recreational, or leisure activities. A simple index card works well to plan a daily schedule, or you may prefer to use a daily planner or organizer. Each night before you go to bed, take a few minutes to prepare your daily schedule for the next day's activities. Keep the schedule in a convenient place for quick reference. After examining the example of the daily schedule on the left, make a daily schedule for yourself in the box on the right.

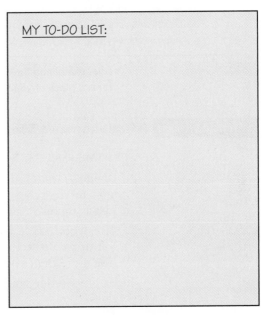

TO DO WED:

8–9:00 AM   Study Psy.
Read & notes for
pages 95–116

CLASSES—Regular schedule

1–3:00 PM   Study Algebra
—Redo Ex. 6 #2–5
—Do Ex. 7 odd numbers
—Make study flash cards

3–5:00 PM   —Start laundry
—Grocery shop
—Read mail
—Finish laundry

MY TO-DO LIST:

Task Schedules

A **task schedule** is a step-by-step plan for achieving a specific task in a specific block of time. You may use a task schedule to complete household chores more efficiently, plan an hour of work at your place of employment, or study productively. For example, if you plan to study math from 10:00 to 11:00 AM, in one or two minutes at the beginning of the study block you can create a plan of action—a task schedule—for the study block. Your task schedule becomes your goal for the hour. (A *goal* is a well-defined plan aimed at achieving a specific result.)

Creating a task schedule is equivalent to setting a goal. You identify specific steps or tasks to complete within the block of time. If you are not able to complete all the tasks you scheduled during the study block, you can transfer the remaining tasks to your next study block or use a flex block of time (see page 78). Task schedules are effective for several reasons:

- They provide structure for the block of time so you do not waste time trying to decide what to do or where to start.

- They give you a purpose and motivate you to stay on task to achieve your goals.

■ They help you learn to estimate more accurately the amount of time required to complete specific kinds of tasks.

■ They provide a form of immediate feedback at the end of the block of time. Your confidence, sense of accomplishment, and feeling of being in control increase when you are able to check off the study tasks you completed successfully.

WED. 10–11:00 AM   Study Math

1. Review class notes.
2. Rework class problems.
3. Read pages 26–32. Highlight key points.
4. Do even-numbered problems on p. 33.
5. Check answers with answer key. Study and rework any incorrect answers.

TIME:_____ DO:_____

After examining the example of the task schedule on the left, make a task schedule for any block of your time in the box on the right.

Group Processing: A Collaborative Learning Activity

Form groups of three or four students for this brainstorming activity.

1. Divide a large chart into two columns. In the left column write all the problems the members of your group have encountered with managing time. List as many different ideas as possible.

2. After you have a list of common problems, brainstorm to find possible solutions. Write the possible solutions in the right column. You may provide more than one possible solution for each problem.

3. Be prepared to share your list of problems and possible solutions with the class.

Reflection Writing 2
Chapter 3

1. For three weeks in a row, create and use a weekly schedule. After you use your first week's schedule, note any time blocks that were difficult to follow. Consider modifying and strengthening your schedule for the second and then the third weeks. If your first schedule was effective, copy the schedule but include any minor changes such as special appointments, social activities, or work schedules. Save all three schedules so you can turn them in with this reflection writing.

2. On separate paper, in a journal, or on this textbook's website, respond to the following questions.

   ■ Draw your original *pie of life* and your current *pie of life*. How has your *pie of life* changed? Be specific.

   ■ What are the most difficult times of the day for you to "stay on schedule"? Why are these times more difficult than others? What strategies are you using to overcome tendencies to abandon your schedule during these times?

   ■ Discuss the effectiveness of your study blocks. Did you use the 2:1 ratio? Did you have adequate time to study and review each week? Did you need to use your flex blocks? Did you use a task schedule for your study blocks?

   ■ Was time management effective for you? What were the benefits? What were the drawbacks? Will you continue to use a weekly schedule this term? Why or why not?

O N L I N E   P R A C T I C E   2

Visit the *Essential Study Skills*, Fifth Edition, website and go to Chapter 3. Click on **Practice 2: Using Schedules**. Complete the ten-question interactive multiple-choice quiz. Upon completion of the quiz, you will receive your score. You can exit at that time, or you can print your results or e-mail them to your instructor.

Applying Time Management

Time management is a highly prized skill in both the work force and the academic world. Learning to manage time effectively will help you meet your goals, be productive, and achieve success in many different avenues of your life. The following strategies will help you apply your time-management skills more effectively and consistently.

Be Flexible

Change is not always an easy process. Self-doubt, frustration, resistance, lack of motivation, or unexpected barriers sometimes crop up when a person attempts to change behavior patterns that have existed for years. Flexibility on your part can make the process of change easier. Be willing to relax your old patterns or ways of doing things, be willing to try new approaches, and be willing to give something new a chance to succeed. Be patient with yourself. As soon as you recognize that you are wandering from your time-management plan, do not be hard on yourself or discard the schedule for the remainder of the day. Simply start in with the task you planned and move forward. The longer you strive to use time management on a daily basis, the easier and more habitual it becomes.

To alter the way you see and handle time, commit to using your schedule for three weeks. During the times when you do not follow your schedule, examine the reasons or the situations. Was there an emergency or situation that was beyond your control that took precedence over your schedule? Did you abandon your schedule by choice? What swayed you from the schedule? Were there other ways you could have dealt with the situation and still followed your schedule? Learning to observe, understand, and monitor your choices is part of learning to use time management successfully.

Inform Others of Your Commitment to Time Management

Inform family members, roommates, partners, or friends about your goals to organize your time more effectively so they can be aware of and support your goals and your time-management plan. Posting a copy of your schedule on the refrigerator helps them know when you are available and when you have set aside special time just for them. Involving family members in the creation of your schedule each week can also add structure to the week and can strengthen communication about activities and events that are important to each person.

Seek Solutions to Time-Management Problems

Some students find that their lives have specific circumstances that make creating a weekly time-management schedule difficult. Be resourceful and seek solutions to your scheduling conflicts. Discuss your circumstances with your instructor or with other students; frequently they will be able to suggest solutions. The following problems and solutions are commonly presented by students who are learning to create weekly time-management schedules.

1. *Rotating work schedules.* If your work schedule varies each week, you should not have a problem because you can adjust your schedule each

week. Write your work schedule first as a fixed activity. Adjust your study blocks and other goals and responsibilities around your work schedule.

2. *Working late-night shifts.* The hours shown on the time-management form on page 81 may not work if you work swing or graveyard shifts. Before you photocopy the weekly time-management schedules, block out the times that are shown in the left-hand column. Write in the times that will fit your awake hours.

3. *Young children at home.* Consider changing your sleep patterns by getting up earlier in the morning before they are awake. If your children attend childcare, consider extending the childcare an hour or two and stay on campus to study during that time. Use all available time between classes to complete as much studying on campus as possible so that more of your time at home can be devoted to your children's needs.

4. *Not on campus five days a week.* If you attend classes only two or three days a week and have the intention of studying on the days you are not on campus, you may find you are not as productive as you had anticipated. Consider coming to campus even on days on which you do not have classes.

Modify Strategies for Independent Study and Online Courses

You can use many of the same time-management techniques discussed in this chapter for independent study or online courses. With these alternative delivery systems, you still have reading and homework assignments and some form of testing or assessment requirements. Even though many students find independent study and online courses appealing, they are sometimes surprised to learn how difficult it is to maintain the self-discipline, dedication, and time commitment required to successfully complete independent study or online courses. Use the following time-management techniques to achieve greater success in your independent study or online courses.

■ **Create a term calendar.** Use the course syllabus to identify due dates for papers, homework assignments, and tests. If the course materials do not include a time line with due dates, create your own by identifying the number of assignments, modules, or units you need to complete to pass the course. On your term calendar, assign completion dates for each component. Also include any orientation, on-site testing, or individual meetings you are required to attend.

■ **On your weekly schedule, write specific times you need to be available.** For example, you may need to view a telecast program or be on the computer to participate in a real-time group discussion.

■ **Commit yourself to work on the course during specific time blocks each week.** Calculate the number of hours you must dedicate to each course, by counting the number of hours that a similar class would meet in a classroom setting, use the 2:1 ratio for studying, and add one to three additional hours. Independent study and online courses often have components that require more time than those included in a classroom approach.

■ **During your study block, limit your use of the television or the computer to the course material you are studying.** Keep your mindset tuned in to the course and your thought patterns focused on the tasks waiting for you. Resist using your study time to check your e-mail or surf the Internet. If you are in online study or discussion groups, strive to keep your contributions related to the topic under discussion. Monitoring your use of the computer during online course time is critical.

■ **Make a task schedule.** Each time you sit down to work on your independent study or online course, create a task schedule for yourself so you have a clear picture of the goals you intend to achieve during the study block. Be vigilant about the passage of time, including the amount of time required to complete various types of assignments.

EXERCISE 3.4   Textbook Case Studies

Read about each of the following student situations carefully. Then, on your own paper and in complete sentences, answer the question that follows each case study. You can also answer these questions online at this textbook's Chapter 3 website. You can print your online responses or e-mail them to your instructor.

1. Cindy always seems to be caught off guard. She is surprised when she arrives in class and hears that a specific assignment is due that day. She seldom has her assignments done on time. Sometimes she does not remember them, and other times she runs out of time. She prefers to do all her studying on the weekends, so when something is due in the middle of or at the end of the week, she never has it completed. What suggestions would you give to Cindy so she might modify her approach to her assignments?

2. Raymond is frustrated by college. He is used to a busy life that includes a variety of activities with his friends. None of his friends are going to college, so they just do not seem to understand. Raymond does not feel like he has time for the things he really loves doing. This frustration is affecting his overall attitude toward school. What strategies could help Raymond?

3. Lydia is a night owl who has to begin her day at 6:30 AM. She is busy during the day taking classes and working thirty hours a week. She arrives home each day at four o'clock and tends to the needs of her three young children. By the time everyone is fed and tucked into bed, it is ten o'clock at night. Too many nights she finds herself falling asleep on her books. She is behind in all her classes and has no energy left for studying or for herself. How can Lydia use the Increase–Decrease Method to examine ways to solve some of these issues?

O N L I N E   C A S E   S T U D I E S

Visit the *Essential Study Skills*, Fifth Edition, website and go to Chapter 3. Click on **Online Case Studies.** In the text boxes, respond to three additional case studies that are only available online. You can print your online responses or e-mail them to your instructor.

O N L I N E   P R A C T I C E   3

Visit the *Essential Study Skills*, Fifth Edition, website and go to Chapter 3. Click on **Practice 3: Applying Time Management.** Complete the ten-question interactive multiple-choice quiz. Upon completion of the quiz, you will receive your score. You can exit at that time, or you can print your results or e-mail them to your instructor.

EXERCISE 3.5 LINKS

With a partner, answer the following questions about the links or relationships between time management and the concepts you learned in Chapters 1 and 2. Write your responses on your own paper. Be prepared to discuss your ideas in class.

1. What is the relationship between the 2:1 ratio for studying and elaborative rehearsal? Can you have one without the other?

2. Which of the four kinds of time-management schedules help students apply the memory principle of time on task most effectively?

Reflection Writing 3
Chapter 3

On separate paper, in a journal, or online at this textbook's website, respond to the following questions:

1. How can learning and using time-management skills affect your life? What are the benefits? What changes will you make as a result of learning how to manage your time?

2. What areas of time management are most difficult for you? What strategies can you use to overcome these difficulties?

SUMMARY

- Learning time-management skills helps you achieve balance in your pie of life in three main areas: school, work, and leisure.

- The Increase–Decrease Method stresses the need to adjust the boundaries that reflect the amount of time you spend in the three areas of your pie of life.

- Using term, weekly, daily, and task schedules helps you organize and control your time. A term schedule outlines important dates on a monthly calendar. A weekly schedule shows specific times for fixed activities; study blocks; flex blocks; goals and responsibilities; and leisure time, which includes friends, family, and recreation. A daily schedule provides a roadmap for the day. A task schedule sets goals for a specific block of time.

- An effective weekly schedule promotes spaced practice, avoids marathon studying (massed practice), reflects the 2:1 ratio for studying, and allows for occasional changes through trading time sparingly.

- Numerous essential time-management strategies exist to help you improve your time-management skills, gain greater control over your time, increase productivity, complete quality work on time, and achieve important goals.

CULMINATING OPTIONS FOR CHAPTER 3

1. Visit this textbook's website and go to Chapter 3 to complete the following exercises:
   a. Flash card review of Chapter 3 terms and definitions
   b. ACE Practice Test 1 with ten fill-in-the-blank questions
   c. ACE Practice Test 2 with ten true-false questions
   d. ACE Practice Test 3 with ten multiple-choice questions
   e. ACE Practice Test 4 with three short-answer–critical thinking questions

2. Go to Appendix C in the back of this textbook for more Learning Options to use for additional practice, enrichment, or portfolio projects.

Chapter 3 REVIEW QUESTIONS

Multiple Choice

Choose the best answer for each of the following questions. Write the letter of the answer on the line.

_____ 1. Using time management effectively
   a. instills a sense of being in control of your free time.
   b. balances the three areas in your *pie of life*: school, social, and family.
   c. frees up your weekends for social, leisure, and recreational time.
   d. provides you with a roadmap to be more productive and in greater control of the main areas of your life.

_____ 2. When you use a fifty-minute study block effectively, you should
   a. spend time reviewing each of your courses.
   b. create a mindset that focuses on only one subject.
   c. cover as many textbook pages as possible by reading fast.
   d. begin by identifying which class has an assignment due the next day.

_____ 3. An effective weekly time-management schedule includes
   a. eight hours of studying on weekends.
   b. adequate time to use the 2:1 ratio, elaborative rehearsal, and spaced practice.
   c. three or more flex blocks, three or more times to trade time, and adequate time for massed practice.
   d. all of your study blocks during your peak hours of alertness.

_____ 4. Marathon studying
   a. is an acceptable practice when you are engaged in creative projects.
   b. occurs when you study for more than three hours in a row.
   c. is the same as massed practice.
   d. All of the above

_____ 5. Which one of the following suggestions should you *not* use when you plan your study blocks on a weekly schedule?
   a. Label each study block by naming the class you will study so you can ensure that you are using the 2:1 ratio each week.
   b. Schedule all your study times Monday through Thursday so weekends are free.
   c. Study your most difficult or your least favorite subject earliest in the day.
   d. Create patterns in the week so your schedule is easier to learn.

_____ 6. The primary purpose of the Increase–Decrease Method is to
   a. help you find ways to increase your social time each week.
   b. find a more satisfying and productive balance in your *pie of life*.
   c. move you toward having a *pie of life* that shows an equal amount of time each week for school, work, and leisure.
   d. All of the above

_____ 7. A task schedule is
   a. a step-by-step plan to achieve a specific task during a specific block of time.
   b. a step-by-step plan that should be used specifically for study blocks.
   c. an approach for planning weekend study blocks.
   d. a plan of action for flex blocks on a weekly schedule.

_____ 8. The fixed study blocks on your weekly time-management schedule should
   a. provide you with ample time to complete assignments and use ongoing review.
   b. not be converted to free time when assignments are done.
   c. identify which course you plan to study during that time block.
   d. All of the above

_____ 9. Which of the following is *not* an effective strategy for planning study blocks on a weekly schedule?
   a. Study during your most alert times of the day when possible.
   b. Study right before a class in which you are expected to discuss information or participate in class activities.
   c. Study right before a class that mostly involves lectures and requires extensive note-taking.
   d. Place a different kind of activity on your schedule after two or three straight hours of studying.

_____ 10. Flex blocks
   a. provide you with blocks of time reserved for extra study time that might be needed to complete assignments or study for tests.
   b. can be converted to free time if they are not needed.
   c. should appear two or three times on your weekly schedule.
   d. All of the above

Short Answer and Critical Thinking

Use complete sentences to answer the following questions. Use terminology and information from this chapter.

1. What common time-management problems can you avoid by using the 2:1 ratio?

2. Why should you use trading time sparingly?

3. What are the main benefits of creating and using each of the following kinds of schedules?
   a. term schedule

   b. weekly schedule

   c. daily schedule

   d. task schedule

CHAPTER 4

Setting Goals

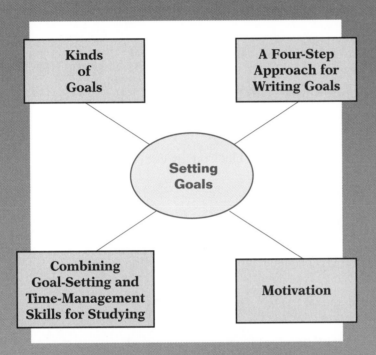

Kinds of Goals

A Four-Step Approach for Writing Goals

Setting Goals

Combining Goal-Setting and Time-Management Skills for Studying

Motivation

Goals—well-defined plans aimed at achieving a specific result—can be long-term, intermediary, short-term, or immediate. Setting goals can help you achieve success in all areas of your life. The four-step goal-setting process includes identifying a specific goal, target date and time, specific steps, and an internal or an external reward. When working on achieving specific goals, you can use a variety of strategies to keep up your momentum and motivation to succeed. Goal setting and time management work in a close partnership; you can use both sets of skills effectively to set academic goals for study blocks, test preparation, and term-long projects.

Chapter 4 Setting Goals Profile

ANSWER, SCORE, and **RECORD** your profile before you read this chapter. If you need to review the process, refer to the complete directions given in the Profile for Chapter 1 on page 2.

ONLINE: You can complete the profile and get your score online at this textbook's website.

	YES	NO
1. I set goals for myself each week.	_____	_____
2. I write goals, but I leave the time to complete the goals open-ended so I can work on the goals at my own pace.	_____	_____
3. It is difficult for me to know specifically what goals I want to reach.	_____	_____
4. I use visualization to see myself achieving the goals I really want to reach.	_____	_____
5. I set goals for myself at the beginning of each study block on my weekly schedule.	_____	_____
6. I tend to set too many goals and then feel overwhelmed.	_____	_____
7. I sometimes lack sufficient motivation to follow through on goals that I set.	_____	_____
8. I identify a reward for myself when I reach a goal, and I deny myself the reward if I do not reach the goal.	_____	_____
9. I always plan my goals in my head and do not feel a need to write them down.	_____	_____
10. I am confident that when something is important to me, I can set a goal and stay motivated long enough to complete the goal.	_____	_____

Reflection Writing 1
Chapter 4

On separate paper, in a journal, or online at this textbook's website, respond to the following questions:

1. What is your profile score for this chapter? What does it mean to you?

2. In what areas of your life have you used goal setting successfully?

3. In what areas of your life has goal setting not worked effectively?

Kinds of Goals

Goals are well-defined plans aimed at achieving a specific result. Goals are your roadmap to become the person you want to be and to create the life you want to live. They reflect your values and priorities about what is truly important to you. When you plan a course of action to achieve a goal and then successfully complete that goal, you feel a sense of pride and accomplishment. You feel more in control of your time, your choices, and your personal life.

One way to categorize goals is to define them by topics such as educational goals, financial goals, or organizational goals. Another way to categorize goals is to define them according to the time frame or length of time established to reach the desired outcome. The following chart defines four kinds of goals defined according to the length of time involved to achieve a specific result.

Kinds of Goals

1. An **immediate goal** is a well-defined plan to achieve a specific result within a few hours or within the next few days.
2. A **short-term goal** is a well-defined plan to achieve a specific result within a relatively short time period, such as within the current week, month, or academic term. A short-term goal may be broken into smaller steps that make the goal easier to accomplish in an efficient, orderly manner.
3. An **intermediary goal** is a well-defined plan that involves completion of a series of short-term goals spread out over a time period of a year or more. These goals serve as benchmarks or motivators to continue to pursue a specific long-term goal. Intermediary goals link the present to a more distant future.
4. A **long-term goal** is a well-defined plan to achieve a specific result at the end of a longer period of time, usually measured in years. Most long-term goals are achieved after the completion of a series of intermediary goals, a lot of hard work, and years of dedication.

What goals have you set for yourself that will lead to graduation?

Your educational plan is an example of a long-term goal comprised of one or more intermediary goals. For example, if you plan to complete a four-year degree, graduation from a university is your *long-term goal*. To reach that long-term goal, you may need to complete a two-year degree, or you may need to complete a series of general requirement courses. These would be your *intermediary goals*. In order to achieve your intermediary goals, you would need to complete a series of *short-term goals* such as completing specific courses, earning a specific number of credits, and establishing an acceptable grade-point average. Throughout your college years, you will face an abundance of *immediate goals*, tasks or assignments that must be done within a short time frame.

The following graphic shows how the long-term goal is the "big picture" to achieve. The intermediary, short-term, and immediate goals are "the smaller pictures," each a subgoal for a higher level accomplishment.

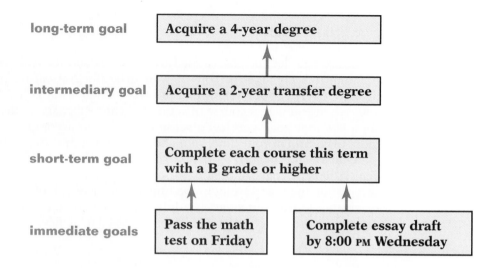

Short-term and immediate goals need not be directly linked to a long-term goal. For example, you may want to create a goal to organize an effective study area, sort your boxes of photographs, change the oil in your car, or plant a vegetable garden. Short-term or immediate goals such as these can be planned, implemented, and achieved within a relatively short period of time without being part of a larger intermediary or long-term goal. You can use the Long-Term and Short-Term Goal-Planning Sheets available on this textbook's Chapter 4 website to identify and set personal goals.

Reflection Writing 2
Chapter 4

On separate paper, in a journal, or on this textbook's website, respond to the following questions.

1. What are your long-term educational goals? What certificate or degree do you plan to obtain?

2. What are the requirements for your program? Locate a printed page of a catalog or brochure that shows the sequence of classes and requirements you need to complete.

3. What is your plan of action? Use the information from question 2 or information you have received from your adviser to develop a plan to reach your long-term goal. List the courses you plan to take each term and any program modifications you plan to implement to finish your certificate or degree.

A Four-Step Approach for Writing Goals

Many people have good intentions and a strong desire or motivation to succeed by achieving their goals; however, many of these same people fall short of making their goals reality. Frequently the inability to achieve goals begins with the lack of a sound process or strategy to write effective goals. You can learn to set and achieve all kinds of goals that will enhance your performance and increase balance in your life by using the following **four-step approach** for writing effective goals.

> ### Four Steps for Writing Effective Goals (STSR)
>
> 1. Set **S**pecific, clear, and realistic goals.
> 2. Set a specific **T**arget date and time to complete each goal.
> 3. Identify the individual **S**teps involved in reaching the goal.
> 4. Plan a **R**eward for yourself when you reach the goal.

Step 1:   **Set Specific Goals** Setting specific goals requires that you take the time to do a personal inventory to identify what it is that you wish to achieve. When your goal is clear, specific, and realistic, you have an exact picture of what you wish to achieve. To simply say, "I will do better" or "I want something new" results in vague goals whose achievements are not easily measured. To say, "I will be a millionaire tomorrow" is not realistic for most people. Before you commit to a goal, evaluate whether the goal is clear, specific, and realistic for you.

Some people shy away from setting specific goals. They may have a fear of failure, or they may think that it is better not to try than to try and not succeed. They may avoid committing to specific goals because they fear becoming discouraged, frustrated, or embarrassed. Fortunately, by learning to write effective goals and to use strategies to achieve goals, you will find that many of your fears and reasons to avoid goal setting vanish. Identifying a *specific*, realistic short-term goal that can be achieved within a few hours and then using strategies for completing the goal are ideal ways to end the pattern of shying away from setting goals and to overcome the fear of failure. One small success, one goal achieved, adds motivation and momentum to create and achieve new goals.

Step 2:   **Set a Specific Target Date and Time** Procrastinators (people who put off doing something) seldom achieve goals. You can reduce or eliminate procrastination by setting a specific target date (deadline) and even a specific time to finish the steps involved in reaching your goal. The target date works as a form of motivation to keep you moving forward and on time.

Step 3:   **Identify Steps** Careful planning of the steps involved in achieving a goal makes it possible for you to allocate enough time to complete each step. Take time to think through the individual steps required. List these steps on paper. If several steps are involved, list specific target dates for completing each step. When you use this method of breaking one large goal into several smaller ones, you can treat this large goal as a series of smaller goals to be accomplished on their own time lines.

Step 4:   **Plan a Reward** You can celebrate the completion of a goal with a reward. You can use that reward as an incentive—a motivation—to meet your goal. There are two kinds of rewards you can include in your goal-setting plan: extrinsic rewards and intrinsic rewards.

Extrinsic rewards are material things or activities that you will give yourself after you reach your goal. The following are examples of extrinsic rewards: buy a CD, go to a movie, go out to dinner, or plan a short trip.

Intrinsic rewards are the emotions or feelings you know you will experience when you reach a goal. Many people can be motivated just by recognizing that when the goal is reached, they will enjoy feelings such as increased self-esteem, pride, relief, joy, more confidence, or immense satisfaction.

A reward is a strong motivator only if you use it *after* you reach the goal. You must also withhold the reward if you do not reach the goal. For rewards to work as motivators, select rewards that truly represent what you *want* and can look forward to receiving.

Example of the Four Steps in Goal Setting

Step 1—Specific goal: Organize my desk to create an ideal study area
Step 2—Target date and time: Have it done by this Sunday at 4:00
Step 3—Individual steps:

1. Separate my bills and mail from the other things on my desk.
2. Sort my notes and homework assignments according to my classes.
3. For each class, put current assignments and notes into my notebooks in chronological order. Put all others into file folders. Label each folder.
4. Organize my textbooks, dictionary, and other references.
5. Organize my supplies into a box or into the drawer.
6. Get rid of any remaining clutter. Empty wastepaper basket.

Step 4—Reward: Extrinsic: Go out for pizza and a movie with friends.

ONLINE PRACTICE 1

Visit the *Essential Study Skills*, Fifth Edition, website and go to Chapter 4. Click on **Practice 1: Goal-Setting Skills**. Complete the ten-question interactive true-false quiz. Upon completion of the quiz, you will receive your score. You can exit at that time, or you can print your results or e-mail them to your instructor.

 EXERCISE 4.1   Achieving an Immediate Goal

Use the four goal-setting steps to tackle a small task that you would like to accomplish but keep putting off doing. Select an immediate goal, one that can be completed within the next few days. (If the goal is larger, such as cleaning the garage, break it down into smaller goals; then, for this exercise, select one of the smaller goals, such as organizing the workbench area.) Complete each step below; write your responses on a separate piece of paper.

1. What is the *specific* goal?

2. What are the *target date* and *time* to complete this goal?

3. What are the individual *steps* you must complete to achieve the goal? List each step.

4. What is your reward?

5. Did you achieve your goal by the target date and time?

   If yes, explain what contributed to your success. If no, describe the obstacles that interfered with the process.

Not achieving a goal by a specific target date and time can become a learning experience and provide you with valuable insights about the process you used. When you do not achieve your specific goal, use the following questions to analyze the situation and adjust your approach to writing and achieving specific goals.

Was the goal that I set unrealistically high? Did I really believe I could achieve the goal?

Could I visualize myself achieving this goal? Was it realistic and within my reach?

Was the goal I set too low? Did I feel a lack of purpose or unchallenged?

Did I adequately estimate the time that would be needed to complete each step?

Was I motivated? Did I really apply effort and follow my plan of action?

Group Processing: **A Collaborative Learning Activity**

Form groups of three or four students. Complete the following directions. Be prepared to share your work with the class.

1. Divide a large piece of paper into two columns. Label the left column *Reasons goals fail.* Label the right column *Reasons goals succeed.*

2. Brainstorm together to make a lengthy list of reasons why some people fail to achieve their goals. Write your ideas in the column on the left.

3. Brainstorm together to make a lengthy list of reasons why some people succeed at achieving their goals. Write the reasons in the column on the right.

4. Discuss how the ideas in the right column could be used to address the problems listed in the left column.

5. List people (public figures, personal acquaintances) whom your group considers to be "successful." What common characteristics, attitudes, or behaviors are shared by these "successful" achievers?

Motivation

Motivation is an integral part of goal setting. **Motivation** is the feeling, emotion, or desire that moves a person to take action. Motivation helps people make changes, learn something new, perform at a higher level, overcome procrastination, and persevere to complete a goal. Motivation is often the factor that begins the process of goal setting. Interestingly, once a person achieves a goal, the accomplishment generates new motivation to tackle other challenges and create new goals. The result is an upward spiral of personal growth, confidence, and success.

Intrinsic and Extrinsic Motivation

Motivation is the driving force behind achieving goals. Motivation appears in two forms: intrinsic and extrinsic. **Intrinsic motivation,** the most powerful and effective form of motivation, comes from within you and becomes your driving force. **Extrinsic motivation** occurs when other people set goals or performance expectations for you, such as may be the case with scholarships or employment duties. At times extrinsic motivation can start moving you to take action, but your greatest performance and success will occur when you convert the extrinsic motivation to intrinsic motivation. Instead of working to please others, you are working to please yourself.

Building and maintaining intrinsic or self-motivation are key components of achieving desired goals. If ever you find yourself quitting before reaching a goal, examine whether or not motivation was a factor. Did you run out of enthusiasm, conviction, or confidence that you could achieve the goal? Did you drop the goal because you allowed other distractions or obstacles to steer you off your course of action? If so, using *The Skill, Not Will Approach* and the *Essential Skills to Build and Maintain Motivation* (see page 101) can help prevent well-planned goals from fading into wishful thinking.

The Skill, Not Will Approach

Dr. Robert Epstein, author of *The Big Book of Motivational Games,* discusses motivation in an excerpt from the article "Getting Psyched! A Playful New Approach."

> *Motivation* is an internal state of arousal that often precedes behavior. If you're already highly motivated but can't find a way to reach your goals, you might want to read books on creativity, career change or, if all else fails, stress management. What can you do

about the opposite problem: the lack of motivation, either in yourself or in those around you? How can you induce an internal state of arousal? In other words, how can you make yourself or others *want* to behave? How can you get people to strive to achieve?

These are important questions because if behavior and motivation aren't in sync—if we drag ourselves through the day or if we lack the opportunity to act on some performance impulse—productivity, mood, health and retention may suffer.

Skill, Not Will

Some self-help gurus will try to persuade you that you can bear down, concentrate, and will yourself to be motivated. But willpower works poorly for most people. Skill, not will, is the best way to change oneself, and anyone can learn and practice new skills.

Skill acquisition has many advantages over willpower. For one thing, it saves you a good deal of grunting and groaning. Second, it prepares you for the long-term; gathering up courage might get you through the new few minutes, but it's hard to count on for the long-term.

Third, the right set of skills will help you deal with changing conditions such as a new boss or a fluctuating economy. Eight types of skills, also called *competencies*, can help you build and maintain motivation. The skilled individual:

1. **Manages the environment:** You create a workspace that helps energize you, and you surround yourself with people who bring out your best.

2. **Manages thoughts:** You use visualization techniques, thought-restructuring techniques, and affirmations to keep yourself thinking positively.

3. **Sets goals:** You make both short-term and long-term goals, and you formulate plans for how to achieve them.

4. **Maintains a healthful lifestyle:** You exercise regularly, get adequate sleep and eat right to keep your energy high.

5. **Makes commitments:** You make commitments to yourself and to others to arrange both positive and negative consequences for your behavior.

6. **Monitors behavior:** You keep records of your progress to bring yourself closer to your goals.

7. **Manages stress:** You practice relaxation techniques, reduce stress in your environment, and plan ahead to stay calm and productive.

8. **Manages rewards:** You seek out people who appreciate you and settings that reward you.

From Robert Epstein with Jessica Rogers, "Getting Psyched! A Playful New Approach," *Psychology Today,* Aug. 2001, pp. 54–55. Adapted from *The Big Book of Motivation Games* by Robert Epstein, © 2001 McGraw-Hill. Reprinted by permission of McGraw-Hill and Sussex Publishers, Inc.

The Power of Positive Words and Beliefs

Intrinsic motivation has a close relationship to *self-talk,* the internal kinds of conversations you have with yourself. Whenever you hear your negative, critical inner voice telling you that you *can't* do something, that you *won't* succeed, that you are *not* skilled enough, or any other similar negative comments about your abilities, intrinsic motivation quickly diminishes. Instantly when you hear negative self-talk, choose to manage your thoughts by turning those statements around and counteracting with **positive self-talk**. Positive self-talk focuses on positive qualities, words of encouragement, and statements that reflect a high self-esteem and **self-efficacy** (the belief in your abilities to achieve at a specific level of performance.) Statements such as *I am capable of doing this, I have what it takes to succeed,* and *I have the intelligence and skills to do well* turn *negative self-talk* into constructive, powerful, positive self-talk.

Using positive self-talk builds and strengthens a person's self-esteem, confidence, and intrinsic motivation. In *Human Relations,* authors Barry Reece and Rhonda Brandt explain the relationship self-talk has with self-esteem.

> People with a strong inner critic will receive frequent negative messages that can erode their self-esteem. It helps to refute and reject those negative messages with positive self-talk. Self-talk takes place silently in the privacy of your mind. It is the series of personal conversations you have with yourself almost continually throughout the day. Just like statements from other people, your self-talk can affect your behavior and self-esteem. Talking back to your inner critic may take the form of words or phrases that are designed to disarm the critic. Figure 3.1 indicates how self-talk is part of the cycle of self-esteem, whether that talk is negative or positive.

From Barry Reece and Rhonda Brandt, *Human Relations: Principles and Practices,* 5th ed. (Boston: Houghton Mifflin Co., 2003), pp. 70–71. Reprinted by permission of Houghton Mifflin, Inc.

Figure 3.1 Self-Esteem Cycles

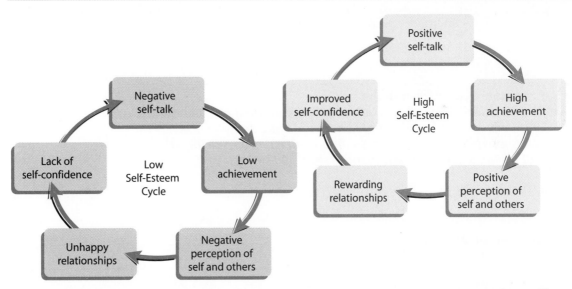

From Barry Reece and Rhonda Brandt, *Human Relations: Principles and Practices,* 5th ed. (Boston: Houghton Mifflin Co., 2003), p. 71. Copyright © 2003. Reprinted by permission of Houghton Mifflin, Inc.

Nathaniel Branden, author of *The Six Pillars of Self-Esteem,* states that the ultimate source of *self-esteem* can only be internal: It is the relationship between a person's self-efficacy and self-respect. **Self-efficacy** is the belief that you can achieve what you set out to do. When your self-efficacy is high, you believe you have the ability to act appropriately. When your self-efficacy is low, you worry that you might not be able to do the task, that it is beyond your abilities. Your perception of your self-efficacy can influence which tasks you take on and which ones you avoid. Albert Bandura, a professor at Stanford University and one of the foremost self-efficacy researchers, views this component of self-esteem as a resilient belief in your own abilities. According to Bandura, a major source of self-efficacy is the experience of mastery, in which success in one area builds your confidence to succeed in other areas.

From Barry Reece and Rhonda Brandt, *Human Relations: Principles and Practices,* 5th ed. (Boston: Houghton Mifflin Co. 2003), pp. 57–58. Reprinted by permission of Houghton Mifflin, Inc.

Use Affirmations

Affirmations are positive statements used as motivators. Affirmations help change your basic belief systems, your self-image, and the direction you are moving to make changes in your life.

Use the following guidelines to write effective affirmations and then repeat the affirmations several times daily:

1. *Use positive words and tones.* Avoid using words such as *no, never, won't.* Say, for instance, "I complete my written work on time," not "I will never turn in a paper late again."

2. *Write in the present tense.* Present tense in verbs gives the sense that the behavior already exists. When you think and believe in the present tense, your actions begin to match your beliefs. Say, for example, "I am a non-smoker," rather than "I will stop smoking soon."

3. *Write with certainty and conviction.* Say, for instance, "I exercise for thirty minutes every day," not "I want to exercise more each day."

4. *Keep the affirmation short and simple.* Brief, simple affirmations are easier to remember and repeat.

EXERCISE 4.2   **Affirmations**

Use the guidelines above to write two effective affirmations that relate to two of your goals. Repeat the affirmation several times daily. Remember to use positive words and tones, write in the present tense, write with certainty and conviction, and keep the affirmations short and simple.

Affirmation 1: _____

_____

Affirmation 2: _____

_____

SET LEARNING GOALS

The following *Essential Strategies to Build and Maintain Motivation* chart highlights nine important strategies to use for motivation. Place a star next to the strategies that you already use. Highlight the strategies that you plan to make a conscious effort to begin using to build and maintain motivation.

Essential Strategies to Build and Maintain Motivation

▶ **Prioritize your goals.** If you try to achieve too many goals at one time, you may feel overwhelmed and frustrated. Make a list of all the goals you want to achieve and then prioritize them according to their importance. After you achieve the higher-priority goals, begin working on the lower-priority goals.

▶ **Evaluate the importance of a goal.** Goals, especially long-term goals, can become outdated. Life circumstances change, and you may need to replace old goals with new, more significant goals. If a goal is no longer of value to you, abandon it. Do not, however, abandon a goal because it is more difficult to achieve or requires more from you than you had originally anticipated.

▶ **Break a larger goal into a series of smaller goals.** If you break a large task or goal into smaller steps or subgoals, achieving your goal feels more possible, realistic, and manageable. Motivation increases as the completion of each of the smaller steps brings you closer to achieving the larger goal. You will also experience less stress and avoid the feeling of being overwhelmed.

▶ **Visualize yourself reaching your goal.** Close your eyes and see yourself succeeding with your goal. **Visualization**, the process of picturing or imagining information or events in your mind, is a powerful tool for learning and goal setting. Visualizing yourself working through the steps, successfully reaching the goal, and enjoying the rewards becomes a powerful motivator to keep you moving forward. If you have difficulty seeing yourself achieving a goal, the goal may not be realistic or right for you. (See Chapter 2, page 52, for more information about visualization.)

▶ **Use positive self-talk and affirmations.** Short, positive statements that are repeated frequently are called **affirmations**. Affirmations, which often reflect personal goals, can enhance self-esteem, build confidence, and increase motivation. To be effective, affirmations must clearly state your goal in positive terms and use the first person (*I*), a present-tense verb, and words that show conviction and certainty.

▶ **Keep your goals in the forefront.** You can write your goals (and affirmations) on index cards and place the index cards around your house and in your notebook as a constant reminder and motivator to spend time each day working toward the outcome.

▶ **Use a goal organizer.** Creating a goal chart, called a **goal organizer**, helps you think seriously about your goal, plan your course of action, predict possible obstacles, and prepare a strategy to deal with the obstacles. Motivation increases as you gain a sense of being in control of the entire goal-setting process. (See Exercise 4.3 for the goal organizer format.)

▶ **Monitor your progress.** Choose an easy-to-use system that you can refer to quickly to confirm that you are meeting your target dates and completing the steps required to achieve your goal. A calendar, a detailed checklist, or a daily or a weekly journal can all help you monitor your progress.

▶ **Acknowledge and praise yourself.** You can be your best cheerleader, supporter, and motivator. Take time to recognize your accomplishments and your daily successes. Pat yourself on the back for each success, whether large or small. For example, when you successfully rework a math problem, tell yourself, "Good job. You got that one right." Saying positive words to yourself reinforces positive actions and provides a steady stream of intrinsic motivation.

CLASS DISCUSSION

Question: Why do you think many of the strategies for building and maintaining motivation relate directly to setting goals?

EXERCISE 4.3 Goal Setting and Motivation

Complete the following directions to show how you could use the motivational strategies to achieve a goal.

1. Identify one short-term goal for this term. With that goal in mind, complete the following goal organizer.

Goal Organizer

1. What is your goal?	
2. What benefits will you gain by achieving this goal?	
3. What consequences will you experience by *not* achieving this goal?	
4. What obstacles might you encounter while working on this goal?	
5. How can you deal with the obstacles effectively if they occur?	
6. What people or resources could help you with achieving this goal?	

2. Visualize yourself reaching this goal by the end of the term. Describe the picture in your mind that appears when you visualize yourself reaching your goal.

3. What method will you use to monitor your progress for achieving this goal by the end of the term?

4. Make a list of five goals that are *not* related to schoolwork and that you would like to accomplish this week. Use the numbers 1 through 5 to prioritize these goals, with 1 the most important and 5 the least important.

5. In the column on the left, give an example of one of your goals that seems too overwhelming to begin. On the right, rewrite the goal as a series of several smaller goals.

   Large Goal _____   Smaller Goals _____

O N L I N E   P R A C T I C E   2

Visit the *Essential Study Skills*, Fifth Edition, website and go to Chapter 4. Click on **Practice 2: Motivation Strategies**. Complete the ten-question interactive multiple-choice quiz. Upon completion of the quiz, you will receive your score. You can exit at that time, or you can print your results or e-mail them to your instructor.

EXERCISE 4.4   Textbook Case Studies
Read about each of the following student situations carefully. Then, on your own paper and in complete sentences, answer the question that follows each case study. You can also answer these questions online at this textbook's Chapter 4 website. You can print your online responses or e-mail them to your instructor.

1. Betty wants to be more efficient and productive. She sets weekly goals, but invariably things happen to disrupt her plans to complete her goals. When these unexpected events crop up, she gets frustrated and says that the goal was not that important. She has more uncompleted goals than she does successfully completed goals. What strategies can Betty use to change this pattern?

2. Ronnie is a "supermom" who "does everything for everyone." She is also an organized goal setter. Every Sunday she writes a new list of goals for the week. She adds more goals on a daily basis. At the end of each day, she often finds that she has to move some of the most important goals to her list for the next day. How can Ronnie improve her approach to writing and implementing goal setting?

3. This is Joel's fifth term in college. He has changed his major four times. His adviser wants him to create a long-term plan, but Joel keeps making excuses, saying he will do it "sometime soon." He resists the idea of goal setting because it makes him uncomfortable. What are some possible reasons why Joel avoids using goal-setting strategies?

ONLINE CASE STUDIES

> Visit the *Essential Study Skills*, Fifth Edition, website and go to Chapter 4. Click on **Online Case Studies**. In the text boxes, respond to three additional case studies that are only available online. You can print your online responses or e-mail them to your instructor.

Combining Goal Setting and Time-Management Skills for Studying

What goal-setting strategies do you think these students used in order to take their tests with minimal stress?

You can combine the four steps for writing effective goals with your time-management skills. The relationship between goal setting and time management is strong. Without time management, you might not find adequate time to work on your goals. Without goal setting, you might not use your time wisely or productively. You can use this combination of goal setting and time management effectively for academic work to

1. Write immediate goals for study blocks.
2. Create a five-day study plan to prepare for a test.
3. Develop a long-term goal for a term-long project.

Immediate Goals for a Study Block

On page 83 you learned to create a **task schedule**, a list of immediate goals to achieve during a specific block of time. A task schedule for a study block shows the specific activities you plan to complete during the study block. You can easily convert your task schedule into a four-step goal. The goal (step 1) and the target date and time (step 2) are built into the task schedule. Your list of tasks provides you with the specific steps for your goal (step 3). All you need to add to the task schedule is your intrinsic or extrinsic reward (step 4). The following example shows a plan for an immediate study block goal.

A Study Block Goal

Step 1—Specific goal: Review math class and do math homework
pp. 26–33.

Step 2—Target date and time: Wednesday, 10:00–11:00

Step 3—Individual steps:
1. Review class notes.
2. Rework class problems.
3. Read pages 26–32. Highlight key points.
4. Do even-numbered problems on p. 33.
5. Check answers with answer key. Study/rework any incorrect answers.

Step 4—Reward: Extrinsic: Watch my favorite show on television.

A Five-Day Study Plan to Prepare for a Test

A **five-day study plan** helps you organize your materials and time to review for a major test, such as a midterm or a final exam. This plan promotes spaced practice and ongoing review; it reduces tendencies to procrastinate, cram, or suffer test anxiety. You can use the same four goal-setting steps to write a five-day study plan.

Step 1:   **Be specific and realistic.**

Begin by making a list of all the topics that you need to review for the test. List the chapters, class lecture notes, homework assignments, lab reports, group projects, or any other materials covered in the class.

Step 2:   **Set target times and dates.**

Days 1, 2, 3, and 4, with specific time blocks, are organized review sessions. Schedule day 5 to be the day before the test; on day 5 dedicate all of your study time to reviewing the special notes you created in the following step 3. Mark these days and times on your calendar or your weekly schedule. Coordinate these times with other students if you are going to review with a study partner or study group.

Five-Day Study Plan

Day 1	Day 2	Day 3	Day 4	Day 5
Monday review:	Wednesday review:	Friday review:	Saturday review:	Sunday final review:
8–9:00 AM	8–9:00 AM	8–9:00 AM	10:00 AM–12:00 PM	2:00–4:00 PM
3–4:00 PM	3–4:00 PM	3–4:00 PM	4:00–6:00 PM	7:00–9:00 PM

Step 3:   **Identify the steps involved.**

This step requires careful planning and completion of four processes:

First, refer to the list of materials you need to review. Group the items in four logical categories; you will review one category of information on each of the first four days of your five-day schedule.

Second, to avoid wasting precious review time, create a pattern or plan for reviewing in your mind or on paper. Perhaps begin by reading the chapter summary, reviewing your textbook notes, reviewing your class notes, reviewing your homework assignment, and reviewing terminology. See the example of the five-day study plan on page 107.

Third, to use your time efficiently, select one or more forms of summary notes to use as you review each chapter. **Summary notes** are special notes that you make for only the materials that need to be reviewed one final time before the test. If you have used effective learning strategies and ongoing review throughout the term, you will already know many concepts and terms; these do not need to appear in summary notes. The formats on page 106 are commonly used for summary notes. (These formats will be discussed further in Chapters 9 and 11.)

Fourth, indicate on your five-day plan what you will review each day. Following is an example of a five-day study plan goal. Note: A Five-Day Study Plan form is available online at this textbook's website, Chapter 4.

Step 4:   **Plan a reward.**

Choose an intrinsic or an extrinsic reward for yourself *after* you complete your five-day study plan *and* after you complete the test.

Goal for a Five-Day Study Plan

Step 1—Be specific and realistic: Prepare for the midterm in sociology scheduled for Monday by reviewing the following items:

Chapters 1–4	The two short papers	Homework questions
Terminology (study guides)	Notes from guest speaker	Notes from video
Lecture notes	Textbook notes	

Step 2—Set target dates and times to study.

Mon. 8–9:00 AM	Wed. 8–9:00 AM	Fri. 8–9:00 AM
3–4:00 PM	3–4:00 PM	3–4:00 PM
Sat. 10–12:00 PM	Sun. 2–4:00 PM	
4–6:00 PM	7–9:00 PM	

Step 3—Identify the steps involved and make summary notes: *Process: Review class work first, then textbook work. Make flash cards for things I need to review again.*

Step 4—Reward: At the end of each daily review time, use the intrinsic reward: the satisfaction that the studying is under control. After the test, use the extrinsic reward: a day trip to the coast next Saturday.

5 Kinds of
Health = vitality

1.
2.
3.
4.
5.

Lists/Categories of
information to remember

Psy. Theory	Who	Type	Char.

Comparison charts to
compare or contrast
different subjects studied

Topic:

Book	Lecture
1.	1. 2. 3. 4.
2.	
3.	EX

Notes based on topics
that include textbook
and lecture information

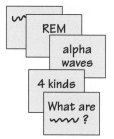

REM

alpha waves

4 kinds

What are ～～ ?

Flash cards of categories,
terminology, and study
questions

III. Chapter Title

A. Heading
   1.
   2. ⟶ Subheadings
   3.

B. Heading
   1.
   2. ⟶ Subheadings
   3.

Chapter outlines made by using
headings and subheadings

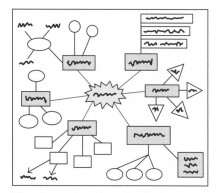

Visual mappings for individual
chapters or topics that appear in several
different chapters

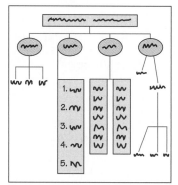

Large hierarchies made on
poster paper to include several
topics or chapters

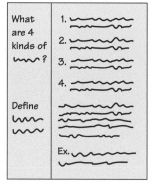

What are 4 kinds of ～～ ?

Define ～～～

| 1. |
| 2. |
| 3. |
| 4. |

Ex.

Cornell notes with study
questions on the left for
self-quizzing (see Chapter 9).

Example of a Five-Day Study Plan

Monday	Wednesday	Friday	Saturday	Sunday
8-9:00 AM (Ch. 1) class study guide homework Q handouts	8-9:00 AM (Ch. 2) study guide homework Q video notes	8-9:00 AM (Ch. 3) class study guide handouts homework Q	10-12:00 PM (Ch. 4) study guide (no handouts) homework Q 2 short papers	2-4:00 PM Review summary notes; self-quiz on Ch. 1 & 2
3-4:00 PM (Ch. 1) lecture notes textbook notes Notes-Guest speaker	3-4:00 PM (Ch. 2) lecture notes textbook notes	3-4:00 PM (Ch. 3) lecture notes textbook notes	4-6:00 PM (Ch. 4) lecture notes textbook notes	7-9:00 PM Review summary notes; self-quiz on Ch. 3 & 4

Goals for Term-Long Projects

Some instructors assign at the beginning of the term a project that is not due until the middle or the end of the term. Many students get a false sense of time; rather than start right away, they put off the assignment until too close to the due date. By doing this, they add unnecessary stress and often neglect study times for other classes so they can finish the project. As soon as you are assigned a **term-long project**, begin planning a schedule for that project.

The following steps can guide you through the process of completing the assignment on time.

1. *Break the assignment into specific tasks.* What are the actual tasks you need to work through from the beginning to the end of the project? Analyze the project carefully until you can identify the individual tasks involved. List these tasks or steps on paper.

2. *Estimate the time needed for each task.* Estimate the number of hours you think you will need to complete each task. Base this estimate on your past experiences with similar projects.

3. *Double the estimated time needed for each task.* You do not want to run out of time. To avoid any tendency to underestimate the amount of time you will need, double your estimate. In that way, you are giving yourself extra time in case you run into unforeseen problems or find that you have to change directions. Following is an example for a long-term assignment for a literature class.

Step 1: List the Tasks	Step 2: Estimated Time	Step 3: Doubled Time
1. Review lists of American poets. Select one I like.	1 hr.	2 hrs.
2. Do library or Internet research on his or her life.	3 hrs.	6 hrs.
3. Read several of the author's poems. Find somethat reflect influences of the author's life.	2 hrs.	4 hrs.
4. Write a draft of the summary of the author's life.	1 hr.	2 hrs.
5. Select two specific poems.	½ hr.	1 hr.
6. Write about the structure and the meaning of poem 1 (draft).	2 hrs.	4 hrs.
7. Write about the structure and the meaning of poem 2 (draft).	2 hrs.	4 hrs.
8. Revise the drafts and integrate into the final paper.	4 hrs.	8 hrs.
9. Proofread. Revise as needed.	1 hr.	2 hrs.
10. Assemble the final project. Include the poems, the research notes, and a bibliography.	½ hr.	1 hr.
Time to plan for project:		34 hrs.

4. *Record due dates on your term calendar for each task.* Consider the number of hours needed for each task and the study block times (and flex times) you have available on your weekly schedules. Set a goal to complete each task by a specific date. Each week when you make your weekly schedule, check this term calendar and add the tasks to your weekly schedule. Following is an example.

   Week 3: Do Tasks 1 and 2 (8 hours).

   Week 4: Do Tasks 3 and 4 (6 hours).

   Week 5: Do Tasks 5 and 6 (5 hours).

   Week 6: Do Task 7 (4 hours).

   Week 7: Do Task 8 (8 hours).

   Week 8: Do Tasks 9 and 10 (3 hours).

   Week 9: I completed the project last week!

5. *Begin right away.* Do not waste time procrastinating. If you finish a task ahead of schedule, it is because you did not need the "doubled time" you allocated. Begin the next task immediately. If you finish your project ahead of schedule, you will have time to revise it again if you wish, and you will be able to breathe a sigh of relief!

You can use the following Long-Term Project Form to plan a long-term assignment. This Long-Term Project Form is available online at this textbook's website, Chapter 4.

Step 1: List the Tasks	Step 2: Estimated Time	Step 3: Doubled Time
1.		
2.		
3.		
4.		
5.		
6.		
7.		
8.		
9.		
10.		
Time to plan for project:		

EXERCISE 4.5 LINKS

Work with a partner or in a small group. Discuss the connections or the relationships between the following paired topics. Be prepared to share a summary of your discussions with the class.

1. goal setting and motivation

2. time management and goal setting

3. visualization and visual learners

4. affirmations and auditory learners

5. goal setting and global learners

6. goal setting and interpersonal intelligence

O N L I N E   P R A C T I C E   3

Visit the *Essential Study Skills*, Fifth Edition, website and go to Chapter 4. Click on **Practice 3: Goal Setting and Time Management**. Type your responses to the five questions. After you type your responses, you can print them or e-mail them to your instructor.

O N L I N E   P R A C T I C E   4

Visit the *Essential Study Skills*, Fifth Edition, website and go to Chapter 4. Click on **Practice 4: All About Goal Setting**. Complete the ten-question interactive true-false quiz. Upon completion of the quiz, you will receive your score. You can exit at that time, or you can print your results or e-mail them to your instructor.

Reflection Writing 3
Chapter 4

On separate paper, in a journal, or online at this textbook's website, respond to the following questions:

1. Which goal-setting strategies in this chapter are potentially the most valuable or important to you? Explain why and how you will benefit from this information.

2. Which strategies will help you build and maintain your motivation to achieve your goals? Explain.

SUMMARY

■ Goals are well-defined plans aimed at achieving a specific result in any area of your life. Long-term, intermediary, short-term, and immediate goals vary in the length of time required to achieve the final result.

■ A systematic four-step approach can be used to write effective goals for all areas of your life:
1. Set **S**pecific, clear, and realistic goals.
2. Set a specific **T**arget date and time to complete each goal.
3. Identify the individual **S**teps involved in reaching the goal.
4. Plan a **R**eward (intrinsic or extrinsic) for yourself when you reach the goal.

■ Motivation is the feeling, emotion, or desire that moves a person to take action. Motivation is an integral part of goal setting.

■ There are two forms of motivation: intrinsic and extrinsic. Intrinsic motivation is the most powerful and effective. *The Skill, Not Will Approach*, which emphasizes eight specific skills, positive self-talk, and nine additional Essential Strategies, provides you with strategies to build and maintain motivation.

■ Time management and goal setting work in a close partnership. For academic work, you can use goal setting for study blocks, to prepare for tests, and to complete term-long projects.

■ You can convert a time-management task schedule to an immediate goal for a study block by listing the individual tasks you want to complete during a study block and identifying a reward.

■ You can use the four steps for writing goals to create a five-day study plan to prepare for a major test. Days 1 through 4 are review days for specific chapters and materials, and for creation of special summary notes. Day 5 of this plan is set aside to review the summary notes you generated on review days 1 through 4.

■ You can use the four steps for writing goals to organize and plan a term-long project. After you identify the specific tasks that you need to do to complete the project, estimate the hours you think you will need for each task. Then double your estimated times and write target dates for each task on a term calendar.

CULMINATING OPTIONS FOR CHAPTER 4

1. Visit this textbook's website and go to Chapter 4 to complete the following exercises:
   a. Flash card review of Chapter 4 terms and definitions
   b. ACE Practice Test 1 with ten fill-in-the-blank questions
   c. ACE Practice Test 2 with ten true-false questions
   d. ACE Practice Test 3 with ten multiple-choice questions
   e. ACE Practice Test 4 with three short answer–critical thinking questions

2. Go to Appendix C in the back of this textbook for more Learning Options to use for additional practice, enrichment, or portfolio projects.

Chapter 4 REVIEW QUESTIONS

True–False

Carefully read the following statements. Write T *if the statement is true and* F *if it is false.*

_____ 1. Setting a specific target date to complete a goal can help reduce or eliminate procrastination.

_____ 2. Extrinsic rewards involve positive feelings, a sense of pride, and renewed motivation to tackle new goals.

_____ 3. Visualizing yourself completing a goal is a technique that helps you keep up your momentum and motivation to achieve success.

_____ 4. Affirmations should include words such as *no, never,* or *won't* so you have a constant reminder of the negative things you want to avoid in your life.

_____ 5. If a goal seems too overwhelming, you should discard it and write only immediate goals that you can achieve in one day.

_____ 6. A person who sets too many goals may benefit from prioritizing the goals so he or she can dedicate time to the goals that are the most important.

_____ 7. A goal organizer helps a person identify the benefits of achieving and the consequences of not achieving a goal, anticipate possible obstacles, and create a plan to deal with obstacles individually or with the help of other people or resources.

_____ 8. Extrinsic motivation is the most powerful form of motivation because it results in approval and recognition from others.

_____ 9. In a five-day study plan, you should create summary notes on the last day of the plan so you have something to review quickly an hour or two before a major test.

_____ 10. When you plan a term-long project, you should double the estimated time to complete each step of the project to compensate for underestimating the time needed to complete individual tasks successfully.

Multiple Choice

*Choose the **best** answer for each of the following questions. Write the letter of the answer on the line provided.*

_____ 1. A long-term goal
   a. often requires completion of one or more intermediary goals.
   b. usually involves a series of short-term goals that must be completed.
   c. may be an educational goal, a financial goal, or a career goal.
   d. is all of the above.

_____ 2. Willpower is
   a. the key element that makes motivation work.
   b. the most effective way to change yourself or aspects of your life.
   c. not as important as skill acquisition for building and maintaining motivation.
   d. all of the above.

_____ 3. Which of the following includes a strategy that is *not* a skill or competency for building and maintaining motivation?
   a. Create an energizing workspace and maintain a healthful lifestyle.
   b. Make task lists for everything you do in school and at home.
   c. Use visualizations, positive self-talk, and affirmations.
   d. Keep a journal and plan rewards for yourself.

_____ **4.** A study block goal
  a. helps you organize the work that you need to do for a course.
  b. includes a task schedule of immediate goals.
  c. identifies a reward to enjoy at the end of the study block.
  d. does all of the above.

_____ **5.** Which of the following is *not* a true statement?
  a. A negative, critical inner voice can have a negative effect on your intrinsic motivation.
  b. You should strive to counteract positive self-talk by replacing it with negative self-talk.
  c. Positive self-talk often reflects high self-esteem and high self-efficacy.
  d. Negative self-talk, low achievement, negative perception of self and others, and lack of self-confidence are components of the Low Self-Esteem Cycle.

Short Answer and Critical Thinking

Use complete sentences to answer each of the following questions. Use information and terminology from this chapter.

1. If a student tries to shorten the four-step process for writing effective goals by omitting one of the steps, the process will be weakened and therefore less effective. What negative outcomes might occur by eliminating any *one* specific step of the process? Identify the step and then the outcomes if the step is omitted.

2. What are the benefits of counteracting a negative, critical inner voice by using positive self-talk?

Increasing Concentration; Decreasing Stress and Procrastination

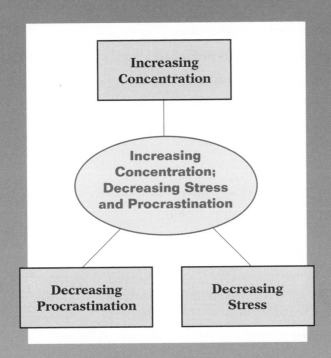

Terms to Know

General Terms

concentration
active learning
external distractors
internal distractors
stress
stressors
self-management
procrastination
fear of failure

Terms for Techniques

take charge
chunking
study ritual
warm-ups
mental rehearsal
say *no*
no need
red bow
checkmark
mental storage box
tunnel vision
emotional *e* words
perfect place
soothing mask
relaxation blanket
breathing by threes
deep breathing
deep muscle relaxation
see success

Concentration is the ability to block out internal and external distractors in order to focus the mind on one specific item or task. A wide variety of strategies are available to use to train your mind and increase your level of concentration. Stress, which is wear and tear on our bodies, needs to be monitored and managed before it becomes excessive. A variety of techniques can reduce the cognitive, physical, behavioral, and emotional effects of stress. Procrastination, the process of delaying what needs to be done, is a self-defeating behavior that you can reduce or eliminate through a variety of effective strategies.

Chapter 5 Increasing Concentration; Decreasing Stress and Procrastination Profile

ANSWER, SCORE, and **RECORD** your profile before you read this chapter. If you need to review the process, refer to the complete directions given in the Profile for Chapter 1 on page 2.

ONLINE: You can complete the profile and get your score online at this textbook's website.

	YES	NO
1. My study area has two sources of light, a low noise level, an adequate work surface, and an availability of materials and supplies.	_____	_____
2. I often study with the radio, stereo, or television turned on.	_____	_____
3. I set individual goals for study blocks before I begin studying.	_____	_____
4. I stop studying when I become uninterested, unmotivated, or bored.	_____	_____
5. I use specific concentration strategies on a regular basis to help me keep my focus when I study.	_____	_____
6. I have difficulty getting started on assignments when I sit down to study.	_____	_____
7. My level of stress often reduces my performance or ability to concentrate.	_____	_____
8. I put my greatest amount of effort into my work at the last minute because I work best under pressure.	_____	_____
9. I tend to procrastinate when faced with unpleasant or uninteresting tasks.	_____	_____
10. I am confident that I have adequate self-management skills to increase my level of concentration and reduce stress and procrastination.	_____	_____

Reflection Writing 1
Chapter 5

On separate paper, in a journal, or online at this textbook's website, respond to the following questions.

1. What is your profile score for this chapter? What does it mean to you?

2. What do you see as your greatest problems with concentration, stress, and procrastination?

Increasing Concentration

Concentration is the ability to block out internal and external distractions in order to focus the mind on one specific item or task. Concentration is a flighty process; you can concentrate one minute and then easily become distracted and lose that concentration the very next. Concentration is a mental discipline that requires a concerted effort to train your mind to keep focused. As discussed in Chapter 2, concentration is also a memory principle and a key element for encoding and processing information in working memory.

Choose An Ideal Study Area

To increase your ability to concentrate, give careful attention to your physical environment. The noise level, lighting, and work space can directly affect your ability to concentrate. An ideal study area has few or no distractions that will affect your concentration.

An Ideal Study Area

1. The noise level is conducive to studying.
2. The lighting includes two or more sources of light.
3. The work space promotes concentration.

The Noise Level   People have different tolerance levels to noise. Some students need a silent environment in order to concentrate; others can tolerate minor sounds or noises without becoming distracted. Some students believe they can study in noisy environments; however, an environment filled with too much noise adversely affects the ability to concentrate, study, comprehend, think critically, and use other complex thought processes. Studying in a noisy environment is neither an efficient nor an effective use of your time. The noise and your attention to the noise take up space in your working memory, thus reducing the amount of working memory available to process information you intend to study. Research shows that excessive noise, music with lyrics and frequent variations in rhythm, and the auditory and visual stimuli from television interrupt thought processes and brainwave patterns, causing concentration to turn on and off and on and off in split-second intervals. Interestingly, however, research shows that soft, classical, and instrumental music (especially baroque music) does not cause the on-and-off pattern. In fact, this type of music is conducive to learning. The music positively alters brainwave patterns (alpha waves) and assists the learning process by creating a relaxed, receptive state of mind. As you become more aware of the noise level in your study environment and how it affects your ability to concentrate, be willing to change your study location and environment until you find one that increases rather than decreases your level of concentration.

The Lighting   Proper lighting is important in any study area. If you have too little light, your eyes can easily become strained and tired. Some lighting can create shadows or glare on your books. To avoid many of the problems created by poor lighting, have two sources of light in your study area. This may include an overhead light and a desk lamp or two lamps in different locations. Two sources of lighting may seem like a minor detail, but sometimes ignoring small details leads to big problems.

Many students have the choice to live in campus dorms or off-campus in their own apartments. What factors might affect the study areas in either of these locations?

The Work Space   Attention to your work space at home and at school results in the most effective and productive use of your study time. Trying to study in an area that lacks sufficient space to spread out your textbooks, open your notebooks, take notes as you read, rework problems and compare them with those in the textbook, or use other study materials and supplies creates distractions that hinder concentration. Your concentration level will also be hindered if your work surface is cluttered with items not related to studying. For an ideal study space, select a desk or table that is clutter free, provides ample space for you to spread out your materials, and is an appropriate height for your size. Use a comfortable, sturdy chair that is also an appropriate height for the table and for your legs. Avoid trying to study on the floor, in a recliner, on a couch, or on a bed. Just as trying to study in a noisy environment is poor for concentration, trying to study without adequate work space also reduces your effectiveness and your ability to maintain a high level of concentration.

Make Adjustments in Your Environment

Each time you sit down to study, assess the noise level, the lighting, and the work space in your study environment. If the noise level, lighting, or work space is not ideal, do not waste your precious time studying in a location that distracts you. Use the **take charge technique** by seeking an alternative place to study or by modifying the existing environment to one that has few or no distractions. Instead of blaming others for distracting noises, getting annoyed by a television or radio, or shifting restlessly in an uncomfortable chair, *take charge* and make the changes necessary to have an ideal study area that promotes higher levels of concentration.

The following examples show ways that students changed or modified their study environments in order to increase their levels of concentration. In each case, students displayed a willingness to try a new approach, to let go of old habits, and to find out firsthand how they could increase their levels of concentration by controlling their environments.

Description of the Student Situation	The Student's Solution
Robert has always had a short attention span and is easily distracted. He tried studying in the library because of the large tables and work surfaces, but ordinary library noises and the movement around him were too distracting and frustrated him.	• Work in a quiet, motionless environment, like an empty office or a conference room. • Move to the large tables in the back of the library away from foot traffic.
Joel grew up in a house with six brothers and sisters, so studying in a noisy environment seemed normal. Joel usually studied in the cafeteria. He was confident in his ability to do well in his classes, but he was missing important details when he studied, and his work was not his best quality.	• Study at home. • Turn on a small fan to provide some background sound that is not distracting.
Heather often studied in a student lounge area. After about a half an hour in that area, her eyes started playing tricks on her. The fluorescent lighting bothered her, and she would see colored streams of light in the air.	• Move to a room with windows so there is a combination of natural lighting and fluorescent lighting. • At home, use a desk lamp and a ceiling light.
Marshall preferred studying at home at his kitchen table, but he soon realized that the kitchen caused distractions. He frequently stopped studying to get drinks or snacks. Work that would normally have taken him an hour to finish at school was taking him much longer at home because of the frequent breaks.	• Modify the environment by removing all kitchen and food items from the table. • Create a box of school supplies for the table to convert it into a work or study area. • Sit facing away from the refrigerator.

⚙ EXERCISE 5.1   **My Ideal Study Area**

In the middle column in the chart below, describe your typical study areas at home and at school. In the right column, describe the changes you could make to create a more ideal study area.

Home	Current Study Area	Ideal Study Area
Noise		
Movement nearby		
Lighting		
Chair		
Work surface		
Supplies		
School	Current Study Area	Ideal Study Area
Noise		
Movement nearby		
Lighting		
Chair		
Work surface		
Supplies		

O N L I N E   P R A C T I C E   1

Visit the *Essential Study Skills*, Fifth Edition, website and go to Chapter 5. Click on **Practice 1: Ideal Study Area**. Complete the ten-question interactive true-false quiz. Upon completion of the quiz, you will receive your score. You can exit at that time, or you can print or e-mail your results to your instructor.

Be an Active Learner

Active learning (the opposite of passive learning) means you are actively involved in the learning process. As you learned in Chapter 1, active learning often occurs when you participate in group activities and use hands-on experiences. Active learning, however, can also occur when you study by yourself and use strategies that discourage you from reading or working in a detached, mechanical way. By using active learning strategies, you can combat many internal distractors, such as feeling sleepy, bored, uninterested, or unmotivated. Active learning promotes critical thinking, multisensory learning, and greater comprehension. The following five active learning strategies keep you involved with the material you are studying, focused, and mentally alert.

1. Have a pen in your hand when you study. Take notes, write questions, or jot down lists of information you need to learn.
2. Use markers to highlight important information in the textbook or in your notes.
3. Talk out loud (recite) as you study to activate your auditory channel and improve both concentration and comprehension.
4. Write summaries or make other kinds of study tools such as visual mappings, hierarchies, flash cards, or comparison charts. (See Chapter 11.)
5. Quiz yourself on the material you are studying. Write or recite questions and answers.

Use Concentration Techniques to Begin a Study Block

The time-management strategies, such as creating *effective study blocks* and *task schedules*, and goal-setting strategies, such as using *positive self-talk* and maintaining your *motivation*, directly improve your level of concentration when you study. In addition to the time-management and goal-setting strategies you learned in Chapters 3 and 4, the following concentration techniques will help you begin your study blocks with a focused and ready mind for studying.

Concentration Techniques to Begin a Study Block

1. Use the **chunking technique** to break large assignments into more meaningful units.
2. Create a **study ritual** to begin each study block.
3. Do **warm-ups** at the beginning of a study block.
4. Use **mental rehearsal** to elevate your performance.

■ *Chunking technique* Long assignments or difficult assignments can create feelings of frustration, confusion, and distraction. To gain control of the situation and get your mind on track, use the **chunking technique** to break the assignments into smaller, more manageable steps. You can also use this technique to divide a long assignment into sections that you can complete in several different study blocks.

■ *Study ritual* You can save time and confusion by beginning each study block with a consistent routine, also known as a **study ritual**. This ritual allows you to get started quickly and move directly into the mindset needed to study and concentrate. For example, your study ritual might be to use a quick relaxation or visualization technique, create a task schedule, and do a *warm-up*.

■ *Warm-ups* When you first sit down to study, you may find your thoughts are on people, events, or things other than studying. A **warm-up** activity at the beginning of a study block is an excellent way to shift your thoughts and create a mindset for studying and concentrating. *Warm-ups* activate your long-term memory, pulling previously learned information back into your working memory or preparing your long-term memory for new learning by setting up frameworks or *big pictures* for new information. Warm-ups include *previewing* (skimming through a new chapter or assignment to get an overview) and *reviewing,* such as taking a few minutes to look over class notes or a previous assignment or to reread a chapter summary.

■ *Mental rehearsal* Use visualization to mentally rehearse your actions and performance. Mental rehearsal is effective because it gives you the opportunity to see yourself responding or performing in advance of the actual situation. Any time you feel apprehension, self-doubt, or low self-confidence, use **mental rehearsal** to create a picture or a movie in your mind that shows you performing effectively. For example, picture yourself beginning an assignment with ease, writing answers on a test with confidence, or studying without distractions. Many athletes have learned the power of mental rehearsal to elevate performance levels. They picture themselves making the perfect free-throw shot, receiving and running with the football, or sinking a long putt.

Deal with Internal and External Distractors

Distractors are elements that break your concentration and congest your working memory. **External distractors** are caused by things in your physical environment, such as noises, people, television, enticing weather, clutter, and lighting. **Internal distractors** are disruptions that occur inside you. Worries, stress, anxiety, depression, sickness, hunger, pain, daydreams, and anticipation of upcoming events are examples of internal distractors that reduce your level of concentration.

When you find yourself distracted and having trouble concentrating, the first step is to analyze the situation to determine the source of your distraction. The second step is to select an appropriate technique to use to address the problem with concentration. The following are effective techniques to deal with distractors; practice using all the techniques so that you will be able to select the most appropriate ones to use for specific situations.

Techniques to Deal with Internal and External Distractors

1. The **say *no* technique** helps you eliminate external and internal distractions.
2. The **no need technique** works to block out minor, familiar distractions.
3. The **red bow technique** discourages others from interrupting you unnecessarily.
4. The **checkmark technique** provides a way for you to score your concentration success.
5. The **mental storage box technique** helps you put internal distractions aside.
6. The **tunnel vision technique** gets your mind back on track instead of wandering.
7. The **emotional *e* words technique** replaces negative emotions with positive ones.

- *Say no:* Sometimes ridding yourself of a distraction is as easy as saying *no.* When friends or family members ask you to drop your study schedule and participate in an activity with them, show your assertiveness by simply saying *no.* Inform them of the times that you *are* available. This technique can also be used to tell yourself to resist the urge to participate in a distraction: no snack, no television now, no daydreaming, or no phone calls.

- *No need:* For minor noises or movement, you can use the *no need* technique to train yourself not to look up and not to break your concentration to attend to minor occurrences that are familiar. For example, if you study in the library, you know that occasionally someone will walk by, pull out a chair, or turn the pages of a book. Without looking, you know the source of the distraction, so force yourself to keep your eyes on your own work. Tell yourself, "There is *no need* to look."

- *Red bow:* Frequently other people are distractors. They interrupt your studying and break your concentration. On your door or in your study area, place a red bow or any other item or symbol to signal to others that you are studying and you want privacy. Ask them to respect your request for no interruptions unless an emergency occurs.

- *Checkmark:* Each time you lose your concentration, make a checkmark on a score card you keep on your desk. At the end of your study block, count the number of checks. Set a goal each time you study to reduce the number of checkmarks.

- *Mental storage box:* Before you begin studying, identify any concerns, worries, or emotions that might interrupt your concentration. Place them inside an imaginary box. Put the lid on the box and mentally shove the box aside for the time being. Tell yourself that you will deal with the contents of the box at a more appropriate time, and then do so.

- *Tunnel vision:* Picture yourself at the beginning of a tunnel that has a yellow line running down the middle. You want to stay on the middle line. As soon as your mind starts to wander, picture yourself swiftly getting back to the middle line before you bump against the walls.

- *Emotional **e** words:* Attitude plays an important role in concentration and learning. Any time you find yourself dealing with negative emotions toward studying a specific subject or an assignment, combat those emotions by refocusing your mind on words with positive energy. Quickly brainstorm and say out loud positive words that begin with *e*. For example, you might say *effortless, enthusiastic, excited, energetic, eager, effective, efficient, essential, excelling, excellent, expert, exhilarating,* or *educated.* In your mind, attach an image of yourself exhibiting these qualities. The result is an attitude adjustment that is more conducive to concentration and learning.

Group Processing: **A Collaborative Learning Activity**

Form groups of three or four students. Then complete the following directions.

1. Divide a large chart into two columns. In the left column, write as many different internal and external distractors as possible in a ten-minute period.

2. After you have a list of distractors, brainstorm techniques to use to combat each distractor. List the techniques in the right column. You may provide more than one technique for each distractor. You may refer to the *Terms to Know* list on page 113.

3. Be prepared to share your list of distractors and techniques with the class.

O N L I N E   P R A C T I C E   2

Visit the *Essential Study Skills*, Fifth Edition, website and go to Chapter 5. Click on **Practice 2: Concentration Strategies.** Type responses to five questions. After you type your responses, you can print them or e-mail them to your instructor.

O N L I N E   P R A C T I C E   3

Visit the *Essential Study Skills*, Fifth Edition, website and go to Chapter 5. Click on **Practice 3: Increasing Concentration.** Complete the ten-question interactive multiple-choice quiz. Upon completion of the quiz, you will receive your score. You can exit at that time, or you can print or e-mail your results to your instructor.

Decreasing Stress

Stress is a reaction or response to events or situations that threaten or disrupt our normal patterns or routines. Stress is the wear and tear on our bodies due to physical, emotional, cognitive, and behavioral responses. The following are important points about stress:

1. Some stress is normal as we move through life making decisions and changing directions in our personal, work, and academic lives.

2. In some situations, stress is beneficial. Stress can compel us to take action and to move in new directions. The increased adrenaline from stress can help us perform at higher levels.

3. As stress increases, our ability to deal with and control the stress decreases.

4. Early warning signs that stress is becoming more intense and moving into the danger level include headaches, backaches, insomnia, fatigue, anxiety attacks, mood swings, depression, forgetfulness, carelessness, and irritability.

5. Excessive stress hinders performance and affects our cognitive abilities. Excess stress affects working memory and long-term memory and reduces our ability to concentrate, solve problems, and make wise decisions.

6. Excessive stress from unresolved issues has physical consequences: increased pulse rate, faster breathing, higher blood pressure, a weakening of the immune system, a decrease in the production of endorphins (a neurochemical that makes us feel happy), ulcers, heart attacks, strokes, and clinical depression.

Learning to manage stress is a lifelong skill that affects the quality of life and longevity. In Appendix D of this textbook, you will find a chapter from a psychology textbook that provides additional information about health, stress, and coping.

Use Self-Management Skills

How you *perceive* and *handle* external situations—rather than the situations themselves—is the cause of stress. People who handle stress best are those individuals who actively look for solutions and use techniques to alter their perception of external situations. When **stressors** (situations or actions that cause stress) enter into your life, often you can take some form of action to reduce or eliminate the stressors. For example, if an upcoming test is a stressor, you can create a plan of action and use specific techniques to take control of the situation. Other stressors, such as the terminal illness of a loved one, are out of your immediate control; the only control you have is how you handle your reaction to the stressor. (Go to Appendix D, on page A-21, Table 10.2, to learn how many potential stressors from this list you have experienced this week.)

Many stress-reduction techniques are **self-management** techniques. *Self-management* involves dealing constructively and effectively with variables that affect the quality of your personal life, your well-being, and your ability to perform regular daily functions. Managing time, goals, concentration, stress, and procrastination are all self-management skills. Using a weekly and a daily time-management schedule, creating task schedules, prioritizing goals, using goal organizers, creating an ideal study area, using a study ritual, doing warm-ups, mentally rehearsing, and using positive self-talk or affirmations are examples of self-management skills that will reduce stress in your life.

In Chapter 1, you learned that interpersonal intelligence deals with your relationship with others; *intrapersonal intelligence* deals with your relationship with yourself. The following *Essential Strategies for Managing Stress* chart shows six techniques that can help you reduce stress by interacting with others and becoming more aware of your inner thoughts and responses.

SET LEARNING GOALS

The following *Essential Strategies for Managing Stress* chart highlights six important strategies to use to manage stress. Place a star next to the strategies you already use. Highlight the strategies you plan to make a conscious effort to begin using to manage stress in your life.

Essential Strategies for Managing Stress

▶ **Interact with others.** Many research studies show the importance of social interaction in reducing stress, improving overall health and the immune system, stimulating cognitive processes, and staving off depression. Make time to spend with a close network of friends, create new friendships, or participate in a student or community organization, a study group, or a church group. Social interaction creates an opportunity for laughter, bonding, and finding a zest for life.

▶ **Redirect your emotions.** Engaging in activities that create positive emotions reduces the intensity of your emotional reaction to stress. Redirect your emotions by spending time on a favorite hobby or craft, listening to music, playing an instrument, singing, dancing, baking, playing a video game, or watching a movie. Continuously dwelling on a negative situation intensifies your emotions; substituting those emotions with positive ones can dissipate the negative energy. When you revisit the problem or issue later, you may see the situation differently and be ready to seek solutions more calmly and with a less negative emotional reaction.

▶ **Discuss your situation with others.** Trying to understand and deal with a stressful situation alone without the input and perception of others or trying to hide your stress and feelings often compounds your stress. The tension and feelings will eventually erupt or intensify. When under stress, you may unintentionally exaggerate the extent of the problem or the hopelessness of the situation. Discussing your situation with others may thwart the tendency to *make a mountain out of a molehill*. If you cannot confide or share your feelings with friends, seek out an advisor or counselor on campus or in the community.

▶ **Take time to center yourself.** Engage in a mind-calming activity such as meditation, yoga, prayer, or biofeedback to center yourself and return to a state of calmness and serenity. Sitting in a sauna, soaking in a hot tub or warm bath, or sitting near a fountain of water can also be a mind-calming experience. Centering activities provide a way to block out and temporarily shield yourself from the rest of the world.

▶ **Take a mental vacation to a perfect place.** The visualization technique called perfect place integrates your imagination with a breathing exercise. To use this technique, close your eyes and breathe in slowly. Start creating a perfect place in the world where you feel relaxed, confident, safe, comfortable, and content. Continue breathing in and out slowly as you let the perfect place unfold in your imagination; add sounds, smells, sights, tastes, and tactile sensations to your perfect place. Make a mental picture of this perfect place. Through the power of association, you can recall the mental picture and the soothing sensations of this perfect place whenever you need to separate yourself in a healthy way from stress and stressful situations.

▶ **Keep a journal.** Journal writing provides a channel to describe your feelings or concerns privately and to tap into some of your innermost thoughts in a nonthreatening way. Putting your emotions on paper often reduces the intensity of the emotions, disperses some of the negative energy, and helps you discover solutions or new directions to take with the situation. There is no right or wrong way to keep a personal journal. You can randomly write down your thoughts and feelings in an unstructured manner, or you can pose a question to yourself and begin writing your response to your own question. Save your journals so you can look back to see how you resolved problems and you can see the changes you have made in your life.

CLASS DISCUSSION

Question: What is the relationship of Howard Gardner's interpersonal and intrapersonal intelligences to the *Essential Strategies for Managing Stress*?

Choose a Healthy Lifestyle

Your lifestyle and the choices you make in your daily and weekly habits and routines influence your level of stress and the way you respond to a variety of stressors. When you feel stress occurring in your life, and especially when you feel the stress is becoming excessive, take time to examine your habits, behaviors, and lifestyle choices. (For additional information, read the section *Risking Your Life: Health-Endangering Behaviors* in the psychology chapter in Appendix D.) A basic look at your lifestyle patterns can begin by looking specifically at the areas of nutrition, exercise, and sleep since these three areas play important roles in reducing and coping with stress.

Nutrition Frequently people experiencing stress turn to fast foods and snacks that are high in sugar and fat. Foods high in sugar often produce a surge in energy as they increase blood sugar in the body. However, the increased blood sugar quickly drops, thus leaving the individual feeling less energetic than before eating the high-sugar foods or snacks. **The following guidelines can help you make choices as part of a healthier lifestyle:**

- Instead of eating foods loaded with sugar, choose foods that break sugars down more slowly and release energy over a more sustained period of time. Complex carbohydrates, such as those found in grains, cereals, rice, pasta, bread, and potatoes, protect blood levels from the roller coaster effect of highs and lows.

- Consume three to four helpings of fruits and vegetables each day. In addition to providing you with essential vitamins and minerals, these foods increase your brain's production of serotonin, a brain chemical that stabilizes mood swings and promotes a sense of happiness. Multivitamins can supplement your dietary needs for vitamins and minerals, although they are not a substitute for good eating.

- Limit your use of nicotine, caffeine, alcohol, and drugs. People often use more of these products when under stress, but they are not effective ways to cope with stress, and their health consequences may lead to more serious problems.

- Set aside fifteen to thirty minutes three times a day to sit down and enjoy a relaxing meal. Put work and other distractions aside so meals become a quiet time to enjoy and digest the food, or a time to socialize with others.

What are the benefits of regular exercise? How often do you exercise to receive these benefits?

Exercise Become more active. Physical activity reduces the physiological effects of stress. Plan twenty to thirty minutes a minimum of three times a week to exercise (walk, run, swim, bike, lift weights, do aerobics, or play basketball, baseball, soccer, or golf). For more structure, sign up for a physical education course, an intramural sport, or a community exercise program or work out with a regularly televised exercise program. In addition to reducing your stress level and giving yourself a mental break from thinking about the stressor, the benefits of regular exercise are many:

1. Exercise gets oxygen moving more smoothly to your brain; your concentration levels will increase, and information will enter and move through your memory system more efficiently.

2. Exercise improves your cardiovascular system, thus reducing your risk of more serious health conditions that may result from prolonged stress.

3. Exercise strengthens your body, making it more resistant to the physical and emotional effects of stress. Your body becomes better equipped to handle stress when stress does occur.

Sleep   Get your sleep pattern on a regular schedule. During times of stress, people's sleep patterns become irregular and often resemble a roller coaster ride. Individuals experience *insomnia,* the inability to fall asleep; their hours of restful sleep are too few, or they do not reserve enough hours per night to get a good night's sleep. Strive to eliminate poor sleep patterns by establishing consistent sleep and waking times. If you experience insomnia, use the time to relax in a prone position. You may want to listen to soft music or spend the time visualizing or practicing relaxation techniques. Resetting your body's time clock requires training and often three or more weeks of scheduling consistency. Your goal is to create a pattern that gives you about eight hours of sound sleep, which results in your awaking each morning refreshed and ready to begin a new day.

Practice Relaxation Techniques

Relaxation techniques can help you reduce your stress levels and improve your emotional health. The goal behind relaxation techniques is to create a state of mind and body that perhaps can best be described as "Ahhhhhhh." In this state, the body is not tense and the mind is not wandering; you are open and ready to receive new information or expand on previously learned information. Relaxation techniques are effective in a wide variety of emotional situations: when you feel anxious, nervous, tense, stressed, apprehensive, hyperactive, restless, defeated, frustrated, or overwhelmed. The following relaxation techniques are easy to learn and require only a few minutes of your time:

Relaxation Techniques

1. **Soothing mask** uses your imagination to block out reactions to stress.
2. **Relaxation blanket** relaxes your body and provides a secure feeling.
3. **Breathing by threes** relaxes the muscles and produces a peaceful feeling.
4. **Deep breathing** relaxes the body and removes tension.
5. **Deep muscle relaxation** reduces tension from the muscles throughout your body.
6. **Yoga** stretches the muscles and produces a state of relaxation.

■ **Soothing mask**   Close your eyes. Place your hands on the top of your head. Slowly move your hands down your forehead, down your face, and to your neck. As you do this, picture your hands gently pulling a **soothing mask** over your face. This mask removes other thoughts, worries, fears, or stresses from your mind. Keep your eyes closed for another minute. Feel the soothing mask resting on your face. Block out thoughts or feelings that are not related to your soothing mask. As you practice this technique, you will be able to do it without using your hands. Your imagination can take you through the same process of pulling the mask over your face.

■ **Relaxation blanket**   Sit comfortably in your chair. Close your eyes. Focus your attention on your feet. Imagine yourself pulling a soft, warm blanket up over your feet. Continue to pull this blanket up over your legs, lap, and chest until the blanket is snuggled around your shoulders and against your neck.

Feel how your body is more relaxed now that it is covered with the blanket. This **relaxation blanket** feels like a security blanket, keeping you warm, confident, and comfortable. Keep your eyes closed for another minute as you enjoy the warmth and comfort of the blanket.

■ **Breathing by threes**   You can do this technique with your eyes opened or closed. Inhale slowly through your nose as you count to three. Gently hold your breath as you again count to three. Exhale slowly through your nose as you count to three. Repeat this several times. Often you can actually feel your body begin to slow down and relax when you are **breathing by threes**.

■ **Deep breathing**   Take a deep breath to fill your lungs. You may think your lungs are full, but there is room for one more breath of air. Inhale once again. Now slowly exhale and feel your body relax. Repeat this **deep breathing** several times. If you feel lightheaded or dizzy after trying this exercise, you might want to select one of the other options.

■ **Deep muscle relaxation**   Stress is often felt in one or more of these muscle groups: shoulders, arms, lower back, legs, chest, fingers, or face. Take a minute to notice the amount of tension you feel in the various locations throughout your body. Then make a clenched fist tight enough so that you can feel your fingers pulsating. Breathe several times and feel the tension in your fingers and your hands. Then breathe slowly and uncurl your fists until they are totally relaxed. Pay close attention to the different sensations as you go from tense to relaxed. Continue this with other muscle groups. Let the feelings of **deep muscle relaxation** and the feelings that the tension is washing away spread throughout your body. Feel the difference!

■ **Yoga**   Sign up for a class or work with someone who knows yoga to learn this Eastern practice, which blends stretching, flexibility, breathing exercises, and meditation. Besides enjoying a sense of calm and relaxation, followers of yoga believe yoga helps the body heal, alleviates various forms of pain, reduces hypertension, and soothes the nervous system.

EXERCISE 5.2   Appendix D Visuals
In later chapters, you will be applying specific skills to the psychology chapter in Appendix D. For now, examine the following visual materials in Appendix D to learn more about stress and its effects on the human body.

O N L I N E   P R A C T I C E   4

Visit the *Essential Study Skills*, Fifth Edition, website and go to Chapter 5. Click on **Practice 4: Decreasing Stress**. Complete the ten-question interactive multiple-choice quiz. Upon completion of the quiz, you will receive your score. You can exit at that time, or you can print or e-mail your results to your instructor.

Reflection Writing 2
Chapter 5

On separate paper, in a journal, or online at this textbook's website, respond to the following questions.

1. What is one specific stressor that you are experiencing now or experience on a fairly regular basis? Take a personal inventory of the ways this stressor is affecting you physically and emotionally. Do *one* of the following and then respond to the second question:

   a. Simply state that you have identified a stressor and recognize the physical and emotional effects it is having on you. You do not need to give any details if you prefer to keep this private.

   b. Discuss the stressor and its effects on you.

2. What specific techniques discussed in this chapter could you use to deal with your stressor more effectively? Explain each technique in your own words and tell how you will use it. The combination of techniques you select creates a "stress reduction plan" that you can begin to implement to gain greater control over your source of stress.

EXERCISE 5.3 Textbook Case Studies

Read about each of the following student situations carefully. Then, on your own paper and in complete sentences, answer the question that follows each case study. You can also answer these questions online at this textbook's Chapter 5 website. You can print your online responses or e-mail them to your instructor.

1. Katlin feels that her life is spinning out of control. She simply cannot find enough time to do quality work in her classes. She feels that she is slapping her work together haphazardly. She makes more mistakes on her assignments than she did in previous terms. She is annoyed with herself and then gets caught up in a lot of negative self-talk. She is too embarrassed about her feelings and stress to talk with anyone. In fact, she finds herself avoiding even her closest friends. She does not know how much longer she can "put on a happy face" in public. What can Katlin do to break this negative pattern?

2. José has a lot of friends and enjoys a wide variety of activities outside school. He was an excellent student in high school but is finding it hard to do well in college. No one told him how much more demanding college would be. His friends come by often to see how he is doing. They usually end up inviting him to go out for a while, and he goes. He tries studying when he gets home later at night. By then he has trouble concentrating. He wastes a lot of time trying to settle down and get assignments started. He feels pressured to do so many things that he has problems deciding where to begin. What strategies can José use to adjust his approach to the demands of college and college-level work?

3. Debbie worked hard to create a weekly schedule with sufficient time to study for each of her classes. She has disciplined herself to sit down to study during the scheduled blocks of time. Frequently, however, an hour passes and she will have accomplished nothing. Her assignments seem long and tedious. She knows she needs to do them, but she cannot seem to gain the momentum, the interest, or the motivation to use her time blocks effectively. What strategies would you recommend Debbie use when she sits down to study?

O N L I N E   C A S E   S T U D I E S

Visit the *Essential Study Skills*, Fifth Edition, website and go to Chapter 5. Click on **Online Case Studies**. In the text boxes, respond to four additional case studies that are only available online. You can print your online responses or e-mail them to your instructor.

EXERCISE 5.4   Partner Discussion

Discuss with a partner ways both of you can use each of the following techniques in your life. Be prepared to summarize your discussion with the rest of the class.

1. Positive self-talk
2. Warm-ups
3. Say *no*
4. Red bow
5. Checkmark
6. Mental rehearsal
7. Breathing by threes
8. Study ritual

Decreasing Procrastination

Procrastination is the process of putting off something until a later time. Procrastinators choose low-priority tasks over high-priority tasks. Procrastination is a learned behavior that can be reduced or eliminated by understanding the reasons for procrastinating and then activating effective strategies to modify the self-defeating behavior. Reducing or eliminating procrastination results in a more productive use of time, improved performance, less stress, and new opportunities and successes.

People who procrastinate frequently to avoid starting all kinds of tasks have created a behavioral and cognitive pattern that is ingrained in their way of "doing life." They accept and even boast about being procrastinators; they pride themselves on being able to do things quickly, at the last minute, and under pressure. They often wait for a "push," a threat of a specific consequence, a crisis, or some outside force to get the momentum to do what needs to be done. Their focus is on completing the task and not necessarily on the quality of the final product. Habitual procrastinators benefit from learning new techniques, such as time management and goal setting, that can replace old, less effective behavioral and cognitive patterns.

Recognize When You Procrastinate

Any time you find yourself avoiding a specific task or making statements such as *I'll do it when I am in the mood, I have plenty of time to do it later, I can let it slide a few more days,* or *I will wait because I work better under pressure,* recognize that you are procrastinating. Become aware of your procrastination patterns by answering the following questions.

1. Are there specific kinds of tasks involved when you procrastinate? For example, do you plan and follow through with studying for your computer class but procrastinate with your writing or your math class? Do you complete specific household chores but procrastinate when faced with the laundry? Identify the specific kinds of tasks that you avoid most frequently; for those tasks, you will want to activate strategies to change your momentum.

2. Do you tend to procrastinate beginning a specific task, or do you begin a task enthusiastically but then procrastinate in the middle of working on the task? For example, do you struggle with setting time aside and sitting down to begin writing a paper? Do you make excuses for not beginning the paper? Or do you begin the paper but lose interest or motivation halfway through the process of writing it? Do you almost have the task or the goal accomplished but find yourself quitting close to the end of the task? For example, do you put off typing the final version of the paper even though you have finished writing it? Understanding *when* in the process of a task you procrastinate can help you select strategies to complete tasks or goals more consistently.

3. Do you start multiple tasks, jumping from one to another, and make less important tasks seem more important or urgent? This behavior is a common sign of the onset of procrastination. Procrastinators can get so caught up in this whirlwind behavior that they do not realize all the busy work is a mask for avoiding specific tasks. When you find yourself scurrying around, sometimes aimlessly keeping busy, take time to identify the task you are avoiding.

Recognize Why You Procrastinate

Causes or reasons for procrastinating vary for different tasks, situations, and individuals. In some cases procrastinating will not have any serious consequences. For example, procrastinating about moving a stack of magazines to the garage or putting your compact discs back in their cases has no dire consequences other than the clutter of magazines or disorganized or scratched compact discs. In many other cases, procrastinating leads to increased stress and additional problems. Procrastinating about paying your bills, studying for a test, or filling your tires with air will have more serious consequences, some of which could alter your goals or course for the future. Learning to reduce or eliminate procrastination can empower you, enhance your self-esteem, strengthen your self-discipline, and put you in greater control of your life. In order to select appropriate strategies to combat procrastination, begin by pinpointing the causes of this learned behavior. The following are common causes:

■ **Lack of motivation, interest, or purpose:** Starting and completing a task is difficult when you harbor negative attitudes and perceive the task as boring, uninteresting, or meaningless. *Intrinsic motivation* is the direct result of showing interest in a task and attaching a purpose, a reason, or importance to completing a task. Using strategies to increase your interest level and give meaning and purpose to your task will increase your intrinsic motivation.

■ **Low self-confidence, low self-esteem, or low self-efficacy:** See Chapter 4, pages 98–100.

■ **Task too difficult or complex:** Some tasks, especially those that involve unfamiliar information or new skills, are perceived as being too difficult or too complex. The thought of beginning the task is too unpleasant, overpowering, or overwhelming. Procrastination is the result of frustration and lack of a solid approach to break the task into smaller, more manageable sections and identify the skills, materials, or information needed to begin and complete the task.

■ **Inaccurate perception of time:** Some people have difficulty estimating the amount of time needed to complete various kinds of tasks. Students may delay starting a project because they believe there is still plenty of time to start and complete the assignment, or they may lack motivation to begin an assignment because they inaccurately assess the time needed. For example, they may put off reading a new sociology chapter because they falsely believe that the assignment will take five or six hours when in reality, they need only two hours to read the chapter.

■ **Overextended and overcommitted:** People who take on too many activities and responsibilities use procrastination as a way to shield themselves from more. They do not feel that they can manage what is currently "on their plate," so they have no desire to add more stress to their lives with more tasks to complete. Procrastination in this situation becomes an attempt to refrain from adding more stress to an already stressful pattern.

■ **Unclear about the task or expectations:** Lack of momentum to act may be due to lack of strategies, understanding, or clarity. In this state of confusion, people lack problem solving or analytical skills to examine the task to determine what needs to be done or which steps to use to tackle the task. To avoid feeling embarrassed or uncomfortable, they shy away from asking for clarification or help.

■ **Unconducive environment:** Some people procrastinate because their work or study environment creates problems and frustrations, and they are not productive. It is difficult to be motivated to work on a task when clutter covers your work surface, lights hurt your eyes, furniture is too uncomfortable, or you are plagued by interruptions from other people. Trying to work in a less than ideal situation becomes too much of a struggle, so tasks are postponed until later.

Author Maia Szalavitz in the following article, "Stand & Deliver," (*Psychology Today*, August 2003, pp. 50–54) provides additional information about procrastination and its causes.

Procrastination is not just an issue of time management or laziness. It's about feeling paralyzed and guilty as you channel surf, knowing you should be cracking the books or reconfiguring your investment strategy. Why the gap between incentive and action? Psychologists now believe it is a combination of anxiety and false beliefs about productivity.

Tim Pychyl, PhD, associate professor of psychology at Carleton University in Ottawa, Canada, tracked students with procrastination problems in the final week before a project was due. Students first reported anxiety and guilt because they had not started their projects. "They were telling themselves[,] 'I work better under pressure' or 'this isn't important,'" says Pychyl. But once they began to work, they reported more positive emotions; they no longer lamented wasted time, nor claimed that pressure helped. The results of this study will be presented at the Third Annual Conference on Counseling the Procrastinator in Academic Settings in August. Psychologists have focused on procrastination among students because the problem is rampant in academic settings; some 70 percent of college students report problems with overdue papers and delayed studying, according to Joseph Ferrari, associate professor of psychology at Chicago's DePaul University.

Pychyl also found that procrastination is detrimental to physical health. College students who procrastinate have higher levels of drinking, smoking, insomnia, stomach problems, colds, and flu. So why can't people just buckle down and get the job done?

False Beliefs

Many procrastinators are convinced that they work better under pressure, or they'll feel better about tackling the work later. But, tomorrow never comes and last-minute work is often low quality. In spite of what they believe, "Procrastinators generally don't do well under pressure," says Ferrari. The idea that time pressure improves performance is perhaps the most common myth among procrastinators.

Fear of Failure

"The main reason people procrastinate is fear," says Neil Fiore, PhD, author of *The Now Habit*. Procrastinators fear they'll fall short because they don't have the requisite talent or skills. "They get overwhelmed and they're afraid they'll look stupid." According to Ferrari, "Procrastinators would rather be seen as lacking in effort than lacking in ability." If you flunk a calculus exam, better to loudly blame it on the half-hour study blitz than admit to yourself that you could have used a tutor the entire semester.

Perfectionism

Procrastinators tend to be perfectionists—and they're in overdrive because they're insecure. People who do their best because they want to win don't procrastinate; but those who feel they must be perfect to please others often put things off. These people fret that "No one will love me if everything I do isn't utter genius." Such perfectionism is at the heart of many an unfinished novel.

Self-Control

Impulsivity may seem diametrically opposed to procrastination, but both can be part of a larger problem: self-control. People who are impulsive may not be able to prioritize intentions, says Psychyl. So, while writing a term paper[,] you break for a snack and see a spill in the refrigerator, which leads to cleaning the entire kitchen.

Thrill-Seeking

Some procrastinators enjoy the adrenaline "rush." These people find perverse satisfaction when they finish their taxes minutes before midnight on April 15 and dash to the post office just before it closes.

Task-Related Anxieties

Procrastination can be associated with specific situations. "Humans avoid the difficult and boring," says Fiore. Even the least procrastination-prone individuals put off taxes and visits to the dentist.

Unclear Expectations

Ambiguous directions and vague priorities increase procrastination. The boss who asserts that everything is high priority and due yesterday is more likely to be kept waiting.

Depression

The blues can lead to or exacerbate procrastination—and vice versa. Several symptoms of depression feed procrastination. Because depressed people can't feel much pleasure, all options seem equally bleak, which makes getting started difficult and pointless.

From Maia Szolovitz, "Stand and Deliver," *Psychology Today*, Aug. 2003, pp. 50–54. Copyright © 2003, Sussex Publishers, Inc. Reprinted with permission.

EXERCISE 5.5   Brainstormings

Work with a partner or in a small group. Divide a large piece of paper into two columns. On the left side of the paper, list the possible causes of procrastination (see pages 129–131). On the right side of the paper, brainstorm possible strategies procrastinators could use to combat each of the causes of or reasons for their procrastination.

SET LEARNING GOALS

The following *Essential Strategies to Combat Procrastination* chart highlights ten important strategies to combat procrastination. Place a star next to the strategies that you already use. Highlight the strategies that you plan to make a conscious effort to begin using to reduce or eliminate the habit of procrastinating.

Essential Strategies to Combat Procrastination

▶ **Use self-management skills and techniques.** Most causes of procrastination relate directly to self-management skills: time management, goal setting, concentration, and stress management. Select appropriate strategies to strengthen self-management skills.

▶ **Face your fear of failure.** Focus on your positive traits, your accomplishments, and the skills you have acquired. Use *positive-self talk*, *affirmations,* and *emotional e words* to negate self-doubts, self-criticism, and **fear of failure**. Build your self-confidence by *mentally rehearsing* the steps of the task several times before you begin.

▶ **See success.** Use the **see success technique**, to create a mental picture of yourself working through a task, feeling positive about your work, and completing the task on time.

▶ **Identify a purpose and create an interest.** As soon as you label information or tasks as "meaningless, stupid, or boring," your processing and memory system starts ignoring the information. To be self-motivated, identify a purpose or significance of the task, focus on its relationship to a larger, more meaningful goal, and use a *goal organizer* to identify the advantages of completing the task and the consequences of avoiding it. To make the task more enjoyable, engage another person to work with you, such as a family member, a tutor, a lab assistant, or a study group. Seek alternative sources of information, such as a video, Internet searches, magazines, or books related to the topic.

▶ **Make a contract with yourself.** When you hear yourself making excuses for your behavior, make a contract with yourself to stop the excuses and get down to creating a plan of action (a *goal*).

Push yourself to "just do it." End your contract with an incentive, such as an *external reward*.

▶ **List your priorities.** When you feel overwhelmed or overextended, make a list of tasks that must be done. Prioritize them by their importance or completion date requirements. Schedule time on your weekly schedule to work on these tasks every day.

▶ **Keep a journal.** Create a *journal* specifically dedicated to procrastination issues. Watch for procrastination patterns: when and why you procrastinate and what kinds of tasks are involved. Create plans to change those patterns of behavaior. Monitor the effects of different strategies so that you know which ones work best for you.

▶ **Set the scene for success.** Gather up all the supplies or materials you need to get started. Select an appropriate work environment. *Take charge* and take responsibility of the situation.

▶ **Relax your personal standards.** If you tend to be perfectionist, examine your standards or expectations for yourself to determine whether they are unrealistically high. Be willing to find a more comfortable, realistic, and typical set of standards that still produce quality work but do not require you to "always be the best." Avoid spending excessive time redoing parts of a task or the final outcome, such as a paper.

▶ **Be willing to change.** Once you have identified yourself as a procrastinator, explore new behaviors to replace the self-defeating behavior of procrastination. Be willing to give up the attitude that "I have always done things this way" and be willing to try new strategies and to create new patterns of behaviors.

CLASS DISCUSSION

Question: Based on other information presented in this chapter, what other strategies could you add to the *Essential Strategies to Combat Procrastination* chart?

ONLINE PRACTICE 5

Visit the *Essential Study Skills*, Fifth Edition, website and go to Chapter 5. Click on **Practice 5: Decreasing Procrastination**. Type responses to the four questions. After you type your responses, you can print them or e-mail them to your instructor.

EXERCISE 5.6 LINKS

Work with a partner or in a small group. Discuss the relationship between the two parts of each of the following paired topics. Be prepared to share a summary of your discussions with the class.

Paired Topics

1. Goal setting and stress

2. Time management and procrastination

3. Procrastination and stress

4. Procrastination and motivation

5. Concentration and stress

6. Stress and working memory

Reflection Writing 3
Chapter 5

On separate paper, in a journal, or online at this textbook's website, respond to the following questions:

1. What strategies in this chapter will help you increase your level of concentration?

2. What strategies in this chapter will help you reduce stress?

3. What strategies in this chapter will help you combat procrastination?

SUMMARY

- Concentration is the ability to block out internal and external distractions in order to focus your mind on one specific item or task.

- An ideal study area has a noise level that is conducive to studying, two or more sources of light, and a work space with adequate room to work. Concentration improves when you use the *take-charge technique* to adjust the noise level, lighting, and work space.

- Active learning occurs when you select learning strategies that actively engage you in the learning process. Active learning combats internal distractors and promotes critical thinking, multisensory learning, and greater comprehension.

- Time-management and goal-setting techniques are directly related to your ability to concentrate. Chunking, task schedules, a study ritual, warm-ups, mental rehearsal, positive self-talk, and affirmations help you maintain your focus.

- To deal with internal and external distractors, you can select from a wide variety of techniques:
  - say *no*
  - no need
  - red bow
  - checkmark
  - mental storage box
  - tunnel vision
  - emotional *e* words

- Stress is a reaction or a response to events or situations that threaten to disrupt normal patterns or routines. Healthy stress can be motivational; excessive stress creates cognitive, physical, emotional, and behavioral consequences.

- Self-management skills, the six *Essential Strategies for Managing Stress*, a healthy lifestyle (exercise, nutrition, and sleep), and the following six relaxation techniques can reduce stress:
  - soothing mask
  - relaxation blanket
  - breathing by threes
  - deep breathing
  - deep muscle relaxation
  - yoga

- Procrastination, a learned behavior, is the process of putting something off until a later time. People procrastinate for a variety of reasons. Low self-efficacy, avoidance of difficult tasks, inaccurate sense of time, fear of failure, perfectionism, and self-control issues are some of the common causes of procrastination. Identifying the cause is the beginning point for combating procrastination.

- The following strategies can help you combat procrastination:
  - Use self-management skills and strategies.
  - Face your fear of failure.
  - See success.
  - Identify a purpose and create an interest.
  - Make a contract with yourself.
  - List your priorities.
  - Keep a journal.
  - Set the scene for success.
  - Relax your personal standards.
  - Be willing to change.

CULMINATING OPTIONS FOR CHAPTER 5

1. Visit this textbook's website and go to Chapter 5 to complete the following exercises:
   a. Flash card review of Chapter 5 terms and definitions
   b. ACE Practice Test 1 with ten fill-in-the-blank questions
   c. ACE Practice Test 2 with ten true-false questions
   d. ACE Practice Test 3 with ten multiple-choice questions
   e. ACE Practice Test 4 with three short answer–critical thinking questions

2. Go to Appendix C in the back of this textbook for more Learning Options to use for additional practice, enrichment, or portfolio projects.

Chapter 5 REVIEW QUESTIONS

Multiple Choice

Choose the best answer to complete each of the following questions. Then write the letter of the best answer on the line.

_____ **1.** Concentration is
    a. the ability to block out distractions and focus on only one item or task.
    b. one of the Twelve Principles of Memory.
    c. a mental discipline that involves training your mind to keep a focus.
    d. all of the above.

_____ **2.** Poor concentration may stem from
    a. stress about personal relationships, worries, or fears.
    b. a lack of motivation.
    c. internal and external distractors.
    d. a noisy studying environment.

_____ **3.** External distractors can include
    a. sunshine, noises, and lighting.
    b. smells, noises, and worries.
    c. negative self-talk, clutter, and people.
    d. the checkmark technique, the red-bow technique, and framing.

_____ **4.** Stressors
    a. are often caused by the way you handle and perceive situations.
    b. require some form of action on your part to be reduced or eliminated.
    c. can sometimes be eliminated by using self-management skills.
    d. involve all of the above.

_____ **5.** Which techniques would work best for a student who wants to stop wasting the first half hour of a study block trying to "get started" on studying?
    a. Warm-ups, chunking technique, and setting goals
    b. Perfect place, red bow, and reviewing
    c. Breathing by threes and relaxation blanket
    d. Tunnel vision, soothing mask, and take charge

_____ **6.** Active learning
    a. occurs when you use a lot of energy reading a textbook nonstop for several hours.
    b. requires a person to walk, pace, or move around the room while studying.
    c. is a type of passive learning in which learning becomes automatic.
    d. requires the learner to use study strategies that require active participation in the learning process.

_____ **7.** Procrastination
    a. may stem from lack of interest, fear of failure, or perfectionism.
    b. occurs when low-priority tasks take the place of high-priority tasks.
    c. is a learned pattern that can be altered by using effective strategies.
    d. is all of the above.

_____ **8.** Which of the following strategies are *not* designed to adjust a person's attitude from negative to positive?
    a. Tunnel vision, intrinsic rewards, and deep breathing
    b. Mental rehearsal and positive self-talk
    c. Affirmations and emotional *e* words
    d. Seeing success and strategies to increase self-efficacy

_____ **9.** Which of the following statements is *not* true about stress?

a. Stress is normal and can help people move in new directions.

b. Prolonged stress can have physical, emotional, behavioral, and cognitive consequences.

c. Excessive stress requires prescription medications in order to avoid physical damage to the body.

d. Excessive stress may affect the functioning of working memory and long-term memory.

_____ **10.** Which of the following helps a person decrease or eliminate the habit of procrastinating about doing important tasks?

a. Taking time to understand *when* and *why* procrastination occurs

b. Using weekly schedules and task schedules

c. Using effective time-management and goal-setting techniques

d. All of the above

Short Answer and Critical Thinking

Use complete sentences to answer the following questions. Use details and terminology from this chapter.

1. What are self-management skills? How do they affect your ability to perform well academically?

2. According to the author, what kinds of choices do you need to make to have a healthy lifestyle that reduces stress?

CHAPTER 6

Boosting Your Memory and Preparing for Tests

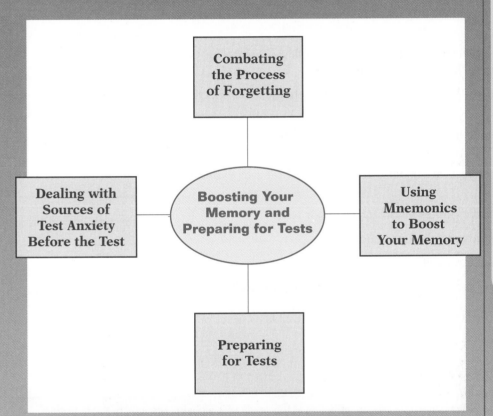

Combating the Process of Forgetting

Dealing with Sources of Test Anxiety Before the Test

Boosting Your Memory and Preparing for Tests

Using Mnemonics to Boost Your Memory

Preparing for Tests

Terms to Know

Five Forgetting Theories
Decay Theory
Displacement Theory
Interference Theory
Incomplete Encoding Theory
Retrieval Failure Theory

Mnemonics
associations
pictures and graphics
acronym
acrostic
rhythms, rhymes, and jingles
stacking
loci
peg systems
   human body peg system
   rhyming peg system
   number shape peg system
cramming
Bloom's Taxonomy
test anxiety
internal locus of control
external locus of control
systematic desensitization

Forgetting is a natural process that occurs throughout the memory system. Five Theories of Forgetting explain why you must strive to use effective study skill strategies to combat the process of forgetting. In addition to an array of study skills strategies, you can use mnemonics (memory tricks) to boost your memory and your ability to recall information that is otherwise difficult to retrieve. Tests in college are a standard method to assess your understanding of course material. In this chapter, you will learn effective strategies to prepare for tests and reduce the occurrence of test anxiety.

Chapter 6 Boosting Memory and Preparing for Tests Profile

ANSWER, SCORE, and **RECORD** your profile before you read this chapter. If you need to review the process, refer to the complete directions given in the Profile for Chapter 1 on page 2.

ONLINE: You can complete the profile and get your score online at this textbook's website.

	YES	NO
1. When I take tests, I tend to forget information I have studied.		
2. I practice predicting and writing test questions as one way to prepare for tests.		
3. I am often nervous, feel sick, or have physical problems (headache, stomachache, clammy hands) right before a test.		
4. I sometimes use memory tricks (mnemonics) to help me learn specific information.		
5. I try to find out as much information as possible about a test before it is given.		
6. Difficulties I have on tests are usually due to factors that are beyond my control.		
7. I make special summary notes before every major test.		
8. I make a five-day study plan before major tests.		
9. I use the survival technique of cramming for most tests.		
10. I am confident that I have adequate skills to prepare effectively for tests.		

Reflection Writing 1
Chapter 6

On separate paper, in a journal, or online at this textbook's website, respond to the following questions.

1. What is your profile score for this chapter? What does it mean to you?

2. Why would you benefit from learning strategies to boost your memory? In what areas do you feel you have the most difficulty remembering information?

Combating the Process of Forgetting

The process of learning involves complex sets of operations that require effort and activity on your part. Unfortunately, the process of forgetting requires no effort on your part and occurs quite naturally in the human memory system. Using the strategies discussed in previous chapters will definitely improve your memory and your ability to recall information, but they will not shield you from the frustrations of "forgetting" or being unable to recall on demand information that you studied or previously learned. By understanding five common causes of forgetting that occur in working memory, you can analyze *what went wrong* or *what broke down* when you find yourself forgetting information or not being able to recall or retrieve it when you need it. You can then use this information to adjust your strategies and to create stronger links or associations to your long-term memory schemas. The Five Theories of Forgetting include the *Decay, Displacement, Interference, Incomplete Encoding,* and *Retrieval Failure* theories.

The following chart shows causes for each type of forgetting and strategies to use to combat the process of forgetting.

	Causes	Strategies to Combat Forgetting
Decay Theory	Sensory stimuli coming into the sensory storage centers or stimuli moving from sensory storage centers into working memory are too weak, get ignored, or are not attended to within the first few seconds. The stimuli fade or decay. True learning never takes place.	1. Be alert and ready to learn. Give your undivided attention to receiving and attending to new sensory stimuli. 2. Make learning the information your intention. Set a learning goal to help you focus on your desire to capture and understand new information. 3. Begin thinking about, working with, or associating the information with familiar ideas as soon as you receive the stimuli.
Displacement Theory	Too much information comes into working memory at too rapid a pace. It overloads the limited capacity of working memory. As a result, some of the information is pushed out of the way, or displaced. True learning never takes place.	1. Slow down the intake process of information. If you are reading, slow down your rate of reading. Allow time to think about or mull over words, ideas, or concepts before you take in more information. 2. Use *spaced practice.* Avoid cramming or using marathon studying (See page 76.) 3. Pause between new pieces or chunks of information. Allow time for your working memory to consolidate or integrate the new information. 4. Select an environment conducive to learning. Avoid environments with excessive, unrelated sensory stimuli (such as noises, sounds, or smells). 5. Free up your working memory from anxiety or intrusive thoughts. (See page 40.)

Causes	Strategies to Combat Forgetting
Interference Theory Confusion occurs between "old" (familiar, previously learned information) and new information. Interference can occur between items studied in the same session or between items studied many years apart. Learning new information may be difficult if it contradicts, differs from, or does not mesh or integrate well with the "old" information. The "old" information is recalled more easily. At other times, new information overrides the ability to recall old information. The new information stays the freshest in working memory.	1. When new information is *similar* to previously learned information, take time to compare the two chunks of information. Examine and recognize their similarities and their differences. For example, if you previously spoke Spanish fluently and are now trying to learn Portuguese, a language similar to Spanish, you can avoid interferences by recognizing ways in which the two languages are similar and are different in terms of sentence structure, verb forms, pronunciation, vocabulary, and diacritical markings above some letters. 2. When new information *differs* from previously learned information, take time to examine and understand the differences. For example, a contemporary, culturally sensitive perspective of American history may differ from what you grew up believing. Your goal is not to erase the previous learning but to understand and integrate it with new information to create a larger, more complex long-term memory schema. 3. When you take a break from studying complex, difficult topics, take a nap or do something quite different before you study the next topic. Providing time between topics establishes a buffer that reduces the possibility of interferences between different topics.
Incomplete Encoding Theory For a variety of possible reasons, information is only partially learned. Incomplete encoding can occur when your learning is interrupted and left unfinished, when you have divided attention during the rehearsal process, or when you use rote memory. Incomplete encoding can also occur when you use an ineffective encoding method: you did not encode an association, a memory cue, a stimulus, a question, or some type of memory trigger with the information.	1. Use elaborative rehearsal techniques to encode information clearly. (See page 37.) 2. Avoid using rote memory or memorization of individual items without attaching meaning to the items. 3. Use self-quizzing and feedback strategies to verify that you have learned the information completely, not just partially. Feedback lets you know when you need to work further with partially learned or vague information. 4. Strive to maintain your focus, to have undivided attention, as you rehearse and associate new information with previously learned information. Do not allow distractions to interrupt your encoding process.

Causes	Strategies to Combat Forgetting
Retrieval Failure Theory The feeling of "going blank" or having information "on the tip of your tongue" indicated difficulties accessing, retrieving, or bringing learned information back into your working memory. Lack of sufficient memory cues or lack of strong associations among chunks of information makes memory searches difficult to conduct successfully. Information randomly "filed" away in long-term memory in an unorganized manner also contributes to retrieval failure.	1. Prepare in advance to prevent retrieval failure. As soon as information comes into your working memory, make a conscious effort to create an association. Practice using the association to recall information at later dates. 2. Prepare in advance by using clear structures or formats to organize information in logical, meaningful ways. By classifying or grouping ideas and details, you create units or chunks of information that are easier to locate in schemas than isolated, disconnected details. 3. Prepare in advance by using ongoing review to practice activating the information and pulling it back into your working memory. When done frequently, the information stays fresh in your mind. 4. Put yourself in *retrieval mode*, a mental state where you intend to recall things. Turn inward and pay attention to your thoughts; start thinking of and watching your mind make associations and activate memory cues. Allow yourself up to a minute to retrieve important information. Retrieval mode requires patience on your part and commitment to the memory process. Some students become too impatient when answers do not instantly pop into their working memories. 5. When you are unable to retrieve a memory, reconstruct your learning situation. Remembering *how, when,* and *where* you learned the desired information can help you find the path into your long-term memory. Reliving the learning experience itself activates your episodic memory.

Working memory (*conscious mind*) involves extensive activity, coordination of processes, integration of information, and transference of chunks of information back and forth between the temporary sensory storage centers, central executive, and long-term memory. Due to the variety of learning environments, learning situations, kinds of content, and personal processing patterns, at some time or another, we all have to make new efforts to find the right combinations of rehearsal and retrieval strategies to use to combat the natural process of forgetting.

Group Processing: A Collaborative Learning Activity

Form groups of three or four students. Then complete the following directions.

1. On a large piece of paper, make a list of different kinds of information members of your group had difficulty remembering this week. Your list may include course-related information, tasks or chores at home, or information or procedures at work.

2. Discuss which type of forgetting possibly occurred in each situation and write the type of forgetting next to each item. The following expressions can serve as quick reminders to help you distinguish among the five kinds of forgetting.

   I wasn't paying attention; I never really learned it. (Decay)
   I was trying to learn too quickly; I never really learned it. (Displacement)
   I can only remember part of it. (Incomplete Encoding)
   I always get these two things mixed up. (Interference)
   I know that I know it, but I just can't remember it right now. (Retrieval Failure)

3. Discuss possible solutions to avoid similar forgetting situations in the future.

ONLINE PRACTICE 1

Visit the *Essential Study Skills*, Fifth Edition, website and go to Chapter 6. Click on **Practice 1: Five Forgetting Theories**. Complete the ten-question interactive multiple-choice quiz. Upon completion of the quiz, you will receive your score. You can exit at that time, or you can print or e-mail your results to your instructor.

Using Mnemonics to Boost Your Memory

Mnemonics are memory techniques or memory tricks that serve as bridges to help you recall specific facts or details that for whatever reason are difficult for you to remember. Mnemonics provide you with an extra clue to help trigger your memory so you can recall information more easily. In this textbook, *SAVE CRIB FOTO* is a mnemonic designed to help you recall the Twelve Principles of Memory accurately. You have most likely created or used mnemonics in the past to learn various kinds of information. For example, think back to how you learned the following kinds of information.

- The number of days in each month of the year
- The direction to move the clock to or from daylight-saving time
- The name of someone whom you just met
- A license plate number or telephone or cell phone number
- An ATM code or an Internet password
- A mental list of items to purchase at the store
- A specific name of a person or a place discussed in class
- A new math equation or formula
- A new vocabulary word or a word in a foreign language

Mnemonics serve an important role in memory, but they have limitations and should be used sparingly. If you use mnemonics too extensively, they become cumbersome and can add confusion to your learning process. If you do not study the mnemonics accurately, they hinder rather than help you recall information accurately. The following chart shows the advantages and disadvantages of using mnemonics.

Advantages of Using Mnemonics	Disadvantages of Using Mnemonics
1. They provide a memory bridge to help you recall information that otherwise is difficult to remember.	1. They must be recited and practiced in a precise manner in order to work correctly.
2. They involve rearranging or reorganizing information, which also helps you personalize the information and be a more active learner.	2. They require time to create, learn, and practice.
3. They add interest to studying by providing you with new ways to work with information.	3. They can become "crutches" and can give you a false sense of security that you know the information.
4. When used properly, they allow you to spend less time retrieving information from your long-term memory.	4. They rely more on rote memory than on elaborative rehearsal, so your actual understanding of the concepts may be inadequate.
	5. Overuse can result in confusion and an excessive expenditure of time reviewing.

Some students use mnemonics quite naturally and on a regular basis. Others shy away from mnemonics because they are foreign or unfamiliar and seem to require too much extra work. However, as with all the other study skills strategies in this textbook, after you learn how to create and study from the following kinds of mnemonics, using them when you study or in your personal life becomes an option that you can use selectively to boost your memory.

Mnemonics

1. Associations
2. Pictures and graphics
3. Acronyms and acrostics
4. Rhythms, rhymes, and jingles
5. Stacking
6. Loci (location)
7. Peg systems

Associations

You learned in Chapter 2 that associating new information with familiar objects, words, pictures, or concepts keeps information active in working memory for a longer period of time. **Associations** also work as memory cues to help you locate information when you conduct a memory search. Most mnemonic associations involve a visual cue or mental image that links a new word, definition, name, or object to a familiar object that will be easy for you to recall. The following steps can help you create vivid images that you can recall more easily.

Steps for Creating Associations

1. Be sure you understand the item (new information) before you create an association. Once you understand the item, actively search for a familiar word, object, picture, or concept that you can link or associate with the item.
2. Visualize the shape and colors of items you plan to use in your association. You can also add sounds and smells to the association when appropriate. Change the actual proportions by exaggerating some part of an object by making it larger than its real size. If you are visualizing letters, use large, bold capital letters.
3. Visually link both items together by blending the two images in the association into one integrated picture.
4. When possible, put action into your image to create a "mini-movie" instead of a still shot.

To use associations effectively, you need to actively look for and think about ways to create simple associations that will be easy to remember and use to recall information. The following examples show several kinds of associations you can create to learn factual information.

1. *Recall a person's name: Associate the name with an object.*

   For example, you want to remember the name of a new classmate, *Annie Carpenter*. Picture Annie as a carpenter wearing a carpenter's apron and holding a hammer in one hand. The name *ANNIE* is printed boldly across the carpenter's apron filled with tools.

2. *Recall a person's name: Think of another person you know with that same name.*

   For example, you want to remember the name of *William Herschel*, an English astronomer who discovered the planet Uranus in 1781. First you think of your uncle William, who was an avid football fan. Then you think of Herschel Walker, a great NFL running back, who retired from the NFL in 1997. Finally, you create an image of your Uncle William with his arms draped over Herschel Walker's shoulders as the two gaze up into the evening sky, wishing they could see Uranus.

3. *Define a new term: Associate the meaning with an object that has a similar characteristic.*

   For example, you have had problems remembering the difference between a *waxing moon* and a *waning moon*. You know that one term means that the illuminated portion of the moon gets larger and that the other term means that the illuminated portion gets smaller. You begin by focusing on the term *waxing*. You immediately think about waxing your car. The more you wax, the shinier it becomes. The shine increases; a waxing moon also increases. This association makes it easy to remember that the illuminated surface of a waxing moon increases, and thus, the illuminated surface of the waning moon decreases.

4. *Spell a word correctly: Create associations by using specific letters within the word.*

For example, to avoid spelling confusions between the words *dessert* and *desert,* just remember that the word with *ss* (*dessert*) is *so sweet*. Also, the plural *desserts* spelled backwards spells *stressed*. To avoid confusion between the homonyms *principal* and *principle*, remember that the only time you use *principle* is when you are referring to a *rule* or a standard, such as the *principles* of accounting or living your life by your own *principles*. You can also remember that a *principal* of a school is your *pal*, but you would also need to remember that there are other meanings of *principal*, such as a principal on a loan or a principal part in a play. To use the correct homonym *piece* or *peace*, remember that *piece* is a portion of something, such as a *piece of pie.*

5. *Remember a specific number: Find number patterns to use in an association.*

For example, you want to remember that Mount Fuji in Japan is 12,389 feet high. Twelve reminds you of 12 months in a year. There are 365 days in a year. You subtract 365 from 389 and get a remainder of 24. There are 24 hours in a day. The association to recall the height of Mount Fuji is $12,365 + 24 = 12,389$ feet.

6. *Remember a specific task to do: Associate the task with an object you will encounter.*

For example, you are in bed when you remember you need to get your gym clothes out of the dryer before you go to school. Since you always begin your day with coffee, you create a clear mental picture of your gym clothes stuffed inside your coffee pot. In the morning when you see your coffee pot, you receive the reminder to get your gym clothes.

7. *Remember a cause-effect relationship: Blend two items into an image of action.*

For example, you want to remember that fertilizer is a petroleum product. You imagine yourself holding a gas can, and as you pour out the contents, you pour fertilizer, not gas. As another example, you want to remember that for some people, rising quickly from bed can cause sudden fainting due to a drop in blood pressure. You picture someone rising quickly, fainting, and dropping to the floor. You can link this to dropping blood on the floor.

Pictures and Graphics

Pictures and graphics are stored differently than words in long-term memory. Visual learners and students with artistic talents often find that converting information into pictures or graphics and using a variety of colors in their study tools help them remember and recall information more efficiently.

To boost your memory, you can add pictures and graphics to any study tools or notes you create. Linking pictures and colors with words often creates a stronger imprint of information in long-term memory. As you experiment with the impact of detailed pictures, whimsical cartoons, basic stick figures, or colorful borders or patterns in your study tools, you create opportunities to add creativity and interest to your work. The following examples show creative ways to combine pictures with information you may need to learn.

■ Five Theories of Forgetting

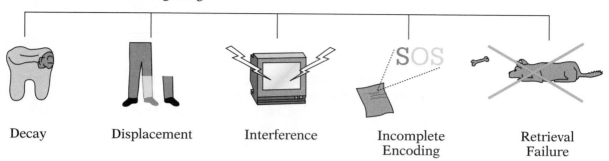

| Decay | Displacement | Interference | Incomplete Encoding | Retrieval Failure |

■ Eight intelligences

Linguistic   Bodily-kinesthetic
Musical   Intrapersonal
Logical-mathematical   Interpersonal
Spatial   Naturalist

■ Penetration of Radiation

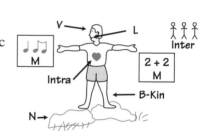

Penetration of Radiation

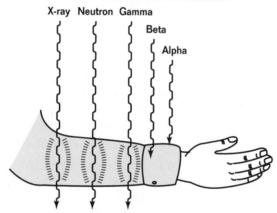

X-ray Neutron Gamma
Beta
Alpha

Acronyms and Acrostics

Acronyms and acrostics are mnemonics designed to help you learn a list of items in either a fixed or a random order. An **acronym** is a *word or group of words* made by taking the *first letter of the key words in a list of items* and using those letters to create a new word or phrase. The new word or phrase is the mnemonic or memory bridge that helps trigger your memory to recall specific information.

The following are examples of *acronyms*:

■ SAVE CRIB FOTO = Selectivity, Association, Visualization, Elaboration, Concentration, Recitation, Intention, Big and little pictures, Feedback, Organization, Time on task, and Ongoing review

■ ARE = Alarm, Resistance, Exhaustion (levels of physical reaction to stress, from Appendix D)

■ GAS = General Adaptation Syndrome (pattern used to adapt to stress, from Appendix D)

■ HOMES = Huron, Ontario, Michigan, Erie, Superior (the five Great Lakes in the northern United States)

Steps for Creating an Acronym

1. Write the list of items you need to remember.
2. Underline the *first letter* of each item in the list. If an item in the list consists of more than one word, select only *one* key word to use; underline the first letter of that key word. *(Note: If you have difficulties creating an acronym in the following steps, return to your items that have two or more words and select an alternative key word and first letter to use.)*
3. Write the first letter of each key word on two separate lines. Place the vowels (*a, e, i, o, u,* and sometimes *y*) on the first line and the remaining letters, the consonants, on a second line. *(Note: Every word must have a vowel, so if none of the key words on your list begins with a vowel, you will not be able to create an acronym.)*
4. Rearrange the letters to form a word or a phrase. A real word is easier to recall than a nonsense word, so strive to rearrange the letters to create a real word or phrase. *(Note: If your list consists of a specific set of steps or items that must appear in an exact order, you cannot rearrange the letters. If the letters in order do not form a word, you will not be able to create an acronym.)*
5. For it to be useful to you, you must now memorize the acronym. Repeat the acronym multiple times and then practice reciting or writing what each letter in the acronym represents. You must be able to attach meaning to each part of the acronym for it to be a valuable memory tool.

The following example shows the application of the five steps for creating the acronym HOMES.

Five Great Lakes

Steps 1 and 2: Make the list. Underline first letter of each key word.

Lake <u>S</u>uperior
Lake <u>H</u>uron
Lake <u>E</u>rie
Lake <u>O</u>ntario
Lake <u>M</u>ichigan

Step 3: Write the first letter of each word on two lines (vowels and consonants)

E   O
S   H   M

Step 4: Rearrange the letters to form a word or a phrase.

HOMES

Step 5: Memorize and practice translating the meaning of each letter.

HOMES

H = Huron   O = Ontario   M = Michigan   E = Erie   S = Superior

An **acrostic** is a *sentence* made by using the *first letters of the key words in a list of items* to create words that form a sentence that helps trigger your memory to recall the items in the list. The following are examples of acrostics:

<u>E</u>very <u>g</u>ood <u>b</u>oy <u>d</u>oes <u>f</u>ine. = E, G, B, D, F (the treble staff lines in music)

<u>K</u>ing <u>P</u>hillip <u>c</u>an <u>o</u>rder <u>f</u>amily <u>g</u>ene <u>s</u>tudies. = Kingdom, Phylum, Class, Order, Family, Genus, and Species (plant and animal classification system)

<u>P</u>lease <u>e</u>xcuse <u>m</u>y <u>d</u>ear <u>A</u>unt <u>S</u>ally. = order of operations in math problems (See the details below.)

Steps for Creating an Acrostic

1. Write the list of items that you need to remember.
2. Underline the *first letter* of each item in the list. If an item in the list consists of more than one word, select only *one* key word to use. Underline the first letter of that key word.
3. Since acrostics work well for a list of items that you need to learn in a specific order, write in order the first letter of each key word, leaving a blank line after each letter so that you have sufficient space to write a word.
4. Using the initial letters as initial letters for words, create a sentence. Sentences that are silly or bizarre or that have personal significance will be easier to remember. *(Note: Do not add any extra words to your sentence; each word in the sentence must represent an item in your original list.)*
5. Memorize the sentence (the acrostic). Accuracy is essential. Repeat the sentence multiple times and then practice reciting or writing what each word in the acrostic represents. You must be able to attach meaning to each part of the acrostic for it to be a valuable memory tool.

The following example shows the application of the five steps for creating an acrostic.

Mathematical Order of Operations

Steps 1 and 2: Write the list of items in order. Underline the first letter of key words.

<u>p</u>arentheses

<u>e</u>xponents

<u>m</u>ultiplication

<u>d</u>ivision

<u>a</u>ddition

<u>s</u>ubtraction

Step 3: Write the first letters of key words, leaving a blank line after each letter.

P_____ e_____ m_____ d_____ a_____ s_____.

Step 4: Create a sentence using the initial letters.

Please excuse my dear Aunt Sally.

Step 5: Memorize the sentence. Practice translating the meaning of each word.

PLEASE EXCUSE MY DEAR AUNT SALLY.

P = <u>p</u>arentheses   E = <u>e</u>xponents   M = <u>m</u>ultiplication

D = <u>d</u>ivision   A = <u>a</u>ddition   S = <u>s</u>ubtraction

EXERCISE 6.1   Working with Acronyms and Acrostics
Use your knowledge of acronyms and acrostics to complete the following directions.

1. Create **acronyms** for the following items. The letters to use appear before the space to write your acronym. In some cases, you have a choice of letters to use for key items; remember, however, to use *one*—not both—of the letters. You can arrange the letters into any order.

   a. A pediatrician's advice for food a child should eat when he or she has a stomach flu: *bananas, applesauce, toast, rice.*

      Letters to use: **b   a   t   r**

      Acronym: _____

   b. What you should do to treat sudden muscle injuries: *compress, elevate, use ice,* and *rest.*

      Letters to use: **c   e   u** *or* **i   r**

      Acronym: _____

   c. Five Theories of Forgetting: *Decay, Displacement, Interference, Incomplete Encoding,* and *Retrieval Failure.*

      Letters to use: **d   d   i   e   r**

      Acronym: _____

   d. Ten body systems in humans: *skeletal, digestive, muscular, endocrine, circulatory, nervous, reproductive, urinary, respiratory,* and *integumentary*.

      Letters to use: **s   d   m   e   c   n   r   u   r   i**

      Acronym: _____

2. Create **acrostics** for the following items. The letters to use to begin words in a sentence appear below; however, if the items do not need to appear in order, you may rearrange the letters.

   a. Four levels of response in order for test questions: *immediate, delayed, assisted,* and *educated guessing*

      I _____   d _____   a _____   g _____.

   b. Steps for writing goals: *Set **specific** goals, set specific **target** date and time, identify **steps**,* and *plan a **reward***

      S _____   t _____   s _____   r _____.

   c. The first ten presidents of the United States in order: *Washington, Adams, Jefferson, Madison, Monroe, Adams, Jackson, Van Buren, Harrison,* and *Tyler.*

      W _____   a _____   j _____   m _____   m _____

      a _____   j _____   v _____   h _____   t _____

   d. Types of contemporary views on motivation: *Equity Theory, Expectancy Theory, Reinforcement Theory,* and *Theory Z*

      E _____   e _____   r _____   z _____.

   e. The five steps in order for the Feedback Model: *goal, action, feedback, comparison,* and *results.*

      G _____   a _____   f _____   c _____   r _____.

Rhythms, Rhymes, and Jingles

Auditory learners and those with strong language or musical skills enjoy learning through **rhythms, rhymes, and jingles** by rhyming words, attaching a catchy tune or rhythm, creating a rap, or thinking up a jingle. Any time you find yourself singing a commercial or repeating an advertising slogan, marketing experts have succeeded in getting information into your long-term memory. The following examples demonstrate the use of rhythms, rhymes, and jingles as mnemonics to learn information.

Many companies have memorable jingles or slogans. What company or product slogans do you know?

- Use *i* before *e* except after *c* or when sounded as *a* as in *neighbor* and *weigh*.
- In fourteen hundred and ninety-two, Columbus sailed the ocean blue.
- Spring forward; fall back (daylight-saving time).
- Thirty days hath September, April, June, and November. All the rest have thirty-one (except February).
- Who invented dynamite? *Alfred Nobel had quite a fright when he discovered dynamite.*
- Which way should you turn to open a jar or tighten a bolt? *Righty tighty, lefty loosy.*
- Stalactites are icicle-shaped deposits that hang down from the roof of a cave. Stalagmites are deposits in a cave that build up from the floor. *When the mites go up, the tights come down.*

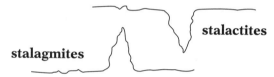

Stacking

The **stacking** type of mnemonic uses pictures and associations to remember a list of specific items in order. You can use this *stacking* technique to memorize a list of items from one of your courses, or you can use it for a daily or personal routine such as grocery shopping. Using this technique can help you strengthen your visual memory and visual sequencing skills.

Steps for Creating the Stacking Mnemonic

1. Make a list of a sequence of items you need to remember.
2. Create a vivid image of the first item. Visualize the size, shape, color, and any other specific characteristics of the item. Mentally place this item on the bottom of the stack.
3. Create an image of the second item. Mentally review the first item; then, stack the second item on top of the first item. Mentally review the image with the first and the second item.
4. Continue this process of visualizing each new item, reviewing the items already stacked, and then placing the new item on top of the stack and visualizing the complete stack.
5. For this mnemonic to work effectively as a memory tool, you need to keep the image of the stack fresh in your working memory by picturing, naming, or reciting all of the objects in order.

The following is an example of using stacking to remember items to purchase at the store without writing and taking a list with you to the store.

cereal

film

apples

toilet paper

watermelon

mayonnaise

milk

shampoo

cabbage

hot dogs

Loci

Loci, which means *locations*, is a mnemonic that dates back to the early times of Greek orators, who could deliver lengthy speeches without any written notes. Orators made mental notes by associating parts or topics of their speeches with familiar rooms or locations in a building. In their minds, as they walked through each room, they visualized items in the rooms that they associated with the topic to be discussed. With this technique they were able to deliver organized, fluent speeches to their audiences.

Steps for Creating a Loci System

1. Make a list of the items you need to remember.
2. Draw a floor plan of a familiar location.
3. On paper or mentally, attach a picture of the first item you need to remember inside the first location or room on your floor plan. You can exaggerate the size or shape of the picture or hang it in an unusual position to make it stand out in your memory.
4. Continue walking through the floor plan, attaching one item to each room.
5. Visually practice walking through all the rooms and reciting the important information associated with the items in the rooms.

For example, you may want to picture the first floor of a building on your campus. The following drawing shows *front doors, hallway, cafeteria, lounge, another hall, lecture hall, foreign language lab,* and *restrooms.* For each of these locations, you could mentally attach a picture that represents the topic you would like to present in a speech, or you could attach pictures that represent a specific event in a sequence of events.

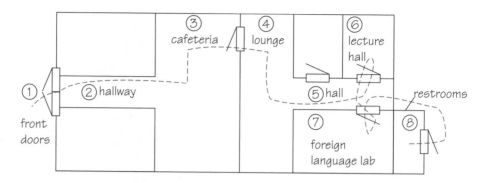

Assume that you are going to give a speech or write an essay for a history class about the end of the economic boom in the 1970s. You need to discuss these topics: 350 percent increase in oil prices; Arab oil embargo; high retail prices; slump in auto industry and manufacturing; high unemployment; easy credit; high costs of health, safety, and pollution controls; and massive government spending. You can picture the following images at each location in the building:

1. At the front door, picture a poster that says "350 percent increase in oil prices."
2. In the hallway, picture a row of oil barrels with large Xs painted on them.
3. In the cafeteria, picture food prices: hamburgers $4.50, milk $3.00.
4. In the lounge, picture posters on the walls of closed auto factories.
5. In the hall, picture people lined up for job interviews.
6. In the lecture hall, picture credit card companies handing out high interest credit cards to students.
7. In the foreign language lab, picture a filthy, unsafe, polluted room with a sign that says, "Too expensive to meet standards."
8. In the restrooms, picture outrageous price tags hanging on fixtures that bear a label that says, "Government property."

EXERCISE 6.2   Using Loci
Complete the following three steps to use the loci system.

1. Select one of the following situations to use with the loci mnemonic technique:

   a. You need to have an important discussion with your roommate concerning five issues.

   b. You have an appointment with your instructor to discuss four topics about the class and your work.

   c. You need to remember the sequence of events or steps for information from one of your courses. There are at least four events or steps in this information.

2. Draw a floor plan of a familiar building. In each room, attach a picture that symbolizes the item you need to discuss or name.

3. Practice mentally walking through your building and reciting the information represented by the pictures in each room. Your instructor may ask you to recite your information in class.

Peg Systems

Several kinds of **peg systems** can be used to help you remember a list of items. The *human body peg system, the rhyming peg system,* and the *number shape peg system* are common peg systems you can learn to use quickly. If you have ever seen a stage performer memorize fifty or even one hundred items that the audience calls out, chances are that the performer used a peg system to memorize the items quickly. The following steps apply to all three peg systems.

Steps for Creating a Peg System

1. Make a list of the items you need to remember. Be sure you have a basic understanding about each item.
2. Memorize the fixed set of pegs. Pegs do not change; only the items that you hang on the pegs change each time you create a new peg system mnemonic.
3. Create a mental picture of the first item on your list. Funny, silly, bizarre, oversized, and colorful pictures work best to hang on the pegs. Mentally hang the picture of the first item on the first peg.
4. Continue adding items, one at a time. After you hang a new item, review all the items in the order in which they are already hung on the pegs.
5. After all the items are hung on the pegs, mentally picture and review all of the items in order. Then, practice recalling items out of order. For example, tell what is on peg 6, then peg 2, and so on.
6. Review the items on your pegs frequently. For academic topics, tell about or recite information about each item.

The **human body peg system** uses parts of the body as pegs; the pegs never change. To use this system, memorize the body parts in order before attaching the mental pictures. In your mind, hang on your forehead the first picture of the item you want to remember. Continue hanging mental pictures on the pegs. After you attach the pictures, practice naming each item in order.

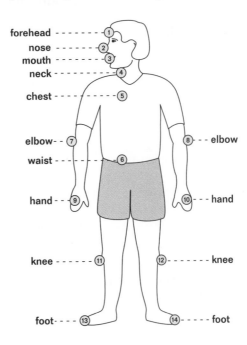

For example, assume you want to use the body peg system to remember six main structures in the human eye: pupil, cornea, iris, lens, retina, and fovea. Picture the following items on the body parts:

forehead	Picture a student	(pupil)
nose	Picture a corn on the cob	(cornea)
mouth	Picture an iris flower	(iris)
neck	Picture sunglasses with large lenses	(lens)
chest	Picture a tin can	(reTINa)
waist	Picture a belt buckle with FOV	(fovea)

The **rhyming peg system** uses a picture that rhymes with a number word from one to ten. This picture is the peg that never changes. In your mind, create a picture for each of the following:

one	= bun		six	= sticks
two	= shoe		seven	= heaven
three	= tree		eight	= gate
four	= door		nine	= vine
five	= hive		ten	= hen

For example, assume you want to use the rhyming peg system to remember eight secondary defense mechanisms discussed in psychology: *displacement, projection, identification, rationalization, intellectualization, substitution, fantasy,* and *regression.* Your task, then, is to link the first mechanism with the bun. Continue to create the visual links; review each peg and defense mechanism before you add a new one. The following example shows the associations you could make to learn the eight secondary defense mechanisms.

Peg Picture	Defense Mechanism	Picture You Create with the Peg
bun	displacement	a hamburger bun being thrown into a garbage can (displaced)
shoe	projection	a shoe thrown through the air as a projectile
tree	identification	a person with a magnifying glass examining a tree
door	rationalization	an opened door with someone being kicked out; the word *but* is written numerous times on the door
hive	intellectualization	surround the hive with "intellectual" facts related to bee hives: drones, worker bees, queen bee, honey
sticks	substitution	show a hand replacing a brown stick with a red stick
heaven	fantasy	show a person fantasizing about life in heaven
gate	regression	show a person walking backward out of a gate

The **number shape peg system** uses a picture in the shape of the number for each peg. A number peg system can go beyond ten pegs. Memorize the first twelve pegs that commonly appear in this system.

1 = pencil	2 = swan	3 = clover	4 = legs	5 = hand	6 = trunk
7 = flag	8 = hourglass	9 = balloon on a stick	10 = ball and bat	11 = ladder	12 = eggs

You can use this number peg system for a list of items in one of your courses, or you can use it for everyday convenience, such as remembering a list of items while grocery shopping or a list of weekend tasks you need to accomplish. For a list of six weekend tasks, begin by memorizing the first six pegs. Then take the first task and associate a mental picture to the pencil. In the following example, your first task is to start the laundry. After you see the picture clearly, work with the second item. Review items one and two mentally. Proceed to add one item at a time. With practice, you can hang items quickly on the pegs.

| laundry | clean bathroom | mow | call parent | dust | bills |

To practice using the number shape peg system, write six tasks you would like to accomplish this weekend. Then visually associate each task to the first six number shape pegs.

1.

2.

3.

4.

5.

6.

⬡ EXERCISE 6.3 Creating Mnemonics

With a partner or by yourself, use any of the seven kinds of mnemonics listed on page 143 to create a mnemonic for each of the following:

1. Planets in order: Mercury, Venus, Earth, Mars, Jupiter, Saturn, Uranus, Neptune, Pluto

2. Eight parts of speech: noun, pronoun, verb, adverb, adjective, preposition, conjunction, interjection

3. The seven coordinating conjunctions used in compound sentences: *for, and, nor, but, or, yet, so*

4. Skeletal (bone) structure of the arm: humerus, ulna, radius, carpals, phalanges

5. Elisabeth Kübler-Ross's stages of facing death: denial, anger, bargaining, depression, acceptance

6. Four types of cloud structures: cumulus, stratus, nimbus, cirrus

7. Five extinct species or races of humans: Java Ape, Peking, Heidelberg, Neanderthal, Cro-Magnon

8. Vertical structure of the atmosphere, beginning with the closest to the Earth: troposphere, stratosphere, mesosphere, and thermosphere.

9. The three stages in the General Adaptation Syndrome: alarm, resistance, and exhaustion.

Reflection Writing 2
Chapter 6

On separate paper, in a journal, or online at this textbook's website, respond to the following questions.

1. Do you enjoy using mnemonics? Why or why not?

2. What are the benefits of using mnemonics? What are the drawbacks?

3. What mnemonics have you learned elsewhere? Do you remember any from elementary, junior high, or high school? What mnemonics have you learned or created in other college courses?

ONLINE PRACTICE 2

Visit the *Essential Study Skills*, Fifth Edition, website and go to Chapter 6. Click on **Practice 2: Using Mnemonics to Boost Your Memory**. Complete the ten-question interactive multiple-choice quiz. Upon completion of the quiz, you will receive your score. You can exit at that time, or you can print or e-mail your results to your instructor.

ONLINE PRACTICE 3

Visit the *Essential Study Skills*, Fifth Edition, website and go to Chapter 6. Click on **Practice 3: Checking Your Memory**. Without referring to the mnemonics used in this chapter, check how well you remember information by typing answers to ten questions. After you type your responses, you can compare your answers with the answer key available online.

Preparing for Tests

In college, tests are a way of assessing your understanding of information presented in your courses. Tests also indicate how well you have prepared, the effectiveness of your study methods, and how well you can take tests. (Chapters 12 and 13 provide you with specific test-taking strategies for objective, recall, math, and essay tests.) Students who do not apply study skills on a regular basis often need to resort to cramming. **Cramming** is an attempt to learn large amounts of information in a short period of time. Cramming is a survival technique that often backfires; frequently, students who cram become even more aware of how much *they do not know*. Feeling underprepared can create test anxiety and lead to poor test performance. As discussed in Chapter 2, working memory needs time to process information, form associations, and assign meaning to concepts and details. Cramming does not provide the brain with time to learn information thoroughly and accurately. The following *Essential Strategies for Test Preparation* will help you prepare for tests and increase your test performance.

SET LEARNING GOALS

The following *Essential Strategies for Test Preparation* chart highlights eleven important strategies to use to prepare for tests. Place a star next to the strategies that you already use. Highlight the strategies that you plan to make a conscious effort to begin using to strengthen your test preparation skills.

Essential Strategies for Test Preparation

▸ **Review your course syllabus and class assignment sheets.** Be certain that you know the chapters or topics that will be included on the test. Plan to review textbook chapters, your notes, and returned homework or lab assignments.

▸ **Find out as much information as you can about the test.** Listen to the instructor's description of the test, the topics or chapters covered, the kinds of test questions, and the length of the test. Talk to other students who have already completed the course; ask them for study suggestions and about the kinds of test questions to expect. Remember, however, that instructors do change test questions and formats, so do not feel overly confident about a test based on information from previous students. If previous tests are available to examine, take the time to look at and practice with the tests.

▸ **Use a five-day study plan to prepare for tests.** For smaller tests, use the same steps but shorten the time period. A five-day study plan provides you with ample time to review. (See Chapter 4, pages 104–105.)

▸ **Review study tools you created for factual information.** Practice associations, relationships, or mnemonics you have previously created. Bringing information back into your working memory activates long-term memory, which increases your ability to access and retrieve information. Always use strategies that include feedback.

▸ **Review procedural information by reworking steps or problems.** Practice writing out the steps to a procedure or process. Identify the kinds of materials or problems that use these steps. Rework previous examples or problems from the textbook and class. Use feedback to check the accuracy of your answers.

▸ **Make summary notes of information you want to review the day before the test.** These special notes should include concepts, steps, and details that you want to review one more time to keep the information fresh in your memory. Summary notes may also include notes that relate to specific information your instructor reminded you to study for the test. (See Chapter 4, page 106.)

▸ **Participate in review sessions.** Review sessions are a powerful way to receive immediate feedback about the topics you understand clearly and those that you need to review further. Review sessions also give you the opportunity to verbalize, explain information in your own words, and answer practice test questions.

▸ **Create a study group if a review group is not available.** Ask each member to write several practice test questions to the group. Ask individual students to come to the session prepared to lead a discussion on a specific chapter. Students could also be asked to provide group members with a set of summary notes for an individual chapter. They can also bring study tools such as flash cards for partner or group drill activities.

▸ **Plan to review the night before a test and an hour or so on the day of the test.** By reviewing close to the test time, you activate course information from your long-term memory and bring it back into your working memory. The information stays fresh, and recall occurs with less effort.

▸ **Predict test questions; write and answer practice test questions.** (See pages 159–160.)

▸ **Deal with sources of test anxiety *before* the day of the test.** (See pages 162–164.)

CLASS DISCUSSION

Question: If you were to use all of the *Essential Strategies for Test Preparation*, would you be activating all twelve of the Principles of Memory?

How can writing practice test questions and answers reduce test anxiety?

Predict Test Questions

Predicting test questions is an excellent method for preparing for tests and reducing test anxiety. Predicting test questions is even easier after you have taken one or two tests from a specific teacher and have a sense of the types of tests he or she uses. Understanding types of test questions is the first step. The following chart shows test formats that are common in college courses.

Kind of Question	Level of Difficulty	Includes	Requires
Recognition (objective)	Easiest	True-False Multiple-Choice Matching	Read and recognize whether information is correct; apply a skill and then recognize the correct answer.
Recall	More demanding	Fill-in-the-Blanks Listings Definitions Short Answers Problem Solving	Retrieve the information from your memory.
Essay	Most difficult	Essays	Retrieve the information from memory, organize it, and use effective writing skills.

Effective test preparation should include studying all the important material thoroughly so you are well prepared for any type of test question. However, many students prefer to modify their test-preparation strategies to reflect specific testing formats when the instructor announces the formats in advance. The following chart provides you with a summary of the types of material you should focus on and practice strategies to include in your review time.

If You Predict . . .	Study This Kind of Information:	Practice May Include:
Objective Questions	• Definitions of key terms • Category flash cards • Details: names, dates, theories, rules, events	• Writing true-false questions • Writing multiple-choice questions • Writing matching questions • Working with a study partner to exchange practice questions

Recall Questions	• Information presented in lists
	• Definition cards
	  —say and spell words on the fronts for fill-in-the-blank tests
	  —three-part definitions on the backs of cards for definition and short-answer tests
	• Category cards
	• Cornell recall columns (Chapter 9)
	• Questions formulated before, during, and after reading
	• Chapter summaries
	• Details on visual notes (Chapter 11)
	• Problem-solving examples
		• Reciting information in full sentences and in your own words
		• Writing a short summary to practice expressing ideas on paper
		• Writing answers to the questions formulated in the reading process
		• Writing fill-in-the-blank listings, definitions, and short-answer questions
		• Reworking math problems
		• Writing the problem-solving steps
		• Working with a study partner to exchange practice questions

Essay Questions	• Themes • Relationships • Major concepts	• Outlining chapters to see headings and relationships • Reviewing notes for recurring themes • See Chapter 13 for strategies.

Write and Answer Practice Test Questions

Writing and answering practice test questions is an excellent way to prepare for an upcoming test. Refer to your textbook and your lecture notes to write objective, recall, and essay questions. Practice answering your own test questions or exchanging questions with a study partner.

On your tests, you will encounter a variety of types of questions. In 1956, a psychologist named Benjamin Bloom developed a classification system with colleagues for levels of questions commonly used in educational settings. This classification system, known as **Bloom's Taxonomy**, begins with the lowest level of questions (recall or recognition of knowledge) and ends with the highest or most complex level of questions (evaluation). The following chart shows the skills that each type of question demonstrates and *question cues* or direction words that each level of question uses. When you write your practice questions, strive to include questions for each of these categories. For example, the following question starters use Bloom's six levels of questions:

1. Define _____
2. Describe _____
3. Calculate _____
4. Classify _____
5. Rearrange _____
6. Compare _____

Bloom's Taxonomy

Levels	Skills Demonstrated and Question Cues
Knowledge	• observation and recall of information • knowledge of dates, events, places • knowledge of major ideas • mastery of subject matter • *Question Cues:* list, define, tell, describe, identify, show, label, collect, examine, tabulate, quote, name, who, when, where, etc.
Comprehension	• understanding information • grasp meaning • translate knowledge into new context • interpret facts, compare, contrast • order, group, infer causes • predict consequences • *Question Cues:* summarize, describe, interpret, contrast, predict, associate, distinguish, estimate, differentiate, discuss, extend
Application	• use information • use methods, concepts, theories in new situations • solve problems using required skills or knowledge • *Question Cues:* apply, demonstrate, calculate, complete, illustrate, show, solve, examine, modify, relate, change, classify, experiment, discover
Analysis	• seeing patterns • organization of parts • recognition of hidden meanings • identification of components • *Question Cues:* analyze, separate, order, explain, connect, classify, arrange, divide, compare, select, explain, infer
Synthesis	• use old ideas to create new ones • generalize from given facts • relate knowledge from several areas • predict, draw conclusions • *Question Cues:* combine, integrate, modify, rearrange, substitute, plan, create, design, invent, what if?, compose, formulate, prepare, generalize, rewrite
Evaluation	• compare and discriminate among ideas • assess value of theories, presentations • make choices based on reasoned argument • verify value of evidence • recognize subjectivity • *Question Cues:* assess, decide, rank, grade, test, measure, recommend, convince, select, judge, explain, discriminate, support, conclude, compare, summarize

*Adapted from Benjamin S. Bloom et al., *Taxonomy of Educational Objectives,* Fourth Edition. Copyright © 1984 by Pearson Education. Adapted by permission of the author and the publisher, Allyn & Bacon, Boston, MA.

Visit the *Essential Study Skills*, Fifth Edition, website for Chapter 6. Click on **Practice 4: Preparing for Tests**. Complete the ten-question interactive multiple-choice quiz. Upon completion of the quiz, you will receive your score. You can exit at that time, or you can print or e-mail your results to your instructor.

Dealing with Sources of Test Anxiety Before the Test

In Chapter 5, you learned that **stress** is defined as your reaction or response to events or situations that threaten to disrupt your normal pattern or routine. With normal stress, a person is aware of the stress, aware of the source of the stress, and still able to control his or her reaction or responses. A student may feel stress related to an upcoming test. That stress actually helps to motivate the student to work hard to try to do his or her best. *Anxiety* occurs when the level of stress is excessive to the point that it hinders one's ability to perform well. During a bout with anxiety, a person no longer recognizes the source of the excessive stress, no longer has control of the situation, and is reactionary rather than problem-solving oriented.

Test anxiety is excessive stress that may occur *before* or *during* a test. Test anxiety hinders performance and immobilizes thinking skills. A student may "go blank," make excessive careless mistakes, mark answers in the wrong place, or quit due to frustration. Symptoms related to test anxiety may appear in physical, emotional, cognitive, or behavioral forms, as shown in the following chart.

Symptoms Related to Test Anxiety

Physical Symptoms of Anxiety	Rapid heartbeat Increased blood pressure Upset stomach, nausea Shakiness Abnormal nervousness Headaches Tight muscles, tension Clammy palms, sweating Blurred vision
Emotional Symptoms of Anxiety	Fear, anger Frustration "Fight or flight" feelings Irritable, short-tempered Anxious, nervous Fatigue Depression Feelings of hopelessness Lack of control of a situation Panic

Cognitive Symptoms of Anxiety	Working memory cluttered with intrusive thoughts Poor concentration, misdirected attention Lack of clear thinking Inaccurate or limited recall "Going blank" Confusion, disorientation Fixating on one item too long Overemphasis on negative thoughts Impulsive responses Careless mistakes
Behavioral Symptoms of Anxiety	Crying, sobbing Procrastination Strained facial expressions Shaky voice Slumped posture Aggression

Sources of Test Anxiety

Test anxiety is a *learned behavior*. As such, it can be unlearned. The first step is to analyze the situation and your feelings to identify when the behavior begins and what triggers the anxiety. The following chart shows the four causes of test anxiety and strategies to use to reduce or eliminate the anxiety.

The Source	Description	Strategies
Underpreparedness	An awareness that you have not put enough time and effort into reading, completing assignments, studying information, or ongoing review.	• Set learning goals. • Use time-management skills. • Include learned study strategies presented throughout this textbook. • Make better use of your working memory. • Use the Twelve Principles of Memory. • Use ongoing review. • Use test-preparation strategies.
Past Experiences	The tendency of hanging on to past test-taking experiences or results and believing you will repeat the negative experiences results in a low level of confidence, low self-esteem, and low self-efficacy.	• Use affirmations and positive self-talk. • Set goals with rewards for yourself to reinforce your ability to succeed. • Use concentration strategies such as *Seeing Success*. • Complete all assignments on time and praise yourself for doing so. • Receive positive feedback by participating in a study group. • Work with a tutor to check your understanding of material. • Learn strategies to shift from internal to external locus of control.

| *Fear of Failure* | Fear of disappointing others, fear of consequences of low grades (scholar-ships, athletic eligibility, financial aid), fear of not living up to personal standards, and fear of being embarrassed by performance result in false thinking that grades reflect one's self-worth and the tendency to over-exaggerate the importance of one test score and to lose perspective of the overall grading system. | • Review the course syllabus to understand how grades are calculated.
• Discuss your realistic level of performance with your instructor.
• Discuss guidelines and requirements for scholarships, eligibility, or financial aid with a counselor to gain a clear understanding of the systems involved.
• Create a plan of action with yourself, your instructor, or a counselor.
• Increase performance in other graded areas such as completion of homework assignments, class participation, attendance, or extra-credit projects.
• Develop personal goals; use the *Skill, Not Will* approach. |
| *Poor Test-Taking Skills* | Limited experience with or under-standing of the various kinds of tests, kinds of test questions, different test-taking formats, and test-taking strategies; limited experience or understanding of how to read and respond to test questions, how to construct strong answers, and how to use test time wisely. | • Use the *Essential Strategies for Test Preparation*.
• Learn how to predict test questions; write and answer practice test questions.
• Look ahead to Chapters 12 and 13 for additional test-taking strategies. |

Locus of Control

Locus of control is a concept that refers to a person's sense of control. An **internal locus of control** means that the individual feels that he or she has the power to control his or her circumstances. An **external locus of control** means that the individual relinquishes control and sees other people or other situations as having the power. Low self-esteem, low confidence in one's abilities, and high levels of frustration blamed on what other people are doing to cause a person's situation are results of an *external* locus of control. To reduce test anxiety, the locus of control needs to shift to the individual, to become an *internal* locus of control. A person who has an internal locus of control has self-confidence and perceives that he or she has the ability to perform well and succeed. The central focus or source of power is in accepting responsibility for events. Notice the difference in power between external and internal centers of control in the following chart.

External Locus of Control	Internal Locus of Control
I did not do well because the teacher does not like me.	My negative attitude is affecting my work.
This test is totally unfair.	I was not prepared for this test.
I could not study because of my children.	I did not remember to study the charts.
All the questions were trick questions.	I need to find more time to myself to study.
I failed the test because it was poorly written.	I need to strengthen my test-taking skills.
The teacher did not even take the time to try to understand what I wrote.	I need to add more review time.
The teacher did not understand my situation.	I need to improve my writing skills.
	I did not know the answer to the essay question.
	I should join a study group.

Convert Negatives to Positives

In Chapters 4 and 5, you learned that many self-management skills involve positive self-talk, affirmations, and visualizations. These positive approaches are aimed at altering the images you have of yourself as a student and converting negative or intrusive self-talk to positive, supportive, motivational, and inspirational self-talk. Using positive self-management skills can help you convert negative past test-taking experiences and fear-of-failure beliefs into more constructive, achievement-based beliefs about yourself and your abilities.

You can also reduce text anxiety before a test by *mentally rehearsing* and using the *See Success* technique. Take a few minutes each day several times a day to visualize yourself studying for an upcoming test with full concentration and understanding, working through your five-day study plan with ease and confidence, and on the day of the test, reading questions carefully, conducting memory searches with little effort, and marking answers with confidence. For procedural information, visualize yourself working through each step of the process or procedure. Converting negative attitudes and feelings about tests into positive attitudes and feelings reduces test anxiety and increases confidence, self-efficacy, and test performance.

Systematic Desensitization

Systematic desensitization is an anxiety-reducing strategy that you can use before the day of a test. This strategy involves a series of exercises or activities designed to reduce strong negative emotional reactions to upcoming tests. With this strategy, you replace fear-based thoughts with positive thoughts that emphasize the successes you have already experienced. You can use *systematic desensitization* in the following ways:

1. Make a list of specific situations or words that trigger your test anxiety. For example, words such as *There will be a test next Monday on Chapters 2 through 5* may trigger early test anxiety. After you have your list of *trigger situations or words,* take time to visualize yourself reacting in a different manner. Perhaps you could visualize your response as *Good. I have time to make a five-day plan,* or *I have stayed current with my work, so I can be ready for this test.* Basically you are creating and rehearsing a script that emphasizes a constructive, positive behavior and self-image.

2. Predict and write practice test questions. Decide on an appropriate amount of time to answer the test questions. Create a test environment as close as

possible to the real thing. If the classroom in which you will take a test is empty, be in that room when you take your practice test. Use relaxation and other study skills techniques you know to work through the test without having a strong negative reaction.

Exercises 6.4 and 6.5 will help you analyze additional information about yourself and your test-preparation skills. The insights you gain from these two inventories can help you unlearn ineffective behavior and attitudinal patterns and learn new behaviors and attitudes to improve your overall test-taking performance.

EXERCISE 6.4   Academic Preparation Inventory

What was the last test you took in one of your classes? _____
Think back to the days prior to that test. Check YES or NO for the following
statements. Be honest with your answers.

	YES	NO
1. I had all the reading assignments done on time.	_____	_____
2. I had all the homework assignments done on time.	_____	_____
3. I reviewed the work on my homework assignments when they were returned.	_____	_____
4. I asked questions about information I didn't understand.	_____	_____
5. I worked with a tutor or a study partner for review.	_____	_____
6. I recited information that I was studying on a regular basis.	_____	_____
7. I followed my time-management schedule and used the 2:1 ratio.	_____	_____
8. I spent time reviewing each week.	_____	_____
9. I attended classes regularly.	_____	_____
10. I was an active learner and used a variety of study methods.	_____	_____
11. I used active reading techniques and took notes.	_____	_____
12. I created study tools that I have found to be effective.	_____	_____
13. I found enough time to read and highlight the textbook carefully.	_____	_____
14. I made a special study schedule for the days prior to the test.	_____	_____
15. I used study techniques that gave me feedback.	_____	_____
16. I was an active listener and participant in class.	_____	_____
17. I was able to stay fairly motivated about the class and the work.	_____	_____
18. I was organized and was able to find the materials I needed to study.	_____	_____
19. I avoided cramming the night before the test.	_____	_____
20. I can honestly say that I gave it my best.	_____	_____

If you answered YES to all or most of the above questions, you used effective study techniques and should have been well prepared for the test. All of the NO answers indicate a need to improve your study methods. Analyze the NO answers to determine which study techniques you need to strengthen. Review the specific skills you need to learn to utilize more effectively.

EXERCISE 6.5 **Test Anxiety Inventory**

Check the response that seems to best *describe you this term.*

	NEVER	SOMETIMES	ALWAYS
1. I procrastinate so much about studying that I am always behind in my assignments.	❏	❏	❏
2. I found it necessary to cram for the last test I took.	❏	❏	❏
3. I read the textbook, but I do not highlight or take any other kind of textbook notes.	❏	❏	❏
4. I have trouble sleeping the night before a test.	❏	❏	❏
5. I fear the consequences of failing a test.	❏	❏	❏
6. I can't help but remember what happened on the last test: I really blew it.	❏	❏	❏
7. My negative voice is quick to tell me what I can't do.	❏	❏	❏
8. I can feel a lot of tension in my shoulders, arms, or face on the day of a test.	❏	❏	❏
9. My heart beats fast during a test.	❏	❏	❏
10. I feel hot, clammy, or downright sick during a test.	❏	❏	❏
11. I am much more hesitant to enter the classroom on a test day.	❏	❏	❏
12. I try to find excuses not to go to school on the day of a test.	❏	❏	❏
13. I am irritable, snappy, impatient, and sometimes even rude right before a test.	❏	❏	❏
14. I make careless mistakes on the test. Sometimes I can't believe the answers that I marked.	❏	❏	❏
15. As soon as I leave the classroom after taking a test, I remember answers that I didn't know during the test.	❏	❏	❏
16. My mind goes blank, but I know that I know the answers.	❏	❏	❏
17. I get distracted and annoyed by the littlest things others do in class during a test.	❏	❏	❏
18. I always worry about not having enough time to complete tests.	❏	❏	❏
19. Without knowing why, I panic and start changing answers right before I turn the test in.	❏	❏	❏
20. I get stuck on one question and become stubborn. I don't want to move on until I remember the answer.	❏	❏	❏
21. I hurry to get out of the room and out of the test as quickly as possible.	❏	❏	❏
22. Enough is enough. I don't even want to think about going back to check my answers or proofread.	❏	❏	❏
23. I turn in tests that are incomplete even when I have more time.	❏	❏	❏
24. I find myself blaming the teacher, my family, or my friends for the fact that I am not prepared for tests.	❏	❏	❏
25. I did not find time to make summary notes or review effectively.	❏	❏	❏

Answers in the NEVER column = No problem; not indicators of test anxiety.
Answers in the SOMETIMES column = Possible indicators; seek ways to alter your behavior.
Answers in the ALWAYS column = Sources of test anxiety; seek strategies to reduce these.

✺ EXERCISE 6.6 Coping with Stress
The psychology chapter in Appendix D deals with health, stress, and coping. With a partner or in a small group, use only charts, diagrams, or information in the margins of the Appendix D chapter to answer the following questions.

1. What are the three stages of reaction to stress known as the General Adaptation Syndrome?

2. After reading the definition of coping, rank the following coping skills in terms of how often you tend to use each skill to manage stress-causing situations. Use 1 to indicate the most frequently used and 8 to indicate the least frequently used.

    _____ confronting

    _____ seeking social support

    _____ planful problem-solving

    _____ self-controlling

    _____ distancing

    _____ positive reappraisal

    _____ accepting responsibility

    _____ escape/avoidance (wishful thinking)

3. What are the six stages used in coping with stress?

4. What is the definition of *cognitive restructuring*?

⊗ EXERCISE 6.7 LINKS
Writing and answering practice test questions is an effective way to prepare for tests. By yourself, with a partner, or in a small group, write one *question for each of the following topics discussed in Chapters 1 through 5. Your instructor may ask you to give your questions to your partner, to another group, or to the class to answer.*

1. Linear and Global Learners (Chapter 1)

2. Multiple Intelligences (Chapter 1)

3. Feedback Model (Chapter 2)

4. Twelve Principles of Memory (Chapter 2)

5. Kinds of Time-Management Schedules (Chapter 3)

6. Essential Strategies for Scheduling Study Blocks (Chapter 3)

7. Motivation (Chapter 4)

8. A Four-Step Approach for Writing Goals (Chapter 4)

9. Self-Management (Chapter 5)

10. Decreasing Stress (Chapter 5)

ONLINE PRACTICE 5

Visit the *Essential Study Skills*, Fifth Edition, website and go to Chapter 6. Click on **Practice 5: Dealing with Test Anxiety**. Type responses to the four questions. After you type your responses, you can print them or e-mail them to your instructor.

EXERCISE 6.8 Textbook Case Studies

Read about each of the following student situations carefully. Then, on your own paper and in complete sentences, answer the question that follows each case study. You can also answer these questions online at this textbook's Chapter 6 website. You can print your online responses or e-mail them to your instructor.

1. Adolpho has not been in school for fifteen years. He was never taught how to study or take tests. He works hard and is able to respond in class and in study groups to questions that are related to the current assignment. However, when it is time to take tests that cover several chapters of information, he freezes and goes blank. What test-preparation and test-taking strategies would you recommend for Adolpho?

2. Jellison does not study much for her communications class because she is taking the class for pass/no pass rather than a grade. As the end of the term approaches, she realizes that she may not have enough points to pass the class. She intends to deal with the situation the way she usually deals with tests—cramming in the day or two before the final exam. What test-preparation strategies would you suggest she use during the last two weeks of the term?

3. Richard enjoys creating mnemonics. He has made more than forty index cards with mnemonics for his biology class. As he prepares for a midterm exam, he starts to panic. Information from one mnemonic is interfering with information from other mnemonics. He is frustrated because his mnemonics no longer seem to be working. What strategies can Richard use to reduce his frustration and prepare more effectively for the midterm exam?

ONLINE CASE STUDIES

Visit the *Essential Study Skills*, Fifth Edition, website and go to Chapter 6. Click on **Online Case Studies**. In the text boxes, respond to four additional case studies that are only available online. You can print your responses or e-mail them to your instructor.

Reflection Writing 3
Chapter 6

On separate paper, in a journal, or online at this textbook's website, respond to the following questions.

1. What strategy works effectively for you to combat forgetting related to the Decay Theory? After briefly discussing your response, continue by discussing one strategy you can use for the other forgetting theories: *Displacement, Interference, Incomplete Encoding,* and *Retrieval Failure*.

2. What conclusions can you draw about your test-preparation skills based on Exercise 6.4, the Academic Preparation Inventory? In your answer, include a brief discussion of the study skills that you need to strengthen or learn to utilize more effectively.

3. What conclusions can you draw about yourself from your answers to the Exercise 6.5 Test Anxiety Inventory? Include in your answer strategies that you could use to increase your test-taking performance with less stress or anxiety.

SUMMARY

■ Five Theories of Forgetting help explain why you may forget information during the learning process: Decay Theory, Displacement Theory, Interference Theory, Incomplete Encoding Theory, and Retrieval Failure Theory. Effective study strategies can combat each type of forgetting.

■ Mnemonics—when used selectively—are helpful for remembering information. Mnemonics provide a bridge when you do memory searches. The following mnemonics may be incorporated into your study skills strategies:

associations	rhythms, rhymes,
pictures and graphics	and jingles
acronyms	stacking
acrostics	loci
	peg systems

■ Cramming is a survival technique in which you attempt to learn large amounts of information in a short period of time. Cramming does not give working memory sufficient time to process effectively.

■ Eleven Essential Strategies for Test Preparation can help you prepare for tests and increase your test performance.

■ Predicting test questions and writing a variety of practice test questions help you prepare for tests and reduce test anxiety.

■ When you write practice test questions, use direction words from each of the levels of Bloom's Taxonomy. Bloom's levels of questions, from most basic to most complex, will prepare you for the kinds of questions you may encounter on tests: knowledge, comprehension, application, analysis, synthesis, and evaluation.

■ Test anxiety, defined as excessive stress, hinders performance and immobilizes thinking abilities. Test anxiety appears as physical, emotional, cognitive, and behavioral symptoms. It is a learned behavior stemming from underpreparedness, past experiences, fear of failure, or poor test-taking skills. You can use strategies to eliminate these sources of test anxiety.

■ In addition to the use of effective study skills strategies, developing an internal locus of control, converting negatives to positives, and using systematic desensitization can reduce or eliminate test anxiety.

CULMINATING OPTIONS FOR CHAPTER 6

1. Visit this textbook's website and go to Chapter 6 to complete the following exercises:
   a. Flash card review of Chapter 6 terms and definitions
   b. ACE Practice Test 1 with ten fill-in-the blank questions
   c. ACE Practice Test 2 with ten true-false questions
   d. ACE Practice Test 3 with ten multiple-choice questions
   e. ACE Practice Test 4 with three short-answer–critical thinking questions

2. Go to Appendix C in the back of this textbook for more Learning Options to use for additional practice, enrichment, or portfolio projects.

Chapter 6 REVIEW QUESTIONS

Multiple Choice

Choose the best answer for each of the following. Write the letter of your answer on the line.

_____ 1. Effective use of mnemonics involves
   a. creating mnemonics only for information that is otherwise difficult to recall.
   b. creating acronyms and acrostics for every chapter in your textbook.
   c. limiting the use of mnemonics to information that appears in lists.
   d. all of the above.

_____ 2. Mnemonics work effectively when you
   a. memorize them with 100 percent accuracy.
   b. practice converting them into the information they represent.
   c. use them as bridges to conduct memory searches for specific information.
   d. do all of the above.

_____ 3. The Memory Principle of Association is used
   a. when you create pictures or graphics for information you need to learn.
   b. in all of the types of mnemonics designed to boost your memory.
   c. each time you create an acronym or use the stacking method.
   d. when you associate a peg with an object you need to recall at a later time.

_____ 4. Effective test-preparation skills
   a. reduce the necessity to cram for tests and use rote memory techniques.
   b. include time-management and goal-setting techniques.
   c. involve working with the information by making summary notes, predicting test questions, and writing practice questions.
   d. do all of the above.

_____ 5. Which of the following statements is *not* true about peg systems?
   a. You must memorize the fixed pegs before attaching items to the pegs.
   b. When using the *human body pegs*, you begin mentally attaching items to the feet.
   c. With practice, you should be able to recall items in and out of their original sequence.
   d. It is important to create strong visual images of the items you attach to the pegs.

_____ 6. Test anxiety can stem from
   a. fear of failure.
   b. underpreparedness and past experiences.
   c. poor test-taking skills.
   d. all of the above.

_____ 7. Cramming
   a. is a survival technique used for underpreparedness.
   b. uses most of the memory principles.
   c. processes large amounts of information efficiently.
   d. can be effective when used the day before a test.

_____ 8. A person with an external locus of control
   a. accepts responsibility for external situations that happen to him or her.
   b. shows a strong sense of self-confidence and control.
   c. blames others for his or her lack of success.
   d. would likely make the following kind of statement: *I need to modify my approach to taking tests so I can increase my test performance.*

Definitions

Write a definition for the following terms. Your answer should include one or two sentences.

1. Internal locus of control

2. Test Anxiety

3. Mnemonics

Short Answer and Critical Thinking

1. Explain the relationship between the Displacement Theory of Forgetting and cramming.

2. How does the use of mnemonics assist the processes of working memory?

3. List the four main sources of test anxiety. After each source, briefly describe one strategy to use to decrease or eliminate that source of test anxiety.

CHAPTER 7

Reading College Textbooks

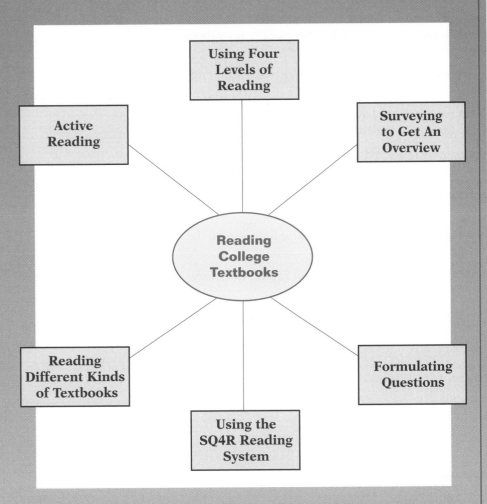

Active reading and essential textbook reading strategies will help you comprehend and master your college textbooks. Reading college textbooks requires a variety of reading strategies and flexibility in using the strategies for different kinds of textbooks and different levels of difficulty. Surveying and formulating questions are two effective strategies to use to familiarize yourself with the textbook and begin the active reading process. SQ4R, a powerful six-step reading system, promotes comprehension, enhances learning, and strengthens the recall of information from long-term memory. You can also improve your reading performance by using specific tips for reading and studying composition, literature, history, math, science, and social science textbooks.

Terms to Know

- active reading
- recreational reading
- overview reading
- thorough reading
- comparative reading
- survey
- title page
- copyright page
- table of contents
- introductory material
- appendix
- glossary
- references/bibliography
- index
- marginal notes

SQ4R system
- Survey
- Question
- Read
- Record
- Recite
- Review

Read-Record-Recite Cycle

Chapter 7 Reading College Textbooks Profile

ANSWER, SCORE, and **RECORD** your profile before you read this chapter. If you need to review the process, refer to the complete directions given in the Profile for Chapter 1 on page 2.

ONLINE: You can complete the profile and get your score online at this textbook's website.

	YES	NO
1. I skim through or preview the front and back sections of new textbooks before I begin the first reading assignment.	_____	_____
2. I adjust my reading strategies for different kinds of textbooks and different levels of difficulty.	_____	_____
3. When I begin reading a new chapter, I always open the book to the first page and read straight through to the end of the chapter.	_____	_____
4. I read the chapter review questions and the summary before I start reading the chapter.	_____	_____
5. I write my own study questions for each heading and subheading in the chapter.	_____	_____
6. I sometimes postpone reading a new chapter because it appears to be difficult or uninteresting.	_____	_____
7. I often finish reading a chapter only to find out that I remember very little of what I have just read.	_____	_____
8. After I read a short section, I stop to highlight, underline, or take notes.	_____	_____
9. When I study, I am quiet because I do all my practicing or reviewing in my head.	_____	_____
10. I am confident in my ability to read all kinds of textbooks without many difficulties.	_____	_____

Reflection Writing 1
Chapter 7

On separate paper, in a journal, or on this textbook's website, respond to the following questions.

1. What is your profile score for this chapter? What does it mean to you?

2. What problems do you frequently encounter when you read your college textbooks?

Active Reading

Active reading is the process of engaging your mind in the reading process with the ultimate goal of understanding, learning, and using or applying information. Active reading, an essential skill for academic success, is a component of *active learning*. As you recall from Chapters 2 and 5, active learning involves using activities that keep you actively involved in the learning process. Active reading places heavy demands on your working memory to understand printed information, associate it with previously learned information, and expand existing schemas in long-term memory by integrating the new information. The following active learning strategies from Chapter 2 and Chapter 5 relate directly to active reading strategies.

1. Have a pen in your hand when you study. Take notes, write questions, or jot down lists of information you need to learn.

2. Use markers to highlight important information in the textbook or in your notes.

3. Talk out loud (recite) as you study to activate your auditory channel and improve both concentration and comprehension.

4. Write summaries or make other kinds of study tools such as visual mappings, hierarchies, flash cards, or comparison charts.

5. Quiz yourself on the material you are studying. Write or recite questions and answers.

As a college student, you will spend thousands of hours reading thousands of textbook pages filled with information you will be required to learn. You cannot afford to spend your valuable time reading page after page in the automatic pilot mode. By setting a learning goal to become an active reader, and then taking action to achieve that goal, you will benefit in the following ways.

- You will be less likely to slip into *automatic pilot,* a state of mind in which you mechanically go through specific motions without registering information into your memory.

- You will be using powerful, multisensory strategies to encode and imprint information in your long-term memory.

- You will increase your reading comprehension, which leads to greater interest and motivation.

- You will feel less stress or frustration with reading assignments because you know how to use a variety of reading skills and strategies to complete the assignment.

- You will know how to select the most effective strategies for specific kinds of reading materials and reading goals.

- You will be actively using the Twelve Principles of Memory and the strategies for processing declarative and procedural knowledge.

- You will be able to apply the following *Essential Strategies for Textbook Reading* to any college textbook situation.

SET LEARNING GOALS

The following *Essential Strategies for Textbook Reading* chart highlights eight important strategies for textbook reading. Place a star next to the strategies that you already use. Highlight the strategies that you plan to make a conscious effort to begin using to strengthen your textbook reading skills.

Essential Strategies for Textbook Reading

▶ **Begin with a clear intention to understand what you read.** Approaching a reading assignment with a negative attitude, a dislike for the subject, a fear of the chapter's level of difficulty, negative self-talk, or an overall lack of interest in completing the reading assignment will give signals to your working memory that the incoming information is not important and does not need attention. The information will rapidly decay or fade away without ever being processed.

▶ **Use an organized system for reading textbook chapters.** Take time to familiarize yourself with a textbook chapter before you begin thorough reading. Surveying a chapter or reading through a chapter to get an overview helps set up a "big picture" or schema to which you can attach important details. Using an organized method for reading textbook chapters creates a reading habit and a system that move you into the reading process without procrastinating or wasting valuable time.

▶ **Be inquisitive.** Create a curiosity about the author's ideas. Ask questions about the information, ponder how to use the information, and seek ways to integrate the information with your own personal experience or knowledge.

▶ **Relate new information to existing schemas in your long-term memory.** Relating new information to previously learned information activates your memory and pulls existing information back into your working memory. Ask questions such as *What do I already know about this topic? How is it like and different from previous learning or what I have experienced?*

▶ **Manage your textbook reading time effectively.** As you tackle a new chapter, set aside ample time to get an overview of the chapter, read the chapter for understanding, mark or annotate the textbook and/or take textbook notes, and study the contents of the chapter. You should not rush textbook reading.

▶ **Use spaced practice or spaced studying.** Spreading the active reading process and activities over several different time periods actually cuts down total learning time. Pause between chunks of new information; give your mind time to mull over, absorb, process, and integrate the new information before you take in more new information. Avoid *marathon studying,* or in this case, *marathon reading,* which can overload your working memory, limit your ability to use the *principles of memory* effectively, and create confusion (interferences) between old and new information.

▶ **Include some form of feedback as you study.** *Recite* small sections of information at a time. Use *self-quizzing* as you read. Use *Look Away Techniques* to see how much you remember. As with all forms of feedback, check the accuracy of your information by comparing it with the original source. Immediately correct any errors or faulty information.

▶ **Encode information from ordinary words into new sensory codes.** As you read, take time to visualize the information, create *movies in your mind,* or create visual images of objects, graphs, charts, or steps in a procedure. Personalize the information by relating it to situations you have experienced, getting in touch with feelings or emotions related to the topic, or imagining how an event or a process would feel physically. Verbalize the information to encode it linguistically. Use multiple sensory codes to create memory cues that can trigger recall at a later time.

CLASS DISCUSSION

Question: Which Principles of Memory are used for each of the textbook reading strategies?

ONLINE   PRACTICE   1

Visit the *Essential Study Skills*, Fifth Edition, website and go to Chapter 7. Click on **Practice 1: Active Reading**. Complete the ten-question true-false quiz. Upon completion of the quiz, you will receive your score. You can exit at that time, or you can print your results or e-mail them to your instructor.

Using Four Levels of Reading

With the multitude of cognitive connections and activities that take place in the brain during the process of reading and understanding printed materials, it should be of no surprise that making sense of what we read does not occur automatically. With some reading materials, we are able to read and quickly grasp the meaning of new information without much effort or struggle, yet with other reading materials, we need to work to understand, process, store, retrieve, and use the information. Recognizing and understanding the four levels of reading as shown in the following chart can explain the differences we experience among different kinds of reading tasks. Using the correct level of reading for your college textbooks reflects your purpose and affects your ability to comprehend and use textbook information.

Kinds of Reading	Description
Recreational Reading	• Read newspapers or magazines to be entertained or stay updated on current events. • Read short stories, poetry, or fiction for pleasure.
Overview Reading	• Skim, scan, or survey textbooks, chapters, essays, or articles to create a *big picture* or framework before reading thoroughly. See *Surveying to Get an Overview*, pages 178–183. • Read through difficult material uninterrupted and without stalling to become familiar with the topic before beginning thorough reading for comprehension. See *Overview Reading*, page 187.
Thorough Reading	• Read slowly and systematically to allow your brain time to acquire and process new information and skills. • Read to understand information presented in sentences, paragraphs, and sections of information (headings, subheadings, or chapters). • Read carefully and adjust your reading strategies for different levels of reading difficulty. See *Reading Flexibility*, page 186. • Use elaborative rehearsal to understand, analyze, associate, and encode information for long-term memory. • Use textbook annotation and notetaking strategies to reflect important information.
Comparative Reading	• Read two or more articles, excerpts, or books on the same subject and then compare or contrast the information. Organize the information and analyze similarities and differences in points of view, rationale, implications, interpretations, models, or approaches.

ONLINE PRACTICE 2

Visit the *Essential Study Skills*, Fifth Edition, website and go to Chapter 7. Click on **Practice 2: Levels of Reading**. Complete the ten-question true-false quiz. Upon completion of the quiz, you will receive your score. You can exit at that time, or you can print your results or e-mail them to your instructor.

Surveying to Get An Overview

To **survey** reading material means to preview or skim through information to get an overview or a *big picture* of the content of a book, a chapter, or an article before you begin reading. As you get the *big picture* of the reading material, you activate existing schemas in your long-term memory and pull previously learned information back into your working memory, or you begin to create a new schema or framework for new, unfamiliar information. As you recall from Chapter 2, attaching information to a larger schema or framework assists the process of creating associations and building accessible memory that you can later recall; it also avoids storing isolated facts or details randomly in your long-term memory. Surveying before beginning the serious process of reading has additional benefits:

How does textbook reading differ from leisure-time reading of magazines or paperback books?

1. It enhances your motivation and your interest in the material.
2. It breaks inertia or the tendency to procrastinate about starting the reading process.
3. It boosts confidence in your ability to master new material.
4. It provides you with a general idea about the length and difficulty level of the material.
5. It helps you set realistic goals and manage your reading and studying time effectively.

Surveying a Textbook

Surveying a complete textbook before you begin reading specific chapters acquaints you with the book's philosophy, organization, and special features and provides you with suggestions for using the book more effectively. Surveying a textbook is a process that usually requires less than thirty minutes of your time at the beginning of the term. The following chart shows the parts of a textbook to survey.

Surveying a Textbook

1. Title page, copyright page, and table of contents
2. Introductory information
3. Appendix
4. Glossary
5. References or bibliography
6. Index

Title Page, Copyright Page, and Table of Contents   The **title page** provides you with the name of the book, the author, the edition, the publishing location, and possibly the author's affiliation with an organization, university, or corporation. If the book is in its first edition, no reference to an edition appears below the author's name. Each edition number indicates that the book has been updated.

The **copyright page** appears on the back of the title page. It shows the publication date of the textbook, which is important when you need to know whether the material in the book is current; the publisher's policy for copying content from the book; and the book's Library of Congress catalog number (or ISBN, International Standard Book Number).

The **table of contents** provides you with an overview of the topics in the textbook, the organization of the topics (chronological or thematic), chapter headings and subheadings, page numbers, and other textbook features. The table of contents is a quick way to check the length of chapters so you can begin to estimate the length of time you will need to work with each chapter.

Introductory Information   The **introductory materials** may include sections titled *Preface, Introduction, To the Teacher*, and *To the Student*. The **preface** (pronounced "pref´is," not "pre-face´") or the *introduction* provides insight into the philosophy, objectives, and structure of the book, and may include background information about the author. The section titled *To the Teacher* provides instructors with information on the teaching/learning approach used by the author, the goals and objectives of the textbook, and suggestions for using the book effectively. The section titled *To the Student* is one of the most important sections for you to read carefully, for it provides you with valuable suggestions, study strategies, and explanations of textbook features that will help you learn the textbook content and use the book effectively.

Appendix   The **appendix**, located in the back of the textbook, contains supplementary materials that can help you throughout the term. It may include useful information that would break the flow of the chapter or disrupt its structure. In a history textbook, for example, the Bill of Rights and the Constitution are important documents; due to their length, however, they may appear as supplementary materials in the appendix. The appendix might also include answer keys; additional exercises; practice tests; supplementary readings; or important tables, graphs, charts, or maps. Textbooks with a wide variety of supplementary materials may have several appendixes.

Glossary   The **glossary** is a course-specific minidictionary located after the appendix. Definitions in a glossary are limited to the word meanings used in the textbook. (Use a standard college dictionary to locate multiple meanings of terminology.) Bold, italic, or colored print within textbook chapters often indicates words that appear in the glossary. If your textbook does not have a glossary, you can create your own glossary for each chapter. Use the following strategies with textbooks that have a glossary.

1. Each time you see words in special print in a chapter, review the glossary definitions; sometimes they provide you with more details or more directly clarify the terminology.

2. As you encounter new terms during the reading process, place a star next to the terms or highlight them in the glossary; use the glossary as a review tool to prepare for tests.

3. Make separate flash cards or study sheets with the definitions of key terms to review to prepare for tests. (See pages 249–250.)

References or Bibliography   The **references** or **bibliography** section in the back of the book cites the titles and authors of books, magazines, or articles that the author used in writing the textbook. (The term *bibliography* comes from the Greek word roots *biblio-*, which means *book*, and *-graphy*, which means *written record*.) If you are working on a paper or a speech, or if you want to pursue a specific topic further, you can use the information in this section to locate the original sources of information.

Index   The **index**, one of the most frequently used sections in the back of a textbook, is an alphabetical listing of the textbook's significant topics. By using the index, you can quickly locate pages throughout the textbook that refer to a specific topic. Some textbooks may have more than one index; for example, you might find a *subject index*, an *author index*, or an *index of illustrations*. Frequently, topics are cross-referenced so they appear in more than one place in the index.

The following strategies will help you use the index effectively:

1. If you are not able to find a term in the index, think of alternative wordings. For example, if you cannot find the term *body rhythms*, try looking under *rhythms* or look for the more formal wording, *circadian rhythms*.

2. During a class discussion or lecture, you may hear others use an unfamiliar word. Write the word in your notes or in the margin of your textbook. After class, use the index to locate the page or pages that explain the term in context. Read the information carefully and then relate the information from the book to the discussion or lecture.

3. When you are assigned a specific topic for a research paper, an essay, a writing assignment, a project, or a test, begin by locating the topic in the index. Then turn to the page numbers provided in the index and read or review the information.

✦ EXERCISE 7.1   Surveying This Textbook
Take 15 to 30 minutes to survey this textbook. Then answer the following questions on separate paper.

1. Read the chapter titles; which chapters contain the skills you feel you most need to learn or improve?

2. What helpful information did you learn from the preface?

3. Did you read the *To the Student* section before you began working in this book?

   If yes, how did the information in this section help you? If no, how could this information have helped you use this textbook if you had read it earlier?

4. *To the Student* provides suggestions on how to start each chapter. Which of these suggestions have you been using each time you began a new chapter?

5. What kind of information appears in the appendixes?

6. This textbook does not have a glossary. Have you started any kind of glossary or system for learning definitions of terminology yourself? Explain.

7. How have you made use of the index so far this term?

EXERCISE 7.2 Using the Table of Contents

After examining the table of contents for this textbook, answer the following questions. Write your answers on your own paper.

1. How are the chapters organized in this textbook?

2. What is the overall theme for Unit Two in this textbook?

3. If you are preparing for an upcoming test and want to read ahead to learn more test-taking strategies, which chapters would you read and why?

4. Which chapter would you refer to if you wanted to learn how to create formal outlines?

5. As you glance through the table of contents, how many different options do you find for taking notes? List the options in your answer.

O N L I N E   P R A C T I C E   3

Visit the *Essential Study Skills*, Fifth Edition, website and go to Chapter 7. Click on **Practice 3: Surveying a Textbook**. Complete the ten-question interactive multiple-choice quiz. Upon completion of the quiz, you will receive your score. You can exit at that time, or you can print your results or e-mail them to your instructor.

Surveying a Chapter

You can also use surveying to look through or preview a chapter. Surveying a chapter before beginning the process of careful, thorough reading is a *warm-up* activity you can use at the beginning of a study block to help you focus your mind and create a *big picture* of the chapter. (See Chapter 5, page 119.)

The benefits of surveying a chapter are numerous, yet doing so generally requires fewer than twenty minutes. For longer chapters, you can modify the process by surveying as many pages of the chapter as you think you can realistically cover in one or two study blocks; survey the remaining pages at the beginning of a future study block. The following chart shows the parts of a chapter to include in surveying.

Surveying a Chapter

1. Read the introductory materials carefully.
2. Read the headings and the subheadings.
3. Look at visual materials such as charts, graphs, or pictures.
4. Read marginal notes.
5. Skim over terminology or information in special print.
6. Read the end-of-chapter materials, including any conclusion, summary, or chapter review questions.

Introductory Materials Read the title of the chapter carefully; take a moment to think about the topic and relate the topic to information you already know. Read any lists, paragraphs, or visual materials that state the objectives for the chapter or introduce the chapter's content.

Headings and Subheadings   Headings and subheadings appear in larger, bolder, or special print; take time to identify the format used to indicate the main headings and subheadings. Begin moving through the chapter by glancing over the headings and subheadings; this step of surveying shows you the "skeleton" structure of the chapter. Later, if you want, you can write the headings and subheadings on paper to make a chapter outline or visual mapping. You can obtain a considerable amount of information by reading the headings and the subheadings in the order in which they appear in the book.

Visual Materials   Visual materials include charts, graphs, diagrams, illustrations, cartoons, and photographs. Read the information that appears next to, above, and below the visual materials. A picture—or in this case, visual materials—may be worth a thousand words, so take time to gather information about the topic by examining the visual materials.

Marginal Notes   **Marginal notes** may be brief explanations, short definitions, lists of key points or objectives, or study questions that appear in the margins of the textbook pages. Marginal notes are designed to draw your attention to important information or to summarize key points. Taking time to read marginal notes during the process of surveying can provide you with background details that will be helpful when you engage in more thorough reading.

Terminology and Special Print   As previously mentioned, terminology (words whose definitions you will need to know) often appears in special print. During the surveying process, skim over the terminology to get a general idea of the number of terms you will need to learn and to gain some familiarity with these key words.

End-of-Chapter Materials   Carefully read the end-of-chapter materials, which may include a conclusion, a summary, a list of key concepts, or chapter review questions. These materials highlight or summarize the important concepts and information you should know and understand after you have read and studied the chapter.

EXERCISE 7.3 Surveying This Chapter
Use the steps on page 181 to survey this chapter. Then answer the following questions. Write your answers on separate paper.

1. How did reading the introductory material help you begin to formulate a *big picture* of this chapter?

2. How long did it take you to survey the entire chapter? If you spent more than fifteen minutes surveying the chapter, did you get sidetracked and begin some in-depth reading?

3. When you surveyed this chapter, which parts of the chapter provided you with the most information and helped you become most familiar with the content?

4. What do you find are the benefits of surveying a chapter before you begin thorough reading?

EXERCISE 7.4   Surveying the Chapter in Appendix D

In twenty minutes or less, survey the psychology chapter located in Appendix D. Use a colored marker or highlighter; place a small check next to each item you skim or examine as you survey. After you finish surveying, work with a partner to complete the following directions.

1. Compare the information you each checked in the process of surveying. Did you tend to check the same information? If not, discuss the differences.

2. Without referring to the chapter in Appendix D, discuss what you learned about stress by simply surveying this chapter.

3. How did surveying the chapter affect your level of interest, curiosity, or desire to learn more?

ONLINE PRACTICE 4

Visit the *Essential Study Skills*, Fifth Edition, website and go to Chapter 7. Click on **Practice 4: Surveying a Chapter in Another Textbook**. After surveying a chapter in one of your textbooks for another course, type responses to the seven questions. After you type your responses, you can print them or e-mail them to your instructor.

Surveying an Article or an Essay

You can also use surveying to preview an article or an essay from a newspaper, a magazine, or a book. Surveying shorter readings requires a minimal amount of time but can provide you with valuable information. Use the following steps to survey an article, an excerpt, or an essay:

1. Think about the title. Without reading the article or essay, what does the title mean to you? What do you predict that the article will be about? What understanding or opinions do you already have about the subject?

2. Identify the author. If you are familiar with the author, think about the information you already know about him or her. If there is a footnote or a byline about the author's affiliations with specific groups or organizations, additional publications, or other personal information, read it carefully and think of ways it might relate to the subject matter.

3. Carefully read and think about any introductory material that appears before the beginning of the article. Such material often provides the reader with background knowledge about the upcoming topic and/or the author.

4. Carefully read the entire first paragraph of the article. The thesis statement, the main point or purpose of the entire article, often appears in this paragraph.

5. Skim through the rest of the article by reading headings, subheadings, and marginal notes (also called *sidebars*).

6. Read the concluding paragraph. The concluding paragraph often restates the thesis statement and summarizes the main ideas in the article.

How can surveying help you save time when you are searching for appropriate articles for a report?

Formulating Questions

Creating questions about the material you are going to read, the material you are in the process of reading, or the material you have already read is an active reading strategy that provides you with a purpose for reading, elevates your curiosity about the subject, increases your comprehension, and helps you maintain a focus on the information. Later, you can use the questions for self-quizzing and feedback. The questions and answers can then work as memory cues or associations to recall the information when you prepare and take tests.

In Chapter 6, you learned about Bloom's Taxonomy, a classification system that orders types of questions according to their level of difficulty. (See Chapter 6, page 161.) When you write questions *before* or *during* the reading process, you will likely focus on knowledge, comprehension, and application-level questions. When you write study questions *after* you have completed the reading process, strive to include higher-level questions that analyze, synthesize, and evaluate information.

Writing Questions Before You Read

Writing questions before you read the printed material is a relatively quick process that you can do by converting the title, the main headings, and the sub-headings into meaningful questions. You can formulate a variety of questions by using the words *what, why, when, where, who,* and *how*. You may write the questions directly in your textbook next to the title, headings, or subheadings, or you may write them on notebook paper or index cards, leaving space to write the answers later. The following is an example of formulating questions before you read. The title, the headings, and the subheadings for the first part of this chapter have been converted into questions by inserting key question words.

Title: *What do I already know about* reading college textbooks?

Heading: *What is* active reading?

Heading: *How do* essential strategies for textbook reading *affect memory*?

Heading: *What are the* four levels of reading?

Heading: *When should I use* surveying to get an overview?

Writing Questions as You Read

The questions you write as you read serve many purposes. They may reflect your curiosity about the topic, your desire to learn implications or applications, questions you want to ask in class, or areas that need clarification or further explanations. As you read, you may also want to predict future test questions and write questions that you can use later for self-quizzing and preparing for tests. Formulating questions as you read, and writing the questions in the margins of the textbook or on separate notebook paper or index cards, is an active reading strategy that keeps your mind focused and holds the information in your working memory.

As you read the following paragraph, many questions may come to mind. You may want to pose a question about specific information in the paragraph, or you may want to pose a question about the implications. A sample question about this excerpt is in the margin.

> Human-made sources of radiation include X-rays and radionuclides used in medical procedures, fall-out from nuclear testing, TVs, tobacco smoke, nuclear wastes, and emissions from power plants. Ironically, because fossil fuels contain traces of uranium and thorium and their daughters, more radioactivity is released into the atmosphere from power plants burning coal and oil than from nuclear power plants.

How does all this radiation affect our bodies?

From Shipman et al., *An Introduction to Physical Science,* 10/e, p. 254. Copyright © 2003. Reprinted by permission of Houghton Mifflin, Inc.

Writing Questions After You Read

Writing questions after you read provides you with study tools to use to rehearse and retrieve information from your long-term memory. These study questions, along with the answers, provide you with feedback to check your accuracy and ability to recall information at a later time. In Chapter 6, you learned that predicting test questions, writing practice test questions, and writing answers to your own questions are excellent ways to prepare for tests. (See pages 159–160.) In Chapter 9, on pages 248–252, you will learn how to use index cards to create study questions and to take textbook notes.

EXERCISE 7.5 Formulating Questions Before You Read

On Appendix D, page A-17, the psychology chapter begins with an outline of the chapter. The outline shows the chapter title, the headings (bold print), and the subheadings (standard print). Convert the title, the headings, and the subheadings into questions. You may write directly on the page. You may be asked to share your questions with a partner, a small group, or the entire class.

Group Processing: A Collaborative Learning Activity

Form groups of three or four students. Then complete the following directions.

1. Individually, think of the last complete chapter that you read in any one of your textbooks. On a piece of paper, make a list of things you do when you read a chapter. Try to explain in chronological order how you go about completing a chapter.

2. Put all the lists together so that you and the members of your group can compare them. Do any of you use the same process? What do the lists have in common? Which approach seems most comprehensive? Be prepared to share your discussion with the rest of the class.

Using the SQ4R Reading System

One of the first textbook reading systems, SQ3R, was developed by Francis P. Robinson in 1941. This system acquired its name by using the first letter of each step in the system: survey, question, read, recite, and review. Other systems have been developed for reading textbooks, but they all basically contain the same essential steps found in SQ3R. The **SQ4R system** in this chapter is based on SQ3R, with a fourth R added for the "record" step. The SQ4R system thus becomes a six-step approach to reading and comprehending textbooks. It includes the previously discussed reading strategies of surveying, formulating questions, and thorough reading.

As with any approach, skipping a step weakens the system. To gain the most benefit from this system, use all six steps on a regular basis. Not only will you comprehend information more readily; you will also not waste precious time rereading chapters to learn new information.

The Steps of SQ4R

1. *Survey* the chapter.
2. Write *Questions* for each heading and subheading.
3. *Read* the information, one paragraph at a time.
4. Select a form of notetaking to *Record* information.
5. *Recite* the important information from the paragraph.
6. *Review* the information learned in the chapter.

Step One: Survey the Chapter

Use the steps for surveying a chapter given on page 181. When you do the **Survey** step, you will use the introductory materials, headings, subheadings, visual materials, marginal notes, terminology, and end-of-chapter materials to create an overview of the chapter.

Step Two: Write Questions

During the **Question** step, formulate a question for each heading or subheading in the chapter. Use the words *which, when, what, why, where, how,* or *who* to turn each heading or subheading into a question. Writing the questions often takes less than ten minutes.

Step Three: Read Carefully

Some students feel that they should be able to "read fast" to get through the chapter. Others read the chapter, only to find at the end of the chapter that they do not remember much of what they have just read; consequently, they must reread at least one more time. The **Read** step of SQ4R encourages you to read *carefully* and *thoroughly*. For most textbooks, you should read *one paragraph at a time* and stop so that you can concentrate and comprehend each paragraph. With careful, thorough reading, you will not need to spend valuable study time rereading chapters.

Reading Flexibility   *Thorough reading* requires some flexibility on your part as you adjust to various levels of difficulty in both content and readability levels. Some textbooks are easy to read and understand; others require a considerable amount of attention and effort. Selecting an appropriate amount of material to read before pausing to think about the information prevents you from going into *automatic pilot,* which results in little or no information registering in your memory. The following chart provides you with guidelines for determining how much information you should read before pausing to think about or to work with the information. Using these general guidelines will keep you from overloading your working memory and displacing information without having sufficient time to process it.

Level of Difficulty	Kinds of Textbook	Reading Length
Easy	Some career guidance, personal growth, developmental writing, and literature textbooks may fall into this category. Reading fiction such as short stories, plays, or poetry may also be included here.	Instead of stopping after every paragraph, stop at the end of each page to think about the information, create a visual image of the material, associate it with other information, formulate questions, or take notes.
Average	The kinds of textbooks that involve an average level of difficulty will depend on your reading skills and familiarity with the subject matter. Generally speaking, writing composition, public speaking, history, and social science textbooks, such as those for anthropology, economics, sociology, business, and political science, fall under the category of average level of difficulty.	Read one paragraph and stop. Think about the information, create a visual image of the material, create associations, formulate questions, look for main ideas, identify important details, look for special terminology, and take notes, which may include highlighting, annotating, or another form of notetaking.

| Difficult | Again, the level of difficulty will be partially determined by your reading skills and your familiarity with the subject matter. Generally speaking, math and science textbooks, such as those for computer science, geology, chemistry, and physics, have the highest level of difficulty for reading and understanding. With these kinds of textbooks, you may find that every sentence contains meaningful and complex information. You may also find that math and science books are more difficult because they require you to work with both *declarative knowledge* (factual) and *procedural knowledge* (steps and processes). | Move through each paragraph sentence by sentence. Strive to understand the information in each sentence. If you have difficulties with a specific sentence, read back and read forward to see if the surrounding sentences add clarity. After you understand the entire paragraph, use the strategies included for textbooks with an average level of difficulty. |

Overview Reading   In the chart on page 177, you learned that **overview reading** is used to survey, but it can also be used to become familiar with a topic prior to reading thoroughly for comprehension or prior to analyzing the contents of the material. When you are reading a short story, an essay, a play, or a short excerpt, you may want to get a sense of the flavor of the writing, allow the words to stir your imagination, and open yourself to the emotional experience created by the writer. Reading this type of material all the way through, without stopping or pausing, immerses you in the writing and keeps the unity of the plot, the characters' actions, and the emotional experience moving steadily forward. Overview reading is also very effective for difficult, complex sections in a textbook. Reading *slowly* all the way through can provide you with basic background information and lay a foundation for more thorough reading. As you read slowly through the complex material, you will also be able to identify confusing, complicated areas that will require your closer attention and scrutiny. Once you complete the overview reading, your task then is to return to the beginning of the writing and begin the process of identifying important details, patterns, and terminology and using elaborative rehearsal strategies, associations, notetaking, and analysis to break the material into smaller, more manageable parts to understand, process, and learn.

Step Four: Record Information

Reading comprehension involves finding main ideas and recognizing important supporting details. After you read a paragraph or a section of information carefully, it is time to use the **Record** step by taking notes of the important information you will need to study, memorize, learn, and use. Taking time to record information, or take notes, benefits you in many ways. First, your notes become a *reduced or a condensed form* of the information you are expected to know. You can save time studying and preparing for tests by using your notes. Second, taking notes keeps you actively involved in the learning process. There is less tendency for your *automatic pilot* to have the opportunity to get turned on. Third, writing the information offers another way for you to hold information in working memory and encode it for your long-term memory.

Many notetaking options exist for you to record important information. After you learn the various notetaking options shown next, you may find that you prefer to use one or two notetaking systems for most of your notetaking needs. You may also find that you prefer to use more than one type of notetaking system for difficult textbooks. Incorporating two different kinds of notetaking systems into your reading and studying strategies makes it possible for you to encode information for your memory in more than one way. You will soon learn the following notetaking options in these upcoming chapters:

Chapter 8   Highlighting, Annotations, and Marginal Notes
Chapter 9   Cornell Notes, Index Card Notes, Two-Column and Three-Column Notes, and Formal Outlines.
Chapter 11 Visual Mappings, Hierarchies, Comparison Charts, and Other Visual Notes

Step Five: Recite

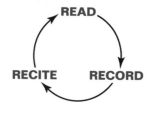

Before you move on to the next paragraph, stop and use the **Recite** step. Recite the information you wrote in your notes. Speak out loud using your own words, and in complete sentences. For math or science chapters with formulas, recite the steps used to solve problems or apply formulas. Convert symbols in equations to English words. Reciting helps you encode the information for memory and creates important retrieval cues.

Reciting is effective because it holds information longer in your working memory. It requires you to explain information clearly and in your own words. Reciting provides you with immediate feedback about your ability to recall the information accurately. Reciting is an important part of active learning; it increases your levels of concentration, participation, and comprehension. Once you have finished reciting the information, continue to move through the chapter by reading the next paragraph (or section) carefully, recording main ideas and important supporting details, and reciting the new information. As you move through the chapter using the **Read-Record-Recite Cycle**, your reading is thorough, detailed, and accurate. Your mind is alert, challenged, active, and focused. By devoting time and effort to this careful method of reading, you do not need to reread the chapter. When you have completed this cycle for the entire chapter, move on to the final step of SQ4R.

Step Six: Review

After you have finished surveying, questioning, reading, recording, and reciting, you do the last step—reviewing. The **Review** step can be accomplished in a variety of ways. The following activities are helpful for both immediate and ongoing review:

- Answer any questions at the end of the chapter.
- Answer the questions that you wrote in the Question step.
- Study and recite from the notes that you took in the Record step.
- Write a summary of the information in the chapter.
- Personalize the information by asking yourself additional questions: *How can this information be used? How does the lecture from class fit in with this information? Why is this important to learn?*
- Create additional study tools such as index cards, study tapes, or visual mappings.
- For math and science textbooks with math problems and formulas, copy the problems from the book. Work the problems; compare the steps you used and your answers with those in the textbook.

EXERCISE 7.6 Knowing the Six Steps

The following chart shows the steps of SQ4R. Fill each box with the name of the step. Then, with a partner, practice explaining each step of the process. Include as many details as you can remember without looking back in the book.

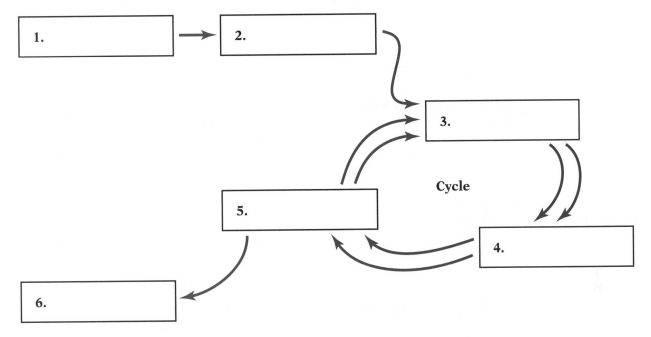

EXERCISE 7.7 LINKS

With a partner or in a small group, discuss which of the Twelve Principles of Memory (SAVE CRIB FOTO) you use in each of the steps of SQ4R. Copy an enlarged version of the following chart. Complete the following chart by listing the principles and brief explanations. Be prepared to share your results with the class.

Steps in SQ4R	Principles of Memory Used
S	
Q	
R	
R	
R	
R	

O N L I N E   P R A C T I C E   5

Visit the *Essential Study Skills*, Fifth Edition, website and go to Chapter 7. Click on **Practice 5: The Steps of SQ4R**. Complete the ten-question interactive multiple-choice quiz. Upon completion of the quiz, you will receive your score. You can exit at that time, or you can print your results or e-mail them to your instructor.

O N L I N E   P R A C T I C E   6

Visit the *Essential Study Skills*, Fifth Edition, website and go to Chapter 7. Click on **Practice 6: Using a Reading System**. Type responses to four questions. After you type your responses, you can print your responses or e-mail them to your instructor.

Reflection Writing 2
Chapter 7

On separate paper, in a journal, or online at this textbook's website, respond to the following questions.

1. What approach did you use to read a new chapter before you learned about SQ4R?

2. What changes will you make in your reading approach now that you know SQ4R?

Reading Different Kinds of Textbooks

All the strategies you have learned thus far for reading a textbook apply to all textbooks. However, understanding the different structures of textbooks from various disciplines will help you select the most appropriate strategies to use. Some textbooks emphasize learning *declarative knowledge* while others focus more on *procedural knowledge*. Some textbooks use mostly expository, or factual, writing styles while others use figurative language that evokes emotional responses. Some textbooks present information as a chronological sequence of events while others present information in themes or units. Understanding the differences among textbooks from various disciplines can help you select the most appropriate strategies to use to increase your comprehension. Visit the student website for Chapter 7 for this textbook to learn more about reading different kinds of textbooks.

 EXERCISE 7.8   Overview Reading
Do an overview reading of the psychology chapter in Appendix D. You do not need to underline, make marginal notes, or record any information at this time. Your goal is to read simply to become familiar with the content.

EXERCISE 7.9   Textbook Case Studies

Read about each of the following student situations carefully. Then, on your own paper and in complete sentences, answer the question that follows each case study. You can also answer these questions online at this textbook's Chapter 7 website. You can print your online responses or e-mail them to your instructor.

1. Justine reads all her textbooks the way that she reads paperback books. She begins at the beginning of the chapter and does not stop until she reaches the end of the chapter. She often finds that she needs to reread chapters two or three times before she can retain the information. What methods can Justine use to comprehend a textbook chapter better and spend less time rereading?

2. The instructor spent half the class time talking about a concept that was unfamiliar to Simon. Simon had not had a chance to read the last three chapters, so he thought perhaps the concept appeared in those chapters. When he sat down to work with a study partner, Simon started flipping through the chapters page by page and eventually located the section of information. What strategies would help Simon be a more efficient reader and student?

3. Because Mikah has always done quite well in math classes in the past, he has developed a habit of saving time by skipping over math problems that he is confident he knows how to solve. The only problems he solves are the ones the instructor assigns for a grade. Midway through the term, Mikah finds himself struggling. He frequently has difficulty solving problems, he confuses rules and equations, and he loses points for not showing the steps in his work. What textbook reading strategies would you suggest Mikah begin using immediately to change his old habits to new habits?

ONLINE CASE STUDIES

 Visit the *Essential Study Skills*, Fifth Edition, website and go to Chapter 7. Click on **Online Case Studies**. In the text boxes, respond to four additional case studies that are only available online. You can print your responses or e-mail them to your instructor.

Reflection Writing 3
Chapter 7

On separate paper, in a journal, or online at this textbook's website, respond to the following questions.

1. What are some of the challenges you encounter when you read your various college textbooks? Be specific; identify definite kinds of problems for specific kinds of textbooks.

2. What are some strategies you learned in this chapter that will help you read your textbooks more efficiently and more effectively?

3. What specific strategies did you learn in this chapter that will improve the way you read and study from math textbooks? Be specific.

SUMMARY

- Active reading is the process of engaging your mind in the reading process by using an array of strategies and skills to understand, learn, and use information. Active reading places a heavy demand on your working memory.

- You can improve your textbook reading skills by using the eight *Essential Strategies for Textbook Reading* and by using the correct level of reading that reflects your purpose for reading. Using the correct level of reading also affects your overall reading comprehension. *Recreational, Overview, Thorough,* and *Comparative* are the four levels of reading.

- Surveying, one form of overview reading, provides you with the *big picture* or framework of a textbook, a chapter, an article, or an essay.

- Formulating questions, which is an active reading strategy that provides you with a purpose for reading, elevates your curiosity level, increases comprehension, and helps you maintain your focus. Formulating questions can occur *before, during,* or *after* the reading process.

- The SQ4R reading system is a highly effective six-step approach to reading: *Survey, Question, Read, Record, Recite,* and *Review.* By using all six steps of SQ4R to read a chapter, you will increase your comprehension and then be able to shift your time and attention to studying your notes, not rereading chapters.

- Surveying a chapter often takes less than twenty minutes. Formulating questions from the headings and subheadings often takes less than ten minutes. The majority of your reading time occurs when you use the *Read-Record-Recite Cycle* to process the information into your memory.

- Thorough reading involves flexibility on your part. You can adjust the amount of information you read based on the level of difficulty of the material, your familiarity with the material, and your reading skill level. For a textbook with an average level of difficulty, pausing after reading one paragraph to think about and work with the information before moving on to the next paragraph is recommended.

- You can use overview reading to read through material without pausing or stopping to analyze or work with the information. This type of overview reading immerses you in the material and provides background information before you return to the material for more thorough reading, elaborative rehearsal, and analysis.

- The *Record* and *Recite* steps of SQ4R are active reading strategies. You can use a variety of note-taking options to capture main ideas and important details on paper. Reciting information you selected during the *Record* step encodes information for your memory and creates valuable retrieval cues.

- Immediate and ongoing *Review* is the final step of SQ4R. You can use a variety of review activities to work with and practice recalling or retrieving information from your long-term memory.

- All of the strategies learned in Chapter 7 work effectively with all kinds of textbooks. However, additional tips for working with specific kinds of textbooks enhance your ability to comprehend, work with, and learn course-specific information.

CULMINATING OPTIONS FOR CHAPTER 7

1. Visit this textbook's website and go to Chapter 7 to complete the following exercises:
   a. Flash card review of Chapter 7 terms and definitions
   b. ACE Practice Test 1 with ten fill-in-the-blank questions
   c. ACE Practice Test 2 with ten true-false questions
   d. ACE Practice Test 3 with ten multiple-choice questions
   e. ACE Practice Test 4 with three short-answer–critical thinking questions

2. Go to Appendix C in the back of this textbook for more Learning Options to use for additional practice, enrichment, or portfolio projects.

Chapter 7 REVIEW QUESTIONS

True-False

Carefully read the following statements. Write T *if the statement is true and* F *if it is false.*

_____ 1. During active reading, new information and previously learned information appear together in working memory.

_____ 2. Formulating questions should only be done before you begin the reading process.

_____ 3. Surveying a chapter before you begin the process of careful reading is a warm-up activity that you can use to focus your mind, increase your interest, and plan efficient use of your time.

_____ 4. You can omit the fourth step of SQ4R without weakening this reading system.

_____ 5. Step 2 of SQ4R provides a purpose for reading, improves concentration, and results in the creation of meaningful questions to use in the Review step.

_____ 6. To read all college textbooks, you should first read through the entire chapter and then reread the chapter, stopping at the end of each page to take notes.

_____ 7. Several options are available for students to use to complete the *question, record,* and *review* steps of the SQ4R reading system.

_____ 8. Overview reading involves identifying key ideas, determining the organization used in the paragraphs, and analyzing the different parts of the overall topic.

_____ 9. Marathon reading may overload your working memory and hinder your ability to process information effectively.

_____10. Creating movies in your mind as you read new information is one way to encode important ideas for your long-term memory.

Definitions

Define the following terms.

1. Overview Reading

2. Comparative Reading

3. Read-Record-Recite Cycle

Short Answer and Critical Thinking

Use complete sentences to answer each of the following questions.

1. When should you use the process of surveying?

2. Explain how to read a textbook without letting your mind slip into automatic pilot, when little or no information registers in your memory as you read.

3. Explain how to use the strategy of formulating questions for textbook materials.

Strengthening Comprehension

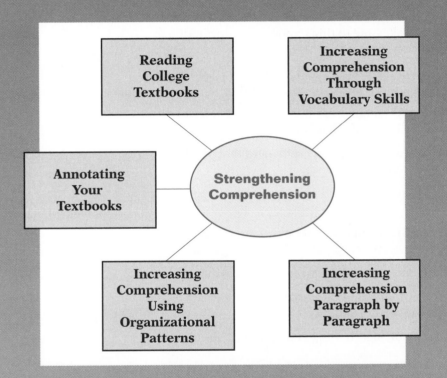

Active reading is an essential skill for college students that requires students to go beyond reading the words printed on textbook pages. You can use many strategies to understand textbook information more thoroughly. Some relate to reading habits, while others relate to vocabulary development and paragraph structure. Annotating, or marking, textbooks helps you comprehend the material more thoroughly and provides study tools for further studying and reviewing. Strengthening reading comprehension is an ongoing process; you will need to continually apply effort and the strategies in this chapter to meet the challenges presented by textbooks of varying complexity.

Chapter 8 Strengthening Comprehension Profile

ANSWER, SCORE, and **RECORD** your profile before you read this chapter. If you need to review the process, refer to the complete directions given in the Profile for Chapter 1 on page 2.

ONLINE: You can complete the profile and get your score online at this textbook's website.

	YES	NO
1. When I read a new chapter, I take time to think about the information in the chapter, analyze it, and work with it in a variety of ways.	_____	_____
2. If I encounter a difficult or confusing paragraph, I skip over it and move to the next paragraph, which may be easier to understand.	_____	_____
3. I use the structure of words and sentences as well as context clues to discover the meanings of unfamiliar words that I encounter.	_____	_____
4. I often highlight or underline several complete sentences that are difficult to read in each paragraph in my textbooks.	_____	_____
5. I reread chapters thoroughly at least three times when I am preparing for a test.	_____	_____
6. After I have read a paragraph in one of my textbooks, I am usually able to identify the main idea and the most significant supporting details.	_____	_____
7. I use the margins in the textbook to write brief notes or draw diagrams.	_____	_____
8. I can usually recognize the primary method a textbook author uses in a paragraph to organize the supporting details.	_____	_____
9. I cannot study from my textbook highlighting and notes because they are too disorganized and difficult to read.	_____	_____
10. I am confident in my ability to use reading comprehension strategies to understand most textbook paragraphs.	_____	_____

Reflection Writing 1
Chapter 8

On separate paper, in a journal, or online at this textbook's website, respond to the following questions.

1. What is your profile score for this chapter? What does it mean to you?

2. What are your greatest challenges or difficulties in the area of understanding the information in your textbooks?

Reading College Textbooks

To read and comprehend college textbooks, you need to use *active learning* and *active reading* strategies to move beyond merely reading printed words. Comprehending what you read is a complex process that involves many skills; it cannot be done quickly or effortlessly. Your working memory requires time to make the following connections:

■ attach meaning to printed words

■ associate pieces of new information with previously learned information

■ analyze information by identifying its individual parts, characteristics, patterns, and relationships

■ integrate information into existing schemas to form generalizations

■ evaluate the logic and accuracy of what you read

■ apply the information to solve problems

This chapter introduces active reading strategies that will help you strengthen your reading comprehension skills. To increase your comprehension and make the reading process more enjoyable, productive, and rewarding, use the *Twelve Principles of Memory* (Chapter 2, page 48), the *Essential Strategies for Textbook Reading* (Chapter 7, page 176), and the *Essential Strategies to Improve Comprehension* (page 198) each time you open a textbook with a learning goal to understand, learn, and process the information.

Group Processing: A Collaborative Learning Activity

Form groups of three or four students. Then complete the following directions.

1. Discuss what *reading comprehension* means to you. As a group, formulate a definition of *reading comprehension*. Write the definition in the following space.

2. Brainstorm a list of reading difficulties you have encountered with some of your college textbooks. List the difficulties in the following space. Be prepared to share with the rest of the class.

SET LEARNING GOALS

The following *Essential Strategies to Improve Comprehension* chart highlights nine important strategies to use to strengthen comprehension. Place a star next to the ones that you already use. Highlight the strategies you plan to make a conscious effort to begin using to improve your comprehension.

Essential Strategies to Improve Comprehension

▶ **Be patient and do not rush the reading process.** If you are reading without comprehending, slow down the intake process, break the text into smaller units, and patiently work your way through the new information. Allow your working memory ample time to process efficiently.

▶ **Stay with a paragraph or section of material until you comprehend it.** When you encounter a confusing or difficult paragraph or section in the textbook, *reread the material* slowly. *Verbalize,* or read out loud; often hearing the words clarifies the information. *Visualize* what you are reading; try converting the information into a *movie in your mind.* Place the paragraph or section in context with the surrounding material. Reread the previous paragraphs and read ahead to the following paragraph or paragraphs to find the natural flow or progression of information.

▶ **Recognize and use different levels of information.** Themes and concepts in textbooks are organized and developed through the use of levels of information. Become an analytical reader by looking for the larger themes or theses; examining the relationships among headings and subheadings; and identifying topics, main ideas, and important supporting details within each paragraph.

▶ **Use knowledge of writing structures to your advantage.** A well-written paragraph has unity (all details relate to the main idea), coherence (ideas flow in a logical sequence), and adequate development (sufficient details to support the main idea). Likewise, paragraphs link together to develop a main point (the thesis, heading, or subheading in a chapter). As an active reader, use this knowledge by asking yourself questions based on these writing structures: *How are the ideas related? How does this information fit with the heading? What logical sequence does the author use? Which details are essential to develop the main idea or main point?*

▶ **Learn the terminology.** Writers use specialized terminology to present and explain information. Understanding and being able to define the specialized terminology lays a foundation for more complex understanding and allows you to communicate on a level above informal conversation. Use study skills strategies, such as creating your own glossary of terms or making vocabulary flash cards, to learn these terms and add them to your working vocabulary.

▶ **Expand your vocabulary.** Do not skip over unfamiliar words. To unlock the meaning of a paragraph, use vocabulary-building strategies to understand the meaning of all the words in the paragraph.

▶ **Get into the writer's head.** Writers select specific organizational patterns to communicate their ideas and present information in a clear, organized way. To improve your comprehension, become familiar with the various organizational patterns and then analyze paragraphs to discover the patterns that the writer used to organize the information.

▶ **Use elaborative rehearsal and active learning techniques as you read.** Work with the information and interact with it in meaningful ways. This may involve highlighting, marking your textbook, taking notes, drawing diagrams, reciting, or formulating questions. You have many elaborative rehearsal options; select ones that are effective for you, and use them on a regular basis as you read.

▶ **Become excited about what you learn.** Reading is a knowledge-broadening experience. Anticipating situations in which you will want to share, explain, or discuss information with someone else becomes motivation to read with greater comprehension. Showing excitement, interest, and enthusiasm about new information helps personalize it and encode it in your memory.

CLASS DISCUSSION

Question: What occurs in working memory and long-term memory as you apply each of the *Essential Strategies to Improve Comprehension*?

Increasing Comprehension Through Vocabulary Skills

Understanding the meanings of course-specific words as well as general words used by the author is essential for understanding information in all college textbooks. Difficulties comprehending the meaning of a paragraph may be related directly to a limited understanding of specific words in the paragraph or to skipping over unfamiliar words. Understanding the terminology and other unfamiliar words used in the textbook lays a foundation for higher-level comprehension skills. The following vocabulary-building strategies will increase your comprehension of textbook information.

> ### Vocabulary-Building Strategies to Increase Your Comprehension
>
> 1. Use **punctuation clues** to identify definitions in context.
> 2. Use **word clues** to identify definitions in context.
> 3. Use **word structure clues** to determine the general meaning of words.
> 4. Use **context clues** to determine the general meaning of words.
> 5. Use glossaries and dictionaries for specific definitions.
> 6. Substitute familiar words for unfamiliar words.
> 7. Use ongoing review to learn terms and definitions.

Use Punctuation Clues

Punctuation clues identify definitions of terminology or general words within the sentence. *Commas, dashes, parentheses,* and *colons* are forms of punctuation that signal definitions. In the following examples (from Appendix D), the terms appear in bold print, and the definitions are underlined. Punctuation clues separate the definition from the other words in the sentence.

commas— Stress may also intensify **functional fixedness**, the tendency to use objects for only one purpose.

dash— **Chronic stressors**—stressors that continue over a long period of time—include such circumstances as living near a noisy airport, being unable to earn a decent living, residing in a high-crime neighborhood, being the victim of discrimination, and even enduring years of academic pressure.

parentheses— Stressors trigger a process that begins when the brain's hypothalamus activates a part of the autonomic nervous system, which stimulates the **medulla** (inner part) of the adrenal glands.

colon— A related phenomenon is **catastrophizing**: dwelling on and overemphasizing the possible negative consequences of an event.

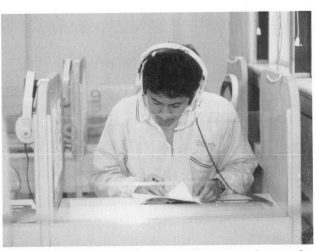

What kinds of vocabulary-building strategies work well for studying a foreign language?

Use Word Clues

Word clues signal definitions within the sentence and link the vocabulary terms to their definitions. Often the term is presented first and then is followed by the definition. However, the order can be reversed. The following word clues are used frequently to define terminology.

also	defined as	referred to as	known as	is/are called
is/are	to describe	mean/means	which is	or

When you search for the words in a sentence that define a word, *be selective;* underline only the words that are a part of a formal definition. In the following examples (from Appendix D), the terms appear in bold print, and the definitions are underlined.

> **Word Clue: known as**
>
> For a time, researchers believed that anyone who displayed the <u>pattern of aggressiveness, competitiveness, and nonstop work</u> known as **"Type A" behavior** was at elevated risk for heart disease.

> **Word Clue: are called**
>
> <u>Efforts to reduce, eliminate, or prevent behaviors that pose health risks and to encourage healthy behaviors</u> are called **health promotion**.

✪ EXERCISE 8.1   Using Punctuation and Word Clues

Work with a partner to complete this exercise. In the following sentences from An Introduction to Physical Science, *use punctuation and word clues to identify the definitions of the words in bold print. Underline or highlight the definitions. Be selective; include only words that are a part of the definition.*

1. The unit of electric charge is called the **coulomb** (C), after Charles Coulomb (1736–1806), a French scientist who studied electrical effects. [p. 167]

2. Waves with relatively low frequencies, or long wavelengths, are known as **radio waves** and are produced primarily by causing electrons to **oscillate**, or vibrate, in an antenna. [p. 122]

3. The fourth and final factor in reaction rate is the possible presence of a **catalyst**, a substance that increases the rate of reaction but is not itself consumed in the reaction. [p. 326]

4. **Thermodynamics** means the dynamics of heat and deals with the production of heat, the flow of heat, and the conversion of heat to work. [p. 107]

5. The **neutron number** (N) is, of course, the number of neutrons in a nucleus. [p. 230]

6. The chemical reactivity of the elements depends on the order of the electrons in the energy levels in their atoms, which is called the **electron configuration**. [p. 272]

7. The outer shell of an atom is known as the **valence shell**, and the electrons in it are called the **valence electrons**. [p. 273]

From Shipman et al., *An Introduction to Physical Science*, 10/e. Copyright © 2003. Reprinted by permission of Houghton Mifflin, Inc.

Use Word Structure Clues

Word structure clues involve using the meanings of word parts (prefixes, suffixes, bases, and roots) to help determine the general meaning of unfamiliar words. For example, if you know the meanings of common *prefixes*—such as *re-, pre-, un-, il-, mis-,* or *ab-* —or you know the meanings of common *roots*—such as *-ject* means *throw, -fer* means *carry,* or *-psych* means *mind*—you can use your knowledge of these word parts to begin to understand an unfamiliar word. (Lists of common prefixes, suffixes, and roots with their meanings are available on this textbook's website.) If using word structure clues results in a vague understanding of the word, you can refer to a dictionary or glossary for a more complete definition. The following chart shows the four word parts that provide word structure clues.

Word Parts

prefixes	Units of meaning attached to the beginning of words
suffixes	Units of meaning attached to the end of words to indicate a specific part of speech (noun, verb, adjective, or adverb)
bases	English words that have meaning and can stand by themselves
roots	Units of meaning (often Greek or Latin) that do not form English words until other word parts are attached to them

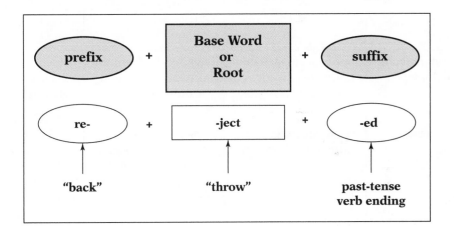

In college textbooks, especially in the fields of science and health sciences, many specialized vocabulary terms have Greek or Latin roots. For example, the Appendix D chapter (page A-24) uses the term *psychobiological model.* You can break the word *psychobiological* into its structural parts: *psycho, bio, log, ic,* and *al. Psycho* refers to the mind or the emotional state of the mind. *Bio* refers to the study of animal and plant life (biology). *Log* comes from *-ology* or *-logy,* which means *the study of.* In this case, it refers to the study of the mind and of life (the body). The suffixes *ic* and *al* convert the noun *psychobiology* into an adjective form. A *psychobiological model,* therefore, is a model that studies psychological and biological variables.

Use Context Clues   **Context clues** provide hints about general meanings of unfamiliar words. The term *context* refers to the words and sentences that surround a specific term or concept. By carefully reading the sentence with the unfamiliar word and then rereading the surrounding sentences, you can often pick up hints or context clues about the meaning of the word. The following chart summarizes kinds of context clues and provides you with an example of each.

Context Clue	Definition	Strategy	Example Sentence
Synonyms	words with exact or similar meanings	Try substituting a familiar word (a synonym) for the unfamiliar word.	*probity:* The judge has a keen sense of recognizing a person's honesty and integrity. For that reason, the *probity* of the witness was not questioned.
Antonyms	words with opposite meanings	An unfamiliar word is understood because you understand its opposite.	*impenitent:* Instead of showing shame, regret, or remorse, the con artist was *impenitent*.
Contrasts	words that show an opposite or a difference	Look for words such as *differ, different, unlike,* or *opposite of* to understand the differences.	*thallophyte:* Because the fungi is a *thallophyte*, it differs from the other plants in the garden that have embedded roots and the rich foliage of shiny leaves and hardy stems.
Comparisons or Analogies	words or images that indicate a likeness or a similarity	Look for the commonality between two or more items.	*cajole:* I sensed he was trying to *cajole* me. He reminded me of a salesman trying to sell me a bridge.
Examples	examples that show function, characteristics, or use of the term	Look for ways that the examples signal the meaning of the term.	*implosion:* *Implosions* are not rare in Las Vegas. The most recent one collapsed an old, outdated casino to make room for a new megaresort. Dust and debris filled the air, but the nearby buildings suffered no damage.

Some context clues may simply be "sensed" by relating the information in the surrounding sentences to common sense, personal experience, or a variety of examples. To use these, and all kinds of context clues, you must keep a focused mind and read slowly to search for useful context clues.

O N L I N E   P R A C T I C E   1

Visit the *Essential Study Skills*, Fifth Edition, website and go to Chapter 8. click on **Practice 1: Increasing Reading Comprehension**. Complete the ten-question interactive multiple-choice quiz. Upon completion of the quiz, you will receive your score. You can exit at that time, or you can print your results or e-mail them to your instructor.

◈ EXERCISE 8.2 Applying Vocabulary Skills

Select one of your textbooks for another course and turn to the chapter that you are currently studying. On your own paper, make a list of ten course-specific terms or unfamiliar words that you encountered when you read this chapter. After each term or unfamiliar word, use the information in the chapter to write a definition. Following each definition, briefly tell what kind of vocabulary clue you used to locate the definition: punctuation, word, word structure, *or* context clue.

Use Glossaries and Dictionaries for Specific Definitions

Glossaries in the back of textbooks provide course-specific definitions for terminology that appears throughout the textbook in bold, italic, or special-colored print. Review Chapter 7, page 179, for effective ways to use a glossary.

As a college student, you know that having reference materials available for your immediate use can save you time and an extra trip to a library or resource center. If you do not already have a collegiate dictionary, make the purchase of a hardback dictionary a top priority. Also explore the possibility of using the dictionary included with many computer software programs, online dictionaries that you can locate by conducting an Internet search, subject-specialty dictionaries available in most libraries and campus bookstores, or a hand-held electronic dictionary and thesaurus that can provide you with a quick method for locating synonyms or short definitions for unfamiliar words.

Substitute Familiar Words for Unfamiliar Words

Once you have identified the meaning of an unfamiliar word, you can use this strategy to convert formal textbook language into a less formal, more personal conversational tone. Above each of the words that was unfamiliar to you, write a more common or familiar word. Reread the paragraph but substitute the common or familiar word for the unfamiliar word. The following example shows how this technique of substituting words adds clarity and improves comprehension of a difficult paragraph.

Few if any philosophies are as <u>enigmatic</u> [puzzling] as *Daoism*—the teachings of the Way (Dao). The opening lines of this school's greatest masterpiece, *The Classic of the Way and Virtue (Dao De Jing)*, which is <u>ascribed to</u> [associated with] the <u>legendary</u> [famous] Laozi, immediately <u>confront</u> [challenge] the reader with Daoism's essential <u>paradox</u> [contradiction]: "The Way that can be <u>trodden</u> [walked] is not the <u>enduring</u> [lasting] and the unchanging Way. The name that can be named is not the enduring and unchanging name." Here is a philosophy that <u>purports</u> [claims] to teach *the* Way (of truth) but <u>simultaneously</u> [at the same time] claims that the True Way <u>transcends</u> [exceeds] human understanding. <u>Encapsulated</u> [Contained] within a little book of some five thousand words is a philosophy that <u>defies</u> [resists] definition, <u>spurns</u> [rejects] reason, and rejects words as inadequate.

From Alfred J. Andrea and James Overfield, *The Human Record*, 3/e, p. 93. Copyright © 1998 by Houghton Mifflin Co. Used with permission.

Use Ongoing Review to Learn Terms and Definitions

Because knowing terminology is a foundation skill for comprehension, take time at the end of a chapter and throughout the week to review terminology and definitions from the current and from previous chapters. Terms and definitions involve **paired associations**, which means two items are linked together in your working memory. When you think of a term, you want to be able to relate that term almost automatically to its definition. When you want to recall the information, either the term (and the spelling of the term) or the definition works as a memory trigger or retrieval cue to recall information from your long-term memory. Each time you practice a paired association, you pull the information back into your working memory and make it possible to integrate that information with additional details or with larger ideas or concepts. The same principle of paired associations applies to learning mathematical symbols and their definitions stated in words.

O N L I N E   P R A C T I C E   2

Visit the *Essential Study Skills*, Fifth Edition, website and go to Chapter 8. Click on **Practice 2: Improving Your Vocabulary Skills**. Complete the ten-question true-false quiz. Upon completion of the quiz, you will receive your score. You can exit at that time, or you can print your results or e-mail them to your instructor.

Increasing Comprehension Paragraph by Paragraph

For most textbooks, *thorough reading* involves reading one paragraph at a time; stopping to understand, analyze, and digest the paragraph; and then moving on to the next paragraph to repeat the process. When you use the SQ4R reading system, after you survey and create questions, you read one paragraph, stop to record information (marking the textbooks or taking notes on paper), and recite the information before moving to the next paragraph. The comprehension skills that follow focus on the structure of individual paragraphs, so emphasis is on learning to slow down the reading process, read one paragraph at a time, and comprehend what you read.

Working with Topics, Main Ideas, and Supporting Details

Being aware of three levels of information used in paragraphs helps you unlock the meaning of paragraphs, tune into the underlying organizational structure, follow the logical flow of ideas, and use active reading skills to increase your comprehension. As you read paragraph by paragraph, you will be working with three levels of information: the topic, the main idea, and the supporting details.

Level 1: The Topic   Every paragraph has a **topic**, which is the subject of a paragraph. The topic is *a word, a name,* or *a phrase* that tells what the author is writing about in a paragraph. Each sentence in the paragraph should tell more about, explain, or give examples of the topic.

Use the following strategies to identify the topic of a paragraph.

1. Use overview reading to read the entire paragraph without stopping.
2. Ask yourself: *In one word or one phrase, what is this paragraph about?*
3. If you cannot state the topic, glance through the paragraph again and ask yourself: *Is one word repeated several times in the paragraph? Does that word work as the topic?*

Level 2: The Main Idea   The **main idea** contains the topic and the author's single most important point about the topic. The sentence that states the main idea is called the **topic sentence**. (Some textbooks refer to the topic sentence as the *main idea sentence*.) The following diagrams show this information.

topic + author's most important point about the topic = **main idea**

sentence with the topic + the main idea = **topic sentence**

Sometimes after you read a paragraph, you can quickly identify the topic sentence; at other times, you may need to reread the paragraph and actively search for the most important sentence that represents the main idea of the paragraph. On occasion, you will encounter a paragraph that has no *stated* main idea, which means you will not find a topic sentence in the paragraph. This occurs when the main idea is *implied* (see page 207).

Use the following strategies to identify the main idea or the topic sentence of a paragraph.

1. The topic sentence is like an umbrella. It needs to be broad enough for all of the other sentences and supporting details in the paragraph to "fit under" it. In a well-written paragraph, each sentence relates to or supports the topic sentence. Ask yourself the following questions to help you identify the topic sentence.
   - What is the topic (subject) of this paragraph? Is there a "big picture" or "umbrella sentence" that contains this topic word?
   - What is the main idea of this paragraph, the idea the author wants to make about the topic? Which sentence states the main idea?
   - Which sentence is large enough to encompass the content of the paragraph? Do all the details in the paragraph fit under this sentence?
2. Use the following positions of sentences to evaluate sentences that may be the topic sentence with the main idea:
   - *First Sentence:* Does the first sentence capture the overall content of the paragraph? In textbooks, the first sentence of a paragraph often states the main idea.
   - *Last Sentence:* If the first sentence is not the "umbrella sentence," check the last sentence. Sometimes the details are presented first; the last sentence summarizes the main points and thus states the main idea.
   - *Other Sentences:* If the first and the last sentences do not state the main idea, carefully examine each sentence in the body of the paragraph.

Level 3: The Supporting Details   The **supporting details** include facts, explanations, causes, effects, examples, and definitions that the writer uses to develop, support, or prove the main idea. The details in each sentence must relate to the topic and the topic sentence, which states the main idea.

> **Use the following strategies to identify the important supporting details in a paragraph.**
>
> 1. Ask yourself: *If I needed to explain the main idea to someone, what details would I want to include in my explanation?* You can underline the key words or phrases in that paragraph that you would use in your explanation.
> 2. Identify specific details that will serve as memory cues or associations to trigger recall of information later from your long-term memory. If the paragraph has multiple examples, select several of the examples as memory cues; you do not need to remember all of them.
> 3. Examine bulleted lists of information and notes written in the margins carefully. Key supporting details often appear in these lists or notes.
> 4. When you highlight or underline supporting details in paragraphs, be selective. Do not mark words such as *to, and, with, also,* and *in addition* because they are not key memory trigger words. You also do not need to underline the same key word, or the topic, multiple times.

In the following examples, the reader identified the topic, located and completely underlined the topic sentence, and identified and underlined key words for supporting details. Study the examples carefully. Notice the *selectivity* used to avoid excessive underlining.

Example 1: In the following paragraph, the main idea is expressed in the second part of the first sentence. The last sentence restates or summarizes the first sentence.

Topic: Order of Plant and Animal Life

Topic sentence

The main forms of plant and animal life may at first glance appear chaotic, but the biologist sees them in a high degree of order. This order is due to an elaborate system of classification. All life is first

Supporting details

grouped into a few primary divisions called phyla; each phylum is in turn subdivided into small groups called classes; each class is subdivided into orders; and so on down through the family, the genus, the species, the variety. This system brings order out of chaos, enabling the biologist to consider any plant or animal in its proper relationship to the rest.

From Louise E. Rorabacher.

Example 2: In the next paragraph, the first sentence introduces the *topic* but does not state the main idea. When this occurs, the next step is to check the last sentence. In this example, the last sentence also does not state the main idea and the topic. To find the main idea and the topic sentence, you now need to examine the sentences inside the paragraph. The second sentence is the topic sentence.

Topic: The Biological Approach

Supporting details

Investigating the possibility that aggressive behavior or schizophrenia, for example, might be traceable to a <u>hormonal imbalance</u> or a <u>brain disorder</u> reflects the biological approach to psychology.

Topic sentence

As its name implies, <u>the biological approach assumes that behavior and mental processes are largely shaped by biological processes.</u>

Supporting details

Psychologists who take this approach <u>study</u> the <u>psychological effects</u> of <u>hormones</u>, <u>genes</u>, and the activity of the <u>nervous system</u>, especially the <u>brain</u>. Thus, if they are <u>studying memory</u>, they might try to identify the <u>changes taking place</u> in the brain as information is stored there. Or if they are <u>studying thinking</u>, they might look for <u>patterns of brain activity</u> associated with, say, making quick decisions or reading a foreign language. . . .

From Bernstein, *Psychology,* 5/e, p. 3

Example 3: On occasion, you will encounter paragraphs that do not directly state the main idea—the main idea is *implied*. In paragraphs with **implied main ideas**, after careful reading, the supporting details in the paragraph should supply you with sufficient information to draw your own conclusion about the main idea. In the following paragraph, if the first sentence were the topic sentence, the entire paragraph would be dedicated to examples of civilizations that left written records that we cannot yet decipher. The last sentence cannot work as the topic sentence because it is an example of mysterious people for whom we have yet to uncover written records. After examining the body of the paragraph, notice how none of the sentences captures the "big picture" of the entire paragraph. After reading the paragraph carefully and thinking about its content, you can formulate a main idea and state it in your own words.

Topic: Written Records

Supporting details

<u>Some</u> of the world's <u>earliest civilizations</u> have <u>left written records</u> that we <u>cannot</u> yet <u>decipher</u> and might never be able to read. These include <u>India's Harappan</u> civilization, which was centered in the Indus valley from <u>before 2500</u> to some time after 1700 BCE; and the <u>Minoan civilization</u> of the Aegean island of Crete, which flourished from roughly <u>2500</u> to about 1400 BCE; and the <u>African</u> civilization of <u>Kush</u>, located directly south of Egypt, which reached its age of greatness <u>after 800</u> BCE; but with much <u>earlier origins</u> as a state. For many <u>other early civilizations</u> and <u>cultures</u> we have as yet <u>uncovered no written records</u>. This is the case of <u>mysterious peoples</u> who, between approximately <u>6000</u> BCE and the first century CE, <u>painted</u> and <u>carved</u> thousands of pieces of <u>art on the rocks</u> of Tassili n'Ajjer in what is today the <u>central Saharan Desert</u>. It is also true of the <u>Olmec civilization</u> of <u>Mexico</u>, which appeared around <u>1200</u> BCE.

From Alfred J. Andrea and James Overfield, *The Human Record,* Third Edition, p. 34. Copyright © 1998 by Houghton Mifflin Company. Used with permission.

Formulated Main Idea: *We cannot use written records to learn about some early civilizations.*

EXERCISE 8.3   Identify Main Ideas/Topic Sentences

By yourself or with a partner, read each of the following paragraphs carefully. Underline the sentence that you think is the topic sentence for each paragraph. Underline key supporting details. Be selective.

1. In a family with two adults and children, for example, one of the adults may already have a job and the other may be choosing between working at home or working outside the home. This decision may be very sensitive to the wage and perhaps the cost of child care or consuming more prepared meals. In fact, the increased number of women working outside the home may be due to the increased opportunities and wages for women. The increase in the wage induces workers to work more in the labor market. Economists have observed a fairly strong wage effect on the amount women work.

    From Taylor, *Economics*, pp. 327, 329.

2. The human brain in late adulthood, however, is smaller and slower in its functioning than the brain in early adulthood. This reduction is thought to be caused by the death of neurons, which do not regenerate. Neurons die at an increasing rate after age 60. The proportion of neurons that die varies across different parts of the brain. In the visual area, the death rate is about 50 percent. In the motor areas, the death rate varies from 20 to 50 percent. In the memory and reasoning areas, the death rate is less than 20 percent. The production of certain neurotransmitters also declines with age.

    From Payne and Wenger, *Cognitive Psychology*, p. 359.

3. A solid has a definite shape and volume. In a *crystalline* solid, the molecules are arranged in a particular repeating pattern. This orderly arrangement of molecules is called a *lattice*. The molecules are bound to each other by electrical forces. Upon heating, the molecules gain kinetic energy and vibrate about their positions in the lattice. The more heat that is added, the stronger the vibrations become. When the melting point is reached, additional energy breaks apart the bonds that hold the molecules in place. As bonds break, holes are produced in the lattice, and nearby molecules can move toward the holes. As more and more holes are produced, the lattice becomes significantly distorted.

    From Shipman et al., *An Introduction to Physical Science*, 10/e, p. 103. Copyright © 2003. Reprinted by permission of Houghton Mifflin, Inc.

4. Finally, having too much support or the wrong kind of support can be as bad as not having enough. People whose friends and family overprotect them may actually put less energy into coping efforts or have less opportunity to learn effective coping strategies. Further, if the efforts of people in our social support network become annoying, disruptive, or interfering, they can increase stress and intensify psychological problems.

    From Bernstein/Nash, *Essentials of Psychology*. Copyright © 2002. Reprinted by permission of Houghton Mifflin.

O N L I N E   P R A C T I C E   3

▲ Visit the *Essential Study Skills*, Fifth Edition, website and go to Chapter 8. Click on **Practice 3: Increasing Comprehension Paragraph by Paragraph**. Complete the ten-question interactive multiple-choice quiz. Upon completion of the quiz, you will receive your score. You can exit at that time, or you can print your results or e-mail them to your instructor.

O N L I N E   P R A C T I C E   4

Visit the *Essential Study Skills*, Fifth Edition, website and go to Chapter 8. Click on **Practice 4: Identifying Main Ideas**. Read each of the four paragraphs carefully. After you read each paragraph, identify the topic sentence, which states the main idea. Then, write your response in the text box. You will also be asked to explain why you selected that specific sentence as the topic sentence. After you write answers for all four paragraphs, you can print your responses or e-mail them to your instructor.

Drawing Pictures of Paragraphs

Converting printed information in paragraphs into pictures improves comprehension. As you work your way through the paragraph by drawing a picture to show significant details, the information in the paragraph becomes clearer and often makes more sense. Converting printed information into pictures has the following benefits as well:

■ The process of drawing helps you create a visual image and encodes the information in a new form.

■ By labeling parts of your pictures with words, you create a strong association between words and pictures. Both the words and the pictures serve as memory cues to recall information later.

■ You hold the information you are reading longer in your working memory, thus reducing the chance that the information will fade or decay before it is processed.

■ You can use this drawing process to solve math word problems. In your picture of the problem, show *what you already know*. Use question marks to show the information that is missing and that you need to discover.

Use the following strategies to draw a picture of a paragraph.

1. Read the paragraph carefully. You should first have an overview of the topic. Underline the topic sentence and the important details.
2. If the information in the paragraph is *sequential* or in a specific order, develop your drawing step by step. Work carefully so that you do not inadvertently skip a step.
3. If the paragraph is not sequential, identify the *individual parts* that together make up the *whole*. As you read the paragraph, add the parts as they are presented.
4. Label all parts of your drawing. Add any other helpful notes, but keep your notes brief.

In the following example, cover up the picture on the left. Read the paragraph slowly, and visualize the information as you read. Then, examine the drawing of the paragraph to see if it clarified or simplified the information in the paragraph.

Greenhouse Effect:

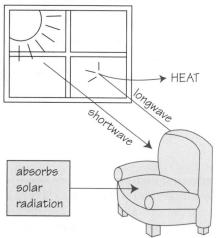

Topic: The Greenhouse Effect

A window pane transmits sunlight. It is nearly transparent, and much of the shortwave energy passes through. Only a little energy is absorbed to heat up the glass. However, the walls and furniture inside a room absorb a large part of the solar radiation coming through the window. The energy radiated from the furniture, unlike the original solar energy, is all long-wave radiation. Much of it is unable to pass out through the window pane. This is why the car seats get so hot on a hot, sunny day when all the windows are closed. Try putting a piece of glass in front of a hot object to see how the heat waves are cut off. A greenhouse traps energy in this way when the sun shines and so does the atmosphere.

From *Investigating the Earth,* American Geological Institute

---

EXERCISE 8.4   Converting Words to Pictures

With a partner or on your own, underline the main idea and the important details in each paragraph. Then, convert the information in the following paragraphs into pictures on separate paper or in the margin.

1.   The human costs of the Civil War were enormous. The total number of military casualties on both sides exceeded 1 million—a frightful toll for a nation of 31 million people. Approximately 360,000 Union soldiers died, 110,000 of them from wounds suffered in battle. Another 275,175 Union soldiers were wounded but survived. On the Confederate side, an estimated 260,000 lost their lives, and almost as many suffered wounds. More men died in the Civil War than in all other American wars combined until Vietnam. Fundamental disagreements that would continue to trouble the Reconstruction era had caused unprecedented loss of life.

From Mary Beth Norton, David M. Katzman, Paul D. Escott, and Howard Chudacoff, *A People and a Nation,* Fifth Edition, p. 437. Copyright © 1998 Houghton Mifflin Company. Used with permission.

2.   The Celsius scale is the temperature scale for general use in much of the world and for scientific use worldwide. On this scale, the freezing point of water is 0°C, and the boiling point of water at normal barometric pressure is 100°C. On the Fahrenheit scale, *the scale in common usage in the United States,* the freezing point of water is 32°F, and the boiling point of water at normal barometric pressure is 212°F. Negative temperatures are possible with both of these scales. For example, liquid nitrogen boils at −321°F and −196°C.

From Darryll D. Ebbing and Rupert Wentworth, *Introductory Chemistry,* Second Edition, pp. 33–34. Copyright © 1998 Houghton Mifflin Company. Used with permission.

3.   The breeding grounds of the hurricanes that affect the United States are in the Atlantic Ocean southeast of the Caribbean Sea. As hurricanes form, they move westward with the trade winds, usually making landfall along the Gulf and south Atlantic coasts. During the hurricane season, the area of their formation is constantly monitored by satellite. When a tropical storm is detected, radar-equipped airplanes, or "hurricane hunters," track the storm and make local measurements to help predict its path. Like that for a tornado, the hurricane alerting system has two phases.

A **hurricane watch** is issued for coastal areas when there is a threat of hurricane conditions within 24 to 36 hours. A **hurricane warning** indicates that hurricane conditions are expected within 24 hours (winds of 74 mi/h or greater, or dangerously high water and rough seas).

From Shipman et al., *An Introduction to Physical Science,* 10/e, p. 536. Copyright © 2003. Reprinted by permission of Houghton Mifflin, Inc.

Increasing Comprehension Using Organizational Patterns

Unlocking the meaning of what you read involves understanding the relationships among the details within a paragraph and discovering the internal logic for the order of the details. For writing to be coherent and make sense, the supporting details within a paragraph need to be organized logically and flow with a natural progression. Seven **organizational patterns** are frequently used in college textbooks to organize details within paragraphs. If you have taken any college composition classes, these organizational patterns are the same ones that you have learned to use in your own writing.

The following charts describe each of the seven organizational patterns. Each chart also provides you with a list of common *clue words* frequently associated with that specific organizational pattern and a diagram that you can use to convert the details of the paragraph into picture form. Following each chart is a paragraph that uses that specific organizational pattern. Read each paragraph carefully and notice how the details are organized. As you read these paragraphs, you may find elements of more than one organizational pattern within a paragraph. In such cases, one pattern is more dominant.

Chronological Pattern	Clue Words	Diagram for This Pattern
• Details are presented in a logical time sequence: *chronological order*. • Details happen in a specific, fixed order to reach a conclusion or an ending. • This pattern is often used to tell a story (a narrative) or explain a sequence of events.	when then before next after first second finally	1. → 2. → 3. → 4. → Conclusion or Ending

Chronological Pattern:

While commercial farming was spreading, cattle ranching—one of the West's most romantic industries—was evolving. Early in the nineteenth century herds of cattle, introduced by the Spanish and expanded by Mexican ranchers, roamed southern Texas and bred with cattle brought by Anglo settlers. The resulting longhorn breed multiplied and became valuable by the 1860s, when population growth increased demand for beef and railroads facilitated the transportation of food. By 1870, drovers were herding thousands of Texas cattle northward by Kansas, Missouri, and Wyoming. On these long drives, mounted cowboys (as many as 25 percent of whom were African-American) supervised the herds, which fed on open grassland along the way. At the northern terminus—usually Abilene, Dodge City, or Cheyenne—the cattle were sold to northern ranches or loaded onto trains bound for Chicago and St. Louis for slaughter and distribution.

From Mary Beth Norton, David M. Katzman, Paul D. Escott, and Howard Chudacoff, *A People and a Nation*, Fifth Edition, p. 496. Copyright © 1998 Houghton Mifflin Company. Used with permission.

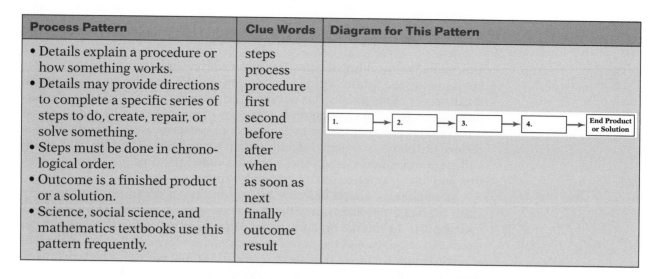

Process Pattern	Clue Words	Diagram for This Pattern
• Details explain a procedure or how something works. • Details may provide directions to complete a specific series of steps to do, create, repair, or solve something. • Steps must be done in chronological order. • Outcome is a finished product or a solution. • Science, social science, and mathematics textbooks use this pattern frequently.	steps process procedure first second before after when as soon as next finally outcome result	1. → 2. → 3. → 4. → End Product or Solution

Process Pattern:

Filtration is a common laboratory and industrial method of physically separating certain mixtures. You can brew coffee by placing ground coffee in a paper filter cup or cone and then pouring hot water over the grounds. The coffee extract passes through the filter paper, leaving the grounds behind. The purpose of the paper cone is to filter the coffee grounds away from the coffee extract. You can use filter paper in the laboratory in a similar way to separate a liquid and a suspended precipitate (a fine crystalline solid formed in solution by chemical reaction). You pour the solution with the suspended precipitate into a filter cone. Clear liquid passes through the filter, and the precipitate remains on the paper. Filtration is a physical process in which a particular mixture (a suspension of precipitate in a liquid solution) is separated into a solid and a liquid.

From Darryll D. Ebbing and Rupert Wentworth, *Introductory Chemistry,* Second Edition, pp. 65–66. Copyright © 1998 Houghton Mifflin Company. Used with permission.

Comparison or Contrast Pattern	Clue Words	Diagram for This Pattern		
• Comparison shows likenesses and/or differences between two or more objects or events (the subjects). • Contrast shows only differences between two or more objects or events. • Several characteristics of "Subject A" and "Subject B" are compared or contrasted.	also similarly likewise but in contrast on the other hand however although while	**Characteristics**	**Subject A**	**Subject B**

Comparison/Contrast Pattern:

To understand leadership, it is important to grasp the difference between leadership and management. We get a clue from the standard conceptualization of the functions of management: planning, organizing, directing (or leading), and controlling. Leading is a major part of a manager's job, yet the manager must also plan, organize, and control. Broadly speaking, leadership deals with the interpersonal aspects of a manager's job, whereas planning, organizing, and controlling deal with the administrative aspects. According to current thinking, leadership deals with change, inspiration, motivation, and influence. In contrast, management deals more with maintaining equilibrium and the status quo.

From DuBrin, *Leadership,* p. 3.

Definition Pattern	Clue Words	Diagram for This Pattern
• Information throughout the paragraph defines a specific term. • Explanations, characteristics, analogies, examples, and negations may be used to define a term. • The term the paragraph defines often appears in bold print in the first sentence.	means is/are is defined as can be considered referred to as	**key points, characteristics, analogies, examples**

Definition Pattern:

Charisma is a quality reflected in your level of energy, enthusiasm, vigor, and commitment. A speaker with charisma is seen as dynamic, forceful, powerful, assertive, and intense. President John F. Kennedy and Martin Luther King Jr. were charismatic speakers who could motivate and energize audiences. So was Adolf Hitler. People can disagree about a speaker's message yet still find that speaker charismatic.

From Daly and Engleberg, *Presentations in Everyday Life: Strategies for Effective Speaking* (Boston: Houghton Mifflin Co., 2001), p. 185. Copyright © 2001.

Examples Pattern	Clue Words	Diagram for This Pattern

• An idea, term, or theory is expanded through the use of examples.
• One extended example may be used throughout the paragraph, or multiple examples may be used.
	for example
	another
	  example
	an
	  illustration
	  of this	

Examples Pattern:

Attitude formation is often related to rewards and punishment. People in authority generally encourage certain attitudes and discourage others. Naturally, individuals tend to develop attitudes that minimize punishments and maximize rewards. A child who is praised for sharing toys with playmates is likely to develop positive attitudes toward caring about other people's needs. Likewise, a child who receives a weekly allowance in exchange for performing basic housekeeping tasks learns an attitude of responsibility.

From Reece/Brandt, *Human Relations, Principles and Practices,* 5/e, p. 111. Copyright © 2003. Reprinted by permission of Houghton Mifflin, Inc.

Cause/Effect Pattern	Clue Words	Diagram for This Pattern
• Show the relationship between two items in which one item causes the other item to happen. • One cause may have more than one effect or outcome. • Several causes may produce one effect or outcome.	because since so therefore caused by result in	

Cause/Effect Pattern:

All humans respond bodily to stress, which is what enables us to mount a defense. Physiologically, the sympathetic nervous system is activated and more adrenaline is secreted, which increases the heart rate and heightens arousal. Then all at once the liver pours extra sugar into the bloodstream for energy, the pupils dilate to let in more light, breathing speeds up for more oxygen, perspiration increases to cool down the body, blood clots faster to heal wounds, saliva flow is inhibited, and digestion slows down to divert blood to the brain and the skeletal muscles. Faced with threat, the body readies for action.

From Brehm, Kassin, and Fein, *Social Psychology,* 5th ed. (Boston: Houghton Mifflin Co., 2002), p. 510. Copyright © 2002.

Whole and Parts Pattern	Clue Words	Diagram for This Pattern

• Focus is on the individual parts, components, or entities that together create the whole object, concept, or theory.
• The details identify, define, and explain each individual part of the whole item.
• Diagrams may include any *whole item* with its *parts* clearly identified and labeled. Science and social science textbooks use this pattern frequently.
	parts
	X number
	  of parts
	categories
	subsystems
	sections
	left
	right
	front
	back
	consists of
	is comprised
	  of
	together
	  make
		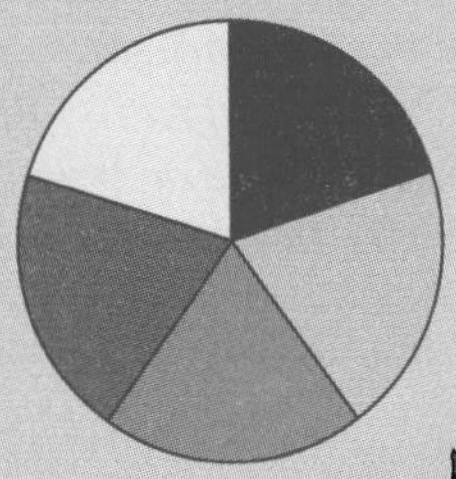 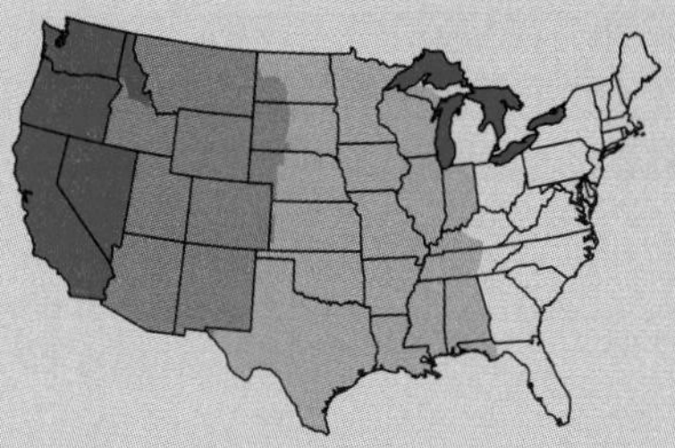

Whole and Parts Paragraph:

Creating a Marketing Mix

A business firm controls four important elements of marketing that it combines in a way that reaches the firm's target market. These are the *product* itself, the *price* of the product, the means chosen for its *distribution*, and the *promotion* of the product. When combined, these four elements form a marketing mix.

From Pride, Hughes, and Kapoor. *Business*, 7th ed. p. 363. Copyright © 2002. Reprinted by permission of Houghton Mifflin, Inc.

EXERCISE 8.5   Summarizing the Organizational Patterns

Complete the following chart to summarize key information about each organizational pattern. Remember to refer to this chart when you review the chapter and prepare for a test on this chapter.

Pattern	Purpose is to show:	Clue Words
Chronological		
Process		
Comparison/Contrast		
Definition		
Examples		
Cause/Effect		
Whole/Parts		

EXERCISE 8.6   Creating Diagrams for Paragraphs
Work with a partner or in a small group. Return to the paragraphs on pages 211–215 that show the seven organizational patterns. Convert the information in each paragraph into diagrams. Refer to the diagram formats in the organizational chart for each type of organizational pattern. When you create these diagrams, be very selective. Use only key words or phrases.

Reflection Writing 2
Chapter 8

On separate paper, in a journal, or online at this textbook's website, respond to the following questions.

1. Why is it important for you to develop a strong vocabulary? In what situations would a strong vocabulary benefit you?

2. Using the paragraph-by-paragraph method for reading textbooks often promotes more critical or analytical reading. In what ways are you a more analytical reader when you use this paragraph-by-paragraph method? What do you look for to analyze? Be specific.

 EXERCISE 8.7   Textbook Case Studies
Read about each of the following student situations carefully. Then, on your own paper and in complete sentences, answer the question that follows each case study. You can also answer these questions online at this textbook's Chapter 8 website. You can print your online responses or e-mail them to your instructor.

1. Cecilia does not have problems reading the textbook words, but she often has problems following the author's line of thinking. She wants to learn new strategies that force her to think about relationships and see "the bigger picture." What strategies will help her tune into the author's logical structures?

2. Lisa has difficulty with reading comprehension. She encounters so many words that are unfamiliar to her; she is not able to understand many of the paragraphs she reads. She feels it will take too much time to use a dictionary to look up all the words. What strategies would you recommend that Lisa use to begin to deal with her problems?

3. Mayumi has a hard time learning the information in textbooks. Some of her difficulties may stem from her reading habits. She reads through several paragraphs at a time at a steady rate. She then returns to each paragraph to look for the main idea; however, all the sentences seem equally important to her. She realizes that she needs to learn how to identify the main ideas in paragraphs. What strategies would you suggest to Mayumi?

O N L I N E   C A S E   S T U D I E S

 Visit the *Essential Study Skills*, Fifth Edition, website and go to Chapter 8. Click on **Online Case Studies**. In the text boxes, respond to four additional case studies that are only available online. You can print your responses or e-mail them to your instructor.

O N L I N E   P R A C T I C E   5

Visit the *Essential Study Skills*, Fifth Edition, website and go to Chapter 8. Click on **Practice 5: Using Organizational Patterns**. Complete the ten-question interactive true-false quiz. Upon completion of the quiz, you will receive your score. You can exit at that time, or you can print your results or e-mail them to your instructor.

Annotating Your Textbooks

Annotating is the active learning process of marking textbooks to show the main ideas and supporting details. The primary goals of annotating are to interact with the printed text, analyze the contents of each paragraph, simplify the structure of the paragraph by selectively identifying the key elements of each paragraph, comprehend the contents, and encode information to store and retrieve from long-term memory.

The following are additional benefits of annotating a textbook:

- You can hold information longer in your working memory, thus reducing the risk of information fading or being displaced before it is processed.
- You have time to think about the information, analyze it, and create meaningful associations that can help you recall the information later.
- You can look for levels of information, relationships among the details, and the parts that comprise the whole main idea or topic.
- You can focus and maintain your level of concentration; you can attend to the information and the task at hand, which assists your working memory.
- You can use motor skills or kinesthetic learning. By using colored highlighters and forms of visual notations, you can also engage visual learning skills.
- You can save yourself time because annotating reduces the amount of information you will need to study or review for an upcoming test. You will not need to reread entire chapters.
- You can personalize or tailor your approach to learning. You can *underline* or **highlight** with colored highlighter pens. Highlighting with colored pens makes different kinds of information and levels of information stand out more clearly.

The following box shows you strategies for effectively annotating your textbooks.

Annotating a Textbook

1. Highlight the complete topic sentence, which states the main idea.
2. Selectively highlight key words or phrases that support the topic sentence.
3. Circle terminology and highlight definitions.
4. Enumerate steps or lists of information.
5. Make marginal notes to emphasize important ideas and integrate information.

Highlight the Topic Sentence

As you have already learned, after you read a paragraph, find the **topic sentence**—the main idea—and underline it completely. When you study, a clearly marked topic sentence helps you keep your focus on the author's main point. This is the *only* sentence in a paragraph that you should completely underline or highlight. Remember that the main idea or topic sentence must serve as an "umbrella sentence." It must be broad enough so that all the other information in the paragraph "fits" under this sentence.

Highlight Key Words or Phrases

You have also already learned that once you find the main idea of the paragraph, you then need to identify the important details that support this topic sentence. Look for key words, phrases, definitions, facts, statistics, or examples to explain the main idea. Locate these **supporting details** or key words and mark them.

How does annotating your textbook save time? Would you find it difficult to study from a textbook that has been marked by another student? Why or why not?

Once you identify specific supporting details, ask yourself whether the details are important. Some details, such as extended explanations of examples, help you understand a concept but are not details you are expected to know. **Selectivity** is essential so that you do not highlight too much unnecessary information. Strive to highlight no more than 40 percent of the paragraph. Overmarking defeats the purpose of annotating, which is to reduce the amount of information you need to learn. Because you are selecting details that will serve as triggers or associations for *your memory*, you may select key words or phrases that other students may not feel are necessary. As long as you are targeting the essential details, do not be concerned if your highlighting is not exactly the same as another student's highlighting.

Most paragraphs that you read will have a topic sentence and supporting details. However, on occasion you may encounter a paragraph that does not seem to have any new information. This may be a **transition paragraph**; the information in it does not need to be marked. Transition paragraphs

- are designed to help ideas from one paragraph flow smoothly into the next paragraph.
- are usually short.
- do not contain strong main ideas or new details.

If the paragraph you are reading is more than a few sentences long and contains new terminology or new ideas, it is not a transition paragraph. Do not skip over it; read more carefully to find the important information to highlight.

Circle Terminology and Highlight Definitions

More than 60 percent of most test questions are based directly on knowing and understanding specialized terminology (vocabulary words). For this reason, it is important to identify and mark the terms you need to define. Words that are underlined or printed in bold, italic, or colored print are usually terms to know.

Circle key terms to make them stand out. Then highlight the main points of the term's definitions. Use word clues, punctuation clues, and context clues to identify the definitions of course-specific terminology.

Enumerate Steps or Lists of Information

A paragraph that has a topic sentence that uses words such as *kinds of, reasons, advantages, causes, effects, ways,* or *steps* often has a list of supporting details. **Ordinals,** or "number words," such as *first, second,* or *third,* may point you in the direction of individual details. Use a pen to write the numerals (1, 2, 3) on top of the ordinals. Also watch for words such as *next, another,* and *finally,* which are **place holder words** used to replace ordinals. Read carefully and write a new numeral on these words as well.

Sometimes ordinals are not used. A clue may be given, however, as to the number of details you should find. For example, saying that there are "five reasons" for something lets you know that you should find five details. You can then number these details clearly. With a pen, write *1* on the first item in the list, write *2* on the second item, and so on, until each supporting detail is numbered. Your final number of details should match the original clue.

Enumerating serves as a memory device, for it is easier to remember a fixed quantity of items than it is an unknown quantity of items. In the following example, notice how the main idea (topic sentence) is *completely underlined,* key words of supporting details are underlined, terminology is circled, and numbers create a list of items. Brief notes in the margins summarize the information.

Earth System

1. atmosphere
2. hydrosphere
3. lithosphere
4. biosphere

The earth system contains a number of interconnected subsystems, often described as "environmental spheres." The four major subsystems are the ① atmosphere, or the ocean of air that overlies the entire earth's surface; the ② hydrosphere, or the water of the surface and near-surface regions of the earth; the ③ lithosphere, or the massive accumulation of rock and metal that forms the solid body of the planet itself; and the ④ biosphere, or the layer of living organisms of which we are a part. All four respond in various ways to the flow of energy and materials through the earth system.

From Holt Atkinson, *Reading Enhancement and Development,* pp. 218–219.

Make Marginal Notes

Marginal notes are *brief* notes that you write in the margins of your textbook pages. Marginal notes give you a glimpse at the important points in a paragraph. You must be very selective and brief when you create marginal notes. Margins with too much information quickly become cluttered and difficult to use effectively.

> **Use the following strategies to create brief, effective marginal notes.**
>
> 1. Be very selective and brief. If the margins in your textbook become filled with too much information, consider an alternative form of notetaking to use.
> 2. Selectively write the following kinds of information in the margins:
>
> | | |
> |---|---|
> | numbered lists of key ideas | key words you need to define |
> | short definitions of terms | definitions pointed to unfamiliar terms |
> | study questions | questions to ask in class |
> | comments or reactions | question marks for unclear information |
> | diagrams or pictures | links to lecture notes |
>
> 3. Use brackets to mark off sections of a paragraph or an entire paragraph that is densely written. Rather than overmark or clutter the margins with too many details, draw a bracket next to the information and add an abbreviation that will draw your attention back to this section when you study. You can also use these abbreviations for sections that you did not place inside brackets but that you want to return to for further study.
>
> | | | | |
> |---|---|---|---|
> | EX. | *example or examples* | DEF. | *lengthy definition* |
> | IMP. | *important to reread* | REL. | *relationship between two items* |
> | RE. | *reasons why . . .* | ? | *information you do not understand* |
> | DIFF. | *differences* | SUM. | *summary* |

The following example shows the various forms of annotation to emphasize main ideas, details, and terminology.

Feminism

DIFF.

Around 1910 some of those concerned with women's place in society began using a new term, feminism, to refer to their ideas. Whereas members of the woman movement spoke generally of duty and moral purity, feminists—more explicitly conscious of their identity as women—emphasized rights and self-development. Feminism, however, contained an inherent contradiction. ① On the one hand feminists argued that all women should unite in the struggle for rights because of their shared disadvantages as women. ② On the other, they insisted that sex-typing—treating women differently than men—must end

IMP.

because it resulted in discrimination. Thus feminists advocated the contradictory position that women should unite as a gender group for the purpose of abolishing all gender-based distinctions.

Norton, *A People and a Nation,* p. 616. Copyright © 1998 Houghton Mifflin Co. Used with permission.

SET LEARNING GOALS

The following *Essential Strategies to Study Annotations* chart highlights six important strategies to use to study annotations you make in your textbooks. Place a star next to the strategies that you already use. Highlight the strategies that you plan to make a conscious effort to begin using to study your annotations.

Essential Strategies to Study Annotations

▶ **Reread, preferably out loud, the information that you marked.** Include highlighted information, numbering used to list ideas, vocabulary terms, and definitions. Read slowly so that your working memory has time to absorb the key points and associate them with each other and with previously learned information. Reading out loud keeps the information in your working memory and maintains your focus on the learning process. When you reread only the marked information, it will sound broken or fragmented; however, you will hear yourself stating only main ideas and important supporting details.

▶ **String the ideas together by inserting some of your own words.** Instead of reading only what you have marked, begin stringing ideas together by inserting some of your own words to convert the information to full sentences and clearer explanations. This verbalizing encodes the information linguistically, personalizes the information, and states the information in your own, often less formal, language.

▶ **Recite the information without looking at the textbook.** Reciting involves explaining information out loud, using your own words and sentences. When you recite from the textbook, you para-

phrase the information (use your own words to say basically the same information as the printed text). Reciting in this manner is a form of *elaborative rehearsal*.

▶ **Get feedback to check the completeness and accuracy of your recited information.** Look at the marked information as well as the marginal notes. If you omitted important points or stated some information incorrectly, redo the reciting process and correct your errors.

▶ **Write summaries that reflect the information you used when stringing ideas together.** After you have practiced stringing ideas together out loud, put your words on paper in the form of a summary. Your summary should include the main ideas and the important supporting details expressed in the form of paragraphs. Use your summary as a study tool to review for a test. Practice rewriting summaries, a skill that is valuable when you are faced with essay tests.

▶ **Review your annotations as a warm-up activity.** Before you begin a new chapter and begin taking in new information, review what you have already learned by rereading the annotations in the previous chapter.

CLASS DISCUSSION

Question: Which Principles of Memory do you use for each of the *Essential Strategies to Study Annotations*?

EXERCISE 8.8   Annotating
Return to the paragraphs on pages 211–215 that show the organizational patterns. Underline the main idea and the important details for each paragraph. Be selective. Use any other forms of annotation to mark these paragraphs. Compare your annotations with another student's markings.

O N L I N E   P R A C T I C E   6

> Visit the *Essential Study Skills*, Fifth Edition, website and go to Chapter 8. Click on **Practice 6: Annotating Your Textbooks**. Respond to five questions by writing your responses in text boxes. You can then print your responses or e-mail them to your instructor.

EXERCISE 8.9   Applying What You Have Learned
Use any combinations of reading and annotating strategies that you learned in Chapters 7 and 8 to read, analyze, dissect, and comprehend one or more of the selections listed next. Your instructor may ask you to discuss your process in class, summarize the strategies that you used, or compare your annotations with another student's work.

Selections: *Chronemics*—Exercise 9.1, pages 234–235
  Kinds of Listening, Chapter 10, pages 267–269
  Characteristics of People with High Self-Esteem—Exercise 11.4, pages 305–306
  Other Solar System Objects—Exercise 11.2, pages 301–302
  Industries That Attract Small Businesses—Exercise 11.10, page 318

 EXERCISE 8.10   LINKS
Apply the reading comprehension and annotation skills to the psychology chapter in Appendix D. (In Chapter 7, Exercise 7.8, you were asked to do an overview reading of the chapter in the Appendix. If you did not do this assignment, you may want to do an overview reading before conducting a thorough reading.) We will continue to work with this chapter throughout this textbook, so the careful reading and comprehension work you do now will facilitate later activities.

EXERCISE 8.11   Defining Appendix D Terminology
On page A-44 of Appendix D, the following fourteen terms followed by the page numbers of the chapter are listed under the Review of Key Terms. *Write definitions for each of the terms. Refer to Appendix D for the definitions.*

1. burnout (p. 356)

2. cognitive restructuring (p. 370)

3. diseases of adaptation (p. 354)

4. general adaptation syndrome (GAS) (p. 353)

5. health promotion (p. 368)

6. health psychology (p. 348)

7. immune system (p. 364)

8. posttraumatic stress disorder (PTSD) (p. 356)

9. progressive relaxation training (p. 371)

10. psychoneuroimmunology (p. 364)

11. social support network (p. 360)

12. stress (p. 350)

13. stress reactions (p. 350)

14. stressors (p. 350)

Reflection Writing 3
Chapter 8

On separate paper, in a journal, or online at this textbook's website, respond to the following questions.

1. Which of the vocabulary development strategies do you find most useful? How will they improve your comprehension in your various courses?

2. How does understanding an author's organizational patterns help you improve your comprehension? Do you now find yourself actively trying to identify the patterns in your textbooks?

3. How have the strategies in this chapter for annotating your textbook changed the way you mark your textbooks? How have the strategies changed the way you study annotations?

SUMMARY

■ Reading college textbooks involves active learning and active reading skills. Active reading moves you beyond simply reading the words printed on the page, promotes comprehension, and lays a foundation for future learning.

■ *Essential Strategies to Improve Comprehension* include slowing down the intake process; rereading, verbalizing, and visualizing difficult paragraphs; working with levels and writing structures of information; learning terminology and expanding your vocabulary; identifying organizational patterns; using elaborative rehearsal and active learning techniques; and becoming excited about what you read.

■ Vocabulary-building strategies include using punctuation, word, word structure, and context clues to unlock meanings of terminology and unfamiliar words. Using reference materials, substituting familiar for unfamiliar words, and using ongoing review to learn terms and definitions are additional vocabulary skills that increase comprehension.

■ Reading and analyzing textbook information paragraph by paragraph increases comprehension. Using the paragraph-by-paragraph method for increasing comprehension involves identifying topics, main ideas, and supporting details. Drawing pictures of information also helps you clarify and understand printed passages.

■ Identifying organizational patterns used to present details logically in a paragraph also increases comprehension. Seven organiza-

tional patterns frequently occur in college textbooks: chronological, process, comparison or contrast, definition, examples, cause/effect, and whole and parts.

■ Annotating textbooks is an active learning process that involves marking significant information that you need to learn. Annotating reduces the amount of information that you need to study and learn.

■ Five active learning strategies can be used to annotate a textbook:
   1. Highlight the complete topic sentence that states the main idea.
   2. Selectively highlight key words or phrases that support the topic sentence.
   3. Circle terminology and highlight definitions.
   4. Enumerate steps or lists of information by using ordinals, place holders, and number word clues.
   5. Make marginal notes to emphasize important ideas and integrate information. Use your annotations as guides for studying and reviewing. Reread the markings, string together the marked information, and then recite the information in your own words to personalize and internalize the information.

■ Annotations can also be used to write summaries or as a warm-up activity at the beginning of a study block.

CULMINATING OPTIONS FOR CHAPTER 8

1. Visit this textbook's website and go to Chapter 8 to complete the following exercises:
   a. Flash card review of Chapter 8 terms and definitions
   b. ACE Practice Test 1 with ten fill-in-the-blank questions
   c. ACE Practice Test 2 with ten true-false questions
   d. ACE Practice Test 3 with ten multiple-choice questions
   e. ACE Practice Test 4 with three short-answer–critical thinking questions

2. Go to Appendix C in the back of this textbook for more Learning Options to use for additional practice, enrichment, or portfolio projects.

Chapter 8 REVIEW QUESTIONS

Multiple Choice

Choose the best answer *for each of the following questions. Write the letter of the best answer on the line.*

_____ 1. Since many students find that writing reinforces the learning of information, they can
    a. write short notes and lists of information in the margins of the book.
    b. transfer the highlighted or underlined information to notes on notebook paper.
    c. verbally string together ideas and then write them in the form of a summary.
    d. do all of the above

_____ 2. Which of the following is *not* true about annotating in a textbook?
    a. It should be done only for textbooks that are difficult to read.
    b. It uses selectivity to reduce the amount of information that a student needs to study.
    c. It reduces overall reading time so students can devote more time to the process of learning.
    d. It can include highlighting, underlining, or making marginal notes.

_____ 3. When you identify important supporting details in a paragraph, you
    a. need to completely underline or highlight the sentence they are in.
    b. select key words or phrases to highlight.
    c. list each of the details in alphabetical order in the margins.
    d. make a mental note to yourself that they support the main idea.

_____ 4. Supporting details
    a. can be words, phrases, definitions, or facts that support the topic sentence.
    b. can sometimes be marked in the text with the use of numbered bullets.
    c. that are words you will need to define should be circled.
    d. are all of the above

_____ 5. When you use careful highlighting and marking in a textbook,
    a. every single paragraph will have important information marked.
    b. approximately 80 percent of the paragraphs should be underlined or highlighted.
    c. transitional paragraphs are the only paragraphs that may not be marked.
    d. all important supporting details will be circled.

_____ 6. If a topic sentence states, "You can use six strategies to strengthen your vocabulary," the reader
    a. should add numbers to his or her marking to indicate each strategy.
    b. should watch for ordinals and use the ordinals to number each strategy.
    c. needs to be aware of the use of "place holders" that replace ordinals.
    d. do all of the above

_____ 7. After the student has highlighted important information in a chapter, the student
    a. then needs to practice rereading the highlighted information out loud.
    b. has learned the information and can begin the next chapter.
    c. needs to reread, string together, and recite the highlighted information.
    d. needs to copy the highlighted information in an outline form.

_____ 8. When highlighted information is "strung together," the student
    a. connects the marked words by adding his or her own words or sentences.
    b. rereads aloud all of the information that was highlighted.
    c. writes the information in phrases on paper in the same order in which they were found in the book.
    d. connects all of the topic sentences together so they appear one right after another.

Locating Definitions

In each of the following sentences, use your vocabulary skills to locate and underline or highlight the definition for the word in bold print. Be selective; underline or highlight only the definitions.

1. The advantage of the **binary system**, which uses only the digits 0 and 1, is that each position in a numeral contains only one of two values. (p. 134)

2. A **point** may be regarded as a location in space with no breadth, width, or length. (p. 253)

3. The property shared by these three numeration systems is that they are **additive**; that is, the values of the written symbols are added to obtain the number represented. (p. 118)

4. We have already studied **perimeter** (the length of the boundary of a polygon) and the area (the space enclosed by the polygon). (p. 395)

5. Primes that differ by 2 are called **twin primes**, and the smallest twin primes are 3 and 5. (p. 160)

From Bellow and Britton, *Topics in Contemporary Mathematics*, 6th ed. (Boston: Houghton Mifflin Co., 1997). Copyright © 1997. Reprinted by permission of Houghton Mifflin, Inc.

Annotating a Textbook Passage

Annotate the following passage by highlighting main ideas and important supporting details. Mark the text in whatever other ways seem appropriate. Create meaningful marginal notes.

Role of Concentration   Undoubtedly one of the most difficult tasks we have to perform as listeners is concentration. Motivation plays an important role in activating this skill. For example, if you really want to listen to a speaker, this desire will put you in a better frame of mind for concentrating than will anticipating that the speaker will be boring.

Two other factors that affect listening concentration are interest level and difficulty of the message. Some messages may be boring, but if you need to get the information, careful concentration is imperative. You also may find the information so difficult that you tune out. Again, if it is imperative for you to understand the ideas, then you have to force yourself to figure out what you do not understand and find a way of grasping the meaning.

We can think three to four times faster than the normal conversation rate of 125 to 150 words per minute. And because we can receive messages much more quickly than the other person can talk, we tend to tune in and tune out throughout a message. The brain operates much like a computer: it turns off, recycles itself, and turns back on to avoid information overload. It is no wonder, then, that our attention fluctuates even when we are actively involved as listeners. A slight gap in your listening at times is a natural part of the listening process. When you tune out, the major danger is that you may daydream rather than quickly turn back to the message. But by taking notes or forcing yourself to paraphrase, you can avoid this difficulty.

Concentration also requires the listener to control for distractions. Rather than attempting to dismiss a whole list of things that you have to attend, control your concentration by mentally setting these other issues aside for the moment to give the speaker your full attention. It takes mental and physical energy to do this, but concentration is the key to successful listening.

Adapted from Berko, Wolvin, and Wolvin, *Communicating*, Eighth Edition, pp. 89–90. Copyright © 2001 by Houghton Mifflin Company. Used with permission.

Taking
Textbook Notes

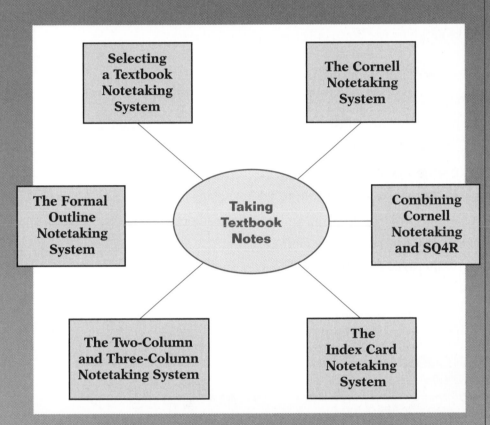

Effective notetaking is an essential skill for college students. In this chapter, you will learn several powerful notetaking systems that lead to greater academic success. The five-step Cornell notetaking system (record, reduce, recite, reflect, and review), the index card system, two- and three-column notes, and formal outlines provide you with notetaking options that you can use to capture main ideas and important supporting details in textbooks and lectures.

Chapter 9 Taking Textbook Notes Profile

ANSWER, SCORE, and **RECORD** your profile before you read this chapter. If you need to review the process, refer to the complete directions given in the Profile for Chapter 1 on page 2.

ONLINE: You can complete the profile and get your score online at this textbook's website.

	YES	NO
1. I am selective when I take notes; I write down only the important ideas and details.	_____	_____
2. I take time to think about and reflect on the information in the chapter.	_____	_____
3. I plan time each week to review notes that I took in previous weeks.	_____	_____
4. I take notes only on the front side of my notebook paper.	_____	_____
5. I use the same notetaking system for all my textbooks.	_____	_____
6. I know how to use the five steps of Cornell notetaking.	_____	_____
7. After I take notes on a paragraph, I recite what I wrote before moving on.	_____	_____
8. My notes summarize important charts, graphs, or pictures in the textbook.	_____	_____
9. I only take textbook notes when I prepare for upcoming tests.	_____	_____
10. I am confident about my ability to take effective notes for all my textbooks.	_____	_____

Reflection Writing 1
Chapter 9

On separate paper, in a journal, or online at this textbook's website, respond to the following questions.

1. What was your profile score? What does it mean to you?

2. How effective is your current notetaking system? Do you understand your notes when you study from them later? Do you have sufficient details in your notes? Are they organized neatly and logically?

Selecting a Textbook Notetaking System

Textbooks are often the starting point for learning the information you are expected to understand and use in your college courses. For that reason, the reading strategies in Chapters 7 and 8 to strengthen your comprehension of textbook information are essential skills. The foundation for most class lectures and activities is the content in your textbooks. Through class lectures, instructors focus your attention on specific concepts or details, provide examples, clarify textbook information, and also possibly expand the topic with new information such as current studies, data, alternative theories, or approaches. When you take notes on textbook chapters, you become familiar with the chapter and are able to follow and understand lectures more easily. Knowing how to take effective notes has additional benefits:

1. You become an *active learner* and use *active learning strategies*.
2. You encode information kinesthetically and visually as you write.
3. You selectively decide what information is important to learn and remember.
4. You focus your attention on ways to organize information logically.
5. You condense or reduce large amounts of information into more manageable units that are easier to study and review throughout the term.

In this chapter, you will learn a variety of textbook notetaking systems that will help you work with and master the information in your textbooks. In Chapter 11, you will learn additional forms of notetaking for even more options. After you learn about the Cornell notetaking system, the index card notetaking system, the two-column and three-column notes, and formal outlines, you will be ready to select the most effective notetaking system, or combination of notetaking systems, for each of your textbooks. The following points about taking textbook notes are important to know.

■ As you take notes on textbook chapters, your goal is to create a comprehensive set of notes that you can use to learn, rehearse, and review textbook information.

■ Outside of class, the majority of your study time will be spent reading and working with textbook information.

■ Studying from well-developed notes is more time efficient than reading and rereading chapters of information.

■ The *Essential Strategies for Textbook Notetaking* provides you with strategies applicable to all notetaking systems.

SET LEARNING GOALS

The following *Essential Strategies for Textbook Notetaking* chart highlights seven important strategies to use to take notes from textbooks. Place a star next to the strategies that you already use. Highlight the strategies that you plan to make a conscious effort to begin using to improve your textbook notetaking skills.

Essential Strategies for Textbook Notetaking

▶ **Understanding what you read is the starting point.** Use effective reading strategies and schedule ample time to understand the information printed in your textbooks. It is very difficult to take accurate and effective notes on information that you do not understand.

▶ **Be selective.** Your notes should not include everything in the textbook chapter. Your goal is to select only the important concepts, main ideas, and supporting details that you need to learn. Do not copy word for word or complete sections. Your notes should be a *condensed* version of the textbook.

▶ **Use a consistent structure in your notes.** Each notetaking system provides you with basic formats or standards to use that give structure to your notes. Strive to use the recommended structure so that the results are organized, easy-to-use notes.

▶ **Label your notes according to textbook chapter.** As you progress through the term, you will have many pages of notes or stacks of index-card notes. To avoid confusion, get into the habit of writing the chapter number on each page or card of your notes.

▶ **Experiment with various forms of notetaking.** Be flexible and willing to try new notetaking methods with your various textbooks. You may find that some forms of notetaking are more compatible with certain kinds of textbooks. You do not need to use the same kind of notetaking system for all your textbooks.

▶ **Use your notes for feedback.** Each type of notetaking system, when used properly, has some form of feedback system built into it that will let you know whether or not you understand and remember the textbook information. Pay attention to the feedback results; if you cannot explain or recite the information smoothly and accurately, spend more time on that section of information.

▶ **Allot time in your study blocks to work with your notes.** You can use your notes as warm-up activities at the beginning of a study block. Schedule time at the end of a study block for immediate review of the notes you made during that study time. Include some time during the week for ongoing review; keep your memory fresh by reviewing notes from previous chapters.

CLASS DISCUSSION

Question: Which *Principles of Memory* do you use when you take textbook notes and study from textbook notes?

The Cornell Notetaking System

The goal of the **Cornell notetaking system** is to take notes that are so accurate and so detailed that you *do not need to go back to the book to study*. Your studying, your learning, can take place by working with your notes as you use the following **five *R*'s of the Cornell system**: record, reduce, recite, reflect, and review. The power of this system is in its steps; if you choose to eliminate any one step, you weaken the system.

> ### The Five *R*'s of Cornell
>
> 1. *Record* your notes in the right column.
> 2. *Reduce* your notes into the recall column on the left.
> 3. *Recite* out loud from the recall column.
> 4. *Reflect* on the information that you are studying.
> 5. *Review* your notes immediately and regularly.

This powerful five-step Cornell notetaking system can be used to take notes from both textbooks and lectures. This notetaking system was designed by Dr. Walter Pauk at Cornell University more than forty-five years ago when he recognized students' need to learn how to take more effective notes. Many college and university teachers consider this the most effective notetaking system for college students.

Setting Up Your Paper

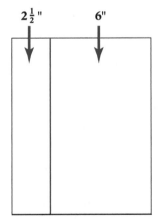

To begin, you need notebook paper with a *two-and-one-half-inch margin down the left side*. Many bookstores now carry Cornell notebook paper with this larger margin or a spiral "law notebook" with perforated Cornell-style pages. If you are not able to find the Cornell notebook paper for your three-ring notebook, draw a margin on the front side of regular notebook paper. All your notetaking is done on the front side only; the back of the paper is used for other purposes.

At the top of the first page, write the course name, chapter number, and date. For all the following pages, just write the chapter number and the page number of your notes. Later you may want to remove your notes from your notebook; having the pages numbered prevents disorganization.

Cornell Step One: Record

The wider right column is for your notes. In this first step—**record**—read each paragraph carefully, decide what information is important, and then record that information on your paper. Your notes should be a *reduced version* of the textbook. Be selective. Use the following suggestions for the first *R* of Cornell.

Do not write in
this column yet.

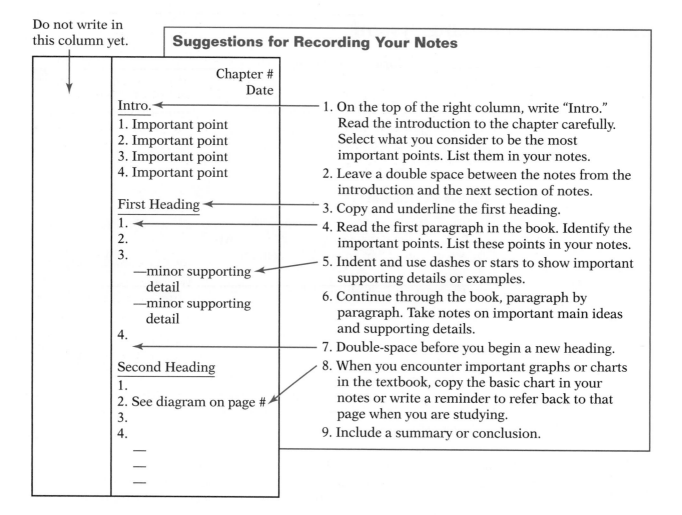

Suggestions for Recording Your Notes

Chapter #
Date

Intro.
1. Important point
2. Important point
3. Important point
4. Important point

First Heading
1.
2.
3.
  —minor supporting
   detail
  —minor supporting
   detail
4.

Second Heading
1.
2. See diagram on page #
3.
4.
  —
  —
  —

1. On the top of the right column, write "Intro." Read the introduction to the chapter carefully. Select what you consider to be the most important points. List them in your notes.
2. Leave a double space between the notes from the introduction and the next section of notes.
3. Copy and underline the first heading.
4. Read the first paragraph in the book. Identify the important points. List these points in your notes.
5. Indent and use dashes or stars to show important supporting details or examples.
6. Continue through the book, paragraph by paragraph. Take notes on important main ideas and supporting details.
7. Double-space before you begin a new heading.
8. When you encounter important graphs or charts in the textbook, copy the basic chart in your notes or write a reminder to refer back to that page when you are studying.
9. Include a summary or conclusion.

Use the Headings   The headings (and subheadings) in the textbook are the *skeleton*, or outline, of the chapter. They serve as guides for identifying main categories of information. By using the following strategies, you can avoid creating an endless stream of details that lacks an organizational structure.

- Use the textbook heading as a heading in your notes.
- Underline the heading so that it stands out as a main category of information.
- Do not number (or letter) the headings.
- Treat subheadings as regular headings if the information will be easier to understand. (See the examples that follow.)
- Create your own headings by regrouping or reorganizing information if your structure makes the information easier to understand or if your textbook does not provide you with headings.

The following example shows modifications made in the headings for textbook notes for the first half of the chapter in Appendix D.

Headings in Notes (Textbook Version)	More Meaningful Headings in Notes (Student Reorganized Version)
Introduction Health Psychology Understanding Stress	Introduction Health Psychology Understanding Stress Stressors Stress Responses Linkages Stress Mediators

Take Notes on the Introduction   The introduction often provides a brief overview of the content of the chapter. By listing the key ideas in your notes, you will be able to see later whether you understood and captured all the key points.

Leave Spaces Between Sections   Notes that are crowded or cluttered are difficult to study. By leaving a double space between each new heading or section of your notes, you are visually grouping the information that belongs together. You are also *chunking* the information into smaller units, which will help your memory.

Record Important Points   Because you will use your notes for studying, you want to see the big picture and the small pictures (details). *Record enough information to be meaningful later:*

- Avoid using only individual words or short phrases that will lose their meaning when you return to them later.
- Use short sentences when necessary to avoid meaningless phrases.
- Do not copy down information word for word. Shorten the information by rewording or summarizing it.
- If you find some sentences or short sections that are so clearly stated that you want to copy them, omit any of the words that are not essential for your understanding.
- If you have already highlighted the information, move the same information into your notes.
- Number the ideas as you include them in your notes. Numbering helps you remember how many important points are under each heading and breaks the information into smaller, more manageable units.
- For math problems or formulas, copy examples or problems and clearly show each step needed to solve the problem or use the formula. Include words next to unfamiliar symbols. (Also see two-column notes on page 252.)

Record Important Minor Details   You will frequently encounter minor details that belong under an idea that you already numbered. Indicate these details by *indenting* and then using *dashes* or *stars* before writing the details.

Include Graphs and Charts   Visual materials such as graphs, charts, and pictures contain valuable information. Usually you are not expected to know every fact or statistic depicted by the graph, chart, or other forms of visual materials. You are, however, expected to identify important patterns, relationships, or trends shown by the visual materials. You can *copy* the graphic material into your notes or *summarize* the conclusions you make by studying the graphic materials. By taking the time necessary to study graphic materials, you will be able to

- Study large amounts of information in a condensed form.

- Identify patterns, relationships, or trends more easily.

- Imprint information in a visual form in your long-term memory so that it serves as a visual memory cue to recall information at a later time.

Include a Summary or Conclusion   Summaries or conclusions pull the main ideas together to help you see the "big picture." If the book has a summary, include the summary as the last heading in your notes. If there is no summary, write your own conclusion to pull the main ideas together.

EXERCISE 9.1   Recording Notes

Read the following excerpt Chronemics: Time as Communication. *Prepare your own paper for taking notes using the Cornell format. (See page 231.) Take notes on this excerpt. Create your own meaningful headings; underline the headings. Under each heading, list and number the important details. You may be asked to share and compare your notes with those created by other students.*

Chronemics: Time as Communication

You communicate to yourself and others by the way you use time. The way people handle and structure their time is known as *chronemics*. "Each of us is born into and raised in a particular time world—an environment with its own rhythm to which we entrain ourselves." Time, as a communication tool, is sometimes greatly misunderstood. Only within certain societies, for example, is precise time of great significance. Some cultures relate to time as a *circular phenomenon* in which there is no pressure or anxiety about the future. Existence follows the cycle of the seasons of planting and harvesting, the daily rising and setting of the sun, birth and death. In *circular time*, there is no pressing need to achieve or create newness, or to produce more than is needed to survive. Nor is there fear of death. Such societies have successfully integrated the past and future into a peaceful sense of the present. Many Native Americans have been raised with this cultural attitude toward time.

Other societies operate on *linear time*, centered primarily on the future. These societies focus on the factual and technical information needed to fulfill impending demands. In most of Western Europe, North America, and Japan, punctuality is considered good manners. . . .

Time has become a critical factor in the U.S. workplace. Throughout a person's career, punctuality is often used as a measure of effectiveness. A person who arrives late for a job interview probably will have difficulty overcoming such a negative first impression, and employees who arrive late or leave early may be reprimanded and even dismissed.

Time is culture based. European Americans, Euro-Canadians, and Western Europeans, in general, are clock bound; African, Latin American, and some Asian Pacific cultures are not clock bound. Time is based on personal systems. European Americans traveling abroad often are irritated by the seeming lack of concern for time commitments among residents of some countries. In Mexico and Central America, tours may be late; guides may fail to indicate the correct arrival and departure times. Yet in other places, such as Switzerland, travelers can set their watch by the promptness of the trains. Businesspeople may get confused over what "on time" means as they meet those from other cultures. "In Britain and North America one may be 5 minutes late for a business appointment, but not 15 minutes and certainly not 30 minutes late, which is perfectly normal in Arab countries." In Latin America one is expected to arrive late to an appointment. This same tardiness for Germans or European Americans would be perceived as rudeness. . . .

In cultures that value promptness, one of the questions raised about time centers on the person who is constantly late. What does habitual tardiness reveal about the person? Chronic lateness, in a formal time culture, may be deeply rooted in a person's psyche. Compulsive tardiness is rewarding on some level. A key emotional conflict for the chronically late person involves his or her need to feel special. Such a person may not gain enough recognition in other ways; people must be special in some way, so the person is special by being late. Other reasons include needs for punishment, power, or as an expression of hostility. Tardiness can be a sign that a person wants to avoid something or that the activity or person to be met is not important enough to warrant the effort to be on time. Procrastinators are often not valued in a linear time-focused culture.

Adapted from Berko, Wolvin, and Wolvin, *Communicating*, 8/e, pp. 61–62. Copyright © 2001 by Houghton Mifflin Company. Used with permission.

Cornell Step Two: Reduce

After you have finished taking notes for the chapter, you are ready to close the book and **reduce**. Now, for the first time, you will be writing in the left column, the **recall column**. Remember, in step one you reduced the textbook information to the most important points and details. In step two, you are going to reduce your notes one step further. These reduced notes will provide you with a feedback system so you will know what information you have learned well and what information needs more practice. You will also refer to this column frequently for review.

Suggestions for Reducing Your Notes

	Chapter # Date
Intro.	Intro.
key word	1. Important point
define:	2. Important point
word	3. Important point
	4. Important point
Heading	First Heading
What are	1.
the 4	2.
ways . . . ?	3.
	—minor supporting detail
Key word	—minor supporting detail
	4.
Heading	Second Heading
Key word	1.
Importance	2. See diagram on page #
of XYZ	3.
chart?	4.
	—
What are	—
the 4 . . . ?	—

1. Copy the heading into the recall column directly across from the heading in your notes. Underline that heading.

2. Reread the notes that are under that heading.

3. Write a study question or a key word to define in the recall column directly across from the notes. Do not write the answers.

4. Be very brief so that you can challenge yourself and get immediate feedback.

Copy the Heading   Using headings in the recall column provides organization. To avoid having rambling, unorganized reduced notes, *place the heading directly across from the heading in your notes.* Make it stand out by underlining it.

Reread the Notes   Learning the information continues as you reread your notes. If your notes seem vague, incomplete, or nonsensical, go back to the book and add any necessary details.

Write Study Questions and Key Words to Define   Directly across from each important detail, write a *brief study question*. You do not need to use complete sentences; abbreviated forms, such as the following, work: *Why? How many kinds of . . . ? Name the 6 . . . . Related to* X *how?* Another option is to simply write *key words* that you will need to define or relate to other ideas.

Be Brief   You will be using this recall column for the next step of studying. It is important that the column not be cluttered with too much information. If you give yourself all the answers, you will end up reading the information and not challenging your memory. *Remember to be selective by focusing only on key words or study questions.* Do not give all the answers!

The following Cornell notes come from the Five Theories of Forgetting in Chapter 6 (pages 139–141). After you read the notes, notice the brief questions and key words that the notetaker used in the recall column.

	Five Forgetting Theories
Introduction	**Introduction**
	1. learning—complex set of operations requiring effort & activity
Forgetting occurs where?	2. forgetting—natural process
	3. forgetting theories—occur in working memory
	4. analyze what went wrong/what broke down when forget
Decay Theory	**Decay Theory**
	1. sensory stimuli too weak, ignored, not attended to within seconds
What happens to stimuli?	2. stimuli fades/decays
	3. learning never occurs
Strategies?	4. strategies
	• alert, ready, undivided attention
	• set learning goal/intention
	• think about/work with info/assoc. to familiar ideas
Displacement Theory	**Displacement Theory**
	1. too much info too rapidly
What happens in	2. working memory overloads/limited capacity
working memory?	3. info pushed out of way/displaced
	4. learning never occurs
Strategies?	5. strategies
	• slow down/read slowly—think
	• use spaced practice—not cramming or marathon studying
	• pause to consolidate/integrate info
	• conducive learning environment
	• free up working memory
Interference Theory	**Interference Theory**
	1. confusion between old and new information
What gets confused?	2. new info may differ from previously learned (old) info
	3. old may be recalled more easily than new
Why does it occur?	4. new may override recall of old
	5. strategies
Strategies?	• recognize similarities and differences; integrate the two
	• take a break (nap or other activity) between different topics
Incomplete Encoding	**Incomplete Encoding Theory**
	1. info only partially learned
Incomplete why?	2. learning interrupted, unfinished, divided attention (rehearsal)
	3. ineffective encoding methods or rote memory
Rote memory	4. strategies
	• elaborative rehearsal for clear encoding
Strategies	• avoid rote memory
	• self-quizzing and feedback strategies
	• maintain focus, undivided attention
Retrieval Failure Theory	**Retrieval Failure Theory**
	1. problems accessing and retrieving info back into working memory
What happens?	(going blank, info on the tip of your tongue)
	2. lack of sufficient memory cues or associations
Why does it happen?	3. info randomly filed in LTM—disorganized
	4. strategies
Strategies?	• create an association and practice it
	• classify/group ideas into meaningful chunks
	• ongoing review to activate info—keep it fresh in mind
	• get into *retrieval mode* = mental state where intend to recall—watch how you think—do memory search for up to one minute
	• reconstruct learning situation: how, when, where learned info

Cornell Step Three: Recite

The third step is to **recite** from the recall column. *Reciting involves speaking out loud and expressing ideas in your own words.* Reciting is a powerful tool for learning information and strengthening memory. If you are able to recite information accurately, you are learning. If you are not able to recite information accurately, you immediately know that more time and attention are needed. This immediate **feedback** is the strong benefit of this third step of Cornell.

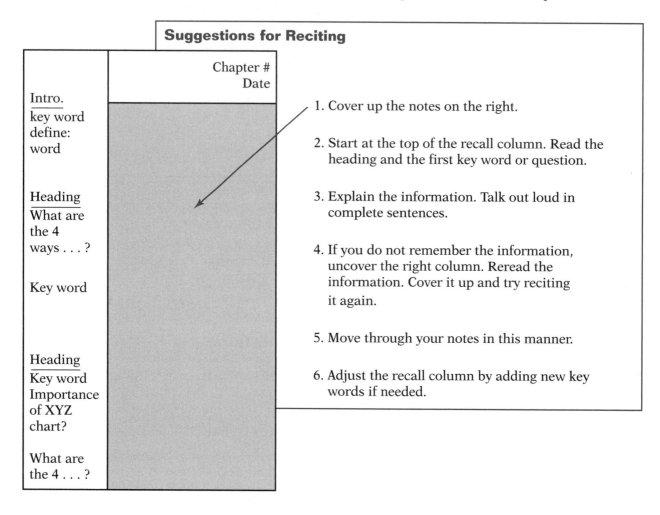

Suggestions for Reciting

Chapter #
Date

Intro.
<u>key word</u>
define:
word

Heading
<u>What are
the 4
ways . . . ?</u>

Key word

Heading
<u>Key word
Importance
of XYZ
chart?</u>

What are
the 4 . . . ?

1. Cover up the notes on the right.

2. Start at the top of the recall column. Read the heading and the first key word or question.

3. Explain the information. Talk out loud in complete sentences.

4. If you do not remember the information, uncover the right column. Reread the information. Cover it up and try reciting it again.

5. Move through your notes in this manner.

6. Adjust the recall column by adding new key words if needed.

Cover the Notes Use a blank piece of paper to cover the notes on the right side. Since you see only the recall column, you can now understand the importance of putting the headings in the recall column to help you remember the overall organization.

Read and Then Recite Read the headings and the key words or questions. Without looking at your notes, answer the questions and tell what you remember about the key words. Use **self-explaining**; pretend you are explaining the information to a friend. *Talk out loud in complete sentences.*

- If you can verbalize the information accurately, you probably understand it.
- If you "go blank," that is valuable feedback that you are not yet ready to move on. Simply pull the paper down, read the information, cover it up, and try again. Reciting after you reread enables your memory to begin processing the correct information.

■ To check the accuracy of the information recited, pull the paper down to check. The positive feedback you receive for correct answers will strengthen your memory and provide motivation.

Continue Reciting   Move through your entire set of notes by reciting, checking accuracy, and reciting again. Remember to take full advantage of this system by using the feedback to look at your notes and recite again.

Adjust the Recall Column   Sometimes it is difficult to know how much and what kind of information to put in the recall column.

■ If you found that you did not give yourself enough cues to recite important points, add more key words or study questions to the recall column.

■ If you found that you wrote all the important information in the recall column and you ended up reading what was there, you had nothing left to recite from memory. Cross out (or white out) some of the details before you recite again.

■ Star the information you did not recall the first time. Pay extra attention to these areas the next time you recite.

 EXERCISE 9.2   Reciting with a Partner
Review the Five Theories of Forgetting *in Chapter 6 (pages 139–141). Then review the notes for the forgetting theories (page 237). Cover up the notes so you only see the recall column. Take turns reciting and explaining the information in the recall column. If the person reciting is not able to recall the information, he or she may pull the paper down, review briefly, cover up the notes, and try reciting again.*

Cornell Step Four: Reflect

To **reflect** means to "think or consider seriously." The reflect step can be individualized and can include a wide variety of activities and study tools. The following are several suggestions for reflect activities.

> **Suggestions for Reflecting**
> 1. Take time to think about the information in your notes.
> 2. Line up your recall columns to see the overall structure of the chapter.
> 3. Write your own summary at the bottom of your notes.
> 4. Use the back side of your notepaper to make lists of information or questions.
> 5. Make study tools such as index cards, visual mappings, or pictures for later reviews.
> 6. For math, make a three-column reflect page for key words, steps for problem solving, or formulas.

Take Time to Think   Reflecting lets the information register and settle in your brain. It also allows you to look at the information from your own perspective and experiences, look for connections or relationships among ideas, and think of ways to extend the information beyond its original context.

Line Up the Recall Columns   To gain an overview of the entire chapter, remove your notepaper from your notebook. Arrange your notes on a table so that you can see all the recall columns lined up in sequence from left to right. By looking at the headings and the details, you will see the entire outline for the chapter. If you enjoy studying from outlines, you could convert this information into outline form to use for review.

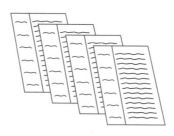

Write a Summary   Look only at the information in the recall columns. Write a summary that explains the important points. Include the main ideas and brief statements of major supporting details. Your summary should be written in full sentences and paragraphs. Save this summary because it is a good review tool to use before tests.

Write on the Back Side of Your Notepaper   The back of your notepaper is now available for you to make additional lists of information or reminders. You can also include diagrams or charts to show how different ideas are related. If you have questions that you would like to ask the instructor, jot them down on the back as well. The backs are convenient and available, so use them as needed.

Make Your Own Study Tools for Later Review   The reflect step is a creative and highly individualized step. No two students will do the exact same activities in the reflect step. This is the time for you to decide *what will work best for you.* Consider the many different kinds of study tools you know how to make (or will be learning how to make). Select one or more that would help you learn the information more thoroughly as well as provide you with study tools to use as you review throughout the term. Here are just a few options:

- Make index cards of all the key vocabulary terms, lists of information, and study questions.

- For math, make a list of symbols and their equivalent English words or make a list of mathematical equations and their equivalent English sentences.

- Make a visual mapping, hierarchy, or outline of the chapter or parts of the chapter. As an option, write a summary of your work.

- Practice drawing or copying diagrams from the chapter.

- Add pictures, cartoons, or stick figures that can serve as memory triggers for parts of your notes later.

- Make study tapes that review the recall column or list the important points you want to remember.

- Use any of the study strategies described for each of the three learning styles (visual, auditory, kinesthetic).

How does taking notes in a math class differ from taking notes in a literature class?

Cornell Step Five: Review

This last step of the Cornell system keeps the information active in your memory. Review provides the repetition you need to retrieve information quickly and accurately from your long-term memory.

Do an Immediate Review   Reviewing actually begins during the reflect step, when you take time to think about the information and create additional study tools. However, **immediate review** goes one step further. Before you close your book and quit studying, take a few additional minutes to review your recall columns. This provides one final opportunity to strengthen your memory.

Ongoing Review   **Ongoing review** means continually practicing learned information. Ongoing review is necessary because you will be storing more and more information in your long-term memory as the term progresses, so you must make sure that you practice "old" information. In addition, by including ongoing reviews in your weekly study schedule, you save time in the long run. When tests, midterm exams, or final exams approach, you won't need to cram, for you will have kept the information active.

Several activities can take place during ongoing review:

- Review the recall columns of your notes. The more frequently you review these, the faster you can move through the columns. Also, as the term progresses, you will find that information placed in your notes early in the term is now clear and easy to understand.
- Review any reflect or review materials that you created earlier.
- If you have a list of questions from the second step of SQ4R or your own written summary, review these.
- Review chapter introductions, summaries, and lists of vocabulary terms for the chapter.

Now that the five *R*'s of the Cornell system have been discussed, take time to learn to use each of the steps. Remember, omitting any one step will weaken the system. The following pictures may help you learn and remember the steps more quickly.

1. Record   **2. Reduce**   **3. Recite**   **4. Reflect**   **5. Review**

✪ EXERCISE 9.3 Applying the Five *R*'s

*Read the excerpt on **Maslow's Hierarchy of Needs** on page 243. If you wish, highlight the important information in each paragraph.*

1. **Prepare:** Draw a two-and-one-half-inch margin down the left side of your notebook paper.

2. **Record:** Use the strategies presented in this chapter for taking notes in the right column. (See the Self-Assessment Form on page 245.)

3. **Reduce:** Reduce the notes in the left column. Write the heading and the key words or very brief study questions. Do not write too much information.

4. **Recite:** Cover up the right side of your notes. Practice reciting your notes out loud and in complete sentences. Check your accuracy.

5. **Reflect:** Do *one* of the following reflect activities:

   Option 1: THINK about the information and answer the following questions:

       a. Do you believe that people are "wanting beings" who seek to fulfill needs?
       b. Do you believe this is really how needs they want to fulfill are arranged?
       c. Could emphasis on the various needs occur in a different order?
       d. Do your needs fall into this sequence? How?

   Option 2: The article suggests ways the business world can meet the different levels of needs of their employees. Brainstorm how colleges and universities strive to meet the different levels of needs of students. Summarize your ideas in paragraph form.

   Option 3: If you were in marketing or sales, how could you advertise in different ways to meet different levels of need? What would advertisements look like for each of the five kinds of needs?

6. **Review:** Review your work so that you will be prepared to discuss this excerpt in class.

> ***Special Note:*** Make multiple copies of the Assessment Forms on pages 245 and 246 so that you will have forms available for various note-taking assignments.

EXERCISE 9.3 continued

Maslow's Hierarchy of Needs

The concept of a hierarchy of needs was advanced by Abraham Maslow, a psychologist. A **need** is a personal requirement. Maslow assumed that humans are "wanting" beings who seek to fulfill a variety of needs. He assumed that these needs can be arranged according to their importance in a sequence known as **Maslow's hierarchy of needs**.

At the most basic level are **physiological needs**, the things we require to survive. These needs include food and water, clothing, shelter, and sleep. In the employment context, these needs are usually satisfied through adequate wages.

At the next level are **safety needs**, the things we require for physical and emotional security. Safety needs may be satisfied through job security, health insurance, pension plans, and safe working conditions.

Next are the **social needs**, the human requirements for love and affection and a sense of belonging. To an extent, these needs can be satisfied through the work environment and the informal organization. But social relationships beyond the workplace—with family and friends, for example—are usually needed, too.

At the level of **esteem needs**, we require respect and recognition (the esteem of others), as well as a sense of our own accomplishment and worth (self-esteem). These needs may be satisfied through personal accomplishment, promotion to more responsible jobs, various honors and awards, and other forms of recognition.

At the uppermost level are **self-realization needs**, the needs to grow and develop as people and to become all that we are capable of being. These are the most difficult needs to satisfy, and the means of satisfying them tend to vary with the individual. For some people, learning a new skill, starting a new career after retirement, or becoming the "best there is" at some endeavor may be the way to satisfy the self-realization needs.

Maslow suggested that people work to satisfy their physiological needs first, then their safety needs, and so on up the "needs ladder." In general, they are motivated by the needs at the lowest (most important) level that remain unsatisfied. However, needs at one level do not have to be completely satisfied before needs at the next-higher level come into play. If the majority of a person's physiological and safety needs are satisfied, that person will be motivated primarily by social needs. But any physiological and safety needs that remain unsatisfied will also be important.

Maslow's hierarchy of needs provides a useful way of viewing employee motivation, as well as a guide for management. By and large, American business has been able to satisfy workers' basic needs, but the higher-order needs present more of a problem. They are not satisfied in a simple manner, and the means of satisfaction vary from one employee to another.

Self-realization needs

Esteem needs

Social needs

Safety needs

Physiological needs

Maslow's Hierarchy of Needs

Maslow believed that people seek to fulfill five categories of needs.

From Pride/Hughes/Kapoor, *Business*, 7/e, pp. 270–271. Copyright © 2002. Reprinted by permission of Houghton Mifflin, Inc.

Group Processing: **A Collaborative Learning Activity**

Form groups of three students. Complete the following directions.

1. Use six index cards or pieces of paper. Write the following on the cards:

   1. Record   2. Reduce   3. Recite

   4. Reflect   5. Review   6. Five *R*'s of Cornell

2. Shuffle the cards and place them face down. Each student draws two cards.

3. The person with card 1 begins by telling everything he or she knows about *Record* (in the Cornell system). Continue with students reciting the cards according to the order above. After a student recites what he or she remembers about the category on the card, other group members may add additional information.

EXERCISE 9.4   **Taking Cornell Notes**

Take a complete set of Cornell notes, including a recall column. Follow your instructor's directions for doing one of the following options.

1. Take notes on a specific excerpt identified by your instructor from any chapter in this textbook.

2. Take notes on the information that appears under *one major heading* of any textbook that you are using this term. If the information under one major heading is less than two pages long, take notes on information under more than one heading. Take notes until you reach the end of that section in the chapter. Your instructor may ask to meet with you to compare your notes to the textbook pages.

EXERCISE 9.5   **Application**

Take notes on the Health, Stress, and Coping *chapter in Appendix D. Be selective. Develop the recall column for your notes. Practice reciting from the recall column. Your instructor may ask you to compare your notes with another student's notes.*

O N L I N E   P R A C T I C E   1

Visit the *Essential Study Skills*, Fifth Edition, website and go to Chapter 9. Click on **Practice 1: Using the Five *R*'s of Cornell**. Complete the ten-question interactive multiple-choice quiz. Upon completion of the quiz, you will receive your score. You can exit at that time, or you can print your results or e-mail them to your instructor.

O N L I N E   P R A C T I C E   2

Visit the *Essential Study Skills*, Fifth Edition, website and go to Chapter 9. Click on **Practice 2: Creating Cornell Notes**. Type responses to five questions. After you type your responses, you can print your responses or e-mail them to your instructor.

Cornell Notetaking Self-Assessment Form

Name _____   Date _____

Topic of Notes _____   Assignment _____

	YES	NO

Record Step

1. Did you clearly show headings in your notes so you can see the main topics?   _____ _____

2. Did you underline the headings and avoid putting numbers or letters in front of the headings?   _____ _____

3. Did you leave a space between headings or larger groups of information so that your notes are not cluttered or crowded?   _____ _____

4. Did you include sufficient details so that you do not need to return to the textbook to study this information?   _____ _____

5. Did you use numbering between the different details under the headings?   _____ _____

6. Did you indent and uses dashes or other symbols to show supporting details?   _____ _____

7. Did you use meaningful phrases or shortened or complete sentences so that the information will be clear at a later time?   _____ _____

8. Did you paraphrase or shorten the information so that your notes are not too lengthy?   _____ _____

9. Did your notes refer to important charts, diagrams, or visual materials in the chapter, or did you make reference to the textbook pages in your notes?   _____ _____

10. Did you write on only one side of the paper, leaving the back side blank?   _____ _____

11. Did you label the first page of your notes (course, chapter number, and date) and use page numbers on the other pages?   _____ _____

12. Did you write your notes so that they are neat and easy to read?   _____ _____

Recall Column (Reduce Step)

1. Did you move each heading into the recall column and underline it?   _____ _____

2. Did you use a two-and-one-half-inch margin on the left for the recall column?   _____ _____

3. Did you include study questions in the recall column for the key points in your notes?   _____ _____

4. Did you include enough information in the recall column to guide you when you recite your notes?   _____ _____

5. Did you include in the recall column some key words that you need to define or explain?   _____ _____

6. Did you write the questions and the key words directly across from the corresponding information in your notes column?   _____ _____

7. Did you avoid writing too much information or giving yourself all of the information in the recall column, thus leaving you with little to recite from memory?   _____ _____

8. Did you try using the recall column?   _____ _____

9. Did you add or delete information in the recall column after you tried using that column for reciting?   _____ _____

Cornell Notetaking Instructor Assessment Form

Name _____   Date _____   Notes for _____

Strengths of Your Notes

Your Notes Column

_____ You clearly showed and underlined the headings.

_____ Your notes will be easier to study because you left a space between new headings or sections of information.

_____ Your notes show accurate and sufficient details.

_____ You used meaningful phrases or shortened sentences effectively so that the information is clear and understandable.

_____ You shortened information effectively and captured the important ideas.

_____ Your notes are well organized. You effectively used numbering and indentations for supporting details.

_____ You included important visual graphics from the textbook.

_____ Your notes are neat and easy to read.

_____ You used notetaking standards effectively: you wrote on one side of the paper, you included a heading, and you numbered pages.

Your Recall Column

_____ You used a 2½-inch column.

_____ You placed your headings, questions, and key words directly across from the information in your notes.

_____ Your questions and key words are effective.

_____ Use the recall column to check its effectiveness. Add more self-quizzing questions, visual cues, or hints to guide reciting if necessary.

Areas for Improvement in Your Notes

_____ Strive to identify and underline headings.

_____ Leave a space before you begin a new heading or section of information so your notes will be less crowded or cluttered.

_____ Include more information in your notes. Your notes lack some important details.

_____ Short phrases or isolated words lose meaning over time. Use more sentences or more detailed phrases to capture important ideas.

_____ Use shortened sentences to capture the important ideas. Your notes are unnecessarily lengthy.

_____ Strive for clearer organization. Number and indent supporting details.

_____ Include graphic information in your notes.

_____ Strive for neater penmanship and readability.

_____ Write on one side of the paper. Include a heading on the first page. Number all the pages of your notes.

_____ Use a 2½-inch column on the left.

_____ Place the headings, questions, and key words directly across from the information in your notes.

_____ You need more meaningful questions and key words in the recall column.

_____ You are giving yourself too much information in the recall column; use questions without answers so that you will have more to recite.

_____ Use the recall column to check its effectiveness. Add more self-quizzing questions, visual cues, or hints to guide reciting if necessary.

Other Comments:

Photocopy this form before you use it.

Reflection Writing 2
Chapter 9

On separate paper, in a journal, or online at this textbook's website, respond to the following questions.

1. What do you see as the greatest benefits of learning to use the 5 *R*'s of Cornell?

2. What, if any, drawbacks do you see for using the Cornell system for taking textbook notes? Be specific.

Combining Cornell Notetaking and SQ4R

You have now learned two very powerful study methods for mastering learning: SQ4R (Chapter 7) and the Cornell system. The following chart shows how you can effectively combine these two methods.

Combining SQ4R and Cornell

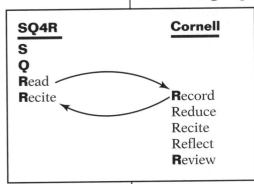

SQ4R	Cornell
S	
Q	
Read	**R**ecord
Recite	Reduce
	Recite
	Reflect
	Review

Begin the SQ4R Steps

1. **Survey:** Do an overview for the chapter.
2. **Question:** Write questions for each heading.
3. **Read:** Read one paragraph.
4. **Record:** Take Cornell notes on separate paper.
5. **Recite:** Recite the important information in the paragraph.
6. Continue to read-recite-record to the end of the chapter.

Continue the Cornell Steps

7. **Reduce:** Make your recall column.
8. **Recite:** Cover your notes and recite from your recall column.
9. **Reflect:** Do one or more reflect activities.
10. **Review:** Review your notes and complete the chapter and the questions you made in the second step of SQ4R.

Note that you begin with the first three steps of SQ4R: survey, question, and read. The Cornell system then merges with the reading system for the record step. (Record is step four of SQ4R and step one of Cornell.)

Once you have completed the reading and have taken the notes, put the book aside. Focus your attention on your Cornell notes and the remaining steps of Cornell: reduce, recite, reflect, and review. Join the review steps in SQ4R with the review step in Cornell. You have now successfully combined two powerful systems for learning.

O N L I N E   P R A C T I C E   3

Visit the *Essential Study Skills*, Fifth Edition, website and go to Chapter 9. Click on **Practice 3: Combining Cornell Notetaking and SQ4R**. Type responses for four questions. After you type your responses, you can print your responses or e-mail them to your instructor.

The Index Card Notetaking System

By now you are aware that one goal of this textbook is to provide you with an array of study tools that meet your learning needs and learning style preferences. The Cornell notetaking system, a very linear, left-brain, systematic approach to taking textbook notes, is one notetaking option you can use for many of your textbooks. The **index card notetaking system**, which involves taking several kinds of notes on 3" × 5" or 5" × 7" index cards, is another option that may be better suited for some textbooks or for your learning style preferences. If you choose a different notetaking system as your primary system, you can create index card notes as a secondary system to use as an elaborative rehearsal or reflect activity. The index card notetaking system incorporates three types of cards to capture the main ideas and important details from your textbook chapters. The *Essential Strategies for Studying Index Card Notes* on page 251 provides you with options for studying from your comprehensive index card notes.

> ### Types of Index Cards for Notetaking
>
> 1. **Question cards** pose study questions for information that you are expected to learn.
> 2. **Definition cards** show key terms (terminology) and their definitions.
> 3. **Category cards** list related items under a specific category or topic.

Question Cards

In the SQ4R reading system, you create main idea questions for the headings and the subheadings in the textbook. In the Cornell notetaking system, you create questions in the recall column of your notes. The kinds of questions you write in SQ4R and in the Cornell recall column, questions that relate directly to the printed information as it is presented by the author, can be used to create **question cards**. Question cards can also include broader questions that involve higher-level reading and thinking skills and questions that explore relationships among concepts, events, or details. The following questions can help you identify information to use for your question cards.

How can I convert this heading or subheading into a study question?

What am I expected to know about the information in this section of the textbook?

What question might appear on a test about this information that I am reading?

What relationships (such as cause-effect, trends, or comparisons-contrasts) are important to know?

What's the author's purpose (or theme) in the short story . . . ?

What events lead up to . . . (a war, a character's situation, an economic situation)?

Once you have identified an important question for your index cards, write the question on the front of the card. On the back of the card, write the correct answer. The answer may be in an abbreviated form or in complete sentences. Continue developing question cards as you read through the chapter. To help with the organization of your index card notes, write the chapter number on the top of each card or use different colors of index cards for different chapters. The following are examples of question cards for information that appears in the psychology chapter in Appendix D.

Front: The Question

> Ch. 10
>
> **Why are some people more strongly affected by stressors than other people?**

Back: The Answer

> Mediating factors affect how people react to stressors. People who have the ability to predict and control stressors, have positive attitudes toward stressors, have social support systems, and have stress-coping skills will react less to stressors than people without these qualities or skills.

Front: The Question

> Ch. 10
>
> **What causes the general pattern known as the** *fight-or-flight syndrome?*

Back: The Answer

> A frightening or dangerous situation causes the *fight-or-flight syndrome* (a physical response that prepares the body to fight or flee the situation). Rapid heartbeat, rapid breathing, sweating, and possibly shakiness occur.

Definition Cards

Understanding and being able to define and explain key words or terminology in any textbook are essential components of comprehension. For this reason, most textbooks use special features to draw your attention to the course-specific terminology. In some textbooks, a list of terms to know appear at the beginning or the end of each chapter. Special print, such as boldface or colored print, often appear in context, accompanied by a formal definition within the sentence or the surrounding sentences. Some textbooks use marginal notes to highlight and define key words. You can use these special features in textbooks by transferring the information to **definition cards**.

To create definition cards, write one term on the front of the card. Include the chapter number on the top of the card. On the back of the card, write the definition and any additional explanations or examples that will help you remember and recall the term. The following are examples of definition cards for various courses.

Front: The Key Word or Term

Ch. 3

Define   ∈

Define   ∉

Back: The Definition

∈ means the element belongs to a set

Example: 4∈A   (4 belongs to set A)

∉ means the element does not belong to a set

Example: 4∉A   (4 does not belong to set A)

Front: The Key Word or Term

Ch. 4

relative pronoun

Back: The Definition

A relative pronoun replaces or refers to a preceding noun in the independent clause.

Example: Lisa, *who* lives in Tucson, breeds dogs.

Relative Pronouns: who, whom, whose,
which, that

Category Cards

Category cards provide you with a study tool to review lists of information. The category is the topic; the items on the list may be steps to complete a process or to apply a formula or details that belong to the given category. To make category cards, place a category or topic on the front. Include the chapter number on the top of the card. On the back, list the individual items without definitions or explanations; items that need to be defined should also appear individually on definition cards. (On the inside back cover of this textbook, you will find many topics that you could include with lists of information on category cards.) The following example is a category card for a math textbook.

Front: The Category

Ch. 1

Three ways to define *sets*

Back: The List

1. Verbal description of the set

2. Roster method listing the elements
   of the set

3. Set-building notation

SET LEARNING GOALS

The following *Essential Strategies for Studying Index Card Notes* chart highlights seven important strategies to use to study from index card notes. Place a star next to the strategies that you already use. Highlight the strategies that you plan to make a conscious effort to begin using to study from your index card notes.

Essential Strategies for Studying Index Card Notes

▶ **Carry your index study cards with you.** Index note cards are portable and convenient to use. Use them to self-quiz between classes, while waiting for transportation or for other events to occur, or any time when you have a few spare minutes.

▶ **Use the cards for quizzing.** You can self-quiz with these cards and receive feedback about the accuracy of your answers. You can practice explaining information clearly by asking friends or family members to use your cards to quiz you.

▶ **Use them as a warm-up activity at the beginning of a study block.** Working with your cards before you begin a new assignment puts you in the mindset for the subject, activates previously learned information, and focuses your mind on studying.

▶ **Study from the front side of your cards.** First, read the front side of a card. Recite an answer to a question, a definition for a term, or the list of items under the specific category without looking at the back of the card. Then turn the card over to receive immediate *feedback* about the accuracy and completeness of your explanations.

▶ **Study from the back side of your cards.** Reversing the previous process by studying from the back side of a card challenges your memory

in new ways and prepares you for test questions that focus on explaining main ideas, recalling terminology, and identifying main categories of information. Read the information on the back. Without turning the card over, state the question, say and spell the key word (term), or name the category that is on the front side. Then turn the card over for immediate feedback about the accuracy of your answer.

▶ **Sort the cards into two piles: the ones you know and the ones you need to study further.** Set aside the pile that contains the cards that you can explain accurately and with confidence. Focus your attention on the pile of cards that you need to study further.

▶ **Create reflect activities with your note cards.** You can use your cards in creative ways for elaborative rehearsal. First, shuffle all your cards together. Begin sorting them by *categories* of information. For example, categories for cards developed for this textbook may include *learning styles, concentration, memory principles, reading strategies,* and so on. Sorting into categories provides practice grouping or reorganizing related items. Second, on a table, spread out all the cards that have been sorted into one of the categories. Make a verbal or written summary that includes information from all of the cards.

CLASS DISCUSSION

Question: How can the *paired associations* used with index cards boost your ability to recall information at a later time?

EXERCISE 9.6   Creating Index Card Notes

Work with a partner or by yourself to create a comprehensive set of index card notes for Chronemics *in Exercise 9.1, pages 234–235. Your set of index card notes should include question, definition, and category cards that cover the important concepts and details discussed in this excerpt.*

 EXERCISE 9.7   Partner Brainstorming

In the following diagram, there are six piles of cards that have been stacked into individual categories of information for topics covered in this textbook. With a partner, brainstorm two question cards, two definition cards, and two category cards that could belong to each pile of cards.

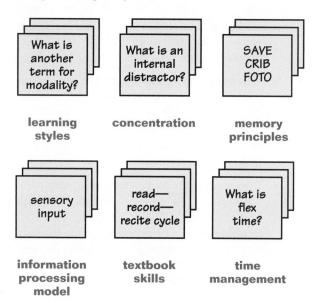

What is another term for modality?	What is an internal distractor?	SAVE CRIB FOTO
learning styles	**concentration**	**memory principles**
sensory input	read— record— recite cycle	What is flex time?
information processing model	**textbook skills**	**time management**

In what ways are index cards more flexible to use for note-taking than marginal notes? When would index cards not be the best option to use for notetaking?

O N L I N E   P R A C T I C E   4

> Visit the *Essential Study Skills*, Fifth Edition, website and go to Chapter 9. Click on **Practice 4: Using Index Card Notes**. Complete the ten-question interactive multiple-choice quiz. Upon completion of the quiz, you will receive your score. You can exit at that time, or you can print your results or e-mail them to your instructor.

The Two-Column and Three-Column Notetaking System

Two-column notes are a modification of Cornell notes. In the left column, place terms to know, key questions to answer, formulas, steps, equations to apply to problem solving, or categories of information. In the right column, place the definitions, answers, examples of problems, or lists of items to remember. You can add items to your two-column notes in any order as the need arises; you do not need to use the formal structure of headings. The following are examples of two-column notes.

Forgetting Theories

Decay Theory	A forgetting theory that occurs in STM; stimuli too weak to process the information
Displacement Theory	A forgetting theory that occurs in STM; too much information comes in too quickly, so some information is shoved aside (displaced)
Forgetting Theories	1. Decay 2. Displacement 3. Interference 4. Incomplete Encoding 5. Retrieval Failure

Sets

Capital letters A, B, C	Used to label sets in math
Lowercase letters a, b, c	Used to label elements of a set
{ }	Show elements in a set $A = \{1, 2, 3, 4\}$

Multiplying Negative and Positive Numbers

When both numbers are positive	Answer is positive Example: $4 \times 9 = 36$
When both numbers are negative	Answer is positive Example: $-20 \div -5 = 4$
When one number is positive and the other is negative	Answer is negative Example: $(-3) \times 4 = -12$

As you learned in Chapter 8, an important reading skill for reading math textbooks involves translating math symbols and math equations into English words. You can use the *two-column notetaking system* to create an ongoing glossary of English words for math symbols and equations. The following are two examples of using two-column notes for these purposes.

Translating English Terms into Algebraic Symbols	
sum	+
add	+
less than	−
subtract	−
times	×
percent of	×
per	/
divide	/
quotient	/

Translating English Words into Algebraic Expressions	
ten more than x	$x + 10$
a number added to 5	$5 + x$
a number increased by 13	$x + 13$
5 less than 10	$10 - 5$
a number decreased by 7	$x - 7$
difference between x and 3	$x - 3$
difference between 3 and x	$3 - x$

Adapted from Paul Nolting, *Math Study Skills Workbook* (Boston: Houghton Mifflin Co., 2000), p. 67. Copyright © 2000. Reprinted by permission of Houghton Mifflin, Inc.

Three-column notes, which can be used creatively for many purposes, work effectively in notetaking situations in which you want to include two kinds of information for a specific topic or subject. For *comparative reading* (comparing information from more than one source), you can use three-column notes to place side by side the information you gathered from two different sources. The following examples show other uses for three-column notes.

Topic/Concept	Textbook	Instructor/Lecture
product life cycle	1. Introduction 2. Growth 3. Maturity 4. Decline	Class example: 3M (Post-it Notes) Sony digital cameras

Topic/Concept	Definition or explanation	Applications—when, where, how to use
infomercial	A form of television advertisement that appears as a 15–30-minute program	Often used with exercise equipment and videos (ex. Tae-Bo), weightloss programs, cosmetics, and "get rich quick" programs

Fold this column back until you rework the problem.

Original math problem	Space to rework the problem	Original solution from textbook or class
Leave the answer in exponential form: $4^5 \times 4^7$		$4^5 \times 4^7 = 4^{5+7} = 4^{12}$

Key Words	Examples	Explanations/Rules
$-n$	$-n$ If $n = s$, Then $-n = -s$ $-(-10) = 10$ $-(-15)(-15) = -15$ Opposite of $-x$ is x	Opposite of any number Count the number of signs; even means +, odd means −

Rational	Rational numbers are
	  fractions (¼, ½, ¾).
		A/B, $B/0$ is rational
		  Division by 0 undefined

Numerator Denominator	numerator/denominator N/D	Numerator on top Denominator on bottom (D = Down)

Adapted from Nolting, *Math Study Skills Workbook*, pp. 50–51.

Just as the uses for three-column notes vary, so do the study methods that you can use to rehearse and study the information in your notes. *Recitation*, a powerful study and review activity that provides you with immediate feedback, works well for most three-column notes. Begin by covering the middle or the right-hand column with a strip of paper. Recite the information that belongs in that column. Then remove the paper to check the accuracy and completeness of your recitation. Continue to study from your three-column notes by covering the remaining columns, reciting the information that is covered, and then checking the accuracy of your explanations.

 EXERCISE 9.8 Group Discussion

Discuss answers to the following questions. Be prepared to share your answers with the class.

1. How are different levels of information used in the index card notetaking system?

2. If your math textbook contains equations, steps to problem-solve, and numerous math problems to be solved, what notetaking system or combination of systems would work effectively to take notes for this type of textbook? Be specific.

3. Which notetaking system would work most effectively for a literature class in which you analyze a short story in terms of its purpose, theme, setting, characters, and plot?

O N L I N E   P R A C T I C E   5

 Visit the *Essential Study Skills*, Fifth Edition, website and go to Chapter 9. Click on **Practice 5: Two-Column and Three-Column Notes**. Type responses to the four questions. After you type your responses, you can print your responses or e-mail them to your instructor.

The Formal Outline Notetaking System

You may already be familiar with formal outlines because many composition instructors require you to include formal outlines with your essays or papers. **Formal outlines** are highly structured, logically organized, detailed notes that show levels of information and relationships among concepts and ideas. Formal outlines provide a *skeleton* or an overview of the basic structure of printed materials, or in this case, of a complete chapter. Some textbooks include chapter outlines as a study tool feature. You can use outlines in the following ways:

■ Create a basic outline of a chapter *before* reading the chapter. By making a basic outline using only the chapter headings and subheadings, you can grasp the big picture or the overall structure of a new chapter.

■ Create a formal outline as you read a new chapter. Use outlining as your main notetaking system.

■ Create a formal outline of a chapter *after* you read the chapter. Outlining a chapter is one form of *elaborative rehearsal,* or one way to reflect on the chapter.

■ Use formal outlining as a lecture notetaking method if you are comfortable with the outlining format and are quickly able to organize information presented by a speaker.

A Formal Outline Structure

In formal outlines you arrange the information in the order in which it is presented. By using *Roman numerals*, capital letters, *Arabic numerals*, lowercase letters, and numerals inside parentheses, you can show the relationship of the larger concepts to the smaller details. Different levels of information appear in the following standard format.

Title:
I.   Main headings or topics appear with Roman numerals.
   A.   Subtopics appear with capital letters.
   B.   Subtopic
      1.   Arabic numerals show important supporting points or details.
      2.   Supporting detail
         a.   Lowercase letters show minor details.
         b.   Minor detail
            (1)   Arabic numerals inside parentheses show subideas of minor details.
            (2)   Subideas of minor details
   C.   Subtopic

The Standard Format to Use

The following points are important to use when you create a formal outline using the standard format:

- *Alignment:* When you indent to show a subtopic of a larger category, place the new letter or the new number directly under the first word that appears above in the larger category.

- *Two or More Subtopics:* Each level of the formal outline must have *at least two subtopics* under each category. If you do not have two items [A, B; 1, 2; a, b; or (1), (2)], try renaming the larger category so you do not end up with only one item under that category. For example, notice how the incorrect form on the left is reworded on the right.

Incorrect	**Correct**
1. Tax benefits a. Individuals	1. Tax benefits for individuals

- *Roman Numerals:* **Roman numerals** are used for main topics. Roman numerals from one to fifteen are written as follows: I, II, III, IV, V, VI, VII, VIII, IX, X, XI, XII, XIII, XIV, and XV.

- *Arabic Numerals:* **Arabic numerals** (1, 2, 3, 4 . . .) are used for supporting details.

- *Wording:* Most outlines consist of key words and short phrases; full sentences are seldom used.

Creating Outlines for Textbook Chapters

Most textbooks provide you with the main headings and the subheadings, so items for the Roman numerals and capital letters are easy to identify and incorporate into a formal outline. More careful thought must be given to the supporting details, the information in your outline that appears with lowercase letters and numerals inside parentheses. Use the following steps to create a formal outline from a textbook chapter.

How to Create Outlines for Textbook Chapters

1. Write the chapter number and title on the top of your paper.
2. Locate the first main heading in your textbook. Label it with a Roman numeral.
3. Locate all the subheadings for your main heading. Label them with capital letters.
4. Use numerals and lowercase letters for supporting details under each subheading.
5. Use numerals inside parentheses for smaller details if needed.

The following is the beginning of a formal outline for the psychology chapter in Appendix D. Notice how this beginning outline provides you with a quick overview of the main ideas (headings), subheadings, and key points. This formal outline uses three levels of information. Level one (Roman numerals) represents the main headings or titles that are placed inside boxes at the beginning of a new section of information. Level two (capital letters) represents the subheadings that appear in larger print on lines by themselves before the paragraph text begins. Level three (minor subheadings) appears in italic print at the beginning of a paragraph. As you examine the following outline, refer to the psychology chapter in Appendix D.

Chapter 10—Health, Stress, and Coping

I. Health Psychology
II. Understanding Stress
    A. Stressors
        1. Psychological Stressors
        2. Measuring Stressors
    B. Stress Responses
        1. Physical Stress Responses: The GAS
        2. Emotional Stress Responses
        3. Cognitive Stress Responses
        4. Behavioral Stress Responses
    C. Linkages: Stress and Psychological Disorders

How to Study from Formal Outlines

Outlines provide an excellent study tool to practice reciting and to give you immediate feedback about your level of understanding and recall of textbook information. Use the following strategies to study from your outlines.

How to Study from Formal Outlines

1. Read one line or item at a time; explain the line or item by reciting.
2. Check your accuracy or completeness.
3. Add clue words to the right of the lines or items.
4. Repeat the process of reciting from the outline.
5. Use the outline to write a summary.

Read and Explain   Begin with the first Roman numeral on your outline. Read the information on that line of the outline. Recite what you know about the topic. Speak in complete sentences; imagine you are explaining the information to someone who is unfamiliar with the topic. Move to the next line of information. Recite what you know; strive to integrate and link ideas together and explain relationships.

Check Your Accuracy or Completeness   As you recite, you will quickly become aware of your level of comfort and familiarity with the topic. Listen to what you say when you recite. If some information does not sound accurate or complete, use this feedback wisely. Refer to your textbook to check your accuracy or to see what kinds of information you did not include in your reciting.

Add Clue Words   You can break away from the formal structure of the outline at this point by jotting down key words or details that you did not initially include in your reciting. These clue words can guide you through the reciting process the next time you use your outline to review the contents of the chapter. You may want to write your clue words in a different color so that they stand out more readily. The following example shows clue words that a student added because of feedback he received during the initial attempt to recite from his outline.

B. Stress Responses

    1. Physical Stress Responses: The GAS *general adaptation syndrome*   — alarm, resistance, exhaustion

    2. Emotional Stress Responses   — fear, anger; diminish, persist, severe

    3. Cognitive Stress Responses   —ruminative thinking; catastrophizing

    4. Behavioral Stress Responses

Repeat the Process of Reciting   Reciting frequently from your outline activates your working memory and assists the process of moving information in and out of your long-term memory. Reciting frequently also provides you with practice explaining, categorizing, and showing relationships.

Write a Summary   Many students learn and remember information more readily when they use their own words to explain and connect information in a logically sequenced manner and when they express themselves in writing. You can use the levels of information in a formal outline to organize and to write a summary. In your summary, briefly discuss or explain each main idea with a brief mention of the most important supporting details in the order in which they appear in the outline. You do not need to include minor details in a summary. A written summary, which is very similar to the summary that you create when you recite from an outline, provides you with practice expressing information in writing and provides you with a study tool to prepare for upcoming tests.

EXERCISE 9.9 Completing the Formal Outline

On your own paper, copy the beginning of the formal outline for the Appendix D chapter (page A-17). Complete an outline for the entire chapter. Use three levels of information: Roman numerals, capital letters, and Arabic numerals (numbers.) If you encounter any difficulties, write them down so that they can be discussed in class.

EXERCISE 9.10 Textbook Case Studies

Read each of the following student situations carefully. Then, on your own paper and in complete sentences, answer the question that follows each case study. You can also answer these questions online at this textbook's Chapter 9 website. You can print your online responses or e-mail them to your instructor.

1. Labrishun learns by writing information and studying from information that she has handwritten. Initially, she thought the Cornell notetaking system would be perfect for her to use with her math textbook. However, after she had taken notes on two different chapters, she noticed that her notes were longer than the textbook chapters and that her hand was getting too tired copying everything from the textbook into her notes. What other notetaking options should Labrishun consider using?

2. With Cornell notes, Joey has learned to condense information effectively into the right column. In his recall column, Joey makes lists of important information, writes definitions for key terms, and writes study questions with their answers. He reads all the information out loud. A tutor suggested to Joey that he practice reciting the information instead of simply reading the recall column. Joey realizes that he does not know the difference between reading out loud and reciting. How would you explain the differences to Joey?

3. In Damon's opinion, his "short-cut method" for taking textbook notes for his biology class results in neat and logically structured notes. He writes the headings and underlines them. He lists the subheadings that appear under each heading. His formal outline shows only two levels of information: headings and subheadings. Damon's instructor announces that the majority of the upcoming midterm will focus on terminology and definitions. Damon realizes that the method of notetaking he has used all term is ineffective. What study tools should Damon create to better prepare for the midterm exam?

ONLINE CASE STUDIES

Visit the *Essential Study Skills*, Fifth Edition, website and go to Chapter 9. Click on **Online Case Studies**. In the text boxes, respond to four additional case studies that are only available online. You can print your online responses or e-mail them to your instructor.

 EXERCISE 9.11 LINKS

Work in a group or with a partner to complete the following chart. The top of the columns are labeled with the letters that represent the Twelve Principles of Memory. The rows show four notetaking options. After discussion, check the boxes to show which principles of memory are used in each of the notetaking systems. Be prepared to explain your answers.

	S	A	V	E	C	R	I	B	F	O	T	O
Cornell System												
Index Card System												
2 and 3-Column Notes												
Formal Outlines												

Reflection Writing 3
Chapter 9

On separate paper, in a journal, or online at this textbook's website, respond to the following questions.

1. Which notetaking system do you find the easiest to use? Explain.

2. Which notetaking system works best for each of your textbooks? Make a list of all the classes you are enrolled in this term. After carefully examining the textbooks for each class, state which notetaking system works best for each textbook and briefly explain why that system is the best choice to use.

SUMMARY

- Effective notetaking is an essential skill for college students. Learning how to use a variety of notetaking systems and then selecting the most effective system for specific textbooks enables you to capture important information from textbook chapters. Comprehensive notes you take on textbook chapters provide you with valuable study tools for ongoing review and test preparation.

- The Cornell system is a five-step notetaking system: *record, reduce, recite, reflect,* and *review.* Begin by taking notes in the right column. After you finish recording notes in the right column, create the left column (the *recall column*) by writing headings, key words and questions. Use the recall column to recite. The reflect step involves selecting one or more activities to work with the information in new ways. The review step promotes ongoing review.

- The Cornell system can easily be incorporated into the SQ4R reading system; thus, two powerful study systems are combined to increase your learning potential.

- The index card notetaking system involves using the fronts and the backs of index cards to create question, definition, and category cards. You may use index card notes as a primary notetaking system or as a reflect activity for both the SQ4R reading system and the Cornell system.

- Two-column and three-column notes, less formal than Cornell notes, provide ways to show different kinds of information for one or more subjects. Three-column notes work effectively for comparative reading, integrating textbook and lecture materials, math equations or terminology, and problem-solving solutions.

- Formal outlines are highly structured notes that reflect levels of information within a chapter. Chapter headings and subheadings provide the skeleton or first two levels of information of a chapter. A standard format for outlines involves use of Roman numerals, capital letters, Arabic numerals, and lowercase letters.

- Cornell notes, index card notes, two- and three-column notes, and outlines are textbook notetaking options that you can use to take effective notes on any of your textbooks.

CULMINATING OPTIONS FOR CHAPTER 9

1. Visit this textbook's website and go to Chapter 9 to complete the following exercises.
   a. Flash card review of Chapter 9 terms and definitions
   b. ACE Practice Test 1 with ten fill-in-the-blank questions
   c. ACE Practice Test 2 with ten true-false questions
   d. ACE Practice Test 3 with ten multiple-choice questions
   e. ACE Practice Test 4 with three short-answer–critical thinking questions

2. Go to Appendix C in the back of this textbook for more Learning Options to use for additional practice, enrichment, or portfolio projects.

Chapter 9 REVIEW QUESTIONS

True-False

Carefully read the following statements. Pay attention to key words. Write T *if the statement is true and* F *if the statement is false.*

_____ 1. The majority of your review time should be spent working with your notes.

_____ 2. All notetaking forms are a reduced version of textbook information.

_____ 3. It is always best to read the whole chapter first and then go back to take notes.

_____ 4. It is not necessary to take notes on graphs, charts, or pictures because they are always easy to remember.

_____ 5. When you integrate the Cornell system and the SQ4R reading system, you begin taking notes during the second step of SQ4R.

_____ 6. Too much information in the Cornell recall column causes you to read and not do much reciting.

_____ 7. You can add more questions or key words to the Cornell recall column if there are too few cues to help you recite.

_____ 8. If you are short on time, it is always best to skip the fourth step of Cornell.

_____ 9. Ongoing review gets you in the habit of using repetition as a regular part of studying.

_____ 10. In formal outlining, the following labels appear in their proper order of importance: I, A, a, 1, 1), and a).

Application

Select one form of notetaking to take a complete set of notes on the following information from a human relations textbook. Organize your notes neatly and logically.

Achieving Emotional Balance

An **emotion** can be thought of as a feeling, such as jealousy, fear, love, joy, and sorrow, that influences our thinking and behavior. It is not an exaggeration to say that much of the human behavior we observe every day springs from feelings. An emotional experience often alters thought processes by directing attention toward some things and away from others.

Throughout each day our feelings are activated by a variety of events (see Figure 8.3). You might feel a sense of joy after learning that a coworker has just given birth to a new baby. Angry feelings may surface when you discover that someone borrowed a tool without your permission. Once your feelings have been activated, your mind interprets the event. In some cases, the feelings trigger irrational thinking: "No one who works here can be trusted!" In other cases, you may engage in a rational thinking process: "Perhaps the person who borrowed the tool needed it to help a customer with an emergency repair." The important point to remember is that we can choose how we behave.

Figure 8.3

Achieving Emotional Balance—A Daily Challenge

The need to discover ways to achieve emotional balance has never been greater. To be successful in these complex times, we need to be able to think and feel simultaneously. People make choices dictated primarily by either their heads (reason) or their hearts (feelings). The thinking function helps us see issues logically; the feeling function helps us be caring and human. Many organizations are spawning fear, confusion, anger, and sadness because the leaders lack emotional balance.

The basic emotions that drive us—such as fear, love, greed, joy, and anger—have scarcely changed over the years. However, we are now seeing enormous differences in the expression of emotions. Today, people are much more likely to engage in aggressive driving, misbehave during commercial airline flights, or become abusive when they are unhappy with service. In the workplace many people experience emotional pain because of disagreeable bosses.

Emotional Intelligence

Daniel Goleman, author of two popular books on emotional intelligence, challenges the traditional view of the relationship between IQ and success. He says there are widespread exceptions to the rule that IQ predicts success: "At best, IQ contributes about 20 percent to the factors that determine life success, which leaves 80 percent to other forces. The focus of Goleman's research is the human characteristics that make up what he describes as *emotional competence*. The emotional competence framework is made up of two dimensions.

Personal Competence This term refers to the competencies that determine how we manage ourselves. Recognizing one's emotions and their effects, keeping disruptive emotions and impulses in check, and maintaining standards of honesty and integrity represent a few of the competencies in this category.

Social Competence This refers to the competencies that determine how we handle relationships. Sensing others' feelings and perspectives, listening openly and sending convincing messages, and negotiating and resolving disagreements represent some of the competencies in this category.

Although IQ tends to be stable throughout life, emotional competence is learnable and tends to increase throughout our life span. The emotional competencies that really matter for work can be learned.

From Reece and Brandt, *Human Relations: Principles & Practices*, 5/e (Boston: Houghton Mifflin Co., 2003), pp. 200–202. Copyright © 2003. Reprinted by permission of Houghton Mifflin, Inc.

CHAPTER 10

Listening and Taking Lecture Notes

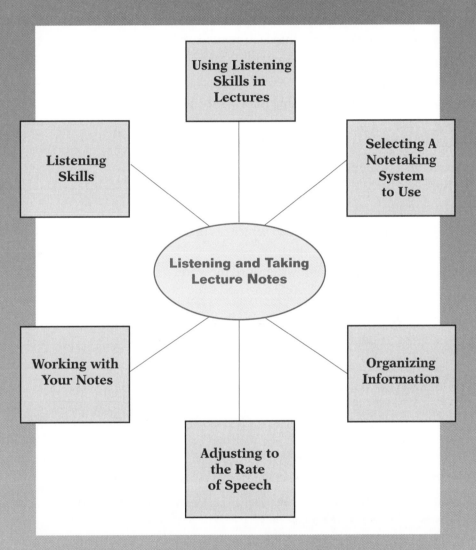

Understanding factors that affect listening and the steps involved in active listening can help you learn to use effective listening strategies. This chapter introduces you to four kinds of listening and strategies for strengthening your listening skills. Strong listening skills are essential for taking effective lecture notes. After learning five kinds of notetaking systems for lectures, you can select the most appropriate system for specific lectures. Notetaking techniques for organizing and recording lecture notes help you keep up with the lecturer's rate of speech, capture important main ideas and supporting details, and produce accurate notes that you can use for studying and ongoing review.

Chapter 10 Lecture Notes Profile

ANSWER, SCORE, and **RECORD** your profile before you read this chapter. If you need to review the process, refer to the complete directions given in the Profile for Chapter 1 on page 2.

ONLINE: You can complete the profile and get your score online at this textbook's website.

	YES	NO
1. I have problems knowing what information to put into lecture notes.	_____	_____
2. I stop taking notes when the speaker sidetracks from the topic, I lose interest in the topic, or I cannot keep up with the pace.	_____	_____
3. I spend time going over my notes and filling in missing information as soon after the lecture as possible.	_____	_____
4. The main ideas and important details are easy to identify in my notes.	_____	_____
5. Internal and external distractors often interfere with my ability to concentrate during a lecture.	_____	_____
6. I can usually take notes that are adequate and easy to use for studying.	_____	_____
7. I frequently use symbols, abbreviations, and shortened sentences in my lecture notes.	_____	_____
8. I reword (paraphrase) what is said so that I do not write word for word.	_____	_____
9. I practice reciting important information in my notes.	_____	_____
10. I am confident in my ability to take effective lecture notes in classes.	_____	_____

Reflection Writing 1
Chapter 10

On separate paper, in a journal, or online at this textbook's website, respond to the following questions.

1. What is your profile score for this chapter? What does it mean to you?

2. In what classes in which you are currently enrolled do you need to take lecture notes?

3. How comfortable and pleased are you with your ability to take effective notes in lecture-oriented classes? After you take lecture notes, how do you use them?

Listening Skills

Of the four verbal communication skills (listening, speaking, reading, and writing), listening skills are often the weakest. You may think that as long as you have ears that work, you can listen. If your auditory channels are functioning, you can *hear*, but that does not necessarily mean that you are *listening*. Listening requires more than taking in sounds and being aware that words are being spoken.

Listening involves understanding what you are hearing and having the ability to hold verbal stimuli in working memory long enough to attach meaning to the words and to interpret what the speaker is saying. Frequently, people incorrectly perceive *speaking* as an active process and *listening* as a passive process. The truth is that *listening is an active process that engages the listener in a variety of mental processes*.

Daly and Engleberg, in the textbook *Presentations in Everyday Life*, state that listening is what audiences are supposed to do when speakers talk. In fact, listening is our number-one communication activity. Although percentages vary from study to study, the following chart shows how most of us divide up our daily communication time.

How do effective speakers draw you in and captivate your attention?

Communication Activity	Percentages
Listening	40–70
Speaking	20–35
Reading	10–20
Writing	5–15

Source: Isa Engleberg and Dianna Wynn, *Working in Groups,* 2nd ed., p. 112. Copyright © 2000. Reprinted by permission of Houghton Mifflin Company.

"One study of college students found that listening occupies more than half of their communicating time. In the corporate world, executives may devote more than 60 percent of their workday listening to others.

"Yet, despite all of the time we spend listening, most of us aren't very good at it. For example, immediately after listening to a short talk, most of us cannot accurately report 50 percent of what was said. Without training, we listen at only 25 percent efficiency. And of that 25 percent, most of what we remember is distorted or inaccurate" (Daly and Engleberg, *Presentations in Everyday Life*, p. 28, © 2001).

Influencing Factors

The poor listening habits that many people have tend not to come from the training given in schools; instead, the poor listening habits often are learned because of the *lack* of training or instruction. A person may begin listening to a speaker with the complete intention of "staying tuned in," listening attentively, following the ideas, and making every effort to understand the information. However, good listening is similar to concentration: it's here one second and then it's gone. All of the following factors can influence your ability to be a good listener.

Factors That Influence Your Ability to Listen Effectively

Your attitude	Your interest level in the topic Your attitude toward the subject Your attitude toward the speaker
The topic	Your familiarity with the words, terminology, or topic Difficulty level of the course Quantity of information presented
The speaker's qualities	Speaker's tone of voice Speaker's rate of speech Speaker's speech patterns and mannerisms Speaker's organization of the presentation Speaker's teaching/lecturing style Speaker's clarity in explaining information, providing examples and/or providing evidence to support a point
External distractors	Noise and movement from people nearby Room temperature or lighting Interruptions by others Outside sounds
Personal factors	Length of time required to remain seated Sitting posture during the lecture Seating location in relation to the speaker Personal physical state at the time Personal emotional state at the time Personal background experiences Cultural background

The way that you approach listening situations will be influenced not only by the many factors noted in the preceding chart but also by your own learning style preferences, which may influence your *listening style*. For example, linear learners often are also **linear listeners**. Linear listeners tend to listen for logical, sequential information; they focus on specific details that support a main point. Linear listeners need to use concerted effort to connect details to see the overall "big picture" and think globally. Global learners, on the other hand, often are also **global listeners**. Global listeners tend to focus on the overall picture supported by vivid examples, discussion, and group interaction. They need to use concerted effort to identify and remember specific details and sequential patterns.

EXERCISE 10.1   Discussion of Influencing Factors
As a class, in small groups, or with a partner, use the previous chart titled
Factors That Influence Your Ability to Listen Effectively. *Answer the*
following questions for each of the categories of factors (attitude, topic,
speaker's qualities, external distractions, and personal factors).

1. How does this factor affect your ability to listen?

2. What personal experience have you had that shows the effect this factor can have on your ability to listen effectively?

Kinds of Listening

Just as there is more than one way to read a book, write a paper, or speak to others, there is more than one way to listen. Each approach to reading, writing, speaking, or listening involves a specific purpose or a goal that you bring to the situation. For example, your purpose for reading varies for reading a movie review, a magazine, a newspaper, a fiction novel, a research report, and a textbook. Your purpose for writing may range from capturing feelings and memories in a diary, expressing yourself through poetry, communicating with a friend, summarizing a short story, answering test questions, or preparing a report. Your purpose for speaking may be to gain someone's support, share personal experiences, vent emotions, teach or inform, clarify a situation, persuade, or promote. Understanding your listening goal each time you approach a listening situation can help you select appropriate strategies to strengthen your listening skills. The following chart shows four kinds of listening and the listening goals associated with each.

Listening

Kinds of Listening	The Listening Goal Is To . . .
Active Listening	Understand and learn new information
Critical Listening	Understand, interpret, examine, and analyze a speaker's message
Empathic Listening	Understand and relate to another person's feelings and emotions
Appreciative Listening	Enjoy, appreciate, and acknowledge a speaker and his or her message

Active Listening   **Active listening** is the process of concentrating intently on information being presented by a speaker. Many of your college *active listening* experiences will occur in classroom settings: in lectures, in labs, in small groups, or in partner activities. Your listening goal in all of these settings is to pay close attention to the information as it enters your working memory and to make a concerted effort to understand and then process the information. You can develop active listening skills by addressing the factors that influence your ability to listen effectively (page 266) and by using the following strategies in active listening situations.

■ Prepare yourself for active listening by familiarizing yourself with the topic *before* class begins. By previewing the chapter that will be discussed in class, reading the chapter if time permits, and reviewing notes and homework assignments, you will become more comfortable and familiar with the terminology, main concepts, and important details.

■ Increase your interest in the topic and your level of intention to learn the new information by preparing a few questions about the upcoming topic before you enter the classroom or listening setting.

■ Show a positive, respectful, and attentive attitude toward the subject and the speaker. Your working memory will be more receptive to the incoming information and will treat it as important.

■ Use concentration strategies to combat external distractors. Sit close to the front of the room near the speaker and any visual materials, and sit with a posture that shows attentiveness and interest.

■ Create a relaxed state of mind and use relaxation techniques as needed before and during a listening activity to free up your working memory for the incoming information.

■ Focus on the speaker's message. Pay attention to the speaker's **verbal clues**—such as tone or pitch of voice, emphasis, volume, and rate of speech—and the speaker's **nonverbal clues**—such as facial expressions, hand gestures, posture, position in the room, and pauses of silence.

■ In small-group activities or class discussions, listen intently to the information presented by other students. Ask clarifying questions and paraphrase what you hear. Be open to other points of view.

■ Participate in the learning process by asking clarifying questions, paraphrasing the speaker to check the accuracy of your understanding, and responding to questions posed directly to you or to the class in general.

Critical Listening   **Critical listening** is a higher, more complex form of listening that involves critical thinking skills. As a critical listener, your focus is on accurately understanding and interpreting the speaker's meaning. This involves examining and analyzing the proof or evidence that the speaker uses to support a specific point of view. Both verbal and nonverbal clues also provide valuable information that can help you interpret the speaker's message, purpose, and point of view.

Many critical listening situations involve personal opinions, differing points of view, and a wide range of emotional responses. Sometimes you will agree with the speaker; consequently, you will understand the message more easily, accept the evidence with less scrutiny, and relate to the speaker in a positive manner. At other times, however, you will disagree with the speaker and possibly experience emotional reactions that actually distort the information and set up barriers to understanding. Separating your emotions and opinions from those of the speaker and allowing the speaker to present all of his or her information before you analyze or evaluate the presentation are essential critical listening skills.

Empathic Listening   **Empathic listening** involves a sincere interest and attempt to *empathize* or understand another person's feelings, emotions, and thoughts related to a specific topic or situation. Empathic listeners pay attention to people's words and nonverbal clues in order to identify the emotion being exhibited (anger, frustration, disappointment, resentment, excitement, enthusiasm, self-pride, and so on) and relate to the speaker's situation, feelings, or point of view. In many empathic listening situations, the speaker wants someone to listen and understand; he or she does not necessarily want to be consoled or given advice.

Empathic listening skills are valuable in college courses that involve group activities, group projects, learning communities, and collaborative learning, for these are situations in which students relate on a more personal level. An atypical or intense emotional response from another student can be an indicator that you need to shift from active listening or critical listening to empathic listening. Listen to and observe what the student wants to communicate to you. Avoid being judgmental, criticizing, making negative comments, or telling the student that he or she is "wrong." Instead, use positive words or gestures to communicate that you *understand* the feeling or the situation (but you do not have to agree with the other person). If the need to be an empathic listener extends beyond a reasonable amount of time, suggest continuing the "discussion" at another time and place, or encourage the person to seek suggestions from the instructor, a counselor, or an adviser.

Appreciative Listening   **Appreciative listening** focuses on enjoying, appreciating, and acknowledging the speaker and the message in positive ways. You most likely used appreciative listening during times when you were drawn into a story by a captivating storyteller, laughed at an instructor's humorous anecdotes or examples in a lecture, marveled at the ease with which a student gave a class presentation, heard an actor practicing a scene from Shakespeare, or listened to a student read his poem in class. Appreciative listening is not a passive, laid-back process. To feel the richness of words, to be moved emotionally by a message, or to experience overwhelming gratitude for a speaker and his or her message all require that you, the listener, take an active role by paying close attention to details, connecting with the speaker, and allowing emotional responses to occur. You can demonstrate your appreciation through nods of agreement, eye contact, facial expressions, compliments or expressions of gratitude, and, when appropriate, applause.

EXERCISE 10.2 Using Four Kinds of Listening

Read the following descriptions of listening situations. Then write one of the following letters to indicate which kind of listening would be the most effective for each situation.

AC = Active   **C** = Critical   **E** = Empathic   **AP** = Appreciative

_____ **1.** A debate about storing the nation's nuclear waste at Yucca Mountain in Nevada

_____ **2.** A lecture that reviews a psychology text chapter—Chapter 10, *Health, Stress, and Coping* (Appendix D)

_____ **3.** Four students' project that involves a ten-minute skit

_____ **4.** A debate in a political science class between two guest speakers

_____ **5.** An instructor's explanation of the steps to use to complete a lab project

_____ **6.** A class discussion about the author's purpose and the thesis of a short story

_____ **7.** A student expressing frustration about a disagreement with a tutor

_____ **8.** An instructor reading three of his favorite poems written by American poets

_____ **9.** A candidate for a county commissioner position giving a campaign speech

_____ **10.** An instructor expressing his or her opinion about job reductions on campus

Steps in the Listening Process

Listening is an active process that occurs in five distinct steps. These five steps, discussed in *Communicating*, a college textbook by Berko, Wolvin, and Wolvin (pp. 52–58), are summarized below.

1. *Reception:* **Reception** involves receiving auditory and visual stimuli, such as facial expressions, body language, and appearance. These stimuli enter your short-term memory, and the process of listening begins.

2. *Attention:* **Attention** involves concentration, selectivity, motivation, and intent. In this step of listening, the stimuli enter the short-term memory system. You must actively focus your attention on the incoming stimuli, block out distractions and other insignificant stimuli, and concentrate on the message with the intent to comprehend what you hear.

3. *Perception:* **Perception** involves an initial attempt to evaluate the information received. During this process, you become aware of the information you understand and the information that does not make sense. Your educational background, your personal experiences, culture, attitude, values, and your mental and emotional states affect how you perceive the information.

4. *Assignment of meaning:* The **assignment of meaning** is the process of interpreting or attaching meaning to what you hear by categorizing the information into schemas. As you interpret information and assign meaning to what you hear, you link the information to existing schemas and associate it with a personal experience. One of the greatest difficulties with this step occurs in the process of interpreting the message as the speaker intended, without distorting or altering the speaker's message by reacting emotionally, being judgmental, or confusing facts and opinions.

5. *Response:* After you assign meaning to the message, the process of listening continues with an intellectual or emotional **response** to the information. Your response may include a nonverbal form of feedback, such as a nod of your head to indicate understanding, or it may include verbal feedback, such as *paraphrasing* the speaker or asking a question. Another form of response may be to link the information with a memory technique that can help you efficiently retrieve the information from your long-term memory at a later time.

Effective listening skills are essential for taking effective classroom lecture notes, participating in classroom discussions, and interacting in small groups. By understanding each listening step, you will be better equipped to analyze your listening patterns, which include your strengths and weaknesses, and to seek strategies to improve your listening skills. The Listening Inventory in Exercise 10.3 will help you analyze your effectiveness in using each of the five steps of listening.

EXERCISE 10.3   Listening Inventory

Janusik/Wolvin Student Listening Inventory

Directions: The process of listening includes the five steps of Reception, Attention, Perception, Assignment of Meaning, and Response. As a process, listening can break down at any of the five steps. This inventory will help you to identify your strengths and weaknesses in terms of the steps within the context of the classroom. After reading each statement below, code the item with the most appropriate response within the context of the college classroom.

Remember, "speaker" can mean the instructor or fellow students, so you may have to average your responses. **(1) almost never, (2) not often, (3) sometimes, (4) more often than not, and (5) almost always.**

_____ 1. I block out external and internal distractions, such as other conversations or what happened yesterday, when someone is speaking.

_____ 2. I feel comfortable asking questions when I don't understand something the speaker said.

_____ 3. When a speaker uses words that I'm not familiar with, I jot them down and look them up later.

_____ 4. I identify the speaker's credibility while listening.

_____ 5. I paraphrase the speaker's main ideas in my head as he or she speaks.

_____ 6. I concentrate on the main ideas instead of the specific details.

_____ 7. I am able to understand those who are direct as easily as I can understand those who are indirect.

_____ 8. Before making a decision, I confirm my understanding of the other person's message with her or him.

_____ 9. I concentrate on the speaker's message even when what she or he is saying is complex.

_____ 10. I really want to understand what the other person has to say, so I focus solely on his or her message.

_____ 11. When I listen to someone from another culture, I understand that the speaker may use time and space differently, and I factor that into my understanding.

_____ 12. I make certain to watch a speaker's facial expressions and body language for further clues to what he or she means.

_____ 13. I encourage the speaker through my facial expressions and verbal utterances.

_____ 14. When others are speaking to me, I make sure to establish eye contact and quit doing other tasks.

_____ 15. When I hear something with which I disagree, I tune out the speaker.

_____ 16. When an emotional trigger is activated, I recognize it for what it is, set aside my feelings, and continue to concentrate on the speaker's message.

_____ 17. I try to be sure that my nonverbal response matches my verbal response.

_____ 18. When someone begins speaking, I focus my attention on her or his message.

_____ 19. I understand that my past experiences play a role in how I interpret a message, so I try to be aware of their influence when listening.

_____ 20. I attempt to eliminate outside interruptions and distractions.

_____ 21. I look the speaker in the eye to focus on her/his message.

_____ 22. I tune out messages that are too complicated to understand.

_____ 23. I try to understand the other person's point of view and why she/he feels that way even when it is different from what I believe.

_____ 24. I am nonjudgmental and noncritical when I listen.

_____ 25. As appropriate, I self-disclose a similar amount of personal information as the other person shares with me.

Scoring the Listening Inventory (Exercise 10.3)

Directions: Write your responses in the appropriate positions. For example, if you gave yourself a "3" for the first statement, transfer the 3 to the first slot under Reception. When you've transferred all of your scores, add up all five scores for each step. The step with the highest score is your strength. The step with the lowest score is the step that can use the most improvement.

Reception	Attention	Perception	Assignment of Meaning	Response
1. _____	5. _____	3. _____	4. _____	2. _____
9. _____	10. _____	6. _____	7. _____	8. _____
12. _____	14. _____	15. _____	11. _____	13. _____
18. _____	20. _____	16. _____	19. _____	17. _____
21. _____	22. _____	23. _____	24. _____	25. _____
Total _____	_____	_____	_____	_____

Now add up your scores for all five steps, and use the following as a general guideline:

125–112 You perceive yourself to be an outstanding listener in the classroom.

111–87 You perceive yourself to be a good listener in the classroom, but there are some steps that could use improvement.

86–63 You perceive yourself to be an adequate listener in the classroom, but attention to some steps could really improve your listening effectiveness.

62–0 You perceive yourself to be a poor listener in the classroom, and attention to all of the steps could really improve your listening effectiveness.

Source: Berko, Wolvin, and Wolvin, *Communicating*, 8/e, pp. 109–111. Copyright © 2001 by Houghton Mifflin Co. Used with permission.

Strengthening Your Listening Skills

Strengthening your listening skills begins with a listening goal. Which of the following is the purpose of listening?

■ To acquire information

■ To analyze and interpret information

■ To empathize with someone's feelings, emotions, or situation

■ To enjoy and appreciate the speaker's message

Once you have identified your listening goal, the next step is to strengthen your ability to move through the steps of the listening process: receive the information, focus your attention, perceive your level of understanding, attach meaning to the information, and finally, respond to what you have heard. By using the *Essential Strategies to Strengthen Listening Skills*, you will strengthen your abilities to listen more effectively in the various listening situations and activities you will encounter in school, at work, and in your personal life.

SET LEARNING GOALS

The following *Essential Strategies to Strengthen Listening Skills* chart highlights nine important listening strategies. Place a star next to the strategies that you already use. Highlight the strategies that you plan to make a conscious effort to begin using to improve your listening skills.

Essential Strategies to Strengthen Listening Skills

▶ **Create an interest or a curiosity about the topic.** Relate the topic to your overall goals and identify ways that the topic is important in your life. Involve yourself in discussions with those who have a natural interest in the topic.

▶ **Strive to develop the mental discipline to stay tuned in to the speaker.** Resist the temptation to tune out when information is too technical, difficult, unclear, or boring. Be nonjudgmental about the speaker and the speaker's clothing, mannerisms, speech patterns, or appearance. Force your mind to stay focused on the information, not on the speaker.

▶ **Attend to levels of information.** Capturing only main ideas is not sufficient; however, focusing on every detail is neither necessary nor realistic. Strive to follow the speaker's ideas by seeing the relationships between the "big pictures," or concepts, and the "small pictures," the details. Think in terms of levels of information as you listen.

▶ **Visualize the topic and the content.** Connecting visualization to the listening process helps imprint the information into your memory. Strive to "make a movie" in your mind as the speaker's information unfolds. Visualize colors, actions, and details. You can imagine sounds and smells, and feelings related to the sequence of events.

▶ **Monitor your emotional responses.** Give the speaker the opportunity to develop his or her ideas; set your personal opinion, point of view, or emotional responses aside. Jot down on paper your emotional responses, in support of or

opposition to the speaker, until the end of the speaker's presentation.

▶ **Ask clarifying questions.** When the time is appropriate to ask questions or when the speaker asks for questions, pose open-ended questions that can provide an opportunity for the speaker to clarify or expand on information. The following are examples of clarifying questions:
What are some ways this could be used to . . . ?
Why is it important to . . . ?
When does this theory not work?

▶ **Paraphrase the speaker.** To check your understanding and to provide the speaker with feedback about the clarity of his or her presentation, rephrase (paraphrase) what you comprehended. The following are examples of paraphrasing:
Do you mean that . . . ?
Am I understanding you correctly when I say . . . ?
Did you say that . . . ?

▶ **Pay attention to nonverbal clues and body language.** Use the speaker's gestures, mannerisms, stance, facial expressions, and pauses in presentation to find signals for important information, shifts in ideas, or emphasis on specific supporting details.

▶ **Discuss or explain the information to someone else.** Report interesting information you learned from the speaker to someone else. Sharing and explaining the information personalizes the listening experience and helps you remember the information at a later time.

CLASS DISCUSSION

Question: Which of the Twelve Principles of Memory do you actively use during the listening process?

Reflection Writing 2
Chapter 10

On separate paper, in a journal, or online at this textbook's website, respond to the following questions.

1. Using the information you have learned in this chapter about listening, on a scale from one to ten, how would you assess your listening skills? What are your strengths, and what are your weaknesses?

2. What strategies can you begin using to become a more effective active listener?

3. Interpersonal skills affect personal relationships as well as work-related relationships. Give an example of a situation in your personal life or your work life in which your role was that of an empathic listener. What empathic listening skills did you use effectively? What empathic listening skills could you have used more effectively?

O N L I N E   P R A C T I C E   1

Visit the *Essential Study Skills*, Fifth Edition, website and go to Chapter 10. Click on **Practice 1: Strengthening Listening Skills**. Complete the ten-question true-false quiz. Upon completion of the quiz, you will receive your score. You can exit at that time, or you can print your results or e-mail them to your instructor.

O N L I N E   P R A C T I C E   2

Visit the *Essential Study Skills*, Fifth Edition, website and go to Chapter 10. Click on **Practice 2: Applying Skills to a Listening Situation**. After completing one of the listening activities, type responses to the ten questions about your listening experience and skills. After you type your responses, you can print them or e-mail them to your instructor.

Using Listening Skills in Lectures

In order to understand classroom lectures and capture the information to place in your notes, you will need strong listening skills. Your auditory memory alone will not suffice to remember information that you hear. Taking notes from lectures places more demands on your working memory than taking notes from textbooks. During a lecture, new information enters your working memory more quickly and you do not control that pace. When you take lecture notes, your working memory needs to hold auditory and visual information in your short-term storage centers long enough to attach meaning to it and to send signals to mobilize your motor skills to write down important information. Using effective listening skills and preparing yourself for lecture situations will ease the demands placed on your working memory. In addition to the *Essential Strategies to Strengthen Listening Skills,* the *Essential Strategies to Prepare for Lectures* will help you become an effective listener and notetaker of lecture information.

SET LEARNING GOALS

The following *Essential Strategies to Prepare for Lectures* chart highlights eleven strategies that you can use to prepare yourself to take effective lecture notes. Place a star next to the strategies that you already use. Highlight the strategies that you plan to make a conscious effort to begin using to prepare yourself for lectures.

Essential Strategies to Prepare for Lectures

▶ **Familiarize yourself with the topic *before* class.** Refer to your course syllabus, any class outlines, and your previous chapter notes so that you know the topic for an upcoming lecture or class discussion. If you do not have time to read a new chapter prior to the lecture, survey the chapter to get the "big picture" or a framework of the topic.

▶ **Familiarize yourself with new terminology, symbols, formulas, and equations.** Identify new terminology, symbols, formulas, and equations in the chapter before you enter the classroom for a lecture. For math and science classes, use a two-column notetaking system to create a quick reference list of new terms, symbols, formulas, and equations. Place this list next to your notes during the lecture.

▶ **Enter the classroom with a positive, receptive attitude.** Your attitude will affect your level of understanding and the quality of the learning experience. Go to class with a sense of curiosity and interest in the topic for the day.

▶ **Leave stress and emotional issues at the door.** Use any of the previously learned techniques to reduce stress and internal distractors, which can reduce your ability to receive information clearly. Your goal is to devote full attention to the listening task.

▶ **Take care of personal comfort needs before you enter the classroom.** Being physically comfortable reduces distractions. Wear comfortable clothing, visit the restroom, get a drink of water, or eat a nutritious snack if needed before you enter the classroom.

▶ **Be mentally alert.** Sound nutrition, adequate exercise, and ample sleep all have positive effects on your ability to stay focused and be mentally alert.

▶ **Sit in the front of the room.** You will encounter fewer distractions and be able to see the board or screen used for visual materials more clearly.

▶ **Identify your listening goal.** For most lectures, your goal is to receive and understand information. You want to capture main points and details and record them in your notes.

▶ **Set goals that include specific listening strategies to implement during the lecture.** Your goals may include asking clarifying questions, paraphrasing, responding to questions, using techniques to eliminate internal and external distractors, or using mental discipline to stay focused and to follow your instructor's lecture.

▶ **Be prepared with appropriate materials.** Have sufficient paper, pencils or pens, and your textbook. Arrive at class with sufficient time to organize your materials and be ready for the beginning of the lecture.

▶ **Begin taking notes as soon as the lecture begins.** The beginning of a lecture often lays a foundation or outline for the upcoming topic. Be ready to capture this information. Continue taking notes through to the end of the class.

CLASS DISCUSSION

Question: How do the *Essential Strategies to Prepare for Lectures* free up space in your working memory?

Selecting A Notetaking System to Use

Being familiar and comfortable with a variety of notetaking systems allows you to select the most appropriate and effective notetaking system to use for the various lecture styles you will encounter in your courses. Unlike taking notes from textbooks, during lectures you will need to organize information quickly and in meaningful ways. Most instructors have their own teaching styles and lecture styles, so after several weeks of a new term, selecting the most appropriate notetaking system for each lecture class becomes easier to do. In Chapter 11, you will learn several visual notetaking systems that you can use for lectures; this chapter focuses on the following five notetaking systems for taking lectures notes:

- The Cornell Notetaking System
- The Two-Column Notetaking System
- The Three-Column Notetaking System
- The Formal Outline System
- The Taking Notes in Your Textbook System

Using the Cornell Notetaking System

The **Cornell Notetaking System** presented in Chapter 9 can be used to take effective lecture notes. For many lecture classes, the Cornell system is the preferred notetaking system because it incorporates the Principles of Memory into the five steps. During step one, *record,* listen carefully for main topics or headings. Write them in your notes and underline them. Then listen for important details and examples; number each point under the main heading. When you hear the speaker shift to a new topic, leave a space before writing and underlining a new heading. Doing this separates units of information and avoids a long stream of continuous, unorganized information. Keep the following format in mind as you take notes.

Recall Column	Notes
	pg. #
	Main Heading
	1. Detail
	2. Detail
	3. Detail
	Main Heading

During the course of a lecture, you may find that the instructor **sidetracks** by discussing information that does not seem to fit within the order or the outline of the topics. When you recognize that the instructor has sidetracked, continue to take notes on the *sidetracked information* as it may be important. On the following page are two ways that you can record sidetracked information.

- Since you are taking notes on only one side of the paper, use the back side of the previous page of notes. Record your sidetracked notes here.
- Continue to take notes in the Cornell column. When you finish taking the sidetracked notes, draw a box around this information to set it off from your regular set of notes.

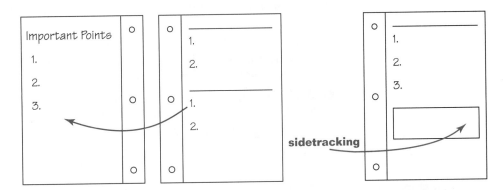

The recall column in Cornell notes, which you develop after the lecture, provides an opportunity to review your notes and condense the information into an effective format to use for reciting and getting feedback on your level of understanding. The reflect and review steps promote elaborative rehearsal and repeated contact with the information you need to learn. The five steps of Cornell that are reviewed below provide you with a powerful notetaking system that promotes understanding and long-term retention of information.

EXERCISE 10.4 Using Cornell Notes to Take Lecture Notes

If your instructor elects to use this exercise in class, he or she will present a lecture on vocabulary skills. As you listen to this lecture, take a complete set of Cornell notes. Your instructor may then provide you with a sample set of notes for comparison. Though your notes will not be identical to the sample notes, they should contain the same main ideas and similar supporting details. See Appendix B for self-assessment and instructor-assessment forms.

Using the Two-Column Notetaking System

The **Two-Column Notetaking System** is an effective notetaking option for lectures that move quickly from one topic to another. You can use the two-column notetaking system for lectures in the following way.

■ Each time the instructor begins a new topic or poses a discussion question, write the topic or the question in the left column.

■ Capture the important points of the lecture or the discussion in the right column.

■ To recite and rehearse from and to review two-column notes, fold your paper and turn the right column back so that it is not visible, or cover the right column with a blank sheet of paper.

■ While looking only at the left column, recite the information or answer the question. Check your accuracy by looking at the right column.

The following example shows two-column lecture notes from a discussion in a literature class.

Topic or Question   **Notes**

Topic or Question	Notes
	Short Story: "The Man to Send Rain Clouds" by Leslie Marmon Silko
What can you infer about Ken and Leon at the beginning of the story based on how they are dressed and what they are doing?	1. basic people—tended to sheep 2. didn't fear death or mourn 3. lived by Nat. Am. beliefs 4. knew the rituals
What are Father Paul's beliefs?	1. Catholic 2. Last Rites and funeral Mass necessary for a death
What is Louise's role in the ceremony?	1. Prepare the clothing for Teofilo to be buried in 2. Sprinkled corn meal on the old man
Do Leon and the priest interpret the sprinkling of water the same way?	1. no—priest sees it as a part of Cath. ritual of Holy water 2. no—Leon sees it as giving the old man plenty of water so he could send thunderclouds
What is the significance of the ending?	1. Christian culture blended into the Nat. Am. culture 2. Shows ceremonies different but both ways honor the dead

Source: Modified from Wiener and Bazerman, *Side by Side* (Boston: Houghton Mifflin Co., 1996) pp. 121–122. Copyright © 1996. Reprinted by permission of Houghton Mifflin Co. Excerpt from *The Man to Send Rain Clouds* by Leslie Marmon Silko © 1969. Reprinted with the permission of the Wylie Agency, Inc.

Using the Three-Column Notetaking System

The **Three-Column Notetaking System** can be used effectively for taking lecture notes in a math class or a science class that involves using formulas or equations to solve problems. During the lecture, copy problems, terms, or equations in the *left* column. Leave the *middle* column empty; this column will be used later to rework the problems. In the *right* column, during the lecture, write the solution for solving the problem, explanations, or rules to apply. After the lecture, fold the right column back or cover up the information so that it is not visible while you rework the problem. After reworking the problem, check the accuracy of your answer by comparing it with the information in the right column. The following is an example of lecture notes from a physical science class; rules for rounding numbers is the topic.

Problem—Directions	Space to Rework the Problem	Solution—Rule
term: s.f.		s.f. = significant figure Method to express measured numbers properly; used in math. operations
6.8 cm/1.67 cm = ?		6.8 cm/1.67 cm = 4.1 cm **Rule:** When multiply or divide quantities, answer has to have as many significant figures as there are in the quantity with the least number of significant figures. 6.8 cm / 1.67 cm = 4.1 ↑ Limiting term has 2 s.f. ↑ 4.0718563 is rounded to 4.1 (2 s.f.)
9.7 m / 4.4 m = ?		9.7 m / 4.4 m = 2.2045454 m = 2.2 m

Source: Modified from Shipman, Wilson, and Todd, *An Introduction to Physical Science,* 10/e (Boston: Houghton Mifflin Co., 2003), p. 15. Copyright © 2003. Reprinted by permission of Houghton Mifflin Co.

Using the Formal Outline Notetaking System

The **Formal Outline Notetaking System** is perhaps the most difficult notetaking system for many students to use effectively *during* a lecture. In a typical lecture situation, instructors present many different topics and supporting details within a relatively short period of time and often at a rapid pace. Students who are not comfortable or experienced in using formal outlining often find themselves overly concerned, confused, or frustrated as their attention shifts to whether or not a piece of information should be a new Roman numeral, capital letter, indented Arabic numeral, or indented lowercase letter. This shift of attention and the decision-making demands overload the working memory, resulting in the loss of attention and the attachment of meaning to new incoming information. However, students who process information in a linear, structured manner and who have learned effective outlining skills may prefer this formal, structured notetaking system for lecture notes.

Formal outlining is an appropriate choice to use for taking lecture notes *when the instructor provides you with an outline of the lecture.* In order to help students take effective notes, some instructors provide an outline of the lecture at the beginning of the class. When this is the case, using formal outlining to take notes is logical, for all you need to do is "fill in" the missing information. You do not need to put organizational demands on your working memory or your *central executive*. The following is an example outline that an instructor might share with the class before beginning a lecture.

Outline for Feb. 5 Lecture

Health-endangering Behaviors

I.   Smoking
        A. Statistics/Studies
        B. Trends
        C. Treatments

II.   Alcohol
        A. Statistics/Studies
        B. Health Consequences
        C. Treatments

Using the Taking Notes in Your Textbook System

An instructor's lecturing straight from the textbook is not very common, but it does occur on occasion, such as in technical, reading, or composition courses. The **Taking Notes in Your Textbook System** works effectively when the instructor presents lecture information by moving systematically through the textbook chapter, discussing various headings and emphasizing certain details. The most appropriate notetaking system in this situation is to follow along with the instructor and work directly in your textbook. Use a specific colored marker to highlight the information the instructor discusses or mentions. Make notes in the margins to reflect any additional information, explanations, or suggestions provided by the instructor. You can also write additional information on small Post-it notes and attach them to appropriate locations in the chapter. After class, you may want to use the textbook markings, marginal notes, and Post-it notes to make a separate set of follow-up notes on notebook paper to use for reflect and review activities.

Group Processing: **A Collaborative Learning Activity**

Form groups of three or four students. Then complete the following directions.

1. On a large chart, make two columns. In the left column, brainstorm problems that students encounter when they take lecture notes. List as many problems as you can think of in ten minutes.

2. In the right column, brainstorm possible solutions for each of the problems. Include solutions you know from personal experience and solutions you have read about in this textbook. You may use information that appears later in this chapter as well.

EXERCISE 10.5 Selecting a System to Take Lecture Notes

Select any one of your classes. Choose an appropriate notetaking system to use to take notes from one of the lectures. On your own paper, identify the class, the topic, and the instructor's name. Then answer the following questions. Turn in your answers with a copy of your lecture notes.

1. What problems did you have taking notes from this lecture?

2. What are possible solutions for the problems you had?

3. How soon after the lecture did you study and review your notes? Were your notes still familiar and clear to you?

4. What method did you use to recite from your notes? How effective was the process of reciting?

ONLINE PRACTICE 3

Visit the *Essential Study Skills*, Fifth Edition, website and go to Chapter 10. Click on **Practice 3: Notetaking Options**. Then type responses to the four questions. After you type your responses, you can print them or e-mail them to your instructor.

Organizing Information

Knowing how to structure notes is sometimes difficult because you do not have a clear sense of the overall organization of the content of the lecture. Most lectures are organized with headings (main ideas) and supporting details; the problem is that you will need to listen carefully for the main headings or shifts in ideas and for the important details.

Selecting the important information and the right amount of information can be challenging. If your notes are too brief and lack sufficient details, they will not be very helpful when you need to study the information or prepare for tests. If your notes are too detailed, you can always reduce them after class, such as during the reduce step of Cornell. Selectivity is the key. If you know that some information is not essential, do not add unneeded information to your notes. If you are not sure if some information is going to be meaningful or essential, try to include it in your notes to be safe. The following techniques will help you organize your notes in meaningful ways.

Techniques for Organizing Your Notes

1. Listen for key words that signal headings and main points.
2. Listen for terminology and definitions.
3. Listen for important details (dates, names, facts, and statistics).
4. Listen for ordinals (number words).
5. Listen for examples.
6. Use verbal clues.
7. Use nonverbal clues.
8. Copy steps and explanations for math problems.

Listen for Key Words	The words in the following list often signal a new heading or a new supporting detail. As soon as you hear these key words, ask yourself if the instructor shifted to a new topic (heading) or to a new supporting detail.

advantages	effects	parts	stages
benefits	factors	principles	steps
causes	findings	purposes	techniques
characteristics	functions	reasons	types of
conclusions	kinds of	rules	uses
disadvantages	methods	solutions	ways

Listen for Terminology	Including terminology and definitions in your notes is important for learning course content. Word clues often signal definitions and signal you to write the information in your notes:

X *means* . . .	X *is defined as* . . .	*The definition of* X *is* . . .
X *is also called* . . .	X, *also referred to as* . . .	X, *also known as* . . .

When you hear these words, use the abbreviation *DEF* to signal that you are writing a definition. Or you may want to use the equal sign (=) as your own symbol to connect a word to a definition. For example, you could write the following definition in your notes.

paraphrasing = rephrasing or saying in your own words

Listen for Details	Notes with material for future use need to include sufficient details. If you find yourself only writing headings or just listing a few points and writing very little, chances are you need to start adding more supporting details to strengthen your notes. Following are important kinds of details to include in your notes to develop or "prove" the main idea.

dates	names
facts	statistics
definitions	examples

Listen for Ordinals	When you hear "first," make that point number 1 in your notes. **Ordinals** (number words) help you organize the details in your notes and confirm that you are selecting the correct number of separate points for your notes. In addition to the ordinals, there are also *place holders,* or words that *represent* a number. The following words are examples of ordinals and place holders.

first	next	in addition
second	also	last
third	another	finally

Listen for Examples	Examples often serve as vivid triggers or memory cues for a specific main idea or concept. Frequently, examples are informative and interesting; association between the example and what you are expected to learn is easier. For that reason, reference to the example should be in your notes. Sometimes, however, the instructor may spend a considerable amount of time on an example, especially if it is an anecdote of a personal experience. Your notes only need to show the basic idea of the example; your notes do not need to "retell the whole story."

Use Verbal Clues

Key words such as *kinds of, steps, advantages of,* and so forth, are verbal clues that signal that the information is important. The following **verbal clues** are even stronger signals of information that should be included in your notes.

> *"This is important. You need to know and understand this."*
>
> *"This will be on the next test."*
>
> *"As I have already said . . ."* (ideas are repeated).
>
> *"Be sure you copy this information (from the overhead or chalkboard)."*
>
> *"If you haven't already done so, be sure you read carefully the information on pages . . . ."*
>
> *"I can't emphasize enough the importance of . . . ."*

During an interview, how are verbal and nonverbal clues used by the interviewer and the person being interviewed?

A person's intonation (pitch of his or her voice), volume of voice, and rate of speech are also verbal clues. Listen to your instructor's patterns carefully. Does he or she speak louder, more enthusiastically, faster, slower, or at a different pitch when giving important information? Many speakers may not even be aware of the verbal patterns they use to emphasize important points, but focused listeners can identify the patterns and use the information to help select the important ideas for their notes.

Information that the instructor writes on the chalkboard or charts or graphs that are displayed on an overhead projector are actually visual clues that information is important. As the information is discussed, you have another verbal clue that the chart, graph, or information on the board is important. If it were not important, why would the instructor spend time displaying it? Information on the board or on overheads should appear in your notes on a regular basis.

Use Nonverbal Clues

Watch your instructor's **nonverbal clues** or patterns as well. Body stance, hand gestures, and facial expressions (forehead wrinkles, eyebrows rise) are nonverbal clues that communicate to observant listeners. If the instructor pauses to look at his or her notes or simply pauses to allow you time to write, the pauses are nonverbal clues. Writing information on the board, pointing to parts of it over and over, and circling words on the board are also nonverbal clues indicating that information is important.

Copy Steps and Explanations for Math Problems

The majority of lecture time in math classes involves the discussion and explanation of solving math problems. As the instructor writes math problems on the board, strive to copy the exact information in your notes. Next to each step of the problem-solving process, write brief explanations or paraphrase the instructor's explanation of the step. Include as much other information as possible, such as when to use a given theorem or sequence of problem-solving steps. If you miss some information, insert question marks; you can return to these question marks after the instructor completes the problem, or you can refer to your textbook to fill in the missing information.

O N L I N E   P R A C T I C E   4

Visit the *Essential Study Skills*, Fifth Edition, website for Chapter 10. Click on **Practice 4: Organizing Information in Lecture Notes**. Complete the ten-question interactive multiple-choice quiz. Upon completion of the quiz, you will receive your score. You can exit at that time, or you can print your results or e-mail them to your instructor.

Adjusting to the Rate of Speech

The major difference between taking textbook notes and taking lecture notes is the rapidity with which you need to respond. With textbook notes, you can read, ponder, organize, and record information at your own comfortable pace. With lecture notes, you lose control of the pace and must adjust to the instructor's **rate of speech** and the rate at which new information is presented. Your **rate of writing** and **rate of thinking** also create discrepancies that contribute to many notetaking difficulties. The discrepancies between the average rate of speech and the average rate of writing, as well as the discrepancies between the average rate of speech and the average rate of thinking, create numerous problems for notetakers. The following chart summarizes these differences.

Average Rates	Words per Minute (wpm)
Average Rate of Speech During Lectures	100–125 wpm
Average Rate of Writing	30 wpm
Average Rate of Thinking	400 wpm

Your goal as an effective notetaker is to use strategies that will help you adjust to the instructor's rate of speech in order to hold important information in your working memory long enough to capture and write it in your notes. Due to the wide discrepancy between the rate of speech and the rate of writing, writing word for word is not possible, nor recommended. The following strategies will help you adjust to the instructor's rate of speech and "keep up" with the process of recording important information.

Techniques for Adjusting to the Rate of Speech

1. Paraphrase the speaker by shortening and rewording.
2. Use abbreviations to reduce the amount of writing.
3. Create a set of common symbols.
4. Use a modified form of printing/writing.
5. Keep writing.
6. Stay focused.

Paraphrase

Paraphrasing means to shorten and rephrase information by using your own words. Paraphrasing is a mental process that must be done quickly. As soon as you capture the speaker's words and interpret the message, write the information in a shortened form. Your sentences do not need to be grammatically correct. Words such as *the, an, and, there,* and *here* may be left out of your sentences, for they do not add to the overall meaning. Paraphrasing is perhaps one of the most difficult parts of notetaking, but with practice and familiarity with different instructors' lecture styles, your skills at paraphrasing will improve.

Use Abbreviations

Many words can be abbreviated to reduce the amount of writing. When you find content-related words that you use frequently, create your own abbreviations for the terms. Other common abbreviations, such as the following, can also be used.

BC. for *because*	**PRES.** for *president*
EX. for *example*	**SOC.** for *social* or *sociology*
IMP. for *important*	**SOL.** for *solutions*
POL. for *politics*	**W/OUT** for *without*

Create a Set of Symbols

You can also use symbols for frequently used words. The following symbols are often used to reduce the amount of writing.

&	and	$\rightarrow$	leads to/causes
@	at	<	less than
$\downarrow$	decreases	>	more than
$\neq$	doesn't equal	#	number
=	equals	+/−	positive/negative
$\uparrow$	increases	$\therefore$	therefore

In lecture notes for a math class, you will often need to use symbols. Become familiar with the frequently used math symbols so you can use them when you take notes. You may want to create an ongoing list of symbols and their English words that you can refer to quickly when needed.

( )	quantity	$p \wedge q$	conjunction *and*
>	greater than	$p \vee q$	disjunction *or*
<	less than	$\sim p$	negation (not *p*)

Use Modified Printing

Lecture notetaking requires quickness; time is of the essence. As a result, many students move toward a style of handwriting that is functional and increases writing speed. A modified form of writing consists of a mixture of cursive writing and printing. Feel free to experiment with this mixture of cursive writing and printing to see if it increases your speed. Since your notes are usually only for you to see, relax your handwriting standards, but maintain legibility.

Keep Writing

If you fall behind, do *not* stop writing and decide to just listen. Instead, leave a gap in your notes and start taking notes again for as long as you can keep up with the instructor. After class, ask another student or the instructor to help fill in the gaps. The more you practice and use the strategies in this chapter, the less frequent and the smaller the gaps in your notes will be.

If you simply cannot keep up with the instructor and organize your notes at the same time, shift to paragraph form. If you find yourself slowing down by trying to decide if a detail is a supporting detail or one that should be indented, shift to writing in paragraph form. Simply keep writing what you hear; paraphrase by restating the information in your own words or write abbreviated sentences. Later, when you have more time, you can reread the paragraph and organize it in a more meaningful way, such as making the recall column in Cornell notes.

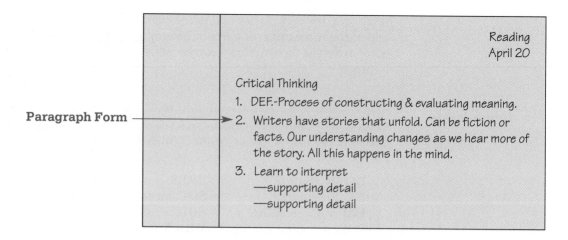

Paragraph Form

Reading
April 20

Critical Thinking
1. DEF.-Process of constructing & evaluating meaning.
2. Writers have stories that unfold. Can be fiction or facts. Our understanding changes as we hear more of the story. All this happens in the mind.
3. Learn to interpret
   —supporting detail
   —supporting detail

Stay Focused

There are times when you may find your mind wandering because the speaker is talking too slowly. Your mind moves much more quickly than the words of the speaker. The discrepancy between the rate of speech and your rate of thinking often leads to daydreaming, doodling, or losing focus. In addition to the listening techniques covered at the beginning of this chapter, the following techniques can help you become an active listener.

■ **Keep Writing**   Even if the details do not seem vital to your notes, write them down anyway. You can always eliminate them later by not including them in the recall column of your notes. By continuing to write, you remain actively involved with the lecture.

■ **Mentally Summarize**   In your mind, run through the main ideas and the supporting details that have been discussed. Try to mentally review and summarize them.

■ **Anticipate the Next Point**   With active listening, you can often tune in to the speaker's outline. Keeping in mind the points that have already been discussed, anticipate or guess the next point. Then listen carefully to determine whether your prediction was correct.

■ **Mentally Question the Information**   Ask yourself several basic questions:

Do I agree with this information?

Does it agree with the textbook?

Does it go beyond the textbook?

How does it relate to other areas previously discussed?

O N L I N E   P R A C T I C E   5

Visit the *Essential Study Skills*, Fifth Edition, website for Chapter 10. Click on **Practice 5: Keeping Up with the Lecture**. Complete the ten-question interactive multiple-choice quiz. Upon completion of the quiz, you will receive your score. You can exit at that time, or you can print your results or e-mail them to your instructor.

EXERCISE 10.6   Textbook Case Studies

Read about each of the following student situations carefully. Then, on your own paper and in complete sentences, answer the question that follows each case study. You can also answer these questions online at this textbook's Chapter 10 website. You can print your online responses or e-mail them to your instructor.

1. Calib has learned the five *R*'s of Cornell. His notes are well organized; his recall columns give complete lists or complete sentences to summarize his notes. To study and review his notes, he rereads the recall column. Calib usually does well on all the test questions that cover the textbook information, but he frequently misses questions that come from lectures. He does not understand why, since it seems to him his notes are thorough, and he spent time reading the recall columns. How does Calib need to modify his approach?

2. Kimberly is very uncomfortable sitting in a classroom. She often feels like other students are watching her, so she sits in the back corner. She has a lot of problems taking notes. Her notes are too brief and ineffective for studying. Sometimes she has problems with her notes because she cannot clearly see what is written on the board. At other times, she simply loses her concentration. When she does try taking notes, she cannot write fast enough to get all of the teacher's words on her paper. What would you recommend?

3. Alex has an outgoing personality. He enjoys discussions and contributing his ideas in class. However, he frequently annoys his classmates and instructors during lectures. He seems to verbalize every thought that enters his head. Thinking that he is participating in class, he often interrupts the instructor with irrelevant questions, or he asks the instructor to repeat information or to slow down. What techniques does Alex need to learn in order to be a more effective listener and positive contributor to the class environment?

ONLINE CASE STUDIES

Visit the *Essential Study Skills*, Fifth Edition, website and go to Chapter 10. Click on **Online Case Studies**. In the text boxes, respond to four additional case studies that are only available online. You can print your responses or e-mail them to your instructor.

Working with Your Notes

Taking lecture notes helps you stay focused on the lecture and keeps your mind from wandering. The most significant purpose of taking notes, however, is to create study tools to use *after* the class has ended. As you learned in Chapter 3, scheduling a study block as soon after a lecture as possible gives you the opportunity to work with your notes while the information is still fresh in your mind. Use the following strategies as soon after class as possible.

Complete Your Notes

Add missing details, fill in gaps, and correct any misspelled key terms that appear in your notes. Confer with other students or your instructor. You can also refer to your textbook for missing information or correct spellings. If you chose to use the Cornell notetaking system, completing your notes will involve creating organized recall columns.

Add More Structure to Your Notes

If your notes seem to lack a clear structure or organization, you can add structure by inserting headings or numbering the individual details. Highlighting specific concepts or key words or using a colored pen to circle terminology also creates more structure or a sense of organization for your notes.

Supplement Your Notes

As you work with your notes, you may want to make lists of information, brief outlines of main ideas, or clarifying questions that you would like to ask in class. Each type of notetaking system recommends that you write only on the front side of your notebook paper. Doing this leaves the back side of the opposing page blank. The back sides are ideal for adding supplementary notes or questions.

Rewrite Your Notes When Justified

Do not spend valuable time rewriting lecture (or textbook) notes simply for the sake of producing a neater set of notes. Instead, use some of the previously mentioned techniques for adding more structure or clarity to your notes. Use your time more wisely for reciting, reflecting, and reviewing activities. You have learned, however, that students who are kinesthetic or highly visual learners may find value in rewriting or typing their notes on a computer. The physical process of rewriting boosts memory and encodes information in a form that is easier to recall. In such cases, rewriting notes, which may include reorganizing information, is a meaningful and effective use of time.

Recite, Reflect, and Review Your Notes Often

As you learned in Chapter 9, reciting, reflecting, and reviewing your notes often strengthens your understanding and recall of information. Reciting encodes the information through your auditory channels and provides you with immediate feedback. Reflecting, thinking about the information, creating additional study tools, and reworking math problems personalizes the information and allows you to use your learning style preferences as you study. Immediate review and ongoing review keep the information alive in your memory and make preparation for tests much easier.

ONLINE PRACTICE 6

Visit the *Essential Study Skills*, Fifth Edition, website and go to Chapter 10. Click on **Practice 6: Working With Your Notes**. Then complete the ten-question interactive multiple-choice quiz. Upon completion of the quiz, you will receive your score. You can exit at that time, or you can print your results or e-mail them to your instructor.

EXERCISE 10.7 LINKS

Work in a group to complete the following directions. In Chapter 1, you learned about the learning styles listed in the following chart. In this chapter, you learned that learning styles can influence listening styles and listening skills. Complete the last two columns on the chart by listing possible notetaking problems and the solutions that each type of learner could use when taking lecture notes.

Learning Styles	Possible Notetaking Problems	Possible Solutions
Visual		
Auditory		
Kinesthetic		
Linear		
Global		
Interactive		
Reflective		

Reflection Writing 3
Chapter 10

On separate paper, in a journal, or online at this textbook's website, respond to the following questions.

1. What specific difficulties do you have taking lecture notes for two or more of your classes?

2. What techniques can you use to overcome these difficulties to create more effective lecture notes?

3. How will you make good use of your lecture notes?

SUMMARY

- Listening is an active process that involves understanding and attaching meaning to what you hear. Listening is our number one form of communication.

- A wide variety of factors influences a person's ability to be a good listener. They include attitude, interests, environment, experiences, learning styles, and personal background.

- Listening goals vary for each of the four kinds of listening: *active listening*, *critical listening*, *empathic listening*, and *appreciative listening*. Most lectures rely heavily on active and/or critical listening skills; however, empathic and appreciative listening skills are also important during lectures and classroom discussions.

- The process of listening occurs in five steps: *reception*, *attention*, *perception*, *assignment of meaning*, and *response*. Using effective listening strategies can help you strengthen your listening skills in all five steps.

- Many strategies exist to strengthen your listening skills and use your listening skills effectively in lectures. Refer to the Essential Strategies charts on pages 273 and 275.

- For success taking lecture notes, select the most appropriate form of notetaking that is suitable for specific lecture classes. You have five options for notetaking systems to use for lectures: Cornell Notetaking, Two-Column Notetaking, Three-Column Notetaking, Formal Outline Notetaking, and Taking Notes in your Textbook.

- Techniques for organizing information involve listening for key words, terminology, important details, ordinals, and examples. You can often get organizational tips through verbal and nonverbal clues.

- The discrepancies between the rate of speech (100–125 wpm) and the rate of writing (30 wpm) create a variety of notetaking problems. The following techniques can help you keep up with the instructor's rate of presenting information: use abbreviations, symbols, and modified printing; shift to paragraph form; or leave gaps in your notes to indicate that information is missing.

- The discrepancies between the rate of speech and the rate of thinking (400 wpm) can cause a loss of concentration when the rate of speech is too slow. The following techniques can help you stay focused on the lecture: keep writing, mentally summarize, anticipate the next point, and mentally question the information.

- After the lecture ends, you should work with your notes as soon as possible. Working with your notes involves adding missing details, adding more structure to your notes, supplementing your notes with condensed lists of important information or questions, and rewriting your notes (only if rewriting is an effective way to encode information into your memory).

- The purpose of lecture notes is to provide you with detailed study tools to use to learn the information and prepare for tests. Lecture notes are valuable only if you schedule sufficient time to *recite*, *reflect on*, and *review* your notes on a regular basis.

CULMINATING OPTIONS FOR CHAPTER 10

1. Visit this textbook's website and go to Chapter 10 to complete the following exercises.
   a. Flash card review of Chapter 10 terms and definitions
   b. ACE Practice Test 1 with ten fill-in-the-blank questions
   c. ACE Practice Test 2 with ten true-false questions
   d. ACE Practice Test 3 with ten multiple-choice questions
   e. ACE Practice Test 4 with three short-answer–critical thinking questions

2. Go to Appendix C in the back of this textbook for more Learning Options to use for additional practice, enrichment, or portfolio projects.

Chapter 10 REVIEW QUESTIONS

Multiple Choice

Choose the best answer *for each of the following questions. Write the letter of the best answer on the line provided.*

_____ 1. Which of the following is the most frequently used form of communication?
    a. writing
    b. listening
    c. reading
    d. speaking

_____ 2. Your listening efficiency or ability may be influenced by
    a. your attitude toward the subject or the speaker and your interest in the topic.
    b. your emotional state, learning style preferences, and cultural background.
    c. the speaker's style of delivery, tone of voice, and rate of speech.
    d. all of the above.

_____ 3. Listening goals
    a. vary for the four different kinds of listening.
    b. involve understanding different kinds of information for different purposes.
    c. for critical listening involve higher-level thinking skills such as analysis.
    d. all of the above.

_____ 4. Which of the following shows the sequence of steps in the listening process?
    a. perception, reception, attention, assignment of meaning, and response
    b. attention, perception, reception, assignment of meaning, and response
    c. reception, attention, perception, assignment of meaning, and response
    d. attention, response, reception, perception, and assignment of meaning

_____ 5. Which of the following is *not* true?
    a. Linear listeners prefer a broad, open-ended discussion of a topic.
    b. Empathic listeners focus on a person's feelings without giving too much input.
    c. Global listeners prefer to get an overview followed by examples and discussion.
    d. Familiarizing yourself with the topic before class promotes active listening.

_____ 6. Underlined headings followed by lists of details can be used in
    a. formal outlines.
    b. Cornell notes.
    c. two-column, three-column, and Cornell notes.
    d. formal outlines and Cornell notes.

_____ 7. The best notetaking system to use in lecture classes is
    a. always the Cornell system.
    b. a notetaking system that works well with the lecturer's style and content.
    c. two-column notes with the topic or question on the right.
    d. a formal outline that shows specific levels of information.

_____ 8. Paraphrasing
    a. involves rephrasing and shortening a speaker's words.
    b. is an effective strategy to use to keep up with the speaker during notetaking.
    c. can be used to pose questions to the speaker.
    d. involves all of the above.

Definitions

Define the following terms:

1. paraphrasing

2. nonverbal clues

Short Answer and Critical Thinking

1. Why is taking notes on lectures necessary and important for the overall learning process?

2. What are two or more major differences between *active listening* and *critical listening*?

3. What listening skills are essential for *empathic listening*?

4. What strategies can you use to combat the effects of a discrepancy between the rate of speech and the rate of writing?

Using Visual Notetaking Systems

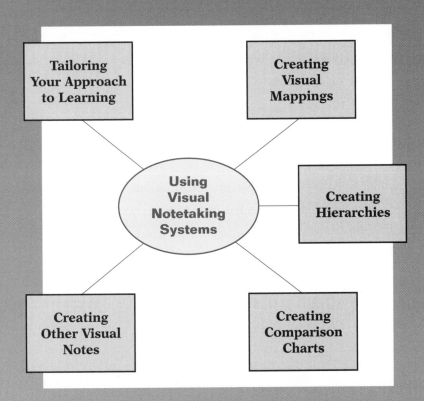

Terms to Know

metacognition
visual notetaking
visual mapping
level-one information
level-two information
level-three information
level-four information
hierarchies

Comparison Charts

columns
rows
cells

Graphic Materials

pie chart
tables
bar graphs
line graphs
flow charts
diagrams
time lines
informational charts

Tailoring your approach to learning involves becoming familiar with an array of strategies, learning to use the strategies, and then selecting those strategies that work most effectively for you and the content or course you are studying. Visual notetaking provides you with an avenue to use your visual skills and creativity to capture important information in the form of visual mappings, hierarchies, comparison charts, and other visual notes for graphic materials. By learning to use all of these notetaking options, you will be better equipped to individualize the process of learning to achieve greater success.

Chapter 11 Using Visual Notetaking Systems Profile

ANSWER, SCORE, and **RECORD** your profile before you read this chapter. If you need to review the process, refer to the complete directions given in the profile for Chapter 1 on page 2.

ONLINE: You can complete the profile and get your score online at this textbook's website.

	YES	NO
1. I often reorganize or rearrange information instead of studying it in the same order in which it was presented.	_____	_____
2. I use one specific notetaking system in all notetaking situations.	_____	_____
3. I draw various kinds of pictures to help me remember what I have read.	_____	_____
4. I understand the concept of different levels of information and know how to show these levels in my notes.	_____	_____
5. I learn main ideas well, but I often overlook important details.	_____	_____
6. I use these two principles of memory frequently when I study: recite and review.	_____	_____
7. I close my eyes or look up into the air to visualize or picture information.	_____	_____
8. When I recite, reflect, and review, I stop to get feedback so that I know whether I am remembering information correctly.	_____	_____
9. I know how to make mappings, hierarchies, comparison charts, pie charts, and time lines.	_____	_____
10. I am confident in my ability to convert printed information into meaningful visual notes.	_____	_____

Reflection Writing 1
Chapter 11

On separate paper, in a journal, or online at this textbook's website, respond to the following questions:

1. What is your score for this chapter? What does it mean to you?

2. What is your current approach to taking notes? Do you use one specific type of notetaking system, or do you use a variety of notetaking methods? Briefly explain.

3. What do you see as benefits you will gain by knowing how to use a variety of notetaking formats?

Tailoring Your Approach to Learning

Learning effective study strategies involves becoming familiar with an array of strategies, learning to use the strategies, and then tailoring your individual approach to learning by selecting strategies that work most effectively for you and the courses that you are studying.

Metacognition is the process of understanding *how* you learn, *what* you need to learn, and finally, *which* strategies or techniques would be the most effective or the best matched to the learning task and your learning process. You have already learned to use an array of powerful study skill strategies or techniques. Needless to say, using *all* of these strategies is not feasible. Instead, after experimenting with the many strategies that you have learned in different learning situations and with different kinds of materials, you should become increasingly more comfortable about *tailoring* or *personalizing* your approach to learning by selecting the combinations that work best for you in particular learning situations.

Notetaking Options

The goal of any notetaking system is to capture important information in notes so that you have a condensed version of lecture or textbook material that you can use to study and review. You will need to determine in each notetaking system which of the many notetaking options seems the most appropriate for the material.

What kind of information is presented in an art history course? Which notetaking system do you think would be most helpful in a course such as this?

Frequently, after you take notes on a lecture or a textbook chapter, you may find that you want to create a second set of notes to *reflect* or *review* the information. Using a different notetaking format for a second set of notes is application of the memory principles of *elaboration* and *organization*. The following list suggests several possibilities.

1. Cornell notes, then index card notes
2. Highlighting, then a formal outline
3. Two-column notes, then a visual mapping, hierarchy, or comparison chart
4. Marginal notes, then graphic notes such as a time line or a diagram

Experiment with the various notetaking systems and combinations until you find the one most suitable to use for each situation and the ones that produce the best results.

Visual Notetaking

In Chapter 1 you explored your learning styles or learning preferences. If you have strong visual skills, **visual notetaking** such as visual mappings, hierarchies, and comparison charts may become your preferred methods for learning new information.

Visual notetaking systems are powerful and work effectively because they are based on memory principles that boost your ability to learn new information. They are also powerful for the following reasons.

■ They incorporate the use of colors, pictures, symbols, and graphic formats that provide you with visual cues and associations to strengthen memory.

- They provide structures to organize and rearrange information logically, show relationships, and record information to use for ongoing review.
- They provide a way for you to personalize information in creative, interesting ways.
- They promote effective recitation, lead to *elaborative rehearsal,* and increase concentration.
- They involve multisensory approaches to learning.

Although visual notetaking is generally used to create reflect activities, some students become so proficient with visual notetaking that it can replace the Cornell notetaking system. Use visual notetaking as your main system of notetaking if it helps you learn and remember new information more easily. Because visual methods involve a relatively new form of notes, you may at first feel uncomfortable with these methods. Give yourself time and practice to learn these tools; they just may be your key to a stronger memory and a system for recalling information quickly.

Studying Visual Notes

As you will recall, effective application of the Cornell notetaking system involves five steps: *record, reduce, recite, reflect,* and *review.* During the *reflect* and the *review* steps in Cornell notes, you may choose to create additional study tools such as visual notes. The following strategies for studying visual notes will be explored in greater detail in the remainder of this chapter.

Strategies for Studying Visual Notes

1. **Imprint** in your visual memory the basic structure (the skeleton) of the visual notes.
2. **Visualize** the skeleton of your notes without looking at the printed information.
3. **Recite** by telling about the basic structure of the notes and then by explaining out loud the main ideas and supporting details for each main idea.
4. **Reflect** through activities that involve elaborative rehearsal.
5. **Review** the visual notes frequently to keep the image and the content fresh in your memory and readily accessible.

Creating Visual Mappings

You have already had some experience with **visual mappings** in this textbook. (Note that visual mappings in other textbooks and websites are also referred to as *cognitive maps, mind maps,* or *clusters.*) You will learn the basic techniques for creating visual mappings in Learning Options, Appendix C.

Mappings can be used in a variety of ways. You can make a visual mapping of

- A paragraph or a group of paragraphs under one heading
- A topic or a subject presented in several chapters and lectures
- Your lecture notes (in addition to Cornell or an alternative notetaking method)
- Information to review for a test
- Each chapter you have covered
- Ideas brainstormed for a paper or a speech

Four basic steps are involved in creating visual mappings. Your choice of borders, shapes, pictures, and colors in each step gives you the opportunity to be creative. The *Essential Strategies* chart on page 307 explains how to study from and visually memorize your visual mappings.

How to Create Visual Mappings

1. Write the topic in the center of your paper (level-one information).
2. Write the main ideas or the main headings; use lines to connect them to the topic (level-two information).
3. Add major details to support the main ideas (level-three information).
4. Add any necessary minor details (level-four information).

Level-One Information: The Topic

Write the Topic   In the center of your paper, write **level-one information—** the topic. The topic can be the title of a chapter, the name of a lecture, or the subject you wish to map.

Border   The border can be a box, a circle, or even a picture. If you are making a mapping of types of real estate investments, you may want the center picture to be a house or a building. If you are making a mapping on memory or on the Brain Dominance Theory, you may want the center picture to be a person's head.

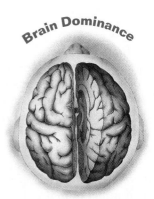

Brain Dominance

Theory

Source: Bernstein and Nash, *Essentials of Psychology*, 2nd ed. (Boston: Houghton Mifflin Co., 2002), p. 59. Copyright © by Houghton Mifflin Co. Used with permission.

Paper size   If you know that your mapping will include many details, you may want to work on legal-size paper (eight-and-a-half by fourteen inches) or drawing paper that is even larger. If your mapping is on a smaller topic, notebook-size paper is sufficient.

Level-Two Information: The Main Ideas or Headings

Write Main Ideas   Next add the **level-two information**, the main ideas of the topic. For a visual mapping of a chapter, use the main headings found in the chapter. For a visual mapping of a topic, carefully consider the different categories or main ideas covered in the textbook, the lectures, and the homework assignments. These will be the level-two information that branches out from the center of your mapping. You may find that your visual mapping of a specific topic may differ from one created by another student because each of you may use different methods for grouping or clustering the information. The following example shows level-one and level-two information for the *Twelve Memory Principles*.

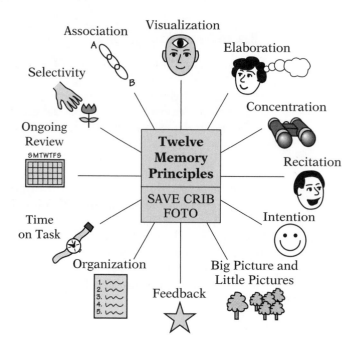

Borders, Shapes, or Pictures   To make the main ideas or categories stand out, you can place a border or shape around each item on level two. You may want to use a different shape than you used for the topic. You can use pictures instead of geometric shapes or pictures placed inside shapes.

Colors   Visual memory is strengthened with the use of color. Experiment with colors by shading in the main ideas. Use different colors for each level of information.

Spacing   Visually appealing and uncluttered mappings are easier to visualize or memorize. Before you begin adding the level-two information, count the number of main ideas to decide how to space them evenly around the page. Place them relatively close to the topic so you'll have room to add details later.

Organization   The most common organization for this level-two information is clockwise, beginning at the eleven o'clock position. If there is a definite sequence to the information, such as steps that you must learn in order, you may want to add numbers to the lines that extend from the topic or inside the borders.

Connections   Draw a line from each main idea to the topic. This gives a visual representation of their relationship. Each main idea is thus represented as a subtopic of the topic in the center of the paper.

Level-Three Information: The Key Words and Details

Add Major Details   Now add the major supporting details for each main idea. This is the **level-three information**. Write only key words that serve as "triggers" for you to recite in full sentences. Avoid the tendency to write long phrases or full sentences; your mapping will become too cluttered. Draw lines from these key words to the main ideas they support. Level-three information does not need to be in clockwise order or to start at the eleven o'clock position. The following visual mapping of SQ4R shows level-three information.

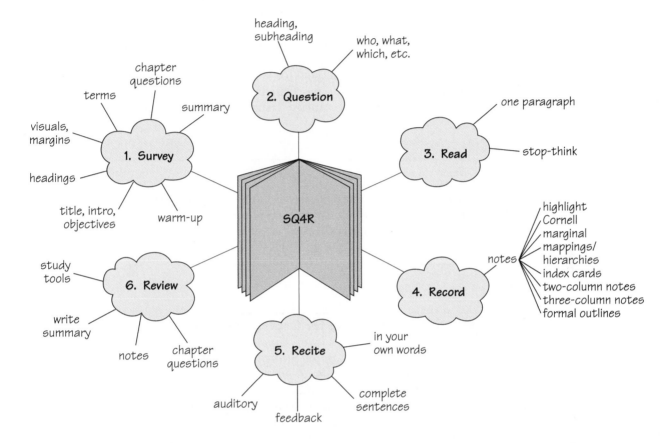

Quantity of Details   Be selective. Include only as many major details as you need to help you remember the important information. You do not need to have the same number of details for each main idea. It is up to you to determine how many details will help your memory.

Horizontal Writing   To make your mapping easy to read, keep all your writing horizontal. Avoid writing at a slant or sideways, or turning the paper as you write, resulting in words written upside down.

Borders   If the mapping details stand out clearly without borders (as shown in the SQ4R mapping), do not include any. If you are color-coding levels of information, you may also want to enclose these major details within a border.

Personalize with Pictures   Pictures help imprint the information in your visual memory. Many times it is easier to recall pictures than it is words, so include pictures when appropriate.

**Level-Four
Information:
Minor Details**

If you need a few minor details, use the same guidelines as for major details. Be very selective; too much **level-four information** results in a cluttered, often distracting, mapping. (Note the level-four details for "notes" in the record step of the SQ4R mapping.) If you find that you need one or more levels of information beyond the minor details, such as may be the case with a long chapter, consider reorganizing the information into several different topics and creating several mappings. You may find that narrowing or limiting the topic of a mapping will be more beneficial for visualizing and studying. By reorganizing, you *chunk* information into more meaningful groups. Your big picture is not so big that it is difficult to memorize, visualize, or comprehend.

O N L I N E   P R A C T I C E   1

Visit the *Essential Study Skills*, Fifth Edition, website and go to Chapter 11. Click on **Practice 1: Creating Visual Mappings**. Complete the ten-question true-false quiz. Upon completion of the quiz, you will receive your score. You can exit at any time, or you can print your results or e-mail them to your instructor.

 EXERCISE 11.1   Creating a Visual Mapping for Coping Strategies
With a partner, in a group, or by yourself, create a visual mapping of the information under the subheading "Developing Coping Strategies," which is located in the sample chapter in Appendix D, on pages A-40–A-41. Begin by carefully reading the information. Identify the main ideas or categories of coping strategies. Then convert the information into a visual mapping with at least three *levels of information. Use colors and/or pictures to add visual appeal and to enhance your visual memory skills. You may create your mapping in the following space or on separate paper.*

EXERCISE 11.2   Creating a Visual Mapping for Other Solar System Objects

Carefully read the following excerpt from Shipman, Wilson, and Todd's
An Introduction to Physical Science, *10th Edition. Include the following information on your visual mapping:*

> Level One (topic): *Other Solar System Objects*
>
> Level Two (headings): *Background, Asteroids, Meteoroids, Comets*
>
> Level Three (details): Key words for pertinent details

Other Solar System Objects

Background

The *solar system* is a complex system of moving masses held together by gravitational forces. At the center of this system is a star called the Sun. Revolving around the Sun are nine rotating planets and over 70 satellites (moons). In addition to the planets and the satellites, the solar system consists of thousands of asteroids, vast numbers of comets, meteoroids, and other solar objects such as interplanetary dust particles, gases, and a solar wind.

Asteroids

Ceres, the first of many planetary bodies between the orbits of Mars and Jupiter, was discovered by an Italian astronomer in 1801. Ceres is the largest of more than 2000 solar objects named and numbered that orbit the Sun between Mars and Jupiter. These objects are called **asteroids**, or *minor planets*.

The diameters of the known asteroids range from that of Ceres (940 kilometers) down to only a few kilometers, but most asteroids are probably less than a few kilometers in diameter. There are perhaps thousands the size of boulders, marbles, and grains of sand.

Asteroids are believed to be early solar-system material that never collected into a single planet. One piece of evidence supporting this view is that there seem to be several different kinds of asteroids. Those at the inner edge of the belt appear to be stony, whereas those farther out are darker, indicating more carbon content. A third group may be composed mostly of iron and nickel.

Like the planets, asteroids revolve counterclockwise around the Sun. More than 26,000 have been cataloged. Although most asteroids move in a orbit between Mars and Jupiter, some have orbits that range beyond Saturn or inside the orbit of Mercury.

Meteoroids

Meteoroids are interplanetary metallic and stony objects that range in size from a fraction of a millimeter to a few hundred meters. They are probably the remains of comets and fragments of shattered asteroids. They circle the Sun in elliptical orbits and strike the Earth from all directions at very high speeds.

A meteoroid is called a **meteor**, or "shooting star," when it enters the Earth's atmosphere and becomes luminous because of the tremendous heat generated by friction with the air. Most meteoroids are vaporized in the atmosphere, but some larger ones survive the flight through the atmosphere and strike the Earth's surface, in which case they become known as **meteorites**. When a large meteorite strikes the Earth's surface, a large crater is formed.

Comets

Comets are named from the Latin words *aster kometes,* which mean "long-haired stars." They are the solar system members that periodically appear in our sky [for] a few weeks or months and then disappear. A **comet** is a reasonably small object composed of dust and ice and revolves about the Sun in a highly elliptical orbit. As it comes near the Sun, some of the surface vaporizes to form a gaseous head and a long tail.

Halley's comet, named after the British astronomer Edmond Halley (1656–1742), is one of the brightest and best-known comets. Halley was the first to suggest and predict the periodic appearance of the same comet (he did not discover it). Halley observed the comet that bears his name in 1682, and correctly predicted its return in 76 years. Halley's comet has appeared every 76 years, including 1910 and 1986.

Adapted from Shipman, Wilson, and Todd, *An Introduction to Physical Science*, 10th ed. (Boston: Houghton Mifflin Company, 2003), p. 381, pp. 404–408. Copyright © 2003. Reprinted by permission of Houghton Mifflin Co.

Creating Hierarchies

Hierarchies are a form of visual mapping that arrange information in levels of importance from the top down. If visualizing mappings with lines extending in all directions is difficult for you, you may prefer the more organized structure of hierarchies. Three different hierarchies for **SQ4R** showing level-one and level-two information follow.

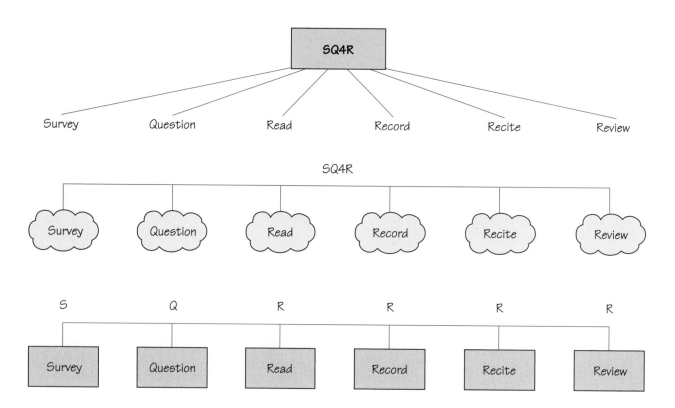

The steps for creating hierarchies are similar to the steps for creating visual mappings. The same levels of information are used: topic, main idea, major details, and minor details. The *Essential Strategies for Studying Visual Mappings and Hierarchies* chart on page 307 explains how to study from and visually memorize your hierarchies.

How to Create Hierarchies

1. Write level-one information (the topic) on the top line of the hierarchy.
2. Draw lines downward from the topic to show level-two information (the main ideas).
3. Under each main idea, branch downward again for level-three information (major details).
4. Add level-four information (minor details) under the major details if needed.

Level-One Information: The Topic

Since a hierarchy uses a top-down structure, place the title (subject) on the top line. If you are creating a hierarchy for a chapter or a heading in a chapter, write the chapter title or the heading on the top line. If you are creating a hierarchy for a specific topic or subject, such as SQ4R, write the topic/subject on the top line. You may add a border or a picture to the line.

Level-Two Information: The Main Ideas or Headings

When hierarchies are created for textbook chapters, the headings in the book become level-two information. When you create a hierarchy for a general topic such as SQ4R, level-two information represents general categories or main ideas.

Determine the number of main ideas to be placed under the topic. Branch *downward* to level two to write the main ideas. Consider using legal-size paper for more extensive hierarchies. Space the main ideas evenly to avoid a cluttered or crowded look. Always write horizontally. Add color coding, shapes, or pictures to strengthen the visual image.

Many textbooks provide informative introductions; these can be included in your hierarchies under a category labeled "Intro." (Level-three information can include key words, concepts, or objectives.) You can also add categories, if needed, to show graphs, visual aids, lists of terminology, or any other information you want to remember.

Level-Three Information: The Key Words and Details

Because level three often has numerous supporting details, you need to consider how you will place the details on the paper. To avoid a cluttered or crowded look, you can stagger or arrange the details in a variety of layouts, as shown in the following illustrations.

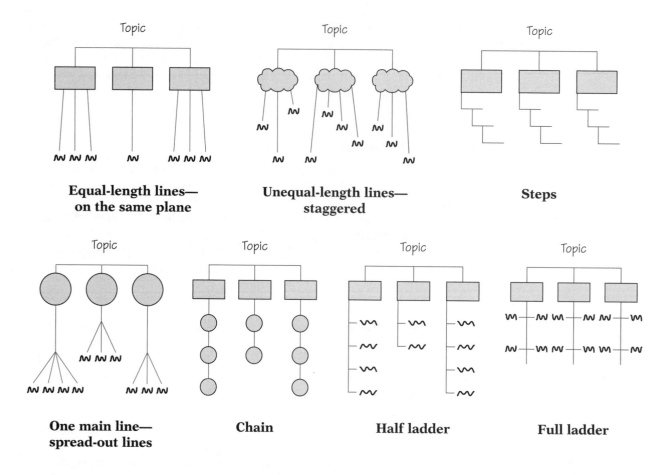

**Equal-length lines—
on the same plane**

**Unequal-length lines—
staggered**

Steps

**One main line—
spread-out lines**

Chain

Half ladder

Full ladder

---

*Level-Four
Information:
Minor Details*

Add minor details by branching *downward* from level three. Be selective. Include only essential key words that you feel you need to help you remember the information. Again, select a layout that will organize the details clearly. You can use borders, pictures, and color coding.

O N L I N E   P R A C T I C E   2

Visit the *Essential Study Skills*, Fifth Edition, website and go to Chapter 11. Click on the **Practice 2: Creating Hierarchies**. Complete the ten-question true-false quiz. Upon completion of the quiz, you will receive your score. You can exit at that time, or you can print your results or e-mail them to your instructor.

⚙ **EXERCISE 11.3 Converting a Visual Mapping to a Hierarchy**
A student made the following mapping during a lecture about vocabulary skills. The instructor began by identifying two kinds of vocabulary: expressive and receptive. The instructor then discussed six strategies for finding definitions for new vocabulary words. On your own paper or on a large chart if you are working in a group, convert this visual mapping into a hierarchy. Show the three levels of information.

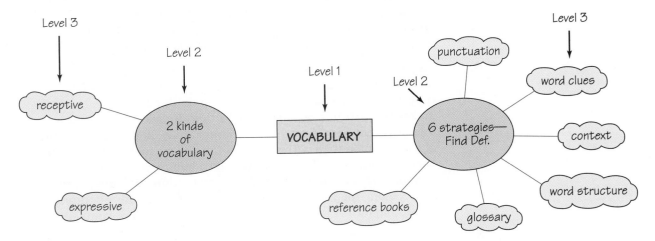

⚙ **EXERCISE 11.4 Creating a Hierarchy**
Read the following excerpt from Reece and Brandt's Human Relations: Principles and Practices. *Then, on a separate piece of paper, convert the information into a hierarchy that has three levels of information. Remember to be selective by using only key words and details.*

Characteristics of People with High Self-Esteem

1. *People with high self-esteem are future oriented and not overly concerned with past mistakes or failures.* They learn from their errors but are not immobilized by them. They believe every experience has something to teach—if they are willing to learn. A mistake can show you what does not work, what not to do. One consultant, when asked whether he had obtained any results in trying to solve a difficult problem, replied, "Results? Why, I've had lots of results. I know a hundred things that won't work!" The same principle applies to your own progress. Falling down does not mean failure. Staying down does.

2. *People with high self-esteem are able to cope with life's problems and disappointments.* Successful people have come to realize that problems need not depress them or make them anxious. It is their attitude toward problems that makes all the difference. In his book, *They All Laughed: From Lightbulbs to Lasers,* Ira Flatow examines the lives of successful, innovative people who had to overcome major obstacles to achieve their goals. He discovered that the common thread among these creative people was their ability to overcome disappointing events and press on toward their goals.

3. *People with high self-esteem are able to feel all dimensions of emotion without letting those emotions affect their behavior in a negative way.* This characteristic is one of the major reasons people with high self-esteem are able to establish and maintain effective human relations with the people around them. They realize emotions cannot be handled either by repressing them or by giving them free rein. Although you may not be able to stop feeling the emotions of anger, envy, and jealousy, you can control your thoughts and actions when you are under the influence of these strong emotions. Say to yourself, "I may not be able to control the way I feel right now, but I can control the way I behave."

4. *People with high self-esteem are able to accept other people as unique, talented individuals.* They learn to accept others for who they are and what they can do. Our multicultural work force makes this attitude especially important. Individuals who cannot tolerate other people who are "different" may find themselves out of a job. People with high self-esteem build mutual trust based on each individual's uniqueness. These trusting relationships do not limit or confine either person because of group attributes such as skin color, religion, gender, lifestyle, or sexual orientation. Accepting others is a good indication that you accept yourself.

5. *People with high self-esteem exhibit a variety of self-confident behaviors.* They accept compliments or gifts by saying, "Thank you," without making selfcritical excuses and without feeling obligated to return the favor. They can laugh at their situation without self-ridicule. They let others be right or wrong without attempting to correct or ridicule them. They feel free to express opinions even if they differ from those of their peers or parents. They are able to maintain an **internal locus of control**—that is, they make decisions for their own reasons based on their standards of what is right and wrong, and they are not likely to comply with the inappropriate demands of others. This internal control helps raise self-esteem every time it is applied.

From Reece and Brandt, *Human Relations: Principles and Practices,* 5th ed. (Boston: Houghton Mifflin Co. 2003), pp. 63–64. Copyright © 2003. Reprinted by permission of Houghton Mifflin Company.

EXERCISE 11.5 Textbook Application

Select a section of information from any one of your textbooks or from a section in the psychology chapter in Appendix D. Then, on separate paper, create a visually appealing, well-organized, meaningful visual mapping or a hierarchy of the information. Use three or four levels of information. Be prepared to share and explain your work to a classmate, members of a small group, or the entire class.

Your Topic: _____

Source of the information: _____

Check which you created: _____ visual mapping   _____ hierarchy

Did you use: _____ pictures?   _____ colors?   _____ borders?

SET LEARNING GOALS

The following *Essential Strategies for Studying Visual Mappings and Hierarchies* chart highlights six important strategies to use to study visual mappings or hierarchies. Place a star next to the strategies that you already use. Highlight the strategies that you plan to make a conscious effort to begin using to study your visual mappings or hierarchies.

Essential Strategies for Studying Visual Mappings and Hierarchies

▶ **Imprint into your memory a visual picture of your mapping or hierarchy.** Look intently (stare) at the level-one and level-two information in your mapping or hierarchy. Carve a mental image of the "skeleton," or first two levels of information. Do *not* focus your concentration on the other levels of information at this time.

▶ **Visualize the topic and the main headings.** Close your eyes, look away, or look "up and to the left" toward the ceiling as you try to recall the visual image of the skeleton. Practice seeing the words, the shapes, and the colors that appear in your visual notes. Look back at your mapping or hierarchy to check your accuracy. Study the skeleton further if necessary.

▶ **Recite the topic and the main headings.** Using only your visual memory picture of the mapping or the hierarchy, name the topic and recite the main headings. For example, you may say, "In SQ4R, six main headings or ideas branch off from the book, which shows SQ4R written in the center. The six branches are survey, question, read, record, recite, and review." Check your accuracy by looking at the mapping or the hierarchy. Rehearse again if necessary.

▶ **Recite the details.** Again, working only with the visual image in your head, begin telling all that you know about the first main heading (level-two information). Your goal is to include all the details you included on your mapping or hierarchy. The details do *not* need to be in the order in which they appear in your visual notes. Look at your mapping or hierarchy to check your accuracy and the completeness of the information stated during reciting. Without looking at your visual notes, visualize and recite again to strengthen your memory of the information.

▶ **Use a reflect activity.** A reflect activity, which provides you with additional practice, is a powerful form of elaborative rehearsal. Experiment with the following four different reflect activities.
1. Copy the skeleton of the mapping or hierarchy onto a piece of paper. Without looking at the original work, write the topic and the main ideas to fill in the spaces on the skeleton.
2. Remove the mapping or hierarchy from your sight; then redraw it and include as many details as possible.
3. Record yourself reciting the entire mapping or hierarchy. The tape becomes a set of auditory notes that you can use for later review.
4. Convert the mapping or hierarchy into a written summary. Use the structure of your visual notes to create paragraphs; each heading should have one or more paragraphs that explain the details for that heading. Writing summaries from mappings and hierarchies begins to prepare you for essay and short-answer questions that may appear on future tests.

▶ **Use ongoing review.** With notes in your visual memory, you can review any time you have a few available minutes. Each time you reconstruct the mapping or hierarchy in your mind, pay attention to areas that are "fuzzy" or unclear; you need to review these areas further in order to create a sharper image. As you remember from Chapter 2, practicing retrieval from long-term memory reactivates the information and the paths to the long-term memory schemas. The more you practice, the sharper the image or visual cue will become, and you will be able to access the information from memory more quickly and accurately.

CLASS DISCUSSION

Question: Which Principles of Memory do you use when you employ these strategies to study visual mappings and hierarchies?

ONLINE PRACTICE 3

Visit the *Essential Study Skills*, Fifth Edition, website and go to Chapter 11. Click on **Practice 3: Studying from Visual Mappings and Hierarchies**. Then type responses to the four questions. After you type your responses, you can print your responses or e-mail them to your instructor.

Creating Comparison Charts

Comparison charts (also known as matrixes, grids, or tables) are designed to organize a large amount of information into a format that is visual and easy to use to compare and contrast information. The title of the comparison chart appears above the chart. The category or characteristics that are being compared or contrasted are placed at the top of each column. The subjects that are being compared or contrasted are placed at the beginning of each row. Whenever you are working with several related subjects that each have specific characteristics, this form of visual notetaking is useful.

Title: _____

Categories → Subjects ↓	Column 1	Column 2	Column 3
Subject A			
Subject B			
Subject C			

In a comparison chart, **columns** run up and down, and **rows** run across the page. Important information about each subject is written inside the boxes (**cells**). The number of columns and rows is determined by the amount of information being covered. The following steps show how to organize information for comparison charts. If you use a computer, these charts can be made through "Table" commands.

How to Create Comparison Charts

1. Identify the number of subjects to be compared or contrasted. Write one subject on each row.
2. Identify the categories of information to be discussed. Write one category at the top of each column.
3. Complete the comparison chart by writing key words in each box where columns and rows intersect.

Identify Subjects and Label Rows

Begin by identifying the number of subjects. Many times the number of subjects (topics) is given in the printed text information. Once you have identified the number of subjects, you can begin to make the rows for your comparison chart. If you have two subjects, your chart will have only two rows. Write the names of the subjects on the rows. In the following comparison chart, the subjects are *asteroids*, *meteoroids*, and *comets*. (See Exercise 11.2.)

Title: Other Solar System Objects

Objects	Location	Size	Origin	Kinds	Also Called	Other Characteristics
Asteroids						
Meteoroids						
Comets						

As you become more familiar with visual materials and recognize different kinds of visual materials from your textbooks, you will note that some tables or informational charts in textbooks use an alternative format. They place the subjects at the tops of the columns instead of at the beginnings of the rows.

Identify Categories and Label Columns

Identifying categories requires you to think carefully about and analyze the information you have read. What categories of information were discussed for all or most of the subjects? You can use the general category "Characteristics," but more specific categories are more useful. The number of categories you select determines the number of columns in your comparison chart. Once you have identified the categories, label the top of each column. In the previous comparison chart on *Other Solar System Objects*, the information was divided into six categories: *Location, Size, Origin, Kinds, Also Called,* and *Other Characteristics*.

If you have difficulties finding appropriate labels for the columns, try using this approach to help you organize important information for the chart:

1. List each of the subjects across the top of a piece of paper.
2. Under each subject, list important details associated with that subject.
3. Look at your list of details. Can you group the details into larger categories?
4. If you see a logical category of information under one subject, is that same kind of information also given for other subjects? If so, you have discovered an appropriate title for a category.
5. Consider the following general categories for specific disciplines. Remember, however, that these are general, suggested categories. In many cases, you may be able to identify more specific categories that are dictated by the information and the subjects that you want to compare and contrast.

literature	author	tone	theme	setting	main plot	characters/traits	actions
sociology and anthropology	culture family	tribe economy	location imports/exports	government foods	religion tools	beliefs transportation	education
history	events	time period	location	leaders/rulers	wars/conflicts	influences	

continued

Chart continued

psychology	kinds/types problems traits frequency duration symptoms causes methods functions uses studies
science	terminology kinds/types causes effects relationships equations theorems problems solution applications

Complete the Comparison Chart

Once you have created the structure or the skeleton of the comparison chart, you are then ready to complete the chart by writing key details in the cells (boxes). To avoid confusion, frustration, or errors with details, approach this task in an organized, systematic manner. The most common approach is to focus on one subject at a time. For example, in the comparison chart on *other solar system objects*, begin by identifying pertinent information about *asteroids*. Reread the textbook or source of your information; then, identify key words or short phrases that tell about the *location, size, origin, kinds, also called,* and *other characteristics*. Write these details in the cells. After you finish the cells for the first subject, move to the second subject (*meteoroids*) and continue the process until you have filled as many of the cells on the chart as possible. An alternative organized and systematic approach begins by focusing on one *column* of information. For example, instead of focusing only on *asteroids*, you would focus your attention first on finding information about the *location* of asteroids, meteoroids, and comets; you would then move to information about the *size* of each of the subjects. The important point to remember is that your goal is to work in an organized, systematic manner to complete the cells in the comparison chart.

The following points about comparison charts are important to remember:

1. Be selective. Include only significant words or phrases. Avoid using full sentences.

2. Use dashes or bullets to separate two or more significant details in one cell.

3. Do not be concerned if information is not available to complete every cell; an occasional empty cell is acceptable. However, if information is not available for numerous cells under one category, the category is ineffective and needs to be changed.

4. Use the *Essential Strategies for Comparison Charts* on page 311 to study and review the information in your comparison charts.

 EXERCISE 11.6   Complete the Comparison Chart for *Other Solar System Objects*

Copy the comparison chart on page 309 onto your own paper. Reread the information in Exercise 11.2, Other Solar System Objects. Using the information from Exercise 11.2, complete your comparison chart by filling in the cells with key words or phrases.

 EXERCISE 11.7   Converting Textbook Information

Create a comparison chart for any topic that you have studied in a textbook for another course or for a topic that appears in the chapter Appendix D. Do not *simply copy a chart that already appears in a book. If you wish to use a textbook chart, find a way to expand it by adding new categories of information or subjects.*

SET LEARNING GOALS

The following *Essential Strategies to Study Comparison Charts* highlights five important strategies to use to study comparison charts. Place a star next to the strategies that you already use. Highlight the strategies that you plan to make a conscious effort to begin using to study comparison charts.

Essential Strategies to Study Comparison Charts

▶ **Imprint into your memory a visual picture of the skeleton of your chart.** Examine, stare at, and memorize the skeleton of the chart (the rows with the subjects and the columns with the categories) with the intent to remember its form. To strengthen the visual image, you can add colors and pictures to your comparison chart.

▶ **Visualize the skeleton of your comparison chart.** Look "up to the left" or close your eyes to visualize the title and the skeleton of the chart. If you do not have a sharp picture of the chart in your visual memory, take more time to imprint the image.

▶ **Recite and check your accuracy.** Recite in a logical order. Begin by reciting information in the chart for one subject. Include details that belong in each of the categories. After you recite, refer back to the chart to check the accuracy and completeness of your information. Then, reverse the order by reciting the information column by column; state the category and explain the information for each of the subjects. Again, refer back to the chart to check your accuracy and completeness of information.

▶ **Use reflect activities.** A reflect activity provides additional practice and promotes elaborative rehearsal. Experiment with three different reflect activities.
1. Redraw the entire chart from memory. Label the rows and the columns. Complete the cells with the important details.
2. Turn on a tape recorder. Read through the chart row by row. Turn the key words and phrases in the cells into complete sentences. Connect the information from one cell to another. Use the taped summary to review. Visualize each part of the chart as you listen to the tape.
3. With the chart in front of you, write a summary that includes all the key points for each subject. Organize your summary by paragraphs, giving one paragraph to each subject. For additional practice, write a second summary organized by the categories of information.

▶ **Use ongoing review.** Review your comparison charts often so that the information stays fresh in your memory and is accessible from long-term memory.

CLASS DISCUSSION

Question: What type or types of organizational patterns would you use when you write a summary based on a comparison chart?

Group Processing: A Collaborative Learning Activity

Form groups with three or four students. Then complete the following directions. Write your work on chart paper or on an overhead transparency.

1. As a group, select a topic from *any section of this textbook* to convert into a comparison chart. You may use specific topics, excerpts used in this textbook from other sources, or a section from the psychology chapter in Appendix D.

2. Work as a group to identify the subjects; label the *rows* in your chart. Then identify the categories of information that relate to each subject; label the *columns* in your chart.

3. Complete the chart by adding details to the cells. Be creative, thorough, and accurate. You may include pictures and colors on your comparison chart. Be prepared to share and explain your final project to the class.

4. If your group needs more time to complete this project than is available in class, arrange for a time to work together on this project outside of class.

ONLINE PRACTICE 4

Visit the *Essential Study Skills*, Fifth Edition, website and go to Chapter 11. Click on **Practice 4: Creating Comparison Charts**. Then complete the ten-question true-false quiz. Upon completion of the quiz, you will receive your score. You can exit at that time, or you can print your results or e-mail them to your instructor.

Reflection Writing 2
Chapter 11

On separate paper, in a journal, or online at this textbook's website, respond to the following questions.

1. What do you like about visual notetaking? What are the advantages of converting information into mappings, hierarchies, or comparison charts?

2. What do you dislike about visual notetaking systems? What difficulties do you encounter with visual notes?

3. What courses are you enrolled in this term? Which forms of visual notes would be most effective for each course?

EXERCISE 11.8   Textbook Case Studies

Read about each of the following student situations carefully. Then, on your own paper and in complete sentences, answer the question that follows each case study. You can also answer these questions online at this textbook's Chapter 11 website. You can print your online responses or e-mail them to your instructor.

1. Monica, a graphic arts student, feels that visual notetaking suits her learning style. The following is her first attempt at creating a visual mapping on *Chronemics* (Exercise 9.1). Monica was disappointed with the results. She found that her mapping was difficult to study from because it seemed "too busy" and "too disorganized." What techniques could Monica try that might result in a visual mapping that might be easier to read and better suited to her?

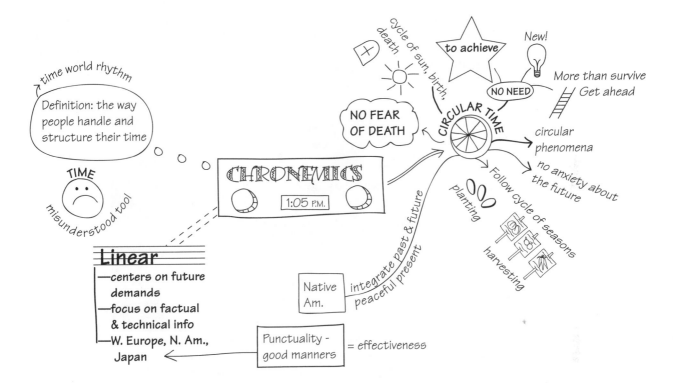

2. Darrel prefers organizing information into comparison charts whenever possible. He finds that comparison charts are logically organized and a perfect way to condense large amounts of information. However, he often struggles with the process of identifying the number of columns he needs and then labeling the columns. What suggestions might help Darrel identify and label effective columns for a comparison chart about three Southwest Indian tribes he is studying in his Native American Studies class?

3. Mickey creates many visual mappings and hierarchies as a second form of notetaking after she has taken Cornell notes for a textbook or a lecture. She finds that the process of reorganizing and writing information in her own handwriting helps her remember better. What memory principles and effective learning strategies does she use by creating a second form of notes?

Creating Other Visual Notes

All forms of visual notetaking involve converting printed information into a more visually graphic form, which may include pictures, drawings, charts, tables, graphs, maps, time lines, or diagrams. For many students, visual notes explain information more succinctly; condense information so that key concepts, patterns, trends, and relationships are easier to understand; and facilitate the process of retrieving information from long-term memory and moving it back into working memory.

What are the benefits of converting textbook information into visual notes? How does the use of pictures and color strengthen visual memory?

Working with Graphic Materials in Textbooks

Many textbooks, especially science, social science, and mathematics textbooks, use the following kinds of **graphic materials** to convey important information, trends, and relationships.

- **Pie Charts** show a whole unit subdivided into its smaller parts.
- **Tables** (also known as *matrixes, comparison charts,* or *grids*) categorize information into columns and rows.
- **Bar graphs** present information in vertical or horizontal bars.
- **Line graphs** (also called *linear graphs*) plot information and connect points to form one continuous line.
- **Flow charts** show the directions in which information flows or how items are related.
- **Diagrams** are pictures that integrate details and label the various parts.
- **Time lines** show a chronological or time sequence of events.
- **Informational charts** compile important concepts and details in a numbered or unnumbered list.

As an active reader, you should read the titles and the captions of the graphic materials, examine the details carefully, and draw conclusions or summarize the significance of the information. As an active learner, you can go one step further by *copying* important graphic materials into your notes (unless the graphic material is too complex); by color-coding the various parts of the visual notes; by *expanding* the graphic materials by adding your own reminders, details, or explanations; and finally, by writing a short summary under the visual graphics in your notes. Actively working with graphic materials is a form of elaborative rehearsal that will strengthen your comprehension and long-term memory.

⊚ EXERCISE 11.9   Expanding Graphic Materials

Refer to the line graph, Figure 10.2, in Appendix D, page A-23. Read the caption to the left of the graph. Then complete the following steps.

1. *Copy* the graph on your own paper.

2. *Expand* the graph by adding your own explanations to the *alarm, resistance,* and *exhaustion* sections of the graph. You may use the information from the caption or information from the text itself.

3. *Summarize* the information presented in the graph. Write the summary using your own words.

Creating Your Own graphic Materials

As you read and study from your textbooks, be alert for opportunities to convert the printed information into forms of visual graphics or notetaking. Pie charts, line graphs, time lines, and diagrams are four common forms of visual notetaking that you can create as you study, so these forms will be discussed in greater detail. Realize, however, that you can also create bar graphs, flow charts, and other informational charts for textbook information.

Pie Chart   A **pie chart**, similar to our Pie of Life (in Chapter 3), represents a whole unit or 100 percent of a category of information. The pie chart then shows how the whole unit is divided into parts. Your pie should reflect the different sizes of each part. Sometimes you can simply estimate where to draw the lines; for example, 39 percent would be less than half of the pie (50 percent) and more than one-fourth of the pie. The dividing line would be placed between 25 percent and 50 percent.

| **25%** | **39%** | **50%** | **75%** | **100%** |

After you have drawn your pie chart, label each section of information. You may add details or explanations within the parts of the pie or outside of the parts of the pie, using arrows to point the information to the correct location in the pie chart. Exercise 11.10 provides you with an opportunity to make your own pie chart for *Kinds of Businesses.*

Line Graphs   A **line graph** connects points on a graph to form one continuous line to show increases, decreases, or changes in the occurrence of a particular action or event. The bottom line, or the *horizontal axis,* is often divided into different time periods (days, weeks, months, or years). The line on the left side of the line graph, the *vertical axis*, shows units such as percentages, quantities, or other labels for the information depicted in the graph. Both the vertical and the horizontal axes must be divided into equal units and labeled. Many line graphs contain multiple lines to plot different patterns or categories of information. (See Appendix D, Figure 10.4, page A-28 for an example of a line graph with multiple lines representing three categories of students.) The following line graph shows one line, indicating only one pattern or category of information.

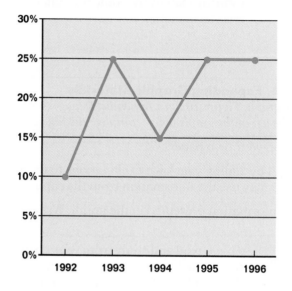

Time lines   A third form of visual notetaking, a time line, shows a chronological order or time sequences of events. A time line consists of one continuous line with equal time intervals marked below the line. Events corresponding to the time intervals are written above the line. More than one event may appear above a specific time period. Time lines are particularly useful study tools for history classes because you will be able to see the relationships among a variety of events: which events occurred at the same time as well as which events occurred before or after a specific time period. As with all visual notetaking systems, avoid producing a difficult-to-read, cluttered time line; use only key words or short phrases. You may add pictures to create a strong imprinting of the information in your long-term memory.

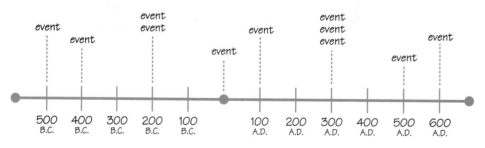

Time periods in equal intervals

Diagrams   **Diagrams** are pictures with labeled parts. In Chapters 1 and 2, you learned that pictures are powerful study tools for imprinting visual images in your memory system. In Chapter 6, you also learned that pictures (diagrams) are one form of mnemonics that assists in the recall of information. One of the techniques for comprehending difficult information is to draw a picture of the information (Chapter 9). Diagrams work well in science, social science, and mathematics courses. In Appendix D, page A-24, notice how the diagram in Figure 10.3 provides a visual explanation of the organ systems involved in the *general adaptation syndrome (GAS)*. In Exercise 11.11, you will have the opportunity to convert the solar system information from Exercise 11.2 into a diagram.

A common technique used to solve math problems is to draw a picture or a diagram with the known variables and then to use the picture or diagram to find the missing information. Use of a diagram can help you understand and solve the following problem.

Problem to Solve: A *liter* is a metric unit used to measure liquids. One liter equals 1,000 milliliters (mL). One quart equals 946 mL. Two pints equal a quart. How many milliliters equal one pint?

Solution: Draw a one-liter container. Divide it into ten equal units (by 100 milliliters). Beside the container, draw a line to show that one quart equals 946 mL. Divide the quart into two pints. You can quickly see from the diagrams that one pint will be half of 946 mL. The answer is 473 mL.

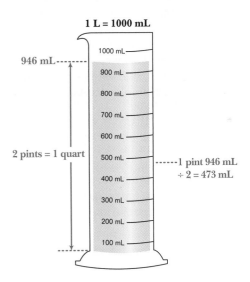

Source: Shipman, Wilson, and Todd, *An Introduction to Physical Science,* 10/e, p. 9. Copyright © 2003. Reprinted by permission of Houghton Mifflin, Inc.

EXERCISE 11.10   Create a Pie Chart
Read the following information about Kinds of Businesses. *Then, on your own paper, convert this information into a pie chart. Divide the chart into its parts and label each part. Use color coding to differentiate the various parts of your chart. Use any method to add useful details that can help explain the chart.*

Industries That Attract Small Businesses

The various kinds of businesses generally fall into three broad categories of industry: distribution, service, and production. Within these categories, small businesses tend to cluster in service and retailing.

Distribution Industries

This category includes retailing, wholesaling, transportation, and communications—industries concerned with the movement of goods from producers to consumers. Distribution industries account for approximately 33 percent of all small businesses. Of these, almost three-quarters are involved in retailing, that is, the sale of goods directly to consumers. Clothing and jewelry stores, pet shops, bookstores, and grocery stores, for example, are all retailing firms. Slightly less than one-quarter of the small distribution firms are wholesalers. Wholesalers purchase products in quantity from manufacturers and then resell them to retailers.

Service Industries

This category accounts for over 48 percent of all small businesses. Of these, about three-quarters provide such nonfinancial services as medical and dental care; watch, shoe, and TV repairs; hair-cutting and styling; restaurant meals; and dry cleaning. About 8 percent of the small service firms offer financial services, such as accounting, insurance, real estate, and investment counseling. An increasing number of self-employed Americans are running service businesses from home.

Production Industries

This last category includes the construction, mining, and manufacturing industries. Only about 19 percent of all small businesses are in this group, mainly because these industries require relatively large initial investments. Small firms that do venture into production generally make parts and subassemblies for larger manufacturing firms or supply special skills to larger construction firms.

From Pride, Hughes, and Kapoor, *Business*, 7th ed. (Boston: Houghton Mifflin Co., 2000), pp. 158–159. Copyright © 2002. Reprinted by permission of Houghton Mifflin Co.

 EXERCISE 11.11   Convert Information into a Diagram
Nine planets revolve counterclockwise around the sun. The order of the planets, beginning with the planet closest to the sun, is Mercury, Venus, Earth, Mars, Jupiter, Saturn, Uranus, Neptune, *and* Pluto. *Use this information to draw a diagram of the solar system. Use the information in Exercise 11.2 to show the location of asteroids, meteoroids, and comets. Remember to label all items in your diagram.*

ONLINE PRACTICE 5

Visit the *Essential Study Skills*, Fifth Edition, website and go to Chapter 11. Click on **Practice 5: Working with Graphic Materials**. Then complete the ten-question true-false quiz. Upon completion of the quiz, you will receive your score. You can exit at that time, or you can print your results or e-mail them to your instructor.

EXERCISE 11.12 LINKS

Work in a small group, with a partner, or on your own to use any form of visual notetaking for the topic Visualization. *Visualization is the process of picturing in your mind events or concepts with details. Create a set of visual notes that shows the many uses of visualization in study skills strategies and study tools. You may use the index in the back of this book to review the use of visualization. You may create your visual notes in the following space or on separate paper.*

EXERCISE 11.13 Selecting a Notetaking System

Select an appropriate notetaking system to use to take notes on the psychology chapter in Appendix D. Unless your instructor assigns only a section of the chapter for this notetaking exercise, take notes on the complete chapter. Your notes should include all of the important main ideas and supporting details such as you would be required to know if you were enrolled in a psychology class that uses this psychology textbook.

Reflection Writing 3
Chapter 11

On separate paper, in a journal, or online at this textbook's website, respond to the following questions.

1. How has this chapter changed your approach to notetaking?

2. Which forms of notetaking do you prefer? Does your preference vary by class? Explain.

3. What do you see at this time as your biggest notetaking challenge or difficulty? What ideas or plans do you have for overcoming this challenge?

SUMMARY

- Tailoring your approach to learning involves understanding and knowing how to use a variety of strategies and then selecting the strategies that work most effectively for you and the courses you are studying.

- Visual notetaking, which includes visual mappings, hierarchies, comparison charts, and other formats for graphic materials, provides you with creative ways to organize and record important information that you need to learn. The use of colors and pictures enhances the effectiveness and recall of visual information.

- You can use visual mappings and hierarchies to record information from individual paragraphs, chapter headings, complete chapters, or lectures or for specific topics to review for tests or to use in papers or speeches. Visual mappings and hierarchies include multiple levels of information. *Level-one information* is the topic. *Level-two information* shows the main ideas. *Level-three information* consists of supporting details. *Level-four information* shows minor details.

- A visual mapping begins with a topic in the center of your paper; main headings branch off from this topic in all directions. A hierarchy arranges information in levels of importance from the top down.

- To study from visual mappings and hierarchies, begin by visually memorizing the skeleton of your drawing (the topic and the main ideas). Recite the details for each main idea; check your accuracy by referring to level-three information in your drawing. Use reflect and review activities.

- Comparison charts organize large amounts of information into columns and rows. List the subjects in the left column. Identify categories of information; label each column with these categories. Use key words or short phrases in the cells of the comparison chart to show similarities and differences among the subjects.

- Additional visual notetaking systems include pictures, drawings or diagrams, charts, tables, graphs, maps, and time lines. You can take notes on graphic materials in textbooks by copying the graphic and then expanding upon the graphic by adding your own reminders, details, or explanations and by writing a short summary for the content of the graphic.

- Pie charts, line graphs, time lines, and diagrams are four forms of visual notetaking that you can use to convert printed information into visual formats that are easier to remember and recall.

CULMINATING OPTIONS FOR CHAPTER 11

1. Visit this textbook's website and go to Chapter 11 to complete the following exercises:
   a. Flash-card review of Chapter 11 terms and definitions
   b. ACE Practice Test 1 with ten fill-in-the-blank questions
   c. ACE Practice Test 2 with ten true-false questions
   d. ACE Practice Test 3 with ten multiple-choice questions
   e. ACE Practice Test 4 with three short-answer–critical thinking questions

2. Go to Appendix C in the back of this textbook for more Learning Options to use for additional practice, enrichment, or portfolio projects.

Chapter 11 REVIEW QUESTIONS

Multiple Choice

Choose the best answer *for each of the following questions. Write the letter of the best answer on the line.*

_____ 1. Visual mappings, hierarchies, and comparison charts can be used to
   a. take lecture notes.
   b. take textbook notes.
   c. make reflect activities.
   d. do all of the above.

_____ 2. Visual notetaking requires the use of
   a. visualization.
   b. creativity.
   c. recitation.
   d. all of the above.

_____ 3. When you visualize your notes, you should
   a. first create a visual image of the skeleton.
   b. be creative and make changes each time you visualize.
   c. stare at the paper for at least fifteen minutes.
   d. keep your eyes focused on the notes the entire time.

_____ 4. Feedback
   a. is nonessential when you work with visual notetaking.
   b. lets you know how well you are learning.
   c. comes only in auditory form.
   d. requires that you work with a partner.

_____ 5. Reflect activities may include
   a. making tapes as you recite in full sentences.
   b. reproducing the visual notes from memory.
   c. summarizing the information in new ways.
   d. doing all of the above.

_____ 6. When reciting is done with visual notetaking, it should
   a. begin from the bottom up.
   b. move counterclockwise.
   c. go from details, to main ideas, to topic.
   d. go from topic, to main ideas, to details.

_____ 7. Which of the following is *not* true?
   a. Comparison charts compare and contrast two or more characteristics of two or more subjects.
   b. Pictures and colors may be added to any form of visual notetaking.
   c. Copying and expanding pie charts, line graphs, and diagrams boost memory.
   d. Most information in textbooks can be converted into pie charts.

_____ 8. Which of the following is *not* true?
   a. Bar graphs and line graphs use labels for the horizontal and vertical axes.
   b. The individual sections of a pie chart must add up to 100 percent or a complete unit.
   c. Most diagrams contain too many details to be visually memorized.
   d. Time intervals frequently appear on time lines and line graphs.

_____ 9. When you need to take notes from a lecture or a textbook, you should
   a. select a notetaking format that seems best suited for the material.
   b. begin with one notetaking format and then consider creating a second type of notes to reflect on or review the information.
   c. include elaborative rehearsal strategies as part of your learning process.
   d. doing all of the above.

Application of Visual Notetaking Skills

Read the following excerpt "Historical Theories of the Solar System." Then select an appropriate form of visual notetaking to record the important main ideas and details of this excerpt. Create your visual notes on a separate piece of paper.

Historical Theories of the Solar System

The rotating and revolving motions of planet Earth were concepts not readily accepted at first. In early times most people were convinced that the Earth was motionless and that the Sun, Moon, planets, and stars evolved around the Earth, which was considered the center of the universe. This concept of the solar system is called the Earth-centered model, or **geocentric model**. Its greatest proponent was Claudius Ptolemy, about AD 140.

Nicolaus Copernicus (1473–1543), a Polish astronomer, developed the theory of the Sun-centered model, or **heliocentric model**, of the solar system. Although he did not prove that the Earth revolves around the Sun, he did provide mathematical proofs that could be used to predict future positions of the planets.

After the death of Copernicus in 1543, the study of astronomy was continued and developed by several astronomers, three of whom made their appearance in the last half of the sixteenth century. Notable among these was the Danish astronomer Tycho Brahe (1546–1601), who built an observatory on the island of Hven near Copenhagen and spent most of his life observing and studying the stars and planets. Brahe is considered the greatest practical astronomer since the Greeks. His measurements of the planets and stars, all made with the unaided eye (the telescope had not been invented), proved to be more accurate than any made previously. Brahe's data, published in 1603, were edited by his colleague Johannes Kepler (1571–1630), a German mathematician and astronomer who had joined Brahe during the last year of his life. After Brahe's death, his lifetime's observations were at Kepler's disposal and provided him with the data necessary to formulate three laws known today as **Kepler's laws of planetary motion**.

Galileo Galilei (1564–1642), the Italian astronomer, mathematician, and physicist who is usually just called Galileo, was one of the greatest scientists of all times. The most important of his many contributions to science were in the field of mechanics. He founded the modern experimental approach to scientific knowledge. The motion of objects, including the planets, was of prime interest to Galileo. In 1609 Galileo became the first person to observe the Moon and planets through a telescope. With the telescope, he discovered four of Jupiter's moons, thus proving that the Earth was not the only center of motion in the universe. Equally important was his discovery that the planet Venus went through a change of phase similar to that of the Moon, as called for by the heliocentric theory, but contrary to the geocentric theory.

The works of Copernicus, Kepler, and Galileo were integrated by Sir Isaac Newton in 1687 with the publication of the *Principia*. Newton, an English physicist regarded by many as the greatest scientist the world has known, formulated the principles of gravitational attraction between objects. He also established physical laws determining the magnitude and the direction of the forces that cause the planets to move in elliptical orbits in accordance with Kepler's laws. Newton's explanations of Kepler's laws unified the heliocentric theory of the solar system and brought an end to the confusion.

Adapted from Shipman, Wilson, and Todd, *An Introduction to Physical Science,* 10th ed. (Boston: Houghton Mifflin Co., 2003), pp. 381–384. Copyright © 2003. Reprinted by permission of Houghton Mifflin Co.

CHAPTER 12

Developing Strategies for Objective Tests

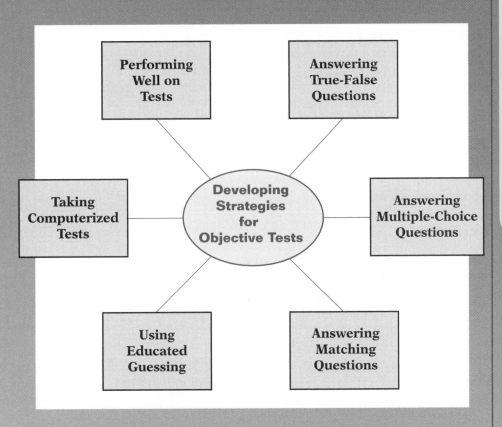

Terms to Know

objective tests
memory search
test anxiety

Four Levels of Response

immediate response
delayed response
assisted response
educated guessing response

negatives
100-percent modifiers
in-between modifiers
definition clues
relationship clues
stem
options
distractors
paired associations
word clues/grammar clues
wild-shot guess

You can increase your performance on tests by using strategies to deal with test anxiety and to answer objective test questions with confidence. This chapter focuses on answering objective questions, which include true-false, multiple-choice, and matching questions. You can use educated guessing strategies for these types of test questions, but you should use educated guessing only as a last resort. Many of the strategies in this chapter apply to computerized tests as well as to handwritten tests.

Chapter 12 Developing Strategies for Objective Tests Profile

ANSWER, SCORE, and **RECORD** your profile before you read this chapter. If you need to review the process, refer to the complete directions given in the profile for Chapter 1 on page 2.

ONLINE: You can complete the profile and get your score online at this textbook's website.

	YES	NO
1. I use other parts of the test to help me find answers I don't immediately know.	_____	_____
2. True-false questions confuse me because I do not understand what they are asking.	_____	_____
3. I read both columns of items on a matching test before I even begin answering.	_____	_____
4. I have a system for answering matching questions so that I do not use an answer twice.	_____	_____
5. I watch for modifiers such as *no, never, some, few, always,* and *often* because they can affect the meanings of questions.	_____	_____
6. I can tell when a question is testing a definition or a cause/effect relationship.	_____	_____
7. I make too many careless mistakes on tests.	_____	_____
8. I turn each part of a multiple-choice question into a true-false question before I select a final answer.	_____	_____
9. The first time I work through a test, I leave blank the answers that I do not know and then return to them when I have time.	_____	_____
10. I am confident in my ability to answer objective test questions without making many mistakes.	_____	_____

Reflection Writing 1
Chapter 12

On separate paper, in a journal, or online at this textbook's website, respond to the following questions.

1. What is your profile score for this chapter? What does it mean to you?

2. What is your general performance level and confidence level for taking tests that involve true-false, multiple-choice, and matching questions? Be specific and give details.

Performing Well on Objective Tests

Objective tests involve *true-false, multiple-choice,* and *matching* questions. Objective test questions are also called *recognition questions* because basically you are required to *recognize* the correct answer or *recognize* whether or not a statement is accurate. To answer many objective test questions, you will need to conduct a **memory search**, which involves thinking through a series of associations until you locate the answer in one of your long-term memory schemas.

Performing well on tests involves an array of skills, many of which begin *before* the actual day of a test. To review strategies to prepare for tests, see the *Essential Strategies for Test Preparation* in Chapter 6 (page 156). Several test-preparation strategies are highlighted below for a quick review.

- Use a five-day study plan to prepare for the test.
- Review study tools for factual information; rework steps or problems for procedural information.
- Create and study from summary notes.
- Participate in review sessions or study groups.
- Predict test questions; write and answer practice test questions.

In the following sections, you will learn additional strategies that will help you stay calm and focused in testing situations, conduct memory searches, use an organized system for answering questions, and increase your performance on objective tests.

Deal with Test Anxiety During a Test

Performing well on tests also involves using strategies to combat **test anxiety**. In Chapter 6, you learned about test anxiety, the four main causes of test anxiety (underpreparedness, past experiences, fear of failure, and poor test-taking skills), and strategies to reduce or eliminate test anxiety that appears *before* the day of a test. **Test anxiety**, the excessive stress that may occur *before* or *during* a test, hinders performance and immobilizes thinking skills. The following chart shows common symptoms of test anxiety that occur *during* a test-taking situation. Carefully read about the strategies you can use to manage and eliminate test anxiety during a test.

Test Anxiety

Symptoms During a Test	Strategies to Use to Combat Test Anxiety During a Test
Go "blank" and are unable to recall the needed information	• Use a quick relaxation technique to calm yourself down. • Use positive self-talk and the *Seeing Success* technique to give yourself encouragement. • Begin thinking about one related idea or item rather than the exact answer. Thinking about a related item, or the situation in which you learned about the item, activates the links of associations required to conduct a memory search. • Move on to another question so that you do not remain stuck on one question for too many minutes.

Test Anxiety, continued

Symptoms During a Test	Strategies to Use to Combat Test Anxiety During a Test
Make excessive careless mistakes in selecting or marking the correct answer	• Slow down the reading and answering process. • Activate your auditory channel by mouthing or quietly whispering the words as you read the directions, questions, and options for answers. • Highlight key words in the questions. Check to ensure that your answer relates to the key words. • Before starting a new question, quickly ask yourself: *Does this answer make sense?* If something seems odd or out of place, slowly reread the question and examine it one more time.
Abandon your regular test-taking strategies; stop answering questions in an organized, logical way	• Use the four levels of response to test questions (page 327). • Use the specific strategies in the following sections of this chapter for *true-false, multiple-choice,* and *matching* questions.
Mind shifts away from the test; concentration on the test fades	• Become more active and interactive with the test. Circle direction words so that they stand out more clearly. Highlight key words in directions and questions. • Use positive self-talk: *I can do this. My eyes and my mind stay focused on the paper. I can figure this out.* • Ignore other students; avoid comparing your test progress with what you perceive to be their progress. Ignore students who finish early and leave early; their early departure often does not mean that the test was easy for them or that they performed well.
Eyes start jumping from line to line of print or skip over words in the reading process	• Use your arm, a blank index card, or a blank piece of paper to block off the rest of the test. Restricting your vision to the question that you are contemplating helps your eyes stay focused on a line of information. • Use your pencil to point to each word as you read silently. Doing this keeps your eyes from skipping words or jumping to other lines of print.
Experience physical, emotional, cognitive, and behavioral symptoms of anxiety	• Briefly pause from the test to use short relaxation techniques to regain a comfortable physical calm. • Use positive self-talk, affirmations, and other concentration and relaxation techniques to manage emotional and behavioral symptoms. • Briefly stop writing. Put yourself in *retrieval mode.* Allow your mind time to search for information, activate "movies in your mind" that might have the information you need, and move through links or associates in your memory to help you locate the correct answer.

Use Four Levels of Response

Some students who have not learned effective test-taking strategies move through a test methodically. They read a question, answer it the best way possible, and move to the next question; this process continues until they reach the end of the test. Performing well on tests is often the result of moving through tests by completing some answers, leaving some questions blank and returning to them later, and changing some answers if proofreading time is available. Performing well also improves when students understand that taking objective tests involves the following **four levels of response.**

Levels of Response	Description
Immediate response	• As soon as you read the question, you immediately know the answer. • The question automatically triggers an association with information in your long-term memory. • This is the payoff for effective studying.
Delayed response	• When you cannot immediately respond, read the question a second time. • Do a quick memory search; try to recall the information by linking or associating key words in the question with information in your long-term memory. • Try *visualizing* the information as it appeared in your notes, in your study tools, in the textbook, or in the lecture. • If no answer surfaces, *place a small checkmark next to the question and move on to other questions.* • Return to the question after you have answered as many questions on the test as possible.
Assisted response	• Return to the unanswered questions. • Use other parts of the test to help you find possible answers. • Skim through the test and look for key words that appear in the question. • Information used in other questions may assist you in finding the information you need or may trigger an association that will lead you to the answer.
Educated guessing	• Use educated guessing strategies only when all else fails. • These strategies are not guaranteed to work all the time, but they may improve your odds in selecting the correct answer. • Educated guessing strategies are *never* more effective than arriving at the answer through other means.

Group Processing: A Collaborative Learning Activity

Form groups of three or four students. Then complete the following directions.

1. As a group, brainstorm to list the kinds of problems you encounter when you take objective tests. List as many problems as possible in random order.

2. Organize your list of problems by creating logical categories for the different problems. On chart paper or on an overhead transparency, rewrite your list of categories and problems. Be prepared to share your work with the class.

O N L I N E   P R A C T I C E   1

Visit the *Essential Study Skills*, Fifth Edition, website and go to Chapter 12. Click on **Practice 1: Using Four Levels of Response**. Then, complete the ten-question interactive multiple-choice quiz. Upon completion of the quiz, you will receive your score. You can exit at that time, or you can print your results or e-mail them to your instructor.

Use Effective Test-Taking Strategies

Feeling slightly nervous or apprehensive when you first enter the classroom or when the instructor distributes the test is a normal reaction to testing situations. Use the following strategies when the class begins:

- Strive to focus your mind on the test and to prepare yourself mentally for the challenge as quickly as possible.

- Use familiar relaxation or visualization strategies to calm your nerves and to begin with a positive state of mind.

- Listen carefully to the directions. Your instructor may announce corrections on the test, suggestions for completing the test, the amount of time available for the test, and other important directions.

- Use the *Essential Strategies for Taking Objective Tests* on page 329 to strengthen your test-taking skills and increase your level of performance.

O N L I N E   P R A C T I C E   2

Visit the *Essential Study Skills*, Fifth Edition, website and go to Chapter 12. Click on **Practice 2: Performing Well on Tests**. Then complete the ten-question true-false quiz. Upon completion of the quiz, you will receive your score. You can exit at that time, or you can print your results or e-mail them to your instructor.

Many professional degree programs require entry-level exams that consist mainly of objective test questions. In what other situations will you frequently encounter objective test questions?

SET LEARNING GOALS

The following *Essential Strategies for Taking Objective Tests* chart highlights eight important strategies to use to take objective tests. Place a star next to the strategies that you already use. Highlight the strategies that you plan to make a conscious effort to begin using to improve your test-taking skills.

Essential Strategies for Taking Objective Tests

▶ **As soon as you receive the test, jot down important information that you do not want to forget.** Jot down formulas, mnemonics, lists, or facts that you may want to refer to quickly during the test. You can jot this information on the back of the test, in the margins, or on a blank piece of paper if your instructor allows you to use your own paper to organize ideas.

▶ **Survey the test.** Glance through the test to become familiar with the types of questions used, the point value of different sections of the test, and the overall length of the test. Be sure to check to see if questions appear on the backs of the test pages.

▶ **Budget your time.** Take a minute to estimate the amount of time you can spend on each section of the test. This is especially important if part of the test is objective and part is short answer or essay because short-answer and essay questions require additional time to organize, develop, and proofread. If you wish, jot down estimated times to begin each section of the test. Push yourself to meet each time line.

▶ **Decide on a starting point.** Many students prefer to work through the pages of the test in the order in which the questions are presented. Recognize, however, that you do not have to do the test pages in order. You may feel more comfortable beginning with one kind of question format, or you may feel more confident about the content of a specific section of the test.

▶ **Read all the directions carefully.** For multiple-choice questions, note whether you can use more than one answer per question. For matching questions, note whether you can use items more than once. If the directions are long or confusing, circle the key words in the directions. Ask for clarification if the directions still are not clear.

▶ **Use your test time wisely.** If you have time available after you have answered all the questions, check your answers. Students often wonder whether they should change answers when they check their work. Do *not* change answers if you are panicking or feel time is running out. *Do* change answers if you can justify the change; perhaps other questions on the test gave you clues or helped you recall information that affects your original answer.

▶ **Do not leave answers blank if you start to run out of time.** You will automatically lose points if you do not choose some kind of answer for one or more questions. When you know you are running out of time, pick up your pace; read faster and spend less time pondering answers. At times you may even need to make an educated guess (or jot down a partial answer on short-answer or essay tests) to avoid leaving blank spaces.

▶ **Use the four levels of response to answer questions.** Using delayed and assisted response is an effective test-taking strategy that can improve your performance. Use educated guessing only as a last resort.

CLASS DISCUSSION

Question: What self-management skills are important to use when you take tests?

Answering True-False Questions

True-false questions are one of the most basic forms of objective questions, for they take less time to read and can easily be scored by hand, by machines (the tests in which you fill in the numbered bubbles to indicate your answer), or by computer. Students sometimes feel that some true-false questions are "trick questions" mainly because they do not know how to read and interpret the questions correctly.

Use True-False Strategies

The following strategies can help you improve your performance on true-false tests:

■ **Read the statement carefully.** If you tend to misread questions, point to each word as you read the statement. *Circle key words used in the question.*

■ **Be objective when you answer.** Do not personalize the question by interpreting it according to what you do or how you feel. Instead, answer according to the information presented by the textbook author or your instructor in class.

■ **Mark a statement as *True* only when the statement is completely true.** If any one part of the statement is inaccurate or false, you must mark the entire statement *False*.

■ **Check items in a series of items very carefully.** Every item must be true for you to mark *T*.

■ **Do not take the time to add your reasoning or argument to the side of the question.** Frequently, the only information that the instructor will look at is the *T* or *F* answer, so other notes, comments, or clarifications will be ignored during grading.

■ **If you are taking a true-false test using paper and pencil, make a strong distinction between the way you write a *T* and the way you write an *F*.** Trying to camouflage your answer so it can be interpreted as a *T* or an *F* will backfire. Answers that cannot be clearly understood are marked as incorrect.

Pay Attention to Key Elements

Pay close attention to four key elements of true-false questions. Learning to identify these key elements will result in more careful reading of true-false questions and more accuracy in your choice of answers.

Key Elements in True-False Questions

1. Negatives in the form of words or prefixes.
2. Modifiers in the form of 100 percent modifiers and in-between modifiers.
3. Definition clues signaling that the definition of a term is being tested.
4. Relationship clues signaling that the relationship between two items is being tested.

Negatives　　As you read true-false questions, pay close attention to any negatives. **Negatives** are words or prefixes in words that carry the meaning of "no" or "not." *Negatives do not mean that the sentence is going to be false.* Instead, negatives affect the meaning of the sentence and require you to read and think carefully. Watch for the following negatives in questions.

Negative Words	Negative Prefixes	
no	dis	(disorganized)
not	im	(imbalanced)
but	non	(nonproductive)
except	il	(illogical)
	in	(incomplete)
	ir	(irresponsible)
	un	(unimportant)

Sentences with negatives can be confusing and can leave you wondering what is really being asked. One method of working with statements that have a negative word or a negative prefix is to *cover up the negative* and read the sentence without it. If you are able to answer *true* or *false* to the statement without the negative, the correct answer for the statement with the negative will be the *opposite* answer.

Modifiers   Modifiers are words that tell to what degree or frequency something occurs. There is a huge difference between saying that something *always* happens and saying that something *sometimes* or *often* happens. You must learn to pay close attention to these words to determine how often or how frequently something actually occurs. As you notice in the following list, there are other kinds of modifiers. Words such as *best* or *worst* show the extremes and indicate that there is *nothing* that is greater or better.

Modifiers can be shown on a scale. The **100 percent modifiers** are on the extreme ends of the scale. They are the absolutes with nothing beyond them. The **in-between modifiers** are in the middle of the scale. They allow for more flexibility or variety because they indicate that a middle ground exists where situations or conditions do not occur as absolutes (100 percent of the time).

Modifiers

100 Percent	In-Between	100 Percent
all, every, only	some, most, a few	none
always, absolutely	sometimes, often, usually, may, seldom, frequently	never
everyone	some/few/most	no one
everybody		nobody
best	average, better	worst
any adjective that ends in *est*, which means "the most," such as *largest, smallest* . . .	any adjective that ends in *er*, which means "more," such as *larger, smaller* . . .	least fewest

Definition Clues   A test writer must find ways to create false statements for true-false tests; one common way to develop false statements is by testing your understanding of the definition of a specific term. The following words, called **definition clues**, often signal that a question is evaluating your understanding of a definition.

Definition Clues

Clues That Signal Definitions		Sentence Pattern Used
defined as also known as		
are/is means		word ⟶ def. clue ⟶ definition
states that which is/are		
referred to as involves		*check carefully*
is/are called		

For definition questions, circle the clue words that signal definitions. Underline the key term that is being defined. Then ask yourself, *"What is the definition I learned for this word?"* Once you can recall the definition you learned, compare it with the definition that is given. If your definition and the test question definition are the same, the statement is *true*. If there is a discrepancy, analyze the test question definition carefully because it may be saying the same thing but simply using different words. If the definitions are not the same, the answer will be *false*.

Relationship Clues   Some true-false questions test whether a certain relationship exists. Relationships often show cause/effect—one item causes another item to occur. Become familiar with the following words for relationships. When you see these **relationship clues** in true-false sentences, think carefully about the relationship being discussed before you decide whether the statement is true or false.

Relationship Clues

Clues That Signal Relationships		Sentence Pattern Used
increases result		
produces since		Subject A ⟶ rel. clue ⟶ Subject B
reason so, so that		
affects creates		*check carefully*
because decreases		
causes effects		

In relationship questions, circle the relationship clues. Underline the key terms that are involved in the relationship. Then ask yourself, *"What do I know about how these two terms are related or associated with each other?"* Once you have a relationship idea in your mind and before you mark *true* or *false*, compare your idea with the one presented in the question.

EXERCISE 12.1 **Answering True-False Questions**

Read the following true-false questions, which test information you learned in previous chapters. Pay close attention to items in a series; when you find negatives, definition and relationship clues, or modifiers, circle them. Write T *for true and* F *for false.*

_____ **1.** You can increase your speed in notetaking by paraphrasing, using abbreviations, and writing sentences that are not grammatically correct.

_____ **2.** The recall column in the Cornell system should have headings, key words, study questions, and all the answers.

_____ **3.** When you create a goal organizer, you identify benefits you will gain, obstacles you may encounter, and resources you could use.

_____ **4.** Ongoing review is essential in the Cornell system but is optional in the SQ4R system.

_____ **5.** Index cards should be used only when you need to learn terminology.

_____ **6.** Reciting is important because it utilizes the auditory channel and provides feedback for understanding.

_____ **7.** Spaced practice is preferred so that the student can usually avoid rote memory and cramming techniques.

_____ **8.** Concentration is defined as the ability to focus on two or more things at one time without being distracted.

_____ **9.** In a formal outline, Roman numerals are never used to label supporting details under a subheading.

_____ **10.** Always begin by studying your favorite subject first so that you can get motivated.

_____ **11.** Reading and speaking are active processes, but listening is an inactive process.

_____ **12.** *Procrastination* is defined as a self-defeating behavior that always occurs when a person has a fear of failure.

_____ **13.** A disorganized desk is not an external distractor.

_____ **14.** The process of selectivity is not used during the fourth step of SQ4R.

_____ **15.** Students should use every concentration technique during a study block.

_____ **16.** Cramming can frequently be avoided if ongoing review is used each week.

_____ **17.** Test anxiety may stem from being underprepared or lacking test-taking skills.

_____ **18.** *Linguistic encoding* is defined as the process of coding words for long-term memory.

_____ **19.** Increasing the amount of information in a schema often makes learning information on that subject easier to do.

_____ **20.** Because test anxiety is a learned behavior, it can be unlearned through the use of strategies, practice, and willingness to change.

Visit the *Essential Study Skills*, Fifth Edition, website and go to Chapter 12. Click on **Practice 3: Answering True-False Questions**. Complete the ten-question true-false quiz. Upon completion of the quiz, you will receive your score. You can exit at that time, or you can print your results or e-mail them to your instructor.

Answering Multiple-Choice Questions

Careful reading is also essential for answering multiple-choice questions correctly. For multiple-choice questions, there are two parts to the question: the stem and the options. The **stem** is the beginning part of the statement. The **options** are the choices for the correct answer. Usually there are four options, and only one of the options is the correct answer. Your goal is to eliminate the options that are incorrect. These incorrect options are referred to as **distractors**.

Use Multiple-Choice Strategies

The following strategies for multiple-choice questions will help you improve your performance on multiple-choice questions.

■ *Read the directions carefully.* Usually the directions say to choose *one answer.* However, variations of this do exist; you may find directions that say you may use *more than one* answer. If no mention is made about the number of answers to choose, always select only one.

■ *Choose the best answer.* One or more of the answers may be correct, but the answer that is the most inclusive (includes the most or the broadest information) is the best answer.

■ *Read all of the options before you select your answer.* Some students stop as soon as they find a good answer. It is important to read all the options so that you are sure you are finding the *best* option.

■ *Write your letter answer on the line.* Some students make careless mistakes and write the incorrect answer on the line. If this is a tendency of yours, first *circle* the letter answer and then write the letter on the line. Using this method, you are able to quickly check to see that you wrote what you circled and what you believe is the correct answer.

Use Two Steps to Answer

The following two steps will guide you through the process of answering multiple-choice questions. Use each step before you write your final answer.

> **Steps for Answering Multiple-Choice Questions**
>
> 1. Read the stem, finish the statement in your mind, and check to see if the answer is one of the options.
> 2. Read the stem with each option as a true-false statement. Eliminate the distractors and select from the remaining options.

Finish the Stem　The first step with a multiple-choice question is to read the stem and finish the stem in your mind. This helps you "get into the correct memory schema" and relate the rest of the question to something you already know. The answer that you get may or may not be one of the answers given as an option, but you will be thinking along the same channels. For practice, how would you complete each of the following stems in your mind?

_____ **1.** The principle of Big Picture–Little Pictures _____

_____

_____ **2.** The five steps of the Feedback Model _____

_____

_____ **3.** Howard Gardner's eighth intelligence is called _____

_____

Read as Four T-F Statements　When you read the stem of a multiple-choice question with just one of the options, the result is a one-sentence statement that you can treat as a true-false statement. This process can continue until you have analyzed each of the options. The strategies you learned previously for true-false statements will be used in exactly the same way for multiple-choice questions. Here is the process:

1. Read the stem with the first option (a).

2. If the statement is false, *cross off the letter of that option*. This is a distractor and will not be the correct answer.

3. If the statement is true, *it may be the correct answer*. You won't know for sure until you have read all the options with the stem. If you would like, you may write a *T* at the end of all the options that make a true answer when they are added to the stem.

The following example demonstrates the use of this strategy:

_b_　　**1.** In the listening process, *assignment of meaning*
　　　　a̸. occurs before the attention and response steps.　F
　　　　b. requires the listener to categorize information into schemas and interpret the message without distorting it.　T
　　　　c̸. requires the listener to check the accuracy of his or her perception by asking a question or providing nonverbal feedback.　F
　　　　d. requires the listener to interpret a message.　T

Both b and d are true statements. Answer b is more comprehensive and inclusive. Answer b includes the information stated in option d.

O N L I N E　P R A C T I C E　4

Visit the *Essential Study Skills*, Fifth Edition, website and go to Chapter 12. Click on Practice 4: Answering Multiple-Choice Questions. Then complete the ten-question interactive multiple-choice quiz. Upon completion of the quiz, you will receive your score. You can exit at that time, or you can print your results or e-mail them to your instructor.

◉ EXERCISE 12.2   Answering Multiple-Choice Questions

For each of the following questions, read the stem and answer the question in your own words. Look to see if your answer matches one of the options. Then make a true-false statement by reading the stem with each of the options. Write T or F at the end of each option. Cross off the false statements. Select the best answer from the remaining options.

_____ 1. Maslow's hierarchy of needs is a theory that explains
    a. people's needs.
    b. how people are motivated by their needs.
    c. why needs are sustained over time.
    d. universal behaviors that exist in all cultures.

_____ 2. It is acceptable to
    a. put many key words in each cell of a comparison chart.
    b. write sideways on visual mappings if necessary.
    c. write a single item under a subheading in a formal outline.
    d. None of the above

_____ 3. When you visualize a mapping, you should
    a. try to see the skeleton first.
    b. always be creative and make changes as you go.
    c. never stare at the paper for as long as five minutes.
    d. add new information that you forgot to put in the original mapping.

_____ 4. Look Away Techniques
    a. always involve reciting.
    b. are used mainly when you read.
    c. help you ignore unimportant information.
    d. provide feedback.

_____ 5. Cramming
    a. is one of the most effective working-memory processing strategies available.
    b. uses all the memory principles.
    c. processes large amounts of information efficiently.
    d. is not a technique used by prepared students.

_____ 6. The five steps in the Feedback Model are
    a. action, goal, feedback, comparison, yes.
    b. goal, action, feedback, comparison, results.
    c. feedback, action, comparison, yes, no.
    d. goal, feedback, comparison, action, results.

_____ 7. Test anxiety can be reduced by focusing on
    a. test-taking tasks such as circling key words or mouthing the question.
    b. outward thoughts and ignoring others.
    c. your strengths and accomplishments.
    d. all of the above.

_____ 8. The principle of Big Picture–Little Pictures
    a. encourages you to memorize individual facts and details.
    b. is based completely on rote memory.
    c. recommends that you process information only in clusters.
    d. recommends that you try to "see the trees" *and* "see the forest" when you study.

Answering Matching Questions

Matching questions consist of two columns of information. The left column contains a numbered list of items; these items are often key words or terminology. A blank line for the respondent to use to identify the answer appears before each of the numbered items. The right column contains definitions, descriptions, or examples that you need to match to the items in the left column. Lowercase letters usually appear before the items in the right column.

Answering on Matching Tests

Use Paired Associations

Matching questions are based on paired associations. **Paired associations** are items that were linked together when you learned the information. For example, a word is linked or paired with its definition. When you think of the word, you associate it with the definition. When you think of the definition, you pair it with the word. Paired associations for matching may include

- Words and their definitions
- People and what they did
- Dates and events
- Terms and their function or purpose
- Problems and their solutions

Use Four Steps to Answer

When you are faced with matching questions on tests, you will see a list of words on the left and their paired associations on the right. The key to answering matching questions is to work through them in a systematic way. The following four steps will help you avoid confusion and perform better on tests that have matching questions.

Four Steps for Working Through Matching Questions

1. Read the directions carefully.
2. Count the number of items in each list to see if the lists are equal.
3. Begin by reading the column that has the shorter entries.
4. Use the four levels of response to match the columns.

Read the Directions   Begin by reading the directions carefully. Usually each item on the right can be used only once; if an item can be used more than once, the directions should say so.

Count the Items   Count the number of items in the left column and then the number of items in the right column. If the lists contain an equal number of items, each item will be used once. Sometimes the list on the right is longer, indicating that some of the items will not be used. Extra items make matching questions a little more difficult because you cannot automatically match up whatever is left over.

Read the Shortest List   Usually the column on the left will have the shortest entries. These may be words (terminology), names, dates, or events. Read these so that you are aware of the choices that are available. Also notice what types of pairing will be used. Are these people, events, dates, or vocabulary terms? Below, the list on the left has shorter entries; read this list first.

———— **1.** intrinsic rewards   **a.** a technique used to switch the time blocks of specific activities

———— **2.** trading time

———— **3.** motivation   **b.** a feeling, emotion, or desire that moves a person to take action

c. feeling proud, relieved, or satisfied

Use the Levels of Response   Now that you are familiar with the items on the left, begin reading the first item on the right. Read the item carefully and quickly search your memory for an association with that item. Look on the left to see whether the associated word is on the list. For example, if the item on the right is a definition, search your memory for the vocabulary term. Then use the **four levels of response:**

Immediate Response   You will use immediate response when you immediately know the answer. Once you see a definite match, write the letter on the line and *cross off the letter you used so you do not reuse it.* If you do not immediately know the answer, move to delayed response. Do not guess or write any answer that you are not absolutely certain is correct.

Delayed Response   Use delayed response when you do not immediately know the answer. In addition to the techniques discussed on page 327, use **word clues** and **grammar clues**. For example, if you see *system, technique,* or *rule,* you would narrow your focus by looking for choices in the shorter list that deal specifically with a system, a technique, or a rule. When you read and connect the item on the left with the item on the right, a meaningful "thought unit" or sentence should emerge. To find this meaningful connection, *mentally chatter your way* to the answer.

If you are not able to identify the correct answer after trying one or more of the previously mentioned techniques, *leave the answer space blank;* do not guess. Use a checkmark in the left margin as a reminder that you need to return to this question later. Move on to the next item. Always work your way from the top down to the bottom of the list.

Assisted Response   Scan through the test to look for any of the key words used on either side of your matching list. Other parts of the test may have information that helps you recall associations or jogs your memory about the information in the matching questions. If you cannot find any clues in other parts of the test, move on to educated guessing.

Educated Guessing   If you have exhausted the previously mentioned techniques and still have not come up with the correct answer, use educated guessing. If you put nothing on the line, it will be wrong; you might as well take the remaining items that you could not match and fill in any empty lines with any of those remaining letters.

The following chart shows the seven steps to use to answer matching test questions. Review these steps by reading through the circled items one through seven.

① Directions say to use each answer once.

② Two answers are extra and won't be used.

Matching

Match the items on the left to the items on the right. Write the letter of each answer on the line. Each item on the right may be used only one time.

③ Read the shorter list. ↷   ④ Start with "a." Do only the ones you know.

_h_	1. working memory	a̸. permanent storage center
___	2. motivation	b̸. associating items together
_a_	3. long-term memory	c. short-term memory and feedback loop
_j_	4. affirmations	d. feeling, emotion, or desire that elicits an action
_f_	5. chunking	e. feedback
___	6. sensory stimuli	f̸. breaking tasks into more manageable units
_b_	7. linking	g. procedural memory
_i_	8. central executive	h̸. conscious mind
___	9. self-efficacy	i̸. manager/organizer of WM
___	10. result of self-quizzing	j. positive statements written in present tense
		k. belief in one's own abilities
		l. words, sounds, pictures

⑤ Use delayed response. Use helper words to try to connect the items that you do not know well.

⑥ Use assisted response. Use the rest of the test for assistance in finding more answers.

⑦ Use educated guessing. Fill in any remaining blanks with letters you did not already use.

ONLINE PRACTICE 5

Visit the *Essential Study Skills*, Fifth Edition, website and go to Chapter 12. Click on **Practice 5: Answering on Matching Tests**. Then type responses to the four questions. After you type your responses, you can print them or e-mail them to your instructor.

EXERCISE 12.3 Matching Problems and Solutions

Read each problem on the left. Then find the solution on the right. Write the letter of the solution on the line. You may use each answer only once.

_____ 1. I highlight too much.

_____ 2. I don't know how to study from underlining.

_____ 3. When I read, I need to find a way to make important terminology stand out more clearly.

_____ 4. I have trouble finding the topic sentence.

_____ 5. I have problems finding definitions for key words in the book.

_____ 6. I don't feel like I really understand how to use the textbook features very well.

_____ 7. I need a fast way to look up page numbers to find information in my book.

_____ 8. The teacher said to check our work with the answer keys in the book, but I can't find any answer keys in my chapters.

_____ 9. I have trouble getting started when I have a reading assignment. I'm just not motivated to "dig right in" and do the serious reading.

_____ 10. I go into "automatic pilot" every time I try to read pages in my textbook.

_____ 11. I can't write fast enough to write down everything the teacher says in a lecture.

_____ 12. When the teacher talks too slowly, my mind wanders to other things.

_____ 13. My notes are a jumbled mess. The information all runs together.

a. Circle the words that you need to be able to define.

b. Survey the book at the beginning of the term.

c. Use punctuation clues, word clues, word structure clues, and context clues.

d. Try to organize with headings and numbered details. Leave spaces between headings.

e. Only mark the main idea and the key words for details.

f. Read one paragraph at a time. Stop. Take time to comprehend what you read.

g. Use your own words to string together the ideas you marked.

h. Use the index.

i. Survey the chapter first as a "warm-up" activity.

j. Paraphrase with shortened sentences. Abbreviate. Use symbols.

k. Check the first and the last sentences to see if one has the main idea that controls the paragraph.

l. Keep writing, anticipate new points, question ideas, or mentally summarize.

m. Check the book's appendix.

EXERCISE 12.4 Textbook Case Studies
Read about each of the following student situations carefully. Then, on your own paper and in complete sentences, answer the question that follows each case study. You can also answer these questions online at this textbook's Chapter 12 website. You can print your online responses or e-mail them to your instructor.

1. Alonzo usually does well on essay tests but has problems on tests with multiple-choice questions. He knows the information; therefore, he believes his errors are simply careless mistakes. Alonzo realizes that he tends to select answers too quickly and that he needs to learn to use a systematic approach to identify the correct answers. What systematic approach would you recommend?

2. Shaina learned long ago that either you know the answer or you don't. Consequently, she works through the test questions in the order in which they are presented. She reads each question once and answers the questions to which she knows the answers. She gets annoyed with herself for not knowing the other answers, so she leaves the remaining questions blank. Which of the four levels of response does Shaina need to learn to use in order to improve her performance on tests?

3. Courtney frequently experiences test anxiety. She often wastes the first five minutes of a test trying to get herself calmed down enough to read the questions. Her anxiety only increases each time she is not able to answer a question. Her eyes dart across the test, and she loses her focus. In her state of panic, she misreads questions, skips over important words, and then randomly selects an answer. Later, when she rereads her test without the time pressure, her comprehension and selection of correct answers improve. What strategies can Courtney use to improve her test performance?

ONLINE CASE STUDIES

Visit the *Essential Study Skills*, Fifth Edition, website and go to Chapter 12. Click on **Online Case Studies**. In the text boxes, respond to four additional case studies that are only available online. You can print your responses or e-mail them to your instructor.

Reflection Writing 2
Chapter 12

On separate paper, in a journal, or online at this textbook's website, respond to the following questions.

1. Examine two or more previous objective tests you completed for any of your classes. Look for the use of *modifiers*, *negatives*, *definition clues*, and *relationship clues* in the questions. Analyze any questions you answered incorrectly. What did you discover by examining your previous tests?

2. How would the objective test-taking strategies in this chapter have helped you achieve a better grade on those tests? What do you notice now about those tests that you were not aware of at the time you took the tests? Be specific in your answers.

Using Educated Guessing

Educated guessing is the fourth level of response for answering objective test questions. Educated guessing involves using specific strategies to improve your odds for supplying the correct answers on objective test questions.

Understanding educated guessing strategies often improves critical reading skills, for you learn to notice the significance of individual words and details in questions. Even though educated guessing strategies may help you gain a few additional points on a test, you need to be aware of the following precautionary notes about using educated guessing

■ The phrase *educated guessing* is used instead of simply *guessing* because you use some background information, logic, and common sense to approach questions that you cannot answer through immediate, delayed, or assisted response.

■ Educated guessing is not foolproof. These strategies only increase the odds that you will reach the final answer.

■ Do not become overly confident about taking tests simply because you know how to use educated guessing. Educated guessing strategies do not guarantee a correct answer.

■ Limit the use of educated guessing strategies to situations in which nothing else has produced an answer. Educated guessing is a last resort!

On page 328 you learned about educated guessing for matching questions. You can also use educated guessing for true-false and multiple-choice questions. The following ten educated guessing strategies apply to true-false and multiple-choice questions. Remember that multiple-choice questions may be seen as a series of true-false questions, so the same strategies used for true-false questions will apply to multiple-choice questions.

Ten Educated Guessing Strategies

1. Guess *false* if there is a 100 percent modifier.
2. Guess *true* if there is an in-between modifier.
3. Guess *false* if there is a relationship clue.
4. Guess *false* if the statement is ridiculous, foolish, insulting, or has unfamiliar terms.
5. Guess *true*, the wild-shot guess, if there are no other clues in a true-false question.
6. If there are numbers as options, eliminate the highest and the lowest; guess one of the options that remain.
7. If there are multiple-choice options that are almost identical (look alike), choose one of those two options.
8. If one multiple-choice option is longer in length or more inclusive in content, choose it.
9. If the last option is "all of the above" and this option is not used throughout the test, choose it.
10. Guess *c*, the wild-shot guess, if there are no other clues in a multiple-choice question.

100 Percent Modifiers (False)

The *100 percent modifiers* are the *absolutes*, meaning that they are the extremes, no exceptions are allowed. Few things happen or exist without exceptions, so the odds are in your favor that questions with 100 percent modifiers will be false. Guess *false*. (See page 331 to review the modifiers.)

Notice how the 100 percent modifiers make the following statements false:

____F____ **1.** Attendance in college is required in <u>every</u> class.

____F____ **2.** <u>Always</u> begin by studying your favorite subject first.

____F____ **3.** <u>Never</u> use a tape recorder in class.

When a multiple-choice option with a 100 percent modifier is added to the stem, a true-false question is created. The true-false guessing strategy for 100 percent modifiers is to guess *false*. Notice how this same strategy works in the following example:

_____ **1.** The prefix *intra-*
    a. is never used in English words.
    b. always means "between."
    c. means "within" or "inside of."
    d. None of the above

____F____ a. The prefix *intra-* is (never) used in English words.

____F____ b. The prefix *intra-* (always) means "between."

Correct Answer → ____T____ c. The prefix *intra-* means "within" or "inside of."

In-Between Modifiers (True)

The *in-between modifiers* make room for exceptions or for the statement to sometimes apply and sometimes not apply. If you are using educated guessing, and you see an in-between modifier, guess *true*. Odds will be in your favor. Notice how the in-between modifiers make these statements true:

____T____ **1.** Reviewing notes from a previous paragraph can <u>sometimes</u> be used to help understand a difficult paragraph.

____T____ **2.** In a sole proprietorship, the person who owns the business is <u>usually</u> the one who operates it.

The same is true for multiple-choice questions because each option can be converted to a true-false statement when it is added to the stem. If more than one option is true, remember to then select the answer you believe is the *best* answer.

_____ **1.** Intrapersonal intelligence is an intelligence that
    a. <u>always</u> shows leadership and group charisma.
    b. <u>often</u> involves a special interest in personal growth and insights.
    c. <u>seldom</u> is combined with linguistic or interpersonal intelligence.
    d. is <u>never</u> taught in schools.

Notice how option *a* and option *d* have 100 percent modifiers. If guessing strategies are used, these would be marked *false*. Both option *b* and option *c* have in-between modifiers. If guessing strategies are used, these would be marked *true*. Therefore, guess one of these two options. However, before you purely guess, think it through more carefully. Option *c* is not accurate information; option *b* makes sense and is the correct answer. If you didn't know this, by reducing the choices to two options, you have a fifty-fifty chance of guessing correctly.

Relationship Clues (False)

True-false questions often test your knowledge of facts; on a higher level, true-false questions can test your understanding of relationships. Two common kinds of relationships questioned on tests are cause/effect and explanation through reason. When you see one of the common relationship clues (*because, since, so, cause, effect,* or *reason*), first try immediate, delayed, and assisted responses. If you cannot figure out the answer, guess *false*. Why? These higher-level thinking skills questions can easily be written to show false relationships. Notice how the two parts of the following questions do not show a true relationship.

__F__ **1.** Lack of motivation is the <u>reason</u> unsuccessful students avoid using time management.

__F__ **2.** Cramming is not recommended <u>because</u> it uses only eight of the Twelve Principles of Memory.

This same strategy can be used for multiple-choice questions. After each of the following options, you will see the true or false answer that would be used for that option.

_____ **1.** Systematic desensitization
    a̸. <u>causes</u> a person to react more mildly to criticism. (F)
    b̸. works <u>because</u> the immune system is strengthened. (F)
    c̸. should <u>never</u> be used to avoid undesirable situations. (F)
    d. helps a person change his or her negative reaction to specific events. (T)

Ridiculous, Foolish, Insulting, or Unfamiliar Terms (False)

If you see statements that are meant to be humorous, ridiculous, or unreasonable, mark them false for true-false questions and mark them as distractors in multiple-choice questions. If you have attended class regularly and have done all the reading assignments, and you encounter unfamiliar terms on a test, odds are in your favor that the statement is false, or it is a distractor in a multiple-choice question. Notice how this works in the following examples.

__F__ **1.** Howard Gardner's multiple intelligences theory applies only to people with IQs over 175. (*ridiculous*)

__F__ **2.** Howard Gardner's Theory of Multiple Intelligences added an eighth intelligence called psychic/intuitive. (*unfamiliar terms*)

__d__ **3.** When you don't know the answer to a test question, you should
    a. try using the rest of the test to trigger your memory. (T)
    b̸. try looking at another student's answers. (*ridiculous*) (F)
    c̸. cry. (*ridiculous*) (F)
    d. use delayed or assisted response before guessing. (T)

__a__ **4.** Interpersonal intelligence is
    a. seen in people with social and leadership skills. (T)
    b̸. associated with immaturity. (*ridiculous*) (F)
    c̸. not a useful quality in school beyond the first grade. (*silly*) (F)
    d̸. a form of type B behavior. (*unfamiliar term*) (F)

Wild-Shot Guess (True)

If there are no modifiers to use, and there is no relationship shown, you will need to take a **wild-shot guess**. If you run out of time on a test and simply must guess, *guess true*. There is a logical reason for this. When teachers write tests, they usually prefer to leave the correct, accurate information in your mind. They know that you are likely to remember what you read. Therefore, they tend to write more true statements than false statements.

Eliminate the Highest and Lowest Numbers

When the options are numbers, chances are better that the correct answer is one of the numbers in the middle range. Therefore, treat the highest and the lowest numbers as distractors. That leaves you with two options. Try to reason through to make the better choice. If any one of the other guessing strategies applies (such as choose *c*), incorporate that strategy as well to choose your answer.

_____ 1. An average rate of thinking speed is
  a. 800 words per minute. (Eliminate the highest.)
  b. 600 words per minute. ⎰Choose between these
  c. 400 words per minute. ⎱two options.
  d. 200 words per minute. (Eliminate the lowest.)

Choose One of the Look-Alike Options

Some questions have two options that look almost the same. Perhaps only one or two words are different. Chances are good that the correct answer is one of these two. Eliminate the other options and focus on these two look-alikes. Carefully think through and associate the information with what you have learned. If you can't decide, choose either one.

_____ 1. Compared to the left hemisphere of the brain, the right hemisphere of the brain
  a. understands spoken language better.
  b. has better logical abilities.
  c. perceives words better.
  d. perceives emotions better.

Focus on *c* and *d* because they are look-alikes. Now try to reason your way through this. You have already eliminated *a*, which deals with language. Because *c* also relates to language, it, too, must be incorrect. This leaves you with *d* as the correct answer, which it is. (Notice in this case how the guessing strategy to use *c* does not work—there are no guarantees!)

Choose the Longest or Most Inclusive Option

This guessing strategy is based on two premises. First, sometimes more words are needed to give complete information to make a correct answer. Second, an answer that covers a wider range of possibilities is more likely to be correct.

You can begin by looking at the *length* of the answer. If one option is much longer than the others, choose it. Also look at the content of the answers. Sometimes two or three answers may be correct to some degree, but one answer contains more information or a broader idea. This answer is the most inclusive. Notice how the *most inclusive answer* in the following example is the best answer.

_____ 1. Test anxiety can be reduced by focusing on
  a. yourself and ignoring others.
  b. outward thoughts and actions.
  c. your strengths and accomplishments.
  d. the four strategies to reduce test anxiety.

All of the answers are correct to some degree. However, *d* is the longest and includes a wider range of information. The answers *a, b,* and *c* fit under the information given in *d*.

Choose "All of the Above"

If you know for sure that two options are correct, but you are not sure about the third option and the fourth option is "all of the above," choose the fourth option. This is a safe guess since you can choose only one answer, and you know that two are correct. If you do not know for certain that two are correct, and you have tried each option in a true-false form and don't know the answer, go ahead and choose "all of the above." This strategy is not very reliable, especially if "all of the above" is used throughout the test. Be sure to check out all other possibilities before you decide to use this strategy.

_____ 1. Cramming is
   a. the result of being underprepared. T
   b. a frantic attempt to learn a lot of information in a short amount of time. T
   c. a method that does not use very many memory principles. ?
   d. All of the above

Your first reaction might be to choose *b* because it is the longest answer. However, if you know that at least two of the choices are correct, your only choice then is to choose *d,* which is correct.

Wild-Shot Guess (c)

Many teachers favor the *c* answer for the correct answer. If you try writing some of your own multiple-choice questions, you may find that you, too, tend to put more correct answers in the *c* position than in any other position. Here are a few explanations for why *c* is the most common answer:

■ *A* is not used as often because many students would stop reading the questions and stop thinking about the answer if the correct answer were given first.

■ *B* is not used as often for the same reason that *A* is not.

■ *C* seems to hide the answer best and force the reader to read through more of the options.

■ *D* seems to be too visible because it is on the last line.

O N L I N E   P R A C T I C E   6

Visit the *Essential Study Skills*, Fifth Edition, website and go to Chapter 12. Click on **Practice 6: Ten Educated Guessing Strategies.** Complete the ten-question interactive multiple-choice quiz. Upon completion of the quiz, you will receive your score. You can exit at that time, or you can print your results or e-mail them to your instructor.

✦ EXERCISE 12.5 Using Educated Guessing on True-False Questions

This exercise has test questions on topics that may not be familiar to you. However, if you apply the educated guessing strategies to answer these questions, you will be correct. Work with a partner and discuss your answers.

_____ **1.** In 1913, President Woodrow Wilson believed that concentrated economic power threatened individual liberty and that the monopolies had to be broken up to open up the marketplace.

_____ **2.** All matter exists in only one of three physical forms: solid, liquid, or gas.

_____ **3.** The liquid form of a given material is always less dense than the solid form.

_____ **4.** Rome's early wars often gave plebeians the power to demand that their rights be recognized, but their demands were seldom met.

_____ **5.** Because monasteries believed in isolation, they never conducted schools for local people.

_____ **6.** In 1013, the Danish ruler Swen Forkbeard invaded England.

_____ **7.** The only objective of medieval agriculture was to produce more cattle for meat and dairy products.

_____ **8.** Historians have determined for certain that the bubonic plague originated in southern Russia and was carried to Europe by traveling soldiers.

_____ **9.** The first movies, which began in the late 1880s, were slot-machine peep shows in penny arcades.

_____ **10.** The Warren Court in 1962 declared that schools would always have the right to require prayers in public schools, but students had the right to refrain from praying.

_____ **11.** The behavioral theory suggests that people learn to use alcohol because they want to become more sensitive to others.

_____ **12.** The Dow Jones Industrial Average, established in 1897, is a stock index still in use today.

_____ **13.** The Standard & Poor's 500 Stock Index and the New York Stock Exchange Index never include more stocks than the Dow Jones averages.

_____ **14.** The Securities and Exchange Commission (SEC) was created in 1934 because stock brokers wanted access to a compiled list of all trading.

_____ **15.** In the 1970s, unemployment was high due mainly to the oil embargo.

EXERCISE 12.6   Using Educated Guessing on Multiple-Choice Questions

Use the educated guessing strategies for the following multiple-choice questions. Remember to convert each option into a true-false question before you select the best answer.

_____ 1. A response pattern known as *cynical hostility*
   a. is linked to coronary heart disease and heart attacks.
   b. develops in childhood years.
   c. is characterized by resentment, frequent anger, and distrust.
   d. All of the above

_____ 2. Signs of post-traumatic stress disorder are
   a. never being able to sleep.
   b. shown in a frequency histogram.
   c. poor concentration, anxiety, and nervousness.
   d. apparent at the time of the trauma.

_____ 3. The domestication of plants and animals began around
   a. 7000 BC.
   b. 4000 BC.
   c. AD 1200.
   d. 9000 BC.

_____ 4. With a *balloon automobile loan,* the
   a. buyer feels stupid when the balloon payment is due.
   b. buyer must sell the car back to the lender at the end of the loan.
   c. first six monthly payments are large, but later payments are reduced.
   d. monthly payments are lower, but the final payment is much greater.

_____ 5. Reinforcement theory is
   a. based on giving rewards for behavior you want repeated.
   b. based on forcing issues.
   c. never to be used by effective managers.
   d. the very best training to use for infants.

_____ 6. In business, the agency shop
   a. never charges dues.
   b. charges annual fees of $10 or less.
   c. requires employees to pay dues even if they do not join.
   d. requires employees to always be union members.

_____ 7. Volcanic mountains are formed from
   a. cinder piles and ash.
   b. cinder piles, lava rock, ash, and shields of magma.
   c. erosion.
   d. sandstone and shale.

_____ 8. Consumer spending reports have shown that _____ percent of Americans' disposable income in 1994 was spent on food.
   a. 5
   b. 9
   c. 15
   d. 28

Taking Computerized Tests

Computerized tests usually consist of multiple-choice questions. These tests may be written by the instructor, but more often they consist of a test bank generated by the textbook publisher. Some of the test banks randomly assign test questions of varying levels of difficulty; other test banks allow the instructor to tag the questions to be used on the test. The following chart shows some advantages and disadvantages of computerized testing.

Advantages	Disadvantages
1. You get immediate feedback and a score on your test.	1. Immediate feedback that indicates your answer is incorrect may cause stress and frustration.
2. Positive feedback that an answer is correct increases your confidence level.	2. Most computerized tests do not allow you to go back to previous questions, so you cannot use the test-taking strategy of assisted response.
3. The time limits to complete the tests are less rigid than when you take a test in class.	3. You cannot go back to previous questions to review or change your answers.
4. You may feel less stress because you can control your pace for answering questions.	4. You usually do not get a printed copy of the test to review or use to study when you prepare for a final exam.

If you have not already experienced computerized testing, chances are good that you will at some time during your college career. When you are faced with taking a test on a computer, gather as much information in advance about the computerized test-taking situation as possible. The following are basic questions you may wish to ask before you enter the computer lab for the test.

Is there a tutorial or practice test?

Is there a time limit for completing the test?

May I take the test more than once?

May I have blank scratch paper and pen to work out problems or to organize my thinking?

Will I be able to preview all of the questions before I begin answering?

Is a hard copy (printed version) available for reference during the test so that I can use some of my test-taking strategies?

Will I be able to get a printed version of the test to use for studying after the test is scored?

Allow yourself ample time to complete the test. For many students, taking computerized tests requires more time than taking tests in the classroom. Therefore, you will want to avoid going into the computer lab when you are rushed or pressed for time. Select a time of day when you feel mentally sharp and best able to concentrate. The following *Essential Strategies for Taking Computerized Tests* will help your overall test-taking performance.

SET LEARNING GOALS

The following *Essential Strategies for Taking Computerized Tests* chart highlights nine important strategies to use to take computerized tests. Place a star next to the strategies that you already use. Highlight the strategies that you plan to make a conscious effort to begin using when you take tests on computers.

Essential Strategies for Taking Computerized Tests

▶ **Create a positive learning goal and intention to do well on this test.** Entering a testing lab feeling confident that you are prepared and will do well on the test will set an effective tone for performing well.

▶ **Understand the computer and the testing software commands.** Ask for help if you are unfamiliar with the computer or do not know how to log on. Read the directions carefully. Be sure that you understand how to enter answers and how to change or delete them. Find out if the software program allows you to return to previous questions.

▶ **Use the multiple-choice strategies.** Read the stem; try to complete the stem in your own words before you read the options. Read the stem with each option before you select the best answer. Pay close attention to key words, modifiers, negatives, and relationship or definition clues. *With your eyes,* eliminate the distractors (false statements).

▶ **Do not answer too quickly.** Once you have decided on your answer, reread the stem with your answer one more time before you make the final selection. You can often avoid careless mistakes by double-checking your answer before selecting it as a final answer.

▶ **If you receive feedback that you selected an incorrect answer, do *not* immediately move to the next question.** Take time to reread the question and learn from your error. Learn what you can from the question because similar information may appear later in the test in another form. Taking time to learn from the question keeps your mind focused on the material and reduces the

tendency to move too hastily to the next question. If you are allowed to have paper and pen, jot down correct answers or reminders to yourself to review that topic later.

▶ **Stop and use a short relaxation technique if you find yourself tensing up, feeling discouraged, or getting irritated.** Remember that working memory needs to remain free of mental clutter; stress or anxiety affect thinking processes. Breathing by threes, using positive self-talk, or stretching your arms, rolling your shoulders, or shaking out your hands can reduce stress. Do not talk to the computer with negative words; instead, talk to yourself with positive words of confidence and encouragement.

▶ **Use concentration strategies to keep a focused mind and deal with distractors.** Your goal is to work as much as possible with a relaxed "ahhhh" state of mind. Try to sit at a computer that is not in the line of a steady flow of traffic. When possible, avoid a high-demand time of the day for testing; concentration is easier when fewer people are in the lab.

▶ **Before you leave the test, jot down any questions that concerned or confused you.** Discuss these questions with your instructor. Make a brief list of topics you want to review further.

▶ **Discuss your computer test-taking skills with the lab assistant or your instructor.** After taking several tests, if you are uncomfortable with computerized tests, ask lab assistants and your instructor for additional test-taking strategies. Find out if other testing options are available. Talk with other students to learn their strategies.

CLASS DISCUSSION

Question: How would studying for a computerized test differ from the way that you would study for an in-class paper-and-pencil test?

What are some of the difficulties with taking computerized tests? How can you effectively deal with these difficulties?

O N L I N E   P R A C T I C E   7

Visit the *Essential Study Skills*, Fifth Edition, website and go to Chapter 12. Click on **Practice 7: Taking Computerized Tests**. Then type responses to the four questions. After you type your responses, you can print them or e-mail them to your instructor.

 EXERCISE 12.7 LINKS

Throughout this textbook, you have worked with the psychology chapter in Appendix D. With a partner, use your test-taking strategies to answer the Multiple-Choice Self-Test at the end of the chapter in Appendix D. Your instructor will provide you with the answer key so you can check your success.

Reflection Writing 3
Chapter 12

On separate paper, in a journal, or online at this textbook's website, respond to the following questions.

1. What solutions could you use to address the problems your group listed for the "Group Processing: A Collaborative Learning Activity" on page 327? If you did not do the activity in class, list the kinds of problems you most frequently encounter with objective questions on tests; then discuss solutions for each of the problems.

2. How do attitude and level of stress affect a person's overall performance on tests?

SUMMARY

■ Objective test questions, also referred to as *recognition questions*, include true-false, multiple-choice, and matching. You often need to conduct memory searches, or think through a series of associations in your memory, in order to answer objective questions.

■ Going "blank," making careless mistakes, not being able to concentrate, and having your eyes jumping around on the paper are some common signs of test anxiety. You can use a variety of effective strategies to manage test anxiety that occurs during a test.

■ Four levels of response should be used to answer objective test questions: *immediate response, delayed response, assisted response,* and *educated guessing.*

■ Eight *Essential Strategies* are recommended for taking objective tests. They include jotting information down when you receive the test, surveying the test, budgeting your time, deciding on a starting point, reading all directions carefully, using test time wisely, writing answers for all questions, and using the four levels of response.

■ Key elements used in objective questions must be read carefully:
1. Definition clues
2. Negatives
3. 100 percent and in-between modifiers
4. Relationship clues

■ Both the stem and all the options in a multiple-choice question should be read as true-false statements before they are answered.

■ A two-step strategy is recommended when you answer multiple-choice questions.

■ A four-step approach is recommended when you answer matching questions.

■ Educated guessing can be used to increase your odds at guessing on true-false and multiple-choice questions.

■ Do not become falsely confident because you know educated guessing strategies; the best approach is to be prepared and learn as much information as possible so that you do not need to use educated guessing on a regular basis.

■ Special strategies can be used to increase your performance on computerized tests.

CULMINATING OPTIONS FOR CHAPTER 12

1. Visit this textbook's website and go to Chapter 12 to complete the following exercises:
   a. Flash-card review of Chapter 12 terms and definitions
   b. ACE Practice Test 1 with ten fill-in-the-blank questions
   c. ACE Practice Test 2 with ten true-false questions
   d. ACE Practice Test 3 with ten multiple-choice questions
   e. ACE Practice Test 4 with three short-answers–critical thinking questions

2. Go to Appendix C in the back of this textbook for more Learning Options to use for additional practice, enrichment, or portfolio projects.

Chapter 12 REVIEW QUESTIONS

True-False

Carefully read the following statements. Write T *if the statement is true and* F *if the statement is false.*

_____ 1. Jotting down reminders on your test can help you keep a calm mind before you begin a test.

_____ 2. The words *reason, because,* and *since* are often relationship clues.

_____ 3. All items listed in a series must be false before you can use a false answer.

_____ 4. True-false statements that use negatives are always false.

_____ 5. The most inclusive option in a multiple-choice question is often the best answer.

_____ 6. You should always work systematically through a test by completing questions in the order in which they appear.

_____ 7. If a multiple-choice question has four options, the question should be read as four true-false statements.

_____ 8. If you cannot give an immediate response, you should use educated guessing.

_____ 9. In matching questions, an item from each column can be formed into a sentence by using helper words during the delayed response step.

_____ 10. If you give an incorrect answer on a computerized test, you should quickly move to the next question to keep your confidence level high.

Multiple Choice

Choose the best answer for each of the following questions. Write the letter of the best answer *on the line.*

_____ 1. If you start to feel anxiety during a test, you can
   a. become more active with the test by circling directions and underlining key words.
   b. activate your auditory channel by rereading questions with a whispering voice.
   c. help keep your eyes focused on the question by blocking off the rest of the test with your arm or a piece of paper.
   d. do all of the above.

_____ 2. The _____ of a multiple-choice question should be used with each option.
   a. distractors
   b. directions
   c. stem
   d. All of the above

_____ 3. Educated guessing should be used after
   a. the recall step of response.
   b. the immediate response step.
   c. all other options have been tried.
   d. the delayed response step.

_____ 4. When you first read the stem of a multiple-choice question, you should
   a. decide you really don't like the question.
   b. turn it into a true-false question.
   c. finish the stem with your own words and then see whether an option matches your words.
   d. identify the distractors immediately by using educated guessing strategies.

_____ **5.** When you are told your answer is incorrect on a computerized test, you should
   a. take a deep breath, relax, and try not to get irritated.
   b. try to remember the test question so you can discuss it later.
   c. take time to learn the information with the correct answer.
   d. do all of the above.

Matching

Match the items on the left to the items on the right, writing the letter answer on the line. You may use each answer only once.

_____ **1.** Paired associations

_____ **2.** 100 percent modifiers

_____ **3.** In-between modifiers

_____ **4.** Relationship clues

_____ **5.** Prefixes with negative meanings

_____ **6.** Recognition questions

_____ **7.** Delayed response

_____ **8.** Assisted response

_____ **9.** Stem

_____ **10.** Distractors

a. words such as *sometimes, often, some, perhaps*

b. units of meaning at the beginning of words that mean "no" or "not"

c. guessing true or the letter *c*

d. the linking of two ideas together

e. the beginning part of a multiple-choice question

f. answers that you immediately know

g. options that are incorrect answers

h. involves rereading, looking for clues, and doing memory searches

i. words that are absolutes

j. objective questions

k. a response you give after you skim the test for clues

l. words that often show cause/effect

Short Answer and Critical Thinking

Answer the following questions in the space below or on your own paper. Use paragraph form for your answers.

1. What are the advantages of using a step-by-step approach for answering objective test questions?

2. Discuss the difference between *delayed response* and *assisted response* that can be used for objective test questions.

CHAPTER 13

Developing Strategies for Recall, Math, and Essay Tests

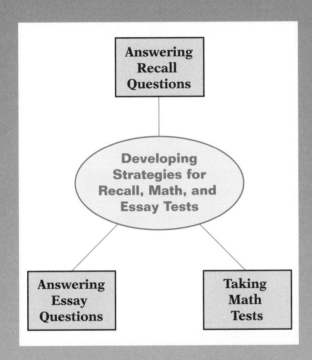

During your college career, you will likely encounter recall, math, and essay tests. In this chapter you will learn effective strategies to answer recall questions, which include fill-in-the blanks, listing, definition, and short-answer questions. You will also learn strategies to avoid common errors on math tests and strategies for increasing your performance on math tests. Essay tests—the most challenging type of test for many students—require you to know the information thoroughly, organize your thoughts logically, and express your ideas in well-written sentences and paragraphs. The strategies in this chapter for answering essay questions will strengthen your performance on essay tests.

Chapter 13 Recall, Math, and Essay Tests Profile

ANSWER, SCORE, and **RECORD** your profile before you read this chapter. If you need to review the process, refer to the complete directions given in the profile for Chapter 1 on page 2.

ONLINE: You can complete the profile and get your score online at this textbook's website.

	YES	NO
1. My answers on questions that require lists of information or short answers are often incomplete or inaccurate.	_____	_____
2. I often have difficulty recalling a specific word to complete a fill-in-the-blank question.	_____	_____
3. Open-ended questions that have many possible answers are difficult for me to answer.	_____	_____
4. I write a one-sentence answer for most questions that ask me to define a term.	_____	_____
5. I understand the different answers required for questions that use the direction words *define, explain, compare, summarize,* or *evaluate.*	_____	_____
6. I know how to analyze my answers on math tests so I can identify my pattern of errors.	_____	_____
7. When I can, I take time to proofread all my answers before turning in the test and leaving the classroom.	_____	_____
8. I use my course syllabus, the table of contents of my textbook, and my class notes to predict themes or topics that might appear in essay questions.	_____	_____
9. I prepare summary notes before major tests, such as midterms or final exams.	_____	_____
10. I am confident in my ability to adequately prepare for recall, math, and essay tests.	_____	_____

Reflection Writing 1
Chapter 13

On separate paper, in a journal, or online at this textbook's website, respond to the following questions.

1. What is your profile score for this chapter? What does it mean to you?

2. What is your general attitude toward tests? How do you react when your instructor announces a test?

3. How do you rate your overall test-taking skills? What are your test-taking strengths and test-taking weaknesses?

Answering Recall Questions

The four most common types of recall questions are fill-in-the-blank, listing, definition, and short-answer questions. Elaborative rehearsal, thorough learning, and efficient long-term memory retrieval techniques are essential for answering such questions. No educated guessing strategies are available for these questions. The following chart summarizes the kind of information to study and forms of practice to include when you prepare for recall questions.

Recall Questions

Study This Kind of Information:	Practice May Include:
• Information presented in lists • Definition cards —say and spell words on the fronts for fill-in-the-blank tests —three-part definitions on the backs of cards for definition and short-answer tests • Category cards • Cornell recall columns • Questions created in the *Q* step of SQ4R • Summaries at the ends of chapters • Details on visual notetaking systems • Mathematical equations • Textbook, class, and homework math problems and solutions	• Reciting information in full sentences and in your own words • Writing short summaries to practice expressing ideas on paper • Writing answers to the questions created in the *Q* step of SQ4R • Writing your own questions for fill-in-the-blank, listing, definition, and short-answer questions • Working with a study partner to exchange practice questions • Writing and explaining the steps in a procedure or equation • Reworking math problems • Grouping or categorizing types of math equations

Fill-in-the-Blank Questions

A fill-in-the-blank question is a sentence with one or more words missing. You must read the sentence carefully and decide which key words will complete the sentence correctly. If you know a test will have fill-in-the-blank questions, you can predict that the majority of answers will relate to terminology. The following strategies provide you with methods for studying and completing this kind of recall question.

Strategies for Fill-in-the-Blank Questions

1. Study from the backs of your index cards.
2. Use immediate response.
3. Use delayed response; search your memory for the category and ask questions.
4. Use assisted response by skimming the rest of the test.
5. Substitute a related synonym or phrase.

Study from the Backs of Your Index Cards   Many fill-in-the-blank questions are based on key vocabulary terms. Spend extra time studying from the *backs* of your index cards so that you can readily recall the terms on the fronts. If you are studying from two-column vocabulary sheets, cover up the left column with the vocabulary words. Read the definitions and practice reciting and spelling the terms in the left column. Your index cards or vocabulary sheets should include all the key terms in the chapter and other terms given in lectures.

Use Immediate Response   If you created, recited, and reviewed vocabulary cards or vocabulary sheets using the method just described, you can often get an *immediate response.* The following points are important to remember when you fill in the blanks.

- Unless the directions say otherwise, write only one word on each blank line.
- The length of the line is not an automatic clue to the length of the word that belongs on the line.
- The completed sentence should make sense and be grammatically correct.
- Blanks that are separated by commas indicate a series of items.
- Several blank lines without commas between them indicate that you will be completing a phrase with a specific number of words.

Use Delayed Response   To use *delayed response,* search your memory for the general category or topic related to the information in the sentence. Once you identify the category, search your memory for the details. Try to recall a specific chapter, a specific visual mapping, a study tool, or a mnemonic you rehearsed for the category. Then ask yourself questions such as *What is . . . What do we call . . . Where is . . . When . . . Who . . . ?* "Talk" your way to the answer.

This *memory search,* or process of thinking back and connecting to information learned, needs to be done quickly. If you have difficulty identifying the category, recalling the study tool used, or answering the questions you formulate, delay your response. Do not spend too much time on one question. If you need to leave the question blank, put a checkmark next to the question so you remember to come back to it later. Move on to the next question.

Use Assisted Response   After you have answered all the questions you can on the test, return to the unanswered ones and apply *assisted response.* Because fill-in-the-blank questions are usually key vocabulary terms, use the rest of the test to look for the terms or their categories. For example, if you know the term belongs to the category "test anxiety," skim through the test looking for other questions about test anxiety. Sometimes you will find the word or an item on the test that will trigger an association to the missing word.

Substitute a Related Synonym or Phrase   You may be able to pick up partial points by writing something in the blank even though you know it is not the correct term. Try one of the following possibilities.

- Use a **synonym** (a word with a similar meaning) or a substitute word. You may not get full points for your answer, but you may be given partial credit.
- If necessary, write a short phrase. Some teachers (though not all) will recognize your effort.

Filling in the blank using synonyms, substitutions, or phrases does show an effort on your part. Be aware, however, that even though you may put effort into using this approach, your answer will be marked wrong because the *exact* answer was needed. Make a mental note to find the correct answers after the test.

EXERCISE 13.1   Filling in the Blanks

Work with a partner. Read the following questions carefully. They are
all review questions based on key terms from previous chapters. First, try
an immediate response; then try a delayed response by doing a memory
search and posing a question.

1. The _____ _____ technique is a concentration technique
   for letting other people know that you do not want to be disturbed.

2. The beginning part of a multiple-choice question is called the _____.

3. _____ time consists of a few hours each week added to your time-management
   schedule to allow for any extra study time beyond your regular study blocks.

4. Howard Gardner's _____ intelligence refers to a person's ability to work cooper-
   atively, understand people, and demonstrate leadership skills.

5. The second step of the Cornell system uses the memory principle of selectivity when information is
   selected to put in the _____ column.

6. The memory principle of _____ is used when two items are linked together in
   memory so one can trigger the recall of the other.

7. A(n) _____ is a "memory trick strategy" that involves making up a word by using
   the first letters of each of the key words that you need to remember.

8. A _____ learner describes a person who is a "right-brain dominant person" and
   tends to be intuitive, creative, and visual.

9. _____ memory occurs when emphasis is on memorizing the exact wording of
   information instead of using elaborative rehearsal for more thorough understanding.

10. _____ is the process of skimming through information before beginning the
    process of careful reading.

O N L I N E   P R A C T I C E   1

Visit the *Essential Study Skills*, Fifth Edition, website and go to Chapter 13. Click on **Practice 1:
Practice Filling in the Blanks**. Complete the ten-question interactive fill-in-the-blank quiz to
review terminology from Chapters 1 through 6. Upon completion of the quiz, you will receive your
score. You can exit at that time, or you can print your results or e-mail them to your instructor.

O N L I N E   P R A C T I C E   2

Visit the *Essential Study Skills*, Fifth Edition, website and go to Chapter 13. Click on **Practice
2: More Practice Filling in the Blanks**. Complete the ten-question interactive fill-in-the-
blank quiz to review terminology from Chapters 7 through 12. Upon completion of the quiz, you
will receive your score. You can exit at that time, or you can print your results or e-mail them to
your instructor.

Listing Questions

Listing questions require you to recall a specific number of ideas, steps, or vocabulary words. The answers are usually key words; full sentences are not generally required. Listing questions often begin with the direction word *list* or *name*. Using the following strategies will improve your performance on listing questions.

Strategies for Listing Questions

1. Predict listing questions when you study.
2. Underline key words and determine whether the question is closed or open ended.
3. Use immediate response.
4. Use delayed response; do a memory search and ask questions.
5. Use assisted response.
6. Substitute a related synonym or phrase.

Predict Listing Questions When You Study   You can predict listing questions as you read, take notes, and create study tools by recognizing or anticipating possible items for listing questions. Lists to study can be found

- on category index cards
- in questions created for headings in the SQ4R system
- in Cornell recall columns
- in chapter objectives and introductions
- in level-one and level-two information in mappings or hierarchies
- in paragraphs that use ordinals (number words)
- in marginal notes written in your textbooks
- in formulas or equations using procedural knowledge

Underline Key Words In Closed and Open-Ended Questions   By underlining the key words in the question, you will be able to focus specifically on the information being asked. Notice how the underlining in the following question helps you focus.

1. Lining up the Cornell columns is one reflect activity you can do during the fourth step of the Cornell notetaking system. List five other study tools that you can make during the reflect step to reinforce the learning process.

Now decide whether the question has specific answers or a variety of possible answers. **Closed questions** require very specific answers, often in a specific order, such as with procedural knowledge. **Open-ended questions** can have many possible answers. You can pull related ideas and information from throughout the term to develop your answer for an open-ended question. The above question about study tools during the reflect step of Cornell is an *open-ended* question. Any five of the following answers would be correct: visual mappings, cartoon/pictures, acronyms, outlines, study tapes, written summaries, predicted test questions, vocabulary flash cards, or hierarchies.

> This is a *closed question*: List the five *R's* of the Cornell notetaking system in the order in which they occur.

> This is an *open-ended question*: List six concentration strategies to reduce attention to external distractors.

Use Immediate Response   After you have underlined the key words in the directions, you may be ready with the answer. Being able to give an *immediate response* indicates that you organized and rehearsed information effectively, which enabled you to quickly bring the information into your working memory and respond.

Use Delayed Response   If necessary, move to *delayed response*. Use association triggers to help you connect the key words in the directions to the information you want to find in your memory bank. Use the following techniques.

■ Focus on the key words you underlined in the directions. These will help you identify the category.

■ Search your memory for study tools that you created to rehearse the information. Try to picture the index cards, the Cornell recall column, the chapter headings, or the main topics in visual notes or outlines.

■ Turn the information into a new *question*. In the preceding example, you might pose the question "What study tools help me reflect on information that I am learning?"

   Because you probably have many other questions to deal with on the test, memory searching and questioning must be done relatively quickly. If you are able to retrieve an answer—or part of an answer—write it down. If you are not able to complete the listing, *place a checkmark next to the question*. You can come back to it later after you have completed as many questions as possible.

Use Assisted Response   When you return to the unanswered or partially answered questions, skim through the rest of the test for possible clues. When the question involves procedural knowledge, skim for related steps or the same kind of problem or equation. Many times important information appears in the test in more than one place but in a different questioning format. Focus on the key words that you underlined in the directions.

Substitute a Related Synonym or Phrase   If you were not able to locate the exact terms for the listing, use synonyms or short phrases. These answers are not as accurate, yet they show your effort and general understanding. An empty space can bring only one result: no points. You may receive full points or partial points for using synonyms or short phrases.

✸ EXERCISE 13.2 Practicing Closed and Open-Ended Questions

Work with a partner. Read the following questions carefully. In the margin, write C if the question is a closed question and O if the question is an open-ended question. On separate paper, list answers for each question without referring to other pages in your textbook or your notes.

_____ **1.** What are the steps, in order, for the Feedback Model?

_____ **2.** List five strategies to reduce or eliminate procrastination.

_____ **3.** List five traits of active listeners.

_____ **4.** What are the eight intelligences in Howard Gardner's Theory of Multiple Intelligences?

_____ **5.** Name the four levels of response (in order) that you can use to answer test questions.

O N L I N E   P R A C T I C E   3

> Visit the *Essential Study Skills*, Fifth Edition, website and go to Chapter 13. Click on **Practice 3: Answering Questions with Lists**. Complete the quiz of ten closed-listing questions to review lists of information from Chapters 1 through 13. Upon completion of the quiz, you will receive the answers for self-scoring.

Definition Questions

Definition questions ask you to define a term. This kind of question asks you to retrieve specific information from your memory and organize the information into sentences. *Paired association* is required and achieved if you have studied from vocabulary cards or vocabulary sheets. You can predict that these questions will come from the course-specific terminology that was defined in your textbook and in lectures. The following strategies will result in well-developed definition answers.

Strategies for Definition Questions

1. Read the question carefully. Underline the term to be defined.
2. Use the three steps for writing definitions.
3. Use delayed response and assisted response if necessary.

Underline the Term   Underline the term in a short definition question to help you keep your focus on that one word. Sometimes definition questions begin by giving background information. Read all of the information carefully and then underline the term to be defined. The following examples are both definition questions.

1. Define the term *neurons*.
2. The human nervous system is comprised of two primary types of cells, the neurons and the glial cells. Glial cells provide physiological support to neurons. Define *neurons* in the central nervous system.

Use the Three Steps for Writing Definitions   For powerful definition answers, include three levels of information. First, name the category associated with the term. Second, give the formal definition. Third, expand the definition with one more detail. The following examples show a weak answer and a strong answer.

Question:	Define the term *distributed practice*.
Weak Answer:	It means you practice at different times.
Strong Answer:	Distributed practice is a time-management strategy that is also related to the memory principle of time on task. It means that study blocks are spread or distributed throughout the week. Distributed practice, also known as spaced practice, is the opposite of marathon studying.

Category ——————
Definition ——————
One more detail ——————

Expanding your definition is the open-ended part of a question that gives you the opportunity to show you know more about a word than just its most basic definition. The following chart shows seven methods, followed by an example, that you can use to expand a definition.

Method	Example
Add one more fact.	*Distributed practice often occurs when the 2:1 ratio is used.*
Give a synonym.	*Distributed practice is the same as spaced practice.*
Give an antonym, a contrast, or a negation.	*Distributed practice is the opposite of marathon studying or massed practice.*
Give a comparison or an analogy.	*Distributed practice is like working on a goal a little every day instead of trying to complete all the steps in one block of time.*
Define the structure of the word.	*The root of <u>neuron</u> is "neuro," which means <u>nervous system</u>.*
Give the etymology.	*The term <u>locus</u> comes from the Latin "loci," which means <u>place</u>, so locus of control refers to a place where there is the control.*
Give an application.	*Surveying can be used to become familiar with a new textbook, chapter, article, or test.*

Use Delayed and Assisted Response   If you are not able to give an immediate response, the questions given for identifying the general category may help you with the delayed response. If your mind is blank, and you cannot write the definition or expand the definition, *place a checkmark next to the question and move on.* After you have answered all the questions you can, skim through the rest of the test to search for additional clues or details to complete your answer. Remember that key terms are frequently used or referred to in other parts of the test in other questioning formats.

EXERCISE 13.3   **Answering Definition Questions**

On your own paper, write a three-part definition answer for the following definition questions. Be sure to use this format for your answer:

category: _____

definition: _____

one more detail: _____

1. Define the term *reciting*.

2. You have learned many study strategies in this course. These strategies have one common characteristic: they all emphasize *elaborative rehearsal*. Define the term *elaborative rehearsal*.

3. Learning involves intellectual and emotional growth. Self-talk has the power to enhance the learning process, but it can also hinder the learning process. In this course, the focus has been on the power of *positive self-talk*. Define what is meant by *positive self-talk*.

EXERCISE 13.4   **Creating Definition Questions**

Work with a partner. Look at the Terms to Know *at the beginning of Chapters 1 through 13. Select any five vocabulary terms for your partner to define out loud using the three-part definition answer. Your partner will then select any five terms for you to give a three-part definition out loud. If you prefer to modify these directions, partners could give each other five vocabulary terms and then* write *three-part definition answers.*

Copyright © Houghton Mifflin Company. All rights reserved.

O N L I N E   P R A C T I C E   4

 Visit the *Essential Study Skills*, Fifth Edition, website and go to Chapter 13. Click on **Practice 4: Answering Definition Questions**. Use the three-part definition answer to type responses to the six definition questions. After you type your responses, you can print them or e-mail them to your instructor.

Short-Answer Questions

Short-answer questions usually require a short paragraph of three to seven sentences for the answer. Sometimes they look like "mini-essays," and at other times they look like expanded "listing questions" that use sentences to explain the items in a listing. With short answers, both the content of your answer and your writing skills are important. Some teachers will grade higher when you use correct grammar, punctuation, and spelling.

As with listing questions, short-answer questions may be *closed questions* in which very specific answers are expected. They may also be *open-ended questions* that require you to connect or relate ideas from different parts of the course, or they may require you to apply your knowledge to new situations. Both types of short-answer questions require sufficient details to show that you know the information. The following steps can help you write an effective answer.

Strategies for Answering Short-Answer Questions

1. Identify the direction word and underline the key words.
2. Make a mental plan or short list of key ideas to use in your answer.
3. Write a strong, focused opening sentence.
4. Add additional sentences with specific details.
5. Use delayed and assisted response if necessary.

Identify the Direction Word and Underline Key Words   The first step is to pay attention to the **direction word** in each question. Each type of direction word requires a specific kind of answer. To get full points for your work, your answer must match the question. The following direction words are common for short-answer questions.

Direction Word	What Is Required
Discuss/Tell	Tell about a particular topic.
Identify/What are?	Identify specific points. (This is similar to a listing except that you are required to answer in full sentences.)
Describe	Give more specific details or descriptions than are required by "discuss."
Explain/Why?	Give reasons. Answer the question "Why?"
Explain how/How?	Describe a process or a set of steps. Give the steps in chronological (time sequence) order.
When?	Describe a time or a specific condition needed for something to happen, occur, or be used.

Circle the key direction word when you first read the question. Review in your mind what is required by this direction word. Because you want to respond quickly, become very familiar with the preceding descriptions of direction words. Then underline key words to use in your answer.

Each of the following test questions has the same subject: visual mappings. However, because of the different direction words, each answer will be slightly different.

(Why) is <u>recitation</u> important to use while <u>studying</u> a visual <u>mapping</u>?

(Explain how) to <u>create</u> a visual <u>mapping</u>.

(How) should you <u>study from</u> a visual <u>mapping</u>?

(When) should you use visual <u>mappings</u>?

Make a Mental Plan or a Short List of Key Ideas   Look at the key words underlined in the step above. These words should be included in your answer. Pause and do a *memory search* for appropriate details for your answer. Either make a mental plan or jot down a short list of points that you will want to present in sentence form. Do only what is expected; do not pad the answer with unrelated information.

Write a Strong, Focused Opening Sentence   Because you will not have much space to write a long answer, begin your answer with a sentence that is direct and to the point. Your first sentence should include the key words of the question and should show that you are heading in the direction required by the direction word. Do not beat around the bush or save your best information for last. The first sentence, when well written, lets the teacher know right away that you are familiar with the subject.

Notice the differences in quality in the following opening sentences. The first one does not get to the point. The second and third examples are direct and show confidence.

Question: Why is recitation important in the learning process?
Weak: Recitation is important because it helps a person learn better.
Strong: Recitation, one of the Twelve Principles of Memory, is important in the learning process for three reasons.
Strong: Recitation is important in the learning process because it involves the auditory channel, feedback, and practice expressing ideas.

Add Sentences with Specific Details   After you write your opening sentence, expand your answer with more information. Give appropriate details to support your opening sentence; try to use course-related terminology in your answers.

Notice the difference between the weak answer and the strong answer in the following example.

Weak: Recitation is important because it helps a person learn. Everyone wants to do the very best possible, and recitation helps make that happen. When you recite, you talk out loud. You practice information out loud before a test.

Strong: Recitation is important in the learning process because it involves the auditory channel, gives feedback, and provides practice expressing ideas. When a person states information out loud and in complete sentences, he/she activates the auditory channel and keeps information active in working memory.

Reciting also gives feedback so that a person knows immediately whether or not the information is understood on the level that it can be explained to someone else. Taking time to recite also provides the opportunity to practice organizing ideas so that they can be clearly expressed.

Use Delayed and Assisted Response   If you are unable to write a strong opening sentence for your short answer, do a memory search for the topic. Frequently, students are able to write the opening sentence but have difficulty with the details necessary to expand the opening sentence. If the delayed response and the memory search do not result in sufficient information or details, place a checkmark next to the question and move on. After you have answered all other questions, skim through the test for related details that you can add to your short answer. Expand your answer with these details.

EXERCISE 13.5   Writing Answers to Short-Answer Questions

Select two questions from the following list. Unless your instructor asks you to write your answers on separate paper, write your answers in the space below. You may be asked to read your answers to other students or to the class.

1. Explain why *rote memory* is not a reliable method for studying most college materials.

2. Explain how *locus of control* affects a person's perception of his or her life.

3. Discuss any one strategy that you can use to comprehend a difficult paragraph.

O N L I N E   P R A C T I C E   5

Visit the *Essential Study Skills*, Fifth Edition, website and go to Chapter 13. Click on **Practice 5: Responding to Short-Answer Questions**. Type responses to the three short-answer questions about information from Chapters 1 through 6. After you type your responses, you can print them or e-mail them to your instructor.

O N L I N E   P R A C T I C E   6

Visit the *Essential Study Skills*, Fifth Edition, website and go to Chapter 13. Click on **Practice 6: More Short-Answer Questions**. Type responses to the three short-answer questions about information you learned from Chapters 7 through 13. After you type your responses, you can print them or e-mail them to your instructor.

EXERCISE 13.6   Textbook Case Studies

Read about each of the following student situations carefully. Then, on your own paper and in complete sentences, answer the question that follows each case study. You can also answer these questions online at this textbook's Chapter 13 website. You can print your online responses or e-mail them to your instructor.

1. Armand takes effective notes in his science class. He does well on multiple-choice tests but frequently has difficulty with fill-in-the-blank tests. He realizes that he needs to adjust his study methods to prepare more effectively for this test format. Which study methods would you recommend that he use to be better prepared for fill-in-the-blank questions?

2. Jessica's sociology instructor writes test questions that require listings and short answers. Jessica decides to form a study group to help her prepare for an upcoming sociology test. She wants the group to be productive, but she needs suggestions on an approach the study group can use to prepare for the test. Which study techniques would you suggest the group implement?

3. Heather studies hard for tests but quickly gets annoyed with herself when she cannot remember information that she studied. When she can't answer a question, the negative self-talk begins. She skips the question and moves on to the next one. The questions that she does answer are usually correct; however, she leaves too many questions blank, which lowers her overall test score. What test-taking strategies can Heather learn to improve her performance on tests?

O N L I N E   C A S E   S T U D I E S

Visit the *Essential Study Skills*, Fifth Edition, website and go to Chapter 13. Click on **Online Case Studies**. In the text boxes, respond to four additional case studies that are only available online. You can print your responses or e-mail them to your instructor.

O N L I N E   P R A C T I C E   7

Visit the *Essential Study Skills*, Fifth Edition, website and go to Chapter 13. Click on **Practice 7: Answering Recall Questions**. Complete the ten-question true-false quiz. Upon completion of the quiz, you will receive your score. You can exit at that time, or you can print your results or e-mail them to your instructor.

Taking Math Tests

Performing well on math tests requires an alert mind ready to manage a variety of thinking processes and tasks that result in an exact correct answer. The test-preparation strategies and test-taking strategies discussed previously apply to test-taking situations for all math tests. The following points about taking math tests can help you achieve better results.

- Preparing for and taking math tests involves both *declarative knowledge* and *procedural knowledge*.

- Using elaborative rehearsal strategies to learn the declarative knowledge, such as knowing the meanings of symbols, translating algebraic symbols into English words, and memorizing formulas, is necessary throughout the term.

- In addition to learning the factual information, you must prepare for math tests by giving adequate time and attention to the procedural knowledge, the steps required to solve an equation or a word problem.

- Because most problems on math tests are patterned after math problems that you worked on in your textbook and in class, reworking problems *multiple times* before a test is essential.

   Using the *Essential Strategies for Math Tests* on the following page can help you improve your test-taking performance on math tests.

How can these students use a completed math test to improve their test-taking skills? What kinds of problem patterns should they look for on the test?

SET LEARNING GOALS

The following *Essential Strategies for Math Tests* chart highlights five important strategies to use to improve your performance on math tests. Place a star next to the strategies that you already use. Highlight the strategies that you plan to make a conscious effort to begin using for math tests.

Essential Strategies for Math Tests

▶ **Read the directions carefully and thoroughly until you understand the type of answer required.** Then, examine the information that is provided and identify what information is missing or what information you will need to supply to solve the problem. Frequently, drawing a simple picture of the problem or expressing the problem in an algebraic formula will help you see the problem more clearly.

▶ **Categorize the problem.** Conduct a *memory search* for similar problems that you solved previously. By categorizing the problem and associating it with previously worked problems, you can think through the problem-solving steps or formula required for this type of math problem. Mentally compare the test problem to problems you practiced and reworked in class and in the textbook.

▶ **Estimate a reasonable answer before you begin solving the problem.** After you work the steps to arrive at your answer, compare your final answer with your estimated answer. A discrepancy between the two answers provides you with feedback telling you to examine the problem more carefully.

▶ **Show your work all the way through to the last step of solving the problem.** Showing all the steps of the process indicates that you understand how to use a set procedure to solve the problem; it can also show you or your instructor where errors occurred if you did not solve the problem correctly. In addition, your instructor may reward points for the work you do show in the individual steps even if the final answer is incorrect.

▶ **Check your work one final time.** Checking your work one final time can help you eliminate common errors such as omitting labels on story problem answers, using the incorrect mathematical sign of operation, or calculating incorrectly when you add, subtract, multiply, or divide numbers.

CLASS DISCUSSION

Question: How do test-taking strategies used for procedural knowledge differ from test-taking strategies used for declarative knowledge?

Six Types of Test-Taking Errors

Recognizing **six types of test-taking errors** can help you strengthen your accuracy on math tests. Use the following information each time you do a math problem for homework as well as on tests. After tests are returned to you, use the information to analyze your errors so you can adjust your strategies for future tests.

Six Types of Test-Taking Errors

1. Misread directions errors
2. Careless errors
3. Concept errors
4. Application errors
5. Test-taking errors
6. Study errors

Adapted from Paul Nolting, *Math Study Skills Workbook*, pp. 92–95. Copyright © 2000. Reprinted with permission of Houghton Mifflin, Inc.

Misread directions errors   occur when you skip directions or misunderstand directions, but you work the problems anyway. To avoid misread directions errors, read all the directions carefully and circle or underline key words. If you do not understand any of them, ask your instructor for clarification.

Careless errors   are mistakes that you can catch automatically upon reviewing the test. Both good and poor math students make careless errors. Students who commit these errors know the math but simply make sloppy mistakes, such as calculation mistakes, or omission of a symbol or the steps used to solve the problem. If a student can point out the mistake upon examination of a problem at a later point, the error is one of carelessness. To reduce careless errors, use all available test time wisely to check your work.

Concept errors   are mistakes made when you do not understand the properties or principles required to work the problem. Concept errors, if not corrected, will follow you from test to test, causing a loss of test points. After the test, go back to your textbook or notes and learn why you missed those types of problems. Rework several problems that use the concept that you need to learn more accurately. In your own words, write the concepts that you use to solve these kinds of problems.

Application errors   occur when you know the concept but cannot apply it to the problem. Application errors usually are found in word problems, deducing formulas (such as the quadratic equation), and graphing. To reduce application errors, you must predict the types of application problems that will be on the test. You must then think through and practice solving those types of problems using the concepts. Application errors can be avoided with appropriate practice and insight.

Test-taking errors   apply to the specific way you take tests. The following list includes test-taking errors that can cause you to lose many points on an exam:

1. *Missing more questions in the first third or the last third of a test:* Errors in the first third of a test (the easiest problems) can be due to carelessness. Errors in the last part of the test can be due to the fact that the last problems are more difficult or due to increasing your test speed to finish the test.

2. *Not completing a problem to its last step:* Take time to review the last step to be sure you show all your work right up to the end of the problem.

3. *Changing test answers from correct to incorrect:* Changing answers without a logical reason for doing so is a sign of panic or test anxiety. Keep your original answer unless you locate an error in your work when you review your work a final time.

4. *Getting stuck on one problem and spending too much time on it:* Set a time limit for each problem. Working too long on a problem without success will increase your test anxiety and waste valuable time that could be better used solving other problems or reviewing your test.

5. *Rushing through the easiest part of the test and making careless errors:* Work more slowly and carefully. Review the easiest problems first if you have time to go back over your work during the allotted test time.

6. *Miscopying an answer from your scratch work to the test:* Systematically compare your last problem step on scratch paper with the answer written on the test. Always hand in your scratch work with your test.

7. *Leaving answers blank:* If you cannot figure out how to solve a problem, rewrite the problem and try to do at least the first step.

8. *Solving only the first step of a two-step problem:* Write *two* in the margin of the test when you first read the problem. This reminds you that you need to show two steps or two answers to the problem.

9. *Not understanding all the functions of your calculator* can cause major testing problems. Take time to learn all the functions of your calculator *before* the test.

10. *Leaving the test early without checking your answers:* Use the entire allotted test time. Remain in the room and use the time to check each problem.

Study errors   occur when you study the wrong type of material or do not spend enough time on pertinent material. Use your time-management skills to allocate sufficient time to review problems and formulas that have been covered in class. Create study tools such as three-column notes and index cards to review frequently before the test.

Adapted from Nolting, *Math Study Skills Workbook,* pp. 92–95.

The RSTUV Problem-Solving Method

In *Topics in Contemporary Mathematics,* the **RSTUV Problem-Solving Method** serves as a model to solve *any* word problem.

RSTUV Problem-Solving Method

1. **R**ead the problem, not once or twice but until you understand it.
2. **S**elect the unknown; that is, find out what the problem asks for.
3. **T**hink of a plan to solve the problem.
4. **U**se the techniques you are studying to carry out the plan.
5. **V**erify the answer.

1. **Read** the problem.

Mathematics is a language. As such, you have to learn how to read it. You may not understand or even get through reading the problem the first time. Read it again and, as you do, pay attention to key words or instructions such as *compute, draw, write, construct, make, show, identify, state, simplify, solve,* and *graph*.

2. **Select** the unknown.

How can you answer a question if you do not know what the question is? One good way to look for the unknown is to look for the question mark "?" and carefully read the material preceding it. Try to determine what information is given and what is missing.

3. **Think** of a plan.

Problem solving requires many skills and strategies. Some of them are *look for a pattern; examine a related problem; make tables, pictures, and diagrams; write an equation; work backward;* and *make a guess.*

4. **Use** the techniques you are studying to carry out the plan.

If you are studying a mathematical technique, it is almost certain that you will have to use it in solving the given problem. Look for procedures that can be used to solve specific problems. Then carry out the plan. Check each step.

5. **Verify** the answer.

Look back and check the results of the original problem. Is the answer reasonable? Can you find it some other way?

From Bello and Britton, *Topics in Contemporary Mathematics*, 6/e, pp. 5–6. Copyright © 1997. Reprinted by permission of Houghton Mifflin, Inc.

O N L I N E   P R A C T I C E   8

Visit the *Essential Study Skills*, Fifth Edition, website and go to Chapter 13. Click on **Practice 8: Taking Math Tests**. Complete the ten-question true-false quiz. Upon completion of the quiz, you will receive your score. You can exit at that time, or you can print your results or e-mail them to your instructor.

 EXERCISE 13.7 Looking at Test-taking Errors on Math Tests

Refer to any previous math test (or a science test with equations) that has been graded. Analyze the kinds of errors that you made by referring to pages 370–371. List the kinds of errors in the following space. Then use the list to write a short summary of the errors you identified. In your summary, include examples that show where you made the errors.

Kinds of errors:

1.

2.

3.

Reflection Writing 2
Chapter 13

On separate paper, in a journal, or online at this textbook's website, respond to the following questions.

1. Which type or types of recall questions have been the most difficult for you in the past? Explain why you feel that they were the most difficult.

2. Which strategies for recall questions do you believe will be the most helpful for you on future tests? Explain why.

3. What math strategies did you learn that are new to you? How will using these strategies change the way you take math tests?

Group Processing: **A Collaborative Learning Activity**

Form groups of three or four students. Then complete the following directions.

1. First, as a group, brainstorm about the ways in which you prepare for essay tests. List all the study strategies or systems that you use.

2. Second, list all the kinds of problems that you encounter or the weaknesses in your answers when you take essay tests. Compile as many different examples as possible.

Answering Essay Questions

Essay questions are demanding; they require that you know the information thoroughly, be able to pull the information from your memory, and write about relationships rather than isolated facts. The way you express the information and the relationships needs to follow a logical line of thinking. For this type of test, your study strategies throughout the term need to include *elaborative rehearsal* of both the textbook and the lecture material. Elaborative rehearsal occurs when you work with the information; rearrange it; look for relationships, patterns, and trends; and work to recognize key concepts, main ideas, and themes as well as significant supporting details for the "big pictures." Essays also require a sound grasp of writing skills (grammar, syntax, and spelling) as well as a well-developed, expressive vocabulary. If essay writing is intimidating to you, be assured that you can strengthen your essay-writing skills by using the following *Essential Strategies for Preparing for Essay Tests* and the strategies for organizing information into essay answers.

SET LEARNING GOALS

The following *Essential Strategies for Preparing for Essay Tests* chart highlights seven important strategies to use to prepare for essay tests. Place a star next to the strategies that you already use. Highlight the strategies that you plan to make a conscious effort to begin using to prepare for essay tests.

Essential Strategies for Preparing for Essay Tests

▶ **Identify major themes developed in the course.** The themes are the *big pictures* that you are expected to know by the end of the term. Essay questions often are based on major themes or on the larger concepts. Examine the course objectives and outcomes stated on your course syllabus or outline. Check your textbook's table of contents; oftentimes the headings of units or chapters form themes. Review the information in the introductory section of your textbook; the author often states the major themes in the introduction. Finally, examine your course notes to identify recurring topics or themes.

▶ **Create summary notes that include textbook, lecture, and homework information for each theme.** Essay questions often require you to compare, contrast, summarize, explain, discuss, or apply information about major themes. Summary notes facilitate the process by compiling and grouping related information to study prior to an essay test.

▶ **Use the list of possible themes and your summary notes to predict and write practice test questions.** Work with a partner or in a study group to create essay questions and answers. Set a realistic time limit to compose your answers. If you practice expressing your ideas on paper *before the test*, dealing with essay questions on the test is much less stressful and intimidating.

▶ **When the *topics* for the essay questions are announced in advance, generate detailed notes on the topics.** Gather pertinent information; use the index of your textbook to locate information on the topic. Reread the pages indicated in the index and prepare a set of summary notes. Predict possible questions. Then organize the information and practice writing answers to the questions you have predicted.

▶ **When the *questions* are announced in advance, gather and organize pertinent information; practice writing essay answers.** Some instructors may provide you with a list of essay questions from which the actual test questions will be selected. Using the index in your textbook, gather pertinent information. Create and memorize an outline or organizational plan for your answers. Write effective answers for each essay question. Without referring to your outline, organizational plan, or initial essay answer, practice writing the essay answer several times.

▶ **Organize materials for an open-book essay test.** Become familiar with the index of your book so you can look up topics quickly. Use a special highlighter to mark important facts (dates, names, events, statistics, and terminology) and quotations you may wish to use in your answer. Use tabs to mark significant pages such as those with important summary charts, tables, lists, steps, or visual materials. Use the previous suggestions for identifying themes, creating summary notes, predicting test questions, and practicing writing answers.

▶ **For take-home essay tests, plan your time well.** A major problem some students face with take-home essay tests is not allowing enough time to develop polished essay answers. Create a study plan that allows ample time to gather information, create summary notes, organize the information logically, and finally, write the essay. After setting the essay aside for a day, reread it; look for ways to strengthen it; proofread for spelling, grammar, and mechanics; and type a final version.

CLASS DISCUSSION

Question: Why are time-management skills essential for preparing for essay tests?

Understanding Direction Words

Some of the direction words used in short-answer questions also appear in essay questions. Understanding the **direction words** is essential for your essay to address the question that was posed. Study the following direction words so that you will know the kind of information that is expected in your answer.

Direction Word	What Is Required
Compare	Show the similarities and differences between two or more items.
Contrast	Present only the differences between two or more items.
Define	Give the definition and expand it with more examples and greater details.
Trace/Outline	Discuss the sequence of events in chronological order.
Summarize	Identify and discuss the main points or the highlights of a subject. Omit in-depth details.
Evaluate/Critique	Offer your opinion or judgment and then back it up with specific facts, details, or reasons.
Analyze	Identify the different parts of something. Discuss each part individually.
Describe	Give a detailed description of different aspects, qualities, characteristics, parts, or points of view.
Discuss/Tell	Tell about the parts or the main points. Expand with specific details.
Explain/Explain why	Give reasons. Tell why. Show logical relationships or cause/effect.
Explain how	Give the process, steps, stages, or procedures involved. Explain each.
Illustrate	Give examples. Explain each example with details.
Identify/What are	Identify specific points. Discuss each point individually. Include sufficient details.
When	Describe a time or a specific condition needed for something to happen, occur, or be used. Provide details and any relevant background information.

As an example of the importance of understanding the direction word, assume that a question on your literature test stated, "Compare the writing style of Homer in *The Odyssey* and John Milton in *Paradise Lost.*" In your essay, you would want to focus on the similarities and differences between the two authors' writing styles. To simply write one paragraph describing Homer and another paragraph describing Milton, and assume that the teacher could infer the differences by reading the two paragraphs would not clearly show the relationships involved. The direction word requires you to identify specific elements of writing styles and compare or contrast the use of each element by Homer and by Milton. Responding appropriately to direction words is an essential key to well-written answers.

EXERCISE 13.8 Analyzing Essay Questions

Work with a partner or in a small group. Read each question carefully. On the line, write C if the question is a closed question and O if the question is an open-ended question. Then circle the direction word and underline key words that you would use in your answers.

_____ 1. Discuss this statement: Business competition encourages efficiency of production and leads to improved quality control.

_____ 2. Is gross national product really a reliable indicator of a nation's standard of living? Explain.

_____ 3. Why should business take on the task of training the hard-core unemployed?

_____ 4. What are the major differences between the economic model of social responsibility and the socioeconomic model?

_____ 5. Define the goal of affirmative-action programs and tell how the goal is achieved.

_____ 6. Explain the differences between general partners and limited partners.

_____ 7. Trace the incorporation process and describe the basic corporate structure.

_____ 8. Discuss the changes made in Washington in the post-Watergate years to place greater restrictions on the executive power of the president of the United States.

_____ 9. Contrast the opinions and sentiments expressed by the people of Panama and the American people in 1977 in regard to the ownership and rights to the Panama Canal.

_____ 10. President Clinton's 1998 visit to China brought the Tiananmen Square event back into the public's awareness. Trace the events in China that led up to and followed the massacre in Tiananmen Square.

_____ 11. In the late 1990s, environmental issues remained high on the international list of global problems. Summarize the global environmental issues that may have the greatest impact on the welfare of the world's population.

_____ 12. Which leadership style or styles most closely conform to supportive communication? Explain.

_____ 13. Think of and then discuss three examples of positive ethnic stereotypes.

_____ 14. Compare the thinking styles of vertical thinkers and lateral thinkers. Include the characteristics of each type of thinker and give examples to clearly show the differences in the way each would operate in day-to-day situations.

_____ 15. What are Piaget's stages of human development? Summarize each stage of his theory.

_____ 16. Trace the path of blood in the circulatory system of mammals.

O N L I N E   P R A C T I C E   9

Visit the *Essential Study Skills*, Fifth Edition, website and go to Chapter 13. Click on **Practice 9: Understanding Direction Words**. Complete the ten-question true-false quiz. Upon completion of the quiz, you will receive your score. You can exit at that time, or you can print your results or e-mail them to your instructor.

Strategies for Answering Essay Questions

The following strategies for answering essay questions are similar to the strategies used for short-answer questions (page 364). The procedures have been expanded to meet the essay requirement that full paragraphs be used to communicate the information. Understanding the general structure of an essay and using the following strategies will result in better performance on essay tests.

Strategies for Answering Essay Questions

1. Identify and underline the direction word and other key words.
2. Write a strong, focused opening sentence called a *thesis sentence* or *thesis statement*.
3. Create an organizational plan for your answer before you begin writing: a brief outline, visual mapping, hierarchy, or list of ideas to develop the body of your essay.
4. Develop the body of the essay. A common format is the five-paragraph essay.
5. Summarize your main ideas in a short concluding paragraph.
6. Proofread and revise.

Identify the Direction Word   The beginning step in writing an essay is knowing what kind of answer is expected. The direction word indicates what is expected and should guide the direction of your answer. Underline the direction word and other key words.

Write a Strong Thesis Sentence   A **thesis sentence** directly states the main point you want to make in the entire essay. The thesis sentence for an essay test should be the first sentence on your paper. This sentence should

- clearly state the topic of the essay
- include key words that are a part of the question
- show that you understand the direction word
- indicate a given number of main ideas you will discuss

The thesis statement is important to you and to your instructor. For you, it serves as a guide for developing the rest of your essay. It provides the basic outline of main ideas to develop with important supporting details. For the instructor, it serves as an immediate indicator that you understand the question and know the answer. Because of the significance of the thesis statement, take time to create a strong, direct, confident opening sentence.

In the chart on the following page, notice how the direction word is identified and circled and how key words are underlined. Thought is given to the type of answer that is expected, based on the direction word. Finally, a possible thesis statement, which would help guide the direction of the body of the essay, is given.

Question	Direction	Possible Thesis Statement
(Discuss) the characteristics of each of Howard Gardner's multiple intelligences.	Discuss = tell about What are the eight intelligences?	*Each of Howard Gardner's eight intelligences has clearly recognizable characteristics.*
(Explain why) elaborative rehearsal is more effective for college learning than rote memory strategies.	Explain why = give reasons What are the reasons? How many reasons?	*Elaborative rehearsal is more effective than rote memory because more of the memory principles are used and information in memory is in a more usable form.*

Create an Organizational Plan for Your Answer Before You Begin Writing
For many students, organizing information is the most difficult part of writing essays. Many students wander off course or are at a loss for ideas to write in essays without first making a plan. Outlines, visual mappings, hierarchies, or basic lists that are not as detailed as outlines are four common **organizational plans** used to organize information for an essay. Explore the different formats and then decide which works best for you. The following examples show the use of a plan in hierarchy form, visual mapping form, outline form, and basic list form.

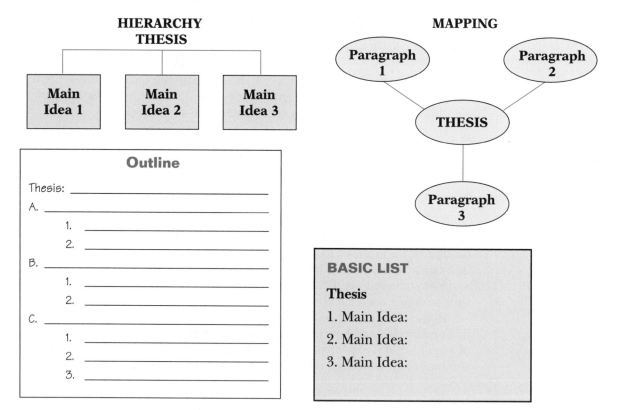

Develop the Body of Your Essay   A strong thesis statement and a plan for the information you want to include in your essay lead naturally to the next step, the actual writing of the **body of the essay.** *Each category or section* of information in your hierarchy, visual mapping, outline, or list can be expanded into sentences and developed into *one paragraph*. Each additional category or section would thus become another paragraph. Remember, however, that a person with strong writing skills is capable of combining ideas in a variety of ways, so other options for developing the body of an essay may also exist.

The following suggestions will help you develop a more effective essay answer.

- Limit each paragraph to one main idea. Shifting to a new main idea is the signal to move to the next line, indent five spaces, and begin a new paragraph.

- Use complete sentences to express your ideas and present your information. Short phrases, charts, or lists of information are not appropriate for an essay.

- Using supporting details is essential, or your essay will be underdeveloped. Include facts such as names, dates, events, and statistics; include definitions, examples, or appropriate applications of the information you are presenting. Do not make the mistake of assuming that information is obvious or that your instructor knows what you are thinking or clearly sees the connection. Write as if your reader is *not knowledgeable* about the subject.

- Use course-specific terminology in your answers as much as possible.

- Use an organizational plan for an essay. The **five-paragraph essay format** begins with the thesis statement, which is then followed by the *body of the essay.* The body often consists of three paragraphs developing three main ideas. Each paragraph includes specific supporting details that show your understanding and knowledge. A short summary or **concluding paragraph** ends the essay. The following organizational plan shows the basic five-paragraph essay format for a sample essay question.

  - Q: *Summarize strategies to use to strengthen a person's vocabulary, textbook reading, and test-taking skills.*

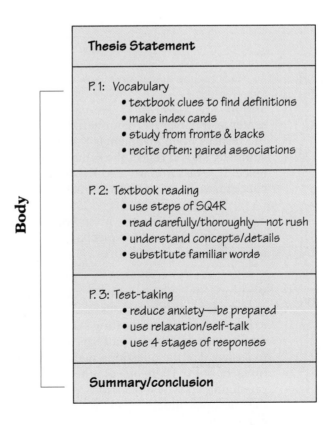

■ Use more than three paragraphs for the body of an essay that has more than three main ideas. The following organizational plan for a sample essay shows a **six-paragraph essay format.**

■ Q: *This term, many study skills were discussed to help you become a successful college student. Select any four skills that you feel are most important for your personal success in college. Discuss the importance of those skills to you.*

Thesis Statement

Body

> **P. 1:** Importance of time management
> - more productive
> - less stress
> - better balance in life
>
> **P. 2:** Importance of concentration
> - make best use of available time
> - learn more thoroughly, less time going back
> - develop mental discipline
>
> **P. 3:** Importance of notetaking
> - select info that needs to be learned
> - puts info in own words
> - steps help memory
> - good ongoing study tool
>
> **P. 4:** Importance of textbook reading
> - read to understand
> - efficient reading—don't need to go back over
> - source of most class info

Summary/conclusion

Summarize Your Main Points   Finish your essay with a short summary sentence or paragraph. Summarizing leaves a clear picture of your main points in the reader's mind and signals that you have finished with your thoughts. Your summary should reflect the same information that you used in your thesis sentence. If your summary and thesis sentence do not focus on the same subject, check to see where you got sidetracked when you developed the body of your essay.

Proofread and Revise   After you have completed your essay, take a few minutes to *proofread* for mechanical errors such as spelling, grammar, word usage, or sentence structure.

Additional Essay Writing Tips

Writing strong essay answers becomes easier with practice. When you get your essay tests back, take time to read the comments and suggestions. You can learn to improve your essay-writing skills by analyzing your essays. Your analysis can also include looking for patterns to the kinds of questions your instructor tends to assign. Are the questions mainly from information in the textbook, in lectures, or both? Then look at other essay test-taking skills. Were you effective in predicting essay test questions? When you wrote your essays, did you answer the questions directly? Were your answers well organized? Did you provide sufficient details?

The following tips will also strengthen your essay-writing skills:

How can you use a computer to plan and develop essay answers? What are the advantages of writing essay answers on a computer?

- If you are given several choices of questions to answer, look at the choices carefully. The majority of students tend to choose the question that is the shortest and looks the easiest. However, these questions are usually more general and sometimes more difficult to answer. Questions that "look the most difficult" because they are longer may actually be more specific and easier to answer. Consider your choice of questions carefully.

- If you are required to do more than one essay question, begin with the one that is most familiar and easiest for you. Your confidence will be boosted, and your mind will shift into the essay-writing mode.

- Strive to write as neatly as possible. Illegible handwriting will hurt your grade. If you need to delete some of the information, delete it by crossing it out with one neat line or by using correction fluid.

- If possible, strengthen your essay by making the following revisions:
  - Replace slang or informal language with formal language or course terminology.
  - Reword to avoid using the word *you*. Replace the word *you* with the word *I* or specific nouns, such as *students*.
  - Replace vague pronouns such as *it* with the name of the specific item.
  - Reword sentences to avoid weak "sentence starters" such as *There is . . . There are . . . Here is . . .* or *Here are.*

- Consider writing on every other line so that you have room to revise or add information if time permits before the test time ends.

- If you were not able to budget your time sufficiently, turn in your organizational plan (hierarchy, mapping, outline, or list). You may earn some additional points for showing that you knew the information and would have included it if you had not run out of time.

- If you have more than one essay to complete on a test, be sure to write something on each question. You will lose too many points by leaving out one question entirely. It is usually better to turn in *some* work on two essays versus only one essay completely developed.

- Weigh the value of different questions. If one question is worth more points, take more time to develop that answer or to return to that answer later and add more information to strengthen your answer.

- If your keyboarding skills are good and you have a laptop computer, ask if you can write your essay on the computer and turn in the disk. Work tends to appear neater and easier to read and is less likely to include spelling errors.

O N L I N E   P R A C T I C E   1 0

Visit the *Essential Study Skills*, Fifth Edition, website and go to Chapter 13. Click on **Practice 10: Strategies for Answering Essay Questions**. Complete the ten-question interactive multiple-choice quiz. Upon completion of the quiz, you will receive your score. You can exit at that time, or you can print your results or e-mail them to your instructor.

EXERCISE 13.9 LINKS

In this textbook, you have learned about the role of stress in the learning process. In Appendix D of this textbook, you learned about the role of stress in your life in general. Refer to Learn by Doing: Put It in Writing *on page A-43 in Appendix D. Then create an organizational plan for an essay answer. (You do not need to actually write an essay unless your instructor extends this exercise to include the actual writing of an essay.)*

EXERCISE 13.10 Writing Essay Answers

Select one *of the following essay questions. Gather appropriate information. Create a hierarchy, visual mapping, an outline, or a basic list of key points to show your organizational plan for your answer. Then write your answer, including an introductory paragraph, paragraphs for the body, and a concluding paragraph.*

1. Define each of the *Five Theories of Forgetting* and discuss strategies that you can use to combat each form of forgetting.

2. Outline ways to use *recitation* in three or more strategies that strengthen the process of learning.

3. We have discussed many forms of notetaking. Some notetaking methods are more appropriate for global learners whereas other forms are more appropriate for linear learners. Discuss the forms of notetaking that are geared toward global learners; then discuss those that are geared toward linear learners. Explain your reasoning.

4. Summarize ways you can use the memory principle of *selectivity* in three or more study skills strategies.

ONLINE PRACTICE 11

Visit the *Essential Study Skills*, Fifth Edition, website and go to Chapter 13. Click on **Practice 11: Five Essay Questions**. Select one essay. After you write your essay, you may print it or e-mail it to your instructor.

ONLINE PRACTICE 12

Visit the *Essential Study Skills*, Fifth Edition, website and go to Chapter 13. Click on **Practice 12: List of Essay Questions**. Use these sample essay questions to prepare for your final exam. No responses are required online for this practice.

Reflection Writing 3
Chapter 13

On separate paper, in a journal, or online at this textbook's website, respond to the following questions.

1. What essay writing skills did you learn in this chapter to address the problems listed in the *Group Processing: A Collaborative Learning Activity* on page 373? If you did not do this activity in class, discuss previous problems you have had with essays and the strategies that you have now learned to address those problems.

2. If you were able to select the type of test to use for any of your courses, what would be your preference? Why?

SUMMARY

■ Recall questions include fill-in-the-blank questions, listing questions, definition questions, and short-answer questions.

■ Fill-in-the-blank questions often require specific vocabulary words as answers.

■ Listing questions require lists of information that you do not need to write as complete sentences.

■ Definition questions require a clear explanation of a vocabulary term. An effective answer consists of three levels of information: a category, a formal definition, and one or more details to expand the definition.

■ Short-answer questions require details, which you can often express in three to five sentences.

■ The four levels of response can be used in recall questions; however, educated guessing is replaced by substituting words or synonyms when you cannot recall the exact answers.

■ Recall questions and essay questions may be *closed* or *open-ended questions*.

■ Math tests involve problem-solving strategies that begin by estimating a reasonable answer. They require application of specific skills and demonstration of the steps involved in solving each problem.

■ Six common test-taking errors on math tests can be corrected through the use of effective studying and test-taking strategies.

■ The RSTUV Problem-Solving Method can be used to solve any math word problem. The steps are *read, select, think, use,* and *verify.*

■ To prepare for essay questions, spend time identifying possible themes for the question, predicting questions, writing your own questions, creating summary notes, creating an organizational plan for your answer, and practicing writing essay answers before the test day.

■ Direction words help you understand the type of answer expected for short-answer and essay questions.

■ A basic essay structure includes a thesis statement, several paragraphs in the body of the essay, and a concluding paragraph.

CULMINATING OPTIONS FOR CHAPTER 13

1. Visit this textbook's website and go to Chapter 13 to complete the following exercises.
   a. Flash-card review of Chapter 13 terms and definitions
   b. ACE Practice Test 1 with ten fill-in-the-blank questions
   c. ACE Practice Test 2 with ten true-false questions
   d. ACE Practice Test 3 with ten multiple-choice questions
   e. ACE Practice Test 4 with three short-answer–critical thinking questions

2. Go to Appendix C in the back of this textbook for more Learning Options to use for additional practice, enrichment, or portfolio projects.

END-OF-THE-TERM CULMINATING OPTIONS

1. Master Profile Chart
Redo the chapter profiles at the beginning of each chapter so you can see the changes and the progress that you have made this term in applying the essential study skills from Chapters 1 through 13. Follow the directions for End-of-the-Term Profile in Appendix A, page A-3. You can also receive scores for all the profiles by completing them online at this textbook's websites for each chapter.

2. Personal Insights Form
Complete the *Personal Insights Form* in Appendix B, page A-9 to summarize the information about yourself as a learner.

3. Portfolio Projects
Organize materials for any portfolio projects your instructor assigned for you to complete over the course of the term. These projects may include writing journals for *Reflection Writing Assignments*, *Appendix C Learning Options*, or a compilation of activities that your instructor assigned to reflect the quality of your work throughout the term. Create an attractive cover for your work; include your name, the course name and term, and a title for your portfolio project.

4. Essential Study Skills Strategy Notebook
Create your own *Essential Study Skills Strategies Notebook* to use as a reference tool for future classes throughout your college years. Remove the pages in your textbook that show *Essential Strategy Charts;* trim the pages and glue them to unlined paper. Then, remove or photocopy any additional charts, forms, diagrams, or lists that you would like to have at your fingertips. Trim and mount them to create additional pages for your *Essential Study Skills Strategies Notebook*. You may wish to insert all the pages into plastic sleeve covers. This notebook is also an ideal place to store any of your exemplary tests, assignments, or creative projects from this term.

Chapter 13   REVIEW QUESTIONS

The following questions will provide you with practice using the test-taking techniques from Chapter 13 as well as provide you with the opportunity to review material from throughout the term.

Fill-in-the-Blank

Write one word on each line to correctly complete each sentence.

1. A _____ is defined as a word that has the same or similar meaning as another.

2. _____ questions on tests are questions that require very specific answers, often in a specific order.

3. A _____ sentence states the writer's main point about an entire essay.

4. A _____ sentence states the main idea for one specific paragraph.

5. _____ are words used in objective tests that indicate how frequently or how completely something occurs. Examples are *sometimes*, *seldom*, *always*, and *never*.

6. When studying math, it is important to practice converting algebraic expressions into English _____ .

7. Students who have test anxiety due to _____ often find the need for last-minute massed practice or cramming.

8. A _____ _____ is a type of visual graphic that organizes information to be compared by using columns, rows, and cells.

9. The _____ step of the Cornell notetaking system is designed for the student to practice information by talking out loud and in complete sentences.

10. _____ can be eliminated by using goal-setting and time-management techniques that encourage a person not to put things off for a later time.

11. The three basic cognitive learning modalities are _____ , _____ , and _____ .

12. When using the SQ4R textbook reading system, the first *R* of the Cornell system would begin during the _____ step of SQ4R.

Definitions

Define the following terms.

1. Memory Principle of Elaboration

2. Central Executive

3. Self-management skills

4. The *reflect* step in the Cornell notetaking system

Listing Questions

Use your own paper to write the answers to the following questions.

1. Name the eight intelligences as defined by Howard Gardner.

2. List the five steps in the Feedback Model.

3. List the steps involved in effective goal setting.

4. Name any six concentration strategies to deal with internal or external distractors.

5. List the Twelve Principles of Memory.

Short-Answer Questions

Write the answers to the following questions on your own paper.

1. Explain how to study from the highlighting done in your textbook.

2. What are the three levels of information in a well-developed definition?

3. How do the discrepancies among the rate of speech, the rate of writing, and the rate of thinking affect a person's notetaking skills?

4. Tell how you can use highlighting or a chapter visual mapping to write summaries.

Essay Questions

Select one *of the following to develop into an essay. Write your answer on your own paper.*

1. Summarize the techniques that you can use to improve comprehension of a difficult paragraph.

2. Explain how to use the RSTUV Problem-Solving Method for math word problems.

3. Discuss the notetaking options that you can use in the fourth step of SQ4R.

4. How does the Working Memory Model differ from the Information Processing Model?

APPENDIXES

APPENDIX A Chapter Profile Materials

Master Profile Chart

	Learning Styles	Processing Memory	Managing Time	Setting Goals	Concentration, Stress, Procrastination	Boosting Memory; Preparing for Tests	Reading College Textbooks	Comprehension	Textbook Notes	Listening and Lecture Notes	Visual Notetaking Systems	Objective Tests	Recall, Math, and Essay Tests
	1	2	3	4	5	6	7	8	9	10	11	12	13
100%	10	10	10	10	10	10	10	10	10	10	10	10	10
90%	9	9	9	9	9	9	9	9	9	9	9	9	9
80%	8	8	8	8	8	8	8	8	8	8	8	8	8
70%	7	7	7	7	7	7	7	7	7	7	7	7	7
60%	6	6	6	6	6	6	6	6	6	6	6	6	6
50%	5	5	5	5	5	5	5	5	5	5	5	5	5
40%	4	4	4	4	4	4	4	4	4	4	4	4	4
30%	3	3	3	3	3	3	3	3	3	3	3	3	3
20%	2	2	2	2	2	2	2	2	2	2	2	2	2
10%	1	1	1	1	1	1	1	1	1	1	1	1	1
0%	0	0	0	0	0	0	0	0	0	0	0	0	0

Beginning-of-the-Term Profile

1. As you begin a new chapter, complete the chapter profile chart. If you prefer, you can complete the profile online and then record your score above.

2. Score your profile. (See Chapter 1, page 2.) Find the chapter number above. Circle your score to show the number of correct responses.

3. Connect the circles with lines to create a graph (your Master Profile Chart).

Profile Answer Keys

1: Learning Styles
1. (Y) N
2. (Y) N
3. Y (N)
4. Y (N)
5. (Y) N
6. (Y) N
7. Y (N)
8. (Y) N
9. (Y) N
10. (Y) N

2: Processing Memory
1. (Y) N
2. (Y) N
3. Y (N)
4. (Y) N
5. Y (N)
6. (Y) N
7. Y (N)
8. Y (N)
9. (Y) N
10. (Y) N

3: Managing Time
1. (Y) N
2. Y (N)
3. Y (N)
4. Y (N)
5. (Y) N
6. (Y) N
7. (Y) N
8. Y (N)
9. Y (N)
10. (Y) N

4: Setting Goals
1. (Y) N
2. Y (N)
3. Y (N)
4. (Y) N
5. (Y) N
6. Y (N)
7. Y (N)
8. (Y) N
9. Y (N)
10. (Y) N

5: Concentration, Stress, Procrastination
1. (Y) N
2. Y (N)
3. (Y) N
4. Y (N)
5. (Y) N
6. Y (N)
7. Y (N)
8. Y (N)
9. Y (N)
10. (Y) N

6: Boosting Memory; Preparing for Tests
1. Y (N)
2. (Y) N
3. Y (N)
4. (Y) N
5. (Y) N
6. Y (N)
7. (Y) N
8. (Y) N
9. Y (N)
10. (Y) N

7: Reading College Textbooks
1. (Y) N
2. (Y) N
3. Y (N)
4. (Y) N
5. (Y) N
6. Y (N)
7. Y (N)
8. (Y) N
9. Y (N)
10. (Y) N

8: Comprehension
1. (Y) N
2. Y (N)
3. (Y) N
4. Y (N)
5. Y (N)
6. (Y) N
7. (Y) N
8. (Y) N
9. Y (N)
10. (Y) N

9: Textbook Notes
1. (Y) N
2. (Y) N
3. (Y) N
4. (Y) N
5. Y (N)
6. (Y) N
7. (Y) N
8. (Y) N
9. Y (N)
10. (Y) N

10: Listening and Lecture Notes
1. Y (N)
2. Y (N)
3. (Y) N
4. (Y) N
5. Y (N)
6. (Y) N
7. (Y) N
8. (Y) N
9. (Y) N
10. (Y) N

11: Visual Notetaking Systems
1. (Y) N
2. Y (N)
3. (Y) N
4. (Y) N
5. Y (N)
6. (Y) N
7. (Y) N
8. (Y) N
9. (Y) N
10. (Y) N

12: Objective Tests
1. (Y) N
2. Y (N)
3. (Y) N
4. (Y) N
5. (Y) N
6. (Y) N
7. Y (N)
8. (Y) N
9. (Y) N
10. (Y) N

13: Recall, Math, Essay Tests
1. Y (N)
2. Y (N)
3. Y (N)
4. Y (N)
5. (Y) N
6. (Y) N
7. (Y) N
8. (Y) N
9. (Y) N
10. (Y) N

End-of-Term Profile

1. Cut a two-inch-wide strip of paper to cover up the original answers on the profile questions at the beginning of each chapter (or complete the profiles on this textbook's website). Redo all the profile questions so you can see the changes that you have made this term. Write **Y** or **N** *next to the number of each profile question.*

2. Score your profile answers using the answer key above.

3. Chart your scores on the Master Profile Chart. Use a different color ink so that you can compare these scores with your original scores.

APPENDIX **B** Useful Forms

Learning Options Assessment Form*

Name _____ Learning Option # _____ for Chapter _____

1. Write a short introduction that states your goals for this Learning Option.

[ ]

2. Write a short self-assessment that states your view of the value and the quality of your work.

[ ]

3. Your instructor will score the quality of your work based on the following criteria:

1	2	3	4	5	Sufficient details
1	2	3	4	5	Accurate information
1	2	3	4	5	Inclusion of required skills
1	2	3	4	5	Neatness, clarity of presentation
1	2	3	4	5	Originality, critical thinking
1	2	3	4	5	Other: _____

Total Points: _____

4. Instructor Evaluation Comments:

*Photocopy this form before you use it.

Class Schedule

List your classes on the following chart.

Reg. #	Course Name	Time	Location/Room	Instructor

Write your classes in the time slots. You may wish to color-code the boxes.

Time	Monday	Tuesday	Wednesday	Thursday	Friday	Saturday
7–8:00 AM						
8–9:00						
9–10:00						
10–11:00						
11–12 noon						
12–1:00						
1–2:00						
2–3:00						
3–4:00						
4–5:00						
5–6:00						
6–7:00						
7–8:00						
8–9:00						

WEEKLY TIME-MANAGEMENT SCHEDULE

For the week of _____ **Name** _____

Time	Monday	Tuesday	Wednesday	Thursday	Friday	Saturday	Sunday
12–6 AM							
6–7:00							
7–8:00							
8–9:00							
9–10:00							
10–11:00							
11–12 NOON							
12–1:00 PM							
1–2:00							
2–3:00							
3–4:00							
4–5:00							
5–6:00							
6–7:00							
7–8:00							
8–9:00							
9–10:00							
10–11:00							
11–12 AM							

Cornell Notetaking Self-Assessment Form

Name _____   Date _____

Topic of Notes _____   Assignment _____

Record Step

		YES	NO
1.	Did you clearly show headings in your notes so you can see the main topics?	_____	_____
2.	Did you underline the headings and avoid putting numbers or letters in front of the headings?	_____	_____
3.	Did you leave a space between headings or larger groups of information so that your notes are not cluttered or crowded?	_____	_____
4.	Did you include sufficient details so that you do not need to return to the textbook to study this information?	_____	_____
5.	Did you use numbering between the different details under the headings?	_____	_____
6.	Did you indent and uses dashes or other symbols to show supporting details?	_____	_____
7.	Did you use meaningful phrases or shortened or complete sentences so that the information will be clear at a later time?	_____	_____
8.	Did you paraphrase or shorten the information so that your notes are not too lengthy?	_____	_____
9.	Did your notes refer to important charts, diagrams, or visual materials in the chapter, or did you make reference to the textbook pages in your notes?	_____	_____
10.	Did you write on only one side of the paper, leaving the back side blank?	_____	_____
11.	Did you label the first page of your notes (course, chapter number, and date) and use page numbers on the other pages?	_____	_____
12.	Did you write your notes so that they are neat and easy to read?	_____	_____

Recall Column (Reduce Step)

1.	Did you move each heading into the recall column and underline it?	_____	_____
2.	Did you use a two-and-one-half-inch margin on the left for the recall column?	_____	_____
3.	Did you include study questions in the recall column for the key points in your notes?	_____	_____
4.	Did you include enough information in the recall column to guide you when you recite your notes?	_____	_____
5.	Did you include in the recall column some key words that you need to define or explain?	_____	_____
6.	Did you write the questions and the key words directly across from the corresponding information in your notes column?	_____	_____
7.	Did you avoid writing too much information or giving yourself all of the information in the recall column, thus leaving you with little to recite from memory?	_____	_____
8.	Did you try using the recall column?	_____	_____
9.	Did you add or delete information in the recall column after you tried using that column for reciting?	_____	_____

Cornell Notetaking Instructor Assessment Form*

Name _____ Date _____ Notes for _____

Strengths of Your Notes

Your Notes Column

_____ You clearly showed and underlined the headings.

_____ Your notes will be easier to study because you left a space between new headings or sections of information.

_____ Your notes show accurate and sufficient details.

_____ You used meaningful phrases or shortened sentences effectively so that the information is clear and understandable.

_____ You shortened information effectively and captured the important ideas.

_____ Your notes are well organized. You effectively used numbering and indentations for supporting details.

_____ You included important information presented in visual graphics from the textbook.

_____ Your notes are neat and easy to read.

_____ You used notetaking standards effectively: you wrote on one side of the paper, you included a heading, and you numbered pages.

Your Recall Column

_____ You used a 2½-inch column.

_____ You placed your headings, questions, and key words directly across from the information in your notes.

_____ Your questions and key words are effective.

_____ Use the recall column to check its effectiveness. Add more self-quizzing questions, visual cues, or hints to guide reciting if necessary.

Areas for Improvement in Your Notes

_____ Strive to identify and underline headings.

_____ Leave a space before you begin a new heading or section of information so your notes will be less crowded or cluttered.

_____ Include more information in your notes. Your notes lack some important details.

_____ Short phrases or isolated words lose meaning over time. Use more sentences or more detailed phrases to capture important ideas.

_____ Use shortened sentences to capture the important ideas. Your notes are unnecessarily lengthy.

_____ Strive for clearer organization. Number and indent supporting details.

_____ Include graphic information in your notes.

_____ Strive for neater penmanship and readability.

_____ Write on one side of the paper. Include a heading on the first page. Number all the pages of your notes.

_____ Use a 2½-inch column on the left.

_____ Place the headings, questions, and key words directly across from the information in your notes.

_____ You need more meaningful questions and key words in the recall column.

_____ You are giving yourself too much information in the recall column; use questions without answers so that you will have more to recite.

_____ Use the recall column to check its effectiveness. Add more self-quizzing questions, visual cues, or hints to guide reciting if necessary.

Other Comments:

*Photocopy this form before you use it.

Personal Insights

1. Learning Style Inventory Score (Chapter 1, page 6)

   Visual _____   Auditory _____   Kinesthetic _____

2. Dominance Inventory—Left/Right, Linear/Global Dominance (Chapter 1, page 17)

   Left _____ Right

         1   2   3   4   5   6   7   8   9   10

3. Multiple Intelligences (Chapter 1, page 21)

   Most developed intelligences: _____

4. Memory Principle Inventory Scores (Chapter 2, pages 43–46)

   Write the numbers to show your Yes and your No scores.

   (Yes = You need to learn to use this principle more effectively when you study. No = You are already using this principle when you study.)

Selectivity	Yes _____	No _____
Association	Yes _____	No _____
Visualization	Yes _____	No _____
Elaboration	Yes _____	No _____
Concentration	Yes _____	No _____
Recitation	Yes _____	No _____
Intention	Yes _____	No _____
Big/Little Pictures	Yes _____	No _____
Feedback	Yes _____	No _____
Organization	Yes _____	No _____
Time on Task	Yes _____	No _____
Ongoing Review	Yes _____	No _____

5. Academic Preparation Inventory (Chapter 6, page 166)

   Yes score _____   No score _____

   (Yes = You use effective study techniques to prepare for a test.

   No = You need to improve your test-preparation study methods.)

6. Test Anxiety Inventory (Chapter 6, page 167)

   Never score _____   Sometimes score _____   Always score _____

   Never = Not indicators of test anxiety

   Sometimes = Possible indicators of test anxiety

   Always = Indicators of test anxiety

7. Listening Inventory (Chapter 10, page 272)

Reception Score: _____

Attention Score: _____

Perception Score: _____

Assignment of Meaning Score: _____

Response Score: _____

Total Score:_____

You perceive yourself to be a (an) _____ listener.

8. Preferred form(s) of notetaking (you may check more than one)

_____ Index cards	_____ Hierarchies
_____ Marginal notes	_____ Comparison charts
_____ Annotations	_____ Formal outlines
_____ Cornell notes	_____ Two-column notes
_____ Visual mappings	_____ Three-column notes

9. The last question in each chapter profile examines your sense of self-efficacy, your belief in your ability to perform specific tasks at an acceptable level. Self-efficacy, which can be learned through the use of effective strategies and recognition of multiple successes, is a powerful influencing factor in achieving success. (See Chapter 4, page 99.) Review question 10 in each of your chapter profiles. Count the number of YES answers and NO answers for question 10. Then write your totals.

Yes answers _____   No answers _____

Yes = You show a strong sense of self-efficacy.

No = You have not yet developed self-efficacy in a specific skill area.

10. Most important concepts you learned about yourself this term:

APPENDIX **C** Standard Learning Options

You can use the following seven Learning Options for every chapter in this textbook.

1. **Expand the chapter visual mapping** on the opening page of the chapter. To expand the mapping, extend lines from each main heading to show key words or concepts that appear under each heading in the textbook. The following example is an expanded visual mapping for Chapter 1.

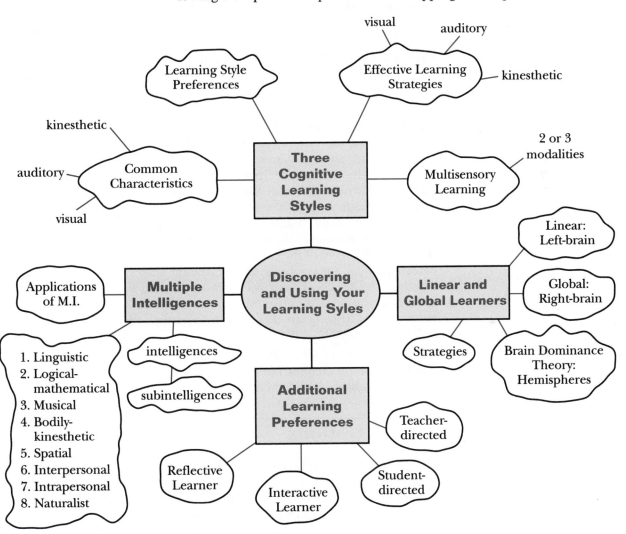

How to Study from the Visual Mapping

a. While looking at the visual mapping, explain out loud and in complete sentences the meaning of the key words and how they relate to the main heading. Strive to connect the information smoothly.

b. Memorize a visual image of the topic in the center and the main headings. Do not attempt to memorize the details. Look away from the visual mapping. From memory, recite each main heading and proceed to tell about the details for each heading. You may glance down at the visual mapping to check your accuracy.

2. **Write a summary** to review the key concepts of the chapter. You may use the *Terms to Know* list at the beginning of the chapter or the *expanded visual mapping* of the chapter as a guide for writing your summary. Strive to include all the key terms in your summary, which you should write in complete sentences and in paragraph form.

3. **Use the Internet links** on this textbook's website to explore other websites with related information. Print the information you wish to use for this project. Prepare a short presentation or written summary of the most significant information you learned. In your presentation or summary, explain how the content on the website relates to the content of this chapter.

4. **Form a study group** with three or more students and meet outside of class to review the content of this chapter, quiz each other on the terminology and general information, and discuss your overall response to this chapter. If you wish, your group could also write practice test questions that you can answer and then use later to review for a test.

5. **Create a personalized study tape** for the chapter. On the tape, summarize or explain the most important points of the chapter and points made in class lectures or discussions. This tape will serve as an excellent review tool later in the term.

6. **Create a set of index cards** (flash cards) for the chapter. On the front of a *definition card*, write one term. On the back of the card, write the definition and any other short explanation of the term. Also make *category cards*, which state the topic on the front and a list of key points, steps in a process, parts of a formula, or items that belong under one category, such as the eight intelligences in the Theory of Multiple Intelligences. Complete your set of index cards by creating *question cards;* write a study question on the front and the answer on the back. To study from your cards, read the information on the front of the card. Recite what you know about the term, the category, or an answer for a study question *without looking at the back.* After you recite, check your accuracy by reading the information on the back. Sort the cards into two piles: cards you know and cards you need to study further. (See Chapter 9 for examples and additional strategies for index study cards.)

7. **Create a poster or a brochure** that explains essential strategies that you learned from this chapter. Devise a plan to share your project with students on campus who are not currently enrolled in a study skills course.

Chapter-Specific Learning Options

Chapter 1

1. The comparison chart on page 25 shows each of the eight intelligences and typical careers. On your own, expand this chart by adding two or more columns: *common characteristics* and *famous people noted for this intelligence.* Complete the chart with relevant details.

2. Create a poster or collage that depicts the various kinds of learning styles and preferences discussed in this chapter. You may use magazine pictures, photographs, or your own drawings to represent the various learning styles and preferences. Organize the information in a logical, appealing manner. People not familiar with this chapter should be able to glean insights about learning styles from your poster or collage.

3. Locate Howard Gardner's *Intelligence Reframed* (Basic Books, copyright © 1999; ISBN 0-465-02610-9). Read and prepare a short report on one of the following:
    a. The eight criteria used to identify intelligences (pages 33–41).
    b. The seven myths and the realities about multiple intelligences (pages 79–92).

Chapter 2

1. Copy the visual mapping of the Twelve Principles of Memory from Chapter 11, page 298. Expand this mapping by adding key words that extend from each of the principles.

2. Create a comparison chart for *all* Twelve Principles of Memory. Use the headings *Definition, Learning Goal, Explanation,* and *Applications.* Fill in each of the spaces by using key words or short descriptions. The beginning of the chart appears below.

Principle	Definition	Learning Goal	Explanation	Applications
Selectivity				
Association				

3. For one week, keep a study log each time you study. At the end of each study session, briefly describe the Principles of Memory that you actively used during that study block. At the end of the week, comment on any study patterns that you saw emerging during the week. For example, are there specific memory principles that you frequently ignore? Which memory principles do you use consistently?

Chapter 3

1. For a week before you go to bed each night, create a daily schedule and at least one task schedule for the following day. Include specific details in both schedules. At the end of the day, check off the tasks that you completed on each schedule. Then compile the seven-day schedules and write a short reaction paper or summary about the successes and the problems that you encountered using both the daily and the task schedules.

2. Interview three people who have three different professions. Create a standard set of questions to ask them about the kinds of time-management problems they encounter in their work, the kinds of time-management strategies that they find effective, and the importance of time management in their line of work. Summarize your findings in the form of a chart or in a paragraph. Include the interview questions and responses.

3. Work with two, three, or four class members to create a five-minute time-management video. Together, write a script that shows students role-playing various kinds of problems related to poor time management. Following each situation in the video, introduce one or more solutions that the student could use to remedy the problems. Be prepared to show your video in class.

Chapter 4

1. For one week, create a task schedule for every study block for any one of your classes. Record your work in a journal. At the end of each study block, write a short statement to praise yourself for your work, use positive self-talk, or comment on the effectiveness of the task schedule for that study block.

2. Create a plan for a term-long project *or* create a five-day study plan for a major upcoming test. Include specific details for each step of your plan. As you move through the plan, keep notes to show your progress and any obstacles that you encounter.

3. Create an inspirational poster that depicts various people who have achieved great successes by setting goals. Use your library periodicals (magazines) and newspapers to locate stories about personal achievements. On your poster, you may photocopy, draw, or use published pictures from magazines you own. Include information about the individual and his or her goals and accomplishments.

Chapter 5

1. Interview five or more adults to find out what kinds of stresses they face in their everyday lives and what strategies they use to reduce their stress levels. Write a separate summary for each of your interviews; you may use fictitious names for the individuals interviewed. Include the list of questions that you used in the interviews.

2. Create a humorous poster that uses one of the following titles: "How to Create Stress in Your Life" or "How to Become a Habitual Procrastinator." On the poster, list techniques to use to add stress to your life or to become a procrastinator. Students who see your poster should be able to understand that effective strategies to reduce stress or combat procrastination are the *opposite* of the strategies shown on your poster.

3. Keep a daily journal for a period of three weeks. In this journal, write a plan of action to increase your concentration while you study, decrease stress, or decrease procrastination. Each day, update your journal by reporting on the progress you made, the problems you encountered with your plan of action, and the decisions or solutions you made to deal with any problems.

Chapter 6

1. Create a portfolio of mnemonics for one of your courses. Use each type of mnemonic discussed in Chapter 6.

2. Create a detailed plan of action to improve your test-preparation skills or to deal with test anxiety before the day of a test.

3. Interview a counselor on campus. Prepare a set of questions related to test anxiety and strategies to combat test anxiety. Take notes during the interview. Then summarize the interview results and be prepared to give a short class presentation if requested by your instructor.

Chapter 7

1. Select a chapter from one of your textbooks. Apply the SQ4R reading system. Begin by surveying; then formulate questions for the title, headings, and subheadings. Use the read-record-recite cycle; use any method that you prefer to record important information. For the review step, write answers to each of the questions that you created for the title, headings, and subheadings in step 2 of SQ4R.

2. Create a mobile (a three-dimensional model) to hang from a ceiling or a light fixture to show the six steps of SQ4R. Your mobile must be informative and instructional so that students who are not familiar with this textbook reading system will be able to identify the steps and understand what to do in each step.

3. Create a *reading plan of action* for each of your textbooks. Look at the structure of the chapters, any special chapter features, and the level of difficulty. Make a list of strategies that you will use for each textbook; strategies should vary from one textbook to another. Follow your plans of action for the remainder of the term.

Chapter 8

1. Create a portfolio of paragraphs taken from your textbooks that show the seven different kinds of organizational patterns. Label each example according to the organizational pattern or patterns that the author used to provide a logical order of information.

2. Use other textbooks or library reference materials to identify additional college reading systems. Compare and contrast the systems with SQ4R. Summarize your findings in a short report.

3. Practice annotating three or more of your textbooks. Photocopy two pages from each textbook to show how you annotated the pages.

Chapter 9

1. Use any form of notetaking to make a comprehensive set of notes for the psychology chapter in Appendix D.

2. Use one or more of your textbooks to create partial notes to demonstrate your understanding and ability to use each of the following notetaking systems: Cornell notes, index card notes, two-column or three-column notes, and a formal outline with at least three levels of information.

3. Select a historical event, a geographic location, an invention, or a geological or meteorological topic (such as volcanoes or earthquakes). Use the Internet or your library resources to locate an informative article about your topic. The article must be two or more pages long. Photocopy or print the article. Then make a complete set of Cornell notes or a formal outline of the article.

Chapter 10

1. Create a listening log for one week. Record the various situations that you encounter in which you need to assume the role of listener. Record the situation and your listening behavior and reactions. Discuss any specific listening strategies that you were aware of using. Then evaluate your effectiveness in each situation; include suggestions for ways that you could have handled the listening situation more effectively.

2. Compile a set of three different kinds of lecture notes for lectures from three different classes. Complete each set of notes, including the recall columns for Cornell notes; then briefly describe the recite, reflect, and review activities you completed for each set of notes.

3. Select an interesting video from your college's library. Use any notetaking system to take a complete set of notes on the content of the video. Then organize and complete your notes. Include the name of the video, its length, and the library call number.

Chapter 11

1. Apply two or more forms of visual notetaking to one of your textbooks from a different class. Take notes on at least five pages from the textbook. Either photocopy the textbook pages to submit with your work or schedule an appointment with your instructor so that he or she can compare your notes to the textbook pages.

2. Use your library to locate a magazine article about a topic that interests you. Photocopy the article. Then select an appropriate form of visual notetaking to use to take notes on the article.

3. Create a three-column set of notes to review ten or more problems from your math textbook or lectures. Fold the right column back before you rework the problems. After you rework the problems and check your accuracy, write a one-paragraph summary of the effectiveness of this system.

Chapter 12

1. Create a chart for one of your classes this term. On the chart, show the test grades you have received. For each test, if possible, show the types of test questions used and the number of correct and incorrect answers for each type of test question. Look for patterns of errors. For example, do you tend to miss more true-false questions than multiple-choice questions? Include a short summary with your chart.

2. Create a portfolio of tests from two or more of your classes. Analyze the tests in terms of correct answers and incorrect answers. Attach a brief summary to each test that tells the results of your analysis and what strategies you could use to improve your performance.

3. Arrange an interview with three instructors on your campus to gain insight into their approaches to tests. Create a standard set of questions to use with each instructor. The following are suggested questions but are not required questions for your interviews.

   What type of questions do you prefer to use on your tests? Why?

   What test-taking strategies or tips do you give to your students?

   Do you use computerized tests? Why or why not?

Chapter 13

1. Identify one major theme from *Essential Study Skills*, Fifth Edition, that you predict will appear on a final exam. Use your class notes, your textbook index, and other related materials to create a set of summary notes for this theme.

2. Write an essay that contrasts your study skills habits or behaviors before you enrolled in this course and your current study skills habits or behaviors. For example, your topic could be your earlier attitude toward learning and your current attitude, or your previous level of self-management skills and your current level of those skills. Refer to your Master Profile Chart (page A-2). Compare your Beginning-of-the-Term Profile scores to your End-of-the-Term Profile scores.

3. Select one essay question from the online list of essay questions. Gather information, create summary notes, create an organizational plan, and write an essay answer.

APPENDIX **D** Psychology Chapter

10

Health, Stress, and Coping

From Bernstein and Nash, *Essentials of Psychology,* 2nd ed. (Boston: Houghton Mifflin Co., 2002), pp. 347–375.
Copyright © 2002. Reprinted by permission of Houghton Mifflin, Inc.

Have you ever gotten a terrible cold "at the worst possible time"—at the end of

the semester, say, or during the holidays, when there's just too much to do and everybody seems to be making demands on you? Most people would answer yes, but a more important question is whether there's anything you can do to avoid getting sick at these times. This is a question of concern to health psychologists. They explore the ways in which health relates to psychological, social, and behavioral factors, and they apply their research to preventing illness and promoting health. They develop programs to help people make lifestyle changes that can lower their risk of illness and premature death. And they study how stress affects people's mental and physical health. Of particular importance is the immune system's response to stress. In this chapter, you will learn about several kinds of stressors, how people respond to them, and the relationship between stress reactions and illness. You will also discover what you can do to protect your own health and change risky behaviors that may affect it.

Reading this chapter will help you to answer the following questions:

- **What do health psychologists do?**
- **How do psychological stressors affect physical health?**
- **How does stress affect your immune system?**
- **Who is most likely to adopt a healthy lifestyle?**

n Bangor, Maine, where snow and ice have paralyzed the community, Angie's headache gets worse as her four-year-old daughter and six-year-old son start bickering again. The day-care center and elementary school are closed, so Angie must stay home from her job at the grocery store. She probably couldn't have gotten there anyway, because the buses have stopped running. During the latest storm the power went out, and the house is now almost unbearably cold; the can of spaghetti Angie opens is nearly frozen. Worry begins to creep into her head: "If I can't work, how will I pay for rent and day care?" Her parents have money problems, too, so they can't offer financial help, and her ex-husband rarely makes his child-support payments. On top of everything else, Angie is coming down with the flu.

How do people manage such adversity, and what are its consequences for the individual? Psychologists who study questions like these have established a specialty known as **health psychology,** "a field within psychology devoted to understanding psychological influence on how people stay healthy, why they become ill, and how they respond when they do get ill" (S. E. Taylor, 1998a, p. 4).

health psychology   A field in which psychologists conduct and apply psychological research to promote human health and prevent illness.

Health Psychology

What do health psychologists do?

The themes underlying health psychology date back to ancient times. For thousands of years, in many cultures around the world, people have believed that their mental state, their behavior, and their health are linked. Today, there is scientific evidence to support this belief (S. E. Taylor, 1998a). We now know that the stresses of life influence health through their impact on psychological and physical processes. Anger, hostility, pessimism, depression, and hopelessness can affect the onset, duration, and outcome of physical illnesses. Similarly, poor health has been linked to behavioral factors such as lack of exercise, inadequate diet, smoking, and use of alcohol and other drugs.

Health psychology has become a prominent field, in part because of changing patterns of illness. Until the middle of the twentieth century, acute infectious diseases such as influenza, tuberculosis, and pneumonia were the major causes of illness and death in the Western world. With these deadly diseases now tamed, chronic illnesses—such as coronary heart disease, cancer, and diabetes—have become the leading causes of disability and death. Compared with acute diseases, these chronic diseases develop more slowly and are more strongly associated with people's psychological makeup, lifestyle, and environment (Lichtenstein et al., 2000; S. E. Taylor, Repetti, & Seeman, 1997; see Table 10.1). The psychological and behavioral factors that contribute to these illnesses can be changed by psychological methods, such as programs that promote nonsmoking and a low-fat diet. Indeed, about half the deaths in the United States are due to potentially preventable health-risky behaviors (National Cancer Institute, 1994).

One goal of health psychology is to help people understand the role they can play in controlling their own health and life expectancy. For example, health psychologists have promoted early detection of disease by educating people about the warning signs of cancer, heart disease, and other serious illnesses and encouraging them to seek medical attention while life-saving treatment is still possible. Encouraging women to perform breast self-examinations and men to do testicular exams are just two examples of health psychology programs that save thousands of lives each year (S. E. Taylor, 1998a). In addition, health psychologists have tried to understand why some people fail to follow prescribed treatment programs for controlling diseases such as diabetes, heart disease, and high blood pressure. Discovering what causes noncompliance with medical advice and creating procedures that encourage greater compliance can speed recovery, prevent unnecessary suffering, and save lives. Health psychologists also study, and help people to understand, the role played by stress in physical health and illness.

TABLE 10.1					
Cause of Death	**Alcohol**	**Smoking**	**Diet**	**Exercise**	**Stress**
Heart disease	x	x	x	x	x
Cancer	x	x	x		?
Stroke	x	x	x	?	?
Lung disease		x			
Accidents and Injury	x	x			x

Lifestyle Behaviors That Affect the Leading Causes of Death in the United States

This table shows five of the leading causes of death in the United States today, along with behavioral factors that contribute to their development.

Source: Data from USDHHS (1990); Centers for Disease Control and Prevention (1999a).

Understanding Stress

■ **How do psychological stressors affect physical health?**

You have probably heard that death and taxes are the only two things guaranteed in life. If there is a third, it surely must be stress. Stress is woven into the fabric of life. No matter how wealthy, powerful, attractive, or happy you might be, stress happens. It comes in many forms, from a difficult exam to an automobile accident, to standing in a long line, to a day when everything goes wrong. Mild stress, like waiting to be with that special person, can be stimulating, motivating, and even desirable, but as stress becomes more severe, it can bring on physical, psychological, and behavioral problems.

Stress is the emotional and physiological process that occurs as individuals try to adjust to or deal with environmental circumstances that disrupt, or threaten to disrupt, their daily functioning (S. E. Taylor, 1998a). Stress thus involves a transaction between people and their environments. The environmental circumstances (such as exams or accidents) that cause people to make adjustments are called **stressors**. **Stress reactions** are the physical, psychological, and behavioral responses (such as nervousness, nausea, and fatigue) displayed in the face of stressors.

Why are some people more strongly affected by stressors than other people, or more affected on one occasion than another? The answer appears to lie in *mediating factors* that influence the relationship between people and their environments. Mediating factors include (1) the extent to which people can *predict* and *control* their stressors, (2) how they *interpret* the threat involved, (3) the *social support* they get, and (4) their *stress-coping skills*. These mediating factors dampen or magnify a stressor's impact. Thus, as shown in Figure 10.1, stress is not a specific event but a *process* in which the nature and intensity of stress responses depend on how stressors are mediated by factors such as the way people think about them and the skills and resources they have to cope with them.

Stressors

Most of the stressors people face have both physical and psychological components. Students, for example, are challenged by psychological demands to do well in their courses, as well as by the physical fatigue resulting from the pressures of academics. Here, we focus on psychological stressors.

stress The process of adjusting to circumstances that disrupt, or threaten to disrupt, a person's daily functioning.

stressors Events or situations to which people must adjust.

stress reactions Physical, psychological, and behavioral responses to stressors.

FIGURE 10.1   The Process of Stress

Stressful events, people's reactions to those events, and interactions between people and the situations they face are all important components of stress. Notice the two-way relationships in the stress process. For example, if a person has effective coping skills, stress responses will be less severe. Having milder stress responses will act as a "reward" that will strengthen those skills. Further, as coping skills (such as refusing unreasonable demands) improve, certain stressors (such as a boss's unreasonable demands) may become less frequent.

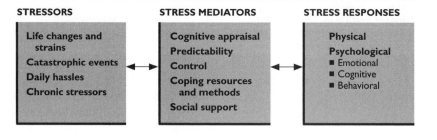

Applying Psychology

ANOTHER CATASTROPHE
Catastrophic events such as explosions, hurricanes, plane crashes, school shootings, and other traumas are stressors that can be psychologically devastating for victims, their families, and rescue workers. As was the case in the wake of this train wreck, health psychologists and other professionals provide on-the-spot counseling and follow-up sessions to help people deal with the consequences of trauma.

Psychological Stressors Any event that forces a person to change or adapt can be a psychological stressor. Even pleasant events can qualify as stressful. For example, a vacation is supposed to be relaxing, but it can be exhausting as well. And though the higher pay of a new job may be desirable, the change may also bring new pressures. Still, it is usually unpleasant circumstances that produce the most adverse psychological and physical effects (Kessler, 1997). These circumstances include catastrophic events, life changes and strains, chronic stressors, and daily hassles (Baum, Gatchel, & Krantz, 1997).

Sudden, unexpected, potentially life threatening experiences or traumas qualify as *catastrophic events.* Physical or sexual assault, military combat, natural disasters, explosions, plane crashes, and accidents fall into this category. *Life changes and strains* include divorce, illness in the family, difficulties at work, moving to a new place, and other circumstances that create demands to which people must adjust (Price, 1992; see Table 10.2). *Chronic stressors*—stressors that continue over a long period of time—

TABLE 10.2

The Undergraduate Stress Questionnaire

Here are some items from the Undergraduate Stress Questionnaire, which asks students to indicate whether various stressors have occurred during the previous week.

Has this stressful event happened to you at any time during the last week? If it has, please check the space next to it. If it has not, please leave it blank.

_____ 1. Assignments in all classes due the same day

_____ 2. Having roommate conflicts

_____ 3. Lack of money

_____ 4. Trying to decide on major

_____ 5. Can't understand your professor

_____ 6. Stayed up late writing a paper

_____ 7. Sat through a boring class

_____ 8. Went into a test unprepared

_____ 9. Parent getting divorced

_____ 10. Incompetence at the registrar's office

Source: Crandall, Preisler, & Aussprung (1992).

include such circumstances as living near a noisy airport, being unable to earn a decent living, residing in a high-crime neighborhood, being the victim of discrimination, and even enduring years of academic pressure (G. W. Evans, Hygge, & Bullinger, 1995). Finally, *daily hassles* involve irritations, pressures, and annoyances that may not be major stressors by themselves but whose effects add up to become significant. The frustrations of daily commuting in heavy traffic, for example, can become so intense for some drivers that they display a pattern of aggression called "road rage" (Levy et al., 1997).

Measuring Stressors   Which stressors do the most harm? To study stress more precisely, psychologists have tried to measure the impact of particular stressors. In 1967, Thomas Holmes and Richard Rahe (pronounced "ray") pioneered the effort to find a standard way of measuring the stress in a person's life. Working on the assumption that all change, positive or negative, produces stress, they asked a large number of people to rate—in terms of *life-change units,* or *LCUs*—the amount of change and demand for adjustment represented by a list of events such as divorcing, being fired, retiring, losing a loved one, or becoming pregnant. (Getting married, the event against which raters were to compare all other stressors, was judged to be slightly more stressful than losing one's job.) On the basis of these ratings, Holmes and Rahe created the Social Readjustment Rating Scale, or SRRS. People taking the SRRS receive a stress score equal to the sum of the LCUs for all the stressful events they have recently experienced.

Numerous studies show that people scoring high on the SRRS and other life-change scales are more likely to suffer physical illness, mental disorder, or other problems than those with lower scores (e.g., Monroe, Thase, & Simons, 1992). However, questions have been raised about whether measuring life changes alone tells the whole stress story (Birnbaum & Sotoodeh, 1991). Accordingly, investigators have developed scales such as the *Life Experiences Survey,* or *LES* (I. G. Sarason, Johnson, & Siegal, 1978), which go beyond the SRRS to measure not just life events but also the respondents' *perception* of how intensely positive or negative the events were. As you might expect, scales like the LES generally show that negative events have a stronger negative impact on health than do positive events (De Benedittis, Lornenzetti, & Pieri, 1990).

The LES gives respondents the opportunity to write in and rate any stressors they have experienced that are not on the printed list. This individualized approach can capture the differing impact and meaning that experiences may have for men compared with women and for members of various cultural or subcultural groups. Divorce, for example, may have different meanings to people of different religious and cultural backgrounds. And members of some ethnic groups may experience prejudice and discrimination that is not felt by other groups (Contrada et al., 2000).

Stress Responses

Physical, psychological, and behavioral stress reactions often occur together, especially as stressors become more intense. Furthermore, one type of stress response can set off a stress response in another dimension. For example, a physical stress reaction such as mild chest pains may trigger the psychological stress response of worrying about a heart attack. Still, it is useful to analyze separately each category of stress responses.

Physical Stress Responses: The GAS   If you have experienced a near accident or some other sudden, frightening event, you know that the physical responses to stressors include rapid breathing, increased heartbeat, sweating, and a little later, shakiness. These reactions make up a general pattern known as the *fight-or-flight syndrome.* As described in Chapters 2 and 8, this vital syndrome prepares the body to face or to flee an immediate threat. When the danger passes, fight-or-flight responses subside. However, when stressors last a long time, these responses are only the beginning of a sequence of reactions.

Careful observation of animals and humans led Hans Selye (pronounced "SELL-yay") to suggest that the sequence of physical responses to stress occurs in a consistent pattern that is triggered by the effort to adapt to any stressor. Selye called this sequence the

FIGURE 10.2

The General Adaptation Syndrome

Hans Selye's research showed that physical reactions to stressors include an initial alarm reaction, followed by resistance and then exhaustion. During the alarm reaction, the body's resistance to stress temporarily drops below normal as it absorbs a stressor's initial impact. Resistance increases and then levels off in the resistance stage, but it ultimately declines if the exhaustion stage is

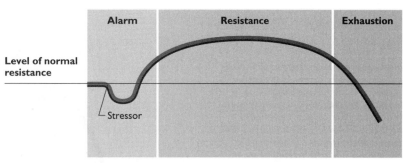

Source: Adapted from Selye (1974).

general adaptation syndrome, or **GAS** (Selye, 1956, 1976). The GAS has three stages, as shown in Figure 10.2.

The first stage, the *alarm reaction,* involves some version of the fight-or-flight syndrome. The reaction to a mild stressor, such as a hot room, may simply involve changes in heart rate, respiration, and perspiration that help the body regulate its temperature. More severe stressors prompt more dramatic alarm reactions, rapidly mobilizing the body's adaptive energy, much as a burglar alarm alerts police to take action (Kiecolt-Glaser et al., 1998).

Alarm reactions are controlled by the sympathetic nervous system through organs and glands that make up the *sympatho-adreno-medullary (SAM)* system. As shown on the right side of Figure 10.3, stressors trigger a process that begins when the brain's hypothalamus activates the sympathetic branch of the autonomic nervous system (ANS), which stimulates the medulla (inner part) of the adrenal glands. The adrenal glands, in turn, secrete catecholamines (pronounced "kat-uh-KOH-luh-meens")—especially adrenaline and noradrenaline—which circulate in the bloodstream, activating the liver, kidneys, heart, lungs, and other organs. The result is increased blood pressure, muscle tension, and blood sugar, along with other physical changes needed to cope with stressors. Even brief exposure to a stressor can produce major changes in these coordinated regulatory body systems (Cacioppo et al., 1995).

As shown on the left side of Figure 10.3, stressors also activate the *hypothalamic-pituitary-adrenocortical (HPA)* system, in which the hypothalamus stimulates the pituitary gland in the brain. The pituitary, in turn, secretes hormones such as adrenocorticotropic hormone (ACTH). Among other things, ACTH stimulates the cortex (outer surface) of the adrenal glands to secrete *corticosteroids;* these hormones release the body's energy supplies and fight inflammation. The pituitary gland also triggers the release of *endorphins,* the body's natural painkillers.

The overall effect of these stress systems is to generate emergency energy. The more stressors there are and the longer they last, the more resources the body must expend in an effort to resist them. If the stressors persist, the *resistance stage* of the GAS begins. Here, the initial obvious signs of the alarm reaction fade as the body settles in to resist the stressor on a long-term basis. The drain on adaptive energy is less during the resistance stage compared with the alarm stage, but the body is still working hard to cope with stress.

This continued biochemical resistance is costly. It slowly but surely uses up the body's reserves of adaptive energy until the capacity to resist is gone. The body then enters the third GAS stage, known as *exhaustion.* In extreme cases, such as prolonged exposure to freezing temperatures, the result is death. More commonly, the exhaustion stage brings signs of physical wear and tear. Especially hard-hit are the organ systems that were weak to begin with or were heavily involved in the resistance process. For example, if adrenaline and cortisol (which help fight stressors during the resistance stage) remain elevated for an extended time, the result can be damage to the heart and blood vessels; suppression of the body's disease-fighting immune system; and vulnerability to illnesses

general adaptation syndrome (GAS)
A pattern of responses triggered by the effort to adapt to stressors. The GAS consists of three stages: the alarm reaction, resistance, and exhaustion.

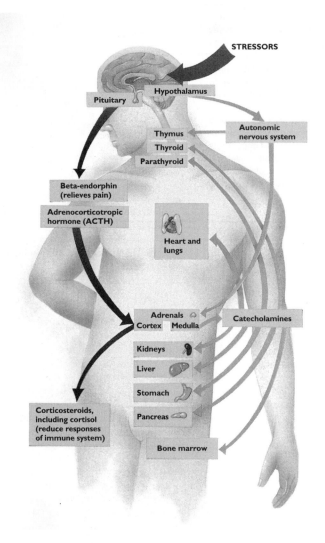

FIGURE 10.3

Organ Systems Involved in the GAS

Stressors produce a variety of physiological responses that begin in the brain and spread to organs throughout the body. For example, the pituitary gland triggers the release of endorphins, the body's natural painkillers. It also stimulates the release of corticosteroids, which help resist stress but, as described later, also tend to suppress the immune system. As described later, some of these substances may interact with sex hormones to create different physical stress responses and coping methods in men and women (S. E. Taylor et al., 2000b).

such as heart disease, high blood pressure, arthritis, colds, and flu (e.g., McEwen, 1998). Selye referred to illnesses caused or worsened by stressors as **diseases of adaptation.**

Although quite influential, Selye's description of the stress process has been criticized for underestimating the role of psychological factors in stress. For example, a person's emotional state or the way the person thinks about stressors can affect responses to those stressors. These criticisms led to the development of *psychobiological models,* which emphasize the importance of psychological, as well as biological, variables in producing and regulating stress responses (R. S. Lazarus & Folkman, 1984; Wickramasekera, Davies, & Davies, 1996). These psychological responses can involve changes in emotion and/or cognition (thinking).

Emotional Stress Responses   The physical stress responses we have described are usually accompanied by emotional stress responses. If someone shows a gun and demands your money, you will most likely experience the GAS alarm reaction. You will also feel some strong emotion—probably fear, maybe anger. In describing stress, people tend to say, "I was angry and frustrated!" rather than "My heart rate increased, and my blood pressure went up." In other words, they tend to mention changes in how they *feel.*

diseases of adaptation   Illnesses caused or worsened by stressors.

High-pressure salespeople know that stress can impair decision making. They take advantage of this stress response by creating time-limited offers or by telling customers that others are waiting to buy the item they are considering (Cialdini, 1995).

In most cases, emotional stress reactions diminish soon after the stressors are gone. Even severe emotional stress responses ease eventually. However, if stressors continue for a long time or if many occur in a short time, emotional stress reactions may persist. When people don't have a chance to recover their emotional equilibrium, they feel tense, irritable, short-tempered, or anxious, and they may experience increasingly intense feelings of fatigue, depression, and hopelessness. These reactions can become severe enough to be diagnosed as major depressive disorder, generalized anxiety disorder, or any of the other stress-related mental disorders discussed in Chapter 12.

Cognitive Stress Responses   In 1995, in the busy, noisy intensive care unit of a London hospital, a doctor misplaced a decimal point while calculating the amount of morphine a one-day-old premature baby should receive. The child died of a massive overdose (C. Davies, 1999). Reductions in the ability to concentrate, to think clearly, or to remember accurately are typical cognitive stress reactions. These problems appear partly because of *ruminative thinking,* the recurring intrusion of thoughts about stressful events (Lyubomirsky & Nolen-Hoeksema, 1995). Ruminative thoughts about relationship problems, for example, can seriously interfere with studying for a test. A related phenomenon is *catastrophizing,* which means dwelling on and overemphasizing the possible negative consequences of events (I. G. Sarason et al., 1986). Thus, during exams, test-anxious college students are likely to say to themselves, "I'm falling behind" or "Everyone is doing better than I am." As catastrophizing or ruminative thinking impairs cognitive functioning, resulting feelings of anxiety and other emotional arousal add to the total stress response, further hampering performance (Mendl, 1999).

Overarousal created by stressors also tends to narrow the scope of attention, making it harder to scan the full range of possible solutions to complex problems (Keinan, Friedland, & Ben-Porath, 1987). In addition, stress-narrowed attention may increase the problem-solving errors described in Chapter 7, on thought, language, and intelligence. People under stress are more likely to cling to *mental sets,* which are well-learned, but not always efficient, approaches to problems. Stress may also intensify *functional fixedness,* the tendency to use objects for only one purpose. Victims of hotel fires, for example, sometimes die trapped in their rooms because, in the stress of the moment, it did not occur to them to use the telephone or a piece of furniture to break a window. Stressors may also impair decision making. Under stress, people who normally consider all aspects of a situation before making a decision may act impulsively and sometimes foolishly (Keinan, Friedland, & Ben-Porath, 1987).

Behavioral Stress Responses   Clues about people's physical and emotional stress reactions come from changes in how they look, act, or talk. Strained facial expressions, a shaky voice, tremors, and jumpiness are common behavioral stress responses. Posture can also convey information about stress, a fact well known to skilled interviewers.

Even more obvious behavioral stress responses appear as people attempt to escape or avoid stressors. Some people quit their jobs, drop out of school, turn to alcohol, or even attempt suicide. Unfortunately, as discussed in Chapter 5, on learning, escape and avoidance tactics deprive people of the opportunity to learn more adaptive ways of coping with stressful environments, including college (M. L. Cooper et al., 1992). Aggression is another common behavioral response to stressors. All too often, this response is directed at members of one's own family (Polusny & Follette, 1995). For instance, in the wake of hurricanes and other natural disasters, it is not uncommon to see dramatic increases in the rate of domestic-violence reports in the devastated area (Rotton, 1990).

LINKAGES
When do stress responses become mental disorders? (a link to Psychological Disorders)

LINKAGES

Stress and Psychological Disorders

Physical, psychological, and behavioral stress responses sometimes appear together in patterns known as *burnout* and *posttraumatic stress disorder*. **Burnout** is an increasingly intense pattern of physical, psychological, and behavioral dysfunction in response to a continuous flow of stressors or to chronic stress (Maslach & Goldberg, 1998). As burnout nears, previously reliable workers or once-attentive spouses become indifferent, disengaged, impulsive, or accident-prone. They miss work frequently; oversleep; perform their jobs poorly; abuse alcohol or other drugs; and become irritable, suspicious, withdrawn, and depressed (S. E. Taylor, 1998a). Burnout is particularly common among those who do "people work," such as teachers and nurses (D. P. Schultz & Schultz, 1998).

A different pattern of severe stress reactions is illustrated by the case of Mary, a thirty-three-year-old nurse who was raped at knife point by an intruder in her apartment. In the weeks following this trauma, she became afraid of being alone and was preoccupied with the attack and with the fear that it might happen again. She installed additional locks on her doors and windows but experienced difficulty concentrating and could not immediately return to work. The thought of sex repelled her.

Mary suffered from **posttraumatic stress disorder (PTSD),** a pattern of severe negative reactions following a traumatic event (R. L. Spitzer et al., 1983). Among the characteristic reactions are anxiety, irritability, jumpiness, inability to concentrate or work productively, sexual dysfunction, and difficulty in getting along with others. PTSD sufferers also experience sleep disturbances and intense startle responses to noise or other sudden stimuli (Shalev et al., 2000). The most common feature of posttraumatic stress disorder is experiencing the trauma through nightmares or vivid memories. In rare cases, *flashbacks* occur in which the person behaves for minutes, hours, or days as if the trauma were occurring again.

Posttraumatic stress disorder is most commonly associated with events such as war, assault, or rape (e.g., Schnurr et al., 2000), but researchers now believe that some PTSD symptoms can be triggered by any major stressor (Ironson et al., 1997). PTSD may appear immediately following a trauma, or it may not occur until weeks, months, or even years later (Heim et al., 2000). The majority of those affected require professional help, although some seem to recover without it. For most, improvement takes time; for nearly all, the support of family and friends is vital to recovery (Foa et al., 1999; LaGreca et al., 1996).

As described in Chapter 12, stress has been implicated in the development of a number of other psychological disorders, including depression and schizophrenia. The *diathesis-stress* approach suggests that certain people are predisposed to these disorders, which they may or may not display depending on the frequency, nature, and intensity of the stressors they encounter.

burnout   A pattern of physical, psychological, and behavioral dysfunctions in response to continuous stressors.

posttraumatic stress disorder (PTSD) A pattern of adverse reactions following a traumatic event, commonly involving re-experiencing the event through nightmares or vivid memories.

Stress Mediators

The interaction of particular people with particular stressors can be important in other ways, too. For example, in Kosovo in 1999, at least one UN air strike was known to have

LIFE HANGING IN THE BALANCE
Symptoms of burnout and posttraumatic stress disorder often plague firefighters, police officers, emergency medical personnel, and others who are repeatedly exposed to time pressure, trauma, danger, and other stressors (DeAngelis, 1995).

killed some of the ethnic Albanians whom the bombing was designed to protect. This "friendly fire" incident occurred because the pilots mistakenly identified the Albanians' trucks as Serbian army vehicles. The stress of combat is partly responsible for similarly tragic decision errors in almost every military operation (Adler, 1993). But why does stress disrupt the performance of some individuals and not others? And why does one individual survive, and even thrive, under the same circumstances that lead another to break down, give up, and burn out? A number of the mediating factors listed in Figure 10.1 help determine how much impact a given stressor will have (McEwen & Seeman, 1999).

Perceiving Stressors　Just as our perceptions of the world depend on which stimuli we attend to and how we interpret, or appraise, them (see Chapter 3, on sensation and perception), our emotional reactions to events depend somewhat on how we think about them. Any potential stressor usually has more negative impact on those who perceive it as a threat than on those who see it as a challenge (Rhodewalt & Zone, 1989). This holds true whether the stressor is a long waiting line or a deskful of work.

A classic experiment by Richard Lazarus demonstrated the effects of people's thoughts on their stress responses. He gave differing instructions to three groups of students who were about to watch a film showing bloody industrial accidents (R. S. Lazarus et al., 1965). One group (the "intellectualizers") was instructed to remain mentally detached from the bloody scenes; a second group (the "denial" group) was instructed to think of the bloody scenes as unreal; and a third group (the "unprepared" group) was not told anything about the film. As Figure 10.4 shows, the intensity of physiological arousal during the film, as measured by sweat-gland activity, depended on how the viewers were instructed to think about the film. The unprepared students were more upset than either of the other two groups. Similarly, physical and psychological symptoms associated with the stress of airport noise or learning about toxins in local soil are more common in people who engage in more catastrophic thinking about these problems (Kjellberg et al., 1996; Matthies, Hoeger, & Guski, 2000).

The influence of cognitive factors weakens somewhat as stressors become more extreme. For example, chronic-pain patients tend to engage in more physical activity if they feel a sense of control over their pain, but this effect does not hold for those whose pain is severe

FIGURE 10.4

Cognitive Influences on
Stress Responses

**Richard Lazarus and his colleagues found
that students' physiological stress reaction to a film showing bloody industrial
accidents was affected by they way they
thought about what they saw. Those who
had been instructed to remain detached
from the film (the "intellectualizers") or
to think of it as unreal (the "denial"
group) were less upset—as measured by
sweat-gland activity—than those in an
"unprepared" group. These results were
among the first to show that people's
cognitive appraisal of stressors can affect
their responses to those stressors.**

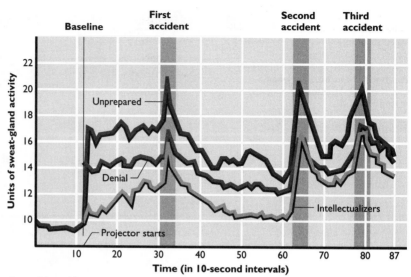

Source: Adapted from R. S. Lazarus et al. (1965).

(M. Jensen & Karoly, 1991). Still, even the impact of major stressors such as natural disasters or divorce may be less severe for those who think of them as challenges to be overcome.
In other words, many stressful events are not inherently stressful; their impact depends
partly on how people perceive them (Wiedenfeld et al., 1990). An important part of this
appraisal is the degree to which the stressors are perceived to be predictable or controllable.

Predictability and Control   Uncertainty about when and if a particular stressor might
occur tends to increase the stressor's impact (Boss, 1999; Sorrentino & Roney, 2000). For
example, wives of American men missing in action during the Vietnam War showed
poorer physical and emotional health than those who knew that their spouses had been
killed in action or were being held prisoner (E. J. Hunter, 1979).

In short, predictable stressors tend to have less impact than those that are unpredictable (R. S. Lazarus & Folkman, 1984)—especially when the stressors are intense and
occur for relatively short periods. For example, rats given a reliable warning signal every
time they are to receive a shock show less severe physiological responses than animals
given no warning (J. Weinberg & Levine, 1980). Among humans, men and women whose
spouses died suddenly tend to display more immediate disbelief, anxiety, and depression
than those who had weeks or months to prepare for the loss (Parkes & Weiss, 1983).
However, predictability does not provide total protection against stressors. Research with
animals shows that predictable stressors can be more damaging than unpredictable ones
if they occur over long periods of time (Abbott, Schoen, & Badia, 1984).

The perception of control also mediates the effects of stressors. Stressors over which
people believe they exert some control usually have less impact (Christensen, Stephens,
& Townsend, 1998). For example, studies of several thousand employees in the United
States, Sweden, and the United Kingdom have found that those who had little or no control over their work environment were more likely to suffer heart disease and other
health problems than workers with a high degree of control over their work environment
(Bosma et al., 1997; Cheng et al., 2000; Hancock, 1996). And at many hospitals, it is now
standard practice to help patients to manage or control the stress of emergency treatment or the side effects of surgery, because doing so helps them heal faster and go home
sooner (Chamberlin, 2000; Kiecolt-Glaser et al., 1998).

Simply *believing* that a stressor is controllable, even if it isn't, can also reduce its
impact (S. C. Thompson et al., 1993). This effect was demonstrated in a study in which
participants with panic disorder inhaled a mixture of oxygen and carbon dioxide that

TABLE 10.3	
Ways of Coping	

Coping is defined as one's cognitive and behavioral efforts to manage specific demands that are appraised as taxing one's resources (Folkman et al., 1986). This table illustrates two major approaches to coping. Ask yourself which approach you usually take when faced with stressors. Now rank-order the coping skills under each major approach in terms of how often you tend to use each. Do you rely on just one or two, or do you adjust your coping strategies to fit different kinds of stressors?

Coping Skills	Example
Problem-focused coping	
Confronting	"I stood my ground and fought for what I wanted."
Seeking social support	"I talked to someone to find out more about the situation."
Planful problem solving	"I made a plan of action, and I followed it."
Emotion-focused coping	
Self-controlling	"I tried to keep my feelings to myself."
Distancing	"I didn't let it get to me; I tried not to think about it too much."
Positive reappraisal	"I changed my mind about myself."
Accepting responsibility	"I realized I brought the problem on myself."
Escape/avoidance (wishful thinking)	"I wished that the situation would go away or somehow be over with."

Source: Adapted from Folkman et al. (1986a); S. E. Taylor (1995).

typically causes a panic attack (Sanderson, Rapee, & Barlow, 1989). Half the participants were led to believe (falsely) that they could control the concentration of the mixture. Compared with those who believed they had no control, significantly fewer of the "in-control" participants experienced full-blown panic attacks during the session, and their panic symptoms were fewer and less severe.

People who feel they have *no* control over negative events appear especially prone to physical and psychological problems. They often experience feelings of helplessness and hopelessness that, in turn, may promote depression or other mental disorders (S. E. Taylor & Aspinwall, 1996).

Coping Resources and Coping Methods　People usually suffer less from a stressor if they have adequate coping resources and effective coping methods. *Coping resources* include, among other things, the money and time to deal with stressful events. Thus, the physical and psychological responses to your car breaking down tend to be more negative if you are broke and pressed for time than if you have the money for repairs and the freedom to take a day off from work.

The impact of stressors can also be reduced by effective *coping methods* (Benight et al., 1999). Most of these methods can be classified as either problem-focused or emotion-focused. *Problem-focused* methods involve efforts to alter or eliminate a source of stress, whereas *emotion-focused* techniques attempt to regulate the negative emotional consequences of stressors (Folkman et al., 1986). These two forms of coping sometimes work together. For example, you might deal with the problem of noise from a nearby airport by forming a community action group to push for tougher noise-reduction laws and, at the same time, calm your anger when noise occurs by mentally focusing on the group's efforts to improve the situation (Folkman & Moskowitz, 2000). Susan Folkman and Richard Lazarus (1988) have devised a scale to assess the specific ways that people cope with stressors; Table 10.3 shows some examples from their scale.

Particularly when a stressor is difficult to control, it is sometimes helpful to fully express and think about the emotions one is experiencing in relation to the stressful event (J. E. Bower et al., 1999; Pennebaker, 1993). The benefits of this coping strategy have been observed among many individuals whose religious beliefs allow them to bring meaning to the death of a loved one or the devastation of natural disasters that might otherwise seem senseless tragedies (Paloutzian & Kirkpatrick, 1995; B. W. Smith et al., 2000). Some individuals who use humor to help them cope also show better adjustment and lower physiological reactivity to stressful events (Lefcourt et al., 1997).

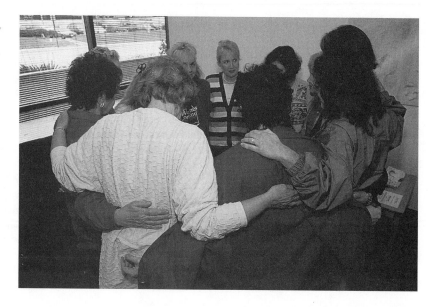

Social Support   Has a good friend ever given you comfort and reassurance during troubled times? If so, you have experienced the value of social support in tempering the impact of stressful events. Social support consists of resources provided by other people; the friends and social contacts on whom you can depend for support make up your **social support network** (B. R. Burleson, Albrecht, & Sarason, 1994). The support can take many forms, from eliminating a stressor (as when a friend helps you fix your car) to lessening a stressor's impact by providing companionship, ideas for coping, or reassurance that you are cared about and valued and that everything will be all right (Sarason, Sarason, & Gurung, 1997).

The stress-reducing effects of social support have been documented for a wide range of stressors, including cancer, military combat, loss of loved ones, natural disasters, arthritis, AIDS, and even ethnic discrimination (e.g., Foster, 2000; Holahan et al., 1997; Penner, Dovidio, & Albrecht, 2001; Savelkoul et al., 2000). These effects were well illustrated in two studies of undergraduate and graduate students (Goplerud, 1980; Lepore, 1995a). Some of the students were part of a supportive network; others were not. Those with the least adequate social support tended to suffer the most emotional distress and were more vulnerable to upper respiratory infections during times of high academic stress. Indeed, one team of researchers concluded that having inadequate social support is as dangerous as smoking cigarettes, because it nearly doubles a person's risk of dying from disease, suicide, or other causes (House, Umberson, & Landis, 1988).

Having strong social support can reduce the likelihood of illness, improve recovery from existing illness, and promote healthier behaviors (Grassi et al., 2000; Uchino, Uno, & Holt-Lunstad, 1999). However, the relationship between social support and the impact of stressors is not a simple one. First, just as the quality of social support can influence your ability to cope with stress, the reverse may also be true: Your ability to cope may determine the quality of the social support you receive (McLeod, Kessler, & Landis, 1992). For example, people who complain endlessly about stressors but never do anything about them may discourage social support, whereas those with an optimistic, action-oriented approach may attract support.

Second, *social support* refers not only to your relationships with others but also to the recognition that others care and will help (Pierce, Sarason, & Sarason, 1995). Some relationships in a seemingly strong social network can be stormy, fragile, or shallow, resulting in interpersonal conflicts that can have an adverse effect on health (Malarkey et al., 1994).

Finally, having too much support or the wrong kind of support can be as bad as not having enough. People whose friends and family overprotect them may actually put less

social support network   The friends and social contacts on whom one can depend for help and support.

energy into coping efforts or have less opportunity to learn effective coping strategies. Further, if the efforts of people in our social support network become annoying, disruptive, or interfering, they can increase stress and intensify psychological problems (Newsome, 1999; Newsome & Schulz, 1998).

Stress, Personality, and Gender   The impact of stress on health appears to depend not only on how people think about particular stressors, but to some extent on how they think about and react to the world in general (Prior, 1999). For instance, stress-related health problems tend to be especially common among people whose "disease-prone" personalities lead them to (1) try to ignore stressors when possible; (2) perceive stressors as long-term, catastrophic threats that they brought on themselves; and (3) be pessimistic about their ability to overcome stressors or other negative situations (e.g., Jorgensen et al., 1996; C. Peterson et al., 1998; Segerstrom et al., 1998).

Other cognitive styles appear to help insulate people from stressors. People who tend to think of stressors as temporary and who do not constantly blame themselves for bringing them about appear to be harmed less by them. This cognitive habit can be especially adaptive when combined with a tendency to see stressors as challenges. Its benefits can also be seen in many devout people whose religious beliefs lead them to think of poverty and other stressors as temporary conditions to be endured until their suffering is ultimately rewarded in an afterlife (McIntosh, Silver, & Wortman, 1993). Whatever the specifics, one important component of the "stress-hardy" or "disease-resistant" personality seems to be *dispositional optimism,* the belief or expectation that things will work out positively (Scheier, Carver, & Bridges, 1994; S. E. Taylor et al., 2000a). For example, optimistic students experience fewer physical symptoms at the end of the academic term (Aspinwall & Taylor, 1992). Optimistic coronary bypass surgery patients heal faster than pessimists (Scheier et al., 1989) and perceive their quality of life following coronary surgery to be higher than do patients with less optimistic outlooks (Fitzgerald et al., 1993). And among HIV-positive men, dispositional optimism has been associated with lower psychological distress, fewer worries, and lower perceived risk of acquiring full-blown AIDS (S. E. Taylor & Armor, 1996). These effects appear due in part to optimists' tendency to use challenge-oriented, problem-focused coping strategies that attack stressors directly, in contrast to pessimists' tendency to use emotion-focused coping such as denial and avoidance (S. E. Taylor, 1998a).

Recent research suggests that gender may also play a role in responses to stress. In a review of 200 studies of stress responses and coping methods, Shelley Taylor and her colleagues found that males under stress tended to get angry, avoid stressors, or both, whereas females were more likely to help others and to make use of their social support network (S. E. Taylor et al., 2000b). This was not true in every case, of course, but why should a significant difference show up at all? The gender-role learning discussed in Chapter 9 surely plays a part (Eagly & Wood, 1999). But Taylor also proposes that women's "tend and befriend" style differs from the "fight-or-flight" pattern so often seen in men because of gender differences in how hormones combine under stress. For example, oxytocin, a hormone released in both sexes as part of the general adaptation syndrome, interacts differently with male and female sex hormones—amplifying men's physical stress responses and reducing women's. This difference could lead to the more intense emotional and behavioral stress responses typical of men, and it might be partly responsible for their greater vulnerability to heart disease and other stress-related illnesses. If that is the case, gender differences in stress responses may help to explain why women live an average of 7.5 years longer than men.

FOCUS ON RESEARCH

Personality and Health

The way people think and act in the face of stressors, the ease with which they attract social support, and their tendency to be optimists or pessimists are but a few aspects of personality (see Chapter 11).

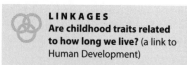

LINKAGES
Are childhood traits related to how long we live? (a link to Human Development)

▪ What was the researchers' question?

Are there other personality characteristics that play a role in people's stress responses? One research team has focused on a more specific version of this question: Are there personality characteristics that help people to live longer in the face of life's inevitable stressors?

▪ How did the researchers answer the question?

Howard Friedman and his colleagues sought the answer to this question by reanalyzing some data from a major longitudinal research project described in Chapter 7 (H. S. Friedman et al., 1995a, 1995b). That project was called the Terman Life Cycle Study because it was begun by Lewis Terman (author of the Stanford-Binet intelligence test). Terman wanted to document the long-term development of 1,528 exceptionally intelligent boys and girls, who came to be nicknamed the "Termites" (Terman & Oden, 1947).

Starting in 1921, and every five to ten years thereafter, Terman's research team had gathered information about the Termites' personality traits, social relationships, stressors, health habits, and many other variables. The data were collected through questionnaires and interviews with the Termites themselves, as well as with their teachers, parents, and other family members. By the early 1990s, about half of the Termites had died. It was then that Friedman realized that the Terman Life Cycle Study could shed some light on the relationship between personality and health, because the various personality traits identified in these people could be related to how long they lived. Accordingly, Friedman gathered the death certificates of the Termites, noted the dates and causes of death, and then looked for associations between their personalities and how long they lived.

▪ What did the researchers find?

Friedman and his colleagues found that one of the most important predictors of long life was a basic dimension of personality known as *conscientiousness,* or *social dependability* (described in Chapter 11). Termites who, in childhood, had been seen as truthful, prudent, reliable, hardworking, and humble tended to live longer than those whose parents and teachers had identified them as impulsive and lacking in self-control.

Friedman also examined the Terman Life Cycle Study for what it suggested about the relationship between health and social support. In particular, he compared Termites whose parents had divorced or Termites who had been in unstable marriages with those who grew up in stable homes and who had stable marriages. He discovered that people who had experienced parental divorce during childhood, or who themselves had unstable marriages, died an average of four years earlier than those whose close social relationships had been less stressful.

▪ What do the results mean?

You may be wondering whether differences in personality traits and social support actually *caused* some Termites to live longer than others. As Friedman's research is based mainly on correlational analyses, it is difficult to draw conclusions about what might have caused the relationships observed. Still, Friedman and his colleagues searched the Terman data for clues to mechanisms through which personality and other factors *might* have exerted a causal influence on how long the Termites lived (C. Peterson et al., 1998). For example, they evaluated the hypothesis that conscientious, dependable Termites who lived socially stable lives might have followed healthier lifestyles than impulsive, socially stressed Termites. Indeed, people in the latter group did tend to eat less healthy diets and were more likely to smoke, drink to excess, or use drugs. But health behaviors alone did not fully account for their shorter average life spans. Another possible explanation is that conscientiousness and stability in social relationships reflect a general attitude of caution that goes beyond eating right and avoiding substance abuse. Friedman found some support for this idea in the Terman data. Termites who were impulsive or nonconscientious were somewhat more likely to die from accidents or violence than those who were less impulsive.

Stress Responses and Stress Mediators	
Category	**Examples**
Responses	
Physical	Fight-or-flight syndrome (increased heart rate, respiration, and muscle tension; sweating; pupillary dilation; SAM and HPA activation (involving release of catecholamines and corticosteroids); eventual breakdown of organ systems involved in prolonged resistance to stressors.
Psychological	*Emotional:* anger, anxiety, depression, and other emotional states. *Cognitive:* inability to concentrate or think logically, ruminative thinking, catastrophizing. *Behavioral:* aggression and escape/avoidance tactics (including suicide attempts).
Mediators	
Appraisal	Thinking of a difficult new job as a challenge will create less discomfort than focusing on the threat of failure.
Predictability	A tornado that strikes without warning may have a more devastating emotional impact than a long-predicted hurricane.
Control	Repairing a disabled spacecraft may be less stressful for the astronauts doing the work than for their loved ones on earth, who can do nothing to help.
Coping resources and methods	Having no effective way to relax after a hard day may prolong tension and other stress responses.
Social support	Having no one to talk to about a rape or other trauma may amplify the negative impact of the experience.

What do we still need to know?

The Terman Life Cycle Study does not provide final answers about the relationship between personality and health. However, it has generated some important clues and a number of intriguing hypotheses to be evaluated in future research with more representative samples of participants. It also stands as an excellent example of how a creative researcher can pursue answers to complex questions that are difficult or impossible to study with controlled experiments.

Our discussion of personality and other factors that can alter the impact of stressors should make it obvious that what is stressful for a given individual is not determined fully and simply by predispositions, coping styles, or situations. (See "In Review: Stress Responses and Stress Mediators.") Even more important are interactions between the person and the situation, the mixture of each individual's coping resources with the specific characteristics of the situation encountered (J. Smith, 1993).

The Physiology and Psychology of Health and Illness

How does stress affect your immune system?

Several studies mentioned so far have suggested that stress shapes the development of physical illness by affecting our thoughts, our organ systems, and our behavior. In this section, we focus more specifically on the ways in which stress can directly or indirectly lead to physical illness. One of the most important connections between stress and illness occurs through the immune system.

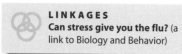

LINKAGES
Can stress give you the flu? (a link to Biology and Behavior)

Stress, the Immune System, and Illness

On March 19, 1878, at a seminar before the Académie de Médecine de Paris, Louis Pasteur showed his distinguished audience three chickens. One bird had been raised normally and was healthy. A second bird had been intentionally infected with bacteria but given no other treatment; it was also healthy. The third chicken that Pasteur presented was dead. It had been infected with the same bacteria as the second bird, but it had also been physically stressed by being exposed to cold temperatures; as a result, the bacteria killed it (Kelley, 1985).

Research conducted since Pasteur's time has greatly expanded knowledge about how stressors affect the body's reaction to disease. **Psychoneuroimmunology** is the field that examines the interaction of psychological and physiological processes that alter the body's ability to defend itself against disease.

The Immune System and Illness   The body's first line of defense against invading substances and microorganisms is the **immune system.** The immune system is perhaps as complex as the nervous system, and it contains as many cells as the brain (Guyton, 1991). Some of these cells are in organs such as the thymus and spleen, whereas others circulate in the bloodstream, entering tissues throughout the body. Components of the immune system kill or inactivate foreign or harmful substances in the body such as viruses and bacteria (Simpson, Hurtley, & Marx, 2000). If the immune system is impaired—by stressors, for example—a person is left more vulnerable to colds, mononucleosis, and many other infectious diseases (Potter & Zautra, 1997). It is by disabling the immune system that the human immunodeficiency virus (HIV) leads to AIDS and leaves the HIV-infected person defenseless against other infections or cancers. The immune system can also become overactive, with devastating results. Many chronic, progressive diseases—including arthritis, diabetes, and lupus erythematosus—are now recognized as *autoimmune* disorders. In these cases, cells of the immune system begin to attack and destroy normal body cells (Oldenberg et al., 2000).

One important facet of the human immune system is the action of the white blood cells, called *leukocytes* (pronounced "LU-koh-sites"), which are formed in the bone marrow and serve as the body's mobile defense units. Leukocytes are called to action when foreign substances are detected. Among the varied types of leukocytes are *B-cells,* which produce *antibodies* to fight foreign toxins; *T-cells,* which kill other cells; and *natural killer cells,* which destroy a variety of foreign organisms and have particularly important antiviral and antitumor functions. The brain can influence the immune system indirectly by altering the secretion of adrenal hormones, such as cortisol, that modify the circulation of T-cells and B-cells. The brain can also influence the immune system directly by making connections with the immune organs, such as the thymus, where T-cells and B-cells are stored (Felten et al., 1991; Maier & Watkins, 2000).

The Immune System and Stress   Researchers have convincingly demonstrated that people under stress are more likely to develop infectious diseases than their less stressed counterparts and to experience flare-ups of the latent viruses responsible for oral herpes (cold sores) or genital herpes (S. Cohen & Herbert, 1996).

These findings are supported by other studies showing more directly that a variety of stressors lead to suppression of the immune system. For example, a study of first-year law students found that as these students participated in class, took exams, and experienced other stressful aspects of law school, they showed a decline in several measures of immune functioning (Segerstrom et al., 1998). Similarly, decreases in natural killer cell activity have been observed in both men and women following the death of their spouses (Irwin et al., 1987), and a variety of immune system impairments have been found in people suffering the effects of divorce or of extended periods of caring for elderly relatives (Cacioppo et al., 1998; Wu et al., 1999).

The relationship between stress and the immune system can be critical to people who are HIV-positive but do not yet have AIDS. Because their immune system is already fragile, further stress-related impairments could be life threatening. Research indicates that psycho-

psychoneuroimmunology   The field that examines the interaction of psychological and physiological processes affecting the body's ability to defend itself against disease.

immune system   The body's first line of defense against invading substances and microorganisms.

YOU CAN'T FIRE ME—I QUIT!
Researchers originally thought that any-one who fit the "Type A" behavior pattern was at special risk for heart disease. More recent research shows, however, that the danger lies mainly in cynical hostility, a characteristic seen in some, but not all, Type A people.

logical stressors are associated with the progression of HIV-related illnesses (e.g., Antoni et al., 2000; Kemeny & Dean, 1995). Unfortunately, people with HIV (and AIDS) face a particularly heavy load of immune-suppressing psychological stressors, including grief, unemployment, uncertainty about the future, and daily reminders of serious illness. A lack of perceived control and resulting depression can further magnify their stress responses.

Moderators of Immune Functioning　　Just as stressors can suppress the immune system, social support and other stress-mediating factors can help to sustain it. For example, students who get emotional support from friends during stressful periods appear to have better immune system functioning than those with less adequate social support (Cohen & Herbert, 1996).

James Pennebaker (1995) has suggested that social support may help prevent illness by providing the person under stress with an opportunity to express pent-up thoughts and emotions. Keeping important things to oneself, says Pennebaker, is itself a stressor (Gross & Levenson, 1997, Pennebaker, Colder, & Sharpe, 1990). In a laboratory experiment, for example, participants who were asked to deceive an experimenter showed elevated physiological arousal (Pennebaker & Chew, 1985). Further, the spouses of suicide or accidental-death victims who do not or cannot confide their feelings to others are especially likely to develop physical illness during the year following the death (Pennebaker & O'Heeron, 1984). Disclosing, even anonymously, the stresses and traumas one has experienced is associated with enhanced immune functioning, reduced physical symptoms, and decreased use of health services (Petrie et al., 1995; J. M. Richards et al., 2000; Smyth et al., 1999). This may explain why support groups for problems ranging from bereavement to overeating to alcohol and drug abuse tend to promote participants' physical health. Future research in psychoneuroimmunology promises to reveal vital links in the complex chain of mental and physical events that determine whether people become ill or stay healthy.

Heart Disease and Behavior Patterns

A number of stress responses, especially anger and hostility, have been linked to coronary heart disease, particularly in men (M. Friedman & Rosenman, 1959, 1974). For a time, researchers believed that anyone who displayed the pattern of aggressiveness, competitiveness, and nonstop work known as "Type A" behavior was at elevated risk for heart disease. More recent research suggests, however, that the danger lies not in these characteristics alone but in cynical hostility—a pattern characterized by suspiciousness, resentment, frequent anger, antagonism, and distrust of others (Helmers & Krantz, 1996).

Does Cynical Hostility Increase the Risk of Heart Disease?

The identification of cynical hostility as a risk factor for coronary heart disease and heart attack may be an important breakthrough in understanding these illnesses, which remain chief causes of death in the United States and most other Western nations. Further, the fact that cynical hostility often develops in childhood (Woodall & Matthews, 1993) suggests a need for intervention programs capable of altering this interpersonal style in time to prevent its negative consequences for health. But is cynical hostility as dangerous as health psychologists suspect?

What am I being asked to believe or accept?

Many researchers claim that individuals displaying cynical hostility increase their risk for coronary heart disease and heart attack. This risk, they say, is independent of other risk factors such as heredity, diet, smoking, and drinking.

Is there evidence available to support the claim?

There is evidence that hostility and heart disease are related, but the exact mechanism underlying the relationship is not clear. There are several possibilities (Helmers et al., 1995). The risk of coronary heart disease and heart attack may be elevated in cynically hostile people because these people tend to be unusually reactive to stressors, especially when challenged (Suls & Wan, 1993). There is evidence, for example, that during interpersonal conflicts, people predisposed to hostile behavior display not only overt hostility but also unusually large increases in blood pressure, heart rate, and autonomic reactivity. More important, it takes hostile individuals longer than normal to get back to their resting levels of functioning. Like a driver who damages a car by flooring the accelerator and applying the brakes at the same time, these "hot reactors" may create excessive wear and tear on the arteries of the heart as their increased heart rate forces blood through constricted vessels. Increased sympathetic nervous system activation not only puts stress on the coronary arteries but also leads to surges of stress-related hormones from the adrenal glands (Suarez et al., 1991). High levels of these hormones are associated with increases in fatty substances, such as blood cholesterol, that contribute to "hardening" of the arteries and coronary heart disease. Cholesterol levels do appear to be elevated in the blood of hostile people (Dujovne & Houston, 1991).

Hostility may affect heart disease risk less directly as well, through its impact on social support. Some evidence suggests that hostile people get fewer benefits from their social support network (Lepore, 1995b). Failure to use this support—and possibly offending potential supporters in the process—may intensify the impact of stressful events on hostile people. The result may be increased anger, antagonism, and ultimately, additional stress on the cardiovascular system (T. W. Smith, 1992; Suls & Wan, 1993).

Can that evidence be interpreted another way?

The studies cited in support of the relationship between hostility and coronary heart disease are not true experiments. Researchers cannot manipulate the independent variable by creating hostility in people; nor can they create experimental conditions in which groups of individuals who differ *only* in terms of hostility are compared on heart disease, the dependent variable. Accordingly, it is difficult to reach firm conclusions about cause-effect relationships in this and many other areas of health psychology.

Some researchers suggest that higher rates of heart problems among hostile people are due not to the impact of hostility on autonomic reactivity and hormone surges but to a third variable that causes the other two. Specifically, it may be that genetically determined autonomic reactivity increases the likelihood of both hostility *and* heart disease (Krantz et al., 1988). There is indeed evidence to suggest a genetic contribution to the development of hostility (Cacioppo et al., 1998). It is at least plausible, then, that some individuals are biologically predisposed to exaggerated autonomic reactivity and to hostility, each of which is independent of the other.

What evidence would help to evaluate the alternatives?

Several lines of evidence could assist in evaluating hypotheses about the relationship between hostility and heart problems. One approach would examine the relationships among hostility, coronary heart disease, and social and cultural factors (Thoresen & Powell, 1992). If the strength of the relationship between hostility and heart disease varied across social or cultural groups, then the theory of biological predisposition would be less defensible.

One way to test whether hostile people's higher rates of heart disease are related to their hostility or to a more general tendency toward intense physiological arousal is to examine how these individuals react to stress when they are not angry. Some researchers have done this by observing the physiological reactions of hostile people during the stress of surgery. One study found that even under general anesthesia, such people show unusually strong autonomic reactivity (Krantz & Durel, 1983). Because these patients were not conscious, it appears that oversensitivity to stressors, not hostile thinking, caused their exaggerated stress responses.

▪ What conclusions are most reasonable?

Most studies continue to find that hostile individuals stand a greater risk of heart disease and heart attacks than their nonhostile counterparts (S. E. Taylor, 1998a). But the causal relationships between hostility and heart disease are probably more complex than any current theory suggests; it appears that many factors underlie these relationships.

A more elaborate psychobiological model may be required—one that takes into account that (1) some individuals may be biologically predisposed to react to stress with hostility *and* increased cardiovascular activity, which in turn can contribute to heart disease; (2) hostile people help to create and maintain stressors through aggressive thoughts and actions, which can provoke others to be aggressive; and (3) hostile people are more likely than others to smoke, drink to excess, overeat, fail to exercise, and engage in other heart-damaging behaviors.

We must also keep in mind that the relationship between heart problems and hostility may not be universal. Some evidence suggests that this relationship may hold for women as well as men, and for individuals in various ethnic groups (e.g., Davidson, Hall, & MacGregor, 1996; Powch & Houston, 1996). Final conclusions, however, must await further research that examines the relationship between hostility and heart disease in other cultures.

Risking Your Life: Health-Endangering Behaviors

As we have seen, many major health problems are caused or aggravated by preventable behaviors such as those listed in Table 10.1.

Smoking   Smoking is the most significant preventable risk factor for fatal illnesses in the United States (Centers for Disease Control and Prevention, 1999a). Even nonsmokers who inhale "secondhand" smoke face an elevated risk for lung cancer and other respiratory diseases (G. Collins, 1997). The American Cancer Society has estimated that if people did not smoke cigarettes, 400,000 fewer U.S. citizens would die in the next twelve months, and 25 percent of all cancer deaths and thousands of heart attacks would never occur. Cigarette smoking accounts for 430,000 deaths each year—which is 20 percent of all U.S. deaths, and more than those caused by all other drugs, car accidents, suicides, homicides, and fires *combined* (Centers for Disease Control and Prevention, 1999a).

Although smoking is on the decline in the United States overall—only about 26 percent of adults now smoke—the habit is actually increasing in some groups, especially Latinos and young African American men (Centers for Disease Control and Prevention, 1999a). Poorer, less educated people are particularly likely to smoke. Conversely, some American Indian tribes in the Southwest and most Asian groups are less likely than other groups to smoke. In many other countries, especially less developed countries, smoking is still the rule rather than the exception.

Breaking the smoking habit is difficult. Only about 10 to 40 percent of people participating in the stop-smoking programs available today show long-term success (Irvin et al., 1999; Klesges et al., 1999; USDHHS, 2000).

Alcohol   Like tobacco, alcohol is a potentially addicting substance that can lead to major health problems. Alcohol abuse is associated with most leading causes of death, including heart disease, stroke, cancer, and liver disease (Centers for Disease Control and Prevention, 1999a). It also contributes to irreversible damage to brain tissue, to gastrointestinal illnesses, and to many other conditions. Both male and female abusers may experience disruption of their reproductive functions, such as early menopause in women and erectile disorder in men. And, as noted in Chapter 9, on human development, alcohol consumption by pregnant women is the most preventable cause of birth defects.

A DEADLY HABIT Today, about 26 percent of U.S. adults are smokers. Health authorities estimate that unless they quit, 25 million of these smokers will die of smoking-related illnesses (Centers for Disease Control and Prevention, 1999a).

Applying Psychology

PREVENTING AIDS   Health psychologists are helping to create adolescent-oriented AIDS prevention programs. These efforts focus on safe-sex media campaigns and studies of the cognitive and emotional factors that can enhance their effectiveness.

More than 100,000 deaths occur each year in the United States as a result of excessive alcohol consumption (U.S. Surgeon General, 1999).

Unsafe Sex   According to the World Health Organization, about 47 million people worldwide are HIV-positive (WHO, 1998). In the United States, more than 600,000 people have been diagnosed as having AIDS, and as many as 900,000 more have been infected with HIV (Centers for Disease Control and Prevention, 1999b). With growing public awareness of how to prevent HIV infection, the rate of new AIDS cases is now falling in the United States, but not everyone is getting the message.

Unsafe sex—especially sexual relations without the use of a condom—greatly increases the risk of contracting HIV. Yet many adolescents and adults continue this dangerous practice (Centers for Disease Control and Prevention, 1999c; Dodds et al., 2000). Like smoking and many other health-threatening behaviors, unprotected sex is more common among low-income individuals, many of whom belong to ethnic minority groups (St. Lawrence, 1993). Among African American men, the risk of contracting AIDS is three times greater than for European American men. The risk for African American women is fifteen times higher than for European American women (Centers for Disease Control, 1998).

Promoting Healthy Behavior

Who is most likely to adopt a healthy lifestyle?

Health psychologists are deeply involved in the development of smoking cessation programs, in campaigns to prevent young people from taking up smoking, in alcohol-education efforts, and in the fight against the spread of HIV and AIDS (Kalichman, Cherry, & Browne-Sperling, 1999; S. E. Taylor, 1998a). For example, they are working on methods for lowering the risk of AIDS among adolescents (St. Lawrence et al., 1995)—an important target group because many sexually active adolescents hold health beliefs that lead them to greatly underestimate the risk of contracting the disease through unprotected sex.

Efforts to reduce, eliminate, or prevent behaviors that pose health risks and to encourage healthy behaviors are called **health promotion** (Taylor, 1998). The aim of health psychologists working in this area is to understand the thought processes that lead people to engage in health-endangering behaviors and, then, to create intervention programs that can alter those thought processes, or at least take them into account (Klepp, Kelder, & Perry, 1995).

health promotion   The process of altering or eliminating behaviors that pose risks to health and, at the same time, fostering healthier behavior patterns.

Health Beliefs and Health Behaviors

This cognitive approach to health psychology appears in various *health-belief models.* Irwin Rosenstock (1974) developed the most influential and extensively tested of these models (e.g., Aspinwall & Duran, 1999). Rosenstock based his model on the assumption that people's decisions about health-related behaviors (such as smoking) are guided by four main factors:

1. A perception of *personal* threat or susceptibility to contracting a specific illness. (Do you believe that *you* will get lung cancer from smoking?)

2. A perception of the seriousness of the illness and the severity of the consequences of having it. (How serious do *you* think lung cancer is? What will happen to *you* if you get it?)

3. The belief that a particular practice will reduce the threat. (Will *your* stopping smoking prevent *you* from getting lung cancer?)

4. The balance between the perceived costs of starting a health practice and the benefits expected from this practice. (Will the reduced chance of getting cancer in the future be worth the discomfort and loss of pleasure from not smoking?)

On the basis of this health-belief model, one would expect that the people most likely to quit smoking would be those who believe that they are susceptible to getting cancer from smoking, that cancer is serious and life-threatening, and that the benefits of preventing cancer clearly outweigh the difficulties associated with quitting.

Other belief factors not included in Rosenstock's model may also be important (Gerrard, Gibbons, & Bushman, 1996). For example, people generally do not try to quit smoking unless they believe they can succeed. Thus, *self-efficacy,* the belief that one is able to perform some behavior, is an additional determinant of decisions about health behaviors (Bandura, 1992; Dijkstra, DeVries, & Bakker, 1996). A related factor is the *intention* to engage in a healthy behavior (Maddux & DuCharme, 1997).

Health-belief models help predict a variety of health behaviors, including exercise (McAuley, 1992), safe-sex practices among gay men at risk for AIDS (W. A. Fisher, Fisher, & Rye, 1995), adherence to doctors' orders among diabetic adolescents (Bond, Aiken, & Somerville, 1992), and the decision to undergo mammogram screening for breast cancer (Champion & Huster, 1995).

Changing Health Behaviors: Stages of Readiness

Knowing *who* is most likely to practice healthy behaviors is important, but health psychologists have also tried to understand *how* people change their health habits. According to James Prochaska and his colleagues, successful change involves five stages (Prochaska, DiClemente, & Norcross, 1992):

1. *Precontemplation.* The person does not perceive a health-related problem and has no intention of changing in the foreseeable future.

2. *Contemplation.* The person is aware of a problem behavior and is seriously thinking about changing it.

3. *Preparation.* The person has a strong intention to change and has made specific plans to do so.

4. *Action.* The person at this stage is engaging successfully in behavior change.

5. *Maintenance.* The healthy behavior has continued for at least six months, and the person is using newly learned skills to prevent relapse.

The path from precontemplation through maintenance can be a rough one (Prochaska, 1994). Usually, people relapse and go through the stages repeatedly until they finally achieve stability in the healthy behavior they desire. Smokers, for example, typically require three to four cycles through the stages and up to seven years before they finally reach the maintenance stage.

Applying Psychology

TAKING TIME OUT Nearly half of all Americans say the workplace is their number one source of stress (NIOSH, 1999). On January 1, 2000, Raymond Fowler, chief executive officer of the American Psychological Association, joined the ranks of those whose elevated blood pressure, heart arrhythmias, and other physical stress responses required a temporary leave of absence from highly stressful jobs (Fowler, 2000). The National Institute for Occupational Safety and Health (1999) suggests a wide range of other behavioral coping options for stressed employees who cannot take time off.

**LINKAGES
How can people manage stress?** (a link to Treatment of Psychological Disorders)

Programs for Coping with Stress

An important aspect of health psychologists' health promotion activities has been to improve people's stress-coping skills. Let's consider a few specific procedures and programs associated with this effort.

Planning to Cope   Just as people with extra money in the bank have a better chance of weathering a financial crisis, people with effective coping skills have a better chance of escaping some of the more harmful effects of intense stress. Like family money, the ability to handle stress appears to come naturally to some people, but coping strategies can also be learned. Programs that teach such strategies move through several stages, which are summarized in Table 10.4.

Bear in mind, however, that no single method of coping with stressors is universally successful. For example, denying the existence of an uncontrollable stressor may be fine in the short run but may lead to problems if no other coping method is used (Suls & Fletcher, 1985). Similarly, people who rely exclusively on an active, problem-focused approach to coping may handle controllable stressors well but find themselves nearly helpless in the face of uncontrollable ones (J. A. Murray & Terry, 1999). Individuals who are most successful at stress management may be those who are best able to adjust their coping methods to the demands of changing situations and differing stressors (S. E. Taylor, 1998a).

Developing Coping Strategies   Strategies for coping with stress can be cognitive, emotional, behavioral, or physical. *Cognitive coping strategies* change how people interpret stimuli and events. They help people think more calmly, rationally, and constructively in the face of stress and may generate a more hopeful emotional state. For example, students with heavy course loads may experience anxiety, confusion, discouragement, lack of motivation, and the desire to run away from it all. Frightening, catastrophizing thoughts (such as "What if I fail?") magnify stress responses. Cognitive coping strategies replace catastrophic thinking with thoughts in which stressors are viewed as challenges rather than threats. This substitution process is called **cognitive restructuring** (Meichenbaum, 1977). It involves first identifying upsetting thoughts (such as "I'll never figure this out!") and then developing and practicing more constructive thoughts (such as "All I can do is the best I can") when under stress. Cognitive coping does not eliminate

TABLE 10.4	Stages in Coping with Stress

Many successful programs for systematically coping with stress guide people through several stages and are aimed at removing stressors that can be changed and at reducing responses to stressors that cannot be changed (R. L. Silver & Wortman, 1980).

Stage	Task
1. Assessment	Identify the sources and effects of stress.
2. Goal setting	List the stressors and stress responses to be addressed. Designate which stressors are and are not changeable.
3. Planning	List the specific steps to be taken to cope with stress.
4. Action	Implement coping plans.
5. Evaluation	Determine the changes in stressors and stress responses that have occurred as a result of coping methods.
6. Adjustment	Alter coping methods to improve results, if necessary.

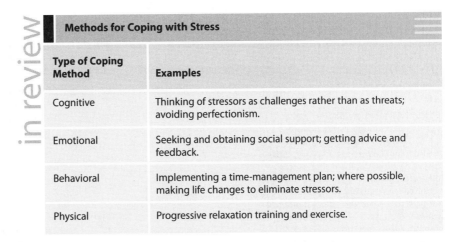

Methods for Coping with Stress	
Type of Coping Method	**Examples**
Cognitive	Thinking of stressors as challenges rather than as threats; avoiding perfectionism.
Emotional	Seeking and obtaining social support; getting advice and feedback.
Behavioral	Implementing a time-management plan; where possible, making life changes to eliminate stressors.
Physical	Progressive relaxation training and exercise.

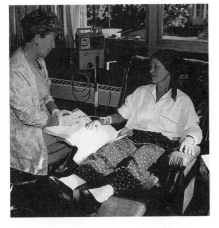

Applying Psychology

DEALING WITH CHEMOTHERAPY
Progressive relaxation training can be used to ease a variety of health-related problems. For example, one study found that this training resulted in significant reductions in anxiety, physiological arousal, and nausea following cancer chemotherapy (Burish & Jenkins, 1992).

cognitive restructuring   A technique for coping with stress that involves replacing stress-provoking thoughts with more constructive thoughts in order to make stressors less threatening and disruptive.

progressive relaxation training   A method for coping with stress that involves tensing a group of muscles, then releasing the tension and focusing on the resulting feelings of relaxation.

stressors, but it can help people perceive them as less threatening and therefore make them less disruptive (Antoni et al., 2000).

Seeking and obtaining social support from others are effective *emotional coping strategies.* The perception that one has emotional support and is cared for and valued by others tends to be an effective buffer against the ill effects of many stressors (S. E. Taylor, 1998a). Having enhanced emotional resources is associated with increased survival time in cancer patients (B. L. Anderson, 1992), improved immune functioning (Kiecolt-Glaser & Glaser, 1992), and more rapid recovery from illness (S. E. Taylor, 1998a).

Behavioral coping strategies involve changing behavior to minimize the impact of stressors. Time management is one example. You might keep track of your time for a week and start a time-management plan. The first step is to set out a schedule that shows how your time is typically spent; then decide how to allocate your time in the future. A time-management plan can help control catastrophizing thoughts by providing reassurance that there is enough time for everything and a plan for handling it all.

Physical coping strategies can be used to alter one's physical responses before, during, or after stressors occur. Unfortunately, the most common physical coping strategy is some form of drug use. Prescription medications are sometimes an appropriate coping aid, especially when stressors are severe and acute, such as the sudden death of one's child. However, people who depend on prescriptions or other drugs, including alcohol, to help them face stressors often attribute any success to the drug, not to their own skill. Furthermore, the drug effects that blunt stress responses may also interfere with the ability to apply coping strategies. The resulting loss of perceived control over stressors may make those stressors even more threatening and disruptive.

Physical exercise is a popular and well-known nonchemical method of reducing physical stress reactions. Another is **progressive relaxation training,** which is learned by tensing a group of muscles (such as the hand and arm) for a few seconds, then releasing the tension and focusing on the resulting feelings of relaxation. This procedure is repeated for each of sixteen muscle groups throughout the body (D. A. Bernstein, Borkovec, & Hazlette-Stevens, 2000). Once people become skilled at progressive relaxation, they can use it to calm down anywhere and anytime. "In Review: Methods for Coping with Stress" summarizes our discussion of stress-coping methods.

active review   Health, Stress, and Coping

Linkages

As noted in Chapter 1, all of psychology's subfields are related to one another. Our discussion of how stressors can lead to the development of mental disorders illustrates just one way in which the topic of this chapter, health, stress, and coping, is linked to the subfield of psychological disorder (Chapter 12). The Linkages diagram shows ties to two other subfields as well, and there are many more ties throughout the book. Looking for linkages among subfields will help you see how they all fit together and better appreciate the big picture that is psychology.

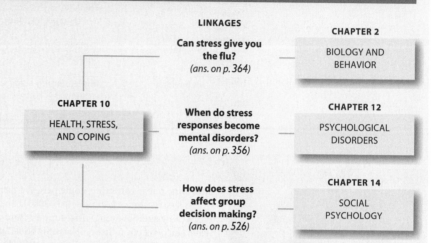

LINKAGES

CHAPTER 10
HEALTH, STRESS, AND COPING

Can stress give you the flu?
(ans. on p. 364)

CHAPTER 2
BIOLOGY AND BEHAVIOR

When do stress responses become mental disorders?
(ans. on p. 356)

CHAPTER 12
PSYCHOLOGICAL DISORDERS

How does stress affect group decision making?
(ans. on p. 526)

CHAPTER 14
SOCIAL PSYCHOLOGY

Summary

HEALTH PSYCHOLOGY

▪ **What do health psychologists do?**

The development of **health psychology** was prompted by recognition of the link between stress and illness, and of the role of behaviors such as smoking, in elevating the risk of illness. Health psychologists seek to understand how psychological factors are related to physical disease and to help people behave in ways that prevent or minimize disease and promote health.

UNDERSTANDING STRESS

▪ **How do psychological stressors affect physical health?**

The term **stress** refers in part to **stressors,** which are physical or psychological events and situations to which people must adjust. The term is also used to refer to **stress reactions.** Most generally, however, stress is viewed as an ongoing, interactive process that takes place as people adjust to, and cope with, their environment. Psychological stressors include catastrophic events, life changes and strains, chronic stressors, and daily hassles. Stressors can be measured by tests like the Social Readjustment Rating Scale (SRRS) and the Life Experiences Survey (LES), but scores on such tests provide only a partial picture of the stress in a person's life.

Responses to stressors can be physical and psychological. These stress responses can occur alone or in combination, and the appearance of one can often stimulate others.

Physical stress responses include changes in heart rate, respiration, and many other processes that are part of a pattern known as the **general adaptation syndrome,** or **GAS.** The GAS has three stages:

alarm reaction, resistance, and exhaustion. The GAS helps people resist stress but, if present too long, can lead to depletion of immune system functions, as well as to physical illnesses, which Selye called **diseases of adaptation.**

Psychological stress responses can be emotional, cognitive, and behavioral. Anxiety, anger, and depression are among the most common emotional stress reactions. Cognitive stress reactions include ruminative thinking; catastrophizing; and disruptions in the ability to think clearly, remember accurately, and solve problems efficiently.

Behavioral stress responses include changes in posture, as well as facial expressions, tremors, or jumpiness, that reflect physical tension or emotional stress reactions. More global behavioral stress responses include irritability, absenteeism, and even suicide attempts. Patterns of response to severe or long-lasting stressors can lead to **burnout** or to psychological disorders such as **posttraumatic stress disorder (PTSD).**

The key to understanding stress appears to lie in observing the interaction of specific stressors with particular people. Stressors are likely to have greater impact if they are appraised as threats, or if they are unpredictable or uncontrollable. The people most likely to react strongly to a stressor are those whose coping resources, coping methods, and **social support networks** are inadequate.

THE PHYSIOLOGY AND PSYCHOLOGY OF HEALTH AND ILLNESS

▪ **How does stress affect your immune system?**

Psychoneuroimmunology is the field that examines the interaction of psychological and physiological processes that affect the body's ability to defend itself against disease. When a person is under stress, some of the hormones released from the adrenal glands, such as cortisol, reduce the effectiveness of the cells of the *immune system* (T-cells, B-cells, natural killer cells) in combating foreign invaders, such as viruses, and cancer cells.

People who are cynically hostile appear at greater risk for heart disease than other people. The heightened reactivity to stressors that these people experience may damage their cardiovascular system.

Most of the major health problems in Western cultures are related to preventable behaviors such as smoking and drinking alcohol. Having unsafe sex is a major risk factor for contracting HIV.

PROMOTING HEALTHY BEHAVIOR

■ **Who is most likely to adopt a healthy lifestyle?**

The process of altering or eliminating health-risky behaviors and fostering healthy behavior patterns is called **health promotion.** People's

health-related behaviors are partly guided by their beliefs about health risks and what they can do about them.

The process of changing health-related behaviors appears to involve several stages, including precontemplation, contemplation, preparation, action, and maintenance. Understanding which stage people are in, and helping them move through these stages, is an important task in health psychology.

To cope with stress, people must recognize the stressors affecting them and develop a plan for coping with these stressors. Important coping skills include **cognitive restructuring,** acting to minimize the number or intensity of stressors, and using **progressive relaxation training** and other techniques for reducing physical stress reactions.

Learn by Doing

Put It in Writing

What is stress like for you? To help you understand the role of stress in your life, write a page or two describing a stressful incident that you had to face in the recent past. Identify what the stressors were, and classify each of them as physical or psychological. List your physical, emotional, cognitive, and behavioral responses to these stressors, and how long the responses lasted. Also include a brief summary of how you coped with these stressors and how successful your coping efforts were. Some research suggests that writing about stressful experiences can help people to deal with those experiences. Did this writing project have any such benefits for you?

Personal Learning Activity

To get an idea of how much people differ in their approach to coping with stressors, create a one-paragraph story of a stressful situation (e.g., losing a job, having one's home destroyed by fire, working with an obnoxious boss, or being overburdened by schoolwork). Now show this description to ten people, and ask each of them to tell you how they would cope with the situation if it happened to them. Classify their responses in terms of whether they were problem-focused or emotion-focused coping methods. Did you notice any relationships between the kind of coping responses these people chose and characteristics such as age, gender, ethnicity, or experience with stress? If so, why do you think those relationships appeared? *For additional projects, see the five Personal Learning Activities in the corresponding chapter of the study guide that accompanies this text.*

Step into Action

Courses

Biological Psychology
Health Psychology
Stress Management
Stress and Coping

Movies

Courage Under Fire (general adaptation syndrome)
Falling Down (behavioral stress responses)
The Deer Hunter (posttraumatic stress responses)
Do the Right Thing (social support networks)
Women on the Verge of a Nervous Breakdown (impact of sudden stressor)
Glengarry Glen Ross (effects of stress in the workplace)
Angela's Ashes (impact of stress on development)
Saving Private Ryan (individual differences in responses to traumatic stress)

Books

Richard Sorrentino and Christopher Roney, *The Uncertain Mind: Individual Differences in Facing the Unknown* (Psychology Press, 2000) (discusses the impact of uncertainty on physical and mental health)

Tony Cassidy, *Stress, Cognition, and Health* (Routledge, 1999) (summarizes research on the effects of stress on thinking and physical well-being)

Jerrold Greenberg, *Comprehensive Stress Management* (McGraw-Hill, 1999) (ideas for stress management)

James W. Pennebaker, *Opening Up: The Healing Power of Expressing Emotions* (Guilford, 1997) (describes research on the benefits of self-disclosure).

The Web

The World Wide Web is a good source of additional information about the science of psychology, provided you use it carefully and think critically about the information you find. The PsychAbilities web site that accompanies this text offers many resources relevant to this chapter. These resources include interactive NetLab exercises; Thinking Critically and Evaluating Research exercises; ACE chapter quizzes; recommended web links; and articles on current events, books, and movies. At http://college.hmco.com, select *Psychology* and then this textbook.

Review of Key Terms

Can you define each of the key terms in the chapter? Check your definitions against those on the pages listed in parentheses below or in the Glossary/Index at the end of the text.

burnout *(p. 356)*

cognitive restructuring *(p. 370)*

diseases of adaptation *(p. 354)*

general adaptation syndrome (GAS) *(p. 353)*

health promotion *(p. 368)*

health psychology *(p. 348)*

immune system *(p. 364)*

posttraumatic stress disorder (PTSD) *(p. 356)*

progressive relaxation training *(p. 371)*

psychoneuroimmunology *(p. 364)*

social support network *(p. 360)*

stress *(p. 350)*

stress reactions *(p. 350)*

stressors *(p. 350)*

Multiple-Choice Self-Test

Select the best answer for each of the questions below. Then check your response against the Answer Key at the end of the text.

1. According to health psychology research,

   a. acute diseases cause more U.S. deaths than chronic ones.

   b. psychological methods cannot change behaviors that contribute to illness.

   c. teaching people to take an active role in protecting their own health has not had a major impact on the death rate.

   d. the stresses of life influence health through their impact on psychological and physical processes.

2. Lila got married, moved to a new city, and took a new job, all in the same month. We would expect Lila to

   a. display physical or psychological stress responses, or both.

   b. experience little stress, because these are all desirable changes.

   c. experience little stress, because these are not chronic stressors.

   d. experience physical stress responses only.

3. Psychological stressors

   a. always stem from a lack of social support.

   b. are by definition long term, or chronic.

   c. result mainly from catastrophic events.

   d. include anything that forces a person to change or adapt.

4. It is 2:00 A.M., and Aaron is lost in a big city with no money. His sympathetic nervous system has initiated the fight-or-flight syndrome. Which stage of the general adaptation syndrome (GAS) is he experiencing?

   a. alarm   b. resistance

   c. exhaustion   d. precontemplative

5. According to Hans Selye, diseases of adaptation occur when the body enters the _____ stage of the GAS.

   a. alarm

   b. resistance

   c. exhaustion

   d. precontemplative

6. While watching TV, taking a shower, or even having dinner with his girlfriend, Enrico finds that he can't stop thinking about all the stressful things happening in his life. Enrico is experiencing _____.

   a. catastrophizing

   b. ruminative thinking

   c. functional fixedness

   d. cognitive restructuring

7. Caitlin just failed her high school math test. She says to herself, "Mom is going to be furious with me! She will probably ground me, which means I won't be able to go to the prom. If I don't go to the prom, I will be a social outcast, and no one will talk to me. I'll never have any friends or find a partner, and no one will ever love me!" This is an example of

   a. cognitive restructuring.
   b. catastrophizing.
   c. posttraumatic stress disorder.
   d. the fight-or-flight syndrome.

8. Dr. Angelica's teenage patient, Juan, is under a lot of stress. If the doctor is most worried about Juan's behavioral stress responses, she would focus mainly on his

   a. depression.
   b. catastrophic thoughts.
   c. blood pressure.
   d. aggressiveness.

9. Shane, a veteran, occasionally experiences flashbacks involving vivid recollections of his wartime experiences. Flashbacks are associated with

   a. generalized anxiety disorder.
   b. posttraumatic stress disorder.
   c. the general adaptation syndrome.
   d. the fight-or-flight syndrome.

10. Robin, Sarah, and Travis all work in the same office complex, which is plagued by temperature-regulation problems. Based on research on stress mediators, which of the three workers will display the most stress responses?

    a. Robin, whose office is always too warm.
    b. Sarah, whose office is always too cold.
    c. Travis, whose office changes from hot to cold without warning.
    d. There is no way to predict who will be most stressed.

11. When postsurgery patients are allowed to adjust their own level of painkillers, they tend to self-administer less pain medication than patients who must ask for it. This phenomenon is consistent with research showing that

    a. people's social support can mediate stress.
    b. predictable stressors are easier to manage.
    c. the perception of control reduces the impact of stressors.
    d. thinking of stressors as threats amplifies their effects.

12. Laton, the head of personnel at his company, knows that the employees have very stressful jobs. Thus, he schedules group picnics and lunches so that employees who don't know each other can get acquainted. Laton is trying to ease the employees' stressors by

    a. promoting cognitive restructuring.
    b. improving social support networks.
    c. increasing employees' sense of control.
    d. helping employees think of their stressors as challenges rather than threats.

13. In the Focus on Research section of this chapter, on the relationship between personality and life expectancy, the researchers found

    a. no relationship between the two.
    b. that conscientiousness was associated with longer life.
    c. that social relationships had no impact on longevity.
    d. that impulsiveness was associated with longer life.

14. Dr. Porter studies immune system cells that have antiviral properties and help prevent tumors. What type of cells does he study?

    a. B-cells   b. T-cells
    c. natural killer cells   d. macrophages

15. Fred is at high risk for coronary heart disease. As his friend, you tell him that current research suggests that he could lower his risk if he

    a. takes up fishing as a hobby.
    b. works at being less cynical and hostile.
    c. reduces his workload.
    d. restructures his thinking about stress.

16. The most significant preventable risk factor for fatal illness in the United States is

    a. smoking.   b. consumption of alcohol.
    c. illegal drug use.   d. unsafe sex.

17. According to Rosenstock's health-belief model, which of the following would most help Bridgit decide to quit smoking?

    a. perceiving a personal threat of getting cancer from her smoking
    b. knowing that smoking causes cancer
    c. knowing that quitting can lower people's risk of cancer
    d. carefully reading the statistics of smoking and health in general

18. Amanda is severely overweight. She knows that for her health's sake, she needs to limit her caloric intake, but she loves to eat and has made no specific plans to go on a diet. Amanda is at the _____ stage of readiness to change a health-risky behavior.

    a. precontemplation   b. contemplation
    c. preparation   d. maintenance

19. Sayumi is trying to control her stress. In response to a hurtful comment from a friend, Sayumi thinks to herself, "Don't jump to conclusions; he probably didn't mean it the way it sounded," instead of "That jerk! Who does he think he is?" Sayumi is using the coping strategy of

    a. cognitive restructuring.   b. emotional restructuring.
    c. catastrophizing.   d. contemplation.

20. Loretta, a marriage counselor, finds her job very stressful. She has found that physical coping strategies help her the most. Loretta most likely engages in

    a. cognitive restructuring.
    b. emotional restructuring.
    c. progressive relaxation training.
    d. problem-focused coping.

Index

Quick Reference List

CHAPTER 1
Cognitive Learning Styles
1. Visual
2. Auditory
3. Kinesthetic

Other Learning Styles
1. Global learners
2. Linear learners
3. Interactive learners
4. Reflective learners

Howard Gardner's
Multiple Intelligences
1. Linguistic
2. Logical-Mathematical
3. Musical
4. Bodily-Kinesthetic
5. Spatial
6. Interpersonal
7. Intrapersonal
8. Naturalistic

CHAPTER 2
Working Memory Model
1. Sensory Input
2. Visuo-Spatial Scratchpad
3. Phonological Loop
4. Central Executive
5. Long-Term Memory

Feedback Model
1. Learning Goal
2. Action
3. Feedback/Self-Quizzing
4. Comparison
5. Results: Yes, No

Twelve Principles of Memory
1. Selectivity
2. Association
3. Visualization
4. Elaboration
5. Concentration
6. Recitation
7. Intention
8. Big/Little Pictures
9. Feedback
10. Organization
11. Time on Task
12. Ongoing Review

CHAPTER 3
Four Types of Schedules
1. Term schedule
2. Weekly schedule
3. Daily schedule
4. Task schedule

Create a Weekly Schedule
1. Fixed activities
2. Fixed study blocks (2:1 ratio)
3. Flex study blocks
4. Goals/responsibilities
5. Leisure/social/family

CHAPTER 4
Goal-Setting Steps
1. Specific goals
2. Target date/time
3. Steps
4. Rewards

CHAPTER 5
Concentration Strategies
Stress-Reducing Strategies
Anti-Procrastination Strategies

CHAPTER 6
Five Theories of Forgetting
1. Decay
2. Displacement
3. Interference
4. Incomplete Encoding
5. Retrieval Failure

Kinds of Mnemonics
1. Associations
2. Pictures or graphics
3. Acronyms and acrostics
4. Rhythms, rhymes, and jingles
5. Stacking
6. Loci
7. Peg systems

Sources of Test Anxiety
1. Underpreparedness
2. Past experiences
3. Fear of failure
4. Poor test-taking skills

CHAPTER 7
Four Levels of Reading
1. Recreational
2. Overview
3. Thorough
4. Comparative

Steps of SQ4R
1. Survey
2. Question
3. Read
4. Record
5. Recite
6. Review

CHAPTER 8
Organizational Patterns
1. Chronological
2. Process
3. Comparison/Contrast
4. Definition
5. Examples
6. Cause/Effect
7. Whole/Parts

CHAPTER 9
5 *R*'s of Cornell
1. Record
2. Reduce
3. Recite
4. Reflect
5. Review

CHAPTER 10
Four Kinds of Listening
1. Active
2. Critical
3. Empathic
4. Appreciative

Steps in the Listening Process
1. Reception
2. Attention
3. Perception
4. Assignment of Meaning
5. Response

CHAPTER 11
Notetaking Options
1. Annotations
2. Marginal notes
3. Cornell notes
4. Index cards
5. Two-column/Three-column notes
6. Formal outlines
7. Visual mappings
8. Hierarchies
9. Comparison charts
10. Graphic notes

CHAPTER 12
Four Levels of Response
1. Immediate
2. Delayed
3. Assisted
4. Educated guessing

CHAPTER 13
Kinds of Recall Questions
1. Fill-in-the-blanks
2. Listing
3. Definition
4. Short answer

RSTUV Problem-Solving Method
1. Read
2. Select
3. Think
4. Use
5. Verify

Essential Study Skills provides in-depth coverage of study skills with ample room for practice and application through a step-by-step, supportive approach. The Fifth Edition includes the contemporary working memory model, helping you take control of your learning potential. Online exercises and case studies from the student website also provide extra practice and application of lessons learned.

Through models, exercises, case studies, and readings, *Essential Study Skills* shows you that academic success is a product of skills and behaviors you can acquire, customize, and effectively apply.

New! Excerpted Psychology Chapter (Appendix D) places study skills in context by showing students how to apply strategies in academic coursework.

New! "Essential Strategies" charts integrated throughout the text offer key strategies and generalized principles in a to-the-point and easy-to-reference format.

Updated! Quick Start Checklist provides tips for surveying your textbooks and improving your note-taking, test-taking, and time-management skills at the start of the semester.

Study smarter, not harder.

To learn more about this text, please visit: http://college.hmco.com/PIC/wongESS5e

For text resources, and more from Houghton Mifflin Student Success, please visit:
http://studentsuccess.college.hmco.com

HOUGHTON MIFFLIN
New Ways to Know ®

ISBN 0-618-52883-0

90000

9 780618 528837

3-60765

Usborne
Understanding your
Brain

Lifting the lid on
what's inside
your head

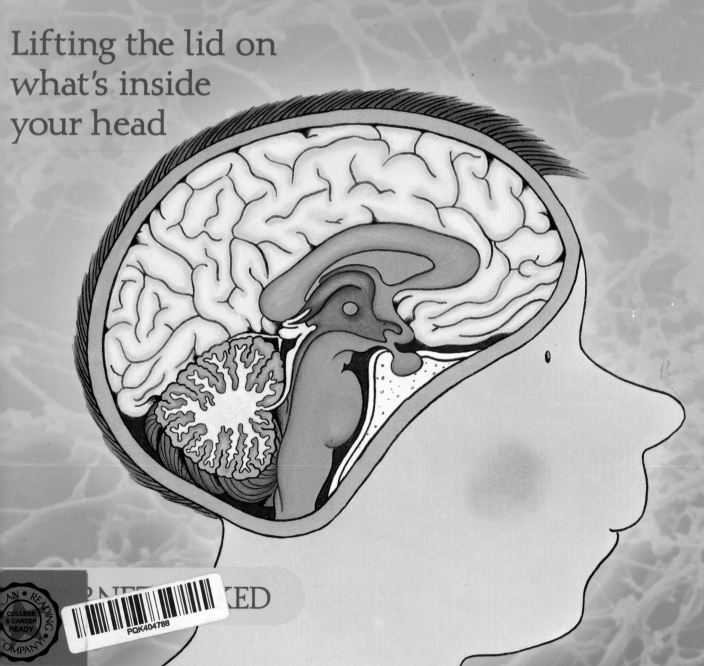

Internet Links

Throughout this book we have recommended websites where you can find out more about the brain. To visit the sites, go to the Usborne Quicklinks Website where you will find links to all the sites.

1. Go to **www.usborne-quicklinks.com**
2. Type the keywords for this book:
understanding your brain
3. Type the page number of the link you want to visit.
4. Click on the links to go to the recommended sites.

Here are some of the things you can do on the websites recommended in this book:
• Build a brain online.
• Watch a cartoon movie about the nervous system.
• Follow a day in the life of a child's brain.
• Play online games about animal intelligence.

Site availability

The links in Usborne Quicklinks are regularly reviewed and updated, but occasionally you may get a message that a site is unavailable. This might be temporary, so try again later, or even the next day. Websites do occasionally close down and when this happens, we will replace them with new links in Usborne Quicklinks. Sometimes we add extra links too, if we think they are useful. So when you visit Usborne Quicklinks, the links may be slightly different from those described in your book.

> ### COMPUTER NOT ESSENTIAL
> If you don't have access to
> the Internet, don't worry.
> This book is a fun, first guide
> to the brain on its own.

Safety on the Internet

Ask your parent's or guardian's permission before you connect to the Internet and make sure you follow these simple rules:

• Never give out information about yourself, such as your real name, address, phone number or the name of your school.
• If a site asks you to log in or register by typing your name or email address, ask permission from an adult first.

What you need

To visit the websites you need a computer with an Internet connection and a web browser (the software that lets you look at information from the Internet). Some sites need extra programs (plug-ins) to play sound or show videos or animations.

If you go to a site and do not have the necessary plug-in, a message will come up on the screen. There is usually a link to click on to download the plug-in. For more information about plug-ins, go to Usborne Quicklinks and click on "Net Help".

Notes for parents and guardians

The websites described in this book are regularly reviewed, but the content of a website may change at any time and Usborne Publishing is not responsible for the content on any website other than its own.

We recommend that children are supervised while on the Internet, that they do not use Internet chat rooms, and that you use Internet filtering software to block unsuitable material. Please ensure that your children read and follow the safety guidelines printed above. For more information, see the Net Help area on the Usborne Quicklinks Website.